H. A. B. Shapiro Memorial Library

NEW HAMPSHIRE COLLEGE

Manchester, N. H.

W9-BCR-598

H. A. B. Shapiro Memorial Library

NEW HAMPSHIRE COLLEGE

Manchester, N. H.

The People
Called Apache

H. A. B. Shapiro Memorial Library
NEW HAMPSHIRE COLLEGE
Manchester, N. H.

The People Called Apache

written and illustrated by

THOMAS E. MAILS

A Rutledge Book
Prentice-Hall, Inc.
Englewood Cliffs, N.J.

Contents

Preface/7

Introduction/11

The Western Apache (Arizona)/23

1 History/23

2 Government and Social Order/52

3 Childbirth/55

4 Childhood, Names, and Training/58

5 Girl's Puberty Ceremony/68

    1901–1902/68

    1920–1930/71

    1930–Present/71

6 Boy's Maturity Rites/85

7 Courtship and Marriage/85

8 Division of Labor/86

9 The Woman's Status/87

10 Mother-in-Law Avoidance/88

11 Personality Characteristics/88

12 Tag-Bands; English Names/90

13 Crime and Punishment/91

14 Social Dances/92

15 Sign Language and Signaling/92

16 Schools/93

17 Dwellings, Furniture, and Utensils/94

18 Food and Drink/96

19 Agriculture/101

20 Tanning/101

21 Apparel and Jewelry/102

22 Hair Dressing and Ornaments/117

23 Tattooing and Body Painting/119

24 Diseases and Cures/120

25 Sweat Bathing/120

26 Religion and Ceremonies/122

    Altars and Sacred Places/126

    The Value of Curing Ceremonials/127

27 The Gans (Masked Dancers, Mountain Spirit Impersonators)/129

28 Medicine Men/142

29 Specific Medicine Items Used by the Western Apache/151

    The Rhombus or Bull-Roarer/151

    Medicine Shirt/151

    Medicine Hat/155

    Medicine Hoops and Effigies/158

    Cross/158

    Medicine Cord/160

    Wooden Medicine Snake/162

    Lizards, Snakes, Bear Claws/163

    Medicine Pillow, Ashes/163

    Roots/164

30 Medicine Ceremonies, a General View/164

31 Medicine Items as Live Objects, 1901–1902/165

32 Ceremonial Dances/170

    The Wheel Dance/170

E
99
.A6
M35
c.1

NOV 18 1974

ISBN: 0-13-656702-9

Library of Congress Catalog Card Number: 74-79603

Copyright 1974 in all countries of the International Copyright Union by The Ridge Press, Inc.–Rutledge Books Division and Prentice-Hall, Inc. All rights reserved, including the right of reproduction in whole or in part

Prepared and produced by The Ridge Press, Inc.–Rutledge Books Division, 25 West 43 Street, New York, N.Y. 10036

Published in 1974 by Prentice-Hall, Inc., Englewood Cliffs, N.J.

Printed in Italy by Mondadori, Verona

Ceremonies for the Sick/170
A Night Dance/170
The Devil's Dance/173
Dance for a Sick Woman/174
Dance for a Sick Child/175
Protection from Ghosts/175
Thank-Offering Dance/176
Dance for Rain/176
Medicine Disk Ceremony/176
The Sickness and Death of Whistling
    Wind/179
33 Death and Burial/179
34 Christian Missions/182
35 Western Apache Life, 1940/186
36 Western Apache Life, 1973/193

The Chiricahua Apache (Arizona)/207
 1 History/207
Color Portfolio/facing page 224
 2 Food Harvests and Agriculture/225
 3 Hunting/227
 4 Tanning/229
 5 Girl's Puberty Ceremony, 1930–1940/233
 6 Religion, Cosmology, and the Supernatural
      Powers/236
    Amulets and Phylacteries/241
    Medicine Shirts and Sashes/243
 7 The Gans/243
    1800s/243
    1930s/248
 8 Raiding and Warfare/252
    Enemies Against Power/260
    The Novice Complex for Raid and War/260
    The Scratching Stick and the Drinking Tube,
      According to Bourke/262
 9 Weapons/263
    Bows and Arrows/263
    Quivers/269
    Lances/273
    War Clubs/273
    Shields/278
    Knives/278
    Stones and Slings/278
    Guns/281
10 Horses, Guns, and Horsemanship/281
11 Time Keeping, 1880s/282

The Mescalero Apache (New Mexico)/285
 1 History/287
 2 Government and Social Order/310
    The Local Group/310
    The Extended Domestic Family/312
 3 Girl's Puberty Rite/313
 4 The Individual Power Quest/324

 5 Death and Burial/326
 6 Division of Labor/327
 7 Dwellings and Sanitation/327
 8 Food and Drink/330
 9 Hunting/331
10 Clothing/332
11 Religion/341

The Jicarilla Apache (New Mexico)/343
 1 History/345
 2 Apparel and Jewelry/365
 3 Religion/381
 4 Ceremonialism/382
 5 Holiness Rite (improperly called Bear Dance)/
    386
 6 Puberty or Adolescence Rite/387
 7 Ceremonial Relay Race/393

Apache Arts, Crafts, and Games/405
 1 Painting/405
 2 Basketry/406
    General/406
    Western Apache Basketry/408
    Mescalero Basketry/410
    Jicarilla Coiled Basketry/410
 3 Beadwork/411
 4 Textiles/412
 5 Pottery/412
 6 Tools/412
 7 Musical Instruments/413
    Drums/413
    Rattles/413
    Violins/414
    Flutes, Flageolets/414
    Rasps/414
 8 Games/414
    Hoop and Pole/414
    Hidden Ball/422
    Foot Races/422
    Shinny/422
    Dice Games/423
    Cat's Cradle/425
    Archery/425
    Bull-Roarer/425
    Wrestling/425
    Tug-of-War/425
    Cards/425
    Moccasin Game/426

Conclusion/427

Bibliography/433
Notes/434
Index/439

To the Apache

Preface

The People Called Apache is about the history and culture of the famed and remarkable Apache peoples of Arizona and New Mexico; more specifically, it is about the Western, Chiricahua, Mescalero, and Jicarilla Apache. For space and other reasons, the Lipan Apache, Kiowa Apache, and Navajo are not included. My hope is to present herein enough written and visual information concerning each of the four individual branches to allow the reader to distinguish one from the others and at the same time to make comparisons among them.

The history of each group will be described in some detail, and also those customs peculiar to it. However, there are numerous areas where practices were so similar that the subject can be covered under the heading of one branch and duplications of material avoided simply by making cross references as they are needed. For example, since the Chiricahua became the best-known raiding and warring group, raid and warfare will be treated extensively in the Chiricahua section, and only briefly if at all in the sections pertaining to the other branches.

Some material, such as that concerning arts and crafts, games, and musical instruments, is so general that it is placed in a separate section under those titles, although with some distinctions as to variations in practice. In doing this I probably run the risk of criticism from those who have special knowledge of the Apache groups, who may correctly say that one custom or another I mention was not practiced by all Apache groups. But a general picture is all I am concerned with, and the lack of total distinctions in the subject matter that I allocate to the chapter on Apache arts, crafts, and games will probably not trouble the book's audience or be of sufficient importance to take issue with. I have tried to select those things that I felt would be of the greatest interest to the Apache and to the general public.

At the time of this writing, no previous single book has been devoted to the renowned Arizona and New Mexico Apache that treats them in written and illustrative detail in a manner that allows for comparisons. Also, with few exceptions—such as the well-done *Warrior Apaches,* by Gordon C. Baldwin—books concerning the individual Apache groups contain remarkably little illustrative material; they are largely devoid of the pictorial details needed to show how the people lived and how they fashioned their instruments, tools, utensils, and ornaments.

When I visited the various museums and laboratories of the West and Southwest in search of Apache artifacts, I was astounded to learn two things: first, that wherever I went—excepting the Arizona State Museum—absolutely no one before me had photographed the Apache artifacts in their collections; and second, that while the Apache population of former days was relatively small, and their material output limited, making questionable how much of it might have survived, there was a surprising wealth of such material collected and available. Accordingly, nearly everything drawn and photographed in these pages will be seen by the reader for the first time, and the Apache life-way should become better known and understood because of this.

In laying out the book, I decided to follow the method employed by Kluckhohn and Hill in *Navaho Material Culture* (Harvard University Press, 1971). Theirs is a splendid material culture study, broken down into numbered sections for easy division and reference.

In compiling the manuscript and the photographs and drawings of the artifacts, I have had the pleasure of extended personal contact with the Apache people of whom I write. Therefore, when I turn to the known authorities for broader information, I find that I am simply confirming what I have already learned through personal experience. The exception, of course, lies with information concerning certain ceremonies and with historic periods that precede my own time and that of my informants. Also, I have not attempted to reconcile the discrepancies between population counts given by authors for various times in history. I have simply cited them as they were set forth.

A few authorities deserve special mention whenever the Apache are considered, since their accumulations of research are the indispensable sources of information to which all others, such as myself, must and do turn, in gratitude. These are the ethnologist Grenville Goodwin, who died in 1940, leaving behind a treasure of information concerning the Western Apache; the anthropologist Morris E. Opler, whose principal published contributions thus far concern the Chiricahua, Mescalero, and Jicarilla; Harry Hoijer, specialist in Apachean languages; and anthropologist Keith H. Basso, whose recent works on the Western Apache I feel are so perceptive as to be of particular significance. (Basso is now engaged in editing for publication the field notes of Grenville Goodwin, thus adding a major contribution to his personal research.) Their contributions will be fully acknowledged. Besides these, I have used the works of John G. Bourke, Captain, Third Cavalry, United States Army, and Albert B. Reagan, a government employee at Fort Apache in 1901 and 1902. Their interpretations of what they saw are frequently in error, but their detailed reports offer rare eyewitness material.

There are many others who have done and are doing important work about and among the Apache, such as Harry T. Getty, Dan L. Thrapp, C. L. Sonnichsen, and Gordon C. Baldwin, but their efforts are of a somewhat different nature from those cited, and far too numerous to include here.

The historic photographs of former times that I have drawn from or adapted came in the main from three sources: the Southwest Museum, Los Angeles, California; the Photo Archives of the Museum of New Mexico, Santa Fe, New Mexico; and the Western History Department, Denver Public Library, Denver, Colorado. These and the artifacts will be individually credited in the captions by letter designations such as "SM" (Southwest Museum). My profoundest thanks are extended to Kathleen Whitaker for the use of her photographs and notes of the Puberty Ceremony taken at San Carlos, in October, 1969.

The photographs of the artifacts are my own. At the time they were taken I did not plan to use them in the book. They were shot in every kind of light, place, and circumstance, and some include more clutter than I would prefer, yet they show the details far better than any drawings I could make. I trust the reader will appreciate their purpose and in this light excuse their shortcomings.

The photographs of present-day reservations are also my own, and the drawings of reservation facilities and living people were begun at the reservations and finished in my studio.

With the exception of a few of my own pieces, the artifacts included in the book are in the collections of the institutions listed below. I express my deepest gratitude to the individuals who treated me so graciously when I examined and photographed these artifacts. Indeed, one of the most heartwarming things one discovers in these pursuits is the endless kindness and cooperation of museum personnel.

The Southwest Museum, Highland Park, Los Angeles,

California: Dr. Carl S. Dentzel, Director; Bruce Bryan, Curator; Kathleen Whitaker, Curatorial Assistant.

The Arizona State Museum, Tucson, Arizona: Dr. Emil W. Haury, Advisor; Wilma Kaemlein, Curator of Collections.

The Heard Museum, Phoenix, Arizona: Patrick T. Houlihan, Director, and Richard Conn, former Director; Randy Morrison.

The Amerind Foundation, Inc., Dragoon Wells, Arizona: Dr. Charles DiPeso, Director; Barbara Powell.

The Museum of Navaho Ceremonial Art, Inc., Santa Fe, New Mexico: Dr. Bertha P. Dutton, Director.

The Museum of New Mexico, Laboratory of Anthropology, Inc., School of American Research, Santa Fe, New Mexico: George Ewing, Associate Director; Nancy Fox; Cordelia Snow.

The Museum of New Mexico, Photo Archives, Santa Fe, New Mexico: Arthur L. Olivas, Curator of Photographic Collections; Dr. Richard Rudisill, Photographic Collections.

My appreciation must also be expressed to certain individuals without whose help this book would not have been possible: to my editor Dennis Fawcett, for his encouragement and patience; to William Eastman, former President of the Trade Book Division at Prentice-Hall, who in learning of my Apache work arranged for its publication; to my friend and agent Clyde Vandeburg, for his constant support; to anthropologist Editha L. Watson, for her enthusiastic contributions; and to J. R. Eyerman, who, as for my previous books, provided me with the excellent color transparencies for the oil paintings included.

My field research methods are hardly comparable to those of the main authorities previously mentioned, and I don't pretend that they are. My preoccupations with my congregation and other pursuits do not allow me the privilege of extended field research, and I have never had an assistance grant to permit prolonged periods of field investigation. Accordingly, I have not deliberately sought out new material, except in the case of the pictorial copy and artifacts, nor have I gone among the Apache people deliberately seeking such information.

Yet I have talked over the years with many Apache, young and old alike. Since I do not speak Apache, many of the conversations with the older people, some of whom were in their seventies and eighties, were carried on with the aid of interpreters, for whose services I am most grateful. Although many of these older people speak and comprehend a surprising amount of English, they still prefer to communicate in Apache, because there are endless concepts for which there are no ready equivalents in English. Even the younger generations prefer to discuss ceremonial things in Apache terms, and will lapse into these as they seek to convey Indian points of view.

The information divulged in such conversations displays a certain amount of personal bias, hence variety—as should be expected, since it is true of all peoples. Nevertheless, over a period of time, basic themes emerge from each group that are held in common. There is always an underlying unity within a seeming diversity.

The elderly people are usually embarrassed about being mentioned by name in regard to information given. There is in this a certain humility that has to be admired. When the idea was broached, one simply smiled, ducked her head, and turned slightly away, as if to say, "Who, me?" Another said, "That's O.K., I don't care about that." Another replied, "How can I do that? I sure don't know everything!" In particular, I found a special reluctance at Mescalero and Jicarilla. Perhaps community pressures and an unwillingness to be named or quoted in something they didn't know the whole of may have been involved.

Nevertheless, there are Apache friends who have been so kind that to not mention them here would be a serious omission. In particular, at Fort Apache Reservation: Edgar Perry, *Jaa Bilataha,* Director of the White Mountain Apache Culture Center, and his lovely wife, Corrine B. Perry; Canyon Z. Quintero, Sr.; and Catherine D. Davenport; at the San Carlos Reservation: Margie Dean, Irma Dean, and George J. Stevens; at Bylas: Burnette Wright; at Mescalero: Bernard Second; at Jicarilla: Herbert Velarde and Sam Elote, Jr.

I am again indebted to my wife for her patience in enduring what an author's wife must as books are brought into being; to my congregation, Christ the Victor Lutheran Church, Pomona, California, for almost the same thing; and to my daughter Allison, who in working on the third Indian book with me has now advanced to the position of a full-fledged research assistant.

Ordinarily, the final stages of a book as large as this are so time-consuming and detailed as to be downright painful, and its completion brings a great sense of relief. It is sent off to the publisher with the attitude that those who like it will feel it is the best there is, and that those who don't will feel that anything else is better. For a while at least after it is mailed you try to tell yourself that you don't really care. In this instance, however, I come to the point of turning it over to the publishers with a feeling of sadness, since I would like to go on with it for a long time to come. I have found the experience of learning about the Apache to be rich beyond belief, and I have come to cherish my friends on the reservations as exceptional people.

In doing a book as comprehensive as this, the writer is forced to choose between what he will include and what he will omit. Time and production costs make this unavoidable. I am aware that certain specialists will wish that I had not omitted one thing or another, or that I had not given so summary—and perhaps, in their view, misleading—a treatment to certain areas. If, however, they are also published, they will sympathize with the problems involved. I have found that those critics who have committed their own work to the public are the most understanding and fair when they consider the efforts of others. In any event, I seek to increase rather than to stem the flow of material about the Apache, and my work is intended as a further stimulant to that end. I trust and hope that whatever is inadequate or missing here will be supplied by someone else at another time, and further, that all who read this book will feel compelled to find and devour the works of Goodwin, Opler, and Basso.

Laguna Niguel, California   Thomas E. Mails
December, 1973

Abbreviations

The following abbreviations are used in the captions:
AF: Amerind Foundation, Inc., Dragoon Wells, Ariz.
ALMN: Museum of New Mexico, Laboratory of Anthropology, Santa Fe, N.M.
ASM: Arizona State Museum, Tucson, Ariz.
BAE: Bureau of American Ethnology
DPL: Denver Public Library, Denver, Col.
HM: Heard Museum, Phoenix, Ariz.
MNCA: Museum of Navaho Ceremonial Art, Inc., Santa Fe, N.M.
MNMP: Museum of New Mexico, Photo Archives, Santa Fe, N.M.
SM: Southwest Museum, Los Angeles, Cal.

Introduction

Of all the Indian nations that inhabit North America, none is better known than the Apache. This is, to me, an astounding fact, for records show that, excluding the Navajo, but counting men, women, and children of the other Apache segments, there were probably never more than ten to twelve thousand Apache living on their early ranges at any one time. Even these were separated as smaller entities in six geographic areas, and the six divisions were further subdivided into virtually independent smaller groups that seldom cooperated in anything, let alone in raids and war. Once settled in their geographic areas, somewhat isolated from one another, these groups adapted to local ecological conditions and developed the linguistic and cultural characteristics that differentiated them in historic times.

Somehow—either from the place where they originated, or by those adjustments made as they migrated, or possibly by experiences undergone as they settled at last into their final ranges—the Apache learned that a most desirable life could be led in localities that combined high and timbered mountains with lush valleys and nearby desert areas. It is believed they came first to the western Great Plains.[1] Sometime later, under pressure from other tribes and perhaps by common agreement among themselves, units whose actual early relationships are not really known formed smaller divisions, which moved apart and searched for geographical areas that provided the desired environment and enough resources so that they could settle down. Each chose, in the end, some of the most spectacular mountain country in North America—for contrary to what is popularly believed, the Apache are mountain people.

As for the desert, it became a resource area for food, and a place one must learn to cross in getting from one mountain range to another. Except in severe winters, the Apache were not by choice on the desert for long at any one time, but since it was essential to be there in growing seasons and for other reasons they learned to exist there incredibly well.

The word perseverence is a key one in coming to know the Apache, since it is a clue to what either always was or later became their basic nature. They learned to survive in every circumstance, and the practicalities of that appear to have become an integral part of the very person and personality of the Apache himself. Scholars who study the people are invariably impressed with their historic tenacity and vitality in the face of adversity. About the only time this weakened was during the darker days of reservation history, when at various times a sense of utter futility forced the Apache into periods of blackest and bleakest despair.

It is important to remember that survival, as it has continuously existed in the mind of the Apache, is understood at the highest level in terms of survival *as an Apache*, and at a secondary level as whatever branch of the Apache people the individual belongs to—Western, Chiricahua, Mescalero, Jicarilla, Lipan, or Kiowa. This identification with a particular Apache group remains in force even when the branches have been mixed because of reservation grouping. For example, when asked what tribe he belongs to, a Chiricahua living at Mescalero today will quickly tell you what he is. I have encountered this response on a number of occasions. In the case where a member of one Apache branch has gone to live with another group, apparently being absorbed in time into the latter, he still displays a few characteristics that set him off from the rest. Even the product of a mixed marriage of Apaches was usually, if not always, viewed with suspicion. Thus the child of such a union was not able fully to become one or the other, a fact that inevitably complicated his life.[2]

The ultimate division of the Apache resulted in, if the Navajo are not counted, what anthropologists have classified as the Western Apache, the Chiricahua Apache, the Mescalero Apache, the Jicarilla Apache, the Lipan Apache, and the Kiowa Apache; six branches in all, each of which was independent of the others and which in time developed certain characteristics that made it different from the rest in some ways. Today the first five are gathered in the main on four reservations, two in Arizona and two in New Mexico. The Western Apache are on the Fort Apache Reservation and the San Carlos Reservation in Arizona. The Jicarilla and the Mescalero, plus some Chiricahua and some Lipan, are in New Mexico, the first on the Jicarilla Reservation, and the latter three on the Mescalero Reservation.

Jicarilla basket maker, 1863 (MNMP).

12

Wherever he is, an Apache is distinctly an Apache, an intensely human and compellingly unique individual. Once thought—and indeed hoped by many—to be on the way to cultural and numerical extinction, his resolute nature is surfacing again today as he moves to gain a solid foothold in the modern world. At the same time he is clinging to, and indeed reinforcing, some aspects of his native culture. His traditional roots and nature, while badly bent and abused in prolonged confrontations with other nations (many of which admittedly were his own fault), were never broken.

The Southern Athapaskans, or Apacheans, are linguistically related to the Athapaskan-speaking peoples of Alaska and Canada. Their time of arrival in the American Southwest is placed by current estimates at between A.D. 1000 and 1500.[3] The exact route they followed and the pace of their migration has not yet been agreed upon by anthropologists. The evidence discovered thus far seems to indicate that the people crossed the Bering Strait and slowly moved south and east. Some anthropologists have speculated that the migration began as much as three thousand years ago, and that hundreds of years were consumed in crossing Alaska and Canada before the people moved to the western Plains and, in the late 1500s, to southwestern North America.[4]

Editha Watson has described the Navajo migration in this beautiful way: "Imagination pictures groups of people, large enough to hold their own against the vicissitudes of an unknown land, following the dim trails laid out by other tribes speaking other languages who had entered the New World before them. No doubt they encountered other peoples here and there, and doubtless added some of them and subtracted some of their own group (or groups) who chose to cast their fortunes in more established areas. They probably traveled as an amoeba moves, expanding and contracting as circumstances dictated. In any case, they kept their language pure enough so that it is still spoken today. What they taught the other tribes they met, and what they learned in exchange, one can only guess."[5]

They called themselves Dine' and Inde', meaning "the people," but others called them Apache; that name, according to John R. Swanton, was probably derived from *apachu*, "enemy," the Zuñi name for the Navajo, who were designated "Apaches de Nabaju" by the early Spaniards in New Mexico. The name has also been applied to some Yuman tribes, the Apache Mohave (Yavapai) and the Apache Yuma.[6]

On linguistic grounds, Harry Hoijer divides the Southern Athapaskans into two main groups: an eastern group, which includes the Jicarilla, Lipan, and Kiowa Apache, with the two former more closely related to each other than either is to the Kiowa Apache; and a western group, with two major subdivisions, the Navajo and the San Carlos-Chiricahua-Mescalero. "The Navajo are always regarded as a distinct tribe."[7]

The term "Apache proper" refers to all those Southern Athapaskan groups other than the Navajo. The Navajo became such an entity during the early years that some once thought they had only a surface relationship with the Apache proper. But subsequent studies have revealed deep and intriguing similarities, and many scholars are increasingly anxious to make detailed and parallel comparisons between the Navajo and other Apache groups.

In 1928, Mooney estimated that the total population of the Apache proper in 1680 numbered 5,000. The census of 1910 listed 6,119 Apache, excluding only the Kiowa Apache, and the 1923 Report of the United States Indian Office showed 6,630 Apache. The census of 1930, including the Jicarilla and Lipan, showed 6,537. The Indian Office Report for 1937 set the population at 6,916, exclusive of the Jicarilla.[8] Other figures for the various groups included in the book will be cited under the individual headings.

In these awesome days in which I write about the Apache, in a time when world events come upon us so swiftly they take our

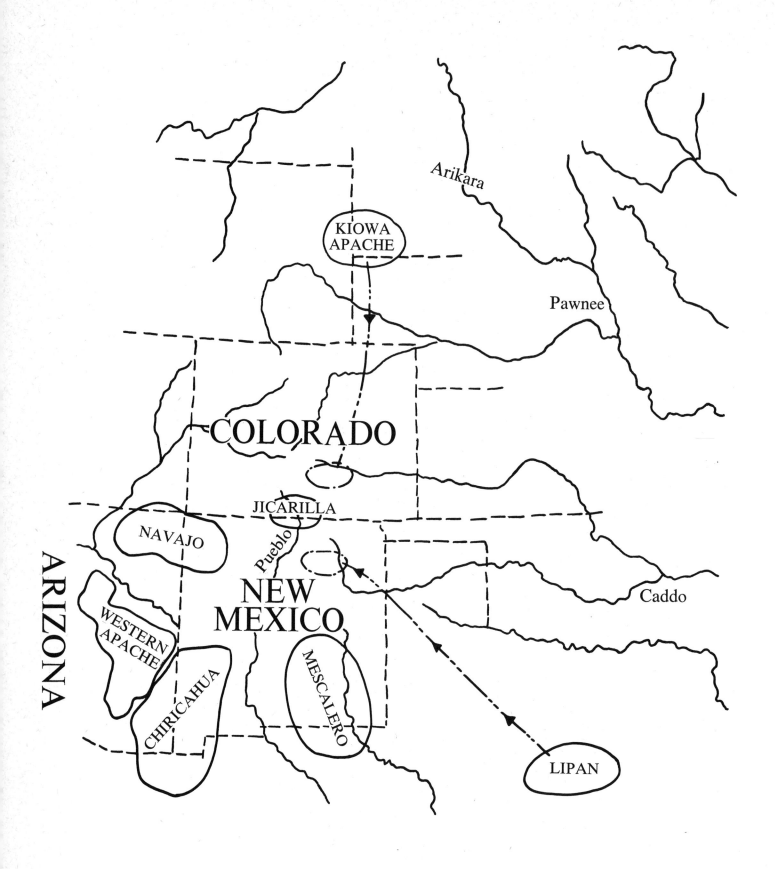

Approximate location of Lipan and Kiowa Apache groups in 1732, with migration traced to areas inhabited in 1800s.

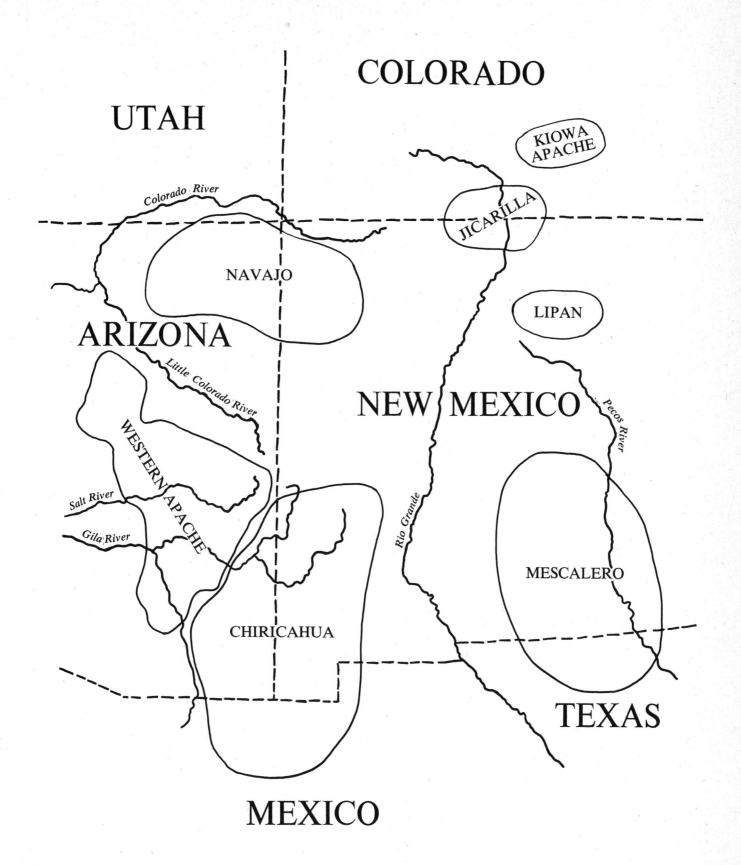

The Apachean groups.

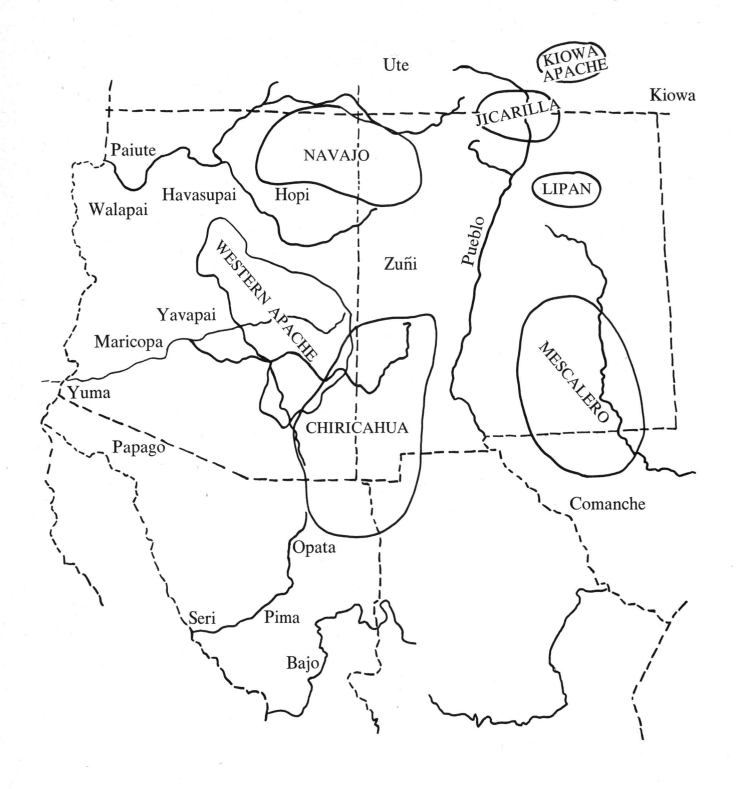

Approximate location of various Indian tribes in relation to the original ranges of the Apachean groups.

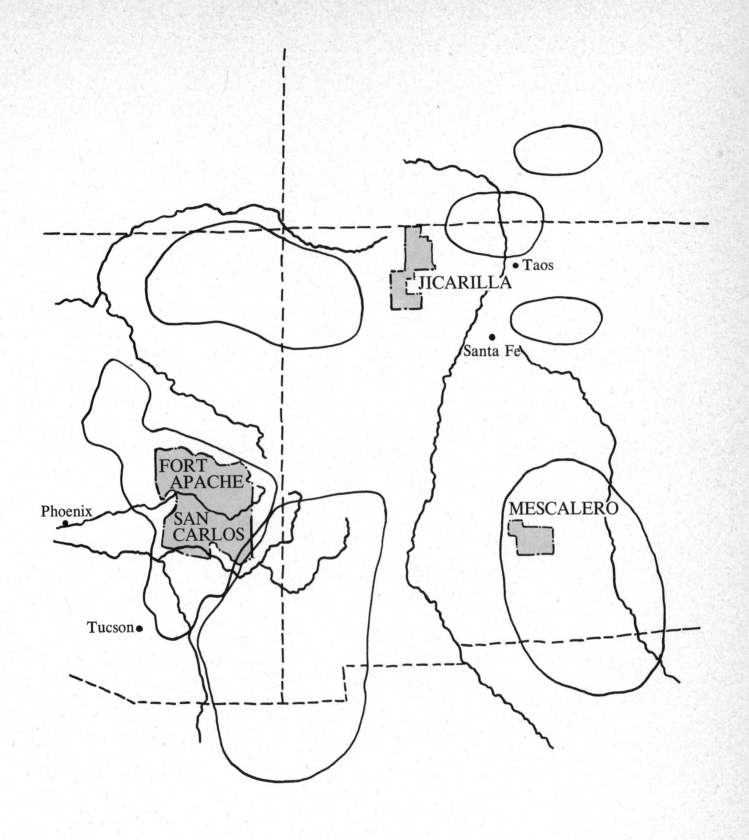

Location of present-day Arizona and New Mexico Apache reservations in relation to original ranges of Apachean groups.

Above: *Mescalero Gan (MNMP).*
Opposite: *White Mountain man in war dress, ca. 1900. Note how breechclout at back wraps around waist.*

breath away and force us to ponder a most questionable future, it might reasonably be asked what value there may be in writing a primarily historical and material-culture study of the Apache.

In my view there are excellent reasons to support it:

First, I am not optimistic about a rapid or equitable solution to the Indian need of adequate compensation for loss of land and near extinction of culture. Nevertheless, I feel that the American conscience must at least view the Apache people as they once were and are now, so as to appreciate why we must continue to render whatever assistance we can muster to the Apache's right to self-sufficiency and self-determination. One cannot know what an Apache is and needs today without knowing what he once was.

Second, since lessons from history are often the best guides to the future, it is my belief that we can find within the Apache lifeways valuable lessons that can be profitably applied to the present and the future. In this unsettling period of history, when most of the earth's peoples may be properly typed as economic beings who are gobbling up the earth's resources at a frantic pace, and as we are at the same time shaken by what such avarice portends, it is probable that we can learn much from all the Indian nations who lived

18

Geronimo holding lance and wearing war cap. From a late photo (SM).

20

in harmony with a Divinely infused nature, revering her, and treating each day as a sacred path to be walked with concern for all created things.

Third, as these things are considered, one comes inevitably to the realization that American Indians were and are, while not devoid of those frailties common to us all, a special people and most worthy of every consideration. Moreover, each nation had special characteristics that gave it its own identity and offered its particular contributions to others. The Apache qualify eminently in this regard, and even though excellent books have been written about them, the Apache people merit being more fully known than they are.

I am often asked how I became interested in Indians. The answer is that I find them unique; they rank among the most interesting peoples in the world. Just to know their life-ways is a growth experience, and every moment of contact is an adventure.

The reader can look for many stimulating things as he encounters the Apache and their life-ways. In particular there are the engrossing mentality and spirit that have enabled the people to survive in the midst of incredible hardships. Their ceremonial practices and their mythology are compelling and filled with important lessons. The ceremonial costumes are splendid and exciting. The Apache war customs have intrigued military students for a century. The history is painful, informative, and rewarding, for it tells us more than we want to know, yet it is precisely that which we must ponder for the valuable lessons it teaches. Finally, it is hoped that the reader will be moved to meet the Apache personally, so that we may all go in closer concert toward the future.

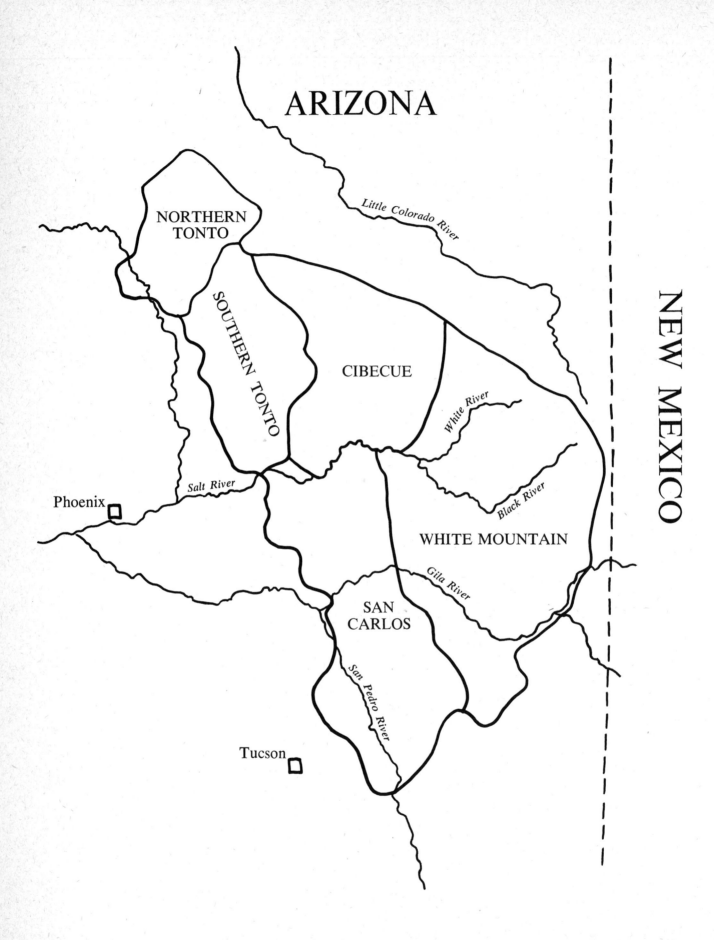

ARIZONA

NEW MEXICO

Little Colorado River

NORTHERN
TONTO

SOUTHERN
TONTO

CIBECUE

White River

Black River

WHITE MOUNTAIN

Salt River

Phoenix

Gila River

SAN
CARLOS

San Pedro River

Tucson

Western Apache subtribal groups.

The Western Apache

Arizona

In the mythological tales of the Western Apache, there is mention of a legendary place in the Little Colorado Valley, north of their historic range, where they claim to have once lived in company with the Navajo and Pueblo peoples. It is an assertion that causes anthropologists and historians to wonder when they moved south to their present locations.[1]

1 History

Writers commonly assign a post-Spanish and relatively late date to the arrival of the Western Apache south of the Mogollon River. The failure of early Spanish expedition documents to mention them is taken as proof that they had not penetrated the area in the A.D. 1540–1604 time period. Goodwin felt, however, that the evidences cited were not conclusive, and he advanced other information to weigh in considering the approximate date of Apache arrival. He noted that the congregation of the Pueblo in a few large pueblos and cliff dwellings may have been a response to the coming-in of the Apache, although he hastened to add that while the Apache attacked these people at times, there were probably long periods of friendly relations. In any event, Goodwin stated it was quite possible that the first of the Western Apache were at the Mogollon Rim by 1400, and he hoped that datable evidence would one day come to light to clarify the question.[2]

There is a theory that the Apache in general probably arrived in the Southwest later than the Navajo, and that they were all congregated as a unit as buffalo hunters on the plains in northeastern New Mexico and western Texas. Under pressure from other tribes, they then pushed southward and westward until the other Apache groups had peeled off and the remaining groups, which became known as the Western Apache, finally settled in the White Mountain area. The only reason for the earlier Navajo arrival theory is that they have absorbed Pueblo culture to a greater degree; and the only justification for insisting that all of the Apache were once on the Plains is that the Coronado expedition of 1540 mentions great numbers of people residing there who probably were "Southern Athapaskans of some sort."[3] Nevertheless, linguistic studies make it clear that the Athapaskan divisions were not as closely related as once thought; the

23

Western Apache, Chiricahua, and Mescalero are more closely related to Navajo than they are to the Jicarilla, Lipan, and Kiowa Apache, and it is not impossible that the Western Apache arrived in the Southwest prior to the Navajo.[4] Also, in considering the Athapaskan movement from north to south, Goodwin feels they may have come down one side of the Rockies, or both.[5]

Morris L. Opler considers the Chiricahua Apache to be the group closest to the Mescalero in language and culture. He emphasizes that the two tribes were normally at peace, had a reasonable amount of contact, and not infrequently offered a haven for each other's members in troubled times.[6] Grenville Goodwin reveals that in prereservation times the Mescalero were known to the Western Apache only "through the intermediate Chiricahua." During the United States Army campaigns against the Chiricahua who had bolted the San Carlos Reservation, Western Apache scouts were sent on several occasions to the Mescalero Reservation in New Mexico, and there saw the Mescalero for the first time.[7]

Goodwin states that the White Mountain and San Carlos subtribal groups had some social contact with the Chiricahua in the prereservation period, and in a general way remained on friendly terms until 1870 or so, when the Western Apache scouts served the Whites against the Chiricahua. Several elements in Western Apache culture are attributed to the Chiricahua, including the making of tulapai, and two important ceremonies for curing venereal diseases. Some intermarriage took place between the two Western Apache subtribal groups and the Chiricahua, resulting in a few members of both groups living in the other's territory. Such marriages resulted from Western Apache group trips to Chiricahua country to exchange gifts and enjoy social relationships. There was no trading, and Goodwin points out that the distinction between gifts and trading was an indication of the "degree of closeness in culture and friendship," for the Apache traded only with people unlike themselves.[8] White Mountain Apache on the way to Mexico to raid were sometimes joined by a few Chiricahua. Nothing is said about joint war parties, presumably because these were the personal duties of clan relatives in avenging the death of a family member.

Taken as a whole, when one considers the overall habits and dress of the Apache, and even allowing for the buffalo hunting expeditions of the Eastern Chiricahua, the parallels seem to have been quite close in early times between the Western Apache and the Chiricahua, and perhaps as close as those between the Chiricahua and the Mescalero.

When the United States government attempted, from 1875 to 1886, to settle the Chiricahua on the Fort Apache and San Carlos reservations, relations between the groups were sometimes friendly, but were also regularly disrupted by the breakouts of the Chiricahua, since these brought inevitable troubles even for those who chose to stay as peacefully as possible on the reservations. In consequence, there were times of bitterness, which varied in intensity according to the overall problems provoked.

Modern contact among the four Apache reservations is infrequent, being limited primarily to occasional social visits between relatives. Political cooperation is nonexistent.

Once the Apache were established in the Southwest, their life-way became a busy one. While the Navajo spoke a language intelligible to any of the Western Apache, relations between the two groups were tenuous, being intermittently friendly or hostile. During peaceful times each side made trading expeditions into the other's country; at other times raiding and war parties invaded the territories of both sides.

The Apache journeyed on occasion to Hopi country to trade. Apache raids were occasionally made against the Hopi, but on the whole relations between the two peoples appear to have been friendly. While it is likely that the Apache attacked the Zuñi at times, relations between them were also largely friendly, and a considerable amount

Western Apache warrior wearing war cap adorned with turkey and eagle feathers.

of trade took place. No intermarriage occurred between the Apache and the Hopi or Zuñi. In their earliest history, there may have been slight contact between the Western Apache and the Rio Grande Pueblo.[9]

Moving southward, the generally friendly Chiricahua were the nearest neighbors of the Western Apache, but beyond them in Northern Mexico were the Opata, considered hostile to the White Mountain, Cibecue, and San Carlos Apache subtribes because they conducted regular raids into Mexico against them.

25

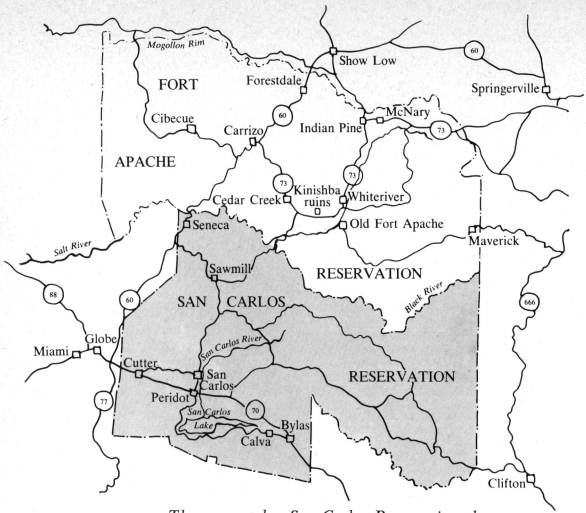

The present-day San Carlos Reservation shown in relation to the Fort Apache Reservation.

The present-day Fort Apache Reservation.

Mexico was far and away the favored raiding territory for the White Mountain subtribal group, and the Cibecue and San Carlos subtribal groups divided their attentions between it and their Indian enemies to the west. The main route to Mexico was through the Arivaipa and San Pedro valleys. Once in Mexico, the parties fanned out in whatever direction they wished, to raid the towns and ranches in the huge territory of Sonora. In time they came to know it as well as their own land, and an Apache raiding party might be operative there for as long as eighty days. Such raids continued for almost two hundred years, beginning about 1690 and lasting until about 1870. The raids are not surprising, for Mexico proved to be a veritable cornucopia of needed supplies.[10]

Also south of the Western Apache were the Apache Mansos of the Tucson area, persistent enemies because they joined the Americans, Mexicans, and Papago in campaigns against the White Mountain and San Carlos subtribal groups. Southwest were the Papago, with whom a state of war always existed, the two sides continually launching raids and war parties against one another.

Westward were other enemies, the Pima and the Maricopa, with whom the Apache battled at every opportunity.

There were other enemies: the Havasupai to the northwest, and the Walapai to the west. These exchanged raids with the Western Apache also.

The Yavapai lived close to the Apache, and were on friendly terms with them. They joined a few of the Apache bands in raids, traded with the Apache, and even intermarried with all but the White Mountain subtribal group.[11]

Below left: *Tonto warrior with painted hide quiver.* Below: *Tonto warrior wearing war cap. Photos by A. T. Willcox (DPL).*

An Apache camp in Cañon de los Embudos, Arizona, 1886 (DPL).

No one seeks to explain the constant animosity between the Apache and their neighbors, and no one can justify its worst aspects, I'm sure. It is not clear who began the hostilities in most instances. Perhaps the Apache displaced some of the tribes as they pushed into the Southwest, or else caused enough shuffling of territories to spur anxiety and increase pressure. The Apache habit had always been to raid; it was part of their economic complex, and that factor assuredly played its inevitable role in the maintenance of a hostile state of affairs.

Goodwin does point out that the Apache raids into Mexico were considered lawful and just, for "did not any people with enemies have the right to raid and kill them?"[12] It may be that there is a key in his statement which sheds some light on the advantages of a hostile state. While with a friend one could only exchange gifts, an enemy became an economic source of some magnitude; enemies were desirable. Thus an Apache boy waited anxiously for the day when he would be old enough to join the warrior force, and a retired warrior spent his evenings in fond remembrances, telling stories about his war and raiding days.

In the 1850s, Mexico's control of her northern frontier had been weakened, while American strength was increasing. It was a perilous time for Mexicans, and the northern presidios in particular were not able to protect the citizens against the marauding Apache, who moved quickly and repeatedly to take advantage of the situation. They struck deep into eastern and northern Sonora gathering food, livestock, and other commodities. They stole or captured horses, mules, burros, cattle, clothing, blankets, cowhide for moccasin soles and other purposes, saddles, bridles, leather, some guns, and metal that could be cut up for arrow points. The cattle were usually killed and eaten in Mexico, since the mobile Apache life-style was not conducive to stock raising. Things were so good for the Indians that there was no incentive to gain territory, to destroy property, or to exterminate the Mexicans, although Lockwood claims that almost four hundred Mexican citizens were killed over the three-year period 1851–1853.[13] The Mexicans were viewed as ongoing economic resources, and enough of a remnant was always left behind to enable the Mexicans to recover and go on producing items that could be appropriated by the Apache later on.

Concern about the Apache pattern of raiding did cause the Commissioner of Indian Affairs to approve, in 1860, a fifteen-mile-square strip of land along the Gila River to serve as a reservation for the Apache. But it was a token gesture, and the Apache who did use

28

it returned to their usual ways with the outbreak of the Civil War.[14]

For a time, the United States forces were also kept busy with the Mescalero, Jicarilla, and Chiricahua, leaving all but a few of the Western bands unmolested and free to continue their Mexican raids. However, the discovery of gold in Tonto territory in 1863 changed all that. Hostilities thereafter were inevitable, and soldiers and citizens alike began to attack the Apache indiscriminately.

On one infamous occasion, a group of Apache was fed poisoned food while participating in what they believed to be a peace conference. Not surprisingly, the Apache responded in kind, and to such a degree that for a time it seemed likely the Whites would be driven out of central Arizona.[15] Arizona was made a United States territory in 1863, and in 1864, Camp Goodwin was established on the Gila River in White Mountain country. Until then the large White Mountain subtribal group had remained comparatively undisturbed by the United States Army, although they were certainly aware of what was going on. In testimony to this their chief, Diablo, hastily accepted the offers of peace put forward by the officers at Camp Goodwin. Thereafter, open conflict with the military was avoided, but the raids into Mexico continued. The treaty itself led to further consequences: first to the unresisted establishment of Fort Ord on the White River in 1868; and second to the willingness of White Mountain and Cibecue warriors to serve as scouts for General George Crook in his later campaigns against the Tonto and the Chiricahua.

By 1870, it was becoming increasingly clear that military means to subdue and control the Apache were lacking. More forts were built, but army manpower was in short supply, and in addition there was no decisive or consistent government plan for dealing with the Apache problem.

In 1871, the Legislature of the Territory of Arizona published a "Memorial and Affidavits showing Outrages Perpetrated by the Apache Indians in The Territory of Arizona during the years 1869 and 1870." It is, in all, a scathing indictment both of the Apache and of the failure of the military forces to protect Arizona's citizens. "A savage war still exists herein, causing the murder of hundreds of our citizens and the loss of a vast amount of property; and that at no period since the settlement of the Territory has the loss of life and property been greater than during the year 1870. . . . Our people have made their homes here, and have no other, but unless protection is given to them, the constant decimation that is made will soon sweep from the country all traces of civilization, except for deserted fields and broken walls."[16] One can easily appreciate such

Western Apache or Chiricahua group, ca. 1880. Photo by Kenneth Chapman (MNMP).

feelings, yet strangely no such views were put forth for the Apache. They had their territory taken from them, they had no other homes to go to, and they might well have questioned the definition of "civilization." It is also true that the Apache, guilty or not, were blamed for every crime perpetrated in Arizona.

Spurred on by such memorials as that just mentioned, in 1871 a body of about 150 enraged citizens from Tucson, with the help of a group of Papago, slaughtered a large group of defenseless Western Apache women and children at Camp Grant, in what became known as the Camp Grant Massacre. Estimates of the actual number of Apache killed have varied, but 120 seems to be an average figure. Besides this, 27 Apache children were taken by the Papago and sold into slavery in Mexico.[17] The public reaction to this outrage caused the federal government to inaugurate a new "Peace Policy" in Arizona, the intent of which was to terminate the indecision in army control of the Apache and to put an end to the White vigilantes and the corruption of civilian agents and contractors.

Western Apache canvas-covered wickiup, 1880 (DPL).

Apache Indian Wickiup, Arizona, 1880.

The Peace Policy called for the placing of all Apache on reservations as a first step toward promoting peace and what the Whites viewed as "civilization" among them. Four areas were set aside for this: one at Fort Apache to house the Cibecue subtribal group and the northern bands of the White Mountain subtribal group; one at Camp Verde in central Arizona to be the home of Northern and Southern Tonto and the Yavapai; one at Camp Grant to provide for the San Carlos subtribal group and the southern White Mountain bands; and one at Ojo Caliente in western New Mexico to house the Warm Springs band of the Chiricahua.[18]

As the ingathering got under way, General Crook was placed in command of the United States forces in Arizona. And while he would ultimately be the man to defeat the Apache who resisted, he nevertheless was among the first to treat them with perception and sympathy. He also had understandable doubts that the reservation policy could bring peace, for while many Apache had come in, a large number were afraid and stayed away.[19] Subsequent developments confirmed his fears, for persistent troubles caused the abandonment of Camp Grant and the establishment of a new headquarters at San Carlos.

Raids continued to occur, and there were ominous omens that the Apache on the reservations would soon bolt and join the others. Crook's answer to this was a campaign to round up all the off-reservation Apache. In the winter of 1872, he began a series of powerful sweeps against the Tonto—whom he would later describe as "in all respects as brutally savage" as the Chiricahua were in 1883—and in a short time dealt them a smashing defeat.[20] Several hundred Tonto were killed, and the rest were captured and placed on reservations. Peace came to Arizona, and General Crook became a hero, although both situations were to last only a brief time, for the federal government soon had another of its characteristic changes of mind.

In 1874, the Department of the Interior came up with a new idea for dealing with the Apache, called a "program of removal." The department would place all of the Western Apache, the Chiricahua, and the Yavapai on a single reservation at San Carlos, consisting of 7,200 square miles and known as the White Mountain Reservation. This would make them easier to administer and protect, and it would reduce the awesome threat they posed to the White settlements of Arizona. It was an idea that would have disastrous consequences for Apache and Whites alike. Some historians say the consequences were unforeseen, but if so, it was because the vast majority of Whites were still not taking the time to understand the Apache divisions and cultural variations.

In February, 1875, more than 1,400 Tonto Apache and Yavapai were moved to San Carlos. A few months later a large group of White Mountain and Cibecue Apache joined them. In 1876, 325 Chiricahua Apache were settled on the reservation, and in 1877, approximately 400 more Chiricahua were brought to San Carlos from the Warm Springs area in New Mexico. By this time, the total number of Apache and Yavapai crowded onto the reservation had reached 5,000.[21]

As indicated earlier, there were inescapable problems. So many centuries had passed since the Apache tribes and subtribal groups had been closely associated that they were virtual strangers now. There was unavoidable distrust and suspicion. They neither knew how to nor cared to cooperate. Disputes arose over how to react to White control, and opinions about this varied even within the single groups themselves. Some found the spartan living conditions at desolate San Carlos unbearable and planned their escape. Others were tired of fighting and wanted peace. Some were certain that peace alone would permit the Apache to survive; others believed that the reservation was a not too subtle device for bringing about the extinction of the Apache peoples. The Whites aggravated the situation by their continued internal struggles for control of reservation policies and by the corruption of White merchants. It was a totally unstable situation, and eventually it exploded.

Some of the Chiricahua began to break out and to kill and raid as in prereservation days, and in no time at all the entire Southwest was again in a state of panic. In 1881, a number of soldiers were killed at Cibecue while attempting to arrest an Apache medicine man named Noch-ay-del-Klinne. This Apache had been an enlisted scout in Crook's 1872–1873 campaign. He had gone to Washington with a group to visit President Grant, gained some stature, and was now stirring up the Apache throughout the area with a prediction that all the Apache dead would return to life and drive the Whites out of their country. During 1881 his influence led to numerous gatherings and an increasing surliness that spread among the Whites the fear of an Apache uprising.

Above: *Western Apache camp scene, 1880. In the background are wickiups and a ramada, or "squaw-cooler," used for outdoor dining and work.*
Opposite top: *Chiricahua Apache prisoners at Fort Bowie, ca. 1886.*
Opposite bottom: *Ration day at San Carlos.*

The military forces were ordered to capture or kill the troublesome medicine man, and a delegation was sent to Cibecue to carry out the order. As soon as they seized him, the troops themselves were attacked. In the battle, seven soldiers were killed; so were Noch-ay-del-Klinne and several Apache. The troops returned to Fort Apache, and were under siege for several days. When quiet finally prevailed, conferences between the military and the Apache revealed that causes ran deeper than the medicine man's prophecies. Inept agents and crooked traders, unnecessary punishment of the Apache, and the encroachments of Whites on Indian land were also involved, and Crook acted late in 1882 to correct these situations.

More Chiricahua fled from San Carlos, and soon it seemed that the program of removal had backfired completely. Alternately thereafter there were periods of peace and turmoil, the records of which are found in Chiracahua history. The worst of the hostilities ended with Geronimo's surrender in 1886, and the shipping off in boxcars to Florida of the remaining Chiricahua. There were a few small breakouts and disturbances after that at San Carlos, but by 1890, the armed conflict between the Apache and the Whites was over, and a tenuous new day began to dawn.[22]

As might be expected, the Western Apache suffered less during the early reservation period than did the Chiricahua. Since with a few exceptions they chose not to resist, relatively few of their people were killed, and most of them were able to remain in their own territory. The Tonto were required to make the greatest changes in location, yet even they recovered and managed to survive. The Cibecue and White Mountain Apache desired peace, and adjusted as well as could be expected to reservation life. Beyond this, it was these sub-tribal groups who furnished General Crook with most of the scouts he needed to bring about the final defeat of the Chiricahua. Both Crook and Grenville Goodwin believed that the Western Apache played a major role in the settling of a wide area of Arizona through their assistance to the United States military forces.[23]

Packing up rations at San Carlos (MNMP).

However, General Crook went on to give special credit to the Chiricahua, pointing out that although Mangus and Geronimo broke out in May, 1885, and one-third of the Chiricahua fighting strength left the reservation with them, over 80 men and 350 women and children stayed peacefully behind on their reservation. Of those Chiricahua remaining, General Crook was able to select what he asserted were 50 "faithful" scouts, and "he could have" selected more, except that he wished the rest of the men to remain to protect the women and children. In this instance the Chiricahua warriors, rather than those belonging to other bands of Apache, were picked as scouts, because they were familiar with the Mexican country in which they would be required to operate. Crook also felt they were superior to any other Indians as soldiers, and fully up to the standard of the renegades.[24] "The Chiricahua Apache, both by nature and education, is beyond cavil, better qualified than anyone else for the warfare which for years past has been carried on in the mountains of Arizona and Mexico. . . . Without the use of the scouts, the surrender of the Chiricahua in 1883 would have been impossible. Without them, the surrender of the whole body of hostiles in March, 1886, could not have taken place."[25]

The enlistment of Apache scouts was authorized by Congress and President Johnson in 1866. They were enlisted for short periods —three months, six months, or a year—and many of them served a number of times. As a precaution, the law stipulated that not more than one thousand scouts could serve at one time. In addition to army pay, the scouts received forty cents a day in return for the use of their own horses. Most wore no uniforms, dressing like all other Apache geared for war.[26] Cloth headbands or stetson hats were used to hold their hair back from their eyes; they wore calico shirts, loose-fitting white cotton trousers, cloth breechclouts, and moccasins or army boots and socks. The White man's vest was also a popular item. They carried army canteens, and awls to repair clothing and equipment. The army equipped them with rifles, some pistols, ammunition, and cartridge belts. To this the Apache scout often added a knife and fire-making equipment. He usually carried his own food.

In 1868, Major John Green, commander of the First Cavalry troops, located Fort Ord at a strategic point midway between Camp McDowell and the Navajo reservation, for at the time the Navajo were the major source of trouble for the United States Government.[27] It is said that the discovery of friendly Coyotero Apache in the area motivated the selection of the site. On January 31, 1870, the War Department declared that their White Mountain homeland would become the reservation for all Apache in Arizona and New Mexico.

The friendliness of the Western Apache made it unnecessary to build an army stockade, and Fort Ord became known as Camp Apache, later to be designated as Fort Apache in 1879.[28] The fort was laid out in garrison fashion without walls. As the scouts enlisted they moved with their families to an encampment near the post, and the fort was soon surrounded by wickiups and by traders and other civilians who came to deal with the army and the Indians. General Crook's headquarters were located at the fort.

Fort Apache was finally abandoned by the military in 1922, and in 1923 it was turned over to the Department of the Interior and converted to the Theodore Roosevelt Indian School. Today the former officers' quarters house the teachers and staff, and students from nine Indian tribes use the sweeping parade grounds for their activities.

Fire destroyed several of the original buildings, and others simply collapsed from age and lack of maintenance. The cavalry barracks, which once stood where the present school building is, were removed. The remains of the infantry buildings can still be seen, but they are in such a dangerous state that the area has been fenced off. The old guardhouse and the commissary buildings serve as warehouses, and two of the three original horse barns and the packers' stables are pressed into service from time to time.

But many of the Fort Apache buildings have been maintained and are in use today. Whenever they are renovated an attempt is made to maintain the original style. The White Mountain tribe's intent is to preserve the fort as a historical landmark.

The large and intriguing log cabin that is said to have served as General Crook's headquarters has become the Apache Culture Center, whose competent and genial director is Edgar Perry. He is ably assisted by his wife, Corrine B. Perry, by Canyon Z. Quintero, Sr., and by Catherine D. Davenport. This is the first attempt of the Fort Apache Reservation people to preserve their heritage, but it is a far-reaching one, and is assuredly an expression of their deep interest in doing so. It is more than a museum by far, for it is a point of assemblage for artifacts, photographs, and accounts of early life. Contacts are being established with the older Apache people and with medicine men, and whenever possible tapes are made to preserve the ancient legends, chants, and rituals before they are lost forever. In the years ahead, some of these will be translated into English. A valuable Apache-English dictionary has also been undertaken, and the handsome and informative first volume was published by the White Mountain Apache tribe in 1972.

While Apache families are involved in all the gainful occupations and activities common to Americans today, a return to the traditional Apache crafts is also being encouraged. The wish is to maintain contact with the past, and to provide the people with additional revenue. An Arts, Crafts, and Bead Association has been organized. Excellent beadwork is being done and sets of puberty dolls are being made; the Association hopes to revive basketweaving and to do work in leather crafts, silversmithing, painting, and carving.

A visit to the sprawling, handsome old Fort Apache evokes a wistful nostalgia. To walk among its gaunt stone structures, the durable witnesses to another period, is to move both back into an awesome time and forward into a splendid future.

A short distance past Fort Apache lies its tiny military cemetery, where on the crown of a small hill Apache scouts, White

soldiers, and civilians lie buried side by side, with white stones and weathered wooden markers placed at the heads of the graves to recall their memorable names. There are Colonel Corydon Eliphalet Cooley, Chow Big, Cody, Dekley, Chissay, Eskehnadestah, and many others, some unknown. The wind blows softly, the junipers bend low over the graves, and over and among the plots are white and blue flowers, yucca, prickly pear, and golden mountain grass. It is a quiet place where everyone who would like to think on things past ought to go, in the late spring or early fall, and spend an hour or two.

In 1897, the White Mountain Reservation was divided into the Fort Apache and San Carlos reservations, each with separate administrative agencies. Present-day Apache living on the San Carlos Reservation are descendants of the San Carlos, White Mountain, Cibecue, Coyotero, Mimbres, Chiricahua, Pinal, Apache Peaks, Arivaipa, Tonto, Mogollon, and Chilecon bands.

At the Fort Apache Reservation, the Apache still retain their old territorial segments. But the placing of other Western Apache groups and bands on the San Carlos Reservation turned it into a melting-pot. Group and band distinctions became blurred, although the White Mountain, San Carlos, and Southern Tonto groups continued to make distinctions among themselves.[29]

Reconstructing a complete history of the Western Apache from 1870 to 1930 is not an easy task. The reports of government officials offer far less than one needs; the Apache themselves kept no written records; most visitors to the reservations came away with superficial accounts.

A *Century Magazine* article published in 1887, which contains some errors and poor word choices—such as labeling the Yuma and Mojave as Apache, and calling the Apache "savages"—nevertheless gives a surface account of how Western Apache life appeared to Whites in 1871–1881. Further on, the meanings of some of the things witnessed will be explained. At the San Carlos Agency the Apache were seen to be "slowly acquiring the arts of peace and will soon be a useful part of the agricultural population of that region." The Indians were "partly civilized, partly barbaric," with

Opposite top: *The nighttime curing ceremony, an important aspect of the life-way.* Opposite bottom: *Man clearing rocky ground at San Carlos for planting, ca. 1900.* Above: *Girls, ca. 1890. Girl at left wears beaded choker necklace; girl at right wears beaded earrings and hair bow.*

"the barbaric element still predominating." The Government had "cultivated their martial feelings, and at the same time turned them (as scouts) to its own account." The author goes on to say that this feat had "thereby lifted [the Indians] a little in their ideas of sovereignty and self-government." And then the author explains the value of this by pointing out that the scouts were being encouraged to spy on even their own families, "acting in the interest of the Government."

Apache accused of crimes were being tried before a jury of Indians, with possible verdicts of three-year sentences at Alcatraz Prison in California, or even death. A guardhouse accommodated the lesser criminals, and "through one of its windows peered the face of an Indian sentenced for life."

The *Century Magazine* writer observed that "superstitions are shown in their dress and ornaments, or rather in the charms which adorn and compose these." He was not, apparently, concerned enough to seek the meaning of these items, or even to ask why they were still being worn by a subject people.

The medicine jacket and belt are common to the whole Apache family, and are about the counterpart of similar dresses so common with savages. From the head of the Chiricahua hangs a single buckskin string about two inches wide and as many feet in length, its upper end braided in the hair. This is ornamented with all the different pieces of shells they can obtain, and for

Above: *San Carlos warriors. Man at right wears a beaded, concho-decorated buckskin war shirt and a war amulet strap in his hair.* Right: *Nalte and Gud-i-zz-ah, San Carlos warriors. Man at left wears medicine cord, for war protection, over right shoulder and diagonally across chest. Photos by Wittick (DPL).*

Mounted woman and child with burden basket hung from saddle.

which they seem to have a reverence, while beads and ornaments of silver and other metals help to cover it with an almost silver coating of decorations.

Maidens may be distinguished from matrons by the peculiar arrangement of their hair, the former wearing what in their language is called a *nah-leen* (*nah-leen* strictly interpreted is maiden). It is flat and of a beaver-tail dumb-bell shape, covered with red, and closely studded with gilt buttons, if procurable, the hair being tied up with this to prevent its flowing over the shoulders as with married squaws. In general, it may be said that the eastern tribes, Sierras Blancas and Chiricahuas, are far finer in dress than those of the western parts, the Yumas and Mojaves, the intermediate tribes of San Carlos and Tontos also being intermediate in dress. Still farther to the east in New Mexico are the Mezcalero and Coyotero Apaches, also very ornamental in dress, but in other respects beyond the ken of this article in their now quiet isolation.

The war-dress of these warm-weather warriors, when actually in a campaign, is not so resplendent in buckskin and beads, nor is it so warm. A gorgeous bonnet of three hawk feathers is about the only display, and the rest has a sort of simplicity known only in the Garden of Eden. An old weapon with them was a heavy round stone at the end of a short stick, the two being wrapped and joined in a common case of rawhide taken from the tail of a horse or ox so as to be continuous and seamless. This was used like a policeman's club, and has its counterpart in the Sioux "skull-smasher," a word which describes it at once. The wild Chiricahuas used the lance, and do some good work with it in a decisive fight. Even the armed warriors use it in killing cattle and stolen stock to save their ammunition thereby, while some of the most horrible tortures practiced on their captives by these fiends are inflicted by this instrument. With the introduction of fire-arms into their warfare fell the shield into disuse. It was a gaudy appendage of the primitive savage, but it exists among the Apaches only as a relic for which they can obtain so much money from the curiosity seeker. They care but little for money, however, except to appease a craving for gambling, or to meet immediate wants.

Top: *Awl case decorated with beads and tin cones.* Above: *Detail, showing draw string.* Opposite: *Woman carrying burden basket by use of head strap.*

They are behind no other savages in their love for the allurements of gambling, and use all sorts of implements, from the most intricate games of cards to the simple throwing of sticks and hoops, and in nearly all of these games their play is one of hazard, in the excitement their horses, rifles, and even the shirts of their backs, changing ownership.

Only in their dances do they excel the physical energy put forth in their gambling plays. From sunset till sunrise can be heard the beating of their drums and tom-toms, and night after night it is kept up. Old squaws and young children dance until they can stand no longer, and cease from exhaustion and fatigue; a cessation of but a few minutes and they are up and at it again. Their medicine dances take place in cases of sickness and distress, to drive away bad spirits or keep them from doing harm. In these the squaws are never allowed to take a part, but in peace, weddings, and feast dances, young and old of both sexes form a conspicuous part. The "corn dance," to make that plant productive, is also a monopoly of the medicine-men, while besides all these there exists the war, the conqueror's and the chiefs' dances, varying in type through all the possible motions and gesticulations of the human body.

The ages which some of them reach appear surprising, considering their rough mode of life in the past, which seems sufficient to end it rapidly when the physical powers begin to fail. Got-ha, a Sierra Blanca, a once famous warrior of their tribe, is probably eighty or ninety years of age, and seems hale and hearty yet. Could this old sage of the sandy deserts concentrate the salient points of his life into a volume, it would rival the tales of Daniel Boone or Kit Carson.

Age, however, finds only a place in their councils of peace, and young blood rules in times of war, unless some mighty chief, with a record of battles that none can gainsay, bears all before him even in his age. It is a keen appreciation of the eternal fitness of things that has helped them in no small way to hold for so long the mastery of the South-west in peace and war. . . .

Railroads run their double bands of iron through their deserts, mines pour their ores from the sheltering sides of their mountain homes, an inexorable decree has cramped them to a corner of their country, where they now wrest a living from the soil they once trod as master, and it may well be said that the Apache sun is near the horizon of their national destiny.[30]

It is certain today that the *Century Magazine* article writer was premature in consigning the Apache to oblivion. He, too, failed to appreciate the survival attributes of the southwestern nations. A decade later, Dr. George A. Dorsey, Curator of Anthropology for the Field Columbian Museum in Chicago, visited the Southwest on several occasions. At the request of the Passenger Department of the Atchison, Topeka and Santa Fe Railway System, he wrote a small book, entitled *Indians of the Southwest,* which included a description of the Western Apache country and the people as they lived in 1903. Dorsey intersperses his comments on living conditions in the early 1900s with descriptions of former customs, and the account, long out of print, provides us with engrossing insights:

The White Mountain Apache Reservation, lying in east central Arizona, is reached by a daily stage from Holbrook to Fort Apache, a distance of ninety-six miles. The trip is made without stop except for change of horses at stage stations, where meals can be procured. Leaving Holbrook about three o'clock in the afternoon, Fort Apache is reached at eight the next morning, the fare for the round trip being fifteen dollars. A far pleasanter journey can be made by private conveyance from the livery stable at Holbrook. A carriage seating four persons and driver costs $5 a day. Meals and lodging en route about $2 a day. Leaving early in the afternoon, Snowflake, on Silver Creek, thirty miles distant, is reached in time for supper at a good hotel. This little Mormon settlement is regularly laid out, with running water through the streets. The houses are built of brick, and the village presents an air of thrift.

41

From the top: *Rawhide saddlebag,
detail (MNMP), fringe detail (MNMP),
and painted buckskin medicine bag,
front and back views (HM).*

Resuming the journey after breakfast, Taylor and Shumway, two small but prosperous Mormon hamlets, four and eight miles distant, are passed. Between Shumway and Showlow, twenty miles from Snowflake, one first encounters that vast region of igneous rock extending from the San Francisco Mountains to Mount Taylor on the southwest. Lava beds three thousand feet in thickness are found in the vicinity of Thomas Peak just off the reservation. Greens Peak, in the extreme northeast corner of the reservation, is the center of an extended basalt area. At Showlow Mr. Adams feeds the hungry man in good western style.

Beyond Showlow, pines appear and beneath their shade one rides to the summit of the divide near Pinetop, a distance of fourteen miles. Below this hamlet, amid the pines, in a beautiful park-like valley, 7,650 feet above the level of the sea, lives genial Colonel Cooley, famous as a guide and scout in Apache warfare. The evening is pleasantly spent in listening to tales of a life of twenty-five years among the Apache.

A drive next morning of twenty miles, through a portion of Black Canyon and along the west bank of the North Fork, brings you to Whiteriver Agency. Here excellent accommodations may be obtained at the home of the Government agent. From the agency a short drive of four miles brings you to Fort Apache, a picturesque military post on the south bank of White River, where several hundred soldiers are stationed.

The White Mountain Apache Reservation is ninety-five miles long from north to south and seventy miles wide from east to west. It contains 2,528,000 acres. The northern portion is drained by the Salt River, with several tributaries emptying into the Gila River. These are fed by the melting snows from the upper mountain ranges. Along their banks are small areas producing abundantly when irrigated. Within the reservation have been gathered at various times the Coyotero, Pinal, Aravaipa, Chiricahua, and other western bands, along with the White Mountain Apache. At an elevation varying from three to eleven thousand feet, we find cactus, yucca, agave, greasewood, sage brush, cedars, pines and firs, and a plant life varying from the semi-tropical to the sub-Alpine. Bear, deer and wild turkey are abundant upon the mountain slopes. The tributaries of the North Fork teem with trout. Along the streams, in groups, are the "campos" of the various bands, each with its petty chief, and designated, for the convenience of the Indian agent, by a letter of the alphabet. There are about 1,850 Apache at Whiteriver Agency, and 2,900 at the San Carlos Agency.

The various bands have intermarried to some extent. A few white men and Mexicans have married Apache women.

Basket-making is the principal industry among the women, two kinds being produced: the bowl-like basket tsa, and the tus, "sewed water jugs." The coils of these baskets are made of either cottonwood or willow. The wrapping of the coils is always cottonwood. Excellently woven burden-baskets are also made. These are ornamented in colored zones, their bases being protected by buckskin, with four strips of the same material extending from the bottom to the rim. They also make water vessels of bottle form. The bush of the squaw-berry is invariably used for this purpose. Some makers of these vessels fill the interstices with the crushed berries of the cedar before coating them with piñon gum. The black designs in the sewed basketry are made from the pod of a species of Martynia. Occasionally very rude baskets are woven of green yucca, the designs in them being made of roots of the Spanish bayonet.

Their houses or "campos" are of a low, oval form, of height sufficient to allow one to stand erect in the center. They are made of poles thrust into the ground and drawn together at the top. With these, twigs and grasses are interlaced and very frequently huge pieces of canvas are stretched over them. Houses of the rectangular form, not unlike those occasionally found among the Navajo, are sometimes seen. These dwellings are usually located along the streams in the vicinity of fields. During the winter season many withdraw to the timber, where houses are constructed from heavier materials. Water in such localities

Top: *Apache group and trader at Old
Fort Apache, ca. 1885. Photo by
Wittick (MNMP).* Above: *Crossing the
Gila River at San Carlos after a heavy
rain, ca. 1890 (MNMP).*

Opposite: *Gen. George Crook and his favorite riding mule.* Right: *Bonito, Apache scout (MNMP).* Bottom: *Mounted White Mountain man, showing horsemanship abilities while aiming gun.*

45

Opposite top: *An Apache to catch an Apache.* Opposite bottom: *White Mountain men crossing the White River, ca. 1890.* Right: *Alchesay, White Mountain chief and scout, with binoculars (MNMP).*

is procurable only from melting snows during the winter season. Where lumber can be had, rude houses or sheds are now being made by the Indians.

Beneath the sloping edges of the "campos" are placed the various house furnishings. In the center is a fireplace, hollowed out of the ground, the smoke escaping through an aperture in the roof. The household utensils are few in number. Saddle bags made of rawhide, of rectangular form and fringed at the ends, usually contain the most valuable and less-used personal effects. These saddle bags are used for storage purposes at home or for pack purposes on the march. Blankets and skins, rolled up when not in use, furnish bedding for the household. At meal time the Apache sit about the vessels containing their food, helping themselves at will. When not thus engaged, they lounge about the "campos." Huge gourds, often provided with a neck of basketry, are sometimes used for the storage of water about the house. Occasionally, decorated gourd dippers are found. These are highly prized and are difficult to obtain. Small circular mortars of malapais are used in preparing paints. Upper and lower mealing stones of the same material are used in grinding coffee, crushing berries and roots for food purposes. The fire drill is occasionally used. The lower stick is made from the stock of the Spanish bayonet, the upper one of greasewood.

The style of moccasins and the women's ceremonial costume that Dorsey describes are the same as those used for centuries:

The moccasins have a hard sole, curving upward above the toe for protection against thorns and cacti. The better moccasins have exceedingly long "uppers," reaching to the thighs, and thus serve as a protection to the legs. Commonly, however, they are worn in three or four folds, reaching only to the knee. As the lower portion is worn out they are drawn down, until from wear, a moccasin formerly reaching the thighs barely covers the ankles. The moccasins are often sparingly decorated with painted designs and beadwork. Those entirely covered with beads are made merely for trade. Men and women wear their moccasins interchangeably. When more completely equipped, they formerly wore over one shoulder a buckskin, which was tied beneath the arm on the opposite side. The women wore on ceremonial occasions a short buckskin shirt or waist, with V-shaped openings at the neck. About the yoke were designs in variously colored beads, usually red, white and black. Below these were one or two rows of tin pendants, either in rows or groups. Upon the open sides of these shirts or waists and extending over the shoulder was an applique design of red flannel. Occasionally brass buttons, of which they are fond, were used in their ornamentation. The buckskin shirts worn with them were very heavy. About the upper portion was a long fringe, and near the bottom two rows of fringe with tin pendants. The portion of the dress below these pendants was often painted with yellow ocher. At the bottom were fringes with tin pendants attached.

Men and women wear necklaces of many-colored beads; some consist of many strands of beads hanging loosely upon the breast, others a flat band of beads in diamond-shaped designs. The women wear ear-rings with several strings of variously colored beads attached. Bead bracelets are worn by both men and women. Copper, brass and iron wire, variously ornamented, is also utilized for this purpose. Maidens wear upon their back hair a highly prized ornament of leather, in the form of a figure eight, more or less heavily decorated with brass buttons. Ornaments consisting of two or more feathers from the tail of the eagle are attached by buckskin thongs to the hair of the men, or are worn upon their hats. In times of mourning the hair is cut squarely off around the head and stands in a disheveled mass.

The faces of men and women alike are frequently tattooed among the Apache. The center of the forehead and the chin are most frequently covered with geometrical designs of a dark blue color. Occasionally a design upon the forehead is produced downward to the end of the nose.

Acorns, sunflower seeds, pine nuts, willow buds, walnuts, juniper berries, mesquite beans, and mescal are eaten. The meat of

the deer and wild turkey is a favorite article of food. Fish and fishing birds are not eaten. The mescal is used in various ways. At maturity, while the flower stock is still tender, the "cabbage" is cut and placed upon a pile of rocks highly heated, covered with bear grass, over which earth is heaped. After twenty-four hours the bear grass and earth are removed, leaving a pulpy mass which contains a syrup of the consistency of molasses. This portion of the plant is highly esteemed. They also crush together mescal and ripe black walnuts, over which they pour water, making a dish of mush-like consistency. The more fibrous portions are bruised, formed into thin cakes and preserved for future use. Squaw-berries are crushed and, with meat, form a dish which they greatly relish. From an early day the Apache

Above: *Apache scouts with army jackets and rifles, ca. 1885 (MNMP).* Opposite top: *Apache scouts, ca. 1885. Note the Plains-like feather-decorated war shield held by warrior in front row.* Opposite bottom: *Scouts in the field, showing how they once prepared for an encounter. Photo by H. F. Robinson, ca. 1906 (MNMP).*

have possessed, in small quantities, corn and melons.

Their game is secured by means of the bow and arrow and traps. Their bows are from four to five feet long, backed with sinew most carefully placed. The arrows consist of a reed-like shaft, a hardwood foreshaft, with a tip of flint, obsidian or chalcedony. The quivers are made of tanned deer-skin or the skin of the mountain lion, with the tail hanging downward.

The weapons of the Apache are the bow and arrow, spear and war club. They made use of poisoned arrows, which were thrust into the liver of a deer that had been bitten by a rattle-snake. The war club consists of an oval boulder encased in raw-hide, with handle attached. The spear has a long wooden shaft, to which has been cleverly hafted by means of the skin of a

49

FORT APACHE
MILITARY CEMETARY

FINAL RESTING PLACE FOR MANY
WHO HELPED WRITE THE COLORFUL
MILITARY HISTORY OF ARIZONA.
INDIANS AND WHITES ALIKE.

THIS HISTORICAL SITE PRESERVED
FOR THE PUBLIC BY THE WHITE
MOUNTAIN APACHE TRIBE. UNLAWFUL
TO DISTURB

cow's tail, a sword-blade, bayonet or other iron object of similar form. The Apache say that a "long time ago" they constantly wore about their waists lariats of horse hair, which they wielded with considerable effect in entangling an enemy.

Like all other Indians, the Apache are great gamblers. The women play the stave game (tsay-dithl) or throw sticks. Three two-faced billets are used, from eight to ten inches long. Within a circle of stones five feet in diameter the staves are thrown upon a rock in the center so as to cause them to rebound, and as they fall, flat or round faces upward, the throw counts from one to ten. Whoever first scores forty points wins. Both men and women play the stave game (haeegohay), using four two-faced staves. One stave of different markings from the rest is called the man; the remaining three, women. The count varies according as the staves fall. The men play naashosh, a variety of the ring and javelin game. Spanish cards are constantly used. Occasionally, at a great expense of time, they have made sets of playing cards of horse hide, with Mexican designs.

Very soon after birth the child is put into its cradle, which consists of a board made of slats, with a hood of the same or lighter material. When once a child has been placed in a cradle, it must thereafter occupy no other. Polygamy prevails, with certain restrictions. Very often a man marries his wife's younger sisters as fast as they mature; or, if she has none, he marries among the members of her clan, to prevent the women from fighting among themselves. If a man marries his brother's widow, he must do so within a year, or she is free to look elsewhere for a mate. Most marriages still take place in the Apache fashion; that is, by purchase.

At death adults are usually interred beneath the ground or in clefts of rocks, in either case being given considerable covering of earthly material. Children are frequently buried in trees, the body being enveloped in clothing and blankets and placed upon a platform of sticks among the branches.

Any young man can enter the ranks of the medicine-men among the Apache if endowed with the requisite natural gifts. Apparently there is no fixed tenet or doctrine among the medicine-men. Each follows his own inclinations, invents his own symbolism. They indulge in no intoxicating decoctions.

The use of charms is wide. Beads of lightning-riven rock and charms made from the wood of a lightning-riven tree are especially powerful in the cure of disease and protection from evil. Stone beads obtained from the graves and ruined pueblos exert powerful protective influences. Charms of various kinds purchased from the medicine-men afford great protection. The symbolism portrayed upon the medicine shirts is little known. The figures of Gans are usually present. The lightning, whose awful power they revere, is also depicted; the storm cloud is occasionally found upon them, also designs representing the four winds and the four world-quarters.

Of the three forms of musical instruments made by the Apache, the most interesting is a violin ("singing wood"), consisting of a hollow cylinder with a single sinew string and a small bow provided with horse hair. Their drums, usually improvised for the occasion, consist of a deer-skin head tightly stretched over an iron pot, galvanized iron bucket or other convenient vessel. These drums are always partially filled with water when in use. They are beaten with a stick having a loop at one end. Three kinds of dances are indulged in, namely, the ordinary social function, in which the men and women take part, the so-called Devil's Dance and the Medicine Dance.

Early writers describe the Apache as being about five feet and five inches high, slimly built and agile, light-hearted, but subject to fits of superstition and timidity. Very often, however, one may see among them men ranging above six feet in height and finely proportioned. The reputation for ferocity and cunning, honestly acquired by one or two bands of the Apache, should not be imposed upon the entire tribe, as is too often done, for no tribe of the great Southwest has been as grossly maligned as the Apache.

The San Carlos Agency of the White Mountain Apache

Opposite top: *Navajo scouts used in the Apache campaigns of 1885–1886. Photo by Wittick (MNMP).*
Opposite bottom: *Entrance to the military cemetery at Old Fort Apache.*

Reservation is situated on a mesa immediately below the junction of the San Carlos with the Gila River, about thirty miles southeast of Globe, on the Gila Valley, Globe & Northern Railway, and about ninety miles north of Bowie on the same line.

Many stories are told of the encounters of the Apache with the Pima and Maricopa, and many localities between their respective reservations are pointed out by knowing ones as scenes of fierce battles between the peaceful Pima and the plundering Apache. In this vicinity was enacted the horrible massacre by the Apache of several members of the Oatman family, in 1851, and the captivity of Olive Oatman, who remained a captive for a year or more and was then sold to the Mohave Indians, by whom she was held until 1856. It was at San Carlos that Mr. Augustus Thomas secured the local coloring for his realistic and admirable play, "Arizona."[31]

2 Government and Social Order

The Western Apache of early times consisted of five distinct *subtribal groups* bearing individual names. They occupied separate re-

Below: Graves of Indian scouts at the military cemetery, Old Fort Apache.
Bottom: Apache ranch and abandoned wickiup north of the town of Whiteriver, 1973.

gions, whose borders joined to form a whole that covered a 90,000-square-mile area, in the eastern and central portions of what later became the state of Arizona. For the present-day orientation, the total territory reached from near Flagstaff in the north to near Tucson in the south.

Ranging in position from north to south, these subtribal groups were: the Northern Tonto, the Southern Tonto, the Cibecue, the White Mountain, and the San Carlos. In population they numbered, all told, about five thousand persons.[1] Despite their proximity to one another, the five subtribal groups did not form a tribe, and they did not become a unified political body. There was no one name to designate the whole.[2] They shared common interests, a common language, and intermarried on occasion, but thought of themselves as distinct entities with peculiarities in dialect and in religious and social practices.[3] The territorial boundaries of each subtribal group were defined by prominent mountains and rivers, and were jealously protected. There were known, although rare, instances wherein circumstances required that Apache trespassers from adjacent areas be expelled, and even killed.

The relationships between the Western Apache groups provide an interesting insight into how separated and individualistic they had become as they settled into their southwestern territories. The Northern Tonto and Southern Tonto subtribal groups were always on friendly terms, and some of their bands exchanged regular visits. Yet other of their bands, while aware of each other's presence and activities, rarely met. The same was true of the Northern Tonto and Cibecue subtribal groups, and while the San Carlos and White Mountain subtribal groups were acquainted with the Northern Tonto, they had no significant contact with them.

The Southern Tonto had little contact with the White Mountain, Cibecue, and San Carlos groups. The San Carlos and Cibecue groups were closely allied in language, custom, and common purpose. The White Mountain subtribal group was in close contact with all the Western Apache save the Tonto groups, which explains why the White Mountain warriors were willing to serve as scouts for Crook during his campaign in Tonto territory from 1871 to 1873. The White Mountain and Cibecue groups and the White Mountain and San Carlos groups joined in conducting warfare against the Navajos, Mexicans, and other enemies. Occasional antagonisms arose between the San Carlos and White Mountain groups because they stole horses from one another, but these were not sufficient to effect a permanent division.[4]

Each of the subtribal groups was divided into smaller units which anthropologists have entitled *bands,* and the bands themselves were composed of *local groups*. Bands had a certain internal unity, but like the subtribal groups they did not participate in joint political action. Each band had a principal chief, and each local group also had a chief whose importance was equal to that of any other chief, including the principal chief. Band sizes varied considerably, ranging from a low of 50 or so to a high of approximately 750 persons.[5] Each band had its own territory within the subtribal area, and stayed for the most part within its own limits, especially in regard to its farming sites. Moreover, band identifications were lifelong; an individual was born a member of a specific band and was always known as such thereafter, regardless of his place of residence.[6] Since intermarriage was common, and clan and blood ties were numerous, the members of bands within the same group visited one another frequently.

Goodwin considered the local groups to be the basic units around which everything in the life-way revolved.[7] Each had exclusive rights to established farm sites and hunting areas, and each was headed by a chief who directed collective enterprises within his own group and enterprises involving other local groups and tribes as well. Local group sizes ranged from 35 to 200 persons.[8]

The local groups were made up of two to six *family clusters.* Most of these were large, matrilocal extended families, consisting of as many as eight individual households, each of which had at least one female member who was related to an older woman in the group and who shared membership in the same clan. The exceptions to this occurred when, in spite of the custom which dictated that married men should come to live with the wife's family, a son might instead choose to remain with his own family and bring his wife to live with them.[9]

Each family cluster was led by a headman—who might even be a male relative by marriage—who had gained the experience and authority for leadership during his years with his wife's family.[10]

The functioning of the local group imparted to the subtribal group the cohesiveness it would otherwise have lacked. Most of the subtribal members were related by blood or marriage and in this wise were obligated, in accord with tradition, to assist each other whenever it became necessary. The solidarity of the local group resulted for the most part from the advantages of remaining in ones' own territory to gather and hunt. The local group also provided a base from which an organized party of men well acquainted with one another could go on raids and war parties. The obvious benefits of remaining in one's own territory also provided the impetus for a substantial number of marriages within the local group.[11]

A further integrating factor for the subtribal bands was the Western Apache *clan system.* There were sixty-two of these clans, whose members were scattered throughout Western Apache country. The members of each clan considered themselves to be related; they were the descendants through the maternal line of a group of ancestors who established farm sites at the clan's legendary place of origin. Persons of the same clan were forbidden to marry, a tradition that regulated marriage. Being related, clan members brought a special strength to the subtribes, because they were expected to aid one another whenever the need arose for more manpower than was available in a single local group.[12]

Goodwin emphasizes the considerable variation that existed between clan members within the subtribal groups. Ritual practices and the words of ceremonial songs were slightly different; there was some variation in dress, and the Apache claimed they could tell the clan of a man or woman by merely scanning their features and mannerisms; for example, by the tilt of a headband.[13] In support of this claim, one cannot avoid noticing, in examining photographs of warriors wearing headbands, a marked difference in their tilts, widths, and methods of wrapping. Beyond this feature, most, if not all, clans had certain clan designs that were used for identification in the early days. These were painted on their water bottles and on their bodies and garments.[14]

All but a few of the sixty-two clans claimed a further affiliation to one of three mythological clans and, on this basis, were grouped into *phratries.* A phratry was composed of clans that were related. Phratry members were, like clan members, forbidden to marry. And, like the sixty-two clans, they were bound by obligations of mutual support in raiding and in war.[15]

Clan relationships, then, cut across the bands and local groups of subtribes to link the whole together in common purpose in certain areas of life. A man of one band in a given subtribe would have relatives in bands in several other subtribes, and this being so he was able to travel throughout the territories of these bands and could expect to receive food and lodging from his relatives. Beyond the obligations mentioned, however, there was little in the way of clan government or law.

The Northern Tonto subtribal group bands, which numbered four, were generally known among the Western Apache as "turquoise boiling up people," a name associated with a spring at their main campsite. In particular, the name was applied to the northernmost band. In summer this foraging band ranged as far north as the foot of the San Francisco Mountains and near the site of the future city of Flagstaff. Goodwin points out they did not go farther up the mountains because they believed (as do the Hopi) that supernatural beings lived on the peaks.[16] During the winter months the northernmost band shifted eastward to the edge of level desert country near the Little Colorado River, but even here very little of the mescal so cherished by the Apache grew. Thus in spring some local groups of this band went south to the Fossil Creek band region where mescal could be obtained, and also east to the Oak Creek band territory where other food plants grew. Being the most exposed of all the Western Apache to the hostile Navajo, Havasupai, and Walapai, the northernmost band was constantly on the move to avoid presenting a stable target, and it depended entirely on hunting and the gathering of wild food plants. The northernmost band was pure Athapaskan linguistically, and did not intermarry with the Yavapai.[17]

The Fossil Creek band of the Northern Tonto was made up of intermarried Yavapai and Apache. These people cultivated a few tiny farms, but were primarily hunters and gatherers. The Bald Mountain band was a very small group that centered around Bald Mountain and made its entire living by hunting and gathering. A few Yavapai were intermarried with the band. The Oak Creek band, whose home was the spectacularly beautiful Oak Creek canyon and the present Sedona area, was another mixture of Apache and Yavapai. They ranged from the present-day Jerome on the west to present-day Flagstaff on the north.[18]

The Southern Tonto subtribal group was divided into the Mazatayal band and six semibands. Their country consisted both of high, pine-timbered areas excellent for hunting and seed gathering and of lower areas suitable for farming.[19]

The three Cibecue subtribal group bands spent a large part of their year farming along creeks in the central section of their country. Mescal was gathered in the southernmost part of their territory, and they hunted game and gathered nuts and berries in the northernmost area, around the present locations of the towns of Snowflake and Showlow.[20]

The White Mountain subtribal group included the 1,500-member Eastern White Mountain Apache, one of the largest and most powerful bands of the Western Apache, and also the Western White Mountain band. Besides possessing a number of farm sites, they ranged north as far as present-day Vernon to hunt and to gather nuts and berries, and also east and southeast into New Mexico to hunt. Mescal grew in the southern portion of their country, and that same area served also as a good base from which to send out raiding parties.[21]

The four bands of the San Carlos subtribal group included wheat among their farm crops. San Carlos country was also an excellent mescal region, and its western mountains provided an outstanding game and wild plant area. The bands were on good terms with the Yavapai, and some intermarriage took place between them.[22]

In summing up his views regarding the various divisions of the Western Apache, Goodwin was not able to arrive at definite reasons for their separate existence. He believed that some of them parted after they arrived in the territorial areas they occupied in historic times. Based upon their social closeness, he made a rough division consisting of three parts, each of which moved as units into the area: the Northern Tonto; the Southern Tonto, Cibecue, and San Carlos; and the White Mountain. Before migrating into their areas, "all three may have formed a whole." Horses may also have promoted the separation, and an increase in population was another probable cause.[23]

3 Childbirth

Since it is impossible to relate all the customs practiced by the Western Apache as they entered the twentieth century, one can only note in passing some of the more interesting things that are known.

According to Reagan, the Western Apache infant of 1901–1902 was brought into the world with a minimum of fanfare. Sometimes the woman in labor was tied to a tree with her hands above her head and her legs spread, and left in this position until the child was delivered by a midwife. The midwife washed the baby by squirting it with water that she had warmed in her mouth. Then the child was rubbed dry with grass, soft moss, or a cloth. The midwife then blew forcefully on the child's body as she sprinkled it with cattail pollen. A cradleboard was made for it, usually by the mother. The wood frame was padded with moss or wrapped with strips of cloth. The child was then placed in it, covered with more moss or cloth, and laced in, "amid much sprinkling of pollen and praying to the gods for the baby's welfare."[1] A few days later a medicine sing was held for the child, at which time it was named.

In more ancient days the Apache had a childbirth ceremony that required the services of several medicine men. Prior to delivery, the shamans were summoned to perform appropriate medicine rites and to use the sacred pollen. Then, as prayers were said, a unique

Methods of carrying cradleboards while on foot or horseback.

maternity belt was put around the woman. It was made of a combination of the skins of the white-tailed deer, the black-tailed deer, the mountain lion, and the antelope, since these were animals that were believed to give birth to their young without difficulty. The belt was worn for a day or two only, and removed immediately after the child was born. Maternity prayers were offered by parents for their pregnant daughter, then by a medicine man, and finally by the woman herself to the gods and elements represented by the symbols on the belt. The symbols themselves were connected to one another by lightning lines. As each power was prayed to in succession, sacred pollen was sprinkled. By 1910, the belts had become so rare that they had to be rented from medicine men.[2]

By 1940, there were no belts. Expectant mothers were attended by elderly women who worked as midwives, or by mothers and other female relatives. The few shamans who were hired remained outside the wickiup rattling their gourd rattles and chanting prayers. The father was usually somewhere alone offering a prayer for the safe delivery of his child. Once the child was born, the father and medicine men were called in to see it.[3]

Whether it occurred in summer or winter, childbirth in 1901 caused the least possible interruption in the daily schedule. Reagan says that on January 14, 1901, the wife of V36 (an identifying "name" given out by the Agency) came with other women to work under Reagan on an irrigating ditch project.

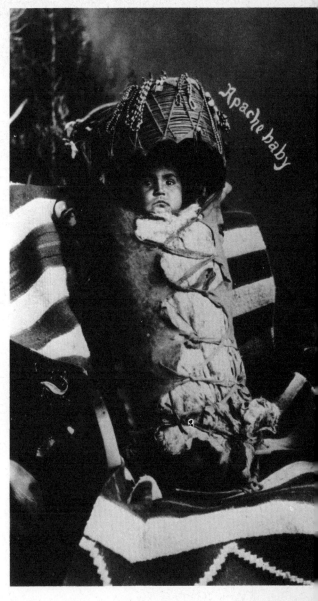

Child in cradleboard with medicine amulets attached to hood (DPL).

> After working an hour, she gave birth to a child, partly standing up and partly sitting on her knees, one of the women aiding her in the delivery. She then stood near the fire and dried herself, while some of the women wrapped the child in a blanket and got the mother a cup of coffee. After dinner, the same day, this woman reported for work on the ditch, but the writer refused to let her work, approved her ration ticket and told her to go home, which she did. Her husband was working on another section of the ditch. On arriving for dinner and noticing the condition of his wife and hearing the child cry, he stood motionless for several minutes. Then, without addressing his wife, he sat down with one of his neighbors and ate dinner. Also after dinner, he rode off to his work on the ditch without saying a word to his wife.[4]

> On September tenth, 1901, at the camp of Z1, Z1's daughter, the wife of Joe V59, gave birth to a baby boy. She sat on her knees while in labor. As soon as the child was born, the sacred dust was sprinkled on it and it was prayed over to the gods. The next day the mother was in a very critical condition and had a medicine singing performed over her which lasted from before noon until dawn the next morning. The sacred dust was sprinkled over her about every fifteen minutes during the ceremony, alternately by the men and women participants.[5]

This particular child was not washed until the day following its birth. "A cradle had been constructed for it by one of its aunts, as its mother was too sick to make it. The woman who washed the child warmed a cup of water in her mouth, then squirted it from her mouth on the part she was washing. The Apache believes that besides warming the water holding it in the mouth gives it certain medicinal properties that will be beneficial to the babe. When she had completed the washing and dried his little body with grass, she sprinkled him all over with the sacred pollen after blowing her breath strongly all over him. She then tied him down in the cradle."[6]

Reagan also attended another birth ceremony, which was something in the nature of a christening.

> The baby was ten days old. A solution of steeped, pounded-up herbs had been prepared the day before. When the solution was a proper temperature, the child was stripped and the medicineman, while singing to his deities, imploring their good will toward the infant, took some of the pounded-up weeds in his hand and using them like a sponge washed the baby all over with the solution, the child, in the meantime, crying and screaming. Then the gray-haired medicineman prayed as he shook the weed-sponge to the noonday sun. During the performance, the father and mother both sang with the medicineman. The mother held the naked child in her lap during the ceremony. After praying, the aged man sprinkled the new cradle with the solution. Then the infant was put in it. The solution was then passed around to all those present and each one sprinkled a quantity of it to the nadir and the zenith and to the gods of the four winds.[7]

Reagan states that the Apache formerly killed feeble children at birth, and that the "cry babies" were also strangled. He met a White man, probably one of the lost Stratton family who had been captured when a child and his identity lost, who still lived among the Apache in 1902. The man had never married, but it was noticed

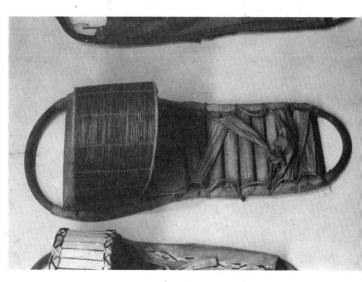

that an apparently full-blooded young Indian man lived with him and called him father. Reagan inquired about the White man and the boy and was told the following story by the White man himself: "One cold chilly morning when I was only about eighteen, I heard an Apache child crying down in the gulch below our house. I went to see what the trouble was and saw a woman strangling her baby to death because it cried. I took it away from her and saved its life, but was ridiculed by the other Indians. No mother would take the little discarded baby. So I told them I would raise it myself. He now considers me his father and he is a good boy to work."[8]

4 Childhood, Names, and Training

Apache children were both wanted and loved, and parents were pleased to have girls as well as boys. A boy was a valuable provider and warrior, but when he grew up and married he went to live with his wife's people, and his own parents might see little of him after that. A girl, on the other hand, remained with her parents even after she married. Her husband came to live with them, and their children grew up in the family complex. Geronimo stated that orphaned children were adopted by the chief or else given away to a family as he desired. Outlawed Apache were permitted to take their children with them, but if they left the children behind with the tribe, the chief decided what would be done with them, and no disgrace was attached to the orphaned children.[1]

By abstinence and care, the Apache mother of former years spaced her children about four years apart.[2] A man who got his wife pregnant too soon was considered irresponsible.[3] Infants received the best care and attention their parents and relatives could give them. An infant was nursed for at least two years, and when the child was able to eat solid food, the best meat and vegetables were given to it. Babies were carefully watched to guard them against injuries, and various religious charms were attached to the hood of the cradleboard to keep evil spirits away. As a rule, the Apache were always kind to all the children in the camp.[4]

The cradleboard was made of split sotol or yucca boughs, cut thin and scraped until they were smooth. A long oak, ash, or willow withe was bent to form an elongated hoop or frame, and the ends were securely fastened to form the bed of the cradle. At the head another loop was secured at a right angle to form a projection, to which a canopy roof was attached to protect the infant from rain and sunlight. The flat roof was made of stretched buckskin, later of cloth, colored yellow, over which still another cloth or blanket could be laid for additional protection. At the foot of some cradleboards there was a small footrest made of ash or oak, that could be lowered to accommodate the growing child. Buckskin sides, colored with yellow ocher, were fastened to the frame for the purpose of holding the baby firmly to the cradle, regardless of position. These were laced together with buckskin or cloth bands after the unclad child was placed on one thick layer of soft, fine grass such as wild mustard, and then covered with another layer of grass. The grass would be discarded and replaced with more as necessary. Chafing was prevented by dusting the child with powder from the bark of the heart-leafed willow. A stuffed pillow was also used to prevent excessive movement of the child's head.[5]

Opler reports that among the Chiricahua, the fourth day after birth was the occasion for a cradle ceremony, although the rite might be delayed for a few days more. A shaman would be hired to perform in order to assure good health for the child. In this case the medicine man made the cradleboard, attending its construction with prayers and ritual. Symbols that had sex indications were cut in the top of the canopy: a full or half moon for a girl, and a cross or four parallel slits for a boy. The protective amulets tied to the canopy by the shaman included bags of pollen, turquoise beads, and pieces of wood that had been struck by lightning. At a public ceremony the child was marked with pollen and held up to the cardinal directions. The mother generally added amulets of her own to the cradleboard, such as the paws and claws of animals and birds, to guard the child against fright, and cholla wood to fend off colds and other sickness.[6] In cold weather a tanned skin or blanket was wrapped around the cradleboard and child for additional warmth. In warm weather the child's arms were left free.

It has been suggested that perhaps no more useful nor comfortable article for the care of an infant has ever been devised than the Apache cradleboard. By placing the carrying strap attached to it about her forehead or shoulders, the mother freed her hands for riding or working. Whether she suspended the cradle from the limb of a tree or the horn of the saddle, stood it up or laid it flat, the baby was always comfortable and protected.

When a child was stillborn or died while it was being carried in the cradle, the body was hastily buried and the cradleboard was damaged by cutting slits in the buckskin. After that it was either hung in a tree near the camp or burned.[7]

If a child was still healthy when the next infant was born, the cradleboard could be used again, although a cradle ceremony was still held. More often, though, a new cradleboard was crafted. In rare situations in late history, twin cradleboards were made. Prior to that time it was the custom to let only one of a set of twins live, because of the problems inherent in attempting to raise two babies at once in the war years.[8]

When it was necessary to bathe a girl infant, the mother would send the older boys away on an errand, for the people were modest and respected the privacy of others. But when the girl was ready to be replaced in her cradle she was sometimes wrapped in

Opposite, top four photos: *Cradleboards.* Opposite bottom: *Cradleboard hung in tree after child had died.*

a blanket and her brother was permitted to hold her. James Kaywaykla tells how he loved his sister dearly, and never forgot how happy he was when she first extended her little arms to him. "She was a strong, healthy little thing. Even on the long, hard trips she seldom cried."[9]

Within the first few weeks or months after birth, the child's mother or maternal grandmother pierced its ears. Something hot was applied to the ear, which was then punctured with a sharp thorn or bone. This was believed to improve the child's ability to hear, and also its behavior. Children with their ears pierced also "grew faster." Earrings of turquoise or white beads were then hung in the child's ears, and he would continue to wear earrings throughout his life.[10]

Infants were given names soon after they were born, but these were not first and last names after the White manner. In the usual instance, a mother would give her child a descriptive name such as "One-who-smiles." These names were seldom retained, since when boys and girls matured they were given new names that were more descriptive of their particular talents. One could not easily tell from an Apache name whether it applied to a boy or a girl. A name was especially respected and valued, for the names in a family were its special property, and with certain exceptions only members of that family could use those names for their children. People outside a given family who wanted to use one of its names had to get permission first. Names could be given as gifts. For example, a renowned hunter could promise his name to a boy he liked. This was a particular honor, and the boy who bore the name of a famous man tried his very best to be like him. Furthermore, it was accepted that the power in the name would help the boy become a great man. Parents were careful to choose the name of a strong, healthy man or woman for their child, for they believed that the choice would assure the strength and health of the child. It was considered unwise to select the name of a deceased person too soon after death, and a number of years would pass before the name was used by the family again.[11]

When parents wanted for a child a particular name that was considered to be the special property of another family, they brought the owners gifts, and usually received permission to use the name. There were, of course, some names common to more than one family. Two women who were both good tanners might be called by the same name, but this would be an instance where the title was associated with a commonly done task. Highly prized names were not shared.[12]

When new names were given to a child, they had to be earned by him. There were certain standards of excellence to which a youngster must attain. The first qualification was obedience, for the choice was often between obedience or death. The next was truthfulness, for human relationships were of no value without it. Known liars could not give evidence against others, and they were not permitted to carry messages. Kindness and friendliness were essential. A youth must become useful and observant. Older boys vied for the honor of serving the warriors. They learned to care for the horses, to run errands, to cook, and to anticipate every need. It was vital to know how to listen and to ask only pertinent questions. They ate the worst food, fasted as necessary, and sought to be faithful, respectful, trusted, and brave. These were, of course, the noble ideals set before the boy who wished status and the valuable name by which others would know him. In practice, the ideal was seldom reached, for the Apache had the same human limitations as others do.[13]

The Apache did not call another person by name unless the occasion was very special. Names could be used at an important ceremony, such as a war dance, or when there was particular danger. By tradition, people could never refuse help to anyone who called them by name. In daily life, the terms "Husband" and "Wife" were used. In speaking of another person, one said "That man," or "His son," or "The old woman's daughter," and children were taught at an early age not to call each other by name. The Apache used warmer terms of greeting than the impersonal "Hello" or "Good morning." A relative or an old friend was welcomed with something akin to "Come in, my brother." If the host had not seen the visitor for some months, they would embrace in silence before conversation began. Equally warm words of parting were used, and in all, one can easily appreciate the good conduct they encouraged. A typical good-bye was "May we live to see each other again."[14]

According to Goodwin, since life was "conceived as a path along which individuals must constantly be helped by ritual devices, and the trail must be followed exactly as the heroes of mythical times journeyed along it, the Chiricahua child's first steps were ceremonially celebrated." This was a symbolic rite celebrated for both sexes, and it took place anywhere between the seventh month and the end of the second year. Once again, a shaman who knew the ceremony must be hired to perform the ceremony, which was done to keep the child healthy and strong, and because Child of the Water, when he first walked, had a similar ceremony. A new buckskin outfit was made for the child. A feast was held at the time of a new or full moon, and many were invited. Besides social dancing, there was considerable ritual. Everyone was marked on the head with pollen. At sunrise, the shaman lifted the child toward each of the four directions four times. Then he made pollen footprints on a piece of white buckskin, and the child was led through the prints, with prayers about good fortune being said for each step. Four times he was walked like this, and then he was walked clockwise four times. Then everyone marked the child with pollen, and there were ritual songs and dancing. Finally the child's first moccasins were put on, and the ceremony ended with feasting and the distribution of gifts.[15] In a general way, the ceremony was much like the girls' puberty rite and had almost the same emphasis. In the spring immediately following the moccasin ceremony, there was a brief hair-cutting ceremony which was associated with the healthy growth of the child and all living things. Ideally the rite was repeated on four successive springs with the same shaman officiating.[16]

Boys and girls played together until they were seven or eight years old. They played house and in general imitated the activities of their parents. They costumed themselves with earrings, necklaces, and bracelets made of grass and pine needles. Slings were fashioned for the boys and elaborate buckskin dolls for the girls. Girls placed their dolls in realistic toy cradleboards made by their mothers or women relatives, and they played at food-gathering near the camp, picking and eating nuts and ground cherries or chewing cottonwood buds. Pet puppies and rabbits were common.

In summer, considerable time was spent swimming and, as a rule, Apache children became good swimmers. The boys made balls of mud or clay which they stuck on the fork of a twig and slung at birds. Some became so expert with these that they could knock a bird off a limb. Children enjoyed making rattles and noise-makers out of gourds. However, it was believed that shaking the rattles might bring on a lightning storm, and the boys were cautioned against using them too near the camps.[17]

John Clum reports how on one particular day his curiosity was aroused

by a succession of mysterious rumblings to the westward, not unlike the reverberations of distant thunder. I mounted my horse and set out to investigate. I had ridden two or three miles to the westward, when, as I rounded the shoulder of a high mesa, the mystery was solved. In the warm sunshine, a dozen of half-naked Apache children were enjoying all the thrills of a genuine toboggan slide. For a toboggan they had a cowhide, dried as hard as a board. Their slide was the steep, gravelly side of a high mesa. The cowhide toboggan was placed on the brink of the slide. It would accommodate half-a-dozen Apache kids. The two in front

61

set their feet in buckskin loops attached to the cowhide, to prevent them from slipping off en route. When the kids were safely adjusted, they let go the moorings and plunged down the steep incline at breath-taking speed. The roar was produced by the swift movement of the hard cowhide over the coarse gravel.[18]

As a brother and sister grew older, they received less encouragement to play with each other, and they learned that they were not to stay in the wickiup together, unless a parent or grandparent was with them. The boy was not required to avoid his sister entirely in order to show his respect for her, as a man was to avoid his mother-in-law. Nevertheless, he followed the custom of not being alone with his sister and of never "joking" with her.[19]

Children were taught to obey their elders. If a child was disobedient and refused to listen, the usual remedy was for the mother to splash cold water in his face. Another treatment was to shun, or ignore the child.[20] A stick was used only when lives were endangered because of the child's behavior. If all else failed, a more extreme measure might be used. This was planned in secret with the help of the boy's grandfather or perhaps an old friend. One night when the fire in the wickiup was almost out and the disobedient boy lay asleep on his bed, a garish, seemingly humpbacked figure suddenly appeared. His long tangled hair hung like a mop over his soot-smeared face; his clothing was in tatters; he carried a huge basket over his shoulder. Hovering over the startled youth he shouted, "Where is that boy I heard about way underground? I've come to take him away with me." The lesson came quickly home, for the man's looks and words were those of an evil ogre about whom every child had heard many times. It was more than enough to reduce any boy to tears, and in return for not being taken away, a promise to behave thereafter was easily extracted. In later years, the old friend or grandfather would tell the boy about the ruse, and it is said that both usually had a good laugh over it.[21]

During the war years it was vital that Apache children were made aware of certain dangers and the need to remain absolutely quiet when necessary. Parents made threats concerning dread beings who preyed upon noisy or disobedient children. The call of the poorwill bird was associated with the impressive masked dancers, and it too was a reminder of the need for proper behavior. In particular, the masked dancer clown was held up to the child as a threat—he was told that misbehavior would cause the clown to come with a huge basket and carry him away in it. When mere warnings were no longer enough, the clown himself, or one pretending to be the clown, appeared at the invitation of the parents and chased the frightened child or children until they were sufficiently subdued. During the masked dancer performances at the puberty rites, clowns who had been retained in advance for the purpose frightened children who needed disciplining. The owl was another culture force that inspired fear, for owls were thought to be ghosts who could harm both children and adults.[22]

By the time Apache boys and girls had reached the age of nine or ten, they were expected to help their parents in the everyday activities of the camp. Girls helped their mothers care for the children, learned to tan and sew, went with their female relatives to gather food plants and firewood, helped erect new wickiups, carried water from the spring, and assisted with the cooking. Since they knew that their lives would be like their mothers' when they grew up, they were anxious to learn to perform every task that was expected of a woman.[23]

A boy assisted his father whenever he could, by watching or catching his horse, by bringing him things he needed, or by holding the end of a bow or steadying the arrow as his father tied the feathers on with wet sinew.

Geronimo said that when he was a child, his mother taught him the legends of their people, tales of the sun and sky, the moon and stars, the clouds and storms. It was she who instructed him how to "kneel and pray to Usen for strength, health, wisdom, and protection." He asserts that the Chiricahua never prayed for Usen's help against others, that if one person had something against another, he took vengeance himself. Children were taught that Usen disliked the petty quarrels of men.[24]

The winter season brought added closeness to the family, since it was an excellent time for discussion and stories. The children listened carefully as their father told them about the brave deeds of the people and about his own hunting, raiding, and warfare.[25] The Apache men enjoyed storytelling, and they were as eager to hear entertaining stories as they were to tell them. If a neighbor's boy interrupted a story by a visit, the family always made room for him by the fire. In such instances, the father would return to the beginning of the story he had been telling, so that the visitor would miss none of it, and when the guest went home, he was given something choice such as piñon nuts and a piece of dried meat to thank him for listening. Opler says that among the Chiricahua, many of the important myths could be told in the winter only. The most vital story was that of the culture hero Child of the Water, also known as Born of Water, and his victorious encounters with the monsters, for this served as a background for many rituals. There were also tales of the supernatural Mountain People, also called Mountain Spirits, who inhabited caves in the sacred mountains and who were impersonated by the masked dancers in order to heal, to bring happiness, and to protect the Apache territory. And there were also the delightful stories about the Coyote—the trickster, who violated all the conventions of society and who was responsible for all the foolish things people do.[26] In the winter camps the child learned reverence for life and nature, and about the substance of supernatural power and the gaining of it for man's good. In the winter the child learned about Apache tradition and the history of his people, of which he was now becoming a part.

A young boy might help his mother with some tasks, but he did not usually work with his father or go hunting for large game with him, and he had to wait until he was fifteen or sixteen before the other men of the camp would take him. This was because he had a great deal to learn before he went along. His grandfather, who remained in camp while younger men were busy elsewhere, was most often his teacher. He talked to the boy about hunting rules and techniques and about the religion and important ceremonials of the Apache. In particular he taught the boy hunting chants and prayers, for almost everything the people did was connected with religion. Ceremonies associated with the hunt, the raid, and the war party must be carried out according to precise custom, for if a man made a mistake in these things, it was believed he would have bad luck and might also bring bad luck to his family and friends. The grandfather taught the boy to study the wild birds and animals intensely; to learn all their habits, what they fed upon and where, and how to track and stalk each species.[27]

A boy who wished to become a good hunter had first to be a good shot. Therefore the grandfather helped his grandson make a bow and some arrows. Ordinarily, these were smaller and cruder than those of adults. A branch of an oak, locust, or maple was cut for the bow and was split, carved down, and scraped smooth. Then the ends were tied together with yucca fiber to give the bow a curved shape, after which it was hung up to season and dry. When the wood was ready, it was greased with fat and worked back and forth to make it flexible. Then the shaft was rubbed in hot ashes to harden the wood. The outside of the bow might be painted black or red, and an incised or painted design might be placed on the inside to identify it and to bring the boy good luck in hunting. The finished bow was about three feet long and had a single, shallow curve. Two or three sinew strips were soaked and rolled together to make the bowstring.[28]

A boy's first arrows were usually little more than self-pointed branches, ranging from a foot and a half to two feet long. The bark was peeled off, and the branches were left in the sun to dry. After this, they were heated and straightened with a stone or bone arrow wrench. As the boy matured, he fashioned better arrows from such woods as mulberry, mountain mahogany, or Apache plume. Boys made wooden war clubs and lances out of the stems of the sotol plant. Hide wrist guards were also made, and sometimes small shields of rawhide, since boys liked to play with shields in imitation of the warriors.

Virtually all of the boys' games and sports imitated their fathers' activities, and as such were a training ground for later life. They went out hunting for small game, such as rabbits, squirrels, grouse, and prairie chickens, in small groups. Sometimes the boys from neighboring camps vied against one another. Boys wrestled, played Indian shinny—a rough game that often ended with a number of casualties—and hide-and-seek, an especially valuable game, since it was so important for a warrior to know how to conceal himself and how to surprise an enemy from ambush.[29]

In some things the girls received the same training as the boys. They too learned to use the bow and arrows, the sling and the lance. Both sexes were taught to mount an unsaddled horse without help. To do this, they caught hold of the mane, dug their toes into the foreleg, and swung themselves astride the animal. After that they learned to leap onto the horse without a handhold. It was difficult to do, but they were able to accomplish it by using a slope for a running jump. At first they just threw themselves face down across the back of the horse, and then wriggled into a sitting position. Sometimes, three months passed before they could perform the same feat on level ground.[30]

There were competitions for distance and accuracy shooting. One boy would shoot his arrow as far as he could and the others would seek to beat him; as was the case with the men, the winner was awarded the losers' arrows. In another game, a boy shot his arrow into a bank, and the others tried to come close enough to touch his arrow feathers with theirs. Whoever did this won the contest. Boys also made a round grass target, which was propped up against a tree and used for practice shooting.[31]

Whenever the warriors were at home, they watched the boys at play and kept score for them. Sometimes they competed with the boys in running races. This was another favorite sport, since boys had to be strong and swift runners in order to survive. When a boy was thirteen or fourteen, it was common practice for his father to make him get up each day before dawn and run up and down a mountainside. And when there were races between boys, fathers coached their sons in their attempts to beat the others. Children were often taken on long, fast hikes to toughen their muscles and feet. The talents shown in the games were often the best indication of when a boy was mature enough to be taken on a large game hunt or on a raid. The consistent winners of races or shooting matches were the first to be invited. Such a privilege meant that the boy was ready to become a man. He would be taken on four raids as a novice, and if he performed well he assumed his place in the tribal complex as a warrior.[32] When a band was moving, young boys served as sentinels along with the men and women. On such occasions they rubbed clay on their bodies and into their breechclouts, and tied bunches of grass or feathers on their heads. Their bodies blended so well with the rock that unless one moved it was impossible to locate them.[33]

Boys were taught to play the hoop and pole game, which was reserved for male contestants only. James Kaywaykla, who is a Chiricahua, says that his father trained him in the use of primitive weapons, of which the sling was his favorite. His father made him one he could use effectively at a hundred yards. Stones themselves were excellent weapons in the hands of an accurate thrower, and when hurled from a sling could be deadly. He mentions that the boys of his band engaged in mock battles with the boys of the White Mountain and Tonto Apache groups. Whenever they saw the signs of others in the evening as they went for the horses, each group scouted for more signs and tried to effect an ambush. As each group advanced toward the other, they threw stones, dodged and twisted to avoid being hit, and made use of whatever cover they could. An outnumbered group sent home for reinforcements, and at times even the men joined them. In one such encounter at Mescalero, one boy had a leg broken, and another's neck was dislocated. Once James himself received a glancing blow and a cut above the eye. He was ashamed to go home till after dark. He appreciated the fact that although his mother noticed the wound the next morning, she made no mention of it.[34]

Occasionally, James Kaywaykla's father took him hunting. If they went far enough from camp and there was little danger of discovery, his father permitted him to practice with his rifle. He knelt behind the boy and held the gun, but let his son sight and pull the trigger. However, the shortage of ammunition allowed little such practice with firearms. The boys were also made to bathe daily, even though in winter it was necessary to break through the ice to gain access to the stream. A fire was built on the bank and their clothing was left by it. They repeatedly went back and forth from the icy water to the fire, yet no one caught a cold or became ill. Kaywaykla adds that the older people bathed as frequently as the children were required to, and in the desert where water was unobtainable they rubbed their bodies with clean sand.[35]

Goodwin reports that Western Apache children never played at being sick or having a shaman come to sing over them and cure them. It wasn't that they were afraid to do it, they just never thought of it. When boys played at deer hunting, they did not pretend to sing the deer songs that gave the men power and success. They did not know real deer songs anyway, and they were afraid of fooling with them because they were dangerous. But they did play at holding the girl's puberty rite. Just as was done at the real ceremony, the boys pretended to butcher meat to feast the people at the ceremony, and the girl for whom the ceremony was given tied in her hair any kind of feather she could find to represent the pubescent girl's eagle-down feather. They also made a cane for her, and a drinking tube and scratcher to hang about her neck. The boys would sing love songs, which were the first songs they learned, and the girl danced to these. When it was time to mold her, four willow sprigs were planted to mark the four directions, and a thick bed of brush was made for her to lie down on. Then she was molded by another girl who took the role of the sponsor. After the molding, the girl ran out to and around each one of the willow sprigs, and, as she did so, the other children chased after her as the people did in the real ceremony. There was even a piece of bark for a ceremonial basket, with small pebbles in it representing corn. This was poured over the girl's head.[36]

The Western Apache children also played at raiding and going to war. The men (boys) would go off and leave the women (girls) behind. When they returned, they sent one boy ahead to tell the girls that they were coming with many cattle and that they wanted tulapai prepared for them. Sometimes they sent word to send other boys to meet them and help them drive the cattle. When the "men" arrived, they might say, "We have killed many enemies." Then the "women" would dance about for joy, just as the old women did at real victory dances. They would call out the name of a certain boy who supposedly had done well and say of him, "Oh, he always does this way." They would sing real victory dance songs and dance about as the warriors did in the victory dance. However, they never painted themselves, nor did the girls dance in only a gee string, as a few of the divorced and widowed women might do at one of the real victory dances.[37]

Goodwin's informants agree with Kaywaykla, claiming that older boys and youths of the Western Apache played a mock war

Top: *Western Apache doll wearing replica of girl's buckskin puberty dress (AF)*. Above: *Detail of head; the hair bow has been tucked into the neck*. Opposite top: *The clown and the disobedient child*. Opposite bottom: *Toy cradleboards made for girls, ranging in length from 3 to 10 inches (SM)*.

game which was fought out in imitation of real warfare. The boys divided into two groups and sent notice when they intended to fight. They used slings and often did considerable damage with them. Older men sat at a distance and watched the sport, encouraging the boys. Sometimes they would fire their guns off in the air to make the "war" seem real. This game trained the boys for actual fighting.[38]

A Western Apache youth sometimes had no experience hunting large game until five or six months after he was married, when he was taken deer hunting for the first time by a male relative. Even those who hunted before marriage probably did not start hunting alone until some time after marriage had taken place. Furthermore, without knowledge of hunting ritual, the Western Apache considered himself to be at a decided disadvantage in hunting. Simple ritual practice that brought good luck, such as placing a shed antler in a tree, praying to a raven flying overhead, setting aside a certain internal organ as an offering to Raven, and the proper method of skinning were usually picked up by a youth shortly after he first started hunting large game. A youth might help with the singing during a hunting ceremony and thus learn some of the songs, but he did not actually acquire hunting power until he was at least twenty years old. Hunting power was dangerous and not a thing for an inept youth to meddle with, for his heart would not be strong enough to withstand it, and it could make him ill or even kill him.[39]

Boys and girls began to take a peripheral part in ceremony at a surprisingly early age, but they did so for pleasure and not with serious intent. Boys of ten or eleven danced with girls of the same age at social dances, and they sometimes tried to help the singers. While boys were not supposed to attend private curing rites, they often did, in order to take part in the feast that the patient's family ordinarily prepared for midnight. At such times they watched, listened to the songs, and sometimes sought to join in the choruses they remembered. At masked dancer performances the singers were accompanied by the beating of wooden switches on a dry cowhide, and almost always it was small boys of eight to twelve who were chosen to do this. They kept perfect time and were intently serious about their job. Thus, in one way and another, children picked up a considerable amount of knowledge concerning ritual form while they were still quite young.[40]

With the onset of puberty, the girl became the center of ritual interest during her rite, and the boy on his first raiding party held much the same position. In addition to the training received, a boy accompanying a war party for the first time was believed to be a source of power for achieving the ends of the raid, and his activities were surrounded by vital restrictions and taboos. His instruction was in the hands of particular relatives, ceremonial paraphernalia was made for him, and various rituals were performed. On his return from the fourth trip he was no longer a boy. It was not until puberty or after it that boys and girls seriously attempted to participate in a curing ceremony by singing, and even then they might be too self-conscious to do so. At puberty, girls could participate by helping in the preparation of ceremony feasts. Certain rites required a given number of participants without sexual experience. Children could not be used, and therefore the choice was confined to youths and maidens.

With occasional exceptions, boys under eighteen were considered too young to impersonate the Gan, who were the supernatural emissaries of the Supreme Being, and those who took part in the masked dances were almost always mature men. Usually, a youth had to be eighteen or more before he was considered old enough or sufficiently confident to introduce, remember, and lead a dance or ceremonial song himself.[41]

Certain minor rites or parts of rites were sometimes learned and even practiced to a limited extent by girls and boys as young as sixteen or seventeen. There were also rare cases in which youths claimed to have acquired power for major ceremonies. Ordinarily

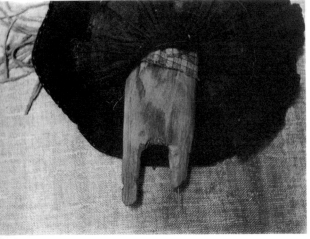

Top: *Wooden doll (MNCA). Small rubber band at upper left gives size comparison.* Above: *Detail of wooden body of doll.* Opposite: *Na-tuen-de, White Mountain girl, in buckskin puberty dress. The edge design consists of cutouts laid over red flannel.*

though, the possession and practice of ceremonies were confined to individuals over twenty-five, and most rites were acquired after thirty. The holy powers active in ceremonies were simply too strong for the hearts of young people to withstand. For the same reason, boys and girls were not often permitted to see curing ceremonial sand painting. Likewise, children were not allowed to look upon the dead, for the fear caused by the dead might prove too much of a shock for their hearts and cause them nightmares or even illness. Mourning for the dead was not usually observed before puberty, and in most instances young people first accompanied burial parties several years after this.[42]

5 Girl's Puberty Ceremony
1901–1902

Reagan observed, in 1901–1902, that when the girl arrived at the threshold of womanhood, she went through more elaborate ceremonies than the boy, though often not of so private a nature. He then gives, as will be seen, a most inadequate description of the event. "The females of the vicinity, and sometimes the males, chased her around, heated her up, and then examined her. Then a new blanket was spread on the ground on which she danced to the beat of a drum made of a pottery vessel with rawhide stretched across the mouth. This was a daytime ceremony. As she danced, the Gans danced around her. . . . These are clowns dressed in the attire supposed to be worn by the great Apache devil, called cheden. Their jokes, grimaces, remarks are stunning." After this ceremony the male admirers gave presents to the girl, and a dance usually followed.[1]

Two such ceremonies—called *Na-ii̇̃-ees* by the Apache—were observed by Reagan:

> At Indian Cooley's camp on Cibicu, April fifteenth, 1901, one of the girls was entering womanhood. Just after breakfast the young people chased her all around the premises and beyond the farmer's residence where the writer was at work. In the final chasing, the girl ran northwestward from her mother's house four hundred yards. Then she returned and ran southeast, east, and then northwest about the same distance in each direction. Then the sacred pollen was sprinkled on her head. While they sprinkled her they prayed to the gods for their ever-protecting care and guidance in her life. A new blanket was spread under an arbor in front of Cooley's house and on this the girl danced the hours away to the tune of the many songs sung. That afternoon a feast was given in her honor, followed by a dance like that described below.
>
> On July twenty-fifth, 1901, John Lupe's niece who had just arrived at the threshold of womanhood had a dance given in her honor that cost not less than sixty-five dollars. Two beeves were killed and the people feasted throughout the day. The Carrizo and Cibicu boys also matched at ball. This furnished the excitement during the daytime hours, except that now and then an old woman would clown to amuse the populace.
>
> About six o'clock in the evening the captain of ceremonies took a large eagle feather and rolled it in the ashes. After holding it toward the sun he tied it in the girl's hair. The feather was placed in the center line back of the crown so that it hung backward. The chief of ceremonies then took another feather and went through a similar performance with the ashes, tying it with a tiny bell on the head of a cane the girl was to dance with that night. In the adolescent ceremony dance the girl does not choose a partner but dances with a cane.
>
> During the ceremonies of the day, a leveled spot of ground was cleared some one hundred yards in diameter in the nearby woods and a great pile of wood was stacked near the center to be used as fuel for light and heat during the dance ceremonies. As night approached, all the populace repaired thither and seated themselves on their various belongings and blankets in a wide circle around the pile of wood. A fire was then kindled just to the west of the pile. The medicinemen gathered west of the

69

Top: *Western Apache Gans and girls
at puberty ceremony (SM). Figure
second from left is the clown.* Above:
*Girl at right holds the pubescent
girl's cane.* Opposite: *The pubescent
girl at the puberty ceremony.*

70

fire and squatted on their blankets and on boughs Indian style, and began to sing medicine songs appropriate for the occasion; two of them beat time on the drum described above. Soon the dance began.

The girls danced first. They formed around the central fire in groups of five to seven, like the spokes in a giant wheel, with the central fire and the musicians for the hub. They all faced inward and danced backward and forward along a radial line from the fire to the outer rim of the cleared area, the girl for whom the ceremony was given leading the dance. After the dance had progressed about twenty minutes, three old women took the cattail-flag pollen, and entering the circle enclosing the dancing area, sprinkled each participant with the sacred pollen, as she made the rounds, beginning at the north side of the enclosure and sprinkling the dancers first as they passed around the circle to the right, after which they sprinkled the musicians.

The sprinkling being completed, the dancing girls went to the group seated outside of the dancing area and chose male partners by slapping them on the shoulder. The girl then returned to her position, followed by the partner of her choice who faced her with his back to the central fire. At no time did the partners touch each other and when the girl advanced in the step her partner danced backward, when he danced forward she retrograded. A set lasted during the continuance of a chanted song, at the close of which the men returned to their seats and the women chose new partners. Thus set after set was danced throughout the night, being varied now and then by drinking tiswin and by the old women dancing singly, as clowns to amuse the on-lookers. One of these clowns had a long, yellow strip of cloth tied around her head with ends trailing on the ground behind her.

At sunrise the dance broke up and the men hurled presents at the feet of the girl—stacks of saddles, blankets and cloth. One man gave her a horse. This act closed the ceremony.[2]

Nearly every girl who arrived at the threshold of womanhood in 1901 went through a set of prescribed ceremonies, including the important puberty rite. Even after this, her menstrual periods remained a matter of special concern in order to prevent injuring her health. In example, Reagan cites an instance when on June 28, 1901, John Lupe's wife was having her menstrual period. "She would not work in the cornfield lest the menses cease prematurely and injure her. The Indians asserted that if a woman goes into the cornfield and works during her period, it always makes her sick."[3]

1920–1930

Goodwin affirmed that the puberty ceremony for a girl was one of the central rituals of the Western Apache, being an important ceremony and social event. The family and relatives of the pubescent girl profited in every way from the ceremony itself, and the local population benefited from the dancing, singing, feasting, and drinking. In the 1930s, poor families were reduced to holding an abbreviated one-day ceremony, but wealthier families held the full four-day ceremonial, in which the pubescent girl, as the central figure, was believed to be filled with power from White Painted Woman (also known as White Shell Woman or Changing Woman), which could be used to ensure the continuance of crops, health, and long life. Gan impersonators were performing at the ceremonies in the twenties and thirties, and the ceremony was often held in connection with the Fourth of July celebrations.[4]

Present-day Apache often refer to the ritual as the Sunrise Dance or Coming-Out Ceremony.

1930—Present

While the decision to hold a Western Apache puberty ceremonial was usually made long before a girl had her first period, the actual preparations were not begun until it occurred. Immediately there-

71

after, her parents selected a group of five or more older people who helped them decide when and where the ceremony would be held and who would serve as the girl's "sponsor." Regardless of when the girl had her first period, the rite was usually held late in June, July, or August.[5] There were no particular religious reasons for this— it was a good weather season, and students were home from boarding school. A friend of mine attended a ceremony at San Carlos held as late as October 3.

When the date had been chosen, the site for the ceremonial was decided upon. It must be large enough for a dance, fairly level, and free of obstructions. There must be an abundant source of water nearby, trees to cut for structures and firewood, and space for temporary dwellings. Next the group selected a medicine man to sing at the ceremony. The girl's father visited him and asked him to conduct the ceremonial. They met just at sunrise, and the father put a pollen cross on the medicine man's hand, on which he placed a gift of money. He also gave him an eagle feather with a piece of turquoise attached to its butt by deer sinew. The woman who was selected to act as sponsor for the pubescent girl played a vital role in the ceremony and, in addition, was expected to make a large financial contribution. However, the principal criterion governing her selection was that she could not be related to the girl in any way. Beyond that she must be of excellent character, good-natured, industrious, wise, and well-to-do. It was preferred that she had gone through the ceremony herself.

Either the father of the pubescent girl or the foreman of the ceremony visited the woman at sunrise and asked her to assume the role. If she accepted, she was given an eagle feather, turquoise, and cattail pollen. This was a significant event, for it began a formal relationship between the pubescent girl, her parents, and the sponsor and her husband, which was binding for life and which was marked by the adoption of special terms of address. Henceforth they would call each other "very close friend," and they were expected to aid each other whenever the need arose. My information is that the girl and her sponsor acted as daughter and mother toward one another thereafter. As in the case of the pubescent girl's parents, the sponsor had to rely heavily on the support of matrilineal kinsmen, since she had to procure enough food to entertain the girl and her relatives at a large feast on the day before the ceremonial. When she agreed to fill the role, she went to the camp of the girl's parents to visit and to discuss the details of the event.[6]

The effectiveness of the ceremony depended upon its being performed according to an established pattern, and anything that disturbed it would be construed by one or more of the powers as signifying lack of respect. Thus, numerous precautions were taken against incidents that would inject an unwelcome element of disorder into a ceremony and, in so doing, threaten its success. As one woman told me, "Everything has to be done just right, there is no other way."

From four to nine structures were erected at the site by the relatives of the girl. These included a temporary wickiup for the pubescent girl and her family, a dwelling for the shaman near the girl's structure, large ramadas in which food would be prepared, and smaller shelters for the storage of groceries and clothing. They were built in two groups placed some distance apart and usually faced each other across the dance-ground. One group was used by the sponsor and her kinsmen, the other by the relatives of the pubescent girl. The sponsor did not arrive at the site until the shade buildings and food shelters were completed.

Since the most important quality bestowed on the pubescent girl during the ceremony was longevity, this was symbolized by a decorated wooden staff or cane with which she danced and which, years later, she might use as a walking stick. The cane varied in length from thirty to fifty inches. The day before the ceremony a male relative of the girl secured a straight piece of wood, stripped off the bark, bent one end over in a curve, and fastened it securely with a raw-

hide thong. Next, at a sweat-bathing ceremony, the medicine man painted the cane with a mixture of yellow ocher and water. Two golden eagle tail feathers were tied to the rawhide thong in an upright position; a turquoise prayer bead was attached to the base of one, and two orange oriole feathers to the base of the other. The eagle feathers were for protection against power-caused illnesses, and the oriole feathers promoted a good disposition—the oriole was a happy bird that minded its own business and behaved well. Four or more colored ribbons were also tied to the thong. The usual four were black, tan, yellow, and green, and they symbolized the cardinal directions. However, one cane I saw at San Carlos had eight ribbons, two each of purple, yellow, white, and black. Small bells were sometimes added to the cane to help the girl keep time while dancing.

Next, a straight drinking tube was fashioned from the stalk of a cattail plant. It was approximately two inches long and painted yellow like the cane. A wooden scratching stick was somewhat longer and also covered with ocher. It was pointed at one end and sometimes carved on the other. Both items were tied to a long strip of rawhide, which the pubescent girl wore around her neck, with the stick and tube hanging on her chest. During the ritual and for four days thereafter, the girl was to drink only through the tube and scratch herself only with the stick. If she drank otherwise she would develop unsightly facial hair. If she touched her face other than with the stick, her complexion would be marred.[7] Certain other important ritual paraphernalia would also be used.

A special buckskin ceremonial dress costume was made for her, and the medicine man covered it with yellow ocher. This was a duplicate of the one worn by Changing Woman, decorated with celestial symbols. To each of its shoulders he attached a small eagle-down feather, which would enable the girl to walk and run as lightly as such feathers floated on the air. Tied to her hair at the forehead was a small abalone shell that would identify her as White Shell Woman or Changing Woman, the mythological figure whose power was involved during the puberty ceremonial. A single eagle feather was fastened to her hair in such a way that it hung down behind her head. This symbolized longevity. It was either white or gray, and it was expected that the girl would live until her hair turned a similar color. There was also a large, tanned buckskin that was painted yellow, to which an eagle feather was attached. This symbolized a plentiful supply of deer meat and assured that the girl would never go hungry.[8]

At dusk on the evening before the event the singer and sponsor presented the girl with her clothing and other items, at which time four songs were sung.

When the ritual paraphernalia was ready, the sponsor presented the pubescent girl and her kinsmen, early in the morning, a gift basket of food for a large feast. And on the following day, after the ceremony had ended, the girl's relatives returned the favor. By exchanging food, the bond of special friendship was formally enjoined and symbolically acted out.[9]

On the night before the dance it was common practice to hold a huge social dance until midnight. It centered around a large bonfire, and there were many singers and drummers.

The Western Apache girl's puberty rite was the only major Apache ceremonial that was not performed at night. Shortly before sunrise, an open tipi was constructed of four spruce saplings, with the leaves either left on or tied on, to house the girl and her attendant. The Western Apache tipi was not nearly so impressive as those of the other Apache branches. A large cover of hide, a blanket, or a canvas was spread on the ground near the center of the dance-ground, and as many as twelve blankets were piled on top of it. The large buckskin was then placed on the pile, with its head end pointing toward the east. Next the gift basket and numerous containers filled with candy, other sweets, and fruit were arranged in two rows directly in front of the buckskin, and two small baskets and four drums

Top: Scratching stick and drinking tube. *Above:* Buckskin hoddentin bag (9th Annual Report BAE, pp. 494, 500).

74

were set to the west. One of these baskets contained tobacco—later cigarettes—and the other, cattail pollen. Before the ceremony got under way a male relative of the pubescent girl addressed everyone present regarding the need for good conduct and good thoughts.

It would not yet be 8:00 A.M. when the shaman and four drummers took their places behind the buckskin and the first song began. At this, the pubescent girl, in her buckskin costume and carrying the cane, came forth from her wickiup, followed by either a maternal aunt or an older sister. The crowd of guests came behind them. The girl and her relative stopped on the buckskin, faced east toward the rising sun, and the guests formed a large circle around the area.

The four-pole puberty tipi at San Carlos.

According to the Western Apache origin myth, there was once a time when Changing Woman lived all alone. Longing for children, she slept with Sun, and not long after gave birth to Slayer of Monsters, the foremost culture hero. Four days later, Changing Woman became pregnant by water and gave birth to Born of Water (also known as Child of the Water). As these half-brothers matured, Changing Woman instructed them how to live. They then left home and, following her advice, rid earth of most of its evil. Unlike certain other figures in Apache mythology, Changing Woman never became old. When she got to be a certain age, she went walking toward the

San Carlos, 1969: Above: *The singer and the musicians.* Opposite top: *Preparing the food for the puberty ceremony.* Opposite bottom: *Food preparation, emphasizing the involvement of everyone in the puberty rite.*

east. After a while she saw herself in the distance walking toward her. When she came together, there was only one, the young one. Then she was like a young girl all over again. Thus the power of Changing Woman offered the pubescent girl longevity and the physical capabilities of someone perpetually young.[10]

The primary objective of the puberty ceremonial was to transform the pubescent girl into Changing Woman. At the invocation of the medicine man, the power of Changing Woman entered the girl's body and resided there for four days. During this period, the girl acquired the surpassing qualities of Changing Woman herself and was thereby prepared for a useful and abundant life.[11]

While in my experience the variance between phases is not such as to be easily noted by the ordinary observer today, Keith Basso states that the Western Apache puberty ceremonial as performed in Cibecue is composed of eight distinct parts or phases. Each phase has its own name, which he sets forth, each is initiated and terminated by a particular group of chants, and each is followed

76

The puberty ceremony at San Carlos, 1969: Above: Temporary dwelling for pubescent girl and family. Opposite: Temporary dwelling for sponsor and family.

by a pause sometimes lasting as long as twenty minutes, during which no chants are sung, and the pubescent girl is allowed to rest.[12]

In my experiences at San Carlos, phases VII and VIII were not so distinguishable as the first six. At Cedar Creek and Whiteriver the format was much like that which Basso gives for Cibecue.

Phase I, "Alone she dances"[13] The pubescent girl dances lightly and alone in place on the buckskin, striking the base of her cane on the skin in time to the beat of the drums. The chants deal with the creation and emphasize the vital contributions made by Changing Woman. By the end of phase I, Changing Woman's power has entered the girl's body. At the same time, the spectators may engage in social dancing.

Phase II, "Kneeling"[14] The pubescent girl's sponsor walks to the buckskin and replaces the woman who first escorted the girl. From here on the sponsor instructs the girl and gives her moral support. Phase II recreates Changing Woman's impregnation by Sun. Prior to its start, the pubescent girl puts her cane down and takes a kneeling position on the buckskin. (In a ceremony witnessed at San Carlos, the cane was stood upright in the ground at the head of the lines of food containers during this phase and phase III.) As the songs begin, she raises her hands to shoulder level and, looking directly into the sun, sways from side to side as she symbolizes the posture in which Changing Woman underwent her first menstrual experience. Her sponsor dances beside her.

Phase III, "Lying"[15] The pubescent girl lies prone on the buckskin, with her arms at her sides and her legs together, while her sponsor, using both her hands and feet, massages the muscles in her legs, back, arms, and shoulders. By these actions Changing Woman causes the girl's body to become soft, so that it can be molded to give her straightness, beauty, and strength. She begins on the left and works to the right, eventually making a circle.

Phase IV, "Cane set out, she runs around it"[16] Before the start of phase IV, food may be distributed to the guests, and the pubescent girl's cane is taken from her by the shaman and stood upright in the ground about twenty-five feet east of the buckskin. As the first of four chants begins, she runs to the cane, circles it once, and returns. She is followed by her sponsor who, after circling the cane, returns with it to the buckskin. The girl's mother and other women may also follow. The sponsor hands the cane to the girl, and the remainder of the chant is danced in place. At the start of each chant, the cane is placed farther away from the buckskin. Each of the four runs symbolizes a stage of life through which the pubescent girl will pass: infancy, childhood and adolescence, maturity, and old age. As soon as the girl circles the cane, she is believed to own the stage of life it stands for. Thus, after completing the final run, the girl has, like Changing Woman, symbolically passed through all the stages of life and is assured of living until she is very old.

Phase V, "Running"[17] Phase V is like phase IV, although its purpose is similar to that of phase III. This time the cane is set out to the east, then to the south, then to the west, and finally to the north. The running in phase V enables the girl to run fast, like Changing Woman, without getting tired.

Phase VI, "Candy, it is poured"[18] The girl stands on the buckskin. The medicine man blesses the girl by sprinkling cattail pollen over her head and shoulders and on the crook of her cane. He then pours the contents of a small basket filled with candy, corn kernels, and coins over her head, and the guests scramble for it. After he pours it over her head, everything in all of the baskets at the ceremony becomes holy. Then the people are assured of food, good crops, and enough money for the future. After this, the male relatives of the pubescent girl carry the candy and fruit containers through the crowd, inviting everyone to take as much as he can.

Phase VII, "Blessing her"[19] The pubescent girl and her sponsor dance in place, while all adults, including outsiders, who so

The puberty ceremony at San Carlos, 1969: Opposite top: The sponsor bringing her gift basket of food to the pubescent girl. Opposite bottom: The food and gift baskets are set out; the ceremony is about to begin. Above: Phase I, "Alone she dances." Medicine man asks for power of Changing Woman to enter girl. Left: Phase III, "Lying." The sponsor massages the girl to give her straightness, beauty, and strength.

Phase IV, "Cane set out, she runs around it."

desire line up before the buckskin and repeat for themselves the blessing with pollen that inaugurated phase VI. This is of great significance, for those who bless the girl may request the power of Changing Woman to grant them a personal wish for help. It is believed that every such wish will come true.

Phase VIII, "Throwing them off"[20] The pubescent girl steps off the buckskin, picks it up with both hands, shakes it, and then throws it toward the east. Following this, she throws a blanket from the pile in each of the other three cardinal directions. This assures that she will always have plenty of blankets and that her camp will always be clean. The thrown buckskin means there will always be deer meat in her camp and good hunting for everyone.

The puberty ceremonial ends with phase VIII. The girl and her sponsor retire immediately, and everyone else goes home. In the one-day ceremony about four hours will have elapsed since the rite began. However, Changing Woman's power continues to reside in the girl for four days and, acting through her, may be used to heal or to bring rain.[21]

In the afternoon of the ceremony, a feast is served and there are social events. At night the Gans, preceded by the clown, perform, and the girl and her companion make an appearance. Social dancing follows, and continues throughout the night as the Apache express their great happiness over the event.

Up until 1900, almost every Western Apache girl had a puberty ceremony. Today it is held only a few times a year, and the dresses are not often as splendid as those of former days. The first reason for its decline has been the White and Indian missionaries who have strongly criticized the "old way religion," causing younger Apache to doubt that the ceremony will actually assure the pubescent girl, among other things, of long life and prosperity. The second

Above: *Phase VI, "Candy, it is poured." The singer blesses the girl with pollen.* Left: *Phase VII, "Blessing her," with pollen.*

reason is its prohibitive cost, for nowadays the expense in money and labor far surpasses what most Apache people are able, or willing, to afford. The cost alone may easily exceed $750. Also, if for one reason or another the pubescent girl herself does not want to have the ceremony, if her parents suggest it, she makes her feelings known and their plans for the ceremony are dropped. Nevertheless, it is a splendid, meaningful and holy event, and its passing as a custom for every girl is to be regretted.

In considering its overall worth in Apache society, the puberty ceremony first of all brought into careful focus a number of critical life-objectives toward which all Apache girls on the threshold of adulthood should aspire. These were positive thoughts about one's own self and value, physical strength, an even temperament, prosperity, and a sound, healthy old age.

The puberty ceremonial also made many contributions to Apache society at large. By stressing the need for close cooperation, ceremonials did much to reinforce clan solidarity. And by demonstrating the practical advantages of extended kinship, they helped confirm the utility and effectiveness of the existing social order.[22] Moreover, in the face of sickness, hunger, and poverty, the ceremony conveyed the comforting message that old age, good health, and prosperity were always within reach. This made the harsh realities of day-to-day existence seem less threatening and easier to contend with. Viewed in this light, female puberty became a means for invoking the benevolence of Changing Woman's power and bringing the prospect of good fortune to everyone in the community.

Taken as a whole, the puberty ceremony symbolized the era of happiness and plenty that the Apache believed existed in mythological times. Thus the myth of Changing Woman, and her presence in the pubescent girl, linked the ritual to the ancient past. Like other Apache rituals, the ultimate justification for the puberty ceremony came not so much from the ceremony itself as from the long cultural tradition of which it was a product.[23]

In visiting the puberty ceremonies of recent years, one can hardly avoid noting that the ready availability of alcoholic beverages has brought enough unhappy consequences to cause serious problems

Below: *Social dancing at the puberty ceremony.* Opposite top: *Painted-hide war medicine amulet worn as necktie (AF). Hoop is 4½ inches in diameter, ½ inch thick. Front view.* Opposite bottom: *Back view.*

for the ritual. On occasion, it has even been sufficient to cause the singer to dispense with or cut short some of his chants. Even the Apache rule about an attitude of happiness and good thoughts is being stretched past its bounds in this regard.

Nevertheless, only a minority are guilty of this. The immediate participants and most of the guests continue to manifest the time-honored reverence and sincerity that has marked the beautiful ceremony over its long and venerable history. And more than once in recent years, a skeptic modern girl who wondered whether the ancient ritual was really worth going through has been literally transformed into a believer by passing through it.

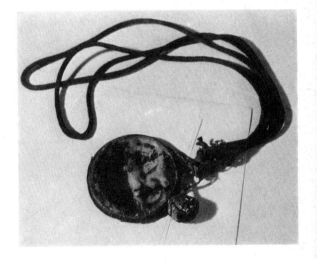

6 Boy's Maturity Rites*

According to Reagan, in 1901–1902, "The boys in the Cibecue area who were entering the period of manhood went off singly or in groups to fast, to pray, and to perform ceremonies prescribed by the medicinemen to make them strong, courageous men, to secure them a suitable wife and healthy offspring. They also received instruction aimed at helping them to choose their adult occupation and to understand their guardian or helper spirit. Hopefully, after prolonged prayer and fasting the spirit would appear to them in a dream as any animate or inanimate thing, or even something purely imaginary." Reagan says, "Having seen his guiding spirit, the seeker for knowledge makes a miniature effigy of it which he wears suspended from his neck ever afterwards. A medicine bag is also given him at this time to ward off sickness and bring him luck. The ceremony is closed with an elaborate feast, usually followed by a prolonged dance."[1]

7 Courtship and Marriage

Albert Reagan presents us with some absorbing insights into Western Apache courtship and marriage customs at the turn of the twentieth century. The female was the aggressor in courtship. By a look, a word, or a light slap as she passed the man of her choice, she indicated that his attentions were welcome. She also chose him at the dances. Once chosen, the male, if he cared to respond, became the aggressor. He sometimes went to her most frequented trail, usually the one along which she carried water, and placed a row of stones on both sides of it for a distance of from five to fifteen feet. Then he hid himself in the immediate vicinity and waited for her to come along, "showing himself to her through the bushes or by peeking over a ridge or behind some obstruction just before she arrives at the line of stones." If she passed around the stones it indicated she had decided to refuse him; but if she walked down the trail between the stones, his advances were welcome.

In some instances, the male then rushed out, seized her, and took her to his camp. Following the more usual custom, however, the girl would slip into his wickiup and stay with him a number of nights, the number of these varying in different parts of the reservation. After the final night she stayed with him, she cooked breakfast in the morning, hung out his bedding to air, and might even catch his horse and saddle it for him. He accepted her as his wife by eating what she cooked and taking the horse she had saddled for him. "He then must buy her from her parents or guardian, or from her former husband's relatives, should she be a widow. The price is usually about one hundred dollars in blankets, ponies, and trinkets." The purchase goods were taken during the night and placed near or against the girl's dwelling. If they were adequate, the girl's family took possession of them and she went, either at once or the very next night, to the man's house to be his wife. If the gifts were not adequate, they were immediately returned.

Sometimes more was demanded. In such instances the suitor would add what he could, and if it was still not enough he or his

* In regard to the boy's maturity, see also the Novice Complex for Raid and War in the Chiricahua section, page 260.

parents or guardians would borrow the balance from relatives. "The Apache are good at helping the aspiring boys in such cases and the writer never knew a case where the borrowed property was not paid back." Sometimes the suitor was flatly rejected, and no amount whatsoever would induce the girl's people to let her become his wife. "For instance, one of the stable boys at the Agency wished to marry a good-looking and well-behaved Apache girl in 1901, but her parents refused to permit the marriage. The suitor was persistent. Five times he took his goods to her home to buy her, increasing the amount each time, but the objection could not be overcome. So he finally married another girl."

The fact that a girl was sold for profit was the cause of considerable trouble for both the Apache and the Agency. The husband felt that since he had bought and paid for his wife he could treat her accordingly. Moreover, when an Apache family was in bad financial straits they often sold their daughters when they were too young to be married—"for example, a marriage of an eight-year-old boy to a girl about the same age. Of course this marriage was not reported to the Agent or approved by him. The Apache marry when too young so that, as a result, there are many separations."

The following courtship and marriage customs in different sections of the reservation in 1901–1902 were related to Reagan by medicine men of the respective sections.

> At Cibicu, when courting, the woman comes to her intended husband's house seven nights in succession. On six mornings she rises before dawn and goes home, but on the seventh morning she stays, hangs out his bed in the sun, cooks his breakfast, and sets it before him, but she herself does not taste it. She then goes home, where she remains some months while he collects property enough to purchase her. When the property is delivered, they have the agent marry them and they live together.

> In courting, at Fort Apache, a girl and boy often slap each other, tap each other, or rap each other over the back or head in a loving way with a stick or anything else which they may have in hand, appearing, to a stranger, as if they were angry at each other. At some gathering, the boy accompanied by another boy or the girl by another girl proceeds to where the other individual is. If there happens to be only one boy at the place, another boy is hunted up for the extra girl. The boy and girl who want to mate go off alone for a friendly chat. After a few such meetings the boy goes to the girl's house, taking another boy with him, for whom a second girl is obtained. Here he has another chat. After he has visited her at home a few times, she, in company with another girl, visits his house. After about five such visits from the girl, a separate house is built for the boy and at nightfall he goes to bed in it. Then, after everyone has retired, the girl slips over to her fiancé's house and crawls in with him, but she does not touch him during the night. In the early morning she slips back to her own house before any of her people are up. The next night she steals to his camp again and sleeps with him, but the next morning she cooks his breakfast and takes his bed out to sun. She does not taste the breakfast and when he has eaten she goes home. This last act shows him that she is willing to take care of him and to live with him. His eating what she has cooked demonstrates his acceptance of her as his wife. He then proceeds to purchase her from her parents or guardian. Then they go to the Agency to be lawfully married.[1]

8 Division of Labor

In the old days, the Apache men went on raids and war parties, hunted, made their weapons and medicine objects, gambled, and sat on the local group councils. In 1902, at the time Reagan wrote, the Apache men worked as White men did when paid for their work, but otherwise were cattlemen, herders, and hunters, and helped a little with the farming work.

The Apache women did the greater part of what might

properly be termed work. To Reagan (although the accounts of Cremony and Goodwin yet to come should be balanced against this), it seemed as if the woman of 1902 was in a very true sense "bought and paid for" by her husband, and he treated her accordingly. "She does his every bidding. Furthermore, at mealtime she must wait until he and his guests have eaten and then eat what is left or do without, if he and his guests have eaten all the food. She even goes to the hills and brings in his horse, saddles and bridles it, and leads it to him, as he lolls outside the house. Her position is the most wretched of any woman yet seen by the writer. Only in drinking tiswin will the husband share equally and at the same time with his wife. He will even offer her a drink first."[1]

The woman usually prepared the man's breakfast for him; then, after putting out water for him to wash in, she went to the hills for his horse, brought it in, and saddled and bridled it. She carried the wood and water, often a half mile or more. Water was transported in a large tus, or water bottle, which she carried on her back and which was supported by a strap that passed from the handles of the tus in a loop across her forehead. The load was so heavy that she had to bow her neck and bend her body forward to carry it. She often handled a monstrous load of firewood, in a large carrying basket suspended at her back much like the tus. She stood the large sticks on end in the basket so that they would lean out from her back, then filled the basket with small sticks. The space between the upright sticks and her back was then filled with poles laid horizontally, as high as she could pile them, placing the poles over her head on the basket.[2]

9 The Woman's Status

While women played the subordinate roles in the social, economic, and religious areas, there were aspects of life in which they exercised control. The wife was a joint owner of family property, and the food was mostly hers, to be disposed of as she saw fit. She was involved in the selection of a mate and in the general control and custody of the children. Marriages, divorces, places of residence, and monetary matters were all subject to the woman's influences.[1] The woman was always a force to be considered in family and camp decisions and in the formulation of the husband's views. Women seldom sat in council, but the men there often spoke for their wives as they advanced their views.

Cremony believed it was a great mistake to suppose that, because Apache men were seemingly indifferent to the condition of their women and forced the burden of hard labor upon them, they were not elated by their praises or humbled by their censures. On the contrary, they were keenly alive to these, and under the mask of apparent indifference and assumed superiority were quite as susceptible to the blandishments and opinions of the female sex as the most civilized and enlightened of their White American friends. After a successful raid the men were received with songs and rejoicings. Their deeds were rehearsed "with many eulogiums," and they became great, in their own estimations, for a while. But if they were unsuccessful, they were met with jeers and insults. The women turned away from them with assumed indifference and contempt. They were upbraided as cowards, as lacking in skill and tact. Further, they were told that such men should not have wives, because they did not know how to provide for their wants. When so reproached, the warriors hung their heads and offered no excuse for failure. To do so would only have subjected them to further ridicule and objurgation. Instead, they simply bided their time and expected to make their peace by a future successful raid.[2]

In another place Cremony claimed that among those who had enjoyed the best opportunities for judging, the award for female chastity was given to the Apache. During a period of about two years, when hundreds of them were under government charge, and during which time they mingled freely with the troops, not a single case occurred, to the best of his knowledge, wherein an Apache woman surrendered her person to any man outside her tribe. Cases of conjugal infidelity were extremely rare among them, and the girls took no ordinary pride in guarding their purity. The art of coquetry was practiced among them with quite as much zest as among the belles of White cities, and with such delicacy and tact that the most refined among others might possibly study at a worse school. On the other hand, the Navajo were "extremely loose and sensuous."[3]

10 Mother-in-Law Avoidance

In 1902, the Apache man continued to observe the custom of not speaking to his mother-in-law, and would turn his back on her as she passed him. He never entered her house, and if it was necessary for her to come to his, he left it and stayed away while she was there. "The Apache say that the mother of the wife is the cause of all domestic trouble and is a woman to be shunned. The Apache woman visits her mother-in-law and in a few cases lives with her. The Apache believe that if a man looks at his mother-in-law he will become blind."[1]

Other information concerning this custom is included in the Mescalero section.

11 Personality Characteristics

Goodwin found the Western Apache to be a happy people who loved to laugh and who had an excellent sense of humor. Other researchers found this to be true of the other Apache peoples as well, and it is so on the reservations today. Goodwin goes on to say that they sometimes laughed until the tears ran down their cheeks, and that young girls often had fits of giggling. Emotions were restrained only when there was danger of hurting someone's feelings. Certain individuals and families gained reputations for their humor, and it appears that this was greatly appreciated by others.[1]

Certain characteristics were believed to be masculine, and certain traits, feminine. The gentler things, such as quiet ways and the quiet happenings in nature, were associated with the woman. Her symbol was the carrying basket, her language was feminine, and she walked and sat in a traditionally modest style. The man was bolder, his symbol was the bow and the gun, and his ways were more boisterous. Now and then an athletic woman would compete with a man in a race just to keep him in his place, and a few women went to war. But these were the exceptions and not the rule.[2]

Goodwin learned that the mental abilities of the Western Apache were like those of other peoples, showing the same trends and qualities as society in general. Some were apt and able, others were limited. It appeared that the children of wealthier families had greater advantages and were usually superior scholastically, reflecting the ability of the rich to expose their children to greater privileges.[3] Irene Burlison found that the Western Apache children of the 1940s were fine students when sensibly approached, and especially talented in art, having excellent creativity and vivid imaginations.[4]

My personal encounters with present-day Apache have revealed them to be quick to comprehend, and to possess incisive minds—in other words, to be people who have common sense and are able to cut quickly to the core of a question in spite of the occasional problem of having to translate it into the Apache concept. They also have a special awareness of others, being concerned to speak and act in such a way as not to shame or embarrass whoever is present at a conversation. This is a special evidence of intelligence on its broadest plane. Unquestionably, there are less capable people on the reservations, but aside from those whose minds have been befuddled by drinking, I've met remarkably few.

As a rule, the poor were considered to be less blessed by the supernatural powers than the rich. But at the same time the rich were expected to be especially generous. Not to be so was considered mean, and in some instances would bring accusations of witchcraft.

There were close bonds of affection between certain kin such as cross-cousins, who were of the same clan, and there were prescribed kinship terms and acts to be employed when such persons met. Kinship terminology was, in fact, amazingly complicated, so much so as to make it impossible to treat the subject here. There was also a distinct type of friendship between close non-relatives. Such persons would be described as "my friend" or "my partner"; the same term could not be used for any one related by blood or marriage or for any member of one's clan, related clans, or paternally related clans. Goodwin explains that if an individual thus addressed becomes a relative-in-law, the term is usually discarded for an affinal one—that is, one pertaining to a relative by marriage. "My friend" is sometimes used between joking cross-cousins, but merely because such improper use of it is a joke. "The word immediately suggests a friendly relationship and interchange of favors and is sometimes used to gain good will, even from a stranger, or to pave the way for some important request."[5]

In portraying the native Apache character and temperament, Goodwin asserts that individual variations among the Apache are just as evident as among the Whites. And it is a matter of extreme importance in social relations to determine just what temperament people are, since this influences others' reactions to them in any given situation.[6]

The average Apache, when sober, was not quarrelsome in Goodwin's day, and that has continued to be so. In fact, the advice usually given is to simply leave an angry person alone until he cools down, since " he's mad and he sure doesn't know what he's doing. If you say something he will only get madder, then he might hit somebody."

While the people have quick tempers, with men being openly hostile when aroused and women likely to cry, blasphemy and profanity have not been a part of the Apache way. Threats made today will probably not be followed up, unless the parties involved are under the influence of liquor. In the old days, drunken brawls often led to the death of several of those involved. It still happens, but less frequently by far.

Apache women love to gossip, but it has always been considered poor conduct to take the names of others in vain. Lying is a terrible fault, punishable by the "powers."[7]

Bravery was a favored quality in the old days, and pride was permissible so long as it was not carried to the extreme. Boasting was acceptable as long as the boast was true.

Modesty in physical habits was expected, although the Apache faced the experiences of living and growing up in a realistic way. Sex and body functions were openly discussed, and without hesitancy, according to Goodwin, in mixed company. Also, obscene jokes were freely told, except in the presence of those with whom there was a respect relationship.[8]

In concluding his remarks concerning the various social concepts and practices among the Western Apache, Goodwin states that in former times the greatest achievement in life that a woman could hope for was to marry a good man, be a fine mother and wife, be economically secure, have good husbands for her daughters, and perhaps own a minor power and ceremony. A man's hopes centered in his becoming a great hunter, warrior, and leader or an influential and successful shaman.[9]

Over the years these aims have changed little for women. Men may still, although more rarely, wish to be shamans, but more often desire to be well-established workers and businessmen. White ideals have become an ever-present part of the life experience, although the present view still favors the conditioning of all things by as much as possible of the old ways, which are still thought good by those who have lived in them and seen the fruit of their blessings.

89

An Apache of former times continued to carry on with his share of the family duties as long as he was physically able. Usually the man, whose tasks required greater physical endurance than those of the woman, retired from active life at a younger age. By this, it is not meant that all activity ceased, but rather that day by day less and less was done, until finally the aged person couldn't keep up anymore.

Very old age was looked upon as a second childhood, and once it was reached the individual did little more than exist until death came. As long as they could follow along on trips, old people did so. At other times they stayed behind to tend the crops. No special favors were shown them, and if an aged person was given help in moving it was as much to speed things along as to show pity. The life was demanding, and people were forced to comply with its demands. There was no other choice.[10]

Sometimes the aged person was given his own wickiup, where time could be spent in drowsing and reminiscing. If he was too weak to cook, food was brought to him from the communal cooking center.

People of influence, such as aged shamans or chiefs, might continue to exercise some influence in the community, and men and women with clear minds would continue to dispense their wisdom in family affairs and in storytelling. Supernatural power itself was believed to wane with the passing of a person's prime years.

If the aged person still shared a family wickiup, he received the poorest location for his bed along with the worst blankets. His clothing was the shabbiest of the family attire, and he received the least desirable portions of food.

Sometimes, when the aged could no longer walk or ride, they were "thrown away." In such instances, the family left a supply of food and water and went away, saying they would return in a few days, but not intending to do so.[11] This was not considered an unkind custom, for the Apache were forced to move to gather food in season, for sanitary reasons, and because a permanent camp would become an easily found target by the enemy tribes. Therefore, in a time of constant moving the aged person became a difficulty of some magnitude, and the old were as well aware of that truth as any of the others, for in their youth they had done the same thing themselves.

12 Tag-Bands; English Names

In the 1800s, the Agency introduced on the Western Apache reservations the use of metal tags for identification purposes. These were employed as a convenient means of administering rations and systemizing daily contacts with the Apache, for English-speaking people were simply not able to use Apache names. In particular, the tags aided the Agency as it began to replace the authority of the local group. Goodwin explains the tag-band system as follows:

> Government usurping of chief's power and function has also helped to liquidate the local group. The government took over supervision of certain irrigation systems, controlled the food supply by rationing, and handled serious social misdemeanors in the reservation courts which it dominated. It did not hesitate to contradict and alter a chief's course of action. It created tag-band chiefs, some of whom were true chiefs, others being merely wealthy men found to be amenable to the whites, and an alien patrilineal system of inheritance for tag-band chieftainships was imposed. In an attempt to recognize some of the already existing social units and to form a method of reservation identification, early governmental authorities on the San Carlos and Fort Apache reservations divided the total population into lettered tag-bands, those on the San Carlos Reservation being listed with double letters, such as "CF" or "SL," etc., and those on the Fort Apache Reservation as A, B, C, etc.
>
> All married men were assigned a number in the tag-band with which they were affiliated, and wives took the same number as their husbands. On the death of a man, his number was held

open for the next man needing one. Tag-band numbers were allotted mainly according to residence after marriage. Each tag-band had a chief selected and recognized by the government, who always was given the number 1. When a tag-band chief died, another man was appointed in his place and given his number. All men were supposed to wear a metal tag about their necks, on which was stamped their number. On the San Carlos Reservation these metal tags are said to have been differently shaped for each tag-band. Actually, tag-bands in the beginning were composed of from one to two or three prereservation local groups coming from the same locality, and in almost all cases the local groups combined in one tag-band came from the same aboriginal band. The tag-band system is rapidly going out of use now [1930–1940], as members are no longer allotted.

Some true chiefs, such as Diablo, were not appointed tag-band chiefs, and though they continued to exert considerable influence among their people, their prestige was seriously damaged. When these chiefs became old, they were not replaced. Thus, formal chieftainship became a thing of the past. Until 1895 tag-band chiefs functioned in many respects as true chiefs. At one time they drew the beef ration for their tag-bands and distributed it. They guaranteed payment on supplies bought by their people in the traders' stores, and credit could be obtained by merely presenting the borrowed metal identification tag of a tag-band chief, against whose account the amount was charged.... By 1895 the change had become so great and government domination so established, there was less and less room for chiefs. In one or two instances tag-band chiefs, too keen and assertive to be duped, were removed from the chieftainship by the agency.... The few tag-band chiefs remaining are old, and when they die they will not be replaced.[1]

Goodwin goes on to state that the Apache copied the Agency in the tag name practice, and that for many years tag-band identifications were often used as names. "However, this custom is gradually passing out of use, for more than twenty years ago the government allotted personal and family names, the use of which has become recognized by both whites and Apache."[2]

An elderly Apache man told Harry T. Getty that "girls used their father's tag-band number until married, then they used their husband's. The boys in a family took successive numbers beyond that of the father, but using the same letters." The Agency superintendent's annual report for 1913 states that a full-blood Apache who was a graduate of Carlisle Indian School had been employed "to take an accurate census of the San Carlos and Fort Apache Indians and to rename them consistently with respect to family relationships, in order to do away with the so-called 'tag-names,' the use of which is repugnant to all ideas of civilization." But Getty found that a 1952 reservation census in the Agency offices at San Carlos still showed the tag-band affiliation of individual Indians.[3]

The Apache received their English names in various ways. Missionaries bestowed some names, and children born in hospitals were sometimes given an English name. Parents named children after Whites they liked, and especially after noted people such as presidents. Some children were named after states. Since the people were often in Mexico, Mexican names became common. Now and then, in utter frustration at trying to pronounce an Apache name, a soldier would give the person an English name or nickname that stuck.[4] In consequence, every conceivable name is found on the reservation today.

13 Crime and Punishment

In former times it had been a Western Apache practice for a husband to cut off the tip of the nose of his wife if she was immoral. It was not often done, but when it was, the man considered that he had only done his duty. Nevertheless, it was a wretched practice, and since the husband was accuser, judge, and jury, his jealousy often caused an innocent woman to suffer. In consequence, the practice was forbidden by the army, and it was not being resorted to in 1901. In those days, the Apache did not as a rule steal among themselves and only rarely took things from White people. Cabins were abandoned for years with things left in them that were never touched. Even a quart of whiskey was left in a certain farmer's residence for seven months while the farmer was serving at the Agency, and it was never touched, though the door of the house was unlocked. So there was no thieving to be punished, although an animal breaking into a field was considered a rogue and his ears were cut off in punishment.[1]

14 Social Dances

At the turn of the twentieth century, social dances were held for amusement whenever the Apache felt like it. No special costume was worn, except that each dancer dressed as well as possible.

There were two styles of social dances. One was similar to the dancing at the puberty ceremonies, except that no girl danced with a cane and the unmarried women all chose male partners. For the second, a central fire was built, to the west of which the musicians, drummers, and all the men who cared to dance were seated. Around them was a large leveled area, on the margin of which were seated the families and spectators. Surrounding the fire were the unmarried women, formed in couples and facing inward. The married women clowned around, but did not dance, lest their ever-jealous husbands beat them even before they got home.

The same girls worked as partners for the entire night. The two girls selected a single boy to dance with in each set. This was done by walking straight to where he was seated and touching him on the shoulder, after which they immediately turned around and walked away. If the boy refused to dance, the masters of ceremony compelled him to do so. Sometimes they took hold of him forcibly and escorted him to the girls who had chosen him. In dancing the girl did not touch the boy but faced him at a distance of about three feet. The dancing consisted of swinging back and forth around the circumference of a great dance wheel, the partners usually taking five steps forward and seven backward, in time with the music of the drum and the singing. When the girls danced forward, the boys danced backward, and vice versa. Reagan says that to see all the radii of the great dance wheel move backward and forward in the light of the huge central fire was a "picturesque sight." The completion of a song marked the conclusion of each dance; then partners were chosen for another set. At intervals there were feasting, visiting, and tulapai drinking. The dance usually continued until dawn.[1]

15 Sign Language and Signaling

When Reagan was with the Western Apache in 1901 and 1902, he found that the people were adept in the use of sign language. One could converse with another and be understood, though neither understood a spoken word of the other's language. They were even more resourceful in their ability to send messages by a signaling system. "At the time of the Battle of Cibicu the scouts with the army advised the Indians just how many soldiers were coming and where they intended to camp, and all arrangements were made for the massacre when the army was still miles away." When Reagan made his first visit to Cibecue in 1902, as the Indians with him "began to descend the Cibicu Range toward Cibicu Valley, the aids began to signal, by flashing sun rays across the intervening space by small reflecting looking-glasses, that the Government party was coming and that the writer was to have charge of the valley, and the reflected glasses of the valley answered back: 'It is well. We are all well. We have plenty to eat.' And so on. About three hours later when the party arrived at the Government quarters in the valley, they found every Indian in the valley there to receive them, having been called together by the signaling." Messages were sent by flashes or mirrors, by smoke and differently arranged fires in the daytime, and by fires at night.[1]

Other means were employed to impart information. A stick laid in a certain way in the trail meant, "You are to go in the direction the sharp end points." If laid at the fork of a trail, it indicated which fork to take. A dead owl placed in the trail meant that some terrible disease was raging in the region toward which the owl's head was turned; sometimes an owl effigy was used instead of a real bird. For this purpose a tree by the trail with all its limbs off except one was used. A mud effigy of an owl, the image of death, was placed on the limb, facing the area where disease was present. Around the tree near the ground a band of grass was wrapped and tied with some weeds to catch the attention of passers-by. When Reagan was at Fort Apache, smallpox broke out at a cow camp on Bonito Creek. "Owl effigies were at once placed in all the trails leading toward the camp and no Indian ventured that way and consequently no one got smallpox."[2]

The signal to advance.

16 Schools

Little is known about the nature of early schooling among the Apache. It is clear, however, that the White man's treatment of the Apache did not encourage them to accept the White man's ways, so that around 1901 most Apache were against the idea of schools. Upon learning that to enter the boarding school at Fort Apache a child had to pass a physical examination at the beginning of the school year, they often did all they could to impair the child's health so that he could not pass the test. Before school began each fall they performed medicine dances and kept the children in constant turmoil in the hope it would exhaust them physically and make them "medicine-proof against the white man's ways and medicines."[1] Sometimes they would dip the children in the cold water of the creeks and hold them there in the hope that they would develop chills, and then be too sick to be admitted to school. It was an effective practice, and it did keep some children out of school, but it also cost the lives of several of them.[2]

Other ruses were employed to frustrate the Agency. Absent children were taught to feign illness when the officers came looking for them. Once Reagan was ordered by the Agent to go to Canyon Creek to get the children of a certain family and bring them to school.

As he approached the place he saw two little girls out in the field working with their mother. As the writer started to descend the canyon, the children spied him and were heard to exclaim, *Indah* (white man). The tortuous trail descending into the valley wound about so that he was out of sight of the field and the children for a moment. When he came in sight again, the children were nowhere to be seen. On arriving at the camp he found them lying on a blanket coughing and breathing hard. They were "awfully sick," said the mother. "All same got pneumonia. Soon die, maybe." The writer said nothing and rode away. Once out of sight he tied his horse and slipped into the canyon on foot. And the children were running about playing with high glee in the field again. Two days later they were in the Fort Apache boarding school.[3]

17 Dwellings, Furniture, and Utensils

In 1900, the Western Apache lived in circular, dome-shaped wickiups, which sometimes had conical tops. San Carlos dwellings were often smaller than those at Fort Apache, because of a poorer supply of materials. The Apache house was erected by the women. It was made of a framework of poles and limbs tied together, over which a thatch of bear grass, brush, yucca leaves, rushes, or flags was placed. A canvas was stretched over this on the windward side. The structure was open at the top to allow smoke to escape from a fire built in a pit near the center of the house. The doorway was a low opening on one side, over which a blanket or piece of skin was stretched. This style of house was reasonably comfortable, but smoke in the eyes was a constant problem. It took about four hours to build such a dwelling.

In summer, the family often built a circular brush windbreak and moved outdoors. They also built a cooler by setting posts in the

Below: Building the wickiup frame *(SM).* Opposite top: *Wickiup covered with melon vines.* Opposite bottom: *Wickiup with bear-grass thatching. Both structures are San Carlos; the front and rear doors of the bottom dwelling are unusual.*

95

ground in the form of a rectangle on which they tied horizontal poles for bracing. On these they interwove twigs and brush to fashion a thatch latticework. They then covered the enclosure with a brush roof. Such a house, called a ramada by Whites and a squaw-cooler by the Apache, made a comfortable work area in summer. Sometimes the posts were set in the ground and only a brush roof was made, forming a more open arbor.

To facilitate easy moving, wickiup furniture was kept at a minimum. Wooden bed frames were sometimes made with a pole base that raised the frame some two or three feet above the ground. On this, brush and dry grass were spread and covered by blankets. For kitchen utensils the woman had a pot, a skillet or frying pan or two, and possibly a dishpan. She also secured a five-gallon coal oil can at the trading post in which to boil meat and soups and make tulapai. She also had a tus (water jug), a few knives, a pounding stone or two, and a pair of stone grinding slabs (metate and mano), which were probably picked up near some old ruin.[1]

Moving camp was a herculean task for the women. The family horse was loaded with as much as he could carry, and the women had to carry the rest.

18 Food and Drink

Corn was harvested in September and October. The Western Apache woman of 1902 ground corn with a metate and mano, but used no grinding box. According to Reagan, to make fine meal she ground the corn twice. By 1902 flour was being purchased at the trader's store and not ground by the Apache. Soups and gravies were common. Corn pone was baked in or under the ashes or in lard in a skillet. A sort of cornmeal pancake was made from cornmeal and water, without salt. When thoroughly stirred, it was baked in a skillet. Mush was prepared much as White women made it, except that it was stirred with two sticks. Wheat flour was made into biscuit bread and fried in the skillet. Dumplings were made without baking powder or soda. A wheat-flour dough bread was baked in or under the ashes. Sometimes it was wrapped in green cornhusks and baked in the ashes, as was corn pone occasionally. In 1902, baking powder and soda bread in flat rolls was baked in Dutch ovens. The principal bread used, however, was the tortilla. To prepare these, a stiff dough was made with flour and baking powder, if available; if not, simply flour, water, and salt. A lump about the size of a biscuit was then pulled off the dough, rolled to biscuit shape, and pressed and flapped between the hands till it was the size and shape of a pancake. It was then baked dry on the bottom of an inverted frying pan placed over the fire. Enough of these were baked for a meal for the whole family, and often this bread with coffee constituted the entire meal.[1]

The bean pod of a species of locust tree was gathered when not quite matured and dried. The pods and beans were then crushed on the metate to a fine sweet powder called "sugar" by the Apache, which was mixed with water and cooked or eaten raw.

The Apache could make a meal of honey and boiled corn smut, a fungus. A beverage was made from walnut meats, hulls, and shells, mashed fine together, covered with water, and boiled. When cooked, the product was filtered; the resulting liquid, which was white and tasted much like milk, was a very nutritious food. Green corn when not yet in the "milk" was boiled and eaten, cob and all, or roasted before the fire. Sometimes it was cut from the cob, mashed on the metate, then boiled. Sometimes it was gathered and thrown into a separate heap. A pit was dug and a large quantity of wood thrown into it. On this, stones were piled. The wood was then ignited. When it had burned down to the live coal stage, wet grass, twigs, or cornhusks were piled in, and the green corn with the shucks still on was hurriedly thrown on. The corn was covered with more wet grass or corn fodder, and about six inches of dirt was heaped over the pile. Just before closing in the top, a quantity of water was poured in, to make steam. The cooking process took about twenty-four hours, after which the dirt was scraped off and the corn taken out. The husks were then stripped and tied together and the ears of corn hung out to dry on the cob. When dried the corn was shelled and stored in hide sacks, large storage baskets, or tus for use when needed. An underground cache was often used for storage. A deep pit was lined with rocks, and the storage containers were placed in it and covered with brush and more rocks. Mud was used to fill the spaces between the rocks, and dirt was smoothed over the top to finish the job.[2]

Roasting corn (MNM, Chapman Coll.).

Mescal was a spring crop. To gather and prepare mescal roots and heads, six to eight women went as a group to the hills where it grew, set up camps, and proceeded to collect the heads. It took them about two days to collect a ton of these. When enough were gathered, a large pit, ten to fifteen feet wide and three to five feet deep, was dug and filled with dry wood, on which a large quantity of stones was piled. The wood was then ignited, and when it had burned down to live coals and the stones were white hot, wet twigs, rushes, or grass were hurriedly placed on them to a thickness of about a foot. The mescal roots were then hurled on the smoking mass, more wet grass and twigs were piled over them, and the whole was covered with a foot or more of earth. A fire was then kindled over this pile and kept burning. The cooking continued for from twenty-four hours to four days, depending on the size of the roots and heads. The pit was then opened and the roots taken out and placed on pack animals or carried by the women to their homes, where they were stored for future use. They tasted like squash, except that they had a slightly burned tinge. They were an excellent food.[3]

Berries were usually eaten without cooking. Reagan, writing in 1902, says there were not many berries in the reservation region.[4] A great variety of cactus fruit did grow in the area, ranging from sour to sweet. The Apache women knew when each kind ripened and they made long trips to obtain it. The fruit was spiny, but good eating when the spines were removed, which was done by rolling the fruit in the sand or rubbing it with a piece of buckskin. It was then eaten like an apple; the sweet kind was made into a sort of butter.

The Spanish bayonet yucca plant growing in the region had a pod which looked something like a very large bean pod. This was gathered by the women and roasted before the fire or in the ashes; the pod, not the seed, was then eaten. It had a burned squash taste, but was relished by the Indians. The pod was also dried after it was split open and the seeds and seed-ribbon were removed. It was then boiled for eating. When thus prepared it had a pumpkin flavor.[5]

In the fall the women went in large numbers to gather piñon nuts. Even whole bands, men and all, would sometimes make up a foraging party. The nuts were gathered in the cone, which was either burned off near where they were gathered or after returning home. As the cone was burned or dried the nuts fell out. These were then collected and placed in storage jars for future use. To prepare them for eating, the nuts were placed among live coals on an open tray, which was shaken and tossed to aid the parching process and to keep the nuts from burning. When done, the nuts were taken from the tray and the charcoal and ashes removed by tossing them in the wind. The nuts were then ground on the grinding slabs, hulls and all, and the flour thus produced was made into soups and also baked like bread cakes.[6]

A certain acorn, called chechil by the Indians, was hulled and the kernel ground and mixed with flour in the proportion of one to five and made into a bread preparation. "Coffee" was also made from this preparation, by browning the acorn. The acorns were also eaten raw. Half-grown pumpkin was sliced and boiled, seeds and all, and eaten unsalted.

Meat was fried, broiled, jerked, or boiled. When boiled, soups and dumplings were often made with it. While formerly eaten raw,

Harvesting grain. Photo by Curtis (MNMP).

beef intestines were washed both inside and out and then broiled over the fire. Stomachs of edible animals were ripped open and washed. They were then cut into sections and broiled over the fire when needed.[7]

Although bears were plentiful in the Fort Apache region, the Western Apache would not eat bear meat. They had the same kind of religious objection to the use of this meat as the Mescalero.[8]

The streams of the region abounded in fish also, but even the Apache school children would not eat them. Reagan says that the fish in the lower country were infected with worms in the summer, and this may have accounted for fish being tabooed, though it was not the reason given by the medicine fraternity. When Reagan asked a medicine man why the Apache would not eat fish, the man replied: "No, we do not eat fish. They are the spirits of wicked women. Do you see the spots on the fish? Once, a long time ago all our people got an 'awful sick.' They were hot. They were burning up with fever. The medicinemen took them all down by the river's brink and there they gave them the 'sick' sweatbath, the hot steam bath of purification. This they all took. Then emerging from the sweathouse, they plunged themselves into the invigorating waters of the river, only to come out on the opposite bank and die. All who were sick died. The people were enraged against the medicinemen. They thought they had intentionally killed the sick. They rose, as one man, to annihilate them all, when the dead people began to turn spotted just like the fish in the river. The explanation was simple. The bad spirits of the fish had entered the people who had bathed and had killed them all. From that day to this no Apache has eaten fish." Reagan adds that few of them have ever bathed either.[9]

The Western Apache women made tiswin or tulapai, intoxicating drinks made from corn or fermented mescal stalk and root.

Tiswin was made from the "heart" or center of the unopened cluster of leaves of the mescal plant. The heart was cooked for about fifteen days until the roots were of a semi-gelatinous consistency. Then they were crushed and the liquor was poured off into retaining receptacles, where it was kept until fermentation set in. At this point friends and relatives in great numbers assembled for a dance that often resulted in a drunken and obscene brawl.[10]

Tulapai was made from corn that was soaked, covered with blankets or hides, dried in the sun, and then ground into meal. Sometimes various perennial weeds and roots were added, also small quantities of the root-bark of the lignum vitae tree and locoweed. The whole was put in five-gallon coal oil cans along with water, and the concoction was boiled for several hours. The "white water" was then poured off into empty cans, and the residue recrushed on the grinding slabs. This residue was then added to the "white water" and the whole reboiled, after which it was set aside and allowed to ferment for sixteen to twenty-four hours, when it was ready to drink.[11]

The day the tulapai fermented a man invited his male friends and relatives from far and near to drink with him, and the women in the immediate vicinity drank as well. The party often lasted throughout the night, with women and men alike getting so drunk they didn't know what they were doing. Besides immoral practices and fights, some would pass out and lie uncovered out in the cold air for hours. Drunken mothers often gave tulapai in large quantities to their children, even babies.

The Indians steadfastly claimed that tulapai was nutritious, but it proved to be a great detriment to the Apache. Not only was it an intoxicant, but the various herbs and weeds undermined the Apache's health. The loss of the grain used to make the drink could be ill-afforded. The drinking caused indolence, and when drinking was going on, fights and immoral practices were indulged in that did not otherwise occur. Over a period of time the drinking lowered the Indian's resistance to disease, and the exposure to the elements so often experienced while drunk led to pneumonia, consumption, and resultant death.

Grinding acorns.

But the constitution of most Apache men was awesome when the corn was in and fermenting. If there was a tulapai drinking party in another area the next day all the men would go to it, while their women, weakened by the previous night's brawl, were left at home to do the farm work. The next day there might be a drinking party in another place, and so it went for as long as the tulapai was available.[12] It surely meant a great deal to the Apache, as liquor seems to to many of them today. The refusal of the White Mountain Reservation Agency at San Carlos to allow the making of tulapai was one of the prime excuses put forth by the Chiricahua for bolting the reservation in the 1880s.

19 Agriculture

Alfalfa and wild hay grew on the Apache reservations. There was not much of the former left in 1902, and what there was, was put up, Reagan says, "somewhat in the ordinary way." The wild hay grew as bunch grass and other grass that filled little vales in the mountains and along the canyon sides. When haying time came, several neighboring families moved together to the hills to cut the hay by hand. This was usually done by the women, with the old-fashioned sickle and even with butcher knives; if a scythe could be obtained, it was usually wielded by the men. When a sufficient quantity was cut, dried, and collected, it was often carried long distances by armloads, then tied on burros and pack horses for transportation to the Agency or military post for sale. Reagan said it was a picturesque sight to see a long train of burros, laden with hay, descending from the mountains. The year he was at Fort Apache, more than two hundred tons were delivered by the Indians in this manner.[1] That's an intriguing figure to consider for those who have been led to believe the Apache were inherently lazy.

Thanks to the persuasion of the reservation Agency, the Apache man of 1902 helped to clear the land and to put in the irrigating ditches on government pay, but he considered agricultural activity to be woman's work and refused to participate in it, if he could avoid it. The Western Apache woman plowed her field with a single-horse plow with a single blade. She either drove the horse with a pair of lines or had one of the children or the husband ride the horse and guide it for her. If corn was to be planted, it was dropped in every third furrow. Small grain was broadcast ahead of the plow. After it was sowed and the plowing completed, the ground was either harrowed with a modern harrow or a brush, or leveled by dragging a log over it. Small grain and corn were both irrigated a number of times between planting and harvest. The little truck garden grown by the Apache was planted in rows and the whole grain plot flooded when irrigating. Potatoes were usually planted and cared for like corn.[2]

In harvesting and threshing, a leveled, circular spot of ground was cleared off near the grain field for a threshing floor. The grain was cut with a hand sickle or a butcher knife. It was either bound into sheaves or piled loosely, then moved to the threshing floor and trampled by horses. The straw was then removed and the grain separated from the chaff by winnowing. Finally it was washed and dried and was ready for use. The woman gathered corn by jerking the ears off and tossing them over her head into the burden basket on her back. When the basket was full, she carried it to a level spot near her wickiup, where she piled the corn. When she had finished jerking the entire field of corn, she shucked the pile, saving the green ears for roasting. The hard corn was piled where it would dry thoroughly. When it was dry, she shelled it and stored it in her storage baskets for future use.[3]

Bourke's San Carlos informants told him that when the Apache planted corn, the medicine men buried eagle-plume sticks in the fields, scattered tule pollen, known as hoddentin, and sang. When the corn was partially grown they scattered pinches of hoddentin over it.[4]

20 Tanning

In 1901, skins were tanned by both the men and the women. If the hair was to be removed, the skin was buried several days in moist earth. It was then soaked in warm water, after which it was stretched over a pole, fur side out, and scraped with a dull knife. It was then spread out to dry in the sun. If the hair was to be left on the hide, this process was omitted. The skin was turned inside out and carefully fleshed with a sharp knife. The brains of the animal were then worked by hand into the skin, which was then allowed to dry,

after which it was pounded and stretched to make it soft and pliable.[1]

21 Apparel and Jewelry

The earlier buckskin clothing has been described by George Dorsey. While in 1901 the style was essentially European, the Western Apache woman's cloth dress was patterned after the old-time buckskin dress. However it had a fuller skirt, made of eight or more yards of vividly colored plain or printed calico, finished off around the bottom with a wide ruffle of a differently colored cloth, itself frequently decorated with three or more contrasting colored bands, though occasionally these bands were simply white. They wore a loose, hip-length, overblouse. The long dresses provided extra warmth in winter, and often one dress was put on over another for better protection.[1]

For mourning, women sometimes wore a poncho-like square of cloth with a hole in the center so that it could be passed over the head. The blouse had no belt to keep it in place and hung loosely over the skirt. Some of the old women wore only the skirt, unless White people were around. When away from home they also wore a rectangular piece of cloth over their shoulders, like a shawl. Some of these were simply flour sacks sewed together; others were of costly cloth. At times they tied two ends of the cloth together to make a loop over the forehead, and then made a carrying bag out of it by holding the other two ends in their hands. In this improvised burden bag they carried all sorts of loads.

Most of the women in 1901, especially the young ones, wore around their necks numerous strands of small and large beads from which mirrors, shell beads, colored Mexican bean beads, fetishes, bear claws, and other medicine tokens were suspended. Earrings were made of pieces of iridescent shell from the Pacific coast. The

arms and wrists were also decorated with wrappings of small beads, trade brass, or silver bracelets, and wrist bands. Most of the women also wore Apache-style bootlike moccasins, made of buckskin and cowhide with turned-up plain, beaded, or painted toe-pieces.[2]

Clothing was made by hand the easiest way possible. No patterns were used for guides. Hide belts and other beadwork were usually well and artistically made by the women. Moccasins were made by both men and women.[3]

The men Bandelier saw in 1883 wore bright headbands with pendants hanging to the waist, often made of a piece of red flannel. Blouses were gaudy calico, and cotton garments were often trimmed in red.[4]

In 1902, the old men dressed as in the old days, simply in a breechclout. The younger generation wore White man's clothing, except that many of them, especially the chiefs, let their shirts hang outside their trousers. When at work on the reservation in hot weather most of the men removed their shirts. Some men wore shoes obtained at the trader's store; some went barefoot; others wore moccasins of a pattern slightly different from those of the women, being hip length when first made. These were soled with bullhide and cowhide and most had the traditional turned-up, rounded toe-piece.[5]

Opposite top: *Puberty dress top edged with cutouts, front view (ASM).* Opposite bottom: *White Mountain girl's puberty dress edged with cutouts laid over red flannel, side and front views.* Below left: *Detail, tin cones.* Below right: *Detail, beading at neck.* Bottom left: *Detail, cutouts and beading.* Bottom right: *Detail, tab with tin cones.*

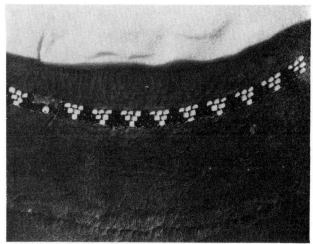

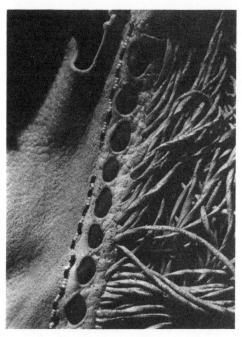

 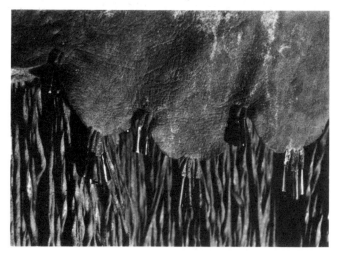

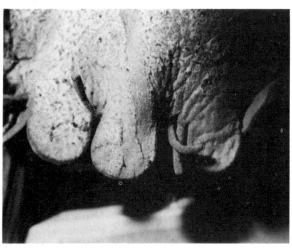 

Top left: *Detail, hem design, fringe, and tin cones.* Top right: *Detail, hem design and fringe.* Above left: *Detail, hem design and fringe.* Above right: *Detail, tab attachment to hem of skirt.* Below: *Puberty dress top, front and back views (ALMN).*

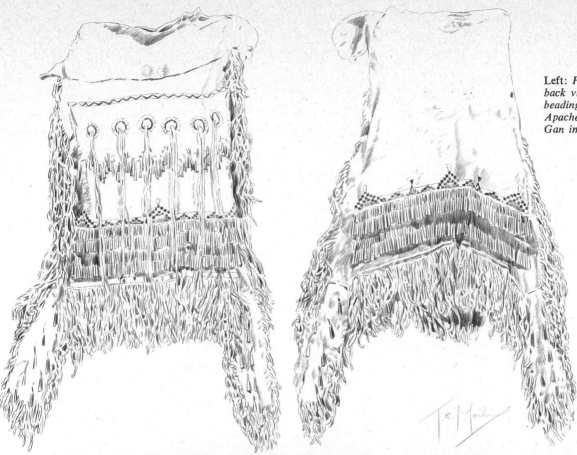

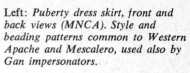

Left: *Puberty dress skirt, front and back views (MNCA). Style and beading patterns common to Western Apache and Mescalero, used also by Gan impersonators.*

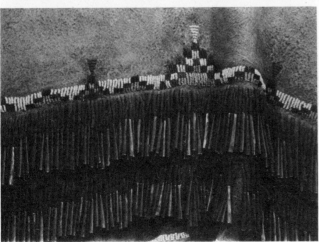

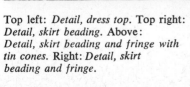

Top left: *Detail, dress top.* Top right: *Detail, skirt beading.* Above: *Detail, skirt beading and fringe with tin cones.* Right: *Detail, skirt beading and fringe.*

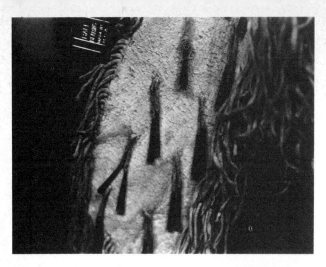

Above left: *Skirt tabs with tin cones.* Above right: *Detail, dress top with tin cones.* Right: *Detail, dress hem with overlapping edge, tin cones, and fringing.* Below left: *Doll dressed in puberty costume (ASM). Originally collected by David J. Yerkes; acquired in 1894 by Mrs. Elizabeth Ducret. Back view.* Below center: *Front view; buckskin dress, hair made of twisted tassel. Dress painting done in red.* Below right: *Child's dress, pink with black rickrack, front view (MNCA). Recently made by Alice Smith, San Carlos.* Bottom: *San Carlos child's dress, white background with red rickrack, front view (MNCA).*

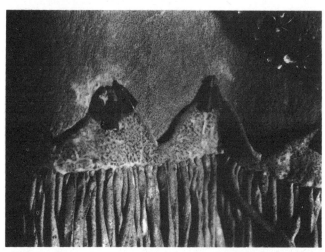

106

Top: *Western Apache man's buckskin war shirt, fringed, beaded, and decorated with German silver conchos and crosses (MNCA). Front view.*
Above: *Back view.*

Details of shirt shown on preceding page: Top left: *Silver crosses, brass tacks, beading, and fringing at neck.* Top right: *Silver conchos, beading, and fringing.* Center left: *Silver crosses, beading, and fringing at back of neck.* Center right: *Brass tacks, beading, and fringing at shoulder.* Above left: *Silver conchos, beading, and fringing at shirt front.* Above right: *Beading of sleeve.*

Western Apache or Chiricahua men at San Carlos, ca. 1885.

Above left: *Western Apache painted moccasins.* Above right: *Western Apache beaded moccasins with toe-piece, worn by Gan dancer (SM).*

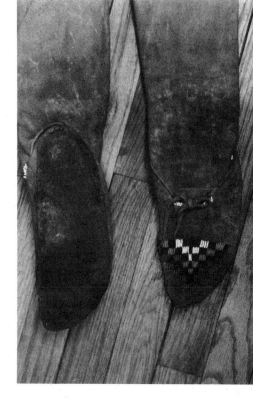

Above left: *Western Apache beaded full-length moccasins, San Carlos design (MNCA).* Above center: *Detail, beading at top of moccasins, front and back.* Above right: *Detail, moccasin sole and beading on toe.*

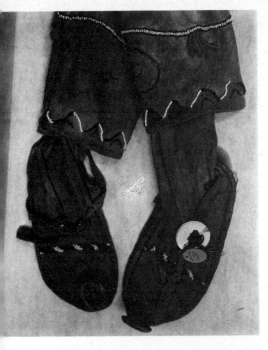
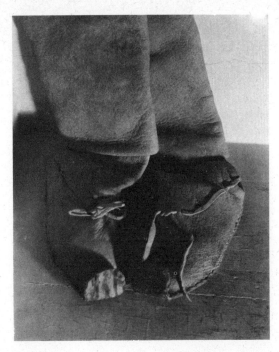
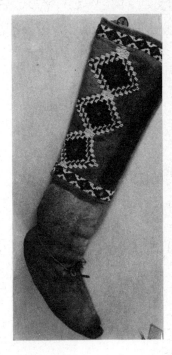

Above left: *Western Apache or Chiricahua dress moccasins (MNCA).* Above center: *Western Apache or Chiricahua moccasins for daily wear, showing method of tying to secure on foot (ALMN).* Above right: *Western Apache moccasin, type often worn by San Carlos girls for puberty ceremony.* Left: *Beaded and fringed moccasins (HM). Possibly Mescalero or Chiricahua, although the Western Apache did some all-over beading.* Below left: *War cap, topped with cut turkey feathers and two golden eagle tail feathers, front view (MNCA). Worn only by experienced warriors.* Below right: *Buckskin war cap, showing metal conchos and tacks used to form symbols, top view (AF).*

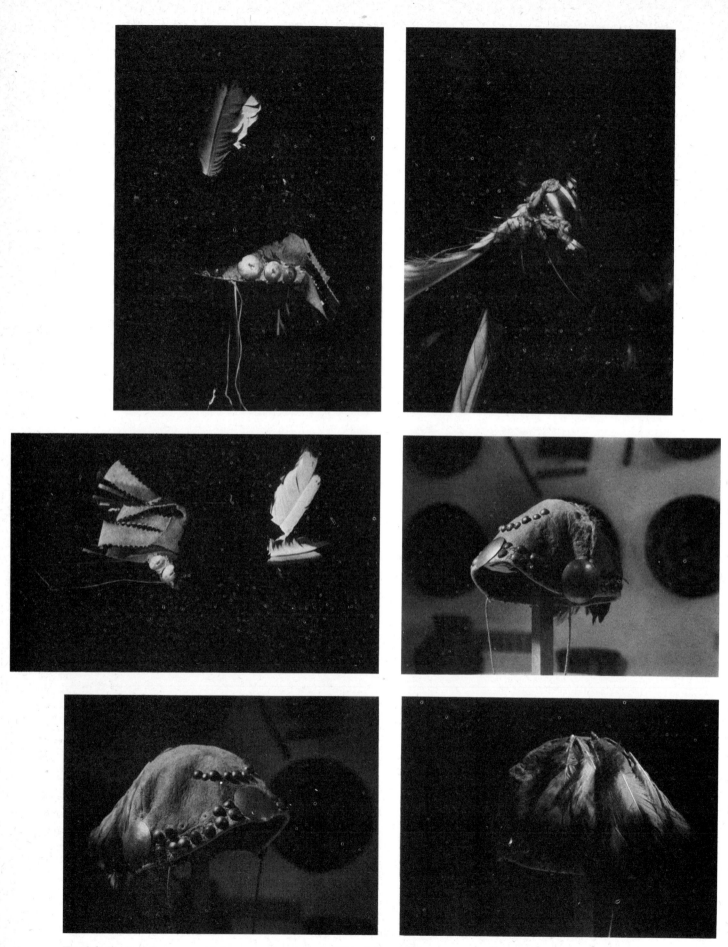

Top left: *Feathered war cap with brass conchos and tabs.* Top right: *Detail,
showing how feathers are attached to inverted metal cup.* Center left: *Back view,
showing scalloped tabs.* Center right: *Buckskin war cap, left side.* Above left: *Right side.*
Above right: *Back view, with golden eagle-down feathers in place.*

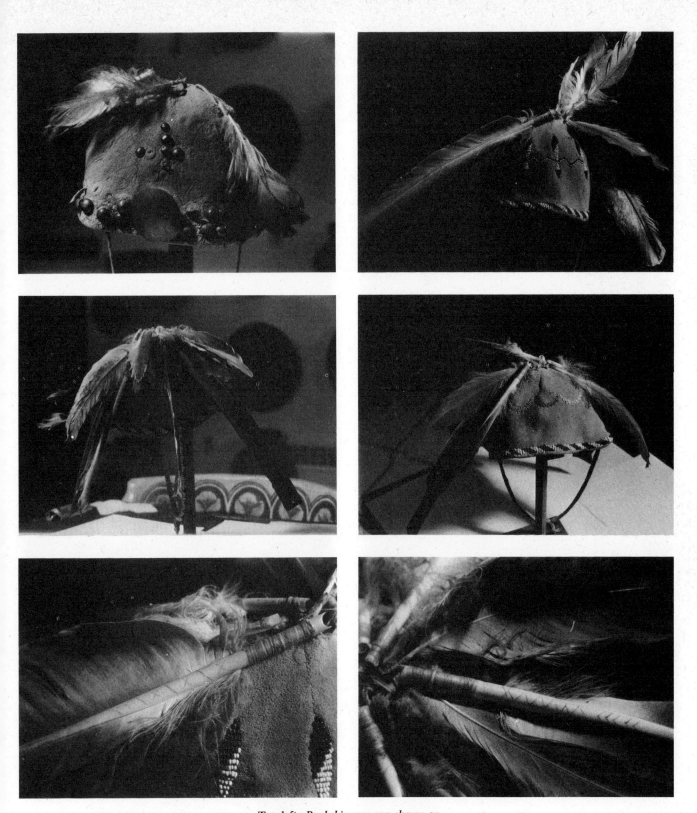

Top left: *Buckskin war cap shown on opposite page, back view, with feathers pushed aside to show cross made of tacks.* Top right: *Buckskin war cap with beaded edging and symbols, topped with golden eagle feathers (AF). The body of the cap is unpainted.* Center left: *Back view, with feathers in place, showing also beaded chin strap.* Center right: *Back view, showing beaded symbols.* Above left: *Detail, top of cap, showing method of attaching feathers with sinew ties and wrapping. Note etched designs on quill butt.* Above right: *Top view, showing etched designs on quill butt.*

Above: *Three views of beaded war
cap with golden eagle feathers (SWM).*

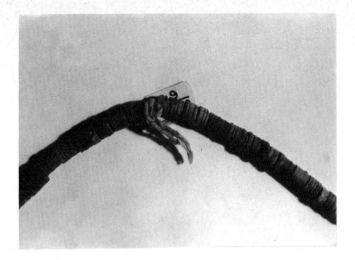

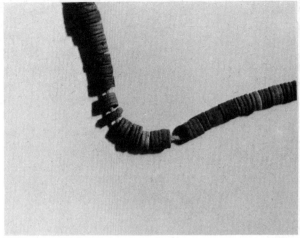

Above left, above right, *and* left: *Bone necklace, type worn by Western Apache and Chiricahua (AF)*. Below left and right: *Seed bead necklace, type worn by Western Apache and Chiricahua (AF)*.

Top left: *Man's war necklace; opaque blue trade beads alternating with seed beads, with two scalloped conchos and pair of tweezers, made from two metal plates fastened together (ASM). Tweezers like these were used to remove facial hair.* Top right: *Back view of conchos, showing method of securing them to the necklace. Small tufts of down feathers are strung through central perforations in conchos.* Left: *War necklace, with scalloped concho, beads, and tweezers, detail (AF). Note etched design.* Above: *War necklace, with scalloped and etched concho beads, shell and metal cross, detail (AF).*

Above: *War necklace tweezers with intricate etching and scalloping. Side view.* Right: *Front view.*

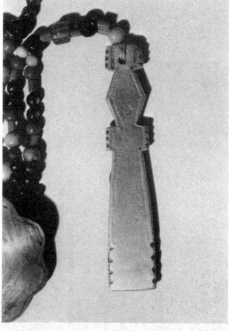

Left: *Brushing Against and Little Squint Eyes, San Carlos women, wearing numerous trade bead necklaces and mirrors. Photo by F. A. Rinehart, 1898 (DPL). Above: Decorative jewelry consisting of trade mirrors and beads (HM). Worn by Western Apache and Chiricahua women.*

22 Hair Dressing and Ornaments

Bandelier describes the Apache he saw in 1883 as "dirty." However, aloe soap weed grew in the region; its roots were collected and taken home to be pounded into pulp and worked into a lather with water. It was used for bathing and especially to shampoo the hair. After shampooing the hair was combed with a bunch of stiff grass tied in a bundle by a cord, the ends used as a comb. The hair was then spread over an uplifted arm to dry in the sun; then it was combed again and arranged according to Apache custom. A single woman dressed her hair in a double, hourglass-shaped roll or fold and a virginity lapel was placed over it. A married woman let her hair hang loosely over the shoulders, cut evenly around at the ends.[1]

The virginity lapel or hair bow was an interesting Western Apache custom. The hair was folded in a perpendicular double loop or "chungo" at the back of the head, and a bow-shaped piece of hide, beaded and/or covered with brass buttons or other bright ornamentation, was tied over it. The cloth ties were left hanging down the back, sometimes reaching to the waist. This hair bow was worn to show that the wearer was unmarried and a virgin. When she married, she destroyed the bow. Any attempt to wear it or keep it would be an indication that she would welcome other suitors, and her husband would roughly take it off her head and probably beat her. Bandelier saw the hair bows, which he called "a convex tongue of red leather," in 1883. They were covered with brass buttons, and the ties hung down the back.[2]

117

23 Tattooing and Body Painting *

Bandelier (1883) saw Western Apache face painting in red, brown, and black, but did not mention tattooing.[1] Dorsey (1903) states that the Apache men and women frequently tattooed their faces. "The center of the forehead and the chin are most frequently covered with geometrical designs of a dark blue color. Occasionally a design upon the forehead is produced downward to the end of the nose."[2] Goodwin's (1930s) Western Apache informants stated that as boys and girls they didn't paint their faces, but used tattoo marks, not letters, on their wrists, hands, and faces.[3] Further on in his notes, the writer adds that boys and girls between the ages of twelve and sixteen tattooed themselves on wrists, arms, and legs. "The present [1930s] use of letters and numbers rather than design elements in general decoration" was due to the shift from general decoration to school year uses. Goodwin adds that tattooing was not a White Mountain trait, but acquired from the Yavapai during reservation life.[4]

Reagan states that in 1902 the younger Western Apache women painted their faces with reddish paint most of the time, but they did not daub it on in large amounts as was customary for many tribes. On special occasions the men painted themselves according to the parts they were to play in the ceremonies.

For the puberty ceremony the girl's sponsor usually painted the girl's cheeks with a yellow or reddish-yellow circle to show that she was ready for matrimony. Sometimes other colors were used, and also decorative symbols for the four directions. The pigments were usually mineral paints that the Apache had compounded themselves, though commercial trade paints and inks were also being used now and then in the early 1900s.[5]

Opposite: *Girls wearing the* nah-leen, *or hair bow, ca. 1880 (MNMP).*
Above: *Preparing the hair for the hair bow (MNCA). The hair was formed into a pony tail, wrapped with a cloth strip, folded up and down, wrapped again, and tied; the hair bow was then tied on with long strips of colorful cloth.*

* For information concerning the use of war paint, see the Chiricahua Raiding and Warfare section.

For information concerning ceremonial painting, see the religion sections for details about the Gans, Clowns, and Wonder Workers.

24 Diseases and Cures

Reagan found the Western Apache of 1901 to be "a much diseased people." Their drinking so much tulapai and tiswin, their exposure to the elements while drunk, their filth, and their sleepless nights at medicine ceremonies were breaking them down physically. The principal diseases were pneumonia and tuberculosis in its various forms, trachoma and other eye diseases. There was also much digestive disturbance. Furthermore, he said, their medicinal practices tended to spread these diseases instead of curing them.

The Apache were able to effect some cures through the use of herbs and minerals. For gonorrhea and syphilis they employed a saline deposit that covered the muddy bank of Carrizon Creek, which seemed to Reagan to consist of sodium magnesium chloride and sodium sulphate. They also used the bark of several herbs and trees, among which was the bark of *Populus tremuloides,* to cure ague, fevers, and also gonorrhea. The bark and herbs were pounded, crushed into a semipulverized condition, then made into a tea and the concoction drunk in great quantities. For the male, in venereal diseases the parts affected were wrapped in the pulverized concoction; in the case of a woman, her vagina was filled with it. A splint made of cedar bark was sometimes used to splint up fractures of legs and arms.[1]

25 Sweat Bathing

It was the custom, in 1901–1902, for the Western Apache to take what Reagan described as "a kind of Turkish bath. Near the river bank they construct a small sweat house about large enough for a man to sit in comfortably. This they cover with blankets. They heat rocks and take them into the house, completely close it, and then pour water on the heated rocks, producing dense steam. Two or more persons take the bath at a time. When the perspiration is pouring from them, they uncover the entrance and jump into the

Below: *Men at left are heating rocks for sweat bathing. The bather, second from right, wears a mud plaster on his head to kill lice.*

cold water of the river. Two or more of these sweats are usually taken before they stop. Both men and women take these baths. These are sweatbaths of purification and are also used in performing over the sick. When used for the latter purpose a medicineman presides over the ceremonies and while the bathing is in progress, sings and dances about the sweatlodge and sprinkles pollen dust to his gods."[1]

In commenting upon Western Apache hygiene in the late 1880s, John P. Clum remarks that since Apache wickiups were not equipped with running water and bathtubs, the Apache occasionally built sweat baths just large enough to hold one person and four or five hot stones. The bather would heat the stones in an adjacent fire, roll them into the hut with sticks, get a bottle of water, discard his clothes, crawl into the hut, and pour the water on the stones. The resulting steam did the cleansing. If by chance a bather happened to sit for an instant on one of the hot stones, a violent exclamation would issue from the hut, and one could learn many new and expressive Apache words merely by listening in on the sweat baths. Nevertheless, the baths "were effective treatment to check a cold or to break a fever."[2]

Clum goes on to say that Apache fleas and kindred small annoying creeping things had the habit of sojourning close to Apache scalps. Since they had no fine-toothed combs, it was not unusual to see two members of a family sitting on the shady side of a wickiup, with one carefully examining and picking the scalp of the other. This was a tedious operation and resulted in only temporary relief. The more positive method of getting rid of these insects was the head pack. A plaster of thin mud was run into the hair until the scalp was completely covered. Then the person would sit in the sunshine until the mud was thoroughly dry and all the unwelcome tenants were suffocated. At this point he ducked his head into the swift waters of the San Carlos River to wash the mud and everything else away.[3]

Ross Santee tells how some of his Apache friends were not as clean "as Old Jim and his family." One night while they were in cow camp together an Apache rode in who had no bedding. Old Jim was wise enough not to offer to share his bed or split his blankets with the visitor, who then curled up by the fire to sleep. Nor did Old Jim say anything when Santee gave the fellow a couple of his blankets to keep him warm. But next morning, when the guest had departed, Old Jim took the two blankets and threw them over a large ant hill. In referring to the overnight guest, Jim said: "Him lousy like what you call pet coon; ants eat lice, ants eat nits, too." In affirming Clum's remarks, Santee also says that it was a common sight as one rode past a wickiup to see squaws and children picking lice from each other's hair. Therefore the White man's short hair and even a bald head were sometimes an advantage.[4]

Grenville Goodwin revealed how the sweat lodge played a further role, as part of the preparation for a council between visiting chiefs. On this occasion four chiefs and their followers came together. The next day they had a sweat bath. All the men went up to it, save one who was sent back to tell the women to cook something and have it brought to the sweat bath. The men stayed at the sweat bath until food was brought to them at noon.

The food was always carried to the sweat bath by youths and maidens, never by married women or old women. At their head walked a youth, and before he started, the women in camp told him that when he arrived at the sweat bath, he was to stick his fingers in the basket of corn gruel he was carrying, put them in his mouth, and say at the same time, "May my food never be exhausted." These words contained power and prevented the food from being used up.

About midafternoon, men were sent again to tell the women to start cooking. The women brought the food this time. Part of it was placed in a pile for each chief, and the chiefs and their people ate in three places. After the meal, the women placed grass around the inside edge of the talk enclosure for the people to sit on. When this was finished, a fire was lighted inside the enclosure. This was the signal that those who were to attend the talk should take their places. Though some of the common women wanted to go and hear the talk, they were not allowed to. The subchiefs and head women of the local group at whose camp the talk was held kept quiet and listened, though the men who came with the visiting chiefs could talk. Each visiting chief and his men sat in a group by themselves, on the side of the enclosure that pointed toward the direction of their home country.[5]

26 Religion and Ceremonies

My general procedure in writing about the Apache is to approach the history of each group chronologically. However, in the case of religion it may be best to reverse the process and begin with an overview of the subject, insofar as one is able to understand it, from the Apache point of view. My hope is that this will make it easier for the reader to pierce through the essentially factual reports of some early writers and so discover at least a sense of the deeper meanings that reside in the ceremonies.

Since the beginning of time for the Apache everything has centered in the matter of power and its important uses. As power sources, supernatural beings and ghosts are just as real as nature's powerful forces. The former also become involved with human affairs, are addressed as human and alive, and are expected to answer in a detectable way. In particular, certain classes of celestial bodies, mythological figures, animals, plants, and minerals possess holy (godiyingo) powers, and by certain means some small part of these powers may be acquired by human beings and put to use. The balance of the power remains with its source, free to help or to harm as the supernatural being wishes, depending upon whether it is pleased or offended by human conduct.

The ancient Apache view, then, is that power pervades the universe. However, man cannot approach it directly. It must work through or come to him through something such as the sun, moon, lightning, bear, eagle, owl, lizard, snake, and so on. And it is man himself who, through contact with the power itself, learns how to apply the power in a beneficial way.[1]

A power and the ability to apply it are acquired either by purchase and instruction from one who has already obtained it or by fasting, prayer, ablutions, a strange event, or the like, which can lead to visions or dreams in which the power presents itself and is imparted. Those who obtain it in the latter way are favored in the people's eyes, for the power came to them voluntarily, even though it might be argued that a power would hardly come to an unreceptive person.[2] Only a few Apache gain, or perhaps better said, serve, a power today, since its acquisition requires more time, energy, expense, and responsibility than most people wish to expend. Power has its rewards, but also its costs, not the least of which may be jealousy. The problem is that people who haven't a power are dependent upon those who have, as they face the inevitable problems life brings. Everyone must reckon with serious predicaments sooner or later, and the price of assistance can be extremely high.

Once a power has given some part of itself to its seeker, the person must determine by trial and error what it is capable of doing through him. Over a long period of time he learns what it can accomplish when correctly used. Although they may have the same type of power, no two men or women will exercise it in the same way.[3] As previously stated, some powers can be called upon to diagnose, cure, and protect against illness. Those who have this gift are commonly known as medicine men or shamans. I would prefer to call them holy men, as it seems more apt. But in discussing this with the Apache I found they felt that the title medicine man was an acceptable one, and in any event they themselves use an Apache term, *diyin*. Aside from medicine men, other men and women have what are considered lesser powers to prophesy and to find lost objects.

In the Apache view, power is by no means a permanent possession or quality—the privilege of being a channel for it can be withdrawn by its dispenser at any time he is displeased, or when he feels an appropriate time has come in its possessor's life to do so. Its presence is in large measure dependent upon the respect accorded it by its holder. He should be concerned about it and keep its welfare foremost at all times. He must never take it for granted. Should he lose it, there is virtually no way to get it back. Its loss brings an understandable fear and insecurity, for the person who had it is now defenseless, and moreover may have forefeited it in such a way as to merit retaliation by the power.[4]

In most instances, power is most effective for men and women in their early thirties, a fact that reveals an association with physical health and prime activity. As this period passes, the ability to use the power is thought to weaken. For many it never passes away entirely. Others are made to understand through dreams, ghosts, or the like that the investor wishes the power to be transferred by traditional means to a more fit recipient.[5]

Since the dawn of time, each power has been so closely associated with a multitude of chants and prayers that these concomitants are considered to be an integral part of it. Therefore the ability to dispense the power is directly dependent upon the capacity of the person to learn and retain its chants and prayers. As implied, these are a part of Apache tradition, and months must be spent in private sessions with medicine men who are able to pass them on. Payment depends upon the amount of work and time involved, but the learning is always expensive. In the old days payment was made in goods; now money is preferred. In truth, cost has become a prime reason for the decrease in the pursuit of medicine powers today. In addition, there is the incredible complexity of the medicine language and ceremonial structure to be mastered, plus the retentive abilities needed, and the sheer physical strength required to sing the exhausting chants for hours on end at a ceremony.

Even considering all this, the rewards outweigh the costs. An individual with power has a prime opportunity for status, social contacts, and respect. He has a sense of personal security and a source of income. Moreover, if the medicine person is prudent and successful in the use of his power, and can avoid charges of witchcraft, the entire community benefits.

To the best of my present understanding, the subject of witchcraft emerged as the Apache sought to explain and to deal with misfortune. Man needed a reason for the tragedies of life, and he needed a way to live with them. Since the powers had the qualities of both benevolence and revenge, it appeared that some had chosen to follow almost exclusively the latter course. Power then is once again at the core of the witchcraft question; in order to practice witchcraft a person must have a power. This means that medicine men and women are the prime suspects, along with private individuals who for obvious reasons have acquired a power but keep it secret, since the application of witchcraft is hardly popular. In all instances, witches have learned their trade from one who already practiced it.[6]

Although the belief in witchcraft is widely shared, as evidenced by the ceremonies held to treat it and the amulets worn to protect against it, the practice remains today a difficult thing to prove. In the old days, informants claimed there were painful trials and punishments for those accused of it, although eyewitness accounts of these are virtually absent. Today the confrontations are less severe, but if guilt is assumed, the result for the accused may be social ostracism and isolation.

There are two classes of witches. The most dangerous of

123

these practice sorcery or voodoo power, which by various and mysterious means (though ones known to all), usually practiced at night, can inflict an individual or his possessions with a "poison" or sickness that has sudden and calamitous results. The second power has to do with sexual practices and is referred to as love magic. It is a bad thing only when applied in full strength, that is, when the normal physical attractions are heightened to the point of lust.[7]

The commonly employed protections against witchcraft are turquoise beads and eagle feathers, which are attached to objects and carried on the person, and cattail pollen. In the event an individual is stricken anyway, he can resort to a curing ceremonial, and lightning, bear, and snake rituals in particular are employed in such instances. In the old days the Gan impersonators were often called in, but now their cost has become almost prohibitive. In a ceremony the shaman pits his power against that of the witch. If he is successful, the sorcerer will die or suffer a tragedy, and the patient will recover.

It should be mentioned that Apache accused of witchcraft who can answer the charges effectively are presumed to be innocent, and their lives will not be seriously jeopardized. They will, however, attempt to live in such a way as not to be liable to such charges again. Accusers, on the other hand, must be careful in registering unjust charges out of anger at someone, for if such is discovered as time passes, that has its penalties too.

As suggested earlier, the survival of the belief in witchcraft is due in large part to the fact that it explains antagonism and adversity, and validates the need for continuing the culture and the traditional ceremonies. Further, it serves as an excuse or explanation for excesses in sexual and social activity. Since those who seem to be blessed economically may be particularly suspected, the belief also encourages them to avoid reactions by sharing what they have with others. In the same way, since offending or arrogant persons are also liable to suspicion, witchcraft provides strong motivation for living in harmony with one's family and others. In substance, then, the presence of witchcraft beliefs has both its negative and positive sides. It can be grievous for those accused of it, but at the same time provides a regulating force in daily life.[8]

It will become clear, as Apache history is considered, that reservation life and Anglo contact has brought a sweeping decrease in ceremonial activity. Most of the profuse rituals that accompanied the vital prereservation life-style have passed out of mind and existence. Some were stamped out by Agency authorities, others were abandoned because they were no longer needed, and some ceased to be practiced because of the complexities involved. Only a few minor personal rites, the curing ceremonials, and the girl's puberty rite are still performed; even these occur less frequently than before. Nevertheless, a number of medicine men are very active today, and many ceremonials are enacted on the reservations in the course of a year. Despite the questions raised by Christianity, the people are, for the most part, reluctant to abandon the ancient rites entirely.

Their faith in the rites is reinforced by continuing diagnoses of ills, by cures, and by effective protections against harm. Furthermore, they understand the ceremonials for what they are, not a replacement for Anglo medical services but a complement to them. They use the medical facilities of the Agencies, but find that the rituals help them to determine the causes of disease and bring protection against recurrences of the same in a way that puts the Apache mind at ease.[9] In claiming to determine causes, it is conceded that shamans are not able to posit the exact nature of an illness as well as a competent physician with his numerous scientific aids. Instead, the ceremonies help to discover the original cause of the problem, that is, what the person did to bring it about; and they might also find the physical or spiritual location of the illness. A cure might be performed, even where physicians have failed; and having recognized where the illness came from—the violation of a taboo or the disrespectful treatment of a power—the shaman can show his patient how to avoid the same difficulty in the future.

Early observers took an almost standard position regarding what they believed was the Apache view of the causes of sickness and death—namely, evil spirits; according to these observers, all medicine was performed to drive the evil away. The reader will find this idea quoted more than once further on.[10]

I feel that illness, with certain exceptions already stated, is more properly viewed by the Apache as the result of violating a power. As mentioned earlier, the powers are free to act as they wish, and they are not always benevolent. When offended, they sometimes retaliate, and illness is one of the ways they do so. Their act is not evil, because men have been forewarned, having been given specific instructions in how to maintain good relationships with the powers.[11] Hundreds of taboos exist, and so long as a person doesn't break one he is safe. For example, one should avoid stepping on a trail made by a snake, and one must not kill a snake, for the snake is a power source. If this sounds simple at first, it is not actually so. While some taboos are practical and can be associated with common sense, most are not, and as such are neither easy to learn nor to remember. Thus the probability of violating by carelessness or error those not known or not remembered is increased. In substance, the power idea serves as a governor for Apache life, since it encourages people to live respectfully and insofar as possible in harmony with their environment. The violated power enters the offender the moment he breaks the taboo. After this it chooses its own time to make him ill. He may then do nothing and take his chances, go to the hospital, or seek the aid of a medicine man or woman.[12]

In earlier times there was a profusion of wondrous and mysterious ceremonies performed for every aspect of life. Scenes from many of these are included in this book to present the reader with an opportunity to experience them. It is everyone's good fortune that Captain John G. Bourke and Albert B. Reagan had the interest and foresight to record the ceremonies they witnessed. Nevertheless, as will be seen, they generally failed, or simply were not able because of circumstances beyond their control, to plumb the deeper meanings in the events.

Nearly all the ceremonies observed by Reagan commenced about nine P.M. and continued until dawn. Other rituals began at dusk. In one instance the daughter of E30 was sung over in the morning. The Medicine Disk ceremony, in which a sand painting was made, was begun and completed in daylight. Some ceremonies continued for several nights, with different, or a progression of, rituals being given.[13]

Nowadays there are two types of curing ceremonials performed: shorter ceremonials to determine the cause of the illness and what to do about it—these usually begin at dusk and close by midnight or shortly thereafter; and longer ceremonials to cure or remove the problem—these begin at dusk and continue until dawn. Some of the latter will go on for more than one night, depending upon the seriousness of the problem, the success of the shaman, and the ability of the patient or his family to pay.

As late as 1940, a typical custom for engaging the services of a medicine man was to make a cross with pollen on the toe of his moccasin or shoe, and then place a down-payment of money, turquoise, eagle feathers, or the like on top of the cross. If the medicine man picked up the offering it indicated that he would perform the curing ceremony. Depending upon the amount of work involved, it was also customary to give more than the initial payment. There was also a practice of drawing a half moon with pollen on the palm of the medicine man's hand when his services were needed. Such customs varied in different parts of the reservations, and depended upon the nature of the illness. They are not always practiced today.[14]

Once the arrangements are made for a curing rite, the age-old traditions come into play. Shortly before the actual ceremony is given, the medicine man or an informed elder meets with the family and friends and describes the mythical origin, the purposes, and the many successes of the rite. Their stories are filled with drama and provide an enthralling preparation for the actual event.

The ceremony itself begins with an exhortation to the people attending to maintain pure and harmonious thoughts. The ritual follows a prescribed structure, which includes the succession of things to be done and the paraphernalia to be employed at specific points. Although chanting is the main device employed, the ritual includes many of the traditional objects set forth in the eyewitness descriptions of Bourke and Reagan. The modern medicine men have only a small white feather pinned to their shirt as a badge of office. In the old days they wore painted medicine hats and shirts, plus other intriguing items such as cords, necklaces, and crosses.[15]

While some ceremonies continue without interruption through the entire night, others reach a midpoint at which everyone rests and eats. The children sleep, adults talk quietly, and for a few hours little is done. Then the fire is stoked up and the ceremony resumes, to continue until dawn, when with appropriate final acts it is over.

The singers who are employed to assist the medicine men are not shamans themselves, and they may not possess a power, although some do. They are those who enjoy singing, and they learn the chants by experience.[16]

Many ceremonials employ specific equipment, such as charms, certain plants, or parts of animals. These contain exorcising power and are applied to the patient to draw out sickness, either being held against the patient's body and drawn away, or used as a brush to sweep the sickness off. Pollen is the most important ceremonial offering; corn is used in some ceremonies. White shell, turquoise, black jet, and catlinite embody power and are of equal importance, each having directional associations. Eagle feathers also form an important part of the religious equipment.[17]

At one time ceremonial hoops were commonly used. Known as *penseh,* they came in two sizes: small ones only a few inches in diameter, and large ones over two feet in diameter. They were made in sets of four, each painted with the color of the direction it represented: green or black the east, blue the south, yellow the west, and white the north. When placed over a patient and taken off, or when passed through by the patient, they removed sickness. White sage, eagle's feathers, stones, and shells were tied to the hoops. Ceremonial staffs, four or five feet long, with a short crosspiece near the top, were also made and were painted with symbolic lines and figures such as deities, animals, cosmos symbols, and lightning lines. Laid on a patient and lifted off, they too removed the "sick." Usually, curing ceremonies were and are held for only one person at a time, but there are rites that can be given in time of epidemics to fend off the disease. Some ceremonies are protective and take place in the spring and summer when lightning and snakes, scorpions, and other poisonous forms of life are present. The lightning ceremony is held for the community when an evil influence is thought to be at work, and also to bring rain.[18]

"Sometimes, when the circumstance warrants it, and when the patient can afford it, the awesome Gan impersonators, or Crown dancers, may be called upon to perform and are prepared for their curing rituals by a medicine man with the power to do so."[19]

Altars and Sacred Places

In 1884, Mr. S. S. Brannan told Bandelier "of the custom of the Apache, whenever they pass one of the artificial stone heaps (as between Show Low and Fort Apache—last year), to deposit on it each one a stone and two twigs placed crosswise, the stone holding down the twigs. Thus their number can be ascertained."[20] Bandelier

126

included a sketch of the stone heap in his original manuscript.

In view of Reagan's more extensive comments on Apache "altars in 1902," it would appear that Brannan's understanding of what went on at the stone heaps in 1884 was lacking; they seem to have represented far more than the number of Apache passing by. It might even be accurate to refer to the stone heaps as the Navajo do theirs, calling them sacred places.[21] Reagan says:

> The altars in various parts of the Reservation usually consist of a pile of stone on which twigs and shingle rock are placed by each passer-by, over which they then sprinkle cattail-flag pollen and pray to the gods of the zenith and nadir and to the gods of the four winds. Many of these altars are of the nature of a thank offering. Such is the altar at the top of the Cibicu divide on the trail in the climb westward out of Carrizo Canyon. On reaching this altar on the writer's first trip to Cibicu, the party paused a moment. In this interval, the Indian guide took a tiny bag from some part of his clothing, and emptying some yellow cattail-flag pollen from it into his hand, sprinkled the altar with the sacred dust, after which he scattered some of the dust toward the four winds, as his lips moved in prayer. Having sprinkled the dust to the gods, he replaced the bag and then broke a twig from a near-by tree. This he laid on the altar and over it he placed a small shingle rock. Out of curiosity, the writer asked him what he was doing. He answered that he was thanking his gods that the miserable hill had been climbed.
>
> Once while on the trail from Carrizo to Cibicu, the writer was accompanied by a boy, a son of V19. At the top of the divide they arrived at a tree cactus around which various kinds of wood were piled. The boy walked around it with his right side toward the tree and deposited more wood in a circle around it. Later on, the party came to an Apache 'post office' altar on which the boy also placed a bunch of juniper twigs as a prayer.
>
> While on his way from Carrizo to Cibicu, July 19, 1902, the writer passed the two oldest daughters of V26 going in the opposite direction. They had evidently been in a rain, judging by the appearance of their apparel, though the rain had passed Carrizo Creek before the writer started. About two miles west of where the writer passed the women, the trail led over a spot of bare, level ground on which it had rained enough to lay the dust. Here these women had established an altar to the gods to thank them for the rain. The altar was made of rock and the offering was piñon twigs. The encircling of the altar and the dancing around it could be distinctly seen in the dust-laid open space. The young women were the only persons who had come over the trail since the rain, as was indicated by their tracks. They were seventeen and twenty-two years old, respectively.[22]

The Value of Curing Ceremonials

When an outsider considers Apache curing ceremonials, there is a tendency to be apologetic. We avoid dealing directly with actual and surprising cures that have taken place in favor of emphasizing the psychological benefits.[23] In other words, since we can't explain the former in conventional medical terms, we let them alone and deal with the latter. This is not to say that the psychological aspect is unimportant. On the contrary, the medical profession has realized for a long time that many physical disabilities are the by-products of psychic disorders.

The Apache learned this too; they also knew that when psychic disorders are breached or replaced by hope, by the conviction that the ceremony will make the patient well, a significant step has been taken toward recovery. The nature of the Apache ceremonial is such that it accomplishes this. It preoccupies the patient in positive ways, bringing him peace of mind, giving him strength by undergirding his will to get well, and assuring him that all his family and friends truly care about him.

Tradition and personal experience have always been the touchstones of healing. The patient learned from childhood on about the firm mythological roots of the Apache beliefs, he participated in numerous ceremonials, and he witnessed cures. The shaman himself was fixed in the life-way as an integral part of the curing process. His "power" was known, and the entire emphasis, once the decision to proceed had been made, was on positive results.

Having procured the shaman, the patient and all who would join in the rite became intensely involved with the traditional details that, if properly carried out, assured success. Everyone was doing something about the illness. The funds to pay for the shaman, his helpers, and the food had to be raised. All activities had to be co-ordinated.

Long before the actual ceremony began, the shaman impressed upon the patient his need to think positive thoughts, infusing into these as he lectured the ancient teachings regarding the ceremony and its benefits. Then, as the time for the event drew near, the place to hold it had to be selected; women cooked, men went for firewood, invitations to guests went out, and the ceremonial paraphernalia was readied.

Those who attended were those who cared. Everyone important to the patient would be present, and everyone who came had something to do. The food preparation went on, and many speeches were made about proper conduct and thinking good thoughts. The men were expected to join in the singing and drumming. Everyone shared in the pollen blessings and in the important social dances.

The stress was on involvement, and this brought about the healthiest possible results. Holding the ritual at night offered the advantage of a time period when people would not be distracted by the usual things they could do and see in the daytime. The darkness formed an aura of wonder and provoked spiritual thoughts. Even the length of time given over to the ceremony was a factor. The ceremony went on all night, lasting long enough for everyone and every aspect of the rite to phase gradually and progressively into what was happening, which was of primary importance. If necessary, it continued for four nights.

As Keith Basso points out, the Apache believed that the powers worked best in a positive atmosphere of happiness. The opposite attitude would convey an impression of doubt and defeat.[24] Therefore, there was little restraint among the guests, and an outside observer without understanding would often criticize their expressions of joy. As the curing ritual went on, the adults not directly involved socialized, laughed, and joked; some men and women searched for tulapai and consumed what they could, and the children ran and shouted freely in the midst of it all.

The curing way is still performed like this today. It has much to recommend to those who ponder the question of determining how a religious ceremony is likely to bear its best fruits.

Goodwin noted that a curing ceremony was often the beginning of a closer and lifelong friendship between the shaman and the patient.[25] Further, when a ceremony failed to effect a cure, the medicine man suffered "irreparable" injury to his reputation only when he had been too confident of success in the beginning. Failures could usually be smoothed over by the suggestion that the shaman had not been retained soon enough, or that witchcraft was involved. Also, the cure might be taking place, yet not show its ultimate effect for some time to come. Therefore the patient must guard against carelessness in the wearing of the protective amulets given him by the shaman, and in the observance of the ever-present taboos.[26]

The people realized that a medicine man might not succeed in every case, and his excuses were actually built into the traditional process. In some instances the services of several shamans were sought before relief was obtained, and sometimes it never came. However, even allowing for the fact that desperation drives people to seek aid, it appears that the curing ceremonies would not have persisted into the present had they not been in some measure effective.

27 The Gans (Masked Dancers, Mountain Spirit Impersonators)

The stories told today by Western Apache informants regarding the origin of the Gans, or Crown Dancers, vary somewhat in minor details, but are similar in substance. A composite of the two most common accounts given in the Whiteriver area is as follows:

In the beginning the Supreme Being, known as Giver of Life, took the Apache from the center or "bowels" of the earth and brought them up to the country where they were to live. Having been placed there, they were instructed to conduct themselves reverently as a part of nature, preserving the land and in particular caring for all living things. But the Apache were limited and vulnerable like all men, and gave in to the corruption and crudeness that the evil powers pressed upon them.

At this point the concerned Giver of Life sent the Gan as his emissaries to teach the Apache how to live a better way. Now they learned in plain terms how to live decently and honorably, how to cure the sick, how to govern fairly, how to hunt effectively and responsibly, how to plant and harvest, and how to discipline those who failed to live as Giver of Life wished them to.

The Gan also revealed that they had the power to assist or to harm the Apache, and the awed people responded by seeking to live as they were instructed to. Once again, though, they gave in to temptations, and gradually backslid into wicked ways. By now the Gan were most unhappy with them, and decided to abandon the Apache and let them reap the bitter harvest they justly deserved. However, they were benevolent spirits and maintained some hope for the people, so before they went away they drew pictures of themselves on rocks near the sacred caves and within the caves themselves. These drawings can still be seen there today. Then the Gan returned through the sacred caves in the sacred mountains, to the place where the sun shone even when the earth was darkened by man's ignorance, and where there was pleasantness and serenity.

The crestfallen and contrite Apache studied the drawings for a long time, and gave much thought to the wicked nature of man and its unhappy fruits. At last they determined to imitate or "impersonate" the Gan in order to live so far as possible as Giver of Life wished them to. They copied the splendid headdresses, skirts, and moccasins depicted on the rocks and used them in performing the power-filled dances the Gan had taught them. In this way the Gan dances came into being.

Once there was an unusual young boy who lived in the Lower Cedar Creek area, west of where Fort Apache was later located. This boy led the men of his camp on four successful hunts in which a specified deer was killed each time. In each instance he gave the men special instructions as to how to butcher the deer, but on the fourth hunt they ignored his directions and broke the hunting "power." Thus the boy had to follow some deer tracks to see where successful hunting could be carried out in the future. He went a long way into the mountains and into a lonely place. There he was startled to hear the sound of drums and noises similar to those made by the Gan. Fascinated by this, he followed the sounds to a cave at the top of a nearby mountain.

When he entered the sacred cave he was astonished to see many Gan dancing. But as he stood there transfixed the Gan also discovered him, and took him prisoner.

By the wondrous mystic powers possessed by the people, the boy's local group learned that he was being held captive by the Gan. So the shaman commanded the lad's grandmother to take his spotted dog with her and sit outside the sacred cave for four days, promising that if she did so the boy would be released. The grandmother went to the mouth of the cave and took up her vigil. The sound of the dancing Gan alarmed her, though, and as they seemed to be coming closer to the entrance each night, she became so frightened that on the third night she fled with the dog to the safety of her camp.

The council listened to her story, and after some deliberation decided that since the Gan had indicated their willingness to release the boy by moving closer and closer to the cave entrance, the people could win his freedom by performing a twelve-night Crown Ceremony near the cave. So they went to the cave, and the spotted dog went with them. For twelve nights the dance was given by four dancers while the people watched, and on the last night, not long before dawn when the rite would end, the Gan came out of the cave and merged with the people.

Opposite *and* above: *Gan
impersonators, showing the typical
positions of the performers.*

The Gan divided themselves into four groups, and each of the four human dancers was invited to join a group. Each group went to a place in the pine trees, so that one group was standing at each of the four cardinal points. Now the people began to pray, and moving in single file passed by each group, sprinkling pollen over them. The spotted dog followed along. As they passed the third group a breathtaking thing happened, for the dog began to cry and wag his tail in recognition, and a Gan bent down and patted the dog's head. The grandmother knew, of course, that this was her grandson, and that he had been transformed into a Gan. True enough, when she spoke to him, she was told that if she had stayed at the cave as instructed, he would have been released. But he could never return now, for he had become a Gan and henceforth would serve as a representative of the Apache among them.

Nevertheless, great benefits had come from the twelve-day ceremony, for the fate of the unusual boy was known, and the Gan had blessed the people by condescending to mingle with them once again. Moreover, before they returned to the cave, they taught the people how to perform the Crown Dancer curing ceremonies.

Dawn was about to break, and it was time for the Gan to leave. Gathering in four groups once more, they danced toward the cave and passed from sight just as the sun broke over the horizon. Only little clouds of dust remained to show where they had been. Finally, the drumbeats and the singing faded away, and all was silent. It was over, and time for the spellbound people to go home.

The White Mountain Apache agree with the Chiricahua concept that the Crown Dancers, also called Mountain Spirit dancers or masked dancers, impersonate the Mountain Spirits, principally for the purpose of curing certain illnesses. Further, the Crown Dance is performed today much as it was originally. There are four dancers in a set, numbered one through four, plus the clown. The identity

The mythological boy and his spotted dog, with Gan.

132

of the performers is kept secret, and those who violate the no-recognition rule "make trouble" and are severely rebuked. According to one informant, at Fort Apache each dancer chooses his own head-dress and costume style, but the medicine man instructs him in what materials to use and how to make the headdress. Informants also speak of the U-shaped bow frame that fits vertically over the head to form the shape of the hood, and of the piece of scrub oak or hide that secures the U-frame by passing laterally across the face under the nose, and which makes it impossible to breath through the nose. This adds a reason beyond the physical exhaustion for the frequent rest periods required by the dancers, who sometimes raise their hoods when away from the crowd. Mask styles differ; the Western Apache model is made of broader segments and is more varied in concept than the Chiricahua and Mescalero styles.

For color and symbols, black, blue, yellow, and white are said to represent the four directions. On every mask there is one charac-ter that indicates the dancer's clan. While one informant claimed that all the decorations are painted on the costume with an eagle feather, which is then washed clean and attached to the mask, others say that regular paintbrushes are often used. A photograph in *Arizona Highways* magazine seems to confirm this.[1] A blue stone is always attached to the butt of the eagle feather used for painting. Black or turquoise stones are sewed inside the mask. In curing, each dancer sometimes carries a stone in his mouth, which he spits on the sick person. Along with other things used, yellow butterflies painted on the wooden part of a dancer's headdress, called the "horns," are said to remind the people that butterflies were among their ancestors. The stars, sun, and moon painted on the back of the mask and the dancer's chest are light to frighten away angry powers. A cross with a red line around it represents Giver of Life and the sun that is coming through Him. The white dots on the headdress frame and on the dancer's body indicate a pure heart. White triangles on the body represent the sacred mountains or dancer's teeth. A red sun painted on the headdress designates dancer number four, and a cross on top of the sun represents the victory of animal horns over the evil powers. A green sun painted on each side of a headdress tells the dancers "which way to go." Inverted triangles on a mask represent the rock that only the medicine man is allowed to sit on. The clown's entire body is painted white with black dots. A snake is sometimes painted down the middle of his mask. On occasion he is the only dancer to have evergreen boughs tied to his waist and wrists. However, the other dancers do wear evergreen while curing some illnesses, and Reagan makes reference to this in his accounts of ceremonial dances.[2] Harmful spirits enter the boughs, and the clown carries them away and burns them. Clown paint symbolizes the deer, which is the clown's symbolic horse.

I have noted that the eye and mouth holes of many hoods have torn edges, indicating that dancers have trouble seeing and breathing, and that as one informant told Opler, the desperate men often tear at the holes while dancing to relieve the problem.[3] An experienced dancer also learns to cut the eyeholes of a buckskin mask at eyebrow level, so that as the mask shrinks the holes come into proper position before the eyes.[4]

Western Apache Gan wands are more ornate than those of the Chiricahua and Mescalero, having crosspieces with pointed or carved ends placed in various numbers at right angles to the main shaft. The wands are either painted in various ways or left unpainted. They are made of sotol stalk or yucca, varying in length from two to four feet, with a slight curve. While the masked dancers' head-dresses were once made of sotol stalk as well, modern versions are often fashioned of thin lumberyard slats and painted with commercial enamel paints. Also, they are seldom as elaborate, delicate, and subtle in design as the stupendous headdresses of early times.

Since the San Carlos and White Mountain masks are quite similar in shape and design, I asked the Apache how they could

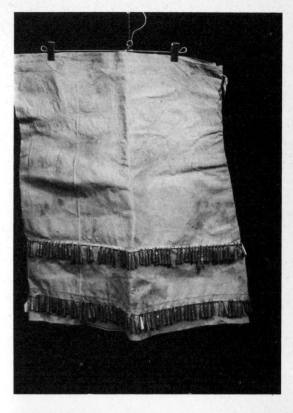

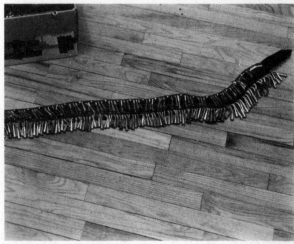

Top: *Modern Gan Dancer skirt made of canvas and decorated with tin cones* (MNCA). Above: *Leather Gan Dancer's belt decorated with tin cones* (MNCA).

tell them apart. The answer was that the San Carlos mask had a snake on it. However, several masks identified as collected in the White Mountain area have snakes on them, and one photograph of a well-known White Mountain shaman painting a mask clearly shows a snake.[5] No doubt there is an explanation for this beyond that which I received.

The dancers of today continue the practice of removing their costumes after dancing and are supposed to hide them away, usually in a sacred cave. Prayers are said over them, and sometimes the knots of the thongs used to assemble the items are untied to prevent their being worn if discovered. This is because Western Apache mythology teaches that if anyone other than a dancer puts on a Crown headdress he will go mad.[6]

The comments of Goodwin in this regard are extremely interesting. He states that boys under eighteen years of age were thought to be too young to impersonate the Gan, and performers were almost always mature men. (Also, a man must be eighteen or more to lead a ceremonial.) He also tells how a certain White Mountain shaman used to paint his own dancers, after which he placed a dot of white paint on each of his cheeks and then made white zigzag lines on the backs of his hands with his fingertips. This same medicine man put on his Gan dance at nearly every girl's puberty ceremony. Afterward, he put the masks away in a certain cave "across the river," which was also used by other shamans as a depository for their ceremonial articles. There was a considerable amount of material stored in the cave, and even though it was a sacred place forbidden to others, adventurous boys would go there, put the masks on, and pretend to dance. However, they never touched the hoops and crosses, for they were really afraid of them. Goodwin adds that such ceremonial objects, once put away, were never used again, for it was very dangerous to disturb them.[7]

Above left: *Detail, Gan belt, back view, showing method of tying cones to belt with buckskin thongs.* Above right: *Detail, Gan belt, front view.* Opposite: *Ancient Gan headdress, ca. 1875, front and back views (SM).*

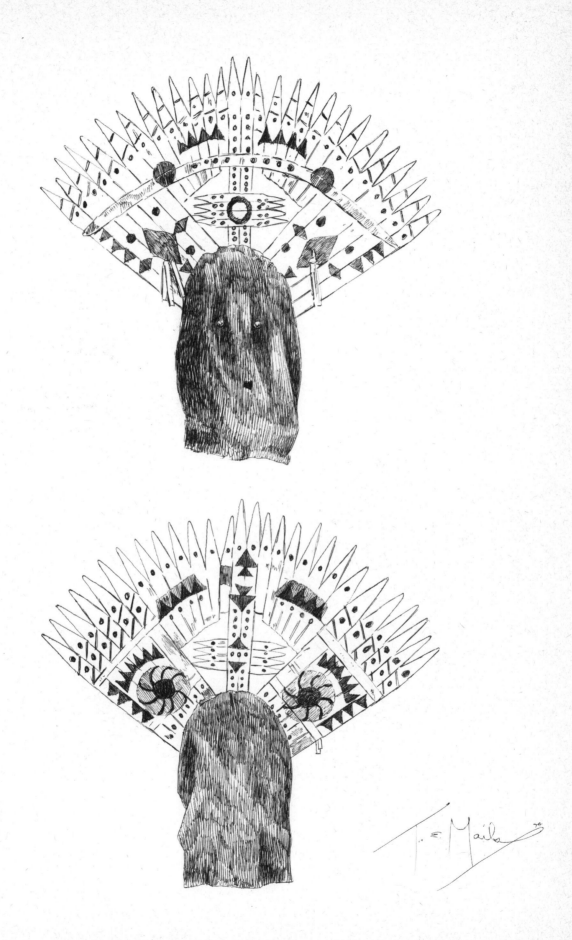

*Ancient Gan headdresses, ca. 1875,
front and back views (SM).*

136

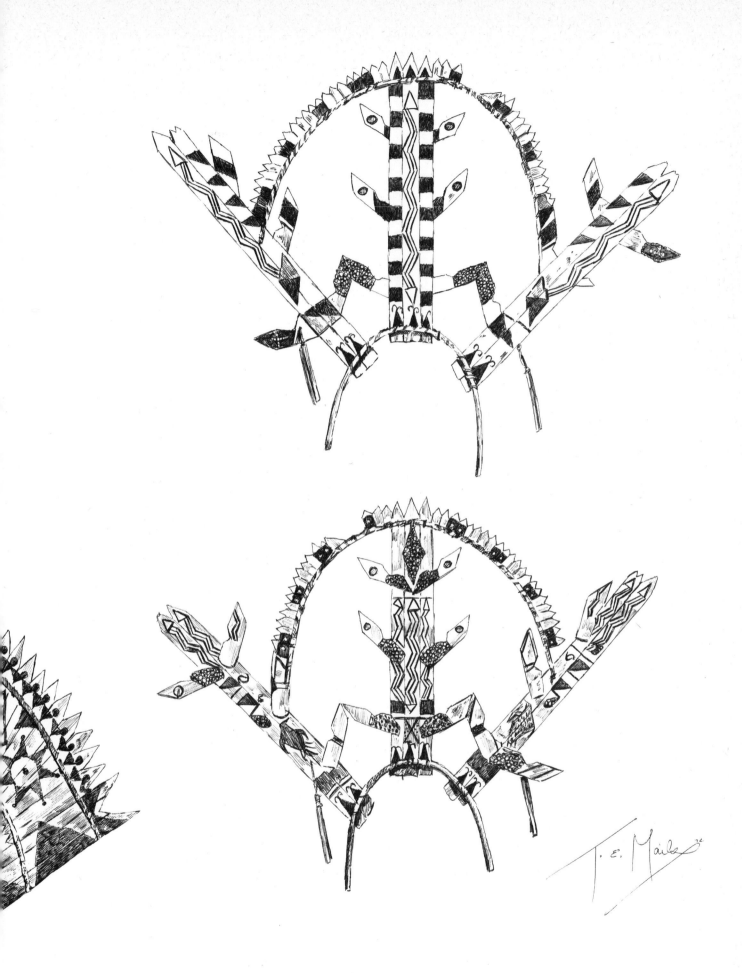

137

Above: *Present-day Western Apache Gans*. Right: *Clown mask, San Carlos (ALMN)*.

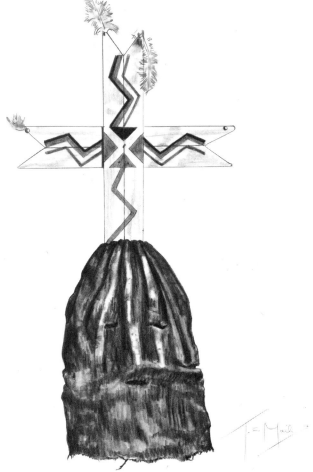

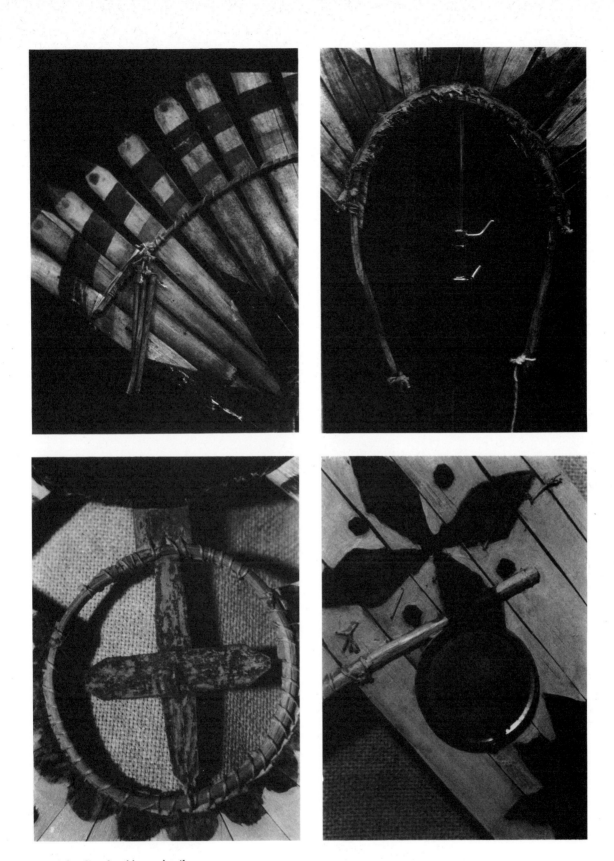

Top left: *Gan headdress, detail, showing pendant hanging and method of securing the slats, or "horns" (MNCA).* Top right: *Detail, showing U-frame used to secure vertical pieces and hold assembly on performer's head.* Above left: *Gan headdress, detail, showing typical open design element made with wooden hoop and cross (ASM).* Above right: *Detail, showing trade mirrors and painted symbols.*

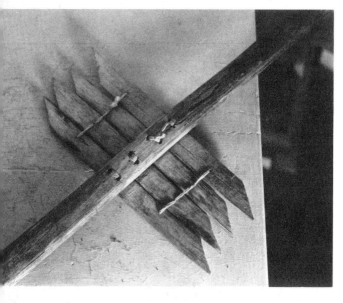
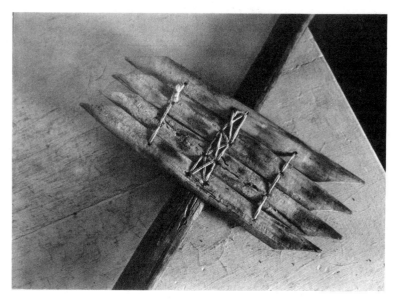

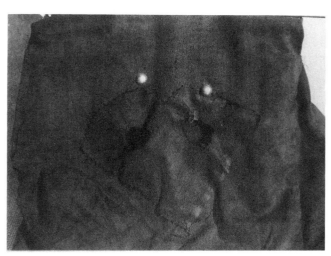

Top left: *Western Apache Gan wand, made of cactus stalk, showing cross-pieces tied with thongs (ALMN). Length of wand, 38 inches. Front view.* Top right: *Back view, showing ties.* Above: *Gan mask, detail, showing method of trimming and tying horns (ASM).* Above right: *Patched cotton face mask, with silver buttons placed above eye holes, detail.* Right *and* far right: *Tridents with owl feathers, carried by clown in curing ceremonies (HM).*

Top left: *Western Apache Gan wand made of sotol (SM).* Top right: *Detail, showing method of securing owl feathers to trident.* Above left: *Gan clown wand listed in museum collection as Apache trident, but probably Pueblo wand used in Matachines Dance or close adaptation thereof (HM).* Above right: *Wand listed in museum collection as Apache trident, but probably a Pueblo wand or adaptation thereof (HM).*

28 Medicine Men

"Probably no tribe with which our people have come in contact has succeeded more thoroughly in preserving from profane inquiry a complete knowledge of matters relating to their beliefs and ceremonials," said Army Capt. John G. Bourke in 1892.

When Bourke first went among the Apache in New Mexico and Arizona in 1869, he "was foolish enough" to depend in great measure upon the Mexican captives who had lived among them since boyhood, and who might be supposed to know the exact explanation of every Apache ceremony. Yet he was repeatedly assured by several of these interpreters that the Apache had no actual religion. The interpreters had no intention to deceive; they were simply unable to disengage themselves from their own prejudices and their own ignorance. They could not, and they would not, credit the existence of any such thing as a valid religion save the little they remembered about the Roman Catholic faith their mothers had taught them in Sonora, Mexico.[1] Bourke was also candid enough to admit that most of his observations were made while the Apache were still actively engaged in hostilities with the Whites, and as such they could not be regarded as, nor were they claimed to be, conclusive on all points.[2] Nevertheless, his observations, which follow, are certainly interesting, although they should be compared with the comments regarding healing in other sections.

The Apache medicine men were not divided into medicine lodges or secret societies, as were their counterparts of the Plains or Eastern nations. The Navajo seemed to have well-defined divisions among their medicine men, and Bourke saw lodges where at least a dozen Navajo shamans were engaged in incantations, but he never witnessed among the Apache any rite of religious significance in which more than six medicine men took part.

Diligent and persistent inquiry of medicine men whose confidence he had succeeded in gaining assured him that any young Apache man could become a "doctor." It was necessary only to convince his friends that he had the gift—that is, he must show that he was "a dreamer of dreams, given to long fasts and vigils, able to interpret omens in a satisfactory manner, and do other things of that general nature to demonstrate the possession of an intense spirituality." Then he would begin to withdraw, at least temporarily, from the society of his fellows and devote himself to long absences, especially by night, in high and remote places conducive to thought and to contact with the supernatural powers.

While the surer mode of learning how to be a shaman was to seek and pay for the guidance and ritual of one who had already gained power and influence as such, nothing prohibited a man from assuming the role of a prophet or healer of the sick, beyond the fear of punishment for failure to cure or alleviate sickness or infirmity. Neither was there such a thing as settled dogma among medicine men. Each followed the dictates of his own inclinations, consulting such spirits and powers as were most amenable to his supplications and charms, and no two appeared to rely upon identically the same influences.[3]

Apache shamans had individual capabilities: there were some who enjoyed great fame as the bringers of rain, some who claimed special power over snakes, and some who professed to consult the spirits only, and did not treat the sick except when no other practitioner was available. There did not seem to have been any inheritance of priestly functions among the Apache or any setting apart of a particular clan or family for the priestly duties.

One of the ceremonies connected with the initiation and with every exercise of spiritual functions by the medicine man was the use of the sweat bath, in which, if he were physically able, the patient also participated. The Apache did not, according to Bourke's knowledge, indulge in the use of poisonous intoxicants during their medicine ceremonies, even though the laurel grew wild on all the

Medicine man wearing owl and hawk
feather hat and painted medicine shirt.

143

Top: *Buckskin medicine hat covered with owl and hawk feathers (MNCA). Front view.* Center: *Back view.* Above: *Right side.*

mountain tops of Sonora and Arizona, and the Apache credit it with the power of setting men crazy; but they never made use of it in their medicine or religion.[4]

"Contrary to what Spencer says," the chiefs of the Apache were not automatically medicine men, although among the Tonto Apache the brother of a head chief named Cha-ut-lip-un was the head shaman, and generally the medicine men were related closely to the prominent chiefs, "which would seem to imply either a formal deputation of priestly functions from the chiefs to relatives, or what may be practically the same thing, the exercise of family influence to bring about a recognition of the necromantic powers of some aspirant."[5]

Medicine men among the Apache claimed the power to shoot off guns without touching the trigger or going near the weapons, and declared they were able to kill or harm their enemies at a distance of 100 miles. In nearly every boast, however, there was included a saving clause to the effect that no witchcraft must be made or the spell would not work, or that no women should be standing nearby who were in a delicate physical state, and so forth. Mickey Free assured Bourke that he had seen an Apache medicine man light a pipe without doing anything but hold his hands up toward the sun, a credible enough story if, as Bourke suspected, the shaman possessed a magnifying glass. The Apache looked upon blacksmiths as being allied with the spirits and called them *pesh-chidin*—the witch, spirit, or ghost of the iron. The Apache did not observe lucky or unlucky days. The recovery of stolen or lost property, especially horses, was one of the principal tasks imposed upon the shamans. They relied greatly upon the aid of pieces of crystal in effecting this. Na-a-cha, a medicine man, could give no explanation of how it was done, "except that by looking into it he could see everything he wanted to see."[6]

The Apache's name, once conferred, seemed to remain with him through life, except in the case of the medicine men, who changed their names upon assuming their profession.

The medicine men were, at least while young, extremely careful of their hair, and Bourke often saw those who were proud of their long, glossy locks. In particular he recalled the "doctor" at San Carlos in 1885, who would never allow his flowing black tresses to be touched. But they did not roach their hair, and they did not add false hair to their own; they did not apply plasters of mud as did their neighbors the Yuma, Cocopa, Mojave, and Pima, and they did not use wigs in their dances.[7]

All charms, talismans, medicine hats, and other sacred regalia were either made or blessed by the medicine men. They were in charge of all ceremonial feasts and dances such as the puberty rite and war dances preceeding battle. Bourke claims that all preparations for war parties were under their control, and that when they were after the enemy their power was almost supreme. Not a night passed on a war journey but that the medicine men got into the sweat bath, if such a thing was possible, and remained there for some minutes, singing and making "medicine" for the good of the party. After dark they sat around the fire, singing and talking with the spirits and predicting the results of the campaign.

When a man was taken sick the medicine men took charge of the case, and the clansmen and friends of the patient were called upon to supply the fire and assist in the chorus. The only musical instrument employed was a flat rawhide drum or a pot drum nearly always improvised from an iron camp kettle, partially filled with water and covered with a piece of well-soaped cloth drawn as tight as possible. The Apache drumstick was a stick curved into a circle at one end; the stroke was not made perpendicular to the surface, but from one side to the other. Bourke states that in the Apache view, all bodily disorders and ailments were attributed to evil spirits who must be expelled or placated. When there was only one person ill, the ritual consisted of singing and drumming exclusively, but dancing was added in all cases where an epidemic was raging or might spread in the tribe. The medicine men led off the singing, and the assistants replied with a refrain that at times appeared to Bourke to be antiphonal. Then the chorus was swelled by the voices of the women and youth, rising and falling "with monotonous cadence." Prayers were recited, several of which were repeated to Bourke and transcribed. Frequently the words were ejaculatory and confined to such expressions as *ugashe* (go away), and there was to be noted the same mumbling of "incoherent phrases" that had been the stock-in-trade of shamans in all ages and places. Bourke calls these phrases "gibberish," and says this was admitted by the medicine men, who claimed that the words employed and known only to themselves (each individual seemed to have his own vocabulary) were mysteriously effective in dispelling sickness of any kind. "Gibberish was believed to be more potential in magic than was language which the practitioner or his dupes could comprehend."[8]

In reading Bourke's comments, I remembered how differently the case of the shaman's phrases was explained to me by a Fort Apache informant in 1972. Far from being "gibberish," the Apache medicine man does indeed have a lucid vocabulary all his own, and it contains phrases that those outside the profession are forbidden to use or to learn. This formed a real barrier to a rounded collection of Apache culture. The informant was not critical of this factor in revealing it, but was simply pointing out some of the difficulties faced in preserving the Western Apache heritage. This leads me to advise the reader to consider all of Bourke's information, invaluable as it may be, in the light of his final comments in this section regarding his true view of the Apache medicine men. He actually held them in contempt, and as such was in no position to evaluate fairly their accomplishments or real worth in Apache society.[9]

Bourke conceded that the monotonous intonation of the medicine man was not without good results, "especially in such ailments as can be benefited by the sleep which such singing induces." At the same time he was forced to recall cases of Apache who recovered under the treatment of their own medicine after White surgeons had abandoned the case, but "this recovery could be attributed only to the sedative effects of the chanting."

Bourke saw a sacred bundle which he was allowed to feel, but not open, and which he learned contained some lightning-riven twigs. It was carried by a young shaman, scarcely out of his teens, during General Crook's expedition into the Sierra Madre, Mexico, in 1883, in pursuit of the hostile Chiricahua. Some of the Plains tribes had a custom of "striking the post" in their dances, especially the Sun Dance, and there was then an obligation upon the striker to tell the truth. Bourke was told that the Apache medicine men used a club to strike the "stagamites" in their sacred caves, but what it meant and what else they did he was not able to learn.[10]

There was little disagreement as to what people would think about a shaman when he failed to cure his patient, but there were conflicting stories about the number of patients he would be allowed to lose before he might be punished. Bourke's own conclusions were that a medicine man would be in danger, under certain circumstances, if only one of his patients died. These circumstances would be the verdict that the shaman was culpably negligent or ignorant. In such instances he could escape death at the hands of the patient's kinsfolk only by fleeing from the camp or by demonstrating that a witch had been the real cause of the death.[11]

Bourke also mentions that the Apache attached great importance to not mentioning the names of their dead. They did not have a clear location in mind for the future world, but did believe that the dead remained for a few days near the place where they departed from this life, and that they attempted to communicate with their living friends through the voice of the owl. If a relative heard this sound by night, or, as often happened, he imagined that he had seen

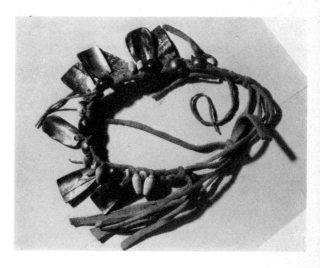

Top: *War medicine necklace, seashells strung on buckskin cord (AF). Front view.* Above: *Back view.*

the ghost itself, he hurried to the nearest medicine man, related his story, and then carried out to the smallest detail the feasting, singing, dancing, and other means that would keep the ghost in good humor on the journey which it would then undertake to the "house of spirits." Nearly all shamans claimed the power to go there at will, and even some who were not medicine men claimed the same power.[12]

Medicine men were paid by each patient or by his friends at the time they were consulted. This was their only means of support. As a general rule, they did not attend to their own families, nor did

Painted medicine bag (SM).

they assist in cases of childbirth unless there was a special need. To both of these rules, however, there were numerous exceptions.

There were medicine women as well as medicine men among the Apache, and Bourke was personally acquainted with two of them. One was named "Captain Jack." She was well advanced in years and quite feeble, but intelligent and well versed in the lore of her people. She was fond of instructing her grandchildren, whom she supported, in the prayers and invocations to the gods worshiped by her fathers. On several occasions Bourke listened carefully and unobserved while she did this, and determined that the prayers were the same as those that had already been given to him as the prayers of the tribe. The other medicine woman was a Chiricahua named Tze-go-juni, a woman with a most romantic history. She had been a captive for five years among the Mexicans in Sonora and had learned to speak excellent Spanish. "A mountain lion had severely mangled her in the shoulder and knee, and once she had been struck by lightning; so that whether by reason of superior attainments or by an appeal to the superstitious reverence of her comrades, she wielded considerable influence."

Bourke asserted that medicine women devoted their attention principally to obstetrics and had many peculiar stories to relate concerning prenatal influences and matters of that sort. Tze-go-juni wore a stone amulet, shaped like a spear point, on a cord around her neck. The stone was silex obtained from the top of a mountain, taken from a ledge at the foot of a tree that had been struck by lightning. The fact that siliceous rock emits sparks when struck by another hard body seemed proof that the fire must have been originally deposited therein by the bolt of lightning. A tiny piece of the woman's amulet was broken off, ground into the finest powder, and then administered in water to women during pregnancy.[13]

Medicine men ate the same food as other people. In the burial ceremonies for deceased medicine men there was "a difference of degree, but not of kind."

Bourke states that "Surgeon Smart shows that among other offices entrusted to the medicine-men of the Apache was the reception of distinguished strangers." Several of the most influential shamans Bourke knew were blind. "Whether this blindness was the result of old age or due to the frenzy of dancing until exhausted in all seasons I am unable to conjecture."[14]

According to Bourke, the Apache would not let snakes be killed within the limits of the camp by one of their own people. However, they would not only allow a stranger to kill snakes, but request him to do so. They made this request of Bourke on three occasions.[15] Albert Reagan adds that the country of the Apache abounded in snakes. There were at least three species of rattlesnakes, all of which were numerous. These were reverenced by the Indians on account of their power to kill. The Apache never killed a snake. When they saw a snake they said to it: " 'Go into your hole, you evil creature, and take the evil world with you.' . . . Most Indians worship evil as well as good, believing it is better to appease the wrath of the evil, than to incur its enmity. They account for unfortunate things by the snakes that died during the summer and left the evil with them. They will not use anything that has been used or touched in any way in connection with a snake. Once the writer got blood on his hands in killing a snake with a spade. He asked one of the Indians to bring a cup of water and pour some on his hands. Reluctantly the Indian did as he was bidden, but none of the Indians would ever use the cup or spade again. An old woman on the Reserve also asserts that her rheumatism was caused by her stepping in some blood where a rattlesnake had been killed."[16]

Reagan also said the Apache had great respect for the crazy and the feebleminded and placed credence in their irrational sayings and acts. They believed that such persons had communication with the mysteries and had power to make people well, to kill, to benefit or harm the tribe, as they asserted in their actions and sayings. He

Top: *Painted buckskin medicine bag (SM). Length including fringe, 12 inches. Front view.* Above: *Back view. Note the corner tabs, typical of such bags.* Opposite: Top left: *Painted buckskin medicine man's bag (SM). Length including tabs, approximately 20 inches. Figure is a Gan symbol. Front view.* Top right: *Back view, with Gan symbol. The background is not painted.* Bottom left: *Carved bone medicine amulet with buckskin loop (AF). Length, 5½ inches. Source unknown.* Bottom right: *Small beaded medicine amulet for hunting use (AF). Hung on buckskin necklace. Source unknown.*

added that many of the medicine men were old and of failing minds, in the dotage stage. Yet the people believed their every saying and action and that they had the power to kill or make live as they chose.[17]

According to Bourke, the items used for curing were at best limited to roots, leaves, and other vegetable matter. In gathering these remedies, the medicine men and medicine women performed no superstitious ceremonies he could detect, although he had not often seen them collecting. He thought they preferred incantation to pharmacy at all times. The main reliance for nearly all disorders was the sweat bath, which generally brought sound sleep.

When a pain was localized and deep-seated, the medicine men resorted to suction tubes placed on the part affected, and raised blisters in that way. After a long march in pursuit of hostiles, he had seen Indians of different bands expose the small of their naked back to the fierce heat of a pile of coals to produce a reddening effect and to stimulate weak backs. They also drank freely of hot teas or infusions of herbs and grasses to cure chills. They were all adept in the manufacture of splints out of willow slats, and had good success in their treatment of gunshot wounds. They did not dress wounds as often as White practitioners, alleging that the latter, by so frequently removing the bandages, unduly irritated the wounds. He knew them to use moxa—herbs applied to the skin—and remembered having seen, upon the left hand of the great Apache chief Cochise, two deep scars caused by this remedy.

While shamans did not cut or gash themselves in the performance of their duties, scarification was quite common among warriors. Exhausted Apache scouts were in the habit of sitting down and lashing their legs with bunches of nettles until the blood flowed, believing that it relieved the exhaustion.

When all other means had failed, the medicine men made "altars" in the sand and clay near the bed of the dying. They portrayed the figures of various animals, then took a pinch of the dust or ashes from each one and rubbed it upon the sick person and upon themselves.[18]

In concluding his report on the medicine men of the Apache, Bourke states that people who carefully read what he says will know what the shamans really were, how tenaciously they remained so, and goes on to assert that the first Spanish writers assessed them correctly,

. . . as the emissaries of Satan and the preachers of witchcraft, and henceforth they appear in the documents as "hechicheros" and "brujos" almost exclusively. Pimentel seems to have derived his information from Cordero, a Spanish officer who had served against the Apache at various times between 1770 and 1795, and seemed to understand them well. "There was no class of persons who so widely and deeply influenced the culture and shaped the destiny of the Indian tribes as their priests. In attempting to gain a true conception of the race's capacities and history there is no one element of their social life which demands closer attention than the power of these teachers. . . . However much we may deplore the use they made of their skill, we must estimate it fairly and grant its due weight in measuring the influence of the religious sentiment on the history of man."[19]

To underscore how completely he agreed with this view, Bourke goes on to add his own questionable conclusion:

It will only be after we have thoroughly routed the medicine-men from their intrenchments and made them an object of ridicule that we can hope to bend and train the mind of our Indian wards in the direction of civilization. In my own opinion, the reduction of the medicine-men will effect more for the savages than the giving of land in severalty or instruction in the schools at Carlisle and Hampton; rather, the latter should be conducted with this great object mainly in view; to let pupils insensibly absorb such knowledge as may soonest and most completely convince them of the impotency of the charlatans who hold the tribes in bondage.

Teach the scholars at Carlisle and Hampton some of the wonders of electricity, magnetism, chemistry, the spectroscope, magic lantern, ventriloquism, music, and then, when they return to their own people, each will despise the fraud of the medicine-men and be a focus of growing antagonism to their pretensions. Teach them to love their own people and not to despise them; but impress upon each one that he is to return as a missionary of civilization. Let them see that the world is free to the civilized, that law is liberty.[20]

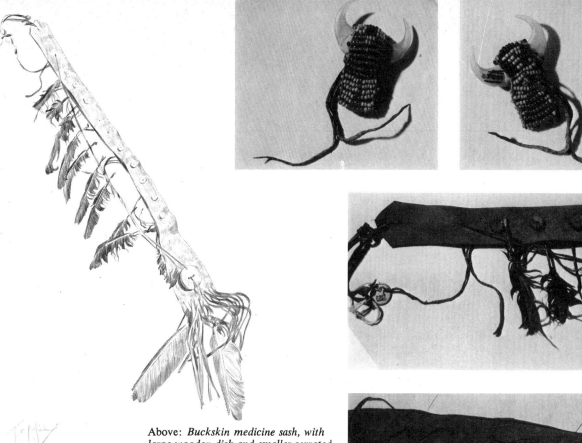

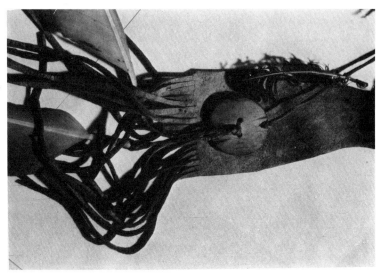

Above: *Buckskin medicine sash, with large wooden disk and smaller serrated disks of rawhide; unpainted except for red edge (AF, Apache Coll.). Length without feather, 30 inches. An unusual artifact, about which there is no information.* Top left: *Tiny beaded war or hunting amulet (AF). Source unknown. Front view.* Top right: *Back view.* Above right: *Detail, front view of sash.* Right: *Detail, back view of sash.* Below: *Detail, end view of sash, showing carved wooden disk and fringing.* Bottom: *Detail, front view of sash, showing method of attaching feathers.*

29 Specific Medicine Items Used by the Western Apache

The Rhombus or Bull-Roarer

The rhombus was first seen by Capt. John G. Bourke at a snake dance of the Hopi in the village of Walpi, Arizona, in 1881. The medicine men twirled it rapidly about the head and from front to rear, with a uniform motion, and succeeded in faithfully imitating the sound of a gust of rain-laden wind. As explained by one of the medicine men, by making this sound they compelled the wind and rain to come to the aid of the crops. At a later date Bourke found it in use among the Apache, and for the same purpose. As the summer season at San Carlos Agency during the year 1884 had been unusually dry, and the crops were parched, the medicine men arranged a procession in which they carried a rhombus and a long-handled cross, upon which various symbols were depicted.

Two examples of the rhombus, or "bull-roarer," front and back views (9th Annual Report BAE, pp. 477–478).

The form of rhombus in use among the Apache at this time was a rectangular piece of wood, seven or eight inches in length, one and a quarter inches in width, and a quarter-inch thick. The extremity through which the twisted cord passed was simply carved to represent a human head. The Apache explained that the lines etched on the front side of the board were the entrails of their wind god, and those painted on the rear side were his hair. The hair was of several colors, and the strands were crooked to represent lightning. The medicine rhombus of the Apache was made by the medicine men, generally of pine or fir that had been struck by lightning on the mountaintops. Such wood was held in the highest estimation among them and was used for the manufacture of amulets with special power. The Apache name given to Bourke for the rhombus was *tzi-ditindi,* "sounding wood."[1]

Medicine Shirt

Reagan witnessed a medicine singing held over a boy of about sixteen years of age at the Camp of C1, May 13, 1901:

> Two pottery drums were used. The medicine man wore a buckskin medicine shirt which had four feathers, each with a piece of clamshell at each side in a perpendicular line, both

front and back. It also had two feathers suspended at the center line in front and two behind and had two medicine god designs in front, one on each side about four inches below the shoulder. The face-head part of one of these medicine designs was a sun disk with rays eight inches long projecting from it. The other head and face design, including the headwear, was a moon mask god design with feather-crested head. Across the lower part of the shirt was a snake design and at the back and just below and back of the arms was a butterfly design, and back of it about two inches in a perpendicular line on each side were three crescent moons. The central back figure was a god design. The sick boy had a green wreath of swamp weed around his head. After they had sung five songs, the old medicine man took the sacred pollen and made a cross first on the sick boy's breast, then on each shoulder, though first, on the left shoulder, as he prayed his deities. He then set the bowl of pollen down and the patient

Painted medicine shirt (9th Annual Report BAE, p. 593).

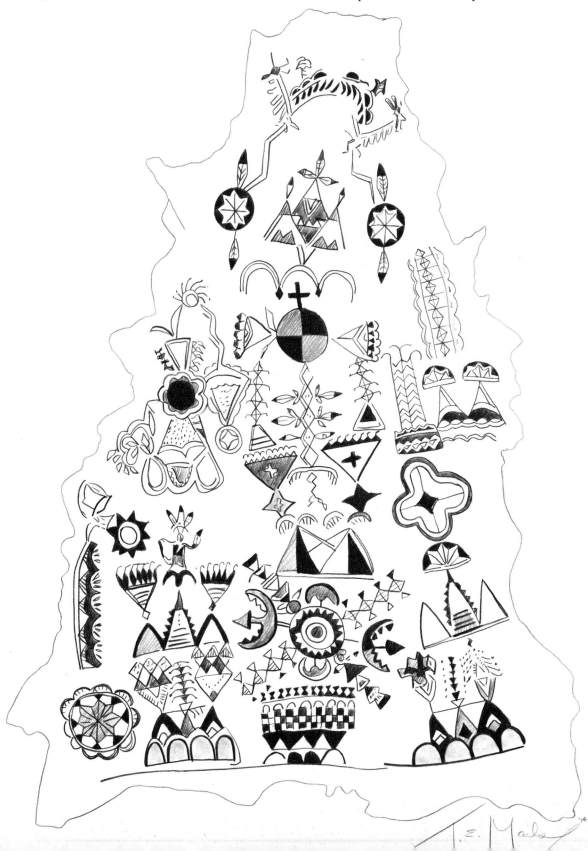

Painted medicine shirt (9th Annual Report BAE, p. 589).

took some of it and placed it in his mouth. The singing continued till morning.

During an interval in the singing, the writer asked the medicine man about the butterfly design on the medicine shirt and he explained its use as follows: "Butterfly antennae are used as medicine. They are placed under the hat band, under the shirt, or in some other place obscured from view, but known only to the Indian himself. The women mix the 'paint' of the butterfly's wing with the common or pounded-up-rock paint and then paint their faces with the concoction. We put the butterfly on our medicine objects because of its medicinal properties."

These ceremonies were held at the camp of C2 on Cibicu in the fall of 1901 over a little girl who was sick. She lay on a pallet to the south of the fire in the center of the house. To the left of this bed was a set of medicine hoops, painted to represent the rainbow. The feathers, which had been removed from them, were wrapped up to show that they were not to be used in this ceremony. A medicine cross was also wrapped up and hung from the house wall. At the head of the bed was suspended a medicine shirt. On the front of this, at the left, were suspended, in succession, five feathers together with five pieces of clam shell, beginning first on top of the shoulder and suspended on down the front about four inches apart. Each clam shell and feather was suspended from a god design. The upper one represented some terrible monster, with claws like a crayfish. The next lower was a human figure with the sun for a head. The

Below: *Painted medicine shirt (9th Annual Report BAE, p. 591).* Opposite top: *Painted medicine hat, front and back (SM).* Opposite bottom left: *Painted medicine hat (SM).* Bottom right: *Painted medicine cross, front and back views (SM). At left, vertical section, 55 inches long, 5⅜ inches wide; cross arm, 33½ inches long, 5¼ inches wide. Zigzag lines from left to right are black, blue, yellow, and white. Holes spaced along bottom of cross arm and down sides of vertical section to receive eagle feathers tied on with thongs. Holes in crown points also.*

others were so covered by the feathers that the writer could not make them out. Between the row of feathers and the center line was another row of emblems. The upper one just below the shoulder line was a huge spider; the next lower, the crescent "dark" moon, the next lower, the crescent "light" moon, the next, the sacred butterfly. On the center line were suspended, in succession, four feathers and four pieces of clam shell, a feather and a clam shell being suspended from the same place. On the right side of the shirt were five feathers and five pieces of clam shells, a feather and a clam shell being hung together, in a perpendicular line on the shirt. Each set of these was suspended from a god design, only one of which could be distinctly seen. It was a human figure with a drawing of the moon for a head. Around the lower margin of the shirt was the great rainbow and just above it was a drawing of the great snake. The shirt was put on the patient and then the usual singing was continued throughout the entire night.[2]

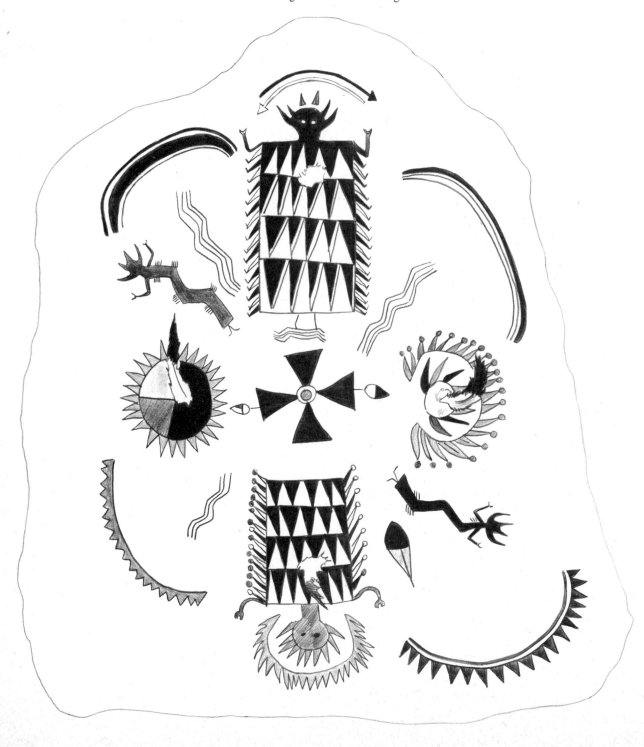

Medicine Hat

According to Bourke, the medicine hat of an old, blind San Carlos Apache medicine man named Nan-ta-do-tash was "an antique affair of buckskin, much begrimed with soot and soiled by long use," which gave life and strength to him and enabled him to peer into the future, tell who had stolen horses from other people, foresee the approach of an enemy, and aid in the curing of the sick. When the old shaman discovered that Bourke had made a rude drawing of it, "he became extremely excited and said that such a delineation would destroy all the life of the hat." His fears were put to rest by several presents, yet as a measure of precaution, he insisted upon sprinkling pinches of hoddentin over Bourke, the hat, and the drawing of it, all the while muttering various prayers. Then he came back a month later and demanded thirty dollars for damages done to the hat, for ever since the drawing was done it had ceased to "work" when needed.

Nan-ta-do-tash explained the symbols painted on the hat and gave Bourke a great deal of valuable information in regard to the profession of medicine men, their specialization, and the prayers they recited.

Bourke was not certain how the buckskin for medicine hats was obtained, but from an incident he saw "in the Sierra Madre in Mexico in 1883, where our Indian scouts and the medicine-men with them surrounded a nearly grown fawn and tried to capture it alive, as well as from other circumstances too long to be here inserted, I am of the opinion that the buckskin to be used for sacred purposes among the Apache must, whenever possible, be that of a strangled animal, as is the case, according to Dr. Matthews, among the Navajo."

The body of the hat was not painted, but the symbols painted upon it were done in two colors, a brownish yellow and an earthy blue, resembling a dirty Prussian blue. The appendages consisted of eagle feathers, both down and black-tipped, pieces of abalone shell, chalchihuitl stone, and a rattlesnake's rattle on the apex. The painted symbols represented clouds, rainbow, hail, the morning star, the God of Wind with his lungs, the black Gan, and great stars or suns.

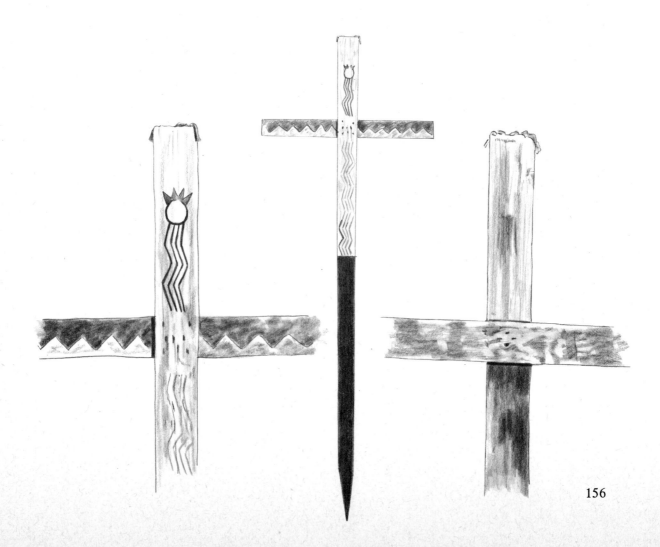

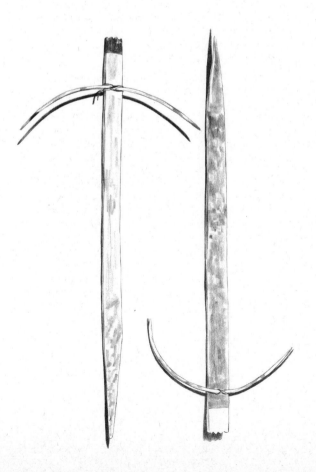

Opposite top: *Gan dancers of Old Fort Apache area performing with medicine cross and trident wands. Usually, only the clown carried the trident.* Opposite bottom: *Ceremonial cross made of sotol (MNCA). Decorated with four zigzag lines of blue, yellow, white, and black; three cross bars; and small circles of black, blue, yellow, and white. Length of cross, 59 inches; 5/8 inch thick. Width of cross bar, 21½ inches. Collected at Canyon Day village near Fort Apache by William Sinten, "used probably in a public ceremony to cure bad sickness in the village community."*

Above: *Medicine man using crescent-crowned crosses to cure a stomach disorder at Canyon Day village.*

Left: *Crescent-crowned crosses made of sotol (MNCA). Black cross, representing the East, has yellow zigzag line on front, black design on back, blue on left side, white on right side. Yellow cross, representing the West, has black design on front, yellow on back, blue on left side, white on right side. Often four such crosses were used in curing stomach disorders and other sicknesses, but never less than two. The tops of the crosses are heads, and around their necks during a ceremony are tied stones appropriate to the colors of the crosses. Eagle feathers were also hung from the ends of the crescents. Length of cross, 31 inches; 1 inch thick. Length of crescent, 19¼ inches. Collected at Canyon Day village by William Sinten.*

Buckskin medicine hat with beaded edge, painted symbols, and owl feathers (AF). From the top: Left side, top, right side. Opposite top: Gans using penseh, *or medicine hoops, to ward off injury by snakes, lightning, or ghosts. The hoops were prayed over, pollen was sprinkled on them, and then they were dropped over the person for whom the ceremony was given. Sometimes the spectators passed through the hoops, particularly when the ceremony was given to protect from lightning. Opposite bottom left: Medicine hoops collected at Canyon Day village by William Sinten (MNCA). When used in a ceremony, the hoops were decorated with eagle feathers, and bunches of white sage tied on in four bundles. Black jet was tied on the black hoop of the East, turquoise on the blue hoop of the South, abalone shell on the yellow hoop of the West, and white shell on the white hoop of the North. Average diameter, 20½ inches; thickness, ½ inch. Opposite bottom right: Detail, showing how ends of hoop are lashed together.*

The appearance of the Gan himself and the shape of the tail of the hat suggested to Bourke the centipede, an important animal god of the Apache. The aged owner of the hat said that the figures represented the powers to which he appealed for aid in his "medicine" and the Gan upon whom he called for help. There were other doctors with other medicines, but he used only those represented in the hat.

"When an Apache or other medicine-man is in full regalia he ceases to be a man, but becomes, or tries to make his followers believe that he has become, the power he represents."[3]

Medicine Hoops and Effigies

In this ceremony held west of the Post January 24, 1902, four hoops were used, painted blue, white, yellow, and green; all had eagle feathers suspended from them. These hoops were supposed to represent the rainbow; the Apache believe that the rainbow is a complete circle of which only a part is ever seen by human eyes. As the singing progressed, the sacred pollen was sprinkled now and then. The ceremony was held in the open. At midnight a snowstorm drove the singers into A56's house, where the singing was continued till morning.

The singing was held over the wife of a brother of Z1, May 16, 1902, who had consumption. The four feathered medicine hoops were placed in pairs opposite each other, against the inside wall of the house, one hoop facing each of the semi-cardinal directions. The northwest one was white, the southeast one black, the southwest one yellow, and the northeast one green. These hoops resembled wooden barrel hoops. Each had a figure like a large inverted V painted in series on the outside. The figures on the white hoop were yellow, those on the green one, red, those of the black-blue one, white, and those on the yellow one, black. When sprinkling the sacred pollen, the leader first held the pollen between the thumb and finger of the left hand as he faced the east and sprinkled it to the wind. Then he repeated the performance as he held his hand toward the northeast, and so on, around the circle of the horizon. He then sprinkled the drummers, medicine men, and singers in the order given, then each of the hoops in succession, beginning with the northwest hoop and going around the circle toward the southwest and south. The sacred dust was sprinkled twelve times during the night. Morning closed the ceremonies.[4]

The daughter of E30 was sung over in the forenoon of February 25, 1902. Several medicine men made a crude image of wood in the likeness of the Gan. When finished, they painted it, drew such designs on it as suited their fancy, and feathered it according to the medicine style for such effigies. At about four P.M. it was finished. The medicine strings were then put in place in the house. A string was tied across the side of the house on the inside, opposite each of the four corners of the earth. Then these were feathered with many war eagle feathers. The medicine god was then brought into the house and placed facing the daughter of E30, who reclined on a blanket south of the central fire of the house; she was suffering from consumption and was the patient for whom the ceremonies were to be performed. The medicine god had the image of an Indian painted on the front. The painting was three inches long, the body green, the hair black, the face worked out in black and white lines, and the hair long and black. The singing lasted all night. At midnight the medicine man placed the effigy face up on the afflicted parts in five different directions, as he prayed to his gods and sprinkled the sacred meal to the deities and the four winds. Four very small medicine hoops were then produced and were manipulated in much the same way as the medicine god. The singing continued throughout the night and was repeated the following night.[5]

Cross

Bourke's observations assured him that the sign of the cross, which was so common in Apache symbolism, was related to the cardinal points and the four winds. It was even painted by warriors upon their

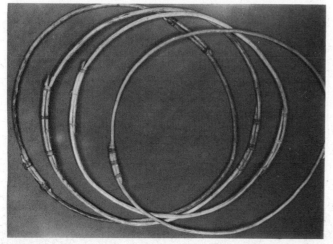

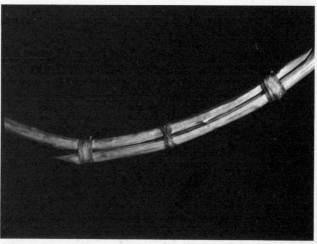

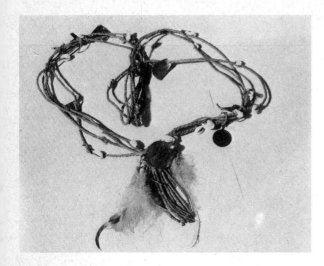

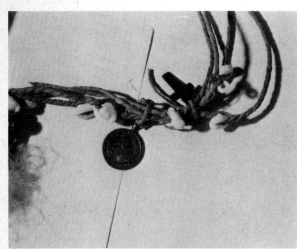

Top: *Four-strand medicine cord (AF).*
Center *and* above: *Details of
medicine cord.*

moccasins upon going into a strange territory, in the hope it would keep them from following the wrong trail.

In October, 1884, Bourke saw a procession of Apache men and women, led by medicine men bearing two wooden crosses. These were made as follows: "The vertical arm was 4 feet 10 inches long, and the transverse between 10 and 12 inches, and each was made of slats about 1½ inches wide, which looked as if they had been in long use. They were decorated with blue polka dots upon the unpainted surface. A blue snake meandered down the longer arm. There was a circle of small willow twigs at top; next below that, a small zinc-cased mirror, a bell, and eagle feathers. Nosey, the Apache whom I induced to bring it to me after the ceremony, said that they carried it in honor of Guzanutli to induce her to send rain, at that time much needed for their crops." Bourke felt it was probable that the Apache wooden cross represented a composite idea of original Apache beliefs modified to some extent by the ideas of the Mexican captives among them. On the other hand, he went on to say, "it is to be remembered that the cross has always formed a part of the Apache symbolism; that the snake does not belong to the Christian faith, and that it has never been allowed to appear upon the cross since the time of the Gnostics in the second and third centuries."[6]

Medicine Cord

Bourke, writing in 1884, believed there was probably no more mysterious or interesting portion of the religious or "medicinal" equipment of the Apache medicine man or member of the laity than the *izze-kloth* or medicine cord. "Less, perhaps, is known concerning it than any other article upon which he relies in his distress."

Bourke regretted very much that he was unable to gain from the Apache the slightest clue to "the meaning of any of the parts or appendages of the cords which I have seen or which I have procured." Part of the problem was that the Apache looked upon these cords as so sacred that strangers were not allowed to examine them, much less handle them or talk about them. So Bourke expended every effort to become friendly "with such of the Apache and other medicine-men as seemed to offer the best chance for obtaining information in regard to this and other matters, but I am compelled to say with no success at all."

Na-a-cha, a prominent medicine man of the Tonto Apache, did at last promise to let Bourke have his cord, but when the Captain was called away from the San Carlos Agency, the opportunity was lost. Ramon, one of the principal shamans of the Chiricahua, made him the same promise concerning the cord he wore. It was unfortunately sent to Bourke by mail, and although one of the best he had ever seen, it was not accompanied by a description of the symbolism of the different articles attached.

There were some things about the cords that Bourke understood from explanations given him at other times. There were one-, two-, three-, and four-strand cords, but whether the difference in the number of strands meant that they belonged to medicine men or to warriors of different degrees was not learned.

The four-strand cord obtained from the Chiricahua named Ramon was the most beautiful and the most valuable. Bourke's attention was called to the important fact that originally each of the four strands had been stained a different color. "These colors were probably yellow, blue, white, and black, although the only ones still discernible at this time are the yellow and blue."

A three-strand cord was sent to Bourke at Washington by his old friend Al Seiber, a scout who had lived among the Apache for twenty-five years. "No explanation accompanied it and it was probably procured from the body of some dead warrior during one of the innumerable scouts and skirmishes which Seiber has had with this warlike race during his long term of service against them."

A two-strand cord was obtained by Bourke "so long ago that the circumstances connected with it have escaped my memory." The

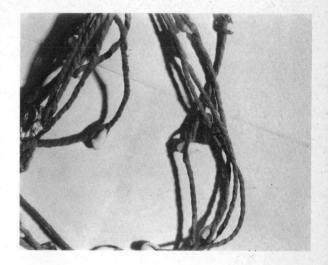

cords were strung at intervals with beads and shells, pieces of the sacred green chalchihuitl, petrified wood, rock crystal, eagle down, hawk or eaglet claws, bear claws, rattlesnake rattles, bags of hoddentin, circles of buckskin in which were enclosed pieces of twigs and branches of trees struck by lightning, small fragments of abalone shell from the Pacific coast, and other sacred paraphernalia of a similar kind.

Bourke declares that no matter what else the medicine man might lack, he would, if possible, have some of the impure malachite known to the Whites of the Southwest as turquoise. "In the malachite veins the latter stone is sometimes found and is often of good quality, but the difference between the two is apparent upon the slightest examination. The color of the malachite is a pea-green, that of the turquoise a pale sky blue. The chemical composition of the former is a carbonate of copper, mixed with earthy impurities; that of the latter, a phosphate of alumina, colored with the oxide of copper." The use of the malachite was widespread, and all tribes possessing it revered it in much the same manner as the Apache. The Apache called it *duklij*, "blue (or green) stone," these two colors not being differentiated in their language. A small stone tied to a gun or bow made the weapon shoot accurately. The stone also had the power to bring rain, and could be found by the man who would go to the end of the rainbow, after a storm, and hunt diligently in the damp earth. Bourke asserts that it was the Apache shaman's badge of office; "without it he could not in olden times exercise his medical functions."[7]

Medicine cords were used for only the most sacred and important occasions, such as war dances, curing ceremonies, and invoking the spirits. At such times every medicine man of consequence would show up with one hanging diagonally over his right shoulder and across his left hip. They were also worn by warriors on war trips.

Bourke claims that only the chief medicine men could fashion them, and when completed and before being put on by the owner

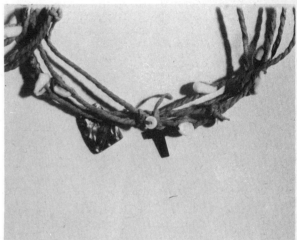

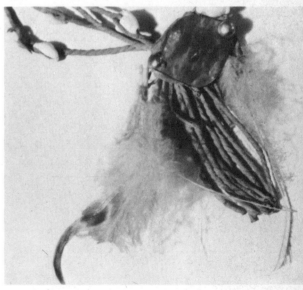

Left: *White Mountain Apache group. Warriors wear medicine cords diagonally across chest, from which circular medicine cases, and what appear to be food bags, are suspended. Note face paint on woman and man in center. Photo by Wittick (MNMP).* Top, center, *and* above: *Details of medicine cord.*

they must be sprinkled, with "heap hoddentin," which meant that there was a great deal of attendant ceremony with the sprinkling.

It was believed that the *izze-kloth* cords would protect a man on a war party. Many Apache were convinced that a bullet would have no effect upon the warrior wearing one of them, that a wearer could tell who had stolen ponies or other property from him or his friends, that a wearer could help the crops and cure the sick. If the small hoop attached to a cord was placed upon a person's head, it would immediately relieve any ache; a wooden cross attached to a cord prevented the wearer from going astray while traveling, for the cross had some connection with cross-trails and the four cardinal points. Bourke was assured that the medicine cords were not memory aids, and that the beads, feathers, knots, and the like attached to them were not for the purpose of recalling to mind some duty to be performed or prayer to be recited.

When he first saw the medicine cords of the Apache, Bourke wondered if they might not be an inheritance from the Franciscans, who, two centuries before, had endeavored to plant missions among the Apache.[8]

John Rope explained the meaning of the medicine cord to Goodwin, calling it a "Slayer of Monster's bandoleer."[9] The full account is included in "Enemies Against Power" of the Chiricahua section.

Wooden Medicine Snake

Reagan describes a medicine singing at the camp of V28 on Carrizo Creek, July 3, 1901, which commenced at about nine P.M.

> Two medicine-men, accompanied by several other persons, entered the camp, and a performance was begun over V28 who was sick. They sang about an hour, each song ending with an accented "hay," followed by each one present spitting in the fire. During this performance a wooden medicine snake lay between the fire and the sick man with its head pointed toward the afflicted parts. It tapered uniformly from head to tail. The head resembled that of a rattlesnake, though in some respects it represented a water snake. The body of the snake had twenty-five black semicircles extending over its body from side to side. The head was spotted, and had two large eyes.
>
> When the performance began, V28 had a high fever and a rapid pulse. After the singing had lasted an hour, the chief medicine man placed the snake on top of the left shoulder with head pointed toward the feet. He then slid it slowly down the arm and down the extended left leg as he continued his singing; the others present did not sing in this case. When reaching the foot he spat in the fire as before, all others present doing the same. He then placed the snake in the hot ashes with its head toward the fire, as he prayed repeatedly to his gods. Then he placed the lower surface of the snake's head on the afflicted parts in five different directions or positions, saying each time as he did so, "Zis, zis, zis, ziz, ziz, ziz," in imitation of the rattling of a rattlesnake. At the close he spat in the fire as before. Then he began on the right leg and shoulder and proceeded as previously. After placing the snake in the five different positions on the afflicted parts, he placed it in five different positions on the top of the patient's head, saying each time as he placed it, "Ziz, ziz, ziz, ziz," etc. This done, he repeated the above described ceremony, beginning again on the left shoulder. The snake performance completed, he threw the snake in the air over the man's body to the other side of the house, where V28's little son placed it in the wall of the wickiup. The chief medicine man then washed his hands. Then all present smoked, while the patient took supper.
>
> At this juncture the writer examined the patient's pulse again and found that it was practically normal; also that his fever had nearly left him.
>
> After the smoke, the singing was resumed and continued till morning.[10]

In treating consumption, a shaman produced toward morning a crudely made, striped wooden snake. He placed this on the afflicted parts of the patient in the four different cardinal directions and sang to the four gods who hold up the four corners of the earth. When finished he burned the snake and sent its hissing spirits away with a harshly blown breath. Then he resumed his singing, and after a considerable time brought out a wooden carving, an effigy of his leading medicine god, which he placed on the patient as he did the snake. When finished he did not destroy it, but instead hid it in a niche in the rocks of a nearby cliff.[11]

Lizards, Snakes, Bear Claws

On Carrizo Creek at the camp of V28, July 18, 1901, the medicine fraternity gathered around the patient in his house at about ten o'clock in the evening and commenced singing, first low and then as the night wore away, with increased intensity. Now and then there was a lull, when all drank liberally of tulapai. At about two in the morning during a pause in the singing the medicine man produced a live sand lizard from some part of his clothes and rubbed it over the afflicted parts of the patient as he spat in the fire and now and then hissed by forcibly sending the air from his mouth. When he had finished with the lizard he had a little boy carry it beyond the house and turn it loose. The singing was then resumed for a little while. Then the medicine man produced a live snake of the striped, harmless kind, and performed with it as he had previously with the lizard. After a short singing spell he produced a bear claw and performed with it over the patient similarly. As he was thus performing he turned to the writer and said:

"Brother, these are good medicine. The lizard remedy is for burns and throat trouble, the snake and bear claws are for swelled legs, rheumatism, etc. The medicine dance is for all cases in which the patient is affected with fits. The medicine men eat fire and pick up red hot rocks to show their power."

A singing was held west of the Post the night of August 16, 1901, over an eighteen-year-old girl who was in the last stages of consumption; her feet were already swollen. She lay on a pallet of willow branches. The eighteen singers were protected from the weather by a circular canvass enclosure about thirty feet in diameter. The remedy was the bear-claw performance previously described.[12]

The same medicine singing in which the medicine snake was used was continued the next evening at about nine o'clock.

The medicine singers were the same as in the previous singing. At the beginning of the performance a bear claw was placed between the patient and the fire. After singing about one hour as on the previous evening, a little boy took the bear claw and dipped it in an herb solution contained in a cup. Then, still holding the claw in the solution, he scraped it with a knife, scraping downward. This finished, he handed the claw to the medicine man, who then commenced practising his art on the patient with it. Beginning at the top of the left shoulder, he slid the claw with its back down, so to speak, from shoulder to toe, as he sang. He then dipped the claw into the ashes three times. Then he proceeded to rub it back down on the afflicted parts, saying as he did so, "You, you, you, you, youm, hah, hah, hah, hah, hah" (the "hah's" being shortened and uttered roughly). When this part was finished he commenced on the right side and proceeded as on the left. Having completed the rubbing on this side he proceeded to rub the afflicted parts as before described. The second application being completed, he placed the claw with back down on five different positions on the head of the patient, saying, "Oo, oo, oo, oo, oom, hah, hah, hah, hah, hah, hah." When this was done, he washed his hands, and all smoked while the patient ate his supper. Then a midnight meal was furnished for those who were waiting on the patient. The singing then continued till morning and at sunrise a second meal was provided for all present. Then, the sacred cattail bloom having been sprinkled over everyone present, everyone set out for home.[13]

Medicine Pillow, Ashes

At the camp of V26, the evening and night of September 3rd, 1901, his second daughter had a hysterical spell, but soon recovered and helped her mother get supper. After supper she had another spell. She became limp and the people of the house stretched her out on a bed near the fire instead of taking her out in the air as they should have done. They then laid her head on what they called a medicine pillow though it looked just like any other pillow. Here she lay for hours. Her body relaxed and became rigid, alternately. Her jaws were set so that a stick was placed between her teeth, thus preventing lockjaw or her biting herself. She lay unconscious on the cot for hours. She was sung over occasionally and now and then ashes were sprinkled over her person and rubbed on her feet and chest. The whole body was also occasionally shaken vigorously. After midnight she gradually recovered and on the following morning she was able to help cook breakfast.[14]

Roots

A young girl of about fourteen was sung over west of the Post February 6, 1902. Medicine was also administered. This was the root which the Indians use for stomach trouble. After the root had been administered, a feather was tied to the stem of the plant from which the root had been cut. The woman of the evening, the mother of the child, had the sacred pollen placed in a circle on each cheek just beneath the eyes. The sacred dust was sprinkled alternately to the four sacred regions by two women about every half hour, each praying at length at each sprinkling. The pollen was sprinkled on the drum first, first across the west drum, from north to south, then from east to west. It was then sprinkled on the medicine man, then over the east drum. The ceremonies closed at dawn.[15]

30 Medicine Ceremonies, a General View

The medicine ceremonies Reagan witnessed from July, 1901, to May, 1902, consisted of medicine singings, medicine dances, and accompanying ceremonies. He attended a considerable number of these ceremonies, perhaps more than any other White man, and as already seen he presented his fascinating observations of each ceremony witnessed. As a prelude to his comments, he stated that "All the Apache believe that evil spirits are the cause of sickness and death and all the medicine, which consists mostly of dancing, is to drive the spirits (sick) away. The ceremonies are usually performed at night."[1] He then goes on to describe the specific medicine items employed in ceremonies, and these are included under that heading in both the Western Apache and Chiricahua sections. The accounts also contain descriptions of "Ceremonial Dances," a summary of which is included in the following material. While authorities such as Goodwin and Opler have valid reservations about Reagan, his accounts represent some of the rarest eyewitness material on the Western Apache available. Moreover, the writings of both Bourke and Reagan make it increasingly clear that the Apache life-way was an extremely involved and active one, since what they saw and recorded represents only a fraction of what was constantly going on at any given time among the people. Reagan's comments are based on what he saw in only nine months on the Western reservations. I stress this because it seems reasonable to bear this in mind when evaluating the Apache life-way and seeking to appreciate it. Accordingly, while Reagan's introduction to his material on medicine and medicine men somewhat duplicates that set forth by Bourke more than a decade earlier, it also reinforces Bourke's reports and in addition shows how consistently the practices were adhered to as time went by.

Perhaps it also would be well to emphasize at this point that Reagan's interpretations of the real meanings and purposes of some acts he saw performed by the medicine men and the Gan dancers should not be taken as gospel. More probably, excepting those instances where acts were explained to him, he was not informed or sympathetic enough to make a reliable and profound statement. I do not, by so saying, profess to do better; I simply affirm, as Bourke did, that the real portent of the acts is known only by the Apache, and even then in its fullness only by the medicine men themselves.[2]

Reagan also gave what he believed was an accurate, but apparently phonetic, representation in English letters of some Apache expressions employed in ceremonies. These appear to be nothing more than rough equivalents, and probably should be taken as such. Nevertheless, I've left them in at certain places where I quote him, for the color and emphasis they provide.

As I was completing my final reading of this manuscript, I obtained a new book, *Grenville Goodwin among the Western Apache*, Morris E. Opler, editor. It consists of a number of Goodwin's letters from the field to Opler. In one of these, dated April 15, 1932, he says he is sorry to say that some of the things Reagan sets forth in his publication "are decidedly cockeyed." He then goes on to cite a few examples of incorrect terms used. In a footnote, Opler agrees, asserting that Reagan was more prolific than accurate in his writings on the Western Apache.[3]

I too had the same feeling about Reagan. Nevertheless, what he saw and was told remains as a valuable collection of eyewitness information, so long as one looks at the details and ignores his explanation of the meanings. I sincerely hope that the notes of Goodwin, now being edited by Basso, will eventually bring the true meaning of the ceremonies, acts, and objects to light.

I am sure that the same thing can be said of Bourke as are said of Reagan. Yet to my knowledge, no one has questioned their honesty or has challenged what they saw. The matter seems more to be that of questioning the interpretations of what Reagan saw. Unfortunately, there are not yet in print any comprehensive accounts of Western Apache ceremonials to lay alongside those of Reagan, so they remain valuable to those interested in Apache lore, and give scholars something worthwhile to consider. More than a few have used his work in their studies.

I note in particular that Goodwin says "some," not all, of what Reagan reports, is "cockeyed."

Undoubtedly, I open myself to criticism by including so much of Reagan's work. Yet I'm expressing the precautions that readers should exercise, and at the same time my gratitude to Albert Reagan for what he provides.

What the Apache will think of all this I don't know. Probably they will smile at some of it to show their skepticism, but then I've seen them do this on several occasions when I advanced for their consideration some of the thoughts of the very best White authorities.

31 Medicine Items as Live Objects, 1901–1902

The medicine or "power" objects common to the Apache medicine men and women that Reagan saw at the turn of the twentieth century were small medicine bags containing holy items, medicine hats, various regalia formerly used in war, medicine crosses and staffs, effigies, wooden carvings, medicine hoops, medicine canes, and other paraphernalia, all of which were used by medicine men in doctoring the sick. These objects were, and still are, sacred to the Apache; and Reagan discovered that it was "with a great deal of reluctance and mental pain that they will part with any one of them."[1] In addition to the objects employed by medicine men and women, every Apache had his personal medicine objects. Some were arrowheads and other relics taken from the ancient ruined villages of the region, others were feathers, bird and animal skins, claws, bear paws, shells, fossils, carvings of parts of trees struck by lightning (wood that lightning had run over being considered sacred), in rare instances the scalps of people killed in long-past war expeditions, rock crystals, and so on. Since it was believed that certain occurrences could cause an item to lose its power, the power could be restored by rubbing it with deer or human blood. The wood carvings were often miniature effigies.

Some of the smaller items might be worn suspended over the chest from a cord around the neck. Animal and bird claws were frequently worn together with beads as a necklace. Some owners placed their medicine powers in a buckskin bag and either wore the bag tied to a cord and suspended over the chest, or else tied the bag to their clothing. The Western Apache believed that when properly used, their medicine gave them power over that specific area of which it was supposed to have control. There were medicines for influencing every undertaking in life, for controlling sickness and death, and for invoking the mysterious powers of the universe.

The usual medicine bag was a little buckskin pouch filled with various powders, cattail pollen, berries, seeds, and other small items seen in the owner's vision. Ordinarily, the bag was concealed somewhere about the clothing in order to have it readily at hand. Its contents were sprinkled in prayer to the gods of the universe, over the altars, over people in ceremonial dances, and over the sick in the medicine ceremonies. "The Apache thinks this medicine has the power to carry the prayers of men to the deities and bring about the desired results."[2]

Cattail pollen or tule rush for ceremonial use was gathered by individual women, and by the medicine men for use in curing ceremonies. "This pollen is called hadn-tin or hoddentin by the Apache and tadatin by the Navajo."[3] It was used in every important ceremony, and even for lesser matters such as sprinkling upon the surface of the water before crossing a stream.[4]

Before moving further into descriptions of specific medicine items that were seen or collected by private parties or museums, it will be worthwhile to consider how terribly important, personal, and alive the objects were to the Apache, and especially how traumatic it was when they were forced by circumstances such as poverty to sell or give them up.

Reagan purchased several medicine hats from Fort Apache area medicine men. The first one he mentions did not want to sell his hat, but the price was raised until the old man agreed to let it go. He wished, however, to retain it a few minutes before releasing it. Before it was handed to Reagan, he apologized personally to the power-infused hat for selling it, explaining that "his poor family needed the things the money would buy, or else he would not part with it. He further begged it not to be angry with him for parting with it and begged it not to harm his family." The medicine man's wife then cried, and he himself carried it to his wickiup while screaming several times. He then returned to Reagan, turned the hat wrong side out, and presented it to the writer.[5]

On August 31, 1901, Reagan purchased the small skullcap-shaped medicine hat of an aged chief medicine man, V25, at Cibecue. It was considered to be the most sacred of all medicine objects the man possessed. Handing the writer the hat to examine, he related its history as follows: "When a boy I desired to be a medicineman and went to the man most skilled in that art and studied under him. I was taught the use of one after another of the medicine things, but my education was not complete until I learned the use of this hat. It was then finally presented to me and it kept me diligently busy two weeks to learn to use it. To it I ascribe my success in the medicine practice. I am now quite old, yet my medicine has always made me a living."

As he presented the hat to Reagan, "the old man shrieked five times so that every nook and corner in the surrounding hills echoed the hissing, blood-curdling sound. The old man then cried. The old woman made a hissing sound like a bull-snake, followed by a similar hissing by the old man, who, at the same time, waved his hands as if asking the heavens to part and swallow him up. He then patted his right shoulder, then his left shoulder with the open palm of his right hand. Then he placed his left hand and then his right over his heart, as he prayed and asked the gods to bless the writer. Then as he sang a song to the gods for the new owner of the hat, the old woman hissed again, putting her hands together in front of her and separating them with a quick sweeping movement to the side. Then she patted her heart and her shoulders. She lifted her hands on high to the gods, first to the right and then to the left, at the same time blowing her breath on the writer."

When Reagan agreed to buy the hat and took possession of it, "V25 asked him to let him have it again for a minute. This was done as wished, and, crying, he took it and held it toward the northeast, the southeast, the southwest, and then toward the northwest, blowing his breath in each respective direction as he held it that way.

Painted bag used by shaman to hold ritual objects (SM).

Then he held it toward the zenith, saying 'Yalan' (good-bye) five times. He then handed the hat to the writer. But he begged to be permitted to retain it forty-eight hours longer until he could sanctify his premises with it and the sacred pollen, which request was granted."[6]

On September 3, 1901, the medicine man whose tag name was V25 brought Reagan the hat that he had sold him on the previous Saturday. On presenting it he raised the hat high in the air, looked toward the zenith, and repeated five times: "Brother *Ako Unzho*," which Reagan understood as a statement that the place where the gods dwell is a good place. The medicine man then looked longingly at the hat and said over and over to it, "Yalan" (good-bye). Then as he presented it to Reagan he blew his breath on it in a hissing manner.[7]

A buckskin medicine shirt, consisting of a front and rear section connected only at the shoulders, was sold to the representative of a museum by V19.

As soon as the Indian had received the money for the shirt he spread it out full length on the ground in an east and west

Ancient medicine object from Fort Apache area (private collection). The bleached stick is covered with a white calcareous stone encrustation. It was originally wrapped with a woven mat of cottonwood.

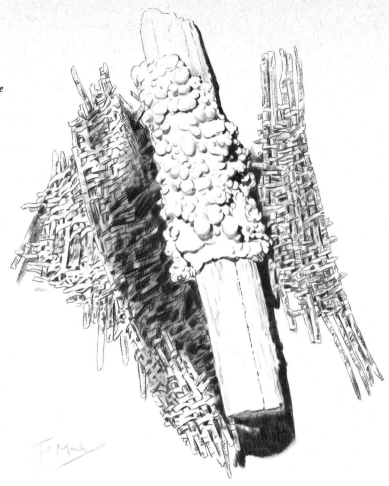

direction. . . . Then after addressing each figure on the shirt in turn, as he stood at the west end of it facing the east, he took the figures from the left in a circle around the neck hole, saying "Dont Zhoda" five times as he held his hand over each figure, medicine button, or feather on the shirt. Then taking a pinch of the cattail-flag pollen in his right hand he sprinkled the first figure on the left shoulder, making a cross on all four sides of it with the pollen. He then made crosses with the pollen around the next figure on the right, which was a god representation. Then he passed the pollen across his right eye, making a mark over it. Then he cast the remainder of the pollen toward the eastern sun. He then put his hand over his mouth and placed his tongue between his thumb and fingers and blew a hissing breath through his hand as he spread it out over the shirt, palm down, and gave it a side sweep to the right, saying "Yalan" (good-bye), five times. He then held the shirt up in his right hand toward the sun with figures in natural position a moment as he again repeated "Yalan" five times. He then turned it wrong side out and said, "It is no good to me any more," as he presented it to the purchaser. [8]

One of the Cibecue Apache sold his war shield to a visiting ethnologist. The shield was purchased in the evening, but the warrior requested that he be permitted to take it home till morning. At about nine o'clock the next morning he brought it back and laid it in the yard at Reagan's home with the decorated side up. "Then he talked to it long and earnestly, telling it that he knew it was wrong to sell it, but his family needed the money. He then begged it not to bring harm to his family because he was parting with it. He then sprinkled it with cattail-flag pollen as he prayed earnestly to his gods. He sprinkled each individual part, drawing, and bunch of feathers decorating its face with the same material. Then he prayed aloud and earnestly to the gods of the four winds and the gods of the zenith and the nadir. He then turned the shield face down, as he said 'Tah unzhoda, tah unzhoda,' (too bad, too bad). He then turned it over to the purchaser; and receiving his money, he at once left the place for home as he kept saying, 'Tah unzhoda.' "[9]

Top left *and* above: *War amulets worn in the hair, the "single buckskin string" mentioned by the* Century Magazine *writer in 1887. Decorated with shells, silver ornaments, and beads. Left:* Amulet strings *(Museum of the American Indian, Heye Foundation).*

32 Ceremonial Dances

Reagan informs us that when the simple singing ceremonies failed to cure the sick, any one of a number of ritualistic dances might be held. Several of these dances were observed by him during the period from July, 1901, to May, 1902. In describing them, he placed them in categories and gave them the following descriptive titles: The Wheel Dance, Ceremonies for the Sick, A Night Dance, The Devil's Dance, Dance for a Sick Woman, Dance for a Sick Child, Protection from Ghosts, Thank-Offering Dance, Dance for Rain, Medicine Disk Ceremony, and The Sickness and Death of Whistling Wind.[1]

The Wheel Dance

According to Reagan, "This ceremony was conducted by Nakai'dok-lin'ni, who is said to have used it to restore two chiefs to life at Cibecue in the summer of 1881, which finally led to the battle of Cibecue and a long series of Apache outbreaks. . . . He also taught the wheel dance that is now the leading medicine dance form of the White Mountain Apache. . . . The performers were arranged like the spokes of a wheel, all facing inward."[2]

Ceremonies for the Sick

Dwachingo is sick. She had a cough. It is that dreaded disease consumption. We hear the drum beating. It is night: the medicine people are at the dwelling of the sick woman. They are going to sing over her. We join the group of singers. The medicineman enters. He goes to the side of the house by the central fire and doubles his feet under him in a sitting position near the patient. Then he bends his body forward; clasps his hands over his face and forehead in the form of a sort of hood and begins to sing, "Go away 'sick.' Go away 'sick.' Go away 'sick.' Go away 'sick,' " as the musicians beat drums. Occasionally, he stops singing, spits in the fire, and sprinkles the sick one with cattail-flag pollen. Then he resumes his singing.

Night after night we visit the medicine singings which are usually similar to the above, though occasionally they are varied. Five hoops, colored like the rainbow which they are supposed to represent, are substituted for the wooden image of a medicine god. Also medicine sticks and medicine canes of various sorts are now and then used. A medicine game is also played with four flat splints. The sticks are bounced on a flat rock in the center of a six-foot circle of forty cobblestones (or pebbles). The sticks falling with a certain side up are favorable to the recovery of the patient. The onlookers, the visitors, also dance through the small hours of the morning. But not withstanding all their performances the patient grows steadily worse day by day and the last, the dramatic ceremonies, must sooner or later be performed.[3]

A Night Dance

At about nine o'clock in the evening of April 28, 1901, five fires were built at the place where the dance was to be held, one fire representing each of the cardinal points and one in the center for the zenith. When the people were assembled, an aged woman arose, and after praying and raising the pollen toward the zenith in her left hand for a moment, she sprinkled everyone present. The pottery drum then began to sound, the beats always being of equal value. The chanters began to sing, and four dancing sections were formed representing the semicardinal directions, with the chanters in the center. "Only women composed the dancing sets. Again the sacred pollen was sprinkled, after which the dancing was begun. Each sector formed in line abreast facing the chanters. The dancing was simply a time-step movement first forward and then backward, but there was some variation. The northwest division took five steps forward and four backward, the northeast six forward and six backward, the southeast seven forward and seven backward, the southwest section seven forward and eight in the reverse direction."

Top *and* above: *Western Apache Gans performing.*

The clown and the masked dancer shaman, who was in charge of the masked dancers, danced singly and usually faced the sector in front of which he danced. The clown wore "a gum coat" and his performance in this instance was unique. The shaman, who also acted as the director for the ceremony, was dressed like the other men, except that he wore a medicine hat. A young woman with a leading role danced in the northeast section. She had a special wand with which she danced. It was four feet long and had three eagle feathers tied to its head.

Nearly all the men joined the singers, and when any woman wanted a partner to dance with, she chose him by going to the singers and tapping her choice with her hand. He could refuse her, but if he accepted, he arose from his sitting position among the chanters and followed her to her division, which now parted to give him space to dance beside his partner. If it was his first dance, he faced his partner and had his back to the singers. If he danced again he faced the chanters, as did his partner.

At daybreak the women dancers all joined the northeast division and danced three sets without partners. At the beginning of the first of these three sets, the shaman held pollen skyward toward the east as he faced the central group. Having said a short prayer, he then took the pollen and gave it to the youngest child present to eat, putting it in the child's mouth with his own fingers. As the second set was closing, he repeated this act and then put pollen into the mouth of the child's mother. At the close of the third set he again held pollen up and prayed. This done, he made a pollen cross on his chest and ended the dance.

Another dance was held on the night of May 2, 1901. After the populace had assembled around the central fire, five mescal-fiber fires were lighted, representing the four semicardinal points and the zenith. This was followed by a series of long prayers and the sprinkling of sacred pollen to the powers. Following this, the music and

Medicine shirt designs, possibly similar to those used for medicine disk paintings (SM).

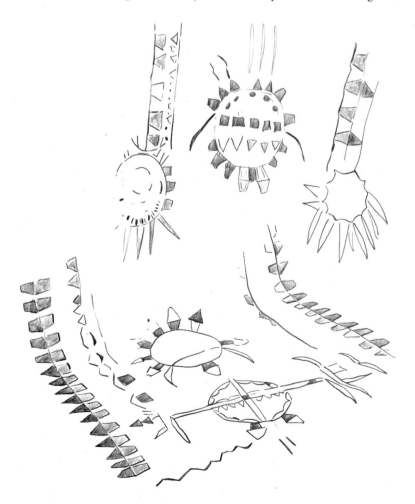

chanting were begun. Soon the dancing commenced. Five women standing abreast danced at a time, keeping step to the music and going five steps forward and five back. Each woman as she entered a dance set took some ashes and sprinkled them to the four winds. She also sprinkled the singer, the dancers, and the assembled people with the sacred pollen twenty-six times during the night, praying and pointing to the five sacred regions each time before the sprinkling.[4]

The Devil's Dance

This is an exceedingly poor choice of title, for what Reagan describes is actually the Gan impersonator dance. This curing dance was rooted in the idea that evil was the cause of sickness and that by ritual dancing and singing it could be extracted and driven away. Reagan describes the atmosphere as "weird, grotesque, picturesque, and spectacular . . . a never-to-be-forgotten sight."

The singers gathered in the early evening and began to sing in a low tone, using a pottery drum for accompaniment. As night approached, the noise and din of the chanting increased in volume and intensity. While they were singing, the Gan impersonators were prepared for the dance.

At one of the dances attended by Reagan, seven torches were seen approaching the central fire from the outer darkness at about 10:30 P.M. The singers at once began to sing with more spirit. The Crown Dancers approached and backed away into the darkness several times, until finally the clown dancer, wearing horns, raced through the throng of singers and sightseers, whirling a bull-roarer. Then he ran away from the crowd and the singers sought to coax him back with their loud singing. In response all seven dancers came; each of the six Gans wore an enormous headdress, each different from the others, made of cloth masks and yucca-lath crests. The body of each of the six was adorned with garlands of evergreen. They wore white skirts and red-tinged moccasins with turned-up toes, and their bodies were painted a reddish brown.

The leader carried a triple medicine cross decorated with feathers. As they danced they offered the cross to the singers, who would reach for it, only to have it withdrawn. This was done several times. Finally, the cross was given to the singers, who sang faster and louder than previously. The Gans then went among the seated spectators and compelled the men to join the singing group. A choosing-partner dance of the wheel type was then begun and continued as a part of the ceremony until its close.

After this the Crown Dancers performed in succession over the patient while the bull-roarer was twirled continuously by the clown. Each Gan placed his pair of yucca-lath wands on the afflicted parts as the patient lay on a blanket east of the central fire. The sickness was believed to be collected on the wands and then dispensed to the four winds as the crossed wands were raised on a level with the face of the dancer, breathed on with a hissing breath, and separated with a quick, sweeping stroke in opposite directions. Sacred pollen was sprinkled by the chief medicine man after each participant had performed. When all seven had finished, they departed in a body, ending the first episode of the dance. Twelve more acts were performed during the night, all similar to the one described above, though with some variations. In the successive sets the Gan impersonators made several little boys dance with them, then old women, then old men, then young girls, and finally they made everyone present dance. Just before dawn, as the last set was danced, everyone made all the noise possible, most of them making a noise like a screech owl. At this time they also danced the hardest and sang the loudest in a last great effort to drive the evil spirit "sick" away.[5]

Another such curing dance for a sick woman was observed at Fort Apache in which twenty-eight young women danced in the form of a whirling five-pointed star. Seven of them carried medicine sticks about eight feet in length, made in the style of the medicine cross. No masks were worn. Besides the women, there were the five

Crown Dancers. In this instance the Crown Dancers' bodies were painted and a Gan was painted on the chest of each.

"Also, at a dance that was held over a sick child, July 30, 1901, the women formed a line abreast, facing the patient, the woman at each end of the line carrying a medicine stick. Five steps each way were danced. It lasted throughout the night, the sacred pollen being sprinkled at regular intervals."[6]

Dance for a Sick Woman

On the evening of March 28, 1901, the Cibecue Apache came together for a medicine dance for a sick woman twenty years old. She had chills, fever, and, as the fever reached its height, recurrent spasms. The people assembled around a huge fire in the center of the flat where the patient had been carried and placed on a blanket. Here they waited, chanted, sang, and beat the drum until after midnight.

Then the Crown Dancers came. There were four Gans and a clown. Their masks in this instance were crested at the front by the spread feathers of a turkey's tail. Each dancer had a thunderbolt, with dart up, painted on his arms from wrist to shoulder and a crescent moon design on his chest. A wreath of spruce twigs girdled each dancer's waist, and each held a wand in each hand. This was a thin stick, about two inches wide and three feet long. It was rounded at each end, with a thunderbolt design drawn down on each side and four feathers suspended from it, two on each side. The clown's mask was similar to that of the Gans, except that the crested feathers were divided into two parts, one on each side of the head, so that they looked like two great ears. In his left hand he held a forked stick, "something like the trident of Neptune." In his right hand he held a bull-roarer, attached to a string that was tied around his wrist. By means of this string he whirled the wand through the air with vigorous force, thus making a peculiar, buzzing noise.

The dancers and the clown approached the people from the southwest, "circling closer and closer, and constantly putting their heads near the ground as if smelling for something and then clucking, sputtering, gobbling, and strutting like a turkey and waving their hands as if imitating a flying bird." At last they came to the patient and, acting as though surprised, danced backward for several yards. This maneuver they repeated seven times. Then they approached the sick woman and strutted around her while the clown performed. When they stopped, the oldest woman present—the "godmother" of the medicine men of the Cibecue area—sprinkled pollen upon them as she blew her breath on each one. This completed the first part of the ceremony, and the Crown Dancers departed.

In the second part of the ceremony, the masked dancers returned and formed in a column facing west, the patient being turned on her blanket so that she faced them. They then pranced up to her and back several times, employing movements and sounds similar to those used before. Then the dancer heading the column came toward the patient like an anxious quail trying to protect her brood. Upon reaching her, he strutted around her, laid the crossed wands on her feet, blew his breath on them, danced backward for twelve or fifteen feet with wands still crossed, and then parted the wands in the familiar way to dispel the sickness. He then repeated the performance by placing the wands on her chest, head, and back. The other masked dancers went through practically the same performance in succession. Then the clown came and besides rolling and tumbling around in the dirt, his performance was practically the same as that of the masked dancers, except that he did not cluck or strut. When finished, he cantered off into the darkness, returning to appear in the third part of the ceremony, in which the sick one faced the north and the medicine column was formed facing her. The overall performance was the same as that previously described. It was repeated four times, but the third time the patient faced the west and the column faced the east; the fourth time she faced the south and the column the north. This closed the second part of the dance, and the Gans pranced off into the darkness.

There were eleven other scenes, all of which were practically the same as the second one, except that whenever the assembled people went to sleep, the clown used his trident to shake them up, jerk them around, and make them dance, there being twenty-seven sleepy people dancing at one time.

Just as the sun broke over the horizon, Gans, clown, and medicine men were again sprinkled with pollen and the dance began in earnest. "Everyone joined in the peculiar drum beat, the loud chanting, and deafening shouts filled the surrounding country with ear-grating sounds. The excitement reached a high pitch of tension. The patient forgot her ailments, picked up her blanket, and walked to her house as if she had never been sick. This closed the dance."[7]

Dance for a Sick Child

Within the wickiup, four variously colored, large medicine hoops and a medicine cross were suspended from the walls. Around the inside of the house and placed on opposite sides were stretched elaborately feathered buckskin medicine cords. Five feathers were suspended from each section of the cords.

To the west of the dwelling, an open, canvas-surrounded enclosure some thirty feet in diameter encircled a level plot of ground. In the center of this was an elaborate sun-disk drawing, which covered an area of approximately sixteen feet in diameter. It consisted of sand paintings of the rainbow, beasts, and Gans. The rings, with the exception of the outer one, were colored black. Early in the morning, the patient, a consumptive little girl about nine years old, was seated in the center. Her mother was sitting behind her and the child leaned on her for support. In front of the child and her mother, facing both, sat medicine man C4, holding in his right hand a piece of clay which he pressed against the child's body at the pit of her stomach. As he held the clay, he sang, chanted, and waved his left hand toward the sun for about two hours. Then the medicine man departed and the child's grandmother, who was a medicine woman, entered the circle. Wetting her hand, she placed it palm down upon each of the disk figures until she had gathered dust from all of them. Then she went to the child and rubbed the dust on the girl's body until she was covered with it. After this, the woman then gathered more sand from several of the designs and put it in a bowl for future use. At this juncture a Gan dancer came from a nearby thicket. Entering the enclosure, he performed over the patient much as the grandmother had done. The grandmother then destroyed all the figures, raking the dust with her hands toward the center of the circle where her daughter and granddaughter were still seated. This closed the performance. Reagan added that the child died that night.[8]

Protection from Ghosts

In this instance the patient had dreamed of seeing "dead people"—ghosts—and the dance was held to keep the ghosts from capturing his soul. It was of the wheel type. The drum was placed on a canvas spread out west of the central fire, and the musicians and male performers in the dance seated themselves around it. One of these was the chief medicine man, who served as the leader for the evening. When all was ready, he removed his hat, then took the pollen, and holding it above his head between thumb and finger of his left hand, prayed to his power for several minutes. Some of the words of the prayer were: "We trade this sacred dust to you to take the evil [death] from our brother." This was repeated six times, after which he sprinkled pollen on the drums. He then made a crescent moon under his left eye with it, a cross on his left cheek, a cross on his left shoulder, and opened his shirt and made a moon design on his chest. At this point he went to the patient and, opening his shirt, made a pollen cross on his chest, beginning with the vertical bar. Then he

175

reversed the action, retracing the cross and finishing with the vertical bar. This was followed by a cross on the patient's left shoulder, then on the right, a sun design on his forehead, a cross on his left cheek, and a crescent moon design on his back between the shoulders. The shaman then seated himself and placed his medicine hat on his head.

Then the leader of the ceremony, and four other men in succession, prayed and sprinkled pollen upon the drums and the medicine man. The leader then made a circular pollen mark just under the eye of the chief medicine man. After this he lectured the people about the dance and the two cows they were to have as a feast at its close. Five women then sprinkled pollen, and then the sponsor of the dance, in this case the mother of the patient, went to the people and ordered them to dance, telling them they must not sleep that night, but must dance till the sun rose and they would feast.

Two old women began the dance with the crow-hop step. Then they chose partners and danced to the four powers that hold up the four corners of the earth, moving from southeast to southwest, then to northwest, and lastly to northeast. This was followed by the choosing-partner wheel dance. Pollen was sprinkled several times between 9:30 P.M. and dawn. At 3:30 A.M., twenty men formed in a curved line on the southwest, between the fire and the musicians, and danced backward and forward, while pollen was sprinkled on them by five women. At the beginning of the next set they changed to the southeast side of the fire and performed as before, then to the northwest, and lastly to the northeast, continuing thus until they had encircled the central fire and the musicians twice. Then they were sprinkled with pollen by about forty women who went through a dance similar to the one the men had just finished. The five old women also continued to sprinkle the pollen as before, dancing round and round the central fire as they carried out the sprinkling act. At several intervals during the night, the chief medicine man lectured the people on the virtue of the powers, exhorting them to behave well and to think good thoughts. A feast at sunrise closed the ceremonies.[9]

Thank-Offering Dance

This dance seen by Reagan was held on August 10, 1901, "to give thanks to the deities for rain." It was opened with a song call, "Yak-say-you-ou-o." Reagan arrived on the scene at dusk, when the singers were being sprinkled with sacred pollen. The sprinklers and praying-group were medicine men, but the performers were mostly women. There were thirteen sets or scenes in all, which, excepting the first three, were practically a repetition of the fourth set.

The chief performer in the Thank-Offering Dance was a woman, who with a man named Loco Jim headed the dancing sets. She carried a medicine stick about two and a half feet in length, four inches wide, made of thin board and variously painted.

Another thank-offering dance was given at Cibecue, in gratitude to the powers for sparing one of the young men of the district near whom lightning had struck. In preparation, all the people had baked enough corn pulp bread for supper and for a night meal. The dance was of the choosing-partner wheel type. It was begun about nine P.M. and continued till morning.[10]

Dance for Rain

"A dance to bring rain was held at Elsesay's camp June 24, 1901. Besides the wheel dance, five Gan dancers in regular costume and headdresses with crescent of feathers falling over the face, acted out clown ceremonies. At sunrise the ceremonies closed."[11]

Medicine Disk Ceremony

The medicine disks must be made, used, and destroyed between the morning and evening of one day. This one, seen and described by Reagan, was to be used in curing a sick woman. It was a sand drawing made on the ground inside a canvas-wall enclosure, being some sixteen feet in diameter and composed of rings surrounding a three-foot circular center. Two major drawings were made in the center circle, a darker one which was a representation of the sun and which occupied the south position, and a symbol of the moon which occupied the north position. A rainbow encircled these in the form of an ellipse, except at the east where an open space was left. The colors of the rainbow, beginning with the inner side, were white, black, green, and red.[12] Standing on the rainbow, painted in the sand, was a circle of fourteen Gans. The four southeast ones were black; a single Gan colored with rainbow ribbons was followed on the southwest and west by four red Gan dancers. The Gans in the north segment were colored green, those on the east white, except the one next to and just north of the open space, which was shown in back view and was all black. In the west and in the north segment was a Gan of the rainbow-colored type. Around the Gans was another rainbow. Standing on it was a duplication of the Gans just described, except that they were double in number. The last figure north of the open space in this circle was a drawing of a goat. One Gan in each circle, in the northeast position, had a peculiar drawing over his head. Around the outer circle of Gans was drawn another rainbow. This completed the disk, which contained fifty objects in all. Each Gan was two feet high; the rainbow circles were about a foot wide. The coloring materials used for the medicine disk were as follows: The white was ground-up limestone; the black was charcoal; the red was ground-up sand rock; the green was ground-up cedar leaves; and the last Gan and the goat were done with a mixture of black and white.

When the disk was completed, a Gan impersonator wearing traditional costume came in. As he approached, the mother of the ill woman entered the canvas enclosure and sprinkled the entire drawing with pollen, moving from the inner to the outer rainbow, and prayed to the gods. She then took a cup partly filled with water, and reversed the procedure, stopping now and then to gather dust from the figures, which she placed in the cup. Then, as she prayed again, she put the cup of wet dust in the center of the sun disk and departed.

The patient then entered the medicine disk, walking around on each circle as she moved from the outer to the inner circle, and sat down facing the east on the rainbow ribbon that connected the sun and moon. At this point the goat and the black Gan were obliterated, and the Gan impersonator danced around the enclosure for a considerable time. Then he entered it and walked around the circles as the sick woman had, till he reached the center circle. Then he approached the woman from behind. He laid down his knife and wand, dipped his hand into the cup, and rubbed the woman's back with his muddy hand. Then, lifting his hands skyward, he sent the "sick" away by blowing a hissing breath through them as he swept them to his side. Employing the same gestures, he then placed his hands on the woman's head, on her chest, and on her arms. As he departed into the hills, the mother sprinkled him with pollen.

When he had gone, the chief medicine man rubbed the woman with mud in the same manner, except that he rubbed her almost all over with the mud as he prayed continually. When he had finished, she arose, retraced her steps around the circles, and departed. Then each spectator who cared to gathered some of the dust as had the mother, after which what remained of the disk was obliterated. A Ghost Dance ceremony for the sick woman was performed the next night.[13]

By sunrise on another occasion observed by Reagan, many people were busy crushing rock on ledges while others were pulverizing charcoal and leaves. By ten o'clock a group of medicine men had gathered on a leveled spot of earth and were also at work making a sand-painted disk on the ground—a likeness of the "sun father," according to their belief. The huge drawing was some sixteen feet in diameter. It was the front view of a massive head, with a crown for a hat and a line of medicine squares like a necktie down from the chin. There was no nose, nor neck, nor body. The eyes and eyebrows were depicted in the same fashion as the mouth, whose lips were drawn in the form of a square set at their proper place on the face. They were parted, showing what Reagan described as an odd-shaped mouth, formed like a diamond and so drawn that each of its respective corners bisected a side of the square that formed the lips. At the left of the mouth was a long-stemmed pipe, on which a lightning line was drawn. From each corner of the lips a funnel-shaped wisp of the sun's rays extended out for some distance. The different parts of the drawing were variously colored in red, white, black, gray, and green.[14] The red coloring matter was made from ground red sandstone; the white from ground limestone; the green from the crushed leaves of a kind of gourd; the black from pulverized charcoal; and the gray from a mixture of charcoal and limestone.

Once the disk was completed a canvas wall was set up around it and the Crown Dancers came. Reagan says the disk was the last curing resort. The patient was presented to the drawing of the god of day, the sun, who would either cure her or take her to his abode in the mysterious beyond.

At this time an old medicine woman carrying a dirty bowl partly filled with water entered the medicine disk by way of the pipe-stem. In a stooping position she passed around within it from left to right, near its outer rim, and took a pinch of the color from each part of the drawing, putting it into the bowl. Then she set the bowl down in the upper corner of the sun's mouth and left the disk drawing by the route she came. At once the medicine men carried the patient from a nearby dwelling to the enclosure, entering the disk by the pipestem, circling the sun's rays from right to left as they moved to the center of the sun's mouth, and placed her there with her face turned toward the afternoon sun.

At this juncture a Gan dancer came from a nearby thicket. His body was painted white, and red lightning lines ran up his arms and down his lower extremities. He carried a swordlike wand in one hand and an old knife in the other. Shrieking, whooping, and occasionally gobbling like a turkey, he crow-hopped around the drawing and the sick woman and then rushed to her. Reaching her, he squatted in front of her, stuck the knife in the ground by her side, and placed the wand on her afflicted parts in each of the cardinal directions. Having gathered the "sick" on the wand in this way, he raised it up in front of his own face, blew a hissing breath on it to drive the "sick" away, then gave an ear-grating howl, seized his knife, and departed.

Now the chief medicine man entered the circle, and rubbed the woman all over with a piece of green gourd rind. Then he did the same with the muddied water from the bowl. This done, he placed the gourd rind against the lower end of the patient's breast bone and sang a song to the gods while musicians with drums accompanied him. After a considerable time the patient was carried from the enclosure and the medicine drawing was at once obliterated.[15]

The closing rites were always performed the night following the medicine disk ceremonies.

By ten o'clock in the evening a huge fire had been kindled in the center of a level area among the hills, and all the people of the valley squatted on deerskins around it in a great circle. At one end, within the circle, were the doctors and musicians. The patient was in an improvised shelter close by, lying face down on a mat while medicine women rubbed her bare back with scorching piñon twigs. Time and again she fainted, only to have more twigs snatched from the blaze and applied to her back.

Now the patient was carried within the circle of people and placed on the opposite side of the fire from that occupied by the musicians. The drums began to beat. The chief shaman leaned forward and covered his face with his hands, being joined by the musicians in a monotonous chant. The Gan impersonators entered the circle of light from the northeast. Each of them carried a wand in each hand, and the clown carried a wand in his left hand, a three-pronged stick or trident in his right. After dancing in single file for a considerable time, while the clown amused the spectators, the Gans approached the patient in single file. Again and again they approached her, then backed away, each time getting closer to her. Finally, the lead dancer moved to the patient, leaned over her, and placed his crossed wands on her head, on her back, on her lower extremities, and on her chest. Then he raised the still-crossed wands toward the northeastern heavens, and parted them with a sweeping motion while emitting a hissing breath from his mouth, thus scattering the "sick." Then, with a shrieking howl, he cantered off into the darkness. The rest of the dancers followed in succession and performed in a similar manner, as did the clown, except that he acted the clown as well as dancer. His principal feat was to kill the "sick" by spearing it with his trident after he had collected it on his wand. His performance completed the first part of the ceremony. The procedure was duplicated three more times: in the second the patient faced the southeast and the performers approached her from that direction; in the third, the patient faced the southwest and the dancers the northeast; and in the fourth, she faced the northwest, and the dancers the southeast. When they departed another set of performers took their places.

The performance continued throughout the night, with the maneuvers described above being repeated thirteen times. Then came the closing scene. As dawn broke, the clown awoke the sleeping people with his trident and compelled them to stand up. The shamans sprinkled everyone with pollen, everyone took another drink of tulapai, and the Gan dancers approached the patient again. As they performed, everyone else joined in a straight backward-and-forward wheel dance within the circumscribed area. The excitement became intense, the hills echoed the shrieking and shouting, and the drums pounded until it seemed to Reagan as if the very poles of the earth had thundered. Finally they raised the patient to a standing position and supported her as she danced. She took a medicine wand in each hand, waved them toward the respective homes of the gods of heaven and earth, swooned, and died. Today her grave marks the spot.[16]

The Sickness and Death of Whistling Wind

Reagan believed that a typical procedure in cases of illness could be outlined in the case of Whistling Wind, a man of twenty-one, who was in the last stages of tuberculosis. A medicine man was called and was paid two blankets, two saddles, three bags of grain, four ponies, and a cow to doctor the man. Many singing ceremonies and several dances had already been held for him. Ceremonial games were played, and even the ceremony with the sun medicine disk was performed, but in vain.

The Ghost Dance was the last resort available to the Apache medicine men. It lasted all night, with five special performers dancing over the patient as he continued to grow worse. Just at sunrise, a circular dance in which everyone joined was instituted. At this point the patient made a heroic effort to rise and join in the dance, but he collapsed, and the dance broke up in turmoil.

"The next day he died. Then, after he was elaborately attired, he was carried to the mountain side and buried with his personal belongings in a niche in the rocks. His stock was then killed and his house burned. This done, the women wailed and mourned for him continuously for thirty days."[17]

33 Death and Burial

When the Apache buried the dead in 1902, they clothed them in the best attire the family could afford, usually the best that the camp was able to furnish. Then they wrapped the deceased in a blanket and carried the body to the hills, where it was either thrown into a crevice in the rocks or placed in a shallow grave. Ashes and pollen were sprinkled in a circle around the grave, beginning at its southwest corner; this act was considered to be a prayer that the soul would safely enter *O'zho,* heaven. Then the grave was filled with earth and stone. A corpse might be pushed into a cavity left by a shifting rock or the fallen stump of a tree, the body being crammed into the smallest space possible. The rock or stump was then moved back into its former position and a number of stones were placed around the base to keep the coyotes out. When an infant died it was often tied in its cradleboard and hung up in a tree, and a tus of water was tied near to it so that the child might drink at will. In 1902, after a burial the Apache still burned the house of the deceased and everything in it; they also killed a man's stock. Mourning continued for a month; at morning, noon, and night in particular, at intervals dismal coyotelike lamentations were uttered.

The Apache of 1902 still believed that after the dead were buried, owls came and called for them and took their spirits away. Apparently, views had not changed much from Bandelier's time in 1883, when an Apache told him that after death "the soul goes into the air."

Reagan attended many ceremonies for the dead while among the Western Apache in 1901 and 1902. His description of the "most conspicuous one" was as follows:

> The person who had died was a young man. The writer was not present when he died at about 8 P.M. one evening, but arrived only about five minutes afterwards. As soon as those present were satisfied that the young man was dead, they wrapped his face in a piece of cloth, folded his arms and covered him with a blanket. Then followed the wake. At intervals during the night the medicineman comforted the relatives, talking for more than ten minutes at one time. Then he went out of the house and talked for a considerable time to the friends and relatives camped outside. He then scampered off into the darkness where he sprinkled ashes to the four sacred directions. He returned and entered the house and seated himself at the head of the bed on which the dead man lay. From then until 3 A.M. everyone remained quiet, except for now and then a wail from a mourning woman. The time was spent in telling stories and in playing jokes on each other, the wake resembling our wakes in many respects.
>
> At 4 A.M. the ceremonial tulapai was passed around and each one drank to the welfare of the dead, all the men and women crying and wailing. The tulapai was drunk because it is believed that it will aid the departing soul in going to the good place. It is drunk to one of the sacred regions, to one of the gods who hold up the four corners of the earth according to the Apache myths. It was drunk again at half past four, at five, and at half past five, once to each of the gods of the sacred regions. It was then morning. Several guns were fired four times in succession, once to each of the regions above mentioned. Then the wailing-howling for the dead began in earnest. The chief medicineman prayed to the gods and again spoke words of condolence. In his prayer he expressed the idea that the Indian did not know where the dead had departed. He used these words: *Hio esken eskingo boyonsidda,* "Where is the child this morning? We don't know." (In translation). "Where will he be day after tomorrow? We don't know." He continued this interrogating and answering until he had asked where he would be ten days from that day and again said: "We don't know." His prayer or sermon was quite lengthy. While he was praying the mourners ceased to howl and wail. At the close of his speech, the women jerked and tore the canvas from the house [wickiup], removed every valuable from inside it that did not belong to the deceased, pulled down the rushes and yucca leaves that formed the wall, and entered the house from the north side.
>
> A sick Apache is usually placed on the north side of the house with his face to the east and when he dies he occupies such a position in the house. When all had entered the house in this way they viewed the corpse. It was then morning and the dressing of the dead began. He was stripped, washed, and then dressed in a full new outfit of White man's attire, even new

shoes. His hair was parted and brushed smooth with a hairbrush. His wrists were covered with bracelets and beads. At his neck he wore a brand new necktie, four strings of beads and one string of his medicine stones, beads, feathers, and fetishes. When dressed, everything which belonged to him, even the letters which he had written home when at school, were wrapped up with him in his blanket-shroud. After the burial, which the writer could not attend, the house and everything belonging to the deceased or which he had used while sick, except what was buried with him, was destroyed, combustible things by fire; his horses and cattle were shot.

After rounding up the grave they sprinkled the sacred pollen over the mound. Then they set the vessel in which the pollen [and ashes] was brought to the place, on the mound at the head of the grave. A month later it was still resting on the grave with ashes in it. The corpse was buried facing the morning sun.

Another funeral was witnessed by Reagan on September 15, 1901, after the granddaughter of C2 by his oldest daughter died. Reagan arrived at the house only a few minutes after she had ceased to breathe and had the privilege of observing most of the funeral and burial ceremonies.

As soon as she died the medicine fraternity sprinkled earth and ashes over her, while practically all present wailed the death lament. The coyotes of the surrounding hills joined this chorus, their howls and the wailing sounded much alike and causing the hills and valleys to resound with ear-grating sounds. At sunrise the next morning the corpse was taken to the hills east of Cibicu Valley and interred. Before the burial, the corpse was dressed in her best attire, then rolled in the best blanket the camp could afford. After the burial, provisions were placed near it to take it on its journey. Then earth and ashes were again sprinkled over it; it was left to journey to the portals of the happy hereafter. After the funeral, the grandfather returned to the camp and burned it and all that was in it except the rock medicine charm which was taken to the hills and deposited among the rocks. The little girl's horses were also killed.[1]

On Sunday February 16, 1902, west of the Post there was a tulapai drunk on the ridge on which D25 lived. The fourteen-day-old baby of D25 was given some of the drink by its mother and died from the effects the next day (the seventeenth). When the writer came from Whiteriver the day the baby died, he found D25 lying face down in the dirt in his yard. A few minutes later he saw Mrs. D25 and noticed that she was crying. He at once went to the house. The little one was still alive. A medicine man was singing over it. At 2 P.M. all hope for its recovery was abandoned and the preparation of the death feast was begun, tulapai, etc., at several of the camps of the ridge. About sunset the baby died. As it was dying nothing out of the ordinary was done, except that ashes were sprinkled on it. For hour after hour before it died all mourned and wailed, the father, twenty-four years of age, out-wailing his wife and mother. At the death of the child, all present, both men and women, joined in the death wail, the man's mother wailing in the house, his mother-in-law outside, as she was not allowed to enter the house while her son-in-law was there—it is forbidden for him to see her at any time even in the presence of the dead. The next morning D25, aided by his wife, dressed their baby for the funeral. D25 then left his house so that his mother-in-law might enter and view the corpse. At about 10 A.M. on the eighteenth the corpse was taken to the hills and buried.[2]

After anyone of the family died, it was the custom of the Apache to set aside a certain part of their fields as the field of the dead. They refused to cultivate this field for a period of three years. Reagan encountered several such cases, one of which was as follows:

"F13, a woman, claimed the entire Glecen flat at Salt River. She said F11 came to Salt River with her many years before and planted all the flat one season. Then one of her children died. So she dedicated most of the flat to the deceased and had let it go to weeds for two years. The writer compelled her either to farm the land or lease it to others, as irrigable land in the section was very scarce. He also compelled her to allow the irrigating ditch to be worked. This she consented to do, but with a great deal of grumbling and abuse of the *Indah* [White man] who she said had no respect for the dead."[3]

Regan described a singing at V19's place, April 30, 1901, in which "At intervals, the medicine man related myths, some of which were as follows: 'The sacred regions are at the four corners of the earth. At each is located a happy hunting ground and the dead may go to which ever place they choose.'

"'Four men made the earth and are now standing at the four corners holding it up. They are four of the gods to whom the Apache pray.'

"In speaking of the dead, he further stated: 'We Apache endow each object with its spirit counterpart and either burn or kill the individual's belongings that they may accompany him on his spirit journey.' "[4]

Goodwin reports that when an aged individual died the body might either be buried or left in the wickiup. In the latter event the structure was pushed in on top of the body, and the family moved to a new location. The exception to this would be an aged chief or medicine man, who would be given a regular burial because of the love and respect felt for him. Goodwin goes on to say that in the Apache view the death of the very old was considered a natural event, and therefore caused little grief and mourning. Also, it was less of an economic blow to the family than the loss of a younger person.[5]

34 Christian Missions

The Lutheran Church was the first to establish missions among the Western Apache, and from 1893 to 1918 theirs was the only Christian Church on the San Carlos Reservation.[1] The most notable of the Lutheran pastors have been Alfred M. Uplegger, who began his work there under the Wisconsin Synod in 1917, and his father, Francis J. Uplegger, who arrived there in 1919.

Francis Uplegger was a man of exceptional talents, and he made a number of special contributions to the San Carlos people. Like all missionaries in those days, his work involved endless hardships and personal sacrifices. The country was primitive; there was the language barrier; and there was the seeming difference in religious views, as symbolized in the view of the missionaries by the Apache medicine man.

Grace Lutheran Church was built at San Carlos in 1921, and the Upleggers' kindness and sincerity won many converts. When tuberculosis struck in the 1920s and 1930s, Francis's tireless ministry to the sick brought him the Apache title of *Iv Nashovd Hastin,* "the Old Gentleman Missionary."

Being a man of unusual linguistic ability, Francis Uplegger learned to understand and speak the Apache language, and more importantly to write it as well. Although he worked with Apache interpreters, none of these was acquainted with grammar or syntax and as such could not explain the structure of the Apachean language. Therefore, Pastor Uplegger turned to the recorded Apache texts that had been phonetically transcribed by the Smithsonian Institution, and in time he was able to compile the first complete Apache dictionary, in four hand-written volumes. The original is now in the Huntington Library in Pasadena, California.[2]

In considering the language, Uplegger noted that certain syllables were repeated after the root word. Applying this principal, he was able to form entirely new words, which the Apache easily understood. The discovery served a double purpose, since he could now explain passages in the Bible that were previously alien to Apache experience, and he could help the Apache at San Carlos formulate new words to describe the new things they were seeing and experiencing in their contacts with the Anglo world.

Francis Uplegger learned to preach fluently in the Apache language, and his sermons are still used as textbooks by missionaries who wish to become proficient in the language. Moving beyond this, the Old Gentleman Missionary wrote and set to music, in Apache and English, twenty-five gospel hymns; and he translated into Apache the Apostle's Creed, the Lord's Prayer, the Lutheran Liturgy, the Baptism and Burial services, certain chapters of the Bible, and most of Luther's Small Catechism.

So respected was Francis Uplegger that when the tribal council decided to adopt a constitutional form of government, they asked him to advise them. In response, he spent days on end explaining the meanings of English words and legal phrases, acted as secretary to the council, and helped them to so fit the words to their particular requirements as to qualify them quickly and easily as a federal corporation under the Department of Interior. For twenty years, Francis was Superintendent of the Apache Indian Mission, which included both the San Carlos and Fort Apache reservations.

Alfred Uplegger has served equally well as a pastor at San Carlos, along with Pastor Henry Rosin and numerous other members of the Uplegger and Rosin families in both the congregations and mission schools. In particular, the mission schools have trained several Apache as teachers, who now instruct both at the reservation and off the reservation.

Today there are fourteen churches on the San Carlos Reservation, serving nine Christian denominations, and over 50 percent of the Apache are church members. In addition, traveling Pentecostal groups or individuals visit the reservation from time to time.

The Church has most certainly played its role in the transitional period of the Apache. As much as any other force, it has conditioned their thinking regarding the role of the medicine man, curing and puberty ceremonies, the keeping of taboos, the preservation of deformed infants and twins, and the welfare of aged people. However much anthropologists and ethnologists may discuss the merits and effectiveness of the change, the missions have been a factor of no small consequence in the life of the Apache.

The first Lutheran mission at the Fort Apache Reservation was established in 1894. At that time the population was 2,500. In January, 1911, Pastor Edgar Guenther and his wife came to serve, and of all the pastors associated with the area, he is the best remembered.

When Guenther arrived at Fort Apache, the mission had made little progress. But being like Francis Uplegger in character, he pitched in and soon had both a church and a school going, having repaired the buildings and built the school furniture himself with the crude materials at hand.

In the beginning he preached and taught through an interpreter, but he soon learned the Apache language. He worked out simple grammar lessons for the school, and he and Mrs. Guenther traveled constantly to every part of the reservation on foot, horseback, and finally by auto, to bring the Gospel, to advise the people, and to give medical aid to the sick. In time, he became known as *Inaschudt Ndaesn*, "Tall Missionary."[3]

Guenther opened the first orphanage for Indians in the Southwest. During the flu epidemic of 1918–1919, a hospital was begun. Of special consequence was his friendship with the important Apache chief Alchesay, who when he became ill and was not cured by the medicine men went out to a lonely place to die. Guenther went after him, administered medicine, and brought him back to health—to the consternation of the shamans and the wonder of the Apache people.

When the new Lutheran Church building was dedicated in Whiteriver in 1923, Alchesay officiated at the dedication, and then led one hundred of his followers into the building to be baptized.[4] With such a testimony as this, the response to Lutheran mission work increased considerably, and over the years nine Lutheran congregations were established on the Fort Apache Reservation. Included are the orphanage, a Home Finding Center, an elementary and high school, dormitories, craft shops, and homes for the large teaching staff, which serves over 250 students. Some of the tribal leaders were brought up in the orphanage and educated in the mission schools. In addition, hundreds of the Apache people have been trained there to take their places as parents and workers in the modern world. By 1962, annual Lutheran support for the mission had reached $150,000.[5]

When Edgar Guenther came at last to the point where he was forced to relinquish leadership and hand it over to his son, Arthur, and others, the grateful Apache adopted him into the White Mountain tribe as the first White man to be accepted as a full brother. In certification of this, they gave him a traditional Apache burden basket and a lifetime permit to hunt and fish on the reservation. He died in 1961, at the age of seventy-five, and when the burial service was held, the church was filled to overflowing with Apache, who came to pay tribute to the Tall Missionary.

This stands in marked contrast to those who, in studying the Apache, have stated that the Christian Church has had little effect upon the people. In evaluating the influence of Christianity, it makes a distinct difference whether one speaks from inside the faith or from outside it. I admit that both parties may read into the situation more than is there from either view, since personal bias assuredly comes into play. It may even be said that one who speaks from either side is hardly capable of understanding the other's position.

In any event, my years in the ministry affirm that those who do not believe in the God of Scripture are not qualified to evaluate the faith and the people who do. The question always is, from whence do they speak? How do they really know? As a rule, a person unacquainted with a given specialized pursuit is not able to make adequate judgments of those who are skilled in that pursuit. If that is so, why should religion be an exception to the rule?

If this is a tenable position, however defensive it may seem, then even the Apache Christian—and indeed the Apache religious view itself—must be judged by those who speak from within the believer's sphere. I do not, in stating this, question the right of others to state their opinions, but rather wish to establish a point I feel should be kept in mind as the views are considered from either side.

For example, what has already been said about the Lutheran missions—which can easily be verified—would certainly call into question such statements as "the Apache simply ignored" the missionaries and that "as late as the mid-twenties, Christian influence on the Western Apache belief system was negligible." The present Lutheran pastors, some of whom have been on the Arizona reservations for forty years or more, by no means agree with such evaluations, and I am forced to wonder whether the matter has even been discussed with them. Irrespective of what a researcher might think of them, they do speak from personal experience, and have historical data to reinforce their claims. And since the Cibecue Apache are the most conservative group today, perhaps a comparison at Whiteriver and San Carlos would add an important balance. It might also be worthwhile to consider Christian progress at Mescalero and Jicarilla in this regard. My personal contacts with informed Apache who consider themselves devout Christians strongly reinforce the argument. Therefore, in the concluding chapter, I will add some thoughts and testimonies in this regard.

Even while I state this, I do agree with most of what Keith Basso has to say in regard to the benefits and nature of curing and puberty ceremonials. His points that the missionaries (some or all?) were critical of customs without seeking to understand the meaning of them, and that they have been in many instances too judgmental, are well taken.[6] So too are the ideas that traditional Apache ritual provides a productive personal involvement for everyone, and that the

Left: *The Lutheran church in the town of San Carlos.* Below: *The Lutheran church in the town of Whiteriver.*

conventional worship service is too short, too one-sided, and too somber for the Apache life-way.[7] This may also be true for Christianity the world over, although with circumstances being what they are, the format the Church has come to is understandable, and in any event it follows Scriptural dictates. Further, I appreciate the fact that the adult Apache, being an intelligent people, would and did properly resent being lectured to as children. These things should have been and should be changed with all Indians, and perhaps especially at Cibecue.

Nevertheless, there is more to be considered regarding the reservation missions than is usually stated. The fact that the transition from complex ancient ways to either Christianity or the modern world is slow should hardly be surprising. In fact, I would consider anything else to be amazing. It has always been so for all peoples. Such changes are usually painful and perplexing, but at whatever points in history they are to be judged, a full evaluation from both sides is only fair and required.

I am of the opinion that in any event conversion is not the primary matter today. The traditional Apache customs and the traditional Christian faith have more in common than first meets the eye, and thus can benefit one another greatly when they are shared by people with open, avid, and sympathetic minds. The Apache have taught me, just as they have taught every researcher, a great deal about many important things in life, including religion. And they have in no small measure enhanced my own appreciation of the God who works simultaneously in nature, in specific teachings, and in the human heart, soul, and mind. It has never occurred to me to believe that He withholds himself from any man who seeks Him by whatever means.

Webster defines pantheism as "the doctrine or belief that God is not a personality, but that all laws, forces, manifestations, etc. of the self-existing universe are God; belief that God is everything and everything is God; the worship of all gods."

The argument of Opler that any vestige of the Christian view appearing in Apache mythology is of late derivation and therefore of foreign origin is well taken and certainly amply documented. I am inclined to believe he is correct, although his own Apache mythology collection affirms one God who is the primary mover in creation; it also attributes a personality to many of the gods and culture heroes.[8] In my experience, the Apache themselves are usually vehement in claiming that they always have believed in a supreme God, under whom there were lesser gods. The argument may never be resolved, and perhaps it is proper or at least acceptable to refer to the original Apache religious view as pantheistic. Of course, even the Bible speaks of God as using angels, humans, and other created items as channels through which His power is dispensed and made available—which is not really so distant from the traditional Apache concept.

35 Western Apache Life, 1940

An overview of Western Apache life as it was being lived in 1940 presents an interesting look at the people in transition. The Apache wickiup was still being built in the traditional fashion by the woman, but she sometimes received the help of the male members of the family. In 1940, the conical framework was being covered with long grass or bundles of straw, over which sheets of canvas were lashed. In the higher elevations of the reservation a small vestibule of sawed planks and a wooden door were added, while at San Carlos a burlap curtain was sufficient to close the entryway. The wickiup was still not wind- or waterproof, but it took only a few hours to erect and could be burned or abandoned without regret. The wickiup dweller still felt himself to be a freer individual than the person with a permanent house. Some wickiups contained modern-style beds, but most of the people spread their quilts and blankets on the floor. During the day

Mother and child, 1935 (MNMP).

187

the bedding was either rolled up and piled against the walls of the wickiup or spread over bushes outside to air.[1]

The Apache woman continued to wear the style of White woman's dress that had been adopted in the 1870s. A voluminous skirt, ground length, was made of about eighteen yards of bright imitation satin or percale, using either a print or a solid color, with flounces and several rows of ornamental braid added for trim. Her overblouse, which hung to the hips, was high-necked, full-sleeved, with more braiding for trim, and almost never belted. Her well-kept hair was long and hung free, and she either went about barefoot or wore buckskin moccasins. A widow added a cape to her outfit, made from a large square of the same material as her dress.[2] A young mother continued to carry her baby about in a cradleboard on her back, with the carrying strap still crossing her forehead.

In 1940, the men wore colored shirts and Levi's for daily wear, but switched to bright colored shirts for dress occasions. The cowboy stetson hat was in standard use. Only a few of the old men still wore their hair long, binding it with a bright-colored silk scarf.

Cooking was done over an open fire, but all the utensils were now metal and were obtained from a trader's store. Almost every family owned a Dutch oven, since it was ideal for cooking beans, meat, and corn bread. In eating, a canvas was spread on the floor as a tablecloth, and the diners sat around the edge of it, holding their plates on their laps. Those who neither had nor preferred to use individual plates ate from a common cooking vessel, using either their fingers or spoons.

In addition to their cultivated crops, the Apache still gathered a wide variety of wild plants to augment their trade store supplies. Tea was made of sycamore bark, the squawberry bush still furnished a medicinal drink and material for baskets, and the reservation was scoured for walnuts, piñon nuts, acorns, and juniper berries. There were wild potatoes, wild onions, and "wild" bananas, and the fruits of the saguaro cactus. Mesquite and other wild beans were gathered, and there was still the favored mescal.[3]

Some beef was jerked, but most was roasted or boiled and used in a stew together with vegetables and corn. The most common way of preparing corn was to roast whole ears of green corn, still in the husk, on a bed of hot embers. Corn bread was made by grinding the corn into coarse meal on a metate, mixing it with water to make a stiff batter, pouring it into an open Dutch oven containing a small amount of hot fat, and then browning it on both sides. The top was then placed on the oven and the corn bread was baked over a slow fire. When jerky was to be eaten, it was placed in a frying pan on a bed of coals, pounded with a pestle, and fried with hominy, chili, or onions. The tortilla was the most popular form of bread. It was made of either cornmeal or white flour, and the grain was ground on the metate. Acorns were also ground in the same manner and made into a bread.[4]

Tulapai was made as usual, but now the ingredients were soaked and cooked in five-gallon oil cans. The Apache continued to claim it was nutritious, and only a mild intoxicant.

Meat, corn, beans, and pumpkins were the staple items of the food supply. Garden vegetables were fairly plentiful and gaining popularity, particularly those that were easy to store. Whereas meat was formerly obtained by hunting, in 1940 it came from the Apache's excellent herds of range cattle. In the more recent years, when cash payments were being received for labor, the diet had been expanded to include most of what the trader's store could provide.

In 1940, the economic unit was the family group, which consisted of grandparents, married daughters and their husbands, unmarried sons, and the daughters' children. The family was still bound together by certain rights and duties. The people lived in large family groups, and the home of the mother continued to be the family center.[5]

By now the numerous activities of the Apache required the

cooperation of several men in a family group; there was land to be cleared, crops to be gathered, and an annual roundup of the cattle. When a man wanted to clear, plant, or cultivate his ground, he invited his friends to come and bring their tools. He provided the tulapai, and the female members of the family cooked large amounts of beef, corn bread, and beans to feed the men at noon and in the evening. The food and drink was the only payment they received for the work. The Apache had become a competent cattleman; 530 men on the San Carlos Reservation owned 25,000 cattle valued at approximately $900,000. A special tribal herd of 3,500 was used to breed cattle, which were issued to individual Indians at cost, and the 700 San Carlos families had an average yearly income of $731. North of San Carlos, on the Fort Apache Reservation, 400 Apache families owned nearly 20,000 head of cattle valued at over $600,000, and the average income was $500 per family.[6] Irene Burlison states that while she was at Fort Apache, one herd there was known as the

San Carlos, 1935.

"Social Security Herd," since the aged, orphans, and widows were supported by funds derived from it.

In land use the Fort Apache and San Carlos reservations differed substantially. The Fort Apache mountain range had numerous valleys, with small but fertile fields watered by perennial streams, which provided over six thousand acres of tillable land. On the other hand, the San Carlos Reservation had only one small year-round river, serving less than a thousand arable acres. Such topographical differences had played an important role in the social culture of the two reservations, but the method of farming was similar. The women still did the bulk of the work where farm machines were not available. Consequently, the fields remained small and the methods simple; a one- or two-horse walking plow was used, and the planting and harvesting were done by hand. The Apache woman still worked exceptionally hard. Besides her housework, she did most of the planting, irrigating, cultivating, and gathering of the crops, although photos show that men did some of the plowing, clearing, or leveling where the ground was rocky and the going especially difficult. The woman also collected and chopped the wood, carrying home on her back an astonishing load of it tied in a shawl or piece of canvas. The Apache woman still engaged in basket making, for while metal utensils served as cooking vessels, the baskets could be traded for food and clothing. And baskets were still used for ceremonies.[7]

By 1940 hunting had become more of a sport than a food source, for game was scarce and beef was easier to obtain. Groups

189

of relatives gathered to hunt rabbits, turkeys, and quail, and these were welcome additions to the diet. Even fish, shunned in the old days, were being caught and eaten.

By 1940 some of the family groups that made up the old local groups had crystallized into cattle associations. There were nine (later just five) of these at San Carlos and eleven of them at Fort Apache, and some of their headmen served as the tribal councils. At this point the Indian Reorganization Act of 1934 had brought about no radical change in the Apache social complex, and even the adoption of formal constitutions did not alter the situation. Infractions of the law were dealt with by Apache judges and order was being kept on the reservations by native police. Court procedures were similar to those of the White man.[8]

The clan system was still operative, linking the group and band. Children were born into the clan of the mother and marriage within the clan was forbidden.

Some of the ancient methods of child training had disappeared by now, since all children entered school at an early age. However,

Pauline's house at San Carlos, 1935. Photo by Margaret McKittrick (MNMP). Several families still live in small one-room houses built in the 1930s.

mothers and daughters remained close and worked side by side in carrying out the household tasks. Medicine men continued to give instructions to younger men to perpetuate the songs, the dances, and the ceremonials. When death occurred, the wickiup and the personal belongings of the deceased were burned, and as always the deceased's name was never spoken again. If the family lived in a house where a person died, it was their custom to move out for a period of six months or longer.[9]

The Apache children imitated their elders' life-style in play. Boys roped dogs, cats, small brothers and sisters, and anything else that moved. Girls played with their dolls, carried them in little cradleboards, and gathered willows for making baskets.

When girls came of age, the elaborate and important puberty ceremony was held if possible, after which they were eligible for marriage. Now, though, a girl might return to school and it would be several years before she actually married. When a young couple did marry in 1940, they lived with whichever family group seemed best. The son-in-law was still forbidden to look upon or speak to his mother-in-law. If the mother-in-law entered a house, the son-in-law had to leave it, and if they rode in the same car, wagon, or truck, a curtain was hung up to separate them. When a girl from a conservative family married in 1940, the marriage would be in large measure a family arrangement. The girl was considered an economic asset, and appropriate gifts were expected from the prospective son-in-law

Top: *The cattleman, 1935.* Above: *Branding, 1935.*

and his family, but the marriage rite itself was performed according to White custom.[10]

The Apache remained an inveterate gambler. Wherever a few men gathered, games and wagers were the order of the day. Men and women alike bet on games, horse races, foot races, and wrestling matches. The bigger the crowd the better, and they were good losers.

The Western Apache continued to be a deeply religious person, and the ceremonies performed were traditional, many, and varied. Custom required that if a certain family member wished to give a dance or a curing ceremony, all the women in the closely related group prepared enough food for everyone expected. Sometimes as many as fifteen hundred people attended rites, and sponsoring these was an expensive and demanding task. Fortunately, it was a shared one, in that most families took their turn as hosts.[11]

Cowboys at the herd camps, 1935.

36 Western Apache Life, 1973

The San Carlos Reservation of 1973 is perhaps the least changed of all the Apache reservations from what it was at the turn of the century. Here it is simple to be part of the past and present simultaneously. The northern mountains with their high plateau areas are covered with rich grasslands and broad forests of ponderosa pine, and they provide a natural habitat for deer, elk, bear, mountain lion, javelinas, and wild turkey. Rainfall can reach twenty-four inches a year, and numerous year-round trout streams wander through the valleys. The southern end of the reservation is arid and relatively flat, supporting little more than sparse grasses, cacti, and scrub growth. The exceptions are the crop areas bordering the San Carlos and Gila Rivers, which flow beneath the surface throughout much of the year. These feed the man-made San Carlos Lake at the southernmost end of the reserve.

Nearly all of the resident San Carlos people live in three communities, with 75 percent dwelling at San Carlos and Peridot on the southwestern part of the reservation, and the rest in the small southern community of Bylas. In 1972, the population was around four thousand, and in addition approximately six hundred tribal members lived and worked off the reservation.

In this day of mixed marriages, an amazing 95 percent of the people are still classified by the BIA as full-bloods (as compared to estimates of only 20 percent in many other Indian tribes today), and more than half the population is under twenty-one years of age.

The primary economic activity at San Carlos is still cattle raising. The present five livestock corporations, composed of tribal members with salaried stockmen, have managed from ten to fourteen thousand head of cattle each year, and have produced gross annual incomes of nearly one million dollars. Nevertheless, the net is such that only one-third of the families each receive an approximate income of $1,000 per year from it. Other contributions to the local economy come from farming, forestry, mining, part-time wage work, and welfare.

The economic gain from the sum of these areas has been consistently hampered by the traditional work and living habits of the Apache. They have tended to retain a work pattern based on periodic and irregular activity, and upon the voluntary cooperation and sharing of surplus within extended kin groups—as opposed to the sustained work pattern so essential to meeting the economic standards of White society. Even the nature of the tribal enterprise system itself has discouraged individual enterprise, since it is always there as a competitor, and one with strong political backing.

Chronic unemployment and low-paying work have drained the strength of the economy for so long that the people are discouraged about life on the reservation itself. At the same time, though, they are unwilling and unprepared to leave it. Thus they have fallen back heavily upon the federal, state, and local agencies for minimal subsistence, and as such pose a serious predicament for the tribal leaders who want to elevate values and better the situation for everyone.

Not the least of the problems has been the substandard level of education attained. Even in the 1960s, White employees holding key positions in tribal enterprises could not be replaced by Apache, simply because the Apache were not qualified for skilled and technical positions.[1] In fact, the lack of adequate educational standards among the Apache themselves was a major stumbling block to improving reservation conditions. In consequence, academic progress is slow; the average level of education in 1962 was estimated to be at the eighth grade, far too low for most skilled jobs. Compounding this has been the serious school drop-out rate, and until recently there was a daily absenteeism problem of some magnitude. There have been only a few high school and college graduates.

At the same time, tribal leaders have long held the opinion

that the Apache young people received inferior training and discriminatory treatment from both public and federal school programs. Moreover, the tribal council was itself utterly dependent upon federal agencies for financial aid and technical assistance for school programs. In consequence, the Apache had little to say about their operation and design. So the basic goals remained Anglo, and the programs moved forward only when the BIA officials saw fit to do so. This led to apathy and ignorance on the part of the Apache people, and on the

San Carlos horses, 1973.

194

broader plane, it became true of virtually all affairs. The BIA and Public Health Service had no part in tribal politics, yet any new program was dependent upon their financial assistance, and the Apache were progressively forced into a way of life not of their own choosing.[2]

It appears then that the primary problems of Apache students have grown out of the almost inevitable conflict between the school systems and the various Apache social, cultural, and economic pressures active on the reservation. In fact, the overall situation has been such that it actually retarded the learning process, and one can easily appreciate the frustrations of Anglo officials and teachers as they have sought to handle the seemingly endless barriers and entanglements that have arisen.

As a further complication, there were mission, federal, and public schools all functioning at once, whose policies and methods varied greatly. In particular, the primary levels of education were not preparing students sufficiently well to enter the high school grades at a competitive level. In addition, the orientation of the entire program continued to be the assimilation of Apache into the Anglo culture.[3] Yet most Apache were utterly opposed to this, and efforts from either side to reconcile the divergent views were virtually nonexistent. For example, Edward Parmee discovered that few public school administrators and teachers ever came to the reservation to see for themselves how it was.[4]

The situation was, of course, rooted in history. The Dawes Act of 1887 provided for the establishment of off-reservation boarding schools. It also passed much of the responsibility for Indian affairs into the hands of religious denominations, who for the most part saw this as an opportunity for the conversion and "civilization" of the red man. By 1900, however, the BIA had changed its mind and had taken over the boarding school operation. Now more and more schools were built on or near the reservations; their programs were such that the Indians considered them a form of captive education and as such a deliberate disruption of traditional family life.

The year 1934 brought some important changes in BIA policies. The Indian Reorganization Act halted the suppression of traditional religious liberties, and while it was to a questionable extent and purpose, the federal schools began teaching what they believed were the "favorable" aspects of the Apache culture. A number of boarding schools were either closed or converted into day schools, and provisions were made for educating Apache children in nearby public schools.[5] After 1950 a few new public schools were built within the boundaries of the reservations, and federal, state, and local agencies cooperated in their administration. In the last fifteen years a stronger emphasis has been placed upon higher education in the areas of academic and vocational training beyond the high school level. The method is that of providing financial aid for those students who will leave the reservation in order to receive outside training that will equip them to return and lead their people into closer alignment with the modern world.[6]

This, to be precise, is where the conflict still lies in 1973. While Anglos continue to view formal education as a process by which the Apache will be peacefully absorbed into White society, the Apache see schooling as a solution to poverty, disease, social disintegration, and political impotence. In short, they recognize the value of achieving a material standard of life equal to that of the White man, but they see little in his cultural heritage for which they wish to trade what is left of their own. Relocation efforts have never succeeded in spite of tribal efforts to support the program. Even economic deprivation is not enough to induce the Apache to leave their communities permanently.

The educational situation has not been helped by the abject poverty of the San Carlos people. In 1963, it was still so grievous the tribal council made a special appeal to the United States Congress. The *Apache Drumbeat* for July, 1963, cited the fact that of the

San Carlos Indian Agency, May, 1973.

San Carlos work force of 1,500 persons, 75 percent were unemployed. "Living conditions on the reservation are equally deplorable, with almost all of the families living in one- or two-room shacks, without electricity, plumbing, a nearby water source, adequate light, heat, or ventilation." At the same time, while aid programs spent large sums of money to alleviate the situation, no effort was made to assist families in efficient management, and unwise buying plus poor financial planning had a demoralizing effect. It should be remembered that as late as 1880 the Apache were operating on a seasonal raiding, gathering, and hunting basis, with relatively little need for thrift. Following this they became in totality the wards of the government, living for almost thirty years on rations. Moreover, the interdependence of the extended family and clan made individual planning unnecessary, and the new need to cope with individual finances was more than most Apache could handle.

In circumstances like these, schooling was bound to suffer, for the problem of the school program itself was simply overwhelmed by the size and complexity of daily life. Even the matter of preparing a child for school involved problems of such dimension as most others in America seldom face. For example, there were the problems posed by the language barrier in a mixed school, by the racial question, by the child seeking help at home from parents without enough formal schooling to assist with lessons or vocational guidance, and by the matter of inadequate clothing and books as compared to the White students who usually had more than they needed. And even recognizing the resistance of adult Apache to Anglo views, in 1964 only two of the sixteen Indian reservations in Arizona had programs for adult education.[7]

This absence of adult education was of greater consequence than educators realized, for it bypassed the fundamental and sensible methods of intellectual growth the Apache life-way had apparently followed since before the time they arrived in their historical territory. Their way was the ongoing and simultaneous growth of all age groups. Everyone kept on learning, and there were always appointed and traditional times for sharing what one knew with others through ritual, stories, and field training.

Thus, when the federal and public education agencies did not capitalize upon this life-way by simultaneously training the child, youth, parent, and grandparent, the best they could achieve was limited success. Edward Parmee is certainly correct when he points out that the program failed to accomplish its objectives of educating and integrating Apache children because "it was not a community-wide program of academic and fundamental education."[8] Without a community-wide program, the adults were neither willing nor able to play an effective part in the education complex.

As previously indicated, the need to adhere to traditional Apache customs and beliefs is an important factor toward being accepted in the Apache community, and entire families find themselves being pressured into retaining Apache ways. This too has resulted in first, a kind of negativistic approach toward all aspects of the non-Indian culture, and second, a passive resistance toward school issues and policies.

The ultimate consequences of the division are exceedingly serious for Apache youth. The Western Apache system of social relationships once found its focus in the interdependent clans and local group, whose responsibility to the child included teaching him what it meant to be and to behave like an Apache. Yet even as Goodwin studied them from 1930 to 1940, he discovered that the clan system was beginning to break down.[9] In 1957, Kaut reported that things were in a state of rapid change, that the younger generation was losing touch with the older generation while it was still not in communion with the Anglo system.[10] Hence the young people at San Carlos floated awkwardly in a middle place, and other studies indicate the identical situation existed at Fort Apache and among the Jicarilla and Mescalero.[11]

Bylas is approximately forty-five miles from the city of Safford. It is made up of small frame houses, somewhat scattered on both sides of U.S. Highway 70. Many of the homes are flanked by the familiar squaw-coolers, which are used for summer work and eating places. The homes have small gardens and shade trees. There are tribal farms in a nearby valley. The town is dominated by its modern general store. There is an Apache Arts and Crafts Association, a BIA School and a Lutheran Mission School, and several churches.

Peridot is named after the semiprecious stones which are found in the area. It consists of an old-time trading post, whose proprietor is Harvey Osborne, and a few frame houses spread out nearby. Since it is located on the San Carlos River, there are cultivated fields of produce crops in the area and a few fruit trees.

In 1927, the name of the Agency headquarters was changed from Rice to San Carlos. The Agency buildings are large, and most are constructed of tufa stone. The same kind of buildings house the tribe's administrative and business offices. A single main highway leads into the town, and the individual homes are mostly to the west and north of it. Large new school buildings are just being completed on the north end. The homes vary in quality. Some of the new ones are of frame or concrete block and, though small and plain, are equipped with all utilities. A number of the homes are still little more than shacks, without running water and electricity, and haven't even a wooden door to close the entrance in winter.

Also in the town are the Public Health Service Hospital, the Government-employees Club House, and Lutheran and Roman Catholic churches. Other church buildings are distributed in the outlying areas. A large rodeo ground is located at the south end of the reservation.

It has already been mentioned that the tribe became a federal corporation, with a tribal council form of government, in 1934. The council is composed of eleven elected members, with a chairman, a vice-chairman, a treasurer, and a general business manager. It is authorized to act in all matters necessary to the welfare of the tribe.

The tribal enterprises—cattle raising, farming, stores, service stations, a garage, and a restaurant—are firmly established, and the excellent timber and recreational potential of the area is being constantly expanded. Two trading posts are leased to concessionaires.

While non-Indians were at first employed to train and supervise Apache, more and more of these are being replaced as time goes by with Apache personnel.

The San Carlos Agency is under the direction of the Phoenix office of the BIA. Its staff, once entirely Anglo, is less than half Anglo today. The rest are Indians, mainly Apache, but including

The newer homes at San Carlos, 1972.

Papago, Hopi, and Navajo. Congressional appropriations for San Carlos reached nearly $1,400,000 by 1962, of which 95 percent was expended for education, welfare, roads, range management, soil conservation, and irrigation.[12]

The Apache at San Carlos are provided with the educational and medical care that were guaranteed in the agreements made when the reservation was first established. Other than this, they receive only the same services and aid available to any United States citizen who qualifies. There is a food stamp program, but interestingly enough, it is difficult to get the families to use it.

Apache are United States citizens and, as such, are subject to all laws, including those regarding military service. Since reservation land is held in trust for them by the federal government, they do not pay taxes on it. But they do pay state taxes on any land owned off the reservation, as well as federal income taxes and social security and sales taxes. A special legislative act of 1924 exempted them from the payment of state taxes.

The average earned income per family at San Carlos is still less than $1,500 per year. Of the 1,750 employable people, approximately 400 have full-time jobs and perhaps twice that number receive part-time employment.

Left: *The desert country at the south end of the San Carlos Reservation.* Below: *Peridot.*

199

Irma Dean, San Carlos, 1973.

Present-day instructors are given special training when they teach on the reservation. Until now, Grades 1 through 4 for San Carlos, Peridot, and Bylas have been taught by BIA and Arizona public school teachers. For Grades 5 through 12, the San Carlos and Peridot children have gone by bus to Globe, and the Bylas children by bus to Fort Thomas.

Six-year-old children who speak only Apache are required to start in a beginner's class for preparatory English, and those who already speak English enter the first grade. Education is reinforced by tribal law, making certain that every Apache child receives the schooling that is available.

The tribal council has a special Education Committee, which oversees the Apache response to the educational program and which purchases school supplies and clothing for needy children. The funds for these are raised by the tribal sponsorship of dances, rodeos, basketball tournaments, and motion picture shows. It also administers a large revolving college scholarship fund which makes loans to students for one semester. The students pay it back either through summer employment or after graduation. In recent years, considerable emphasis has been placed on vocational training at off-reservation locations under BIA auspices.

Much of the foregoing applies also to the Fort Apache Reservation, home of the White Mountain Apache tribe, which lies immediately north of the San Carlos Reservation and is separated from it by a common east-west boundary. It is an absolutely magnificent mountain retreat of 1,664,872 acres, surrounded on three sides by natural forests. Two-thirds of it lies in the White Mountains and is covered with rich stands of aspen, spruce, fir, and Ponderosa pine. The other third, at the south end, consists of rolling foothills spotted in different places with scrub oak, cactus, juniper, cedar, manzanita, and piñon pine. The high point, Mount Thomas, soars to 11,459 feet, and the low point at Salt River Canyon is 2,700 feet high.

There is no question that the White Mountain Apache possess the ideal land in Arizona for some purposes, for they control the last perfect wilderness area in the state. In truth it is a vacation paradise, with prime hunting, fishing, and camping facilities.

The central town is the bustling community of Whiteriver, and there are several smaller but growing communities scattered around the reservation. Just south of Whiteriver is Old Fort Apache with its Culture Center, already discussed in some detail. Whiteriver houses the BIA and tribal buildings, a government hospital, stores, schools, courts, police and fire departments, churches, and residential dwellings. In the last decade, numerous new homes of excellent quality have been built at Whiteriver and in other areas along the main paved U.S. Highway 73 that cuts through the reservation. There is also a large and well-equipped rodeo and ceremonial ground.

On the far west side of the reservation is the settlement of Cibecue, located in a spectacularly beautiful valley. Included in the village are a large new day school with accommodations for three hundred students in Grades Beginner through 8. There is housing for the teachers, and Apache homes include thirty modern three-bedroom houses with all utilities. There are municipal and community buildings, five churches, stores, trading posts, a rodeo and ceremonial ground, a sawmill and logging business, and three cattlemen's associations. Grasshopper is a well-known archeological site.

The tribal council form of government was established at the Fort Apache Reservation under the provisions of the Indian Reorganization Act of 1934, and the Tribal Constitution, patterned after the United States Constitution, was ratified in 1938. The residents of reservation districts elect nine councilmen to represent them. The council has a chairman, vice-chairman, secretary, and treasurer. Members of the council make up the various committees needed to serve the numerous affairs of the tribe. These include such things as

Health, Education and Welfare; Law and Order; Budget and Finance; Land Uses; Roads; Cattle Raising; and Recreation.

There is also a judicial branch with a chief justice and an associate justice, a fire department, and a modern police force with radio-equipped cars.

The tribal council makes up its own budget for the fiscal year, which has now passed the $750,000 mark and which is addressed to administration, welfare, and special projects having to do with the maintenance of tribal properties. An additional $1,000,000 is applied to revenue-producing enterprises.

One of the important tribal businesses is its herd of pure-bred registered Herefords, which are grazed at the southern end of the reservation. The beef cattle herd itself numbers twenty thousand head. Another enterprise at Whiteriver is the tribal sawmill and wholesale lumber company, the Fort Apache Timber Company, which has a present capacity of over twenty million board feet. The reservation contains a stand of some 300,000 acres of Ponderosa pine and is part of the world's largest western yellow pine forest. Its harvest and manufacture has become the single greatest producer of revenue for the tribe, with ninety-two million board feet of lumber being harvested annually. The annual net for the past five years has exceeded $1,100,000 per year and employment is provided for over two hundred men.

The tent evangelists at San Carlos, 1973.

Careful management is exercised in the cutting, with a grid of plots being used to assure that each plot will be harvested only every twenty years. The harvest is planned to make certain the esthetic values of the mountain area will be retained, as well as to preserve the excellent hunting and fishing areas.

Besides the sparkling trout streams which crisscross the reservation, the tribe has built twenty-six recreation lakes with docks, boats, and other facilities, and hundreds of smaller ponds. More than a thousand well-equipped campsites have been installed for fishermen. Marshy places provide the cattails from which the pollen so valuable for ceremonies is obtained.

Hunters can obtain permits for big game animals such as elk, deer, antelope, and mountain lion and for small game animals and game birds.

The newest industry for the White Mountain tribe is its splendid 104-room, year-round resort complex at Sunrise Park. Combined with this are all the other modern facilities needed by the tourist, including a 6,800-foot chair lift on Mount Thomas for winter sports.

202

Leases are being offered for hundreds of cabin-home sites, in conjunction with a construction enterprise. In all, such a superb job is being done that representatives from over forty Indian tribes have come to Fort Apache to study it with an eye to doing the same.

The Theodore Roosevelt School at Old Fort Apache serves now as the BIA elementary boarding school. The children of nine different tribes of the west are presently educated and boarded there; BIA elementary schools are at Cedar Creek and Cibecue; a public elementary school and Alchesay High School are located in Whiteriver. In addition to these, there are several mission schools in the various communities of the reservation.

Higher education was slow in coming to the White Mountain people. For many years, federal and state grants were available, but they covered only part of the expenses, and the Apache were so poor they couldn't supply the difference. Of course, there were also the ideological complications mentioned earlier. But the formation of the Tribal Education Committee with a full-time education coordinator changed the picture graphically. For example, while in 1967 there were only five White Mountain Apache youth in college, by 1972, with the encouragement and financial help of the committee, that number had risen to more than one hundred. As at San Carlos, vocational training is also being emphasized to prepare the students for employment in the various types of work now available on the reservation.

Of some importance on the reservation is the Pueblo ruin known as Kinishba, "Brown House." It is estimated that as many as two thousand people once lived there and that it was inhabited until sometime after A.D. 1350. It is presently registered as a National Historic Landmark by the National Park Service.

It is at the Fort Apache Reservation that one sees the stirring picture of the modern Apache emerging, with enough of the old way still present to measure the compelling contrast. The strong spirit of the Apachean is there, and as it is applied the promise of a glowing future is clearly seen. The old pride and determination are being asserted in a new way, but within the sphere of living and functioning

Jimmy Dean, San Carlos, 1973.

as an Apache in the modern world. The Apache at least see themselves as a contributing unit in American society, and it is rewarding to know this is so.

San Carlos is somewhat quieter than Whiteriver, more as it was long ago, and a visit there, like a visit to Old Fort Apache, carries one swiftly back to how it was in the tumultuous early days. At home on both reservations the women still wear the colorful voluminous dresses of eighty years ago. On certain occasions, the girls may don them, too. But there are miniskirted secretaries and high school girls, young people in Levi's, and kids mounted on everything from burros to motor scooters. There are football, basketball, and baseball games, rodeos, movies, and tribal fairs. The men prefer cowboy clothes, boots, and stetson hats, but when necessary wear business suits.

But the Gans still dance, the puberty ceremonies are held, there are curing rites, and there are many who cling to all they can of the ancient and good life-way.

Some women can and still do make cradleboards, burden baskets, coiled baskets, the tus, and saddlebags in the old way. Young girls bead the beautiful T and apron necklaces for the puberty rite.

Diet includes the same food everyone else eats, with a special love for candy by all ages. But the traditional acorn stew is still

Bylas, 1973.

around, along with roasted corn, pinto beans, potatoes, tortillas, and Apache fry bread. Harvests gathered by the women include squash, melons, corn, grain, beans, carrots, onions, chili peppers, piñon nuts, acorns, walnuts, apples, and pears. Meat is still jerked, and cactus fruits, wild grapes, and berries are picked. Even nowadays a great deal of canning is done by those who are not able to buy all they need from the stores.

It takes a great deal of looking to find wickiups, although there are still a few, including those abandoned ones still standing. One has even been built at the Culture Center so that visitors can see how they looked and were made. The squaw-cooler remains popular, and is often the center of social life as families gather around open fires to prepare everyday meals.

Out of the particular concern for the problems caused by drinking, and especially among the young men, a Tribal Alcoholism Program has been begun, in which counseling and other services are available. The *Fort Apache Scout* carries articles regularly about its programs—articles that exhort the citizens to higher standards of living.

For the old people, the living is not easy, although they remain remarkably genial as they face the continued problems they must. In discussing the forthcoming winter season with some at Old Fort Apache recently, I asked whether they had enough wood to get them through. All answered that they hadn't nearly that amount, even though the first snow had already fallen. Why not? It cost too much for a load, $20 now on the mountain reservation. I received little comfort from knowing it had jumped to $120 a load where I live; $20 was still too high a price there. Average family income at the Fort Apache Reservation appears to have passed that of the people at San Carlos, but it is still far less than that of the average American. Of course, they have no corner on poverty, but I assume that the difference is they have been immersed in it for well over a hundred years now, and with health and material comfort problems such that in early reservation days from three to four hundred Apache might die in a single severe winter.

The Chiricahua Apache

Arizona

The Chiricahua range before White contact included what is now known as southwestern New Mexico, southeastern Arizona, and the northernmost parts of the Mexican states of Sonora and Chihuahua. Opler notes that the Chiricahua say the entire tribe once lived in the vicinity of Hot Springs, New Mexico, and from here spread out into bands.[1] While there was no true tribal name for the nation, one of the bands of the tribe often took refuge in the Chiricahua Mountains of southeastern Arizona, and others applied the name "Chiricahua" to them because of this. Later on, the term was transferred without distinction to all bands of the tribe.

1 History

Opler says that the Chiricahua bands were three in number: the Eastern band, whose territories joined that of the western Mescalero; the Central band, whose territory was southwestern New Mexico and southeastern Arizona; and the Southern band, whose home was northern Mexico.[2]

The Chiricahua name for the Eastern band was "red-paint people." They are referred to in literature by several titles: Warm Springs, Ojo Caliente, Mimbreños, Mogolones, and so forth. Well-known leaders included Victorio, Nana, Mangus Colorado, and Loco.

The Central band is best known for its leader Cochise, his son Natchez, and for its strongholds in the Dragoon, Chiricahua, and Dos Cabezos Mountains. Their spectacular defense of their country caused some Whites to refer to them as "the Wild Apache."

The Chiricahua name for the Southern band was "enemy people." Juh was its best-known leader, and the notorious Geronimo was born into this band.[3]

It is never prudent to differ with Opler, and I'll assuredly not do so. However, it might be worthwhile to mention that James Kaywaykla, a Warm Springs Apache who was born about 1887 and died in 1963, divides the tribe known as Chiricahua into four bands that were "closely associated":

ARIZONA

NEW
MEXICO

Rio Grande

EASTERN BAND

CENTRAL
BAND

TEXAS

SOUTHERN BAND

MEXICO

*Approximate location of the Chiricahua
bands within their original Southwest
range.*

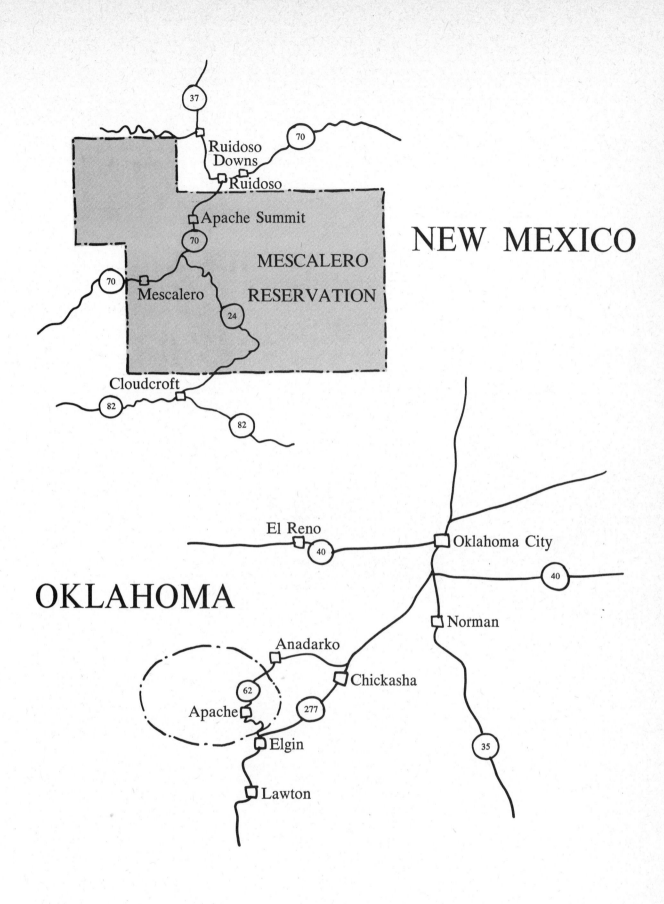

Present-day location of the Chiricahua on Mescalero Reservation and at Apache, Oklahoma.

The true Chiricahua, which were the groups led by Cochise and Chihuaha.

Warm Springs; the *Chihinne*, or "red people," a name derived from the traditional band of red clay drawn across a warrior's face.

Nednhi; Juh was their leader, and their stronghold was in the Sierra Madre Mountains of Mexico.

Bedonkohes; Geronimo was a minor leader, "but not a chief"; and their territory was around the headwaters of the Gila River.[4]

Whichever the proper division may be, once the wars with the Whites erupted, the bands put aside their territorial distinctions in favor of a fierce military alliance, and the title "Chiricahua" became an apt appendage for them all. The Mescalero may well have fought as long and as hard against the successive enemies of the Apache as the Chiricahua, but the Chiricahua battled the Whites, and as such their powerful stand is better attested to in the Arizona, New Mexico, and United States media and government records. It is, by any measure, a stunning account. Yet in the end the Chiricahua paid dearly for the defense of their homeland, for not a single reservation bears their name today, and aside from their warrior image as still seen in motion pictures, they are close to being a forgotten people.

Endless numbers of books and articles have been devoted to the ferocious stand of the Chiricahua; some of them are so well done and complete that it would be an injustice for me to attempt a comparable task or to set forth more than a summary here. For those who desire more information, I recommend in particular the three splendid volumes of Dan L. Thrapp, which treat in great detail the crushing defeat of the Apache people.[5]

Nor do I intend to eulogize the Apache warriors of those days. Both their desirable and undesirable qualities in warfare continue to speak for themselves.[6] They are called a terror, treacherous, frustrating, vexatious, cruel, naked savages, incomparably efficient, and lastly, the "Tigers of the human species," by General George Crook, the man who, with Apache help, finally brought them down. Fair men who later evaluated the situation that developed would counter that treachery and cruelty in equal measure were committed by supposedly civilized Whites who opposed them. However one might seek to justify it, it became plain that hate was not a quality restricted to the Chiricahua alone; "civilized" men and women were capable of it too. An editorial in *The Arizona Citizen* of April 15, 1876, stated: "The kind of war needed for the Chiricahua Apaches is steady, unrelenting, hopeless and undiscriminating war slaying men, women and children . . . until every valley and crest and crag and fastness shall send to high heaven the grateful incense of festering and rotting Chiricahuas."

The Chiricahua and other Apache had been locked in bitterest combat with the Spanish, Comanche, and Mexicans for three long centuries before the Americans came. Precious little peace was theirs from 1540 on. There is assuredly evidence to support their heartfelt wish that things would be different with the Whites.[7] In particular, they hoped an alliance might be made that would protect them against the Mexican army. When it was plain that no such possibility existed, they realized that if they were to survive where they were, as a people, it would mean an all out retaliation against every invader. Therefore, it was not long before Arizona and northern Mexico were bathed in blood. The potential odds against the Apache were more formidable than they had first realized; never, of course, did all the bands join together at any one time, yet even if they had, the sum of the warriors who could be mustered from all the branches put together would not have exceeded 2,500 men. For a brief time in the beginning, the Apache outnumbered the United States troops in the field. It was a plurality that quickly evaporated, though, and the Apache endured, not because of numbers, but because of their

211

Top: *Chiricahua country, east of Cochise stronghold.* Above: *Chiricahua country, north of Cochise stronghold.*

astounding ability to thrive in their rugged land where others couldn't. By the time they were controlled in 1886, forty years of savage war had passed.

Sad to say, the Apache were never able to comprehend the persistent and contradictory nature of those who came in steady swarms to seize their land, and who did it without the slightest regard for Indian rights.[8] They kept asking what or whom it was that gave men the right to act in such a way. Had their God told them to behave so? If that were the case, they certainly wanted nothing to do with Him! Again, when the Whites dug up the apparently precious yellow iron and then fashioned gleaming crosses out of it, was that really their god? The Whites plundered their land, stole their horses, killed their people, and destroyed their villages; why then did the Whites find it so strange when the destitute Apache raided in return? Finally, the Whites said they would give them reservations. Yet how could they give the Apache that which already belonged to them in the first place? Was there any recourse but to fight with such a peculiar foe?[9]

As mentioned earlier, Fort Apache, Arizona, was established in 1870 as an army camp from which to control the Navajo and Apache. In 1871, after numerous campaigns in which hostile Apache bands were subdued, the army, with General George Crook in charge, set up four major reservations for the Apache. These were located at Fort Apache, Camp Verde, and Camp Grant in Arizona, and in the Tularosa Valley of southwestern New Mexico. The Chiricahua branch, numbering 1,675, was settled on the Chiricahua reservation in southeastern Arizona. However, for better control, and for other reasons too numerous to mention, all the Arizona Apache were forcibly moved in 1875 to a single, desolate, restricted area in the White Mountains of Arizona, later to be known as San Carlos.[10]

Had the authorities known or cared about the ancient differences and animosities among the Apache tribal branches themselves, they might have followed another and wiser course. Whatever tragedy the Apache branches had shared under White domination, it was not sufficient to bring them together. Besides this, the branches held different views as to how their problems with the Whites might best be solved. And each branch seemed to disdain the positions of the others, especially if a view favored peace with the Whites. Developments in methods of control by Washington aggravated conditions further.

The military command of the reservation was partially replaced by the civilian Office of Indian Affairs. Soon thereafter, the two services were bickering among themselves and jousting for control. Meanwhile, there was grievous graft and fraud in the purchase of food and supplies for the Apache. Prospectors and cattlemen moved onto the reservation and unlawfully took possession of large parcels of land. Incredibly, but predictably, the authorities in Washington confirmed the settlers' right to the Apache land, and the seizures continued until the reservation had dwindled from its original 7,200 square miles to only 2,600 square miles, and that the poorest property in the area.[11]

The Apache were anxious, restless, and angry. In particular, the Warm Springs Apache and the Cochise Apache bands chaffed at the constricting and uncertain bit and wished to be free. Soon groups of Apache, led by strong and experienced leaders, began to escape repeatedly from San Carlos. Once away, they brutally plundered and killed whomever they encountered, as they raced through Arizona and New Mexico on their way to strongholds in the remote Sierra Madre Mountains in northern Mexico.

In 1882, General Crook was ordered to return to Arizona as head of the Military Department in order to reestablish control of the marauding Apache. Upon assessing the situation, he placed the blame where it really belonged. "Greed and avarice on the part of the Whites, in other words, the almighty dollar, is at the bottom of nine-tenths of our Indian troubles." His method of ending the conflict was

212

Below: *Mountain forest area in heart of Cochise stronghold. The renowned Chiricahua chief probably camped here many times.* Bottom: *Wash area in heart of Cochise stronghold.*

the only one that ever could have worked. It would take an Apache to catch an Apache. So he organized and enlisted forces of friendly (as opposed to hostile) Apache warriors to serve as scouts for the army troops.[12] Realizing that continued battles kept things in unrelenting turmoil for those still on reservations, and that if things went on as they were a time might come when all the Apache would be destroyed, even prominent leaders willingly became scouts. Even then, it would require the services of hundreds of Apache and five thousand United States soldiers for over four years in order to end the conflict. The magnitude of their task can be seen by citing only a few details concerning the nature of the Apache they pursued.

Victorio, leader of the Warm Springs Apache, was more than fifty years old when he escaped and led his group into hiding in the Dragoon Mountains of southeastern Arizona in 1880. With a force that never exceeded three hundred warriors, Victorio slaughtered over two hundred New Mexican citizens, over a hundred United States soldiers, and two hundred Mexicans before he was shot and killed by a Mexican Indian in October of 1880.[13]

In July, 1881, a seventy-three-year-old infirm leader named Nana led a two-month-long, thousand-mile raid in which the forty warriors who followed him off the San Carlos reservation killed forty Whites and wounded many more. He was victorious in eight pitched battles, captured two enemies and two hundred horses, eluded 1,400 army troops and armed civilians, and withdrew to his Mexican hideout without losing a man.[14]

In 1883, Chatto, Benito, and twenty-six warriors made their way across four hundred miles in six days without once being seen by a soldier. They did lose one man, themselves killing twenty-eight victims. Others who made the trip reported that except for naps on horseback, Chatto went sleepless for the entire period. That same year, a minor leader named Geronimo led a band off the reservation to raid throughout Sonora, Mexico. In May they surrendered to General Crook and were returned to San Carlos.[15]

In 1885, Geronimo and his followers were off and raiding again, with thirty-five warriors, eight boys, and a hundred or so women and children. He was wounded several times; he lost six men, two boys, a woman, and a child, but they killed seventy-five civilians, twelve Apache, two officers and eight United States soldiers, and over a hundred Mexicans.[16]

In November, 1885, Josanie and ten warriors traveled 1,200 miles in a month, wore out 250 stolen horses, killed thirty-eight people, and escaped into Mexico with the loss of one warrior. The more amazing fact is that they moved through an area patrolled by eighty-three companies of United States troops.[17]

Geronimo was the final holdout, surrendering with his small group of followers for a second and final time to the forces of General Miles near the Mexican border on September 4, 1886.[18]

The surrender terms Crook offered to Geronimo and his followers were two years confinement outside the territory, after which they would be free to return to the reservation. But General Sheridan, being consistent with Washington's typical disregard of promises, insisted on unconditional surrender and permanent removal. Crook replied that he could not go back on his word to the Apache and asked to be relieved of his command. In less than a day he was replaced by General Nelson Miles.

Four days later the entire Chiricahua tribe was packed aboard a train and shipped off to prison in Florida. Loyal Chiricahua scouts, including the two who had negotiated Geronimo's surrender, were imprisoned along with the hostiles. As the train pulled out of Bowie Station, the Fourth Cavalry band played "Auld Lang Syne." Some say it was only the beginning of one of the blackest periods of injustice in American history.[19]

Geronimo went with the last group to be confined in prison in Florida. He remained there for two years and then was reunited with his family in an Alabama prison camp. In 1894 they were all

Dahteste, Chiricahua, who was on the
warpath with Geronimo (Smithsonian).

215

transferred to the military reservation at Fort Sill, Oklahoma, where Geronimo remained under loose confinement until he died on February 17, 1909.

Approximately 340 Apache were shipped to Florida. The environment was so alien there that they died in alarming numbers. Within a year they were moved to Mount Vernon Barracks, Alabama, where they were kept for seven more years, during which time they begged continually to be allowed to return to Arizona. Finally, White humanitarians took up their cause with Washington, and in 1894 they were brought by train to Fort Sill, Oklahoma Territory. Those who witnessed their arrival described them as a pitiful sight, wretchedly poor. They numbered approximately 296 persons at this time, of which only 50 or so men were well enough to work. During their stay in Oklahoma, they became known as the Fort Sill Apache. Their first winter, in hastily prepared wickiups, was an extremely difficult one, but the next spring they were put to work as army scouts and at farming and raising cattle, producing excellent results in these occupations in the years that followed. The Dutch Reformed Church began mission work among them in 1899. Geronimo himself finally joined that denomination in 1903, but historians feel the evidence shows he remained a nominal convert.[20]

Despite their improved living conditions, the Chiricahua Apache population continued to decline, and leaders such as Naiche (Natchez) and Geronimo pleaded with the authorities to allow them to return to their home country in Arizona or New Mexico. Meanwhile, Apache children who had been born in captivity in Florida or Alabama grew to maturity as prisoners of war.

Finally, in 1913, after twenty-seven painful years of confinement, the Chiricahua were released by an act of Congress and given the choice of either taking up residence on the Mescalero Reservation of New Mexico or accepting allotments of land in Oklahoma. Their population now was down to 258 persons; 87 of these made the painful decision to remain, and the other 171[21] were sent in boxcars to join the Mescalero. For all intents and purposes, their fortunes merged with the Mescalero tribe from then on, and Mescalero history from that date is theirs as well. One might note, in passing, the awesome difference between the large Chiricahua population of 1,675 in 1873, and the small group of 258 surviving in 1913.

The Apache cattle herd at Fort Sill was sold, and the proceeds were divided among those remaining so they could purchase land from the Kiowa and the Comanche. There was enough to provide for an eighty-acre homestead for each with the town of Apache, in Caddo county and close to Fort Sill, as their center. Today they are "Christianized," with some still holding membership in the Dutch Reformed Church. There is no tribal organization. They are a rural people who follow modern practices in agriculture and the raising of livestock. Two-thirds are full-bloods, the rest are mixed blood. The old Apache arts and crafts are no longer practiced, although Chiricahua Gan dancers still perform in the annual American Indian Exposition at Anadarko.[22]

Chato, Chiricahua of the Warm Springs band, who later enlisted at San Carlos as a scout.

Above: *Child in cradleboard, Wichita Mountains, Oklahoma (DPL). Right: Taz-ayz-Slath, wife of Geronimo, and child (DPL). Opposite: Nai-chi-ti, or Naiche, son of Cochise. Photo by Wittick (MNMP).*

Top: *Chiricahua camp. Photo by A. T. Willcox (DPL).* Above: *Chiricahua camp. Photo by Wittick (MNMP).* Right: *The Yellow Coyote, Chiricahua scout, called "Dutchy." Said to be one of the Chiricahua accused of numerous "murders" of White people (DPL).* Opposite top: *Attack on the miners.* Opposite bottom: *The war party.*

Above: *Doll showing woman's style of dress (HM)*. Above right: *Back view of head, showing beaded hair bow*. Right: *Detail of head, showing construction details and bead wrapping*. Below right: *Side view of head, showing method of attaching hair bow*.

Left: *Painted war shirt attributed to Chiricahua (Museum of the American Indian, Heye Foundation)*.

222

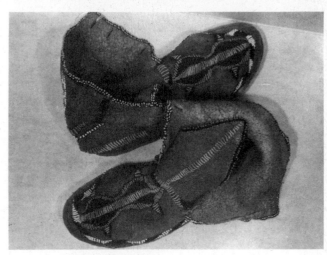

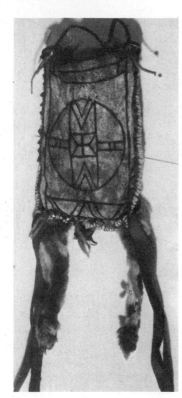

Top left: *Moccasins, possibly Eastern band of the Chiricahua (MNCA). Actual group unknown.* Top right: *Moccasins, possibly Chiricahua (ALMN). Actual group unknown.* Above left: *Moccasins, possibly Eastern band of the Chiricahua, possibly Mescalero (MNCA). Actual group unknown.* Above right: *Moccasins, possibly Eastern band of the Chiricahua, possibly Mescalero (MNCA). Actual group unknown.* Far left: *Beaded pouch (AF). Group unknown.* Left: *Painted deer-hide pouch with weasel feet attached, deer hair left on and turned inside pouch; front view, back undecorated (AF). Group unknown.*

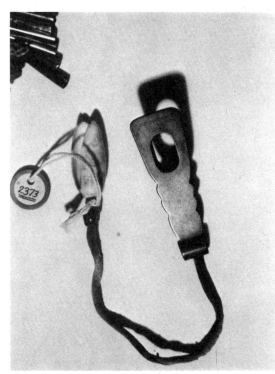

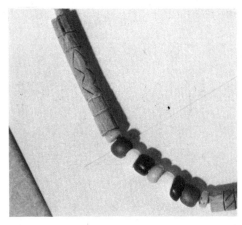

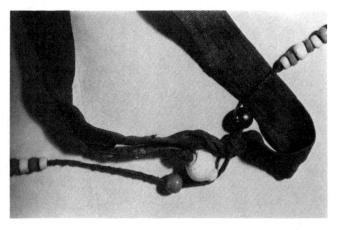

Top left: *Buckskin awl case decorated with beads, tin cones, and red flannel (ASM). Front view.* Top right: *Back view.* Center left: *Metal tweezers, beaded ration-ticket bag, beaded awl case, and bone awl (AF).* Center right: *Detail of tweezers, showing scallop*

design and shell. Above left: *War necklace with engraved bone beads (AF). Photos show Chiricahua men wearing this type.* Above right: *Detail of war necklace, showing cloth strip tied on for added decoration.*

Above: *Apache girl in puberty
ceremony dress. (Composite employing
Curtis photo.)* Following pages:
White Mountain interlude.

Above: *Mopquo, the White Mountain
hunter.* Opposite: *The Chiricahua sentinel.*

Above: *The trident used in curing ceremonies by the Western Apache clown. Opposite: Western Apache puberty ceremony. (Adapted from Arizona Highways.)*

Opposite: *Elote, subchief of the Jicarilla, 1900.* Above: *Warrior of
1880s showing method of holding bow and arrow, and colors of typical clothing.*

Recounting the victories and the losses.

Below: *Western Apache painted moccasins (SM)*. Bottom: *Western Apache painted rawhide medicine bag (HM)*. Opposite: *The Gans emerging from the sacred cave*.

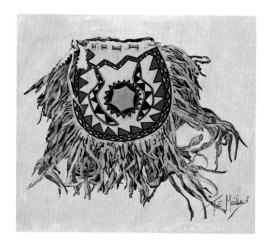

Below: *Apache women with the tus,*
or water jars, at San Carlos, ca. 1890.
Opposite top and bottom: *The Jicarilla*
beaded adolescence rite cape (ALMN).

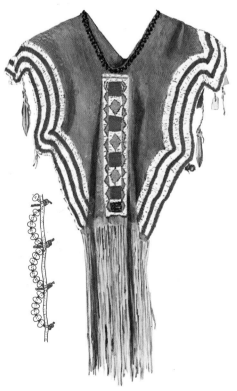

The Western Apache medicine man.

2 Food Harvests and Agriculture

The gathering of food was a major and vital responsibility of the Chiricahua woman. Not surprisingly, then, the Chiricahua year was divided into six time-periods, each of which was closely related to the various foods to be gathered. For example, mescal was gathered and stored in the spring. Then acorns were collected and placed in bags. By the time that was done the yucca fruit, sumac berries, and other things would be ready.[1]

Food that was near the camp would be gathered by a woman working alone or with a female member of her family. Journeys to favorite but more distant harvest areas called for a party of several women. If the trip took the women a long way from camp and exposed them to danger, men went along to assist and protect them. Pack horses were also taken on long trips to carry the harvest home.[2]

Stored vegetables, nuts, fruits, and meat carried the family through most of the winter and up until midspring, when the harvesting could begin.

The green and tender central stem of the narrow-leafed yucca was the first food to be gathered at the spring harvest. Its stems were roasted in a pit for a day, then sun-dried and stored in a rawhide container. Before being eaten they would be softened by soaking in water. During this same time period, white rootstocks and tule shoots were accumulated, to be boiled with meat and made into a soup.

Next came the white flowers of the narrow-leafed yucca. These were boiled with meat or bones, any surplus being boiled, dried, and stored. Other yucca buds were opened and dried for use as sweetenings for tea drinks. Hot teas and liquids made of herbs and grasses were one of the common treatments for chills.[3] One informant speaks of "a strong black tea."[4]

The century plant, or mescal, was now ready. Before any blossoms appeared, its stalks and crowns were cut and roasted or pit-baked like the yucca stalks. Long trips were necessary to obtain mescal, requiring the establishment of a temporary camp while it was harvested. That which was not eaten immediately was sun-dried and given a preservative glaze made of mescal juice. Like the yucca stalk, it was soaked in water before eating. For variety, it was sometimes mixed with berries or nuts. Several trips would be needed to collect enough mescal. By summer the plant would flower and was unfit for further use.

In early summer, locust-tree blossoms and wild onions were picked. When food was scarce the inner surface of western yellow pine bark was scraped and provided a sweet material. One variety of sumac berry was picked, washed, and sun-dried. Later it was ground and mixed with mescal to form a mixture that did not spoil.

Midsummer was the time to collect berries and seed-bearing plants. The seeds were boiled and either eaten whole or dried and ground to flour for making bread. Grapes were also gathered; some were eaten, others dried and preserved. Raspberries were crushed, dried, and kept in a caked form. A crude type of baked bread was made from a paste formed by ground acorns, hackberries, mesquite beans, and other berries not edible in the raw state.[5]

Late summer found women and children in the mountains collecting chokecherries and potatoes.[6] The chokecherries were dried and stored. The potatoes were placed in a cave if possible, then ground into flour for making bread.[7] Certain lowland plants also bore fruit at this time, which was dried, caked, and stored.

Important fall foods included the screw bean, the fruit of the giant cactus, the broad-leafed yucca fruits, prickly-pear cactus fruits, mesquite beans which made pancake flour, sweet berries, currants, walnuts, piñon nuts, and acorns. Acorns were used in making a kind of pemmican. To do this, the acorn meats were mixed with jerked deer meat and some fat, then rolled into little balls that kept all winter and served as premium emergency food for trips.[8]

Late in the year the women gathered greens and harvested wild grasses and plants for their seeds. Seeds made a gravy and flour for baked bread. Grass seeds were gathered by holding a bucket under the heads and striking the grass sharply.[9]

Some of the Chiricahua branches obtained salt from "a little lake in the Gila Mountains." The water was too salty to drink, and the bottom of the lake was covered with a brown crust. When the crust was broken, the salt stuck to it. The salt pieces could only be washed clean in the lake itself, for the salt dissolved in clear water. The site was a kind of holy ground where enemies and game alike could come and go without being molested.[10]

The Apache often spoke of how food supplies and other commodities were cached in secret caves, usually located near a water hole. Even clay cooking pots were left in the caves, and some of these were described as having a semicircular base so perfectly balanced that they righted themselves when they were tipped. Even bolts of calico cloth were deposited in these caves to be utilized in making clothing. Cached supplies like these served as emergency supplies when the Apache moved from one location to another during peaceful times and when they were on the run from enemies.

Once they were in dangerous territory, the women always checked the water jars and food bags before sleeping, so as to be ready to flee on a moment's notice. Also, each individual carried small emergency ration bags attached to his belt.[11] James Kaywaykla told Eve Ball that when the people went south for the winter they harvested food as they found it and stored the supplies in caches in caves. The White man's cooking utensils were also left there, because they did not break like pottery; and also blankets and bales of calico that had been taken from the enemy.[12]

The Chiricahua considered honey a delicacy, and when hives were discovered a smudge fire was employed to smoke the bees out so that the honey could be collected. It was mixed with drinks and eaten with bread.[13] Another method was to spread skins on the ground, and then shoot arrows at a hive till chunks of comb fell off. These were squeezed and the honey extracted was dripped into skin bags with small mouths.[14]

When the tule became yellow with pollen in the fall its tops were cut off, dried, and then shaken over an outspread buckskin. Cloth, of course, wouldn't hold the fine pollen, but the Apache felt it would be wrong to use anything but buckskin bags for the substance used in rituals.

While the Chiricahua did not cultivate tobacco, they found small supplies of it growing wild. It was cut and cured in autumn, and when the leaf supply ran out even the stalks were used. All Apache smoked, although a boy was forbidden to smoke until he had hunted alone and killed large game, and an unmarried girl was considered immodest if she picked up the habit. In smoking, cigarettes were fashioned by rolling the tobacco in wrappers of oak leaves. Tobacco was not used in Apache councils or ceremonies as was the custom on the plains.

Geronimo stated that there were times of particular need when his people settled for a short while in valley areas suitable for farming. It was common then for a number of families each to cultivate about two acres of unfenced ground, and the burden of guarding the entire cultivated area against animals was shared by all those involved. Parents and children joined in the work of planting, breaking the ground with wooden hoes. Corn was planted "in straight rows, beans among the corn, and the melons and pumpkins in irregular order over the field."

When the melons were ripe they were gathered as needed and eaten. Pumpkins and beans were collected in the autumn in bags and burden baskets; the harvested ears of corn were tied together by the husks, and all the produce was placed on pack animals for delivery to the home village. The corn was shelled on arrival and together with the other crops was cached in caves or other places to serve as winter supplies.[15] Corn was not fed to horses; in winter they ate fodder.

Niño Cochise confirms the above when he speaks of a time in August, 1889, when the corn was "as high as a man." In the same garden were many vegetables, including melons and potatoes. They had also planted about an acre of pinto beans. All the crops were doing very well, and guards watched the fields around the clock to keep the rabbits and deer away. He also mentions how a field of half-grown corn became an excellent hunting ground when deer and other animals were drawn to its inviting produce.[16]

3 Hunting

Hunting was the man's responsibility, although Chiricahua accounts do reveal that women hunted when circumstances made it necessary.[1]

Deer was the most sought-after difficult to kill game animal for the Chiricahua, and because of this specific thoughts and cere-monies preceded a hunt.[2] Fasting increased one's chances for success; onions were not to be eaten, and a man should not wash himself or put on anything aromatic that the deer might smell.[3] It is clear that while the Chiricahua considered these things in ritual terms, they also made good sense.

The hunter must be both reverent and generous. The kill must be shared with others; no baskets were to be brought along as evi-dence of overconfidence.

Even if men went in a group to a favorite site, once arrived the men separated and hunted alone. Most deer were killed with bow and arrow. Sometimes mounted men or relays of men on foot ran deer till the animals were exhausted, then roped and strangled them.[4] But running the game did affect the meat, and it was not a preferred method.

Deer-head and antelope-head masks were used in stalking, but not elk-head masks, since the hunters felt they were not needed. To make a deer-head mask, the head was mounted on a circular stick that rested on top of the hunter's head. The features were filled out with grass, and the skin was tied or sewed together at the sides to fit it to the head and make it stay on. Jason Betzinez, who was with Geronimo, mentions a mask that slipped over the hunter's head and shoulders.[5] The hunter also wore clothing or a covering the color of the deer, and in stalking acted like a grazing deer. Deer were ap-proached against the wind. If the deer was in the open the hunters crawled long distances on the ground, keeping brush in front of them for a shield.[6] To call the deer, a leaf whistle was made by holding the leaf horizontally along the lips.[7]

The hunter skinned and cut up his kill immediately. This, too, was done according to traditional rules as to where to begin and ceremonial gestures to be used. To assure future luck, the head and hoofs must be brought home with the meat.[8] Deer meat was jerked by cutting it into long thin strips "with the grain," and then spreading it over bushes (mesquite is mentioned) to dry. When it was dry, it was pounded until it was compact and stored in cowhide bags. One method of cooking the deer meat was to roast it on a spit hang-ing over a dry cedar fire.[9] Another was to make a venison stew.[10]

There were few elk on the Southern Chiricahua range, but plenty in the Central area. Mountain sheep and goats were taken when possible. Opposum and wood rats were regular diet supple-ments. Other game mentioned were jaguar, skunks, coatis, and moles.[11] Cottontail rabbits were eaten, but not jackrabbits.[12] Young boys hunted the rabbits and squirrels and had several techniques for capturing them.[13] Wild hogs and prairie dogs were not eaten because they ate snakes. Dogs were not consumed either.[14] Some Chiricahua believed that wildcat meat was forbidden, and did not eat it. Moun-tain lions were eaten, and the hides were used for quivers.[15] Geronimo claimed he killed several with arrows and one with a lance.[16]

Buffalo were not present in most of the range, and in conse-quence are thought to have played but little part in the general

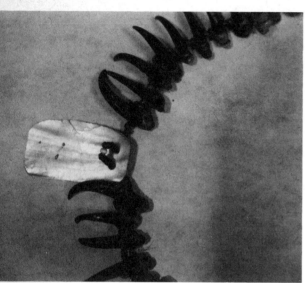

Top: *Bear claw necklace, with yellow and green trade beads (MNCA).*
Above: *Detail of necklace, showing method of attaching claws and shell.*

economy of the Chiricahua. Geronimo states, however, that he began to follow the chase "out on the prairies" when he was only eight or ten years old. The game captured there included deer, antelope, elk, and buffalo as they were needed. Usually buffalo were hunted on horseback with bows and lances. The meat was eaten; hides were used to make tipis and bedding.[17]

When Betzinez was a boy, the buffalo had virtually disappeared, but on rare occasions his people traveled eastward to find them. Both men and women went, and the trip took several days. The leaders planned the hunt and sent parties out to scout for buffalo. During the chase, men rode by guiding the horses only with their knees so that hands were free for lances or bows and arrows. This suggests that trained horses were used. The women skinned the carcasses, cut up and dried the meat in regular Plains fashion.[18] In late history, cattle, horses, burros, and mules were regularly consumed.

Some animals, such as badger, beaver, and otter were hunted for their fur.

It appears that birds were hunted more for their feathers than they were for food, the feathers being used for ritual purposes and for fletching arrows. Informants differed as to whether and what birds were actually eaten; the conclusion is that some Chiricahua ate them and some didn't. Geronimo's people caught great numbers of wild turkeys by driving them into an open area, and then either riding up and catching the tired ones by hand, or else clubbing those that flew out of the air.[19] Betzinez states that contrary to what is often said, the Apache liked turkey and ate so little of it only because they didn't have an opportunity to get more. His group shot them with arrows on moonlit nights when they could creep up on their roosts.[20] Niño Cochise speaks of roasting four turkeys they had shot along the canyon rim.[21] Boys hunted birds with bows and arrows and with slings. Men sometimes fashioned bird traps to lure them close enough to shoot.[22]

Eagle feathers were prized and the bird was trapped.[23] To do this, a circle of separate sinew loops, with lines running out to limbs so that they would pull tight with pressure, was set around a dead animal, used for bait. When the eagle alighted and, in walking around, stepped into a loop, it caught itself. It was then clubbed to death. On rare occasions eaglets were taken from their nest and raised in small cages until their feathers were ready for plucking.[24]

The Chiricahua expressed a strong dislike for pork, fish, and frogs, the latter two being classified with snakes. "Usen did not intend snakes, frogs, or fishes to be eaten."[25] Small boys sometimes threw rocks at them for enjoyment or practiced their archery by shooting arrows at them. "To Apaches, eating the flesh of fish or dog is repugnant."[26]

Despite the many taboos reported by informants concerning the bear, who was like a person because it walked upright, and some Chiricahua believed that when the wicked died their spirits returned to the earth in the body of a bear, it appears that bears were hunted by the Chiricahua, considered good for food, and thought to have a valuable skin. This is true at least of Geronimo's band. He claims he killed several bears with a lance and was never injured in a fight with one.[27]

Niño Cochise speaks of the *maba,* or annual bear-hunting time, when they went to obtain bear grease to use for oiling guns and greasing women's hair. [28] He adds that bear skins were used to keep warm in winter.[29]

Betzinez describes an awesome experience when a large bear crossed the trail in front of his father and himself. His father gave chase; when the bear turned to fight, he killed it with an arrow in the side. But the bear was not skinned, because of the strong superstition of the Apache concerning the bear, that perhaps he was some kind of ancestor associated with their ancient history.[30] Betzinez goes on to say that while numerous brown, black, and silvertip grizzlies infested Apache country, they were given a wide berth, although a warrior fought an angry grizzly when he had to rather than show cowardice. Some were killed even with a knife, and a necklace of bear claws usually testified to this accomplishment.[31]

Early winter was, apparently, a good hunting time. An instance is mentioned when heavy snows and cold drove the bears into hibernation and the deer down into the flats. In three days, forty hunters had taken fifty-four deer, five bighorn sheep, and nine mountain lions.[32]

4 Tanning

Geronimo reports that deer hides were soaked in water and ashes, after which the hair was removed. "Then the process of tanning continued until the buckskin was soft and pliable."[1]

Tanning was woman's work, although a man helped with the stretching of big hides.

In the early days, the hides of deer, antelope, and elk were fleshed with a sharp deer bone or stone; later on a scraper with a metal blade was employed. Using a stiff rawhide for a basin, the hide was then soaked in water for two or three days. The wet hide was laid over a pole that had been leaned against a tree (see the Mescalero section for a drawing of the procedure); the hair was removed with a horse's rib, which served as a beaming tool. Now a cushion of grass was spread on the ground, and the skin was laid on it, inner side up. Pegs were driven around the edge to hold it down, and it was left in the sun for several days. During this time, lumpy or thick places were thinned and pounded with a rough stone. Thus far, rawhide had been made.[2]

To turn the rawhide into buckskin, boiled deer brains and warm water were worked into it with the hands. When the hide was soft, it was hung in the sun to dry a little, then stretched by holding one end on the ground and pulling on the other. This process was repeated until the desired effect was obtained. It took about half a day to complete.[3]

Warm weather was best for tanning, since once begun the cold made it impossible to stop and affected the quality of the work. In summer a hide could be worked in easy and smooth stages, and whenever possible the task was put off until then.

The thick hides needed for moccasin soles were not stretched in this manner. Opler's informants stated that the hair was removed from hides to be used for soles.[4] This could be only partially true, since museum collections contain many soles with the hair left on the bottom of the sole for added wear and padding.

Water caused buckskin garments to turn hard, and it was a sad moment when one was caught out in the rain. The hide could be softened again with a rough stone, but it never returned to its original softness and velvet quality.

Hides to be utilized for robes or blankets received the fleshing, pounding, and deer-brain treatment on the inside, but the hair was left on the outside. In very cold weather the hair side was turned in for added warmth.

To make a saddlebag, a woman staked out the hide hair side down over a bed of grass. When the exposed side was dry, the hide was turned over, scraped, fleshed, and treated in the usual way with deer brains. It was not, however, soaked in water. It was cleaned and fashioned into a bag shaped like a large, flat envelope.[5] When its form was complete, a slit was cut across the middle on one side and dirt fill put in each end to shape the pockets. Elaborate cut-out decorations were often added to these, and the rawhide saddlebag was one of the most beautiful Apache creations.

The Plains-style parfleche, or rawhide container, was a late addition to the Chiricahua household, and even then it was not employed by every branch. The Southern Chiricahua didn't make it at all, the Central group made some slight use of it, and the Eastern

Top: *Old Army McClellan saddle used by Geronimo and left at Fort Sill, Oklahoma.* Above: *Knife used by Geronimo for skinning and for carving bows and walking canes that he sold as souvenirs at Fort Sill, Oklahoma.*

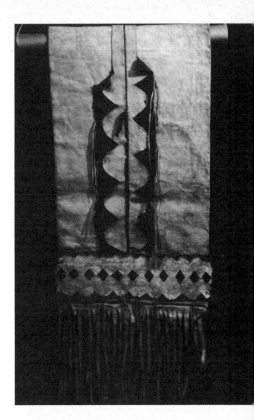

Top left *and* top center: *Rawhide saddlebags (ASM).* Top right: *Rawhide saddlebag (MNCA). Length, 6 feet, with 14-inch fringe at each end; width, 18 inches.* Above left: *Rawhide saddlebag (MNCA). Length, 4 feet 10 inches, with 16-inch fringe at each end; width, 15 inches.* Above center: *Rawhide saddlebag (MNCA). Length, 2 feet 10 inches, with 24-inch fringe at each end; width, 12 inches.* Above right: *Detail, showing scalloped design and painting of tabs.*

Top left: *Rawhide saddlebag made for a child (MNCA). Front view.* Top right: *Back view.* Center left: *Detail, showing intricate cutouts laid over red cloth.* Center right: *Detail, showing tabs and fringe.* Above left: *Painted buckskin medicine bag (MNCA). Front view.* Above right: *Back view.*

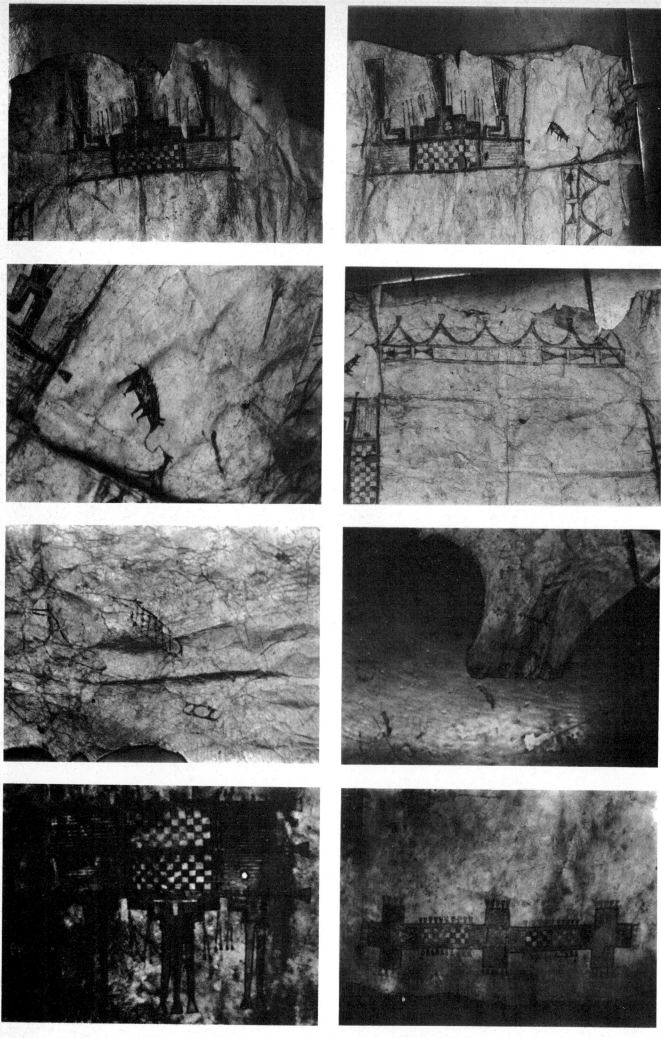

Details of painted hide (SM). Possibly an Eastern parfleche, although no evidences of folding are visible; therefore, possibly a ceremonial item.

232

branch, which had more contact with Plains culture, seems to have made many parfleches.[6] While the Central band model was left plain, the Eastern women painted involved geometric designs on theirs. Men were not allowed to be present while parfleches were crafted and finished, a practice that seems to be clear testimony that it was woman's work.[7] It is noteworthy that Eastern Chiricahua women employed only geometric designs in their painting, while men drew freehand figures; this was also the practice of the Plains tribes.

Beautiful buckskin awl cases adorned with beads, tin cones, metal discs, and buttons were crafted by the women. They also made buckskin and beaded bags for pollen, food, and other items and cut out and shaped rawhide pieces for bowls and water carriers.

For thread, the Chiricahua women used sinew taken from alongside the backbone and leg bones of large animals. Mescal fibers could also be used for this purpose. Deer sinew was preferred, but the material was also taken from horses and steers. Awls for punching holes for sewing were made from wood and from the sharpened leg bone of the deer.

Color was obtained by soaking the hides in dyes. Dark brown was obtained from walnut juice, red from boiled root and bark of mountain mahogany, yellow from soaked algerita roots. Yellow ocher from clays was rubbed on the surface of garments, with added treatments required as the color wore off.[8]

Top: *Beaded buckskin medicine bag with tin cones (MNCA). Fairly recent make. Front view.* Above: *Back view, showing painted symbol.*

5 Girl's Puberty Ceremony, 1930–1940

First menstruation was cause for great rejoicing on the part of the family of the girl. Even though all might not be in readiness for the prolonged puberty ritual and celebration, the family and close neighbors gathered for a feast and a token ceremony, called the Little Rite. In the 1930s, this daytime celebration was a reduced version of the full ceremony to follow: the girl might wear her buckskin dress, finished or not; an attendant might knead her body; songs would be sung to lead her through four steps. Then a basket with the bag of pollen and an eagle feather in it would be put to the east and she would run around it clockwise and return to her place four times. Each time the basket was brought nearer. As she returned the last time, tobacco, fruits, and other presents were thrown into the air as soon as she reached the buckskin. Then the girl marked the singer across the nose with pollen, and he marked her the same way. Next she marked the women and children, also across the bridge of the nose, and they marked her. Then she marked the men on the side of the face. After that she picked up the buckskin and shook it to the four directions, beginning with the east. Then more presents were given out.[1]

White Painted Woman is usually credited with the establishment of the puberty ceremony, and her son, Child of the Water, is often associated with her in this undertaking. After Child of the Water had dispatched the monsters and there were many people and different tribes, the girl's puberty rite became known. There was a woman who had a daughter who was almost grown and ready for her first flow. Child of the Water and White Painted Woman taught them what to do. They gave a little feast the day she menstruated. Then they prepared a big feast. They obtained a man to sing for her in the big tipi. The best masked dancers were prepared off in the mountains and led in. Spruce trees were cut down for the tipi. When all was ready, everyone was invited, and they came from every direction and far away places. The celebration was held for four days. The people had a good time at the dancing. First came the masked dancers, followed by the partner dances.[2]

During the ceremony, the pubescent girl became White Painted Woman. During the four days and nights of the rite and for four days thereafter she was addressed and referred to only as White Painted Woman. Her dress and decoration were a duplication of the costume White Painted Woman wore during her stay on earth, and

Emma Tuklonen in puberty dress.

Daughter of Naiche, chief of the
Chiricahua, in puberty dress.

her very name was symbolic of the body paint she wore. At one point in the ritual the initiate was painted with white clay so that the promise of her name might be actualized. The acts, the songs, and the prayers associated the girl with her divine namesake; the ceremonial tipi itself was described as "the home of White Painted Woman"; and the young girl became the image of the real White Painted Woman.[3]

First menstruation and the puberty ceremony, or Sunrise Ceremony, were vital transition points in a Chiricahua girl's life. Before this she was called a girl, afterward, a woman, and was considered of marriageable age.

The ceremony was a social, economic, and ritual center for the entire community, and it was expected that every girl would go through the Sunrise rite. A girl who failed to do so was not discriminated against, but it was said that she would not be healthy and would not live long. Only a poor or foolish girl would pass through this phase of her life-journey without the proper ceremonial help and the accompanying popular recognition. Preparations for the rite began as soon as it became evident that the girl was becoming a young woman, and they were such as to tax the resources of any family. Therefore, individuals outside the relationship group would also lend aid, and exceptional generosity was the order of the day.[4]

The dress that the girl always wore during the ceremony in early days was made from five doeskins or buckskins: two for the top, two for the skirt, and one for the moccasins. The girl's mother, grandmother, or a close female relative might make the outfit, or if any of these lacked the required skill an outsider would be hired. Prescribed rules were followed. The tail suspended from the back hem of the top must be that of a black-tailed doe. For the upper garment the skin side of the top faced outward; for the skirt the flesh side was out. As deer skins became harder to obtain, an adjustment was sometimes made wherein a skin top was worn over a regular but attractive full and colorful cloth skirt.[5]

All the garments were decorated with beaded or painted designs symbolizing the powers that would be appealed to on behalf of the girl. These included the morning star, the crescent moon, a stepped design for the puberty dwelling, circles for the sun, and arcs for the rainbow. The buckskin dress itself was colored yellow, the hue of pollen, by either rubbing yellow ocher on the skin or dying it in a liquid prepared from algerita roots. When completed, the dress was blessed by having someone sing for it. Men sometimes did this, but the singer was usually an old woman who sang for as long as two months. She was paid for these services, tying on amulets and singing for every piece of fringe.[6]

Three principal people were retained to play lead roles in the ceremony: an attendant, a singer, and a masked dancer shaman.

Since, in 1913, the Chiricahua fortunes began to merge with those of the Mescalero, and because their puberty ceremonies were quite similar anyway, it will suffice to describe the ritual itself in the Mescalero section.

Those who would like comprehensive details of the Chiricahua ceremony will find them beautifully set forth in Morris Opler's *An Apache Life-Way*, pages 82–134.

For many years now the Mescalero and Chiricahua have joined together in their annual celebrations of the Sunrise ritual.[7]

6 Religion, Cosmology, and the Supernatural Powers

Chiricahua ritual, poetry, and prayer often refer to the time "when the earth was new" or "when the earth was created," yet there is no tale that describes the event. Life Giver is given credit for the creation of the universe, but there are no details about the act. Ideas concerning the relations of the earth, the heavenly bodies, and the forces of nature are often mixed with those about personal supernatural power or folk beliefs. Feminine qualities are attributed to the earth, and in all ceremonial contexts the earth is called by a term that is said to mean "Earth Woman." But, except as it is thought of and expressed by the few shamans who obtain supernatural power from it, the earth is not personified, nor does it appear as a Supernatural in the myths. Some people gain supernatural power from the sun, stars, and constellations. Others use them for the practical purpose of computing the passage of time and the change of seasons.[1]

Lightning and thunder are thought of as persons from whom power can be obtained. Thunderstorms are good when they are mild, bad when they do harm. Lightning is the arrow of the Thunder People, the flash is the flight of the "arrow," and the noise is the shouting of the real person, the one who is back of lightning and thunder. Long ago the Thunder People acted as hunters for humans and with their arrows killed all the game the tribe could use. Human ingratitude moved them to withdraw their assistance. One must be very careful about offending Thunder People, and prayers are offered

Killer of Enemies, Child of the Water, and the giant.

to them during a storm. Sickness can be induced by or through Thunder, and special observances and curative rites exist to cope with it.[2]

There is a mythological association between water and lightning. In the most common version of the birth of the culture hero, his mother is impregnated by Water. In a variant, Lightning strikes at the mother four times and thus causes her to conceive Child of the Water. Another version adds that after the impregnation, Lightning tests the hero, discovers him to be his son, and later helps him conquer a giant. In another myth there is a quarrel and division

237

between Thunder and Wind concerning their respective abilities. When they separate, the earth suffers from alternate floods and droughts. Finally a meeting is arranged, and, with Sun as mediator, they agree to work together once more. Thunder then creates four persons and sends them out in the four directions. They are told that whenever the earth trembles, they should come together at the center. Now Lightning and Wind use their power to make the earth as it was before, with green grass and the proper amount of water.[3]

At this point the animals of the mythological period appear, looking and speaking like men. Coyote is a trickster with few redeeming qualities. He turns benefactor by stealing fire from those who've hoarded it and spreading it throughout the world, but, by opening a bag that he has been told to leave untouched, he looses darkness. Only the night creatures enjoy this; the rest do not. The moccasin game is arranged to determine whether day shall come and which side, day or darkness, will be vanquished. The side of the day creatures wins, the horizon to the east brightens, but a few of the losers escape—the snake, the owl, and the bear—and these are still considered power creatures that can harm men. During this period Coyote makes death inevitable for mankind by throwing a stone into the water and declaring that, if it sinks, living beings shall experience physical death. In fact, Coyote's behavior creates a "path" that man has been obliged to follow. All the wicked things that man does "Coyote did first." Gluttony, lying, theft, adultery, incest, and the like were introduced by Coyote and have become inescapable for those who "follow Coyote's trail."[4]

White Painted Woman has existed from the beginning. Killer of Enemies is variously described as a brother of White Painted Woman, an older son, a twin brother of Child of the Water, and even as the husband of White Painted Woman and therefore the stepfather of the culture hero. In the most common versions he appears as an older and already grown brother of Child of the Water when the culture hero is born. During this period White Painted Woman and Killer of Enemies share the earth with human beings and with monsters who prey upon the human beings and prevent them from thriving. One of them, Giant, consumes a number of White Painted Woman's children as she attempts to rear them. Finally she is impregnated by Water and gives birth to Child of the Water, who is protected from Giant by being hidden from him on numerous occasions. Child of the Water grows with miraculous speed, and soon the brothers hunt together. One day they encounter Giant, and Child of the Water slays his colossal foe. After this he kills or conquers other monsters, birds, and animals. Those he lets live he forces to serve man. For example, he uses the feathers of the monster eagle to create the birds that exist today. Now, White Painted Woman and Child of the Water instruct the Chiricahua in the girls' puberty ceremony, and Killer of Enemies frees the game animals from an underground "animal home" in which they have been kept by Crow. When the survival of mankind is guaranteed, the supernaturals retire to their sky homes.[5]

Opler believes that Christian influence and White contact have brought certain additions to the Chiricahua world-view. One of these is a flood story, which has been "incompletely synchronized" with other mythological events. Another is the story of the creation of man. "In keeping with the feeling that actual deeds are to be attributed to the culture hero rather than to Life Giver, it is said that Child of the Water shaped people from mud or produced them from a cloud . . . [creating] the White man at the same time as the Indian. In the division of the goods of the earth, Child of the Water chooses for . . . the Chiricahua, and Killer of Enemies for the white man—the former selecting the bow and arrow, the forested mountains, and the wild foods; the latter choosing mineral-rich lands, the gun, and agricultural food staples." Understandably, then, Killer of Enemies is considered the less heroic of the two brothers and even cowardly. Missionary teachings concerning the importance of the

Bible are also included in folklore. A man, sometimes named Herus, whose name Opler thought to be a corruption, through the Spanish, of the name Jesus, comes into possession of a book whose "loss will result in the captivity and misfortune of his people. At his death the book is burned, according to custom, with the rest of his possessions, and the dire results foretold come to pass."[6]

The Supernatural Mountain People "are of more importance than any so far mentioned, with the possible exception of Child of the Water and White Painted Woman." They are not made known during the period when the animals spoke like people but appear in a separate series. "They live in the mountains and have many children. There are girls, boys, women, and old men there. The real masked dancers are the masked dancers of these people." Opler employs the name Mountain People in reference to the total population of mountain-dwelling Supernaturals, and the term Mountain Spirits in speaking of those of the Mountain People who act as dancers. "It is the Mountain Spirits who are impersonated by the masked dancers of the Chiricahua."[7]

Two kinds of Water Beings are also mentioned. One, a beneficent Supernatural, is called Controller of Water. He lets the rain loose or shuts it off. Men sing to him if they know his song. If people believe and learn his song, they can get rain. Water Monster is a fearful being who appears either in human form or as a large serpent. He is responsible for anything that disappears in the water.[8]

The important functions of the Mountain People and of their most important representatives, the Mountain Spirits, are set forth in several myths. One describes the curing of two children, one legless and one blind. Abandoned, these two try vainly to follow their people, with the blind boy carrying the cripple and being guided by his directions. Then the Mountain People find them and take them to their holy mountain home. Here the boys are cured and they return to their parents. Another myth describes how they assist a man who is being pursued by many enemies. He runs, praying, toward a home of the Mountain People. In response the Mountain Spirits rush out, surround the enemy, and drive them into a cave which then closes upon them. This tale emphasizes the role of the Mountain People in guarding the tribal territory and defending the people from enemies and epidemics.[9]

A third myth reveals the care that must be exercised during the masked dancer ceremony and explains the prominent place of the clown. A medicine man informs the people that he is going to paint masked dancers at a distant mountain. He advises everyone, except the dancers and those who will assist him in preparing them, to stay on the flats below, and he tells them that they are not to call out the names of the dancers when the performance begins. But a little girl disobeys and is caught by the Mountain People. The shaman tries to intercede for her and finally hides her under the dance fire. The displeased Mountain Spirits now come and take the place of their impersonators in dancing. On each of the first three nights a Mountain Spirit of a different color leads the search for the girl but does not find her. On the fourth night the clown heads the line. He finds her, and for her disobedience the girl is slain. A fourth myth explains the penalty for disrespect toward the Mountain Spirits and indicates what happens when it occurs. When masked dancers are joined by two mysterious strangers who are excellent performers, the people seek to learn their identity. When the last dance of the fourth night is completed, riders stationed on swift horses pursue the two strangers. But a rock wall opens to receive the two beings, and the men realize that they have pursued actual Mountain Spirits. "Not long after that disease broke out among them and killed many of them."[10] It is easy to see why the Mountain Spirits are held in such fear and reverence that those who have no ceremony for them are hesitant even to discuss them.

Masked dancer ceremonies always originate in a personal supernatural experience, though those who possess them may later teach them to others. A shaman with Mountain Spirit power can perform his rite without dancers if there is a sudden emergency or if the full ceremony would be too costly for his patient. Also, if he is not able to find enough dancers, he uses only their headdresses, placing them against the body of his patient and then holding them out to the cardinal directions to dispatch the sickness.[11]

There are numerous ceremonies to cure sickness, but the prevention of epidemics is a main function of the Gan impersonators. In such instances the clown, whose role is that of messenger and funmaker at the girl's puberty rite, fulfills the important role and reveals his power. At times of special danger, such as an epidemic, another masked dancer, Black One, is sometimes made. There are three different grades of masked dancers. There are the regular Gans; there is the clown, who is "dangerous"; and there is Black One, who is supposed to be "very dangerous." His headdress does not have the usual wooden frame above his black buckskin or cloth face mask. He just has feathers in a bunch at the top of the mask. His body is painted black all over. He carries spruce in his hands and has spruce tied to each arm. Sometimes he carries wands. He wears a skirt of woven yucca, which reaches almost to the ground. He does not dance, he remains silent, and he does not mix with the others. Any who touch him will be harmed. Only one Black One is made for something bad, "to keep everything bad away."[12]

All three types of masked dancer may appear in the same ceremony to stave off epidemics. On occasion the Mountain People transmit their messages to the people through the Black One. But more often it is the leader or one of the members of the regular masked dancer group who fulfills this role by receiving a vision while dancing. Ceremonies conducted for the public good are usually undertaken in response to requests from a group of people. The masked dancers act to both keep illness away and diagnose the trouble when people are sick. If witchcraft is discovered, the impersonators may have to expose a sorcerer by pointing him out with their wands. Usually the leader of the group does this. The dancers are also called upon to control the weather. When the performance of the masked dance at the girl's puberty rite is threatened by stormy weather, a shaman will gesture to the directions with a headdress in order to drive the clouds away.[13]

There is a present belief in "animal homes," places within caves or mountains where game is hidden when it is hard to find. Opler feels it is evident that the Mountain People are considered "not only the denizens of a given mountain but also the custodians of the wild life ranging in a vicinity. Often the power-acquisition stories [of the Chiricahua] have the 'holy homes' of the Mountain People richly populated with game animals. . . . Anyone who is in the vicinity of a home of the Mountain People, whether he has power from them or not, sprinkles pollen toward the holy place" and prays for protection against enemies and other harm while they are near him. Those who are in need are advised to pray to the Mountain People, and are assured they will come from the mountains and protect them. If a man is in trouble he might ask Life Giver to help him, but if he gets a ceremony in answer, it will come from some other source, like lightning or an animal, and not directly from Life Giver. Nevertheless, it is his prayer to Life Giver that starts it. When a person has a special ceremony such as Lightning, he will pray directly to Lightning and will not call on Life Giver. But many feel that Life Giver is answering through this other source. Opler feels certain that Life Giver is a response "to European doctrine." However, his informants claim that "Life Giver was an old conception. The very old Indians pray this way. Some old Indians who don't know the first thing about Christianity the way the preacher speaks of it, pray this way. . . . We think of Life Giver as a spirit of no particular sex. We do not attribute deeds to Life Giver. No pollen would be thrown to Life Giver."[14]

"Child of the Water figures prominently in [Chiricahua] religious traditions and ritual. However, it is believed that his work was largely completed when he departed from earth. . . . Now he is almost a sky-god, magnificent and rather remote. Occasionally, someone believes that Child of the Water has 'talked' to him . . . through the medium of dreams." The situation of White Painted Woman is much the same. "Perhaps the most important use of this supernatural in rites now is a symbolic one." For instance, in a certain Lightning ceremony dramatizing the legend of the birth of the cultural hero, the earth is referred to as White Painted Woman. It is an association found in more than one context. In any political or religious speech the earth is called "Earth Woman" and in reality the reference is to White Painted Woman.[15]

Amulets and Phylacteries

According to Bourke, in the 1880s both men and women wore amulets, called *tzi-daltai,* made of wood which had been struck by lightning, generally pine, cedar, or fir. Such wood was highly valued and not to be sold. The pieces were shaved very thin and carved in a simple semblance of the human form. They were much like the rhombus, but much smaller, and were also decorated with incised lines representing lightning. They were often attached to cords around the necks of children or to their cradleboards. They were all unpainted. An Apache named Deguele consented to exhibit to Bourke a Gan, or god, that he carried about his person. He said the Captain could have it for three ponies. It was made of a flat piece of lath, unpainted except for the designs. The figures were drawn upon it in yellow, with a narrow black band, excepting three snake heads, which were black with white eyes. Flat pearl buttons were fastened at two points and a small eagle-down feather was tied on each side of the board. The rear of the amulet was almost an exact reproduction of the front. Its owner assured Bourke that he prayed to it at all times when in trouble, that he could learn from it where his ponies were when stolen and which was the right direction when lost, and that when drought had parched his crops the amulet would never fail to bring rain in abundance to revive and strengthen them. The symbols consisted of the rain cloud, serpent lightning, the rainbow, raindrops, and the cross of the four winds.

Small amulets such as these were also to be found within the buckskin medicine cases that the shamans wore suspended from cords around their necks or waists.[16]

Bourke used the term "phylactery" to describe any piece of buckskin or other material upon which were inscribed certain characters or symbols of a religious or "medicine" nature, and which was worn attached to the person seeking to be benefited by it. The phylactery differed from the amulet in that it was concealed and kept as secret as possible. The phylactery, itself a medicine, might also be employed as a wrapping for other medicine and thus increase its own power. The Apache in general objected to having their "medicine" scrutinized and touched, and Bourke had no end of difficulty in convincing the owners to let him have even a glimpse of their phylacteries.

The first phylactery he was allowed to examine was tightly rolled in "at least a half a mile" of orange-colored silk cloth obtained from some of the cavalry posts. After being uncovered, it was found to consist of a small folded piece of buckskin two inches square, upon which were drawn red and yellow crooked lines, which the Apache owner said represented the red and yellow snake. Inside the buckskin were a piece of green chalchihuitl, a small cross made from a lightning-riven pine twig, and two very small perforated shells. The cross was called *intchi-dijin,* the black wind.

The second phylactery he examined consisted of a piece of buckskin of the same size as the other, "but either on account of age or for some other reason no characters could be discerned upon it." It was wrapped around a tiny bag of hoddentin, which in turn held a small but clear crystal of quartz and four eagle-down feathers. The

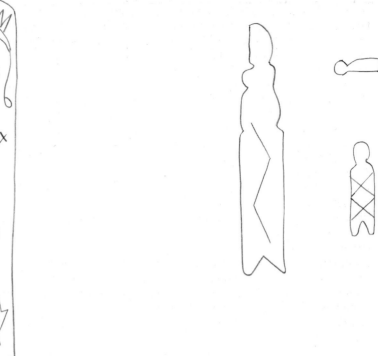

T.E.Mails

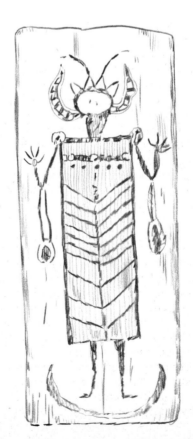

242

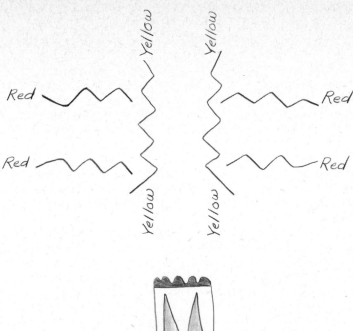

Opposite: *Amulets (9th Annual Report BAE, pp. 587–589)*. Left: *Phylacteries (9th Annual Report BAE, p. 592)*. Below: *Medicine sash (9th Annual Report BAE, p. 593)*.

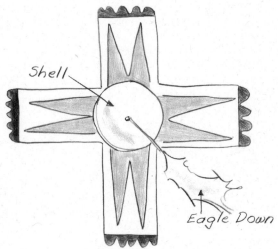

owner explained that this phylactery "contained not merely the 'medicine' or power of the crystal, the hoddentin, and the *itza-chu*, or eagle, but also of the *shoz-dijiji*, or black bear, the *shoz-lekay*, or white bear, the *shoz-litzogue*, or yellow bear, and the *klij-litzogue*, or yellow snake, though just in what manner he could not explain."[17]

Medicine Shirts and Sashes

Bourke, writing in the 1880s, believed that the medicine shirts of the Apache did not require an extended description. The symbolism was different for each one, but might be generalized as typical of the sun, moon, stars, rainbow, lightning, snake, clouds, rain, hail, tarantula, centipede, and some one or more of the Gan or gods.

The medicine sashes followed the pattern of the medicine shirts, being smaller in size but with the same symbolic decoration. Similar ornamentation was found upon the amulets that were made of lightning-struck pine or other wood. All of these were believed, among their other virtues, to protect the wearer from the arrows, lances, or bullets of the enemy.[18]

7 The Gans
1880s

Captain Bourke was once with a party of Apache young men who led him to one of the sacred caves of their people, in which they found a great quantity of ritualistic paraphernalia of all sorts. They told him that in former times they stood down there and looked up to the top of the mountain to watch the Gans come down.

The Gan dancer headdress was known to the Chiricahua, in

Bourke's interpretation, as the *ich-te,* a contraction from *chas-a-i-wit-te.* Some of the symbols painted on the headdresses meant the following: The round piece of tin in the center was the sun; the irregular arch underneath it was the rainbow; stars and lightning were depicted on the side slats and under them; parallelograms with serrated edges were clouds; the pendant green sticks were raindrops; snakes and snake heads were painted on both horizontal and vertical slats, the heads on the horizontal slats being representative of hail.

The feathers of the eagle were used to conciliate that powerful bird; turkey feathers were an appeal to the Mountain Spirits; and white gull feathers appealed to the Spirits of the Water. Small pieces of nacreous shell were also attached, as well as one or two fragments of the chalchihuitl stone.

The Gan or Mountain Spirit Dance itself was called *cha-ja-la.* Bourke described a Chiricahua dance he saw at Fort Marion, St. Augustine, Florida, in 1887, when the Apache were confined there as prisoners. A great many of the captives had been suffering from sickness of one kind or another, and twenty-three of the children had died; as a consequence, the medicine men were having the Mountain Spirit Dance. A huge fire had been built. Ramon, the old medicine man, was beating violently upon a drum, which had been improvised of a soaped rag drawn tightly over the mouth of an iron kettle that held a little water. Although acting as leader, he was not painted or adorned in any special way.

Three dancers were having the finishing touches put to their bodily decoration. They were given an undercoating of greenish brown, and a yellow snake was painted on each arm, the head toward the shoulder blade. The snake on one arm of one of the men had a head at each extremity. Each man had a design in yellow placed on his back and chest, but no two designs were exactly alike. One man had a yellow bear on his chest, four inches long and three inches high, and on his back a Gan of the same color and dimensions. The second man had a similar bear on his chest, but a zigzag for lightning on his back. The third man had the zigzag design on both back and chest. All three wore fringed buckskin dance skirts and

Above: *The clown, or "Gray One."*
Right: *The Gan impersonator at a Chiricahua camp.*

244

Flashlight photo of Sacred Dance of the Geronimo Apache Indians, only Photo made of this dance Copyrighted E Bates

moccasins reaching to the knees. Each man held, one in each hand, two four-foot-long wands ornamented with lightning lines in blue.

As they began to dance, the dancers emitted a peculiar whistling noise, bent slowly to the right, then to the left, then frontward, then backward, until their heads were level with their waists. Then they spun round in full circle on the left foot, back again in a reverse circle to the right, and raced around the little group of tents in their camp, "making cuts and thrusts with their wands to drive the maleficent spirits away." These preliminaries occupied a few moments only; then the medicine men advanced to a mother who was holding up her sick baby in its cradleboard. The mother remained kneeling while the dancers thrust their wands at, upon, around, and over the cradleboard.

The baby was held toward each of the cardinal points, so as to face the point directly opposite. While at each position, each of the Gan dancers in succession made all the passes and gestures just described, then took the cradleboard in his hands, pressed it to his chest, lifted it to the sky, next to the earth, and finally to the four cardinal points, all the time dancing and making noises, while the mother and her women friends added to the din with piercing shrieks and hoots.

That ended the ceremonies for that first night so far as the baby was concerned, but the dancers continued to dance. Bourke's understanding was that the dancing had to continue until the firewood was completely consumed; any other course would entail bad luck.

The dance was continued for four nights, and the colors and the symbols painted upon the Gan dancers' bodies varied from night to night. Each Gan had long strips of red flannel tied to his arms just above the elbow. The headdress of the first of the dancers, "who seemed to be the leading one," was so elaborate that the swift movements and the meager light supplied by the flickering fires made it impossible to portray. "It was very much like that of number three, but so fully covered with the plummage of the eagle, hawk, and, apparently, the owl, that it was difficult to assert this positively." The hide mask was spotted black and white and shaped in front like the snout of a mountain lion. The dancer's back was painted with large arrowheads

The caption reads, "Flashlight photo of Sacred Dance of the Geronimo Apache Indians, only photo made of this dance. Copyrighted E. Bates." No date given (DPL). The event is actually a puberty rite. The clown is mimicking a White soldier. The horns of the Gan mask are very similar to Mescalero designs.

in brown and white. The second dancer had on his back a figure that terminated between the shoulders in the form of a cross. The third man's back was simply whitened with clay.

The Gan headdresses "were made of slats of the Spanish bayonet, unpainted, excepting that on number two was a figure in black, which could not be made out, and that the horizontal crosspieces on number three were painted blue."

The masks covering the dancers' heads were of blackened buckskin for the two men whose masks were fastened around their necks by sashes. The neckpiece of the third Gan was painted red; the two false eyes appended to the masks seemed to be glass knobs or brass buttons.[1]

Left: *Drawing based on a sketch reported to be of a Chiricahua Gan headdress (MNMP). No authentication available.* Below: *Drawing based on a sketch reported to be of a Chiricahua Gan headdress (MNMP). No authentication available.*

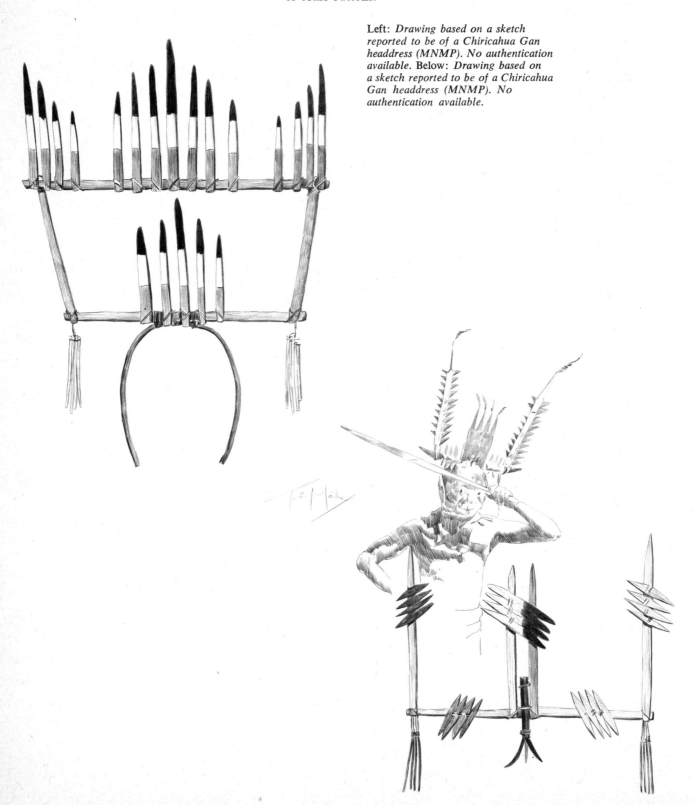

Chiricahua Gan impersonators.

247

1930s

Opler is the major source of information about the Chiricahua Gan dancers at this time. According to his account, the painting and dressing of the masked dancers began at sunset. The men who were to dance assembled at a brush shelter erected some distance from the place where they were to perform, for it was dangerous, especially to the women and children, to have them "made" close to the camps. Since the dancers were impersonating Supernaturals who dwelt in the mountains, a place in the foothills was most likely to be chosen. There the masked dancer shaman waited, with dancing costumes and paints. The medicine man rarely painted the dancers himself. He directed helpers who did this while he prayed and sang, accompanying himself with a buckskin-covered pottery drum. Upon this drum he drew symbols with pollen, such as that of the sun, to keep his throat from becoming hoarse.[2]

The masked dancer shaman might have some trouble assembling his dance group, for the impersonator of the Supernatural had to follow stringent rules. He couldn't wash his paint off—it either had to be sweated off while he was dancing or rubbed off. If he washed, it would cause a big rain to come. If the dancer made a mistake and didn't perform properly, he was certain to get sick. It was dangerous for one dancer to touch another who had been made by a different shaman. Also, the power of one masked dancer maker might be stronger than that of another and cause a spasm in the mouth or ear, or eye trouble, or a swollen face. The only way to cure this was to go through a ceremony and have the masked dancers blow the sickness away. If a dancer placed his mask over his head without the proper ritual gestures, he might go mad temporarily. He must show the proper reverence for the power of the office. If any of the violations led to trouble, the dancer must turn for help to his shaman, who always had certain things he could do to correct the situation. The dancer had to observe suitable modesty and remember that he was but an instrument of the rite and not its owner, else he too was in serious trouble. No one should make his own costume, and only those who were given the right to paint the dancers should do so. The dancer worked for the one who had the power to do the ceremony. Furthermore, a man must have natural aptitude and special physical condition to become a successful dancer. Some excelled from the beginning, and others remained mediocre performers for their entire careers. The amount a man earned and the number of requests for his services were largely determined by his talents.[3]

The virtuoso among dancers could on occasion be particular about the conditions under which he would perform. One might demand long wands so that he wouldn't have to bend much to place them on the ground. Another might insist on a new mask for every performance. Within his own sphere the masked dancer was relatively independent. Sometimes there were as many as sixteen masked dancers performing for the puberty rite, and men resented dancing where it was crowded. Therefore they could dance about four times and then stop if they wanted to. In such instances they simply removed their costumes and joined the spectators at the dance. Also, they could ignore the calls from the people to return and dance while they were in the woods resting between performances. After all, at puberty rites they were just entertaining the people.[4] Like all things the Apache did, Gan preparations and activities had their humorous moments. Opler records an instance wherein a leader on the way to the dance-grounds stumbled into an arroyo in the dark, to the utter delight of his dance group and of the people when they learned of it the next day. In fact, the pleasures of dancing were such that accomplished dancers, in spite of the strenuous nature of the task, were reluctant to withdraw even when they grew old and had to pull their skin smooth to put the paint on. Also, if a dancer wished to become a ceremonialist of the rite, his experience as an impersonator made it easier for him to learn.[5]

Chiricahua or Mescalero Gan impersonator.
(After Opler, Apache Life-Way, *p. 101).*

249

Chiricahua or Mescalero Gan mask (Museum of the American Indian, Heye Foundation).

The clown—"Gray One," "Long Nose," or "White Painted" —was prepared at the same time as the other performers. He wore a mask of scraped rawhide, sometimes made with a big nose or big ears. He wore only moccasins and a breechclout; his body was covered with white paint. It was said that it was good to be a clown before one danced as a masked dancer in order to get used to the dances. For social occasions, it was not necessary to have a clown with each set of dancers, and sometimes the shaman did not paint a clown. But when they danced to cure sickness, the clown became the most important dancer, for he had more power than any other masked dancer.[6] Except when he carried messages for the Gans, the clown would not talk to the people when he danced at the time of the puberty rite, for it was dangerous to do so while impersonating a supernatural power. He only motioned, and he was just there to make fun. The people gave him directions, and he followed them, making a fool of himself just for the fun of it. He had no special position in the line of dancers, and it was not dangerous to touch him. During the puberty performances, the clown was the servant and messenger of the masked dancers, carrying requests to the musicians for certain dance songs and to spectators with personal items.[7]

Opler says that in preparing for their performances, the men who were to dance stripped, put on their skirts and moccasins, and stood or sat facing the east. The medicine man then blew smoke to the directions while reciting an extemporaneous prayer about the relationship of the Mountain Spirits and the performers. The painting was begun with the leader, but it didn't matter which dancer was finished first. Helpers applied the paint with sticks that had been pounded, softened, and sometimes turned back at the end. Even the fingers were used if the work had to be done quickly. The helpers were usually familiar with the designs; what information they lacked was supplied by the shaman. Sometimes the dancers assisted by painting each other.

While the painting was going on the medicine man sang and beat his pottery drum. If these songs were not sung in the right way, a masked dancer would drop like a man knocked out if he should touch another masked dancer while performing. The songs also called on the Mountain Spirits to give the dancers endurance. They were sung in no particular order. In general, songs for a puberty rite dealt with the holy home where the ritual was learned from the Mountain Spirits, with the sounds made by the pendant sticks of the headdress and by the bells or tin cones of the skirt as the dancers moved to the fire, and with the cardinal directions from which the Mountain Spirits guarded the Chiricahua against sickness and danger. When the body painting was finished, the dancers ate a generous meal that had been provided for them by the sponsors. It would be. nearly dark now, and soon the great fire would be kindled below for the entrance of the masked dancers.

As the shaman chanted a set of four ancient songs, the dancers lined up in a row facing the east, headdresses in hand, praying and asking to be blessed. Then they turned clockwise, calling out at each mention of the Mountain Spirits and motioning with their headdresses to the directions. The buckskin masks had been moistened so that they would be pliable. When the singing ended, each dancer, including the clown, spat into his mask four times, made three ritual feints toward himself with the headdress, and pulled the mask over his head the fourth time. At this point the group was ready to move in single file down the hillside, led by their most experienced dancer.[8]

Their splendid costumes consisted of high moccasins and yellow-colored buckskin skirts. The skirt was held in place by a broad hide belt ornamented with brass tacks or silver conchos. From the skirt were suspended horizontal bands of fringe of various lengths. Some skirts also had narrow strips of beading, and in later days tin cones were added to the ends of the fringe. The arms and upper part of the body, except for the face, were entirely covered with clay and

250

Chiricahua Gan performers;
artifacts from Fort Sill, Okla.

charcoal paint. Black, white, brown, and yellow were the usual colors; sometimes blue was added. The designs consisted of narrow bands of contrasting color, a branching design to represent cactus, a saw-toothed element, a stepped line, a zigzag line, the triangle, the Greek cross, a pattée type cross, and a four-pointed star that symbolized the basic design for the horns of the headdress. The designs could be the same for all four nights, the same design might be used the first and third nights and another the second and fourth nights, or different designs could be applied each evening. Occasionally, the painted designs on the leader varied slightly from those of the others.[9] Each dancer carried painted wooden wands in each hand; one or both of those carried by the leader might have a cross-piece at the handle, but the others had no cross-pieces (as did those of the Western Apache), and they were pointed at the end opposite the handle, like a sword. Four- to six-foot-long narrow buckskin streamers with eagle feathers were tied to the upper arms. In later days, when hides were harder to obtain, colorful blankets or shawls were wrapped around the waist for skirts, and after that canvas was used.

The lower part of the mask was a buckskin hood, later cotton cloth, which fitted snugly over the head and was gathered at the neck by a drawstring. Two tiny round holes were cut for the eyes, and sometimes one for the mouth. The buckskin or cloth was usually painted black, but yellow, blue, or two tones were also used. When they were not a solid color, the design elements employed were the same as those mentioned for the body. A piece of abalone shell or turquoise might be tied to the outside front of the hood at the forehead or nose. The abalone shell was strong, and the masked dancers were supposed to have the same physical strength as the abalone.[10]

Attached to the top of the Chiricahua hood were the uprights or "horns," so called because the Mountain Spirits were associated with the protection and guardianship of game animals, the most important of which had horns. They were made from pieces of oak, split, soaked in water, and heated until they could be fashioned into spread and curved prongs. The spread lower end was secured to the

251

top of the cloth hood. The upper end was connected to the huge but light yucca or sotol frame that rose above it. A bunch of turkey feathers or green juniper was tied to the oak and the frame at the point where they were joined. The superstructure of wooden slats strongly resembled a great candelabra balanced on the top of the dancer's head. The usual Chiricahua version was basically a horizontal bar to which vertical pieces of varying heights were tied with thongs at the two ends and in the middle. From each end of the horizontal support two or four short lengths of wood called "earrings" were hung in a pendant group by a thong. These struck against one another like soft chimes, making a sound that signaled the approach of the dancers. The sound was associated with the Mountain Spirits themselves as they moved about. Eagle-down feathers were tied to the tops of the vertical pieces. The colors used for the uprights were black, yellow, and green; red would be used only by a witch on a Chiricahua masked dancer horn. To make the colors, the juice of the yucca leaf was mixed with charcoal, yellow ocher, a decoction of algerita root, and turquoise. The addition of the yucca juice made the colors permanent. Green and blue were not differentiated in Chiricahua terminology; both colors were used and both were referred to as blue.[11]

8 Raiding and Warfare

Until the Chiricahua were sent off to prison in Florida, raiding was viewed as a regular and legitimate part of the Chiricahua economy. When the people were in need, they raided other nations or other tribes, so that raiding was essentially an economic pursuit. Raiders went out in small numbers seeking horses, cattle, or whatever else the families required; they attempted to avoid encounters with the enemy.

Raids were organized by the camp leader, who called for volunteers. Five to ten men were enough. Equipment mentioned by various sources consisted of weapons, a robe or two, and a plaited rawhide rope. A small bag of food with three days' rations was tied to the belt, and it is said that water, in a bag made from an animal's intestines, was carried in the hand. At least one man would bring a fire drill. Booty was evenly divided among the participants, with the leader often getting less because he was supposed to be generous.[1]

Sometimes raiding parties were discovered by the enemy, and Apache warriors might be killed. This called for a revenge war party in return.

All large war parties were undertaken to avenge deaths. Usen, the Supreme Being, the one Geronimo and Niño Cochise describe as the Creator and Ruler, had not commanded the Apache to love their enemies, and it was a sacred obligation to avenge the wrongs done to them. Nor was a life for a life enough to compensate for a loss. For every Apache killed, many lives would be required. In the end, the Apache came to believe that their point of view was little different from that of the Whites who said one thing, yet who slaughtered Apache men, women, and children at every opportunity. The difference was that the Indians were honest about it.

A relative of the deceased got the expedition under way by asking the leader to organize it. If he agreed, requests for volunteers went out, while relatives of the dead enlisted as many as possible of their own families. It seems that the size of the response was often determined by the importance of those who asked. If there was an experienced leader among the families of those slain, he would be in charge of the war party. Not the least of his abilities would be knowing where the caches of food and ammunition were stored that would be needed along the way.

A war dance would be held that night in preparation for departure the next day. It was a dramatization of warfare itself, and when a warrior joined in, it served as his pledge to go and to fight bravely. The war dance was considered a plea for success and safety in the coming conflict, and as such was considered a profound religious experience.[2]

The war dance called for a principal singer of war songs whose supernatural power was associated with wars and raiding. Male singers assisted him and also served as drummers. The songs were prayers that called for manliness, and the participants were expected to respond affirmatively. Songs also named the enemy and expressed the hope that he would be defeated.

The men sang softly, accompanied by drums. They never shouted, since to do so in battle meant certain death, although guns were fired. The spectators were permitted to shout, however. Some men who danced carried ceremonially made items like lances, war caps, or shields. No paint was worn. Hair was held in place with a headband; moccasins were worn over bare legs. The typical Chiricahua breechclout, which consisted of a long, narrow strip in front coming almost down to the knees and a broad strip in back that came down farther, was pulled through the legs and tucked in the belt for the dance, for it was fixed like that in battle to get it out of the way. Shirts were also worn, but not tucked in.

Four men started the dance in fixed traditional fashion, then the others who intended to go along joined in. Those who had boasted they would go while they were drunk, but held back now, were taunted and called out by name. It is said that few refused.[3]

Women at the war dance were all called White Painted Woman, and they could not be referred to by their own names.

The dance ended when the bonfire had been circled four times. It was followed immediately by a round dance, and after that a partner dance of the kind that took place during the nights of the girl's puberty rite. Social dancing continued until morning.[4]

Informants differ as to precisely how long each war dance was continued. Many referred to a four-day dance as opposed to the one-night dance. Also, the party did not always start off the next morning. A day to go was set, and it might be five or six days before they left.

Certain protective steps were taken before departure to assure the success of the war party. Amulets were procured; protective war caps and jackets were fashioned or refurbished; medicine men were consulted as to the probable outcome of the expedition. The shaman conducted his ceremony; if the result was favorable, the party went— if not, the party stayed home. He also gave the participants small bags of pollen, and herbs for sickness.[5]

Since raiding and warfare were both the special interests of those who had supernatural power to find and frustrate the enemy, one or more shamans were sure to accompany a large war party. The party leader himself might have this power. In all instances the shaman's advice and predictions would receive great respect during the journey, and his ceremonies would be performed regularly as guidance from his "power" was sought.[6] Several testimonies were given in evidence of Geronimo's amazing ability to predict events accurately.[7]

The actual war journey got under way early in the morning, and the entire camp gathered to see the party off. Wives had certain ritual customs to observe while their husbands were away. Some prayed, and all relatives had to be on good behavior, as it was believed that bad behavior would bring the men bad luck.

While certain tragedies might cause the warriors to throw caution to the winds, most war excursions followed a disciplined order. When they felt secure, the warriors would sing to keep up the group's spirits.[8] In traveling, they usually took to the rocks and the mountaintops. The traveling was more difficult there, but the Apache had the stamina for it and by it evaded all but the most stubborn pursuers. Also, there were more springs and water holes in the mountains, and the army troops, burdened as they were with wagons, had to travel in the flats where they were more easily seen from the peaks.

Seldom did the war party move in a straight line. Captain Bourke testified in writing to the effectiveness of the Apache method:

Above: *Beaded buckskin war cap, front view (HM). Group unknown.* Right: *Geronimo in the last years of his life in Oklahoma (DPL). The eagle feather and cap decorations are late additions for showmanship purposes.* Below: *Apache camp during the war years, ca. 1880 (MNMP).*

"A number of simultaneous attacks were made at points widely separated, thus confusing both troops and settlers, spreading a vague sense of fear over the territory infested, and imposing on the soldiery an exceptional amount of work of the hardest conceivable sort. . . . He is fiendishly dexterous in the skill with which he conceals his own line of march. . . . He will dodge, twist and bend in all directions, doubling like a fox, scattering his party the moment a piece of rocky ground is reached."[9] Scouts were placed ahead, behind, and alongside the main body. In open areas an advance detachment was sent far ahead of the main body.[10]

A final search in all directions was made for enemies before camps were established, and in the morning another search took place. Each day the leader designated an assembly point ahead. High ground with a water supply was preferred, because it made for better observation and helped to avoid the party's being taken by surprise. If they were caught by a surprise attack, they scattered in every direction to make pursuit difficult and met at the assembly point later on. When under close pursuit, they would sometimes make an imitation camp at the assembly point, arranging shelters and small fires, and even tying up a worn-out horse. Then they would move on for several miles before actually bedding down for the night.[11] Another device was to have a few warriors drive all the animals several miles beyond where they intended to camp. Then they all climbed to a high peak and made camp, secure in the belief that pursuers would follow the animal tracks past them and not notice the camp.[12] Geronimo says that in the days of conflict with the Whites, they never camped while on a march without putting scouts out.[13]

The men of each family cluster marched with their own leader, but provided for themselves. Some might ride on horseback; others went on foot. Each man carried his own provisions in a bag held by a shoulder strap. It usually included mescal, jerky, and a fire drill. Sometimes water was carried as a shoulder loop in the intestines of animals with the ends tied. Unless women were along, each man cooked for himself. Informants claimed that men on the warpath made every effort to avoid being seen, always covering their tracks or disguising them to look like something else.[14] In an open area where the ground was soft, they sometimes walked on their heels or toes, leaving only little round holes instead of tracks.[15]

Face painting was an individual choice, but a leader of note with power might paint his men as his power directed him. It is said that Geronimo marked his men on the forehead, the sides of the face, and across the nose.[16] Hide or cloth war headbands were worn to keep the long hair out of a man's eyes in a battle.[17]

Novices, called Child of the Water, were taken along on the less hazardous raids. They were required to use a stick for scratching themselves and a reed for drinking water. They also had to use a sacred language.

If time permitted, men about to do battle removed their shirts and tucked them under their belts. That way the shirts wouldn't be lost, and the men of their party could be differentiated from the clothed soldiers. It is also suggested that the Indians' copper-colored skins blended in better with the rocks and earth as they crawled about.[18] Photographs often show a warrior with a blanket wrapped around his waist. Blankets were hard to replace and necessary equipment for travel, so they were always kept securely at hand. Geronimo mentions that the Apache even went north to trade for blankets with the Navajo.[19] The large Apache breechclout also served as a blanket in a pinch.[20] Apache moccasins were designed for easy repair, but became useless when wet: in that case emergency footgear was fashioned by tying grass to the feet with strips of yucca.[21]

The preferred attack was made quietly and early in the morning, with just enough light to see a few hundred feet. Hand-to-hand encounters were considered the best. Once the enemy was engaged, the leader and the shaman had central roles to play, with the leader

"Pickets in Victorio's stronghold, 1880–85." Photo by Wittick (MNMP).

255

Apache Indian Panti

setting an example of heroism and the shaman at the rear praying to the four directions and exhorting the men to charge. Fighting was voluntary, though, and no leader could order his men to fight. Men fought to protect their families, for revenge, and to avoid accusations of cowardice.[22] As much strategy as possible was employed in a fight, and when things went badly, a retreat was both sensible and in order.[23] Personal names were not ordinarily used, but a warrior in trouble could call another's name, and the man could not deny him. In doing battle, some men crawled along, rolling rocks the size of their heads before them for protection.[24]

If a party was forced to flee, the usual procedure was to scatter, running on rocks as much as possible to avoid leaving tracks. Clumps of grass and brush were also used to wipe out tracks. Wolf and bird calls were sometimes simulated to keep contact in a scattered group.[25] The call of a night bird and a white-winged dove are mentioned in particular.[26]

Certain traps were set to ambush pursuers: a large party traveling as a unit might divide, with half taking cover and the rest luring the enemy on until caught between the halves of the party; another device was to hide all but two men, who would decoy the enemy into following them into the midst of the rest. On occasion everyone just hid and waited.[27] Sometimes large rocks were rolled to a ridge above a trail and then pushed down upon the enemy.[28]

Signs and signals served to transmit messages, and warriors were always watching for them. Items might be tied in a tree, stones piled or pointed a certain way, and lines or sticks laid on the ground to indicate a direction. Smoke signals and mirrors were used to convey only limited amounts of information.[29] Smoke from a mountaintop meant enemies were around, and called for a careful investigation; smoke sent up from a valley meant that sickness was present. It was said that an Apache party at some distance from another group could easily determine whether or not it was friendly. If both parties built a fire to the right of where they stood, they were friends. Some experienced men could make use of the stars to travel by night. Counts of days were kept with rocks, marks on a stick, or beads on a string.[30]

In the desert, lack of water was a constant problem. Stones or sticks were placed in the mouth to start saliva. Cactus was a good moisture source. The inner parts were chewed, and the barrel cactus was like a watermelon; the top was knocked off and the pulp squeezed. A reed made a good tube to suck out the liquid. Bourke may have been right in feeling that the requirement that a novice carry a drinking tube had something to do with teaching him to have one on hand when he was on a journey. The Plains Indians were known to obtain water by riding their horses back and forth along a dry creekbed that was bordered by a still-green line of cottonwoods.[31] The Apache knew the technique, but found it easier to get water by digging with their hands in a rock basin at the foot of a dry waterfall.

It was an accepted rule among the Apache that a man should not sacrifice his life needlessly. But when the situation was hopeless, the Chiricahua stripped to his breechclout—if he had not already done so—and threw caution to the winds. Attempts were made to bring the wounded home, with medicine men applying herbs and treatments along the way. The Apache did make a truce on occasion, and were said to carry a piece of white buckskin to use as a white flag.[32]

The Chiricahua seldom took scalps because of their fear of death and ghosts.[33] Scalping was done only in retaliation after the Mexicans inaugurated the tactic. Those who had been particularly troublesome might be scalped, or perhaps the leader of an enemy party.[34] Only the Eastern band was known to display scalps or to hold scalp dances.[35]

Adult male prisoners were usually questioned and killed; occasionally they were brought back to camp, where the women carried out the execution in vicious ways. Young male prisoners might be permitted to grow up and even marry in the tribe. Women and children were usually let go. If women were taken they were

Opposite top: *U.S. Army encampment during Apache wars (MNMP).* Opposite bottom left: *"Painting for the warpath, U.S. Army scouts in Apache wars, c. 1885." Photo by Wittick (MNMP).* Opposite bottom right: *War bonnet (Apache Coll., AF). If it is Apache, possibly Eastern band. Eagle wing feathers, with silver conchos on headband.* Above: *Chiricahua medicine cap (Museum of the American Indian, Heye Foundation).*

257

Top: *Detail of war bonnet shown on page 256, showing silver conchos used on headband.* Above: *Detail of war bonnet, showing method of securing horn and feathers.*

not molested sexually, because that brought bad luck. Some informants claim that captives who stayed with the Apache for even a short time preferred to remain with them even when they were free to go.[36]

Much has been written about the Apache custom of mutilating their victims. Vivid descriptions include such reports as people being hung alive head down over a fire, stretched out and staked down in the sun to roast, buried up to the neck in the center of an anthill; of eyes being gouged and tongues torn out. The accounts stand. An infuriated Apache was indeed a remorseless foe. Some say their harsh environment and painful history fashioned them into a people without pity. The question is whether the brutal acts were a common custom, truly an Apache trait, that always asserted itself. A Warm Springs Apache claims that he saw hundreds of people killed, but "nobody tortured, nobody scalped."[37] He was with Victorio's band until he died, and never saw a scalp taken.

Geronimo explained why a group of Apache on the run usually killed even people who offered no resistance. The Apache did not want to be caught. Therefore, no witnesses, whether accidental or not, could be left alive to report their position or direction of travel to the military of either the United States or Mexico.[38] However, not everyone encountered was killed. Geronimo stated that where the Indians met with no resistance, the inhabitants were not disturbed, and only part of their possessions were taken.[39]

During the period when groups of Chiricahua broke out of the San Carlos Reservation, entire families were frequently included in the war party. In such instances the women played anything but a passive role. On one occasion, when the Apache were surrounded by Mexicans, the women dug entrenchment holes for the warriors to fight from.[40] On another, a grandmother took her place as a lookout to watch for an enemy group known to be in pursuit.[41] A third account mentions two women who accompanied a group of men. They were efficient fighters and highly skilled in dressing wounds and, as such, were exempted from the cooking and other chores ordinarily done by the women and boys.[42] In a further instance, the women in a fleeing party distributed ammunition and loaded rifles during a battle.[43]

When victorious war parties returned home, there was a great celebration. After a feast, at which time some of the pack mules might be killed and eaten, horses and cattle taken were distributed equally among the entire band.[44] However, each warrior kept the enemy items he had taken personally.[45] Victory dances lasted at least one full night, and usually continued for four days and nights, with warriors dressing as they did in battle. Dances followed the same pattern as those held before the departure of the war party. Each man had a chance to dance, and the singers described the meaning of the dancer's actions. When all the warriors had been recognized, a round dance and a circle dance followed. On the fourth night the men and women danced in separate lines, alternately approaching and moving apart, as in the girl's puberty rite. One informant mentioned a "holy singing walk" done with a single line of individuals. Conventional morality was not discarded on such important occasions as this, but more freedom than usual was allowed, as appropriate to the moment.[46]

The warriors who had died on the journey were not mentioned; no deaths were formally announced. Families received such news privately, and any ghost medicine employed thereafter to fend off evil effects was an individual matter.[47]

When a group returned home from a raid or war party without a victory or spoils to divide, the expedition was considered a disgrace. Families were pleased to know the men were safe, but there was no celebration. They were likely to be taunted by their wives and by other warriors, and would be motivated to go out again soon and do better.[48]

Harmony and singleness of purpose did not always reign

among the transient groups. Betzinez was honest enough to reveal that while sentry duty was a demanding task and a great responsibility, some of the men performed it poorly on occasion. Understandably enough, they were criticized for this by the others, and bad feelings resulted. A further cause of insecurity was the struggle for superiority that went on between leaders as they sought control. Apparently, some of these disputes were intense enough to jeopardize the expedition, and an influential and cooler man would be called upon to act as peacemaker. Betzinez goes on to say that the indifference and selfishness of different leaders, which prevented the tribe from ever becoming a strong confederation, was "a common subject among the Indians of those days."[49] However, Geronimo includes in his own story the description of an instance in the summer of 1859, when three divisions of the tribe joined in a revenge war party against the Mexicans. The Bedonkohe Apache were led by Mangus Colorado, the Chokonen Apache by Cochise, and the Nedni Apache by Whoa (Juh). They marched on foot about fourteen hours a day, made three daily stops for meals, and averaged from forty to forty-five miles a day.[50]

Since the groups that included men, women, and children who escaped from San Carlos were as much a war party as any other expedition, their mode of procedure deserves recognition here.

They moved from one range to another, following the ridges as best they could. They crossed the open areas at night, although not by preference, and fought at night only when they were unable to avoid it, for some Apache believed that one who was killed at night would walk in darkness after his death. A strong advance guard of warriors was placed in front, the women and children were in the middle, and another detachment of warriors brought up the rear. The children were tied to their horses by a rope passed under the horse's belly, or else rode behind and were tied to older youths or adults.

The horses were prodded along steadily at a fast walk or a slow trot, maintaining a pace of five or six miles an hour for half a day or night. When the horses were exhausted, the Apache stole others wherever they could. The tired horses that were trained would follow along; the rest would be herded. Women and boys, as well as men, participated in the horse thefts, and some women were as skilled in the practice as the warriors.

If there were no mountains to move in, they traveled in arroyos. Out on the desert they dug shallow trenches to hide in. The ability of all Apache to scale cliffs was taken for granted. Here the plaited rawhide ropes were put to special use. When pursuers left them no other course, the Apache killed their horses and scaled cliffs "no enemy could climb." The men tied ropes to the women and children, and hoisted them from ledge to ledge until the top was reached. Then, while the women and children moved on ahead, a few of the men remained behind to see if they could shoot the Apache scouts who always preceded the army troops.[51]

Wherever they went in perilous times, the Apache took advantage of every object they might hide behind. Silence was imperative. Babies were watched carefully, and if they cried the mothers or girls were quick to smother the sound. Others kept their hands near the nostrils of the horses to keep them from betraying a hiding place. It is said that above all, the Apache knew how to be quiet.[52]

Those who went on such trips, traveling across mountains and deserts for weeks on end, make it clear that the journeys were filled with misery and pain. There was little food, extremes of heat and cold, often no fires, and constant fatigue. The difference between the Apache and others who could not have accomplished it lay in attitude, the determination to endure whatever came without complaint. Even children carried their own emergency ration bag of food and a blanket, and neither of these things would leave their side, day or night, for months on end.[53] Sometimes the aged, or mothers caught in childbirth along the way, had to be dropped off at cave retreats known to the band, but the rest went on until a safe stronghold was reached. Not the least of their resilient qualities was the ability to laugh heartily at themselves, or at any happening that gave them an opportunity to break the misery for a moment.[54]

Enemies Against Power

Apache informants refer frequently to "enemies against power." It was of mythological origin, and thus the most important power a man could have for raiding and war. It was a personal thing. That is, men learned it on their own in communion with the Supernaturals, and each man applied it in his own way.

Grenville Goodwin collected several accounts concerning its use, which can be found in *Western Apache Raiding and Warfare*, edited by Keith H. Basso. In essence, enemies against power could be called upon by using certain sacred words, either before a raid or war party got under way, while on the journey toward the objective, or in the midst of an engagement with the enemy. There were different powers for different purposes: to bring success, to make an arrow or bullet miss its mark,[55] to avoid exhaustion, to catch horses or cattle, to provide running power, and the like.[56]

In *The Social Organization of the Western Apache*, Goodwin records John Rope's account of his receipt of a very strong war power. A great shaman bestowed it upon him, using holy words, for Rope was to be a chief. "He used all the different war-power words" on Rope for protection against guns and bullets, and also taught Rope some of his power so that he would understand it and know how to use it.

While this was going on, Rope was chosen to lead a raiding party into Mexico as part of his preparation for replacing the old chief. Then when he was actually made chief he received a war-charm bandolier, known as the "Slayer of Monsters bandoleer." It was made of four strands of buckskin, with two pairs of already twisted strands being twisted about each other. On it were tied eagle feathers—each one representing holy words—and turquoise and obsidian, standing for the swordlike weapon that Slayer of Monsters used in war. As the "bandoleer" was placed on the new chief, words were spoken over him, which he was also taught to use, for protection by the sky and by bats when he went into battle.[57]

Opler found evidence among the Chiricahua of the use of power against enemies that was similar to that of the Western Apache. It was invoked for protection, for finding and weakening the enemy, for influencing the weather, and even for controlling the length of day or night.[58]

The Novice Complex for Raid and War

When a Chiricahua boy reached puberty, the age at which the girl was elevated to womanhood by the puberty rite, he was still undergoing the training process. But unlike the girl, he was not permitted to move quickly from childhood to maturity. The duties allotted to the young woman could be graduated according to her strength. But a man had to confront the dangerous realities of warfare; the young man on a raid or war party had to cover the same distance and suffer the same hardships as the strongest member of the group.

By the time he was about sixteen, the youth was approaching the required standards. Now he was ready to serve as a novice on raids or warring expeditions, of which he must complete four before he could be accepted as a man. During this period, though he was exposed to a minimum of danger, he acquired the experience that would enable him successfully to undertake the hazards of war.[59]

Even before the boy was accepted as a novice, he was taught how to care for himself on the march, and especially what to do if he should become separated from the others. In effect, his relatives and other experienced men gave him a course in survival in every possible circumstance. There was no definite age at which a boy must join his first expedition. When he was old enough and felt ready, he volunteered. Opler states that though none were required to participate, those who wished to enjoy material benefits had hardly any other choice. Because of the practical and ceremonial ramifications, the apprenticeship trips were necessary for successful warfare, and the man who had not undergone them was not welcomed by members of a raiding party he sought to join. Some did not volunteer for the novice experience, and they were thought badly of for it. Yet the youth who was slow to volunteer was not goaded into it prematurely. If a boy felt he couldn't make it, he didn't go.[60]

Once a boy declared his intention to become a novice, he was instructed as to his conduct during the four expeditions. If a youth proved to be unreliable and disobedient these first four times, he would remain that way in expeditions and battles. So he must try to be at his best during this time. A novice had to watch his morals. If, when he returned from one of the expeditions, he had more than what was considered a proper amount of sexual intercourse, this would be his nature through life. And other things were impressed on him, such as, "Don't be a coward; don't be untruthful; don't eat too much when you come back to camp between raids, or that will be your nature." During the entire period the boy did his very best to comply with the rules. One informant told Opler that the necessary information was imparted to each boy by his father. Another claimed that a relative taught the boy, and that a special man was not needed. Still other accounts indicated that "bow" shamans, whose rites centered about the location and frustration of the enemy and the granting of invulnerability in battle, often prepared the youths for the four journeys.[61] They also made the war shirts and other things that protected a man in battle. Often, several young men of the same age were put in the care of one shaman. He taught them the warpath words and how they should conduct themselves.[62]

The inexperienced boy was given a certain kind of war hat, which among the Western Apache differed from the hat of the warrior. The latter was plain, with just eagle tail feathers on it. The novice's cap had four types of feathers on it—hummingbird, oriole, quail, and eagle—but it was without "power."[63] The novice also received a drinking tube and, attached to the same cord, a scratching stick, about five inches long and made from the wood of any fruit-bearing tree. The shaman made the hat, tube, and scratcher, with no charge for the service. As he made them, he put a lightning design on the tube and scratcher, and offered prayers and threw pollen to the directions. When the boy finished his apprenticeship he returned these articles to the shaman, who could use them again for other novices.

The novice was different from the other men, first of all in a ritual sense. The older men treated a novice reverently because the young man was under holy restrictions. Like the pubescent girl, he was identified with a Supernatural. When a party was under close pursuit, he might even be called upon to perform certain rituals for its safety.[64] On raids and war parties the men called him Child of the Water.

Sacred aspects were further emphasized by behavior and food restrictions. The novice could not turn around quickly and look behind him. He must glance over his shoulder first. When he faced the other way he had to turn toward the sun first, the way the Apache threw pollen. Bad luck would come to the party if this was not done. If the boy did not use the scratcher, his skin would be soft. He had to use the tube for all drinking. If he did not use the scratcher and tube, his whiskers would grow fast. There was also a strict rule against a novice having sexual intercourse while he was out on a raid. He must also use the special war language that had been taught him. If he disobeyed in all this, he would be very unlucky.[65]

A novice was not allowed to eat warm food. If he had to cook the food, he must let it get cold before he ate it, or horses would not be worth anything to him. He was not allowed to eat entrails either, for if he did, he would not have good luck with horses. The novice was cautioned against overeating lest he become gluttonous, and he was forbidden to eat choice parts of the meat or meat from the head of an animal. The novice should not gaze upward when he was on a raid or a heavy rain would come. He should be discreet in all things. He should not laugh at anyone, no matter how amusing the situation. He was not to speak to any warrior except in answer to questions or when told to speak. He must speak respectfully to all the men and must not talk freely or obscenely about women. He must stay awake until he was given permission to lie down, for to go to sleep before the others would show contempt and would cause all the members of the party to be drowsy. Above all, he should show courage and bear all hardships uncomplainingly. Before the boy left on his first trip, the women and men of the camp formed a line and put pollen on him to guard him on his journey. They also told him to return in a specific period of time, and he had to promise he would.[66]

Although his conduct was vital to the success of the expedition, the novice was required to gain his practical experience in a subordinate capacity. He worked, but he couldn't fight. He carried only a bow and four blunt arrows for hunting.[67] Novices went for the water and wood and did the heavy work around the camp at night. The men ordered them around as they wished. They arose early in the morning, built the fire, and cared for the horses. They did the cooking and made the beds for the men. Sometimes they carried provisions for the men too. They were the only ones who did guard duty.

The special words that the boy learned and that he was instructed to use during his first four raiding journeys constituted a vocabulary that replaced ordinary forms of speech. These were ceremonial words, and according to Opler's informant, only the novice was allowed to use them, and only while he was out on the raid.[68] As an example, the term for heart became "that by means of which I live." Geronimo stated, however, that once the tribe had entered upon the warpath, no common names were used in anything pertaining to war, for war was a solemn religious matter.[69]

While the novices were expected to share the hardships of the journey, they were protected from danger by the experienced men. The loss of a novice reflected badly upon the leader of the raid, for the youth was under the protection of ritual and was present primarily for experience. Nevertheless, raiding in enemy country was hazardous work at best, and sometimes the group had to leave the novice some distance behind so that he would not be involved in battle. On occasion they were not able to get back to him again. Novices left alone in this way sometimes perished or else suffered great hardship before reaching their homes.[70]

No special raiding parties were organized for the novice; the trips depended upon the needs of the encampments and the state of intertribal relations, and as much as a year might elapse between the first and the fourth journeys. Unless there was particular criticism of the young man's conduct on his fourth journey, he joined to the ranks of the men when he returned home from this trip.[71] According to Geronimo, he still had to be admitted to warrior status by vote of the council. If any warrior objected, the novice might be subjected to further tests before acceptance. Even then he began as a warrior of lowest rank, progressing upward by his accomplishments and wisdom.[72] He no longer had to stay at home: he was free to do what he wished and to have his own views. He could smoke now, and he could marry. When the next raid or war party was announced, he could participate in the war dance and commit himself to the undertaking as a warrior.[73] The system had its obvious benefits, since it provided capable and resourceful warriors.

The Scratching Stick and the Drinking Tube, According to Bourke

When General Crook's expedition against the Chiricahua Apache reached the heart of the Sierra Madre, Mexico, in 1883, Bourke said that it was his good fortune to find on the ground in Geronimo's rancheria two insignificant looking articles of personal equipment, to which he learned the Apache attached the greatest importance. One of these was a scratching stick, a small piece of hardwood, cedar, or pine, about two and a half to three inches long and half a finger in thickness; the other was a drinking tube, a small section of the cane indigenous to the Southwest and of about the same dimensions as the scratching stick.

The first four times a young man went out with a war party, he was not allowed to scratch his head with his fingers or let water touch his lips. "He does not scratch his head with his fingers; he makes use of this scratch stick. He will not let water touch his lips, but sucks it into his throat through this tiny tube." A single, long buckskin cord was used to tie the stick and tube together and to the novice's belt. Bourke was not able to determine whether the stick and tube "had to be prepared by the medicine-men or by the young warrior himself; with what ceremonial, if any, they had to be manufactured, and under what circumstances of time and place."[74]

> Exactly what origin to ascribe to the drinking reed is now an impossibility, neither is it probable that the explanations which the medicine-men might choose to make would have the slightest value in dispelling the gloom which surrounds the subject. That the earliest conditions of the Apache tribe found them without many of the comforts which have for generations been necessaries, and obliged to resort to all sorts of expedients in cooking, carrying, or serving their food is the most plausible presumption, but it is submitted merely as a presumption and in no sense as a fact. It can readily be shown that in a not very remote past the Apache and other tribes were compelled to use bladders and reeds for carrying water, or for conveying water, broth, and other liquid food to the lips. The conservative nature of man in all that involves his religion would supply whatever might be needed to make the use of such needs obligatory in ceremonial observances wherein there might be the slightest suggestion of religious impulse. We can readily imagine that among a people not well provided with forks and spoons, which are known to have been of a much later introduction than knives, there would be a very decided danger of burning the lips with broth, or of taking into the mouth much earthy and vegetable matter or ice from springs and streams at which men or women might wish to drink, so the use of the drinking reed would obviate no small amount of danger and discomfort.[75]

Since the significance of the drinking tube has just been given in the material concerning the Novice Complex, Bourke's information is included because it is interesting, yet it is an example of how easy it is to guess incorrectly at the purpose of an item. And it is another good reason for the student to turn to Goodwin and Opler for the better or at least fuller information needed. Informants do mention that reeds were sometimes used to drink from water holes, but no reference is made to the drinking tube as being employed for this purpose.

9 Weapons

Before they obtained guns, the Chiricahua used the bow and arrows, war clubs, knives, lances, and shields. In addition to these, boys were skilled in the use of rocks and slings.

Bows and Arrows

The usual Chiricahua bow was a self- or one-piece bow. The preferred wood for Western Apache and Chiricahua bows was wild mulberry cut from second growth trees. A straight piece without knots was procured. It was trimmed with a knife while still green, and then hung up to dry for several weeks. Some men made their own bows, and others purchased theirs from men who were especially skilled at the task.[1]

Bows were made in two shapes, a single arc and a double arc. The single arc was considered best because it was easier to place an

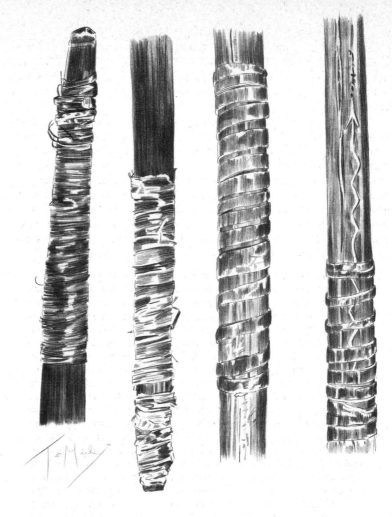

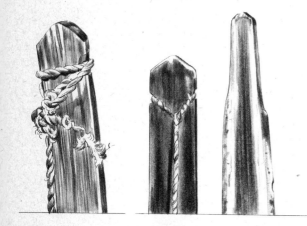

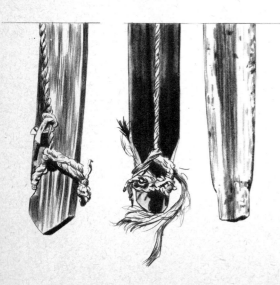

Right: *Bow details, showing ends wrapped with sinew and grip wrapped with rawhide (ASM). Note incised arrow mark on bow at right. Bow has many small holes once inlaid with turquoise. Length, 120 cm.; diameter, 2.5 cm. Collected by Ernest Davies, whose father was acquainted with Geronimo and visited him while he was in prison, where Geronimo gave him the bow in exchange for tobacco. Below: Bow notch details (ASM).*

arrow on it. Most specimens in collections are single arc, and exceedingly flat in comparison to the Plains bow.

Arrows were of two types: a one-piece shaft of hardwood such as desert broom, and a cane shaft with a hardwood foreshaft. The shaft tip was fire-hardened, set into the cane foreshaft with pitch, and bound with sinew. Three feathers were attached with sinew to guide the arrow in flight. Painted bands, primarily red and black, were used to mark the arrows for identification. Goodwin mentioned that the "horizontally red people" clan painted their arrows all red.[2] Arrow shafts were heated for straightening and smoothed with a pair of soft stones with grooves cut in them.[3]

Arrow poison was made in several ways: deer's blood was mixed with poisonous plants and allowed to rot before being placed on the points; deer spleen was mixed with spit;[4] poisonous insects were mixed with putrifying liver. One Opler informant reported that arrow poison for hunting was made by pounding the prongs of plants like prickly pear, mixing it with deer stomach and blood, and then allowing it to spoil. It was claimed to work without spoiling the meat.[5]

Four kinds of arrow points were made: stone (white flint), trade metal, self-hardened wood, and a four crosspiece for shooting birds. The end of the arrow shaft, which received a separate point, was split or grooved, and the point was bound to the shaft with sinew.[6]

Bowstrings were usually made from deer sinew, although certain cactus fibers could be used temporarily in an emergency. The sinew came from alongside the backbone and hind legs of a deer. The ends of two or three wet pieces were spliced or stuck together to form a long string. This was doubled over and the two parts were twisted together by putting a stick through the looped end. The finished string was placed on the bow and its length was adjusted as

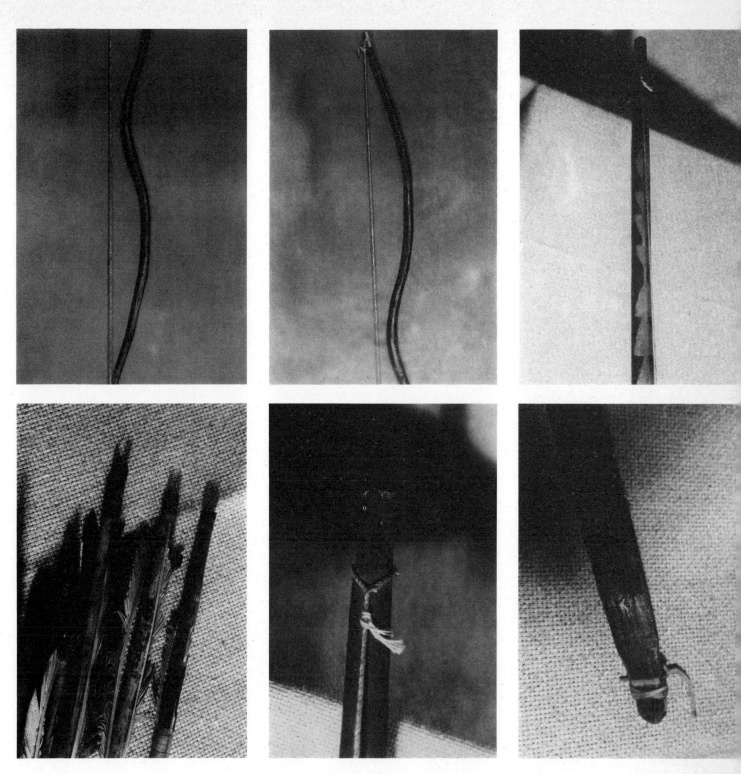

Top left: *Recurved bow bottom (MNCA)*. Top center: *Recurved bow top.* Top right: *Painted bow (ASM). Triangles are green, grip is red.* Above left: *Arrow nock and fletching detail showing markings and sinew wrapping (ASM).* Above center: *Bow tip, showing method of stringing loop end of string (ASM).* Above right: *Bow tip, showing notching for tied end of string (ASM).*

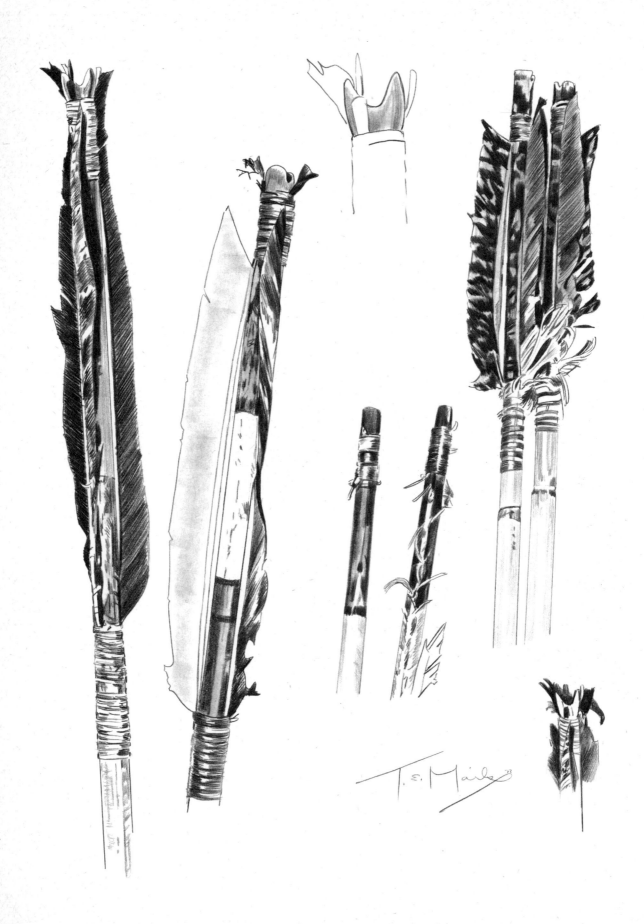

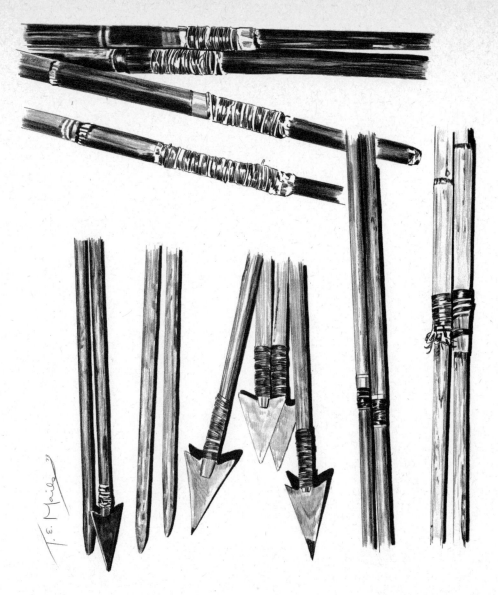

Opposite: *Arrow fletching, marking, and nock details (ASM). Markings are red and/or black. Above: Top and right, method of securing hardwood foreshaft in cane shaft with pitch and sinew. Bottom, self-points and metal points (ASM). Right: Left, one-piece hardwood arrows; right, cane arrows (ASM). Average length of cane arrow, 34–36 inches.*

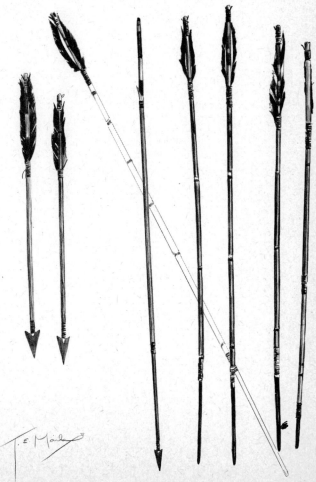

Apache method of holding bow and arrow (SM).

it dried. Lumps in the string were chewed to smooth them out.[7]

Wristguards of rawhide or buckskin were worn to protect the wrist while shooting. The bow was held in the middle with the thumb of the left hand braced vertically against it. The arrow went to the left side of a vertically held bow and rested on the first finger. The arrow nock was held by the right hand. The first finger was above the nock, and either the second or the second and third fingers were below it. In either case, those fingers also held the bowstring. A Goodwin informant reported the three-finger method for the Western Apache,[8] but my Apache photographs clearly show instances where only two fingers were used to hold the arrow and pull the string.

For close shots the bow was held vertically. For long shots it was held horizontally. In a battle, it was held any way possible!

Quivers

Bows and arrows were carried either in a single-piece self-quiver which held both bow and arrows, or in a two-piece quiver and bow case whose shape was like that of the Plains Indians, but ornamented in a uniquely Apache way. The most typical markings were red flannel cutouts and lines of paint. An Apache quiver can also be recognized by a center boot with scalloped and painted tabs pendant from it. Mountain lion was favored as quiver material, but horsehide, cowhide, deer, wolf, fox, wildcat, and ocelot were also used.

The bow case was usually carried on the back with the top at the right shoulder, but like the Plains Indians, when the Apache went into action they shifted the case (except for left-handed warriors) into a position under the left armpit for easier access.[9] Sometimes they carried the case over the chest.[10] The average quiver held from twenty to forty arrows, plus an extra string.[11]

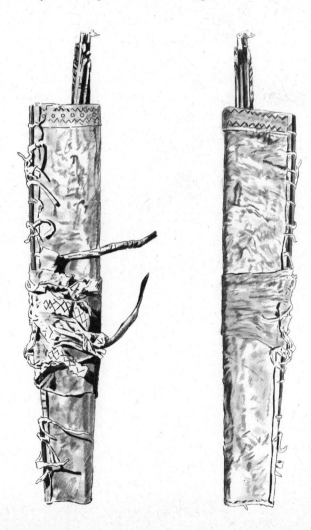

Left: *Front and back views of Western Apache quiver (SM). Bow was sometimes inserted through the boot and carried in that manner.*
Above: *Painted deer-hide quiver (SM).*

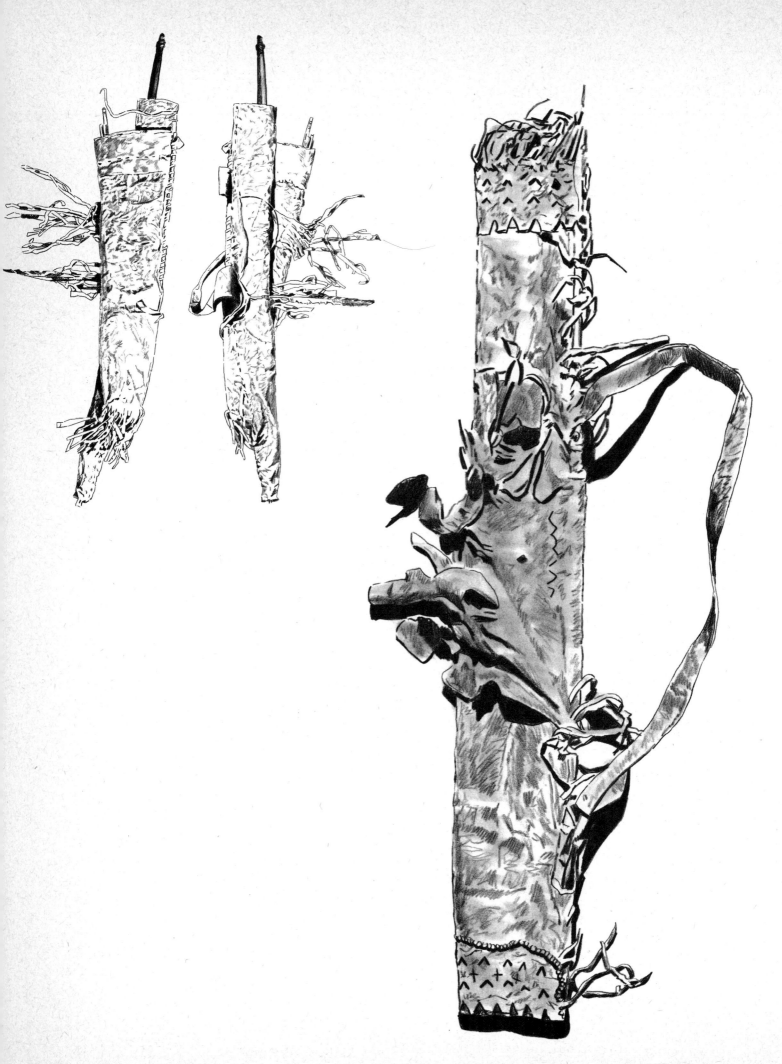

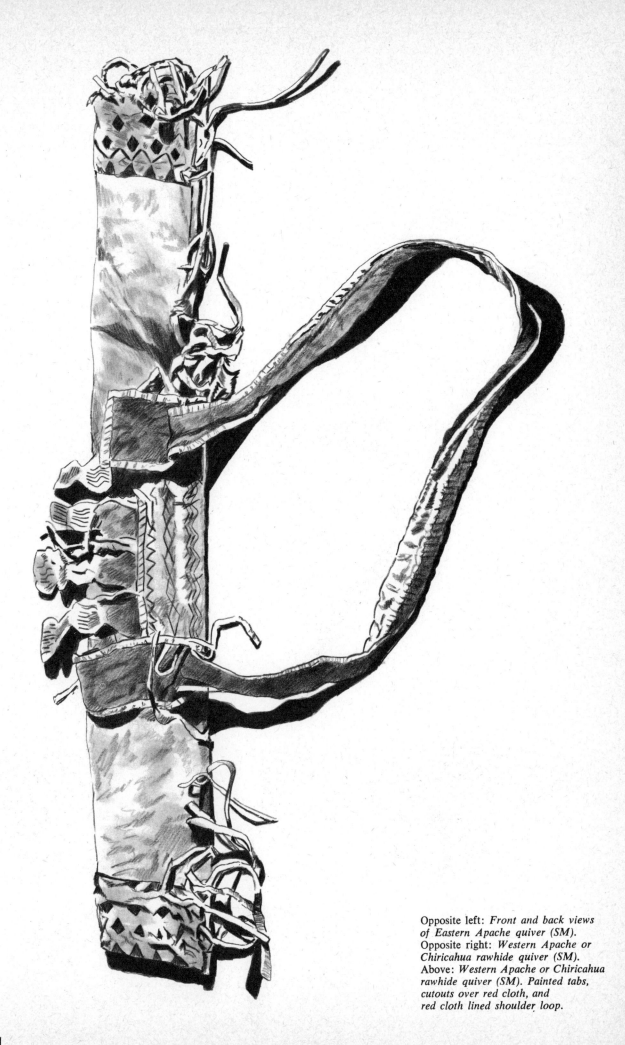

Opposite left: *Front and back views of Eastern Apache quiver (SM).*
Opposite right: *Western Apache or Chiricahua rawhide quiver (SM).*
Above: *Western Apache or Chiricahua rawhide quiver (SM). Painted tabs, cutouts over red cloth, and red cloth lined shoulder loop.*

Top: *Mescalero quivers and bow cases (from old photo of artifacts, MNMP). Top, deer hide. Bottom, mountain lion.* Above left: *Rawhide Chiricahua quiver and bow-case cutouts over red cloth (HM).* Above right: *Detail of quiver and bow case.* Right: *Detail of quiver and bow case showing method of securing shoulder loop.*

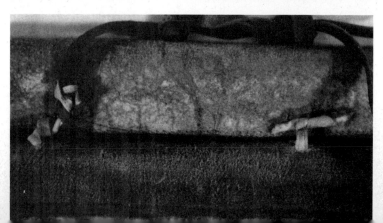

Lances

Lances were most often made for others by medicine men who had weapon power. The best material was dead stalks of sotol, which were heated, straightened, and smoothed. In the earliest days they had a fire-hardened self-point. Some mountain mahogany points were made.[12] Later, knives and bayonets were employed as points, and regular lance points were obtained from the Spanish and Mexicans. Sometimes entire lances were obtained.[13] A common method of hafting was to slit the butt of a piece of cow's tail and slip it over the point to cover the place where the point was inserted in the split end of the sotol stalk.[14]

Informants stated that war leaders used lances to prove their bravery. The lance was a favorite weapon to be employed by a swift man on foot when an enemy was forced to pause to reload his breech-loader.[15] James Kaywaykla remarks that the lance was a formidable weapon, noiseless, and effective in killing game.[16] Lances were also used to prod stolen cattle to keep them moving.[17] The length of most lances was eight or nine feet, but some shown in photographs are easily twelve feet long.

Western Apache lance shafts were sometimes painted. The upper half to the point was blue or black, and the lower half was either red or left plain. Two eagle feathers were tied at the point end.[18]

Jicarilla lance shafts received more ornamentation than those of the Western Apache. Some had numerous feathers tied to them, and others had pendant tabs that were both beaded and painted. A few shafts also received wrappings of beads. As a rule, the Jicarilla lances were about the same size as those of the Western Apache.

Most informants reported that lances were thrust with one or both hands, and never thrown.[19] Apache lances had no wrist loops like those of the Plains nations.

Several photographs of Mescalero lances are available to researchers. These reveal that the weapon consisted of a five- to eight-foot-long wooden shaft, which by reservation times was usually fitted with a Spanish or Mexican metal lance point nearly two feet in length, making a total length of seven to ten feet. Shafts were approximately one and a half inches in diameter. They were seldom bead-wrapped until the late 1800s, but now and then had an enemy scalp attached for dramatic effect. Some had a short wrapping of fur or a pendant tab, with painted and/or beaded symbolic designs on it for medicine power, placed toward the butt of the lance.

When in camp, the Mescalero warriors formed tripods by placing three lances together, and then used these as racks upon which to hang shields, quivers, and items of apparel.

In a winter campaign against the Mescalero, Captain Richard S. Ewell reported that one of his dragoons was "surrounded and lanced after killing an Indian."[20] Another time a detachment that went in pursuit of Apache raiders, who had stolen horses and oxen, found twenty of the oxen "speared to death."[21]

War Clubs

The usual Apache war club consisted of a short wooden stick for a handle, and a round stone head, over which a single piece of cow's tail or hide was slipped or wrapped and sewed with sinew.[22] A loop was passed through the handle to slip the wrist through.

Sometimes the cow's tail was left attached to the hide as a pendant. A few of the clubs were painted with symbolic designs on the handle and head and were handsome in appearance. The usual colors employed were a dull red and yellow and black. Some late-date clubs received a short, two- or three-inch-long wrapping of beads, with white and blue beads predominating.

A unique feature of the Apache club was a connecting tab, two or three inches in length, between the handle and the head. This was either a flat single or double piece, or a slit and twisted segment, either of which provided a flexible movement to the head as it struck an object. This prevented the head from breaking off. Because of this tab, the club style is known as the "flop head."

Many clubs in museum collections are identified as Apache, but none I saw were identified as Mescalero. One Mescalero warrior was photographed holding a club whose wooden shaft and stone head are wrapped with one continuous piece of rawhide; it has a long horsetail pendant. The stone head itself is separated from the shaft by a flat V-shaped rawhide connector, which provided the previously mentioned "flop" or flexible action to the head when it struck an object. No painted designs are apparent on the club, and it is a type common to the Apache in general.

War club with yellow horse-tail pendant and painted designs, and detail of head connected with twisted strips of rawhide (MNCA). Length, 18 inches, plus tail.

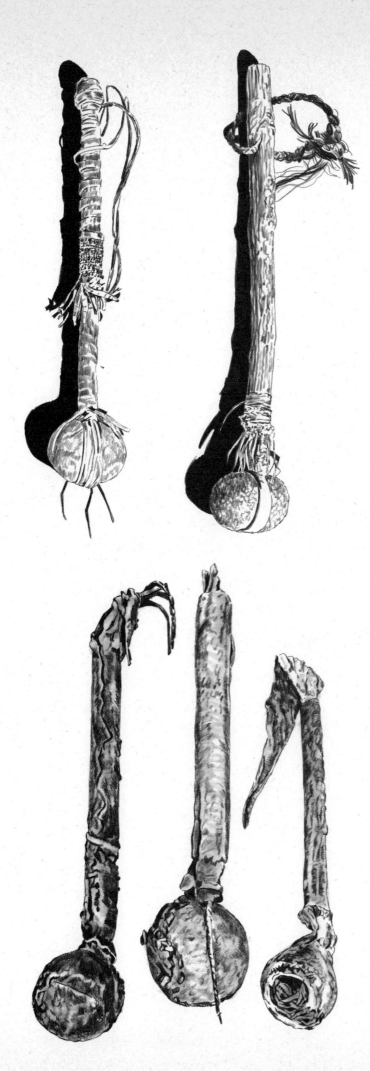

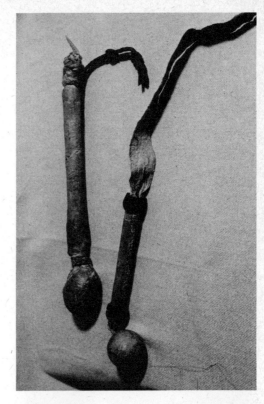

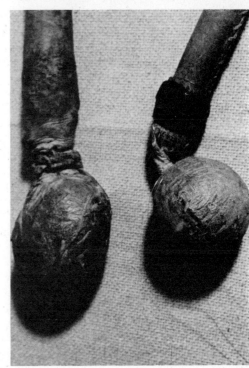

Top left: *War clubs, oldest type*
(SM). Top right: *War clubs (ASM)*.
Left: *War clubs, oldest type (HM)*.
Above: *Detail of rawhide-encased*
stone heads of flop knob type.

Above: *War clubs. Left (AF), length, 23 inches, including pendant.* Right top: *War clubs. Left, beaded; middle, rawhide-encased; right, plaited (SM).* Right bottom: *Rawhide-encased war clubs (SM).* Opposite: *Painted war clubs. Left, tab of red cloth, red and blue paint used for designs, gray-white horse's tail. Length, 15 inches plus tabs. Right, red and black paint used for designs, blue and white beads used to edge tab; length, 22 inches including tab. Center, detail showing method of attaching (MNCA).*

Shields

Chiricahua shields were carried by a few men for defense in battle. The inference in most accounts is that one who had weapon power had to be retained to make a shield. Most were plain and of late date, being made of painted cowhide, with a few feathers in the center and a buckskin edge. The shield was held over the arm by one or two straps. There was no buckskin cover as was usual on the Plains. The shaman who made it performed his ceremony over it and put his own symbols on it.[23]

Mescalero shields were, by contrast, always painted with various combinations of symbolic designs, and in some instances compared favorably with the splendid Plains shields, which had pendant medicine items and felt and feather trims. The pictures in this book show several of these. They had a shoulder loop like the Plains shield.

The Western Apache shields were convex, being formed in a shallow pit scooped in the ground. Some were painted on the front, and a stiff hand handle was put in the exact center of the back. Some had feathers attached, and some a flannel trim piece. The usual material was cowhide or horsehide. Some covers were made. One photograph of a group of scouts shows a warrior holding a shield decked with golden eagle feathers in the usual Plains style, but whether he was Western Apache or Chiricahua is anyone's guess.

Knives

The earliest Apache knives were made of white chert or flint.[24] Most of the Western Apache and Chiricahua men and women had "belt knives,"[25] and these were carried in, for the most part, plain rawhide cases. Some of the plain cases were painted with a few lines. A few warriors made more elaborate cases, which approximated the shape and ornamentation of those of the Plains warriors. Decorations consisted of paint and/or brass tacks. Most men slipped their knife cases under their belts; they did not pass the belt through a cut-out in the case, as did many of the Plains men.

Jicarilla women wore a sumptuously decorated, thick, broad hide belt from which the knife case was hung by a loop.

The Mescalero adopted the Plains style of knife and case. Stone and bone knives were originally used; later they were replaced with trade knives, the Mescalero sometimes fashioning their own handles.

Rawhide knife cases used by warriors were made in both plain and painted models. Some were covered with beads on the front side in the late 1800s and had long beaded pendants attached. Those beaded cases that I have seen were the type hung from the belt by a loop, and most made no provision for the belt to pass across the case and through a triangular or rectangular hole in it as was usually done on the Plains.

Mescalero women were frequently seen with a butcher knife simply thrust under their belt.

Stones and Slings

The Apache boy considered stones to be a weapon for hunting, becoming expert at throwing them and thus managing to kill small animals.[26]

Boys also fashioned a hide sling for hunting. It was a formidable weapon and used extensively.[27] The pocket was a diamond-shaped piece of buckskin about four inches long, with holes in each corner. Sinew was used for the throwing string. Only one whirl was made before the stone was released.[28]

Top: *Lance head and point (SM).*
Above: *Beaded and fringed rawhide knife case (SM).*

Far left: *Painted rawhide knife case (SM). Front view.* Left: *Back view.* Below: *Western Apache painted war shield (Coll. Rev. Guenther, White-river, Ariz.).*

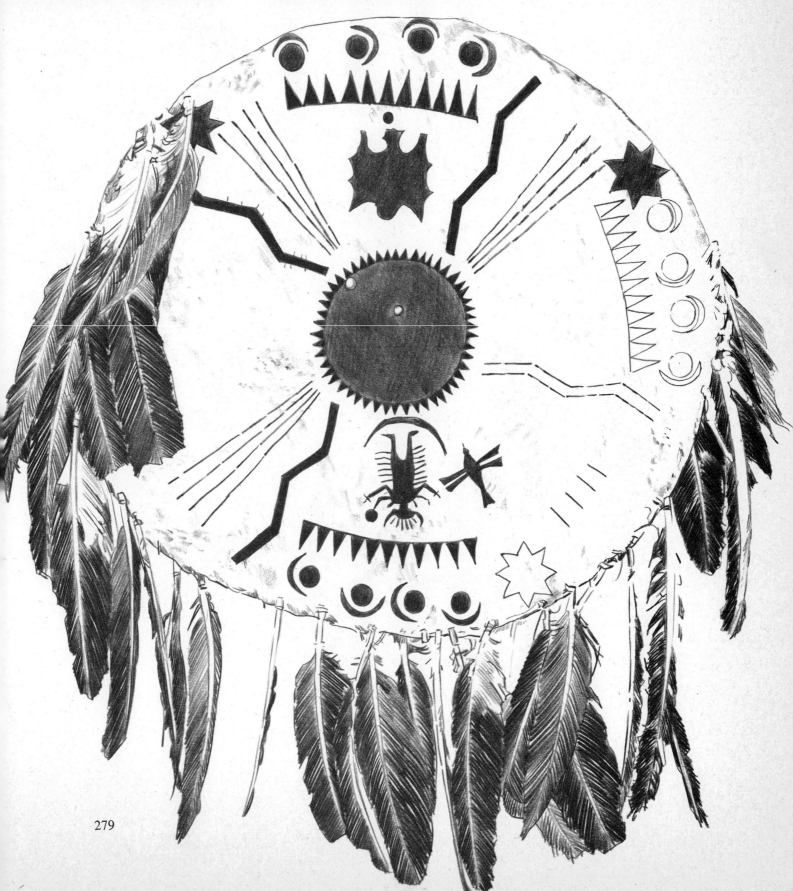

279

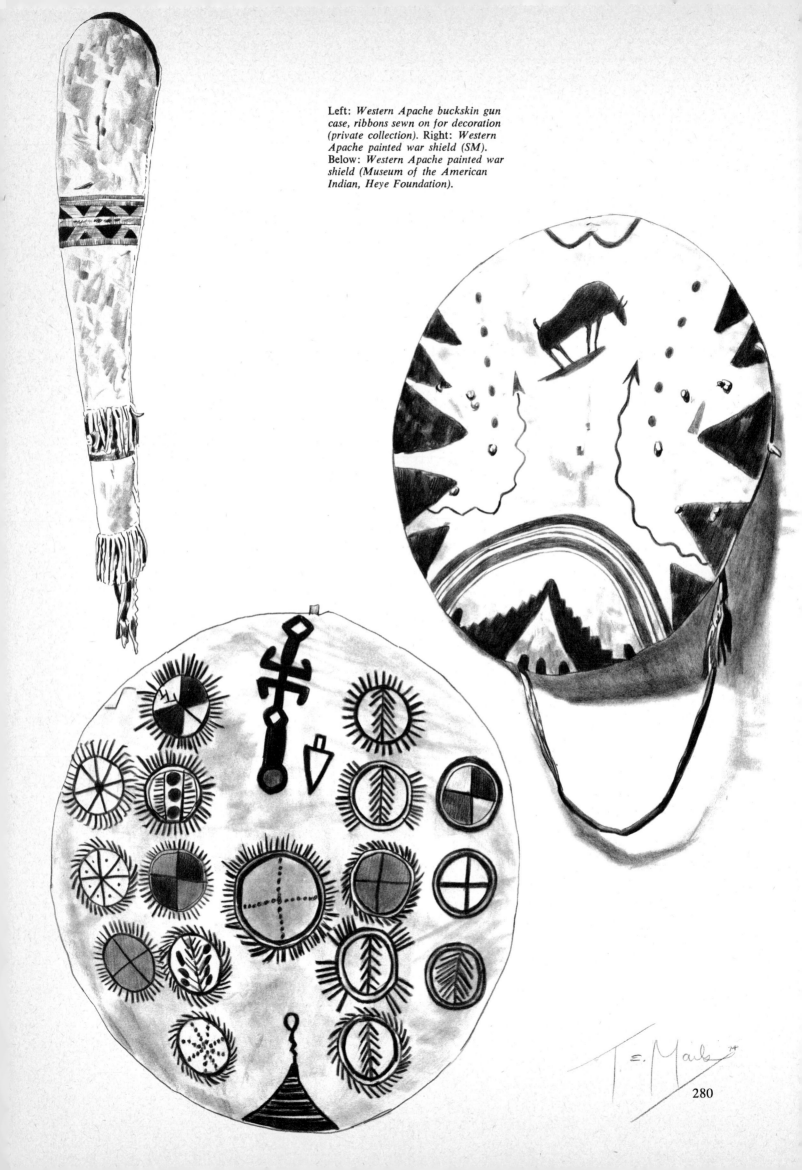

Left: *Western Apache buckskin gun case, ribbons sewn on for decoration (private collection).* Right: *Western Apache painted war shield (SM).* Below: *Western Apache painted war shield (Museum of the American Indian, Heye Foundation).*

Guns

Jason Betzinez insists that by 1882, the Apache were well supplied with guns obtained in trade or taken from the enemy in battle. From this time forward, bows and lances were seldom used. "The Apache never did use tomahawks."[29]

A Warm Springs Apache explained that Victorio had many ways of obtaining arms and ammunition. Some came from traders, some, which were given in return for "protection," from the villages along the Rio Grande, and some from sources in Mexico. The rest were stolen or taken from the bodies of victims. This source agrees with Betzinez that the primitive weapons were seldom used, but served in training boys in the art.[30]

The Apache made few gun cases, but I have one in my own collection, made of buckskin and covered with strips of cloth for color and design.

10 Horses, Guns, and Horsemanship

In early times, the Eastern Chiricahua bands, the Mescalero, and the Jicarilla hunted buffalo on horseback, in virtually the same manner as the Plains Indians.[1] To accept this requires one to accept that the Apache buffalo hunters trained their horses for this task, since a rider on an untrained horse was not likely to survive in a mass of running buffalo.[2]

By 1660 the Apache in western Texas possessed enough horses to merit being called Horse Indians.[3] And as the Spanish continued to push northward, they abandoned more and more mounts or lost them in various ways. From 1650 to 1670, mounted Spanish expeditions of various types traveled north of the Platte River, and within a few more years even the people of the northern Great Plains had become mounted Indians.[4]

The Apache of the southern Great Plains were equally eager to acquire horses, and before many years had passed they owned great herds and were trading the animals to other tribes. Their struggle to monopolize this commerce would be one of the causes of their downfall as rulers of the southern Plains.

The ranges of the Apache country were a natural home for the horse, and the horse migrated, something like the buffalo, following the grass and the seasons. The gun came to the Apache with the horse, but its adoption was much slower. A gun without powder and lead was not as good a weapon as those they already had, and although guns were stolen or captured, obtaining sufficient quantities of powder and lead was extremely difficult. Long after the Whites had begun to push westward from the Mississippi, the Apache continued to use their traditional weapons.[5] However, the gun was in general use by 1870 or so, and together, the horse and the gun transformed the Apache warrior into one of the most formidable and skillful warriors the world has ever known.[6]

Rabbits and turkeys were hunted by the Chiricahua on horseback as well as on foot. Horses were trained to follow rabbits at full speed, and as the rider came alongside he would swing down and strike the rabbit with a "hunting club." A rabbit at a distance would be killed with a "throwing stick." Turkeys were herded into an open area and slowly pushed till they were tired out. Then riders swooped in and caught them. Those who could still fly were knocked out of the air with a hunting stick.[7]

John C. Cremony describes a mounted antelope hunt with

Apache as follows: The Apache was reticent, and by no means given to talking. Conversation was only indulged in while in camp, and amidst friends during a period of apparent security. But upon this occasion the Apache gave full vent to their joy and satisfaction. The group rode for five miles until the top of a hill was reached, from which they could obtain a good view of the surrounding country. Here a short consultation was held among them, during which Cremony smoked a "cigarito" and gave several to those close to him. Having chosen the field of operations, the party went on, and after having progressed about two miles, the band formed into two lines, the first being about six hundred yards in advance of the second. These two bodies then extended their lines so that no two individuals were closer together than forty or fifty yards, which stretched each line to the distance of something like three thousand yards, covering a large area, and yet remaining close enough to prevent the escape of an antelope between the huntsmen. In this formation they moved forward until a herd was seen about half a mile ahead. Instantly the two wings of the first line rode forward at full speed and cut off the retreat of the animals by completing a circle; at the same time the gaps between the men were rapidly closed, and the circle narrowed with amazing celerity and dexterity. The terror-stricken antelope were soon trapped. Bewildered, panting with agony and fear, enclosed on all sides, they were then killed with perfect ease. The few that managed to break through the first line met death at the hands of the second. Not one in fifty escaped, and in this way the party managed to destroy eighty-seven antelope on that expedition.[8]

While crossing the desert, the people lived mostly on cactus fruit, and fed cactus pulp to their horses. One informant, in referring to such a trip, says that upon arrival the horses were scrawny.[9] During the winter, horses were given fodder to eat.[10]

Ross Santee states that it was hard for him to accept the fact that the Apache was a timid person. But this he seemed to be insofar as horses and roping were concerned. "The white cowpunchers would dab their lines on anything that moved, no matter how wild and big the steer or how rough the country; and some of them rode horses when they did it that an Apache would not even approach in the corral. Once an Apache rode a horse, it was seldom the pony ever got his head up again. It was the Apache's custom to tie up a wild one he had caught and give him no feed or water for several days. Then the Indian would lead the pony to the creek and let him drink his fill. With a paunch full of water and in deep sand, halfway to the pony's knees, the Apache would saddle him and crawl aboard."[11]

The Apache groups developed little in the way of horse gear of their own. The Mescalero did make a Plains-like saddle which varied from the standard Plains model in that the cantle was wide, flat, and fan-shaped. A saddle of this type is in the Mescalero Culture Center, and another is in one of the photographs in my collection. Opler states that Chiricahua men made saddles. Generally though, American, Spanish, or Mexican gear was used, being obtained by trade, conquest, or theft. When this was not available the Apache either rode bareback or draped a blanket or skin over the horse.[12]

According to Dan Thrapp's research, it meant little to Apache who were being pursued to lose their horses and camp equipment. Davis is recorded as reporting that seven times in fifteen months this happened to a particular group, "and seven times within a week or ten days they re-equipped themselves through raids on Mexican settlements or American ranches."[13]

Opler's Chiricahua informants told him they used rawhide "horse moccasins" to protect their horses' hoofs.[14] He also learned that they either stabbed or shot some of a deceased man's horses at the grave, and cut the manes and tails of the rest of his herd.[15]

11 Time Keeping, 1880s

During his years of service with General Crook in the Southwest, in the 1870s and 1880s, Captain Bourke was surprised to learn that the Apache scouts kept records of the time of their absence from home on campaign by several means; one method being that of colored beads on a string—groups of six white ones to represent the days of the week, separated by one black or other colored bead for each Sunday. This method gave rise to some confusion, for the Apache had been told that there were four weeks and four Sundays in each moon. Therefore, most warriors found that their own method of determining time by the appearance of the crescent moon was more satisfactory. Another Apache method of indicating the passage of time was that of drawing a horizontal line on a piece of paper and then placing along this line individual circles or straight lines to represent the full days which had passed. A broad, straight line was drawn for each Sunday, and a small crescent line for the beginning of each month.[1]

*The present-day Mescalero Reservation
(includes Chiricahua and Lipan).*

The Mescalero Apache

New Mexico

Approaching the Mescalero Reservation from the west, as I most often do, the last day's drive through southeastern Arizona and southwestern New Mexico can be a long and dreary one for those who have no fondness for sweltering deserts. One speeds as rapidly as possible along the broad, smooth Highway 10, passing through mile after mile of flat, essentially barren country. It is a land bordered on one or both sides by almost treeless mountain ranges, hazy and blue or purple in the distance, and so rugged as to make the viewer shudder at the thought of having to climb a single peak, let alone having to make his way through the ranges on foot as the Apache once commonly did.

Summer days in this desolate territory can be simply blistering, with even the shady places offering scant comfort. While they probably aren't really, the small towns encountered seem lazy places. No tourist would blame the residents if they were so, for eking out an existence in southern Arizona and New Mexico, let alone building and maintaining the towns, could never have been an easy task.

The motels look attractive enough from the street, but are always less luxurious than one might hope for—as if they know that travelers will be happy to leave them as quickly as possible.

The towns are virtually the only patches of green one sees, even in winter. Yet between them on warm summer nights, swarms of insects come hurtling in from every direction to plaster auto windshields almost solid.

The Rio Grande river, and seventy miles further on, the sprawling city of Alamagordo, New Mexico, bring the first hint of a change; although these remain only a hint. Alamagordo is a welcoming and friendly place, yet it would not be the preferred city for most Americans who have been elsewhere in scenic country. It is expanding and progressing of course, but not even the Mescalero would have chosen it as a central year-round location in preference to other parts of their early mountain range.

Mescalero warrior wearing war paint (DPL).

Highway 54 climbs immediately on leaving the city. Three miles north, you can, if you choose, swing abruptly right on Highway 82, proceed twelve vertical miles or so into spectacular forested country to 8,600-foot-high Cloudcroft, then turn left on Highway 24 and go sharply down into a rich valley, where you come to the southern end of the Mescalero Reservation. A large, bold sign marks the point of entry. It says "Welcome to the homelands of the Mescalero Apache Tribe."

The alternate and better route, however, is to go twelve miles north of Alamagordo to Tularosa, then right on Highway 70 and straight up into the mountain home of the Mescalero. Now one begins to see why they chose it and love it. The thirteen miles to the town of Bent includes a climb of nearly three thousand feet, and it accomplishes a swift transition, from arid desert to luxurious valleys surrounded by aspen, juniper, spruce, cedar, piñon, Ponderosa pine, Douglas fir, and the towering peaks of the Sierra Blanca range. In two more miles the same type of Mescalero sign mentioned earlier is passed, and just two miles beyond that is the town of Mescalero, which houses most Mescalero, the Indian Agency, and the school.

Most tourists who are unacquainted with the advances being made by the Apache would be unprepared for what they may see in the town. In my view the sprawling civic center, with its large modern structures and expansive parking areas, is architecturally the most impressive of all those newly built by the Apache on the different reservations. Clearly, there is desire, foresight, capability, and a spirit of progress at Mescalero.

Yet it's at the sleek new cultural center itself that something begins to trouble the visitor. The old Mescalero artifacts one expects to see are not present. The waiting showcases are so far virtually empty, and the Mescalero hosts can as yet give no indication of when, if ever, they will be filled. Something else is missing as well—the genial hospitality that even a casual visitor may find at San Carlos and Fort Apache. Obviously, while a vibrant step forward under able leadership is being made at Mescalero, underneath it all runs a powerful current of discontent, and of coolness toward the casual non-Indian visitor. When one asks why this should be so, history ancient and recent holds the answer. As with other Southern Athapaskan nations, the lot of the Mescalero during foreign incursions and domination has not been and still is not a happy one. Thus, an overview of that history will be helpful to those who wish to understand. But bear in mind as it is reviewed that in contrast to the experiences of the casual visitor, some Whites who went to live among the Mescalero as agents, friends, and missionaries have spoken of a warm love that developed between them.[1] There was and is a broad difference between the passing touch and the shared life in the Mescalero mind.

1 History

The name Mescalero means "gatherer (or eater) of mescal," an agave or century plant; it reflects the extensive use of mescal for subsistence. The present Mescalero Reservation encompasses 460,177 acres. Here the visitor will find Apache men who have uniformly adopted western clothing for everyday dress. Many of the older women still wear the modes of dress associated with the early 1900s, a loose, hip-length

blouse overhanging a full skirt, or a one-piece dress of the Mother Hubbard style. Most young girls wear non-Indian attire in keeping with current styles. The women wear their hair long and loose, most older men no longer wear braids, but some of the young men have gone back to the shoulder-length or longer fashion common to the Apache of earlier days. It looks splendid and natural for them, and I am pleased to see it and to know what it represents. Moccasins are no longer worn, except at ceremonial events.

The Mescalero, using tribal funds, have built four-room frame cottages for most of their families. A few families who live in and away from Mescalero have larger homes, including log outbuildings to house farm or ranch equipment. A relatively few families still employ canvas-covered tipis and brush wickiups for shelter, but these are off the main highway and seldom seen.

Those looking for cradleboards, basketry, or old-style water jars will find that such craftworks are available. Some basketry is being made and some beadwork is done, but while people enjoy fashioning items in identification with their culture, there is not enough profit to encourage large-scale production.

The Mescalero men and women have taken up nearly all the occupations common to United States citizens. Fire fighting is a Mescalero specialty; since they began in 1948, the Indian crews, with their distinctive red-striped steel helmets, have become famous for their success in this field, matched in this regard only by the Zuñi.[2] Mescalero also serve as fire guards and fire lookouts.

The tribe itself operates a number of profitable industries in which every effort is made to give employment to qualified numbers. There is a tribal store and Summit enterprise; there is a lumberyard and a Christmas tree operation; there is a Ruidoso recreation area, a soil conservation project, a cattle enterprise, a fish hatchery, and road building and repair work. Besides these, fees are derived from permits for hunting, fishing, and prospecting on the reservation. Most Mescalero funds, however, come from timber sales, the income from which is deposited in trust with the United States Treasury. Some Mescalero are employed by the BIA, the Public Health Service, and at nearby Holloman Air Force Base. Some Mescalero leave the reservation intermittently to work.[3]

The Mescalero operate under a federal charter as a federal corporation in Otero County. They are governed by a ten-person Tribal Business Committee, which is elected by the tribe. They have their own criminal laws and police and administer their own government. The present president, Wendell Chino, is a very talented man, and their government is noted for its smoothness and efficiency, their constituents being among the best informed of all those tribal members on reservations today. There are about 1,650 members in all, consisting of Mescalero, Chiricahua, Lipan, and Kiowa, in addition to Comanche, who are included as legal members of the Mescalero tribe.

Almost 60 percent of the population is under nineteen years of age. Approximately 15 percent of the enrolled population lives off the reservation. Of those on the reservation, 95 percent dwell in or near Mescalero, with other small settlements at Three Rivers, Elk-Silver, Carrizo, and Whitetail.[4]

It is accepted that while poverty has been a nagging problem in the past, the Mescalero are moving effectively toward cultural, social, and economic solidity. They do, however, have a long way to go by comparative standards. The infant mortality rate is over three times the national average. Life expectancy is thirty-nine years as opposed to sixty-eight for non-Indians. Sixty-five percent of the work force is either underemployed or not employed at all. Drinking is a distinct problem. Housing and sanitation are substandard for almost all home situations; refrigeration is a rarity, and 75 percent of the families have incomes of less than $3000 per year. A ten-year planning program for economic development was inaugurated in cooperation with the United States Government in 1964, with the main emphasis upon the development of tourist and recreation facilities. The majestic country is ideal for this enterprise, being high, forested, rich in historic sites, and surrounded on three sides by the Lincoln National Forest. Public Works funds got the program under way, and good progress has been made. An efficient sawmill operation is also hoped for, as well as improvements in the cattle industry. Thus far

Opposite: Mescalero village, ca. 1906 (MNMP). Below: Mescalero camp, ca. 1908 (MNMP). Note brush ramadas used for outdoor work.

the BIA has expended more than $200,000 in range improvement.[5]

All Mescalero Apache children have been attending public school since 1953. Although the tribe offers scholarships to high school graduates, many have started college only to drop out. Mescalero children and those under forty years of age usually speak good English, but the Apache language is still widely used.[6]

The suppression and decay of the ancestral Mescalero religion has reduced their practices in this sphere to the occasional employment of shamans, and to the annual celebration, in the first week of July, featuring the girl's puberty rite. While drinking and other problems tend to reduce and complicate the ceremony, one finds here the only visible replica of the ancient culture. Nevertheless, many Mescalero are no more firm in the non-Indian religions than they are in their own. Several hundred tribesmen are what would have to be classified as nominal Roman Catholics, and the beautiful Catholic Church building, erected by Father Albert Braun, is one of the structural features that dominates the town of Mescalero. The Reformed Church has a small group of followers, as do the Mormons, who came in 1954, and the Assembly of God.

One of the primary activities of the Mescalero today is that of joining with other Apache branches in seeking by legal means to collect adequate damages from the United States Government for land losses and the "alleged atrocities" that decimated their people in early times. In response, the Indian Claims Commission has already awarded millions of dollars, but appeals for more have been filed.

Once there were a number of Mescalero bands living in the Sierra Blanca, the Guadalupes, and the Davis Mountains—groups that moved out fanwise from their mountain home, going southeast

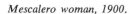

Mescalero woman, 1900.

Mescalero group, 1900.

to raid into the Texas Panhandle and the Big Bend country of Texas, and south into Mexico on trips with the Lipan Apache. The bands had common speech, dress, and custom.

   The original Mescalero Apache range placed them in constant contact with widely divergent cultures. To the immediate south were the Spanish and Mexicans, to the west other Apacheans, to the north were the Pueblo, and to the east the Plains dwellers. Finally the Americans came. Faithful to their heritage, the Mescalero held on to certain central concepts that were in keeping with the general Apachean life-way; yet many of their activities were molded and restructured by other groups, in subtle and interesting fashion, as the years went by.

   For instance, they became acquainted with the agricultural practices of the Pueblo, Spanish, Mexicans, and Americans, and did some farming when the situation permitted it. Yet uncertain weather conditions and frequent water shortages forced them to depend to a greater extent upon hunting and the gathering of wild harvests so common to the Western Apache and Chiricahua. Groups shifted to the lower elevations in winter and to the higher areas in the summer. They hunted all sorts of game: deer, elk, bighorn sheep, and smaller animals, and, at one time, buffalo as well. Until the southern herds were killed off in 1875, they spent most of the summer and probably some part of each fall on the buffalo-covered plains. Thus, photographs taken on their New Mexico reservation around the year 1900 reveal certain similarities to the habits of the middle and southern Plains Indians, as far as housing, clothing, and some other aspects of the Mescalero way of life were concerned. The moment we make this statement, however, we must go on to admit that the Mescalero culture of 1900 had actually become a composite of a number of influences.

   Among the Mescalero, the dress and war clothing, hair styles and jewelry of the men were unique, being Plains-like, and distinctly different from those of the Western Apache and Chiricahua, and intriguingly enough even somewhat different from those of the buffalo-hunting Jicarilla, Lipan, and Kiowa Apache. Women's styles of 1900 were quite like those of the Western Apache, and most ceremonial clothing was also akin to that of the Western and Chiricahua Apache.

The preferred housing was a tipi. Its structure was similar to that of the Plains tribes, yet the Mescalero version was apparently never so well designed or painted as the regal Sioux, Crow, or Blackfoot versions. Opler believes that while the tipi was used on the flats, it was usually replaced in the foothills and mountains by a brush-covered wickiup.[7] However, numerous photographs show that during the early reservation period the tipi was in extensive use both on the flats and in the mountains, with typical Apache-style brush ramadas, rather than wickiups, placed alongside of or connected to the tipi as structures to work in when the weather was pleasant. No doubt the Mescalero used wickiups, but probably not on so broad a scale as the Western Apache groups. A dog-, and later horse-drawn, travois was used to transport the tipi poles and cover in the buffalo hunting areas, but poles were so readily available in the heavily forested mountains that travois were less needed there. The people simply cut poles at whatever place they decided to settle for the moment and left them when they moved on.

Since the Mescalero were a highly mobile people, some other aspects of Plains culture were adopted. Lightweight rawhide and buckskin containers were fashioned to carry medicine items, food, weapons, and clothing, and some of these bags were painted with distinctly Apache designs. In general, though, the social customs, religious practices, and material possessions of the Mescalero remained simple and few compared to those of most Plains nations. Their total environment demanded such an immediate response to seasonal needs, that it frequently called for a ready willingness to give up and replace almost any material possession.

Mescalero camp, 1908. Tipi-style brush ramada.

The Mescalero warrior picked up most of the war customs of the Plains. He employed the painted hide shield with medicine appendages, the lance, the bow and arrow with a Plains-style bow case and quiver, and the war club and sheathed knife. As for the headdress, he made a few of the traditional golden eagle war bonnets, usually without the trailer, and a few bonnets with groups of feathers and a pair of cow horns. Buffalo headdresses with buffalo horns are not visible in the photographs of warrior groups. The more usual head piece, and the one seen most often in pictures, was the fur turban-with-pendant type, similar, after a fashion, to that worn by the southeastern Plains warriors. In fact, such a cap on an Apache almost certainly identifies its wearer as a Mescalero.

Moccasins were often beaded, dyed, and fringed in the southern Plains style, as were the small bags for carrying personal medicines, flints, and ration tickets.

Opler says that Mescalero warriors employed the Plains manner of publicly describing their successful war deeds when they returned from battle and of having these verified by eyewitnesses.[8] The Plains Indians described this as "coup counting," and awarded specific honors for each deed accomplished. But the Mescalero apparently had no such award system. Victory dances were held to celebrate successful war parties and raids, but scalps taken played a less important role than on the Plains. As mentioned earlier, scalping was never popular with any of the Apache, and it seems to have been done in reaction to the bounties offered by the Mexicans for Apache scalps. In 1835, the state government of Sonora inaugurated a scalping project in which Apache scalps would be paid for as follows: adult male, 100 pesos ($100); adult female, 50 pesos; child, 25 pesos. The state of Chihuahua adopted the plan two years later, and bounty hunters combed the area with terrible results.[9] Indian foes were only infrequently scalped by the Apache, for the Mescalero feared both

Mescalero scouts, 1885. Identified by Anton Mazzanovich, Trailing Geronimo, *as "Mescalero Apache scouts and Sergeant F. W. Klopfer of Troop H, 6th U.S. Cavalry. Taken near Fort Stanton, N.M."*

294

death itself and touching the dead. Authorities have said that enemy scalps were not stretched on hoops, kept, or preserved, being discarded as hastily as possible after serving their primary purpose as proofs of victory. Nevertheless a careful look at Mescalero photographs will show that some scalps were kept, were stretched on small wooden hoops, and in certain instances, even if rarely so, were appended to the shafts of Mescalero lances.

While the Mescalero held a Plains-like belief in the acquisition of spiritual power through visions, the visions did not lead them to establish warrior societies, civil societies, cults, or women's guilds. The Sun Dance as a form of sacrifice and thanksgiving never made its appearance among them. Nor did they, in the mountains at least, camp in the manner of the familiar Plains tipi circle, although informants state that dwellings were oriented with the entrance facing toward the east and the rising sun.[10]

In the area of religion and ceremony, Mescalero practices remained Apachean in nature, with Pueblo customs shaping these to some extent over a long period of time. Opler attributes the Mountain Spirit dancers to this source, as well as the ritual of color-directional symbolism and the employment of pollen, stones, and shells. He feels further that witchcraft beliefs might also be traced to Pueblo sources, along with certain other material traits.[11] If these speculations are valid, it would follow that since parallel customs were common to all reservation Apacheans in variant forms, the rest were also influenced by Pueblo contacts. An intriguing question then, regarding the Western and Chiricahua Apache, is when and how? So far, researchers have not been able to say.

Opposite: *Mescalero women, ca. 1900.*
Below: *Mescalero woman at the government Agency, 1906 (MNMP).*

Mescalero warriors. Foreground figure is San Juan, chief. Note the stacked lances, one with a bunch of cut feathers and cloth pendant attached. On the front stack is a shield, bow case and quiver, and a fur turban. From Wittick photo (MNMP).

Historians who have studied the cultural development of the Plains Indians agree that the advent of the horse played a major role in the redirecting of their life-way.[12] Whatever the little known life-pattern of the Mescalero might have been before that animal arrived, it is certain to have affected them as much and as well. The Mescalero obtained their first horses before the end of the seventeenth century, and the equestrian molding process was begun. A hundred years later, the advancing American colonists were pushing the central and southeastern Indian tribes westward and southward, including the large Comanche nation. Numbering some two thousand or more agitated members, and already at odds with the Mescalero, the Comanche then became a dominant pressure factor in the lives of all of the Eastern groups: Kiowa Apache, Lipan, Jicarilla, and Mescalero. A prolonged succession of conflicts between them broke out as contention for territory, horses, and buffalo became constant.

By 1598 the Spanish were pushing their frontier northward, and Roman Catholic missionaries were in Mescalero territory. The new colonists recognized no Indian claim whatsoever to Indian land. Disagreements over this view led inexorably to armed encounters, and as Spanish soldiers were sent to protect the settlers, an ever-accelerating series of battles took place. The most savage of these occurred in 1789, and even worse things would have come to pass at once had not a change at home for the Spanish altered the course of events and presented the Mescalero with a thirty-year breathing period.

The Spanish themselves were now under siege by the Mexican independence movement, which finally triumphed in 1821. Mexico declared her independence in 1822, and in consequence, in 1824, what is now known as New Mexico was declared to be a territory of the Mexican Republic. Hastening then to blunt the rapid movement of American colonists into the area, the Mexicans themselves moved swiftly to settle the territory inhabited by the Mescaleros. Once again the clashes between the Indians and the settlers took place with mounting frequency. Many were killed on both sides, and this was only a portent of tragic events to come.

The Republic of Texas was created in 1835, and it laid claim at once to some of the Mescalero tribal lands. The fruits of this fateful act were, however, delayed for a brief time. The annexation of Texas by the United States in 1845 fostered an immediate quarrel over the western boundary of the new state and precipitated a war between the United States and Mexico. It mattered little to the disputants that much of the territory being fought over was considered by the Mescalero to be theirs alone. The war raged on for three tumultuous years, until the 1848 Treaty of Guadalupe-Hidalgo, together with the Gadsden Purchase of 1853, gave victory to the Americans, and a huge section of the Mescalero range came with it as well.

Even while the war raged, the inevitable confrontation between the American settlers and the Mescalero began. By 1849 an Indian agent had been appointed for the Mescalero by the United States Government, and in 1850 the United States Territory of New Mexico was created, with its governor being named to the additional post of Superintendent of Indian Affairs.

Even before this time, hordes of zealous American prospectors were crossing Mescalero territory on their way to west-coast gold fields. Inevitable clashes brought cries of protest from the heedless seekers, and they implored the government to control and contain the Apache. Several deceptive means were used to accomplish this. Between 1852 and 1855, numerous peace treaties were negotiated, none of which were approved or implemented by the United States government officials—or by the Mescalero for that matter. Instead, several forts were constructed for the protection of travel routes and settlements. By 1853, army units were moving out from these to badger and to shut the Mescalero up in their mountain strongholds, and the idea of isolating and confining the Apache had really taken root. In 1855, a treaty was made in which the Mescalero agreed to exchange all their land for a reservation. Fort Stanton was established, and a reservation nearby was set aside for the Mescalero. The treaty was neither ratified nor enforced, but an agency was opened at the location and maintained for some time thereafter. In 1856 the territorial legislature began petitioning Washington for the establishment of Indian reservations. In reply, the federal appropriation acts of 1856 and 1857 provided for the reserves desired in New Mexico.[13]

Immediately prior to the outbreak of the Civil War, gold was discovered in Colorado, and more than a hundred thousand miners led a horde of settlers to the area. Some of these found their way to New Mexico, and the increased activity in settlement and trade routes brought additional violence to the area. When the tormented and pinned-down Mescalero attempted to farm or ranch in obedience to agents' requests, their stock and produce were often stolen by Whites, and when the Mescalero expressed their resentment in any way, White vigilante groups responded by attacking them. It is fair to say that the Mescalero did not behave particularly well either during this time.

The beginning of the Civil War brought another brief respite from army pressure to the Mescalero, giving them an opportunity to strike back with enthusiasm at the prospectors and settlers. This, however, boomeranged more powerfully than expected, for in 1862, United States General James H. Carleton was persuaded to turn his full attention to the Mescalero. He swiftly planned and executed a massive three-pronged attack into their favorite mountain retreats, ordering the routed warriors to surrender immediately for their own

Mescalero policeman with mountain lion bow case and quiver (DPL). Note length of bow typical of Mescalero.

298

protection at Fort Sumner, alternately called Bosque Redondo, and directing that all who failed to do so should be killed outright. The order itself proved to be a thinly veiled ruse, for many Mescalero were slain as they attempted to comply. Some others, in discovering this, escaped to the Plains or to northern Mexico.[14]

Finally, 472 Mescalero men, women, and children were collected at the fort, where they were set to agricultural work under strict military supervision. Now General Carleton set out to subdue the huge Navajo nation. Ignoring his promise to the Mescalero that Bosque Redondo would belong to them alone, and heedless of the inevitable consequences, he brought nearly ten thousand subdued Navajo to the fort. Neither the land nor the resources were sufficient for so many. Beyond that, the Navajo and the Apache did not prove to be compatible peoples, and when a series of natural disasters compounded their difficulties, desperation surfaced and pitched battles broke out. Late one night in 1865, the miserable Mescalero sneaked away, leaving behind only nine of their number who were too old or ill to go with them.

Carleton's policies had already been under attack, and the escape sealed the end of his work at Bosque Redondo. In September of 1866 he was relieved of command. For the next four years the smarting and angry Mescalero remained in hiding in the mountains. An agency was kept open for them, but they stayed away from it. Not until 1870 were any of them willing to entrust themselves to White protection again. In 1869, Lt. A. G. Hennisee became the Mescalero agent. His attempt to persuade them to come to Fort Stanton failed, but he did propose a reservation be established for the tribe in their favorite mountains.[15]

The executive order of President Ulysses S. Grant established the Mescalero Reservation on May 27, 1872. In 1873 the boundaries were set in the White and Sacramento mountains, and while a final survey was not filed until 1876, the Mescalero were directed to confine themselves to it. Even though the tribe was now reduced in size, the reservation was an extremely small area compared to their natural and original range, not large enough for successful hunting. They were not given enough food or clothing, and the reservation forced them into an entirely new pattern of life. Five different agents with five frustrated opinions governed the Mescalero from 1871 to 1881. Compelled to remain and subsist in the high mountains even in severe weather, they suffered much and complained bitterly, but the boundary lines were patrolled by the army. To leave the reservation a Mescalero had to have a pass, and any Apache found outside without one was considered hostile and fair game. The pass system remained in force until 1898. It has been fairly said that the United States Government did not give the Mescalero a reservation; it took all their land save half a million acres.

At the same time no restrictions whatsoever were being applied to White miners and settlers. Crooked contractors defrauded the Indians; Mescalero horses were stolen time and again, as were other commodities. White hostility remained at a constant pitch, gangs terrorized and killed unarmed Indians, and, responsible or not, the Apache were blamed for every crime that took place.[16] The severe confinement also made the Mescalero prime targets for disease. In 1877 an outbreak of smallpox struck down dozens of Mescalero, and from then on recurring attacks of it decimated the tribe time after time. That same year the Desert Land Act of 1877 opened more Western lands to settlement. This demanded an even greater concentration of Indians on fewer reservations than before in order to get them further out of the way. Until this time the Warm Springs segment of the Chiricahua had been promised their own reservation. Now they were ordered to move to the miserable confines of San Carlos, Arizona, to live with the Western Apache. Over four hundred complied, but some eighty warriors angrily refused, and under the leadership of the renowned Victorio fled to the vicinity of the Mescalero reservation in New Mexico.

Natzele, Mescalero warrior, in buckskin war dress, carrying lance and shield (DPL).

Shortly thereafter, Victorio decided to move south into Mexico, and an undetermined number (some say two hundred, some say only a few) of unhappy Mescalero decided to go with him. It is asserted that some went because Victorio threatened to come to the agency and kill all the Mescalero if they didn't.[17] Believing, perhaps correctly, that the entire Mescalero tribe was assisting and supplying Victorio in various ways, the ever impulsive United States military command decided in April, 1880, to disarm and imprison those remaining. Gathered under false pretense of "protection," they were quickly surrounded by a thousand troops and Indian scouts, disarmed, shot at, shot down, and herded like cattle into a horse corral whose floor was covered with fresh manure three to six inches deep.[18] Two hundred Mescalero horses were confiscated and sold. Fourteen Mescalero found it too much to bear, resisted, and were instantly killed. The rest were forced to live there for four months, until sickness spread among them to such a degree that even their captors couldn't stand it anymore. In total they were cooped up for nine months. Yet the wretched Indians were not permitted to leave the immediate area to hunt or gather in order to supplement their meager rations. Every plea fell on deaf ears, and the dirty, vermin-infested Mescalero remained under tight control, until at last Victorio was killed in battle in 1880 and the danger of his concord with the Mescalero was past. All in all, it was an event that, writers often say, some White men still blush to think about.[19]

Perhaps it is fair to say that while the general fortunes of the Mescalero had, at this point, reached bottom, a few things of a more hopeful nature were taking place. Carter gives us some interesting insights into life at Mescalero in those days. Agency buildings were built of pine or cedar slabs cut from trees with the bark still intact. The boards were placed in a vertical position against a framework, and the spaces between the boards were filled with mud. The floors in the rooms were of dirt, on which water was sprinkled to pack it down. Where no carpet was available, gunny sacks were sometimes tacked to the floors. Carter says there were two seasons: wet, and dry and windy. During the rainy season it poured unceasingly. Roofs leaked, and at other times dust blew into the building so thickly as to cover everything. Her mother tacked muslin to the walls and ceiling, but when the dust blew it came in so heavily that the muslin was "filled and sagging."[20] By 1880, seven or eight steers were being brought to the Agency and issued to the Indians every two weeks or so. These were herded into a corral, and the Indian men were allowed to shoot them. The hides were stripped off, and the meat was cut up and taken to the ration center for distribution. Whole families came and stayed throughout the day to receive their share, building small fires in the vicinity upon which to cook their meals. As a special treat, children were given pieces of raw liver, and they ran about eating it while the blood ran down their faces and bodies. No part of the butchered animals was wasted: the hides were tanned and used for tipi covers, clothing, and containers; the entrails were rinsed in a stream, cooked, and eaten.[21] In 1881, what turned out to be excellent agent, W. H. H. Llewellyn, arrived at Mescalero. He associated closely with the Indians and won their respect. He organized an Indian police force and persuaded the Apache to work at herding and farming. He sought diligently to understand the Indian mind, made some progress, and saw finally that their religion appeared to bear as much good fruit as that of others.

In 1881, the Albuquerque Indian School was founded for the education, albeit in the White man's ways, of Mescalero and Pueblo children especially. In 1882, after much persuasion, the Mescalero leaders sent their first three children to the institution. The following year, Agency buildings were renovated and enlarged, and the first concerted attempt to missionize the Mescalero was made. There were 462 Mescalero then, and 173 of them were baptized by the Roman Catholic Church. This remains the religion to which most Mescalero adhere today, although any such statement must be made with quali-

Mescalero warrior with lance, bow case,
and quiver, wearing beaded war cap with
cow horns and golden eagle feathers.

301

Mescalero artifacts (MNMP): Stacked lances, fur turbans, beaded bags, beaded bow cases, and quivers. Lower middle, two toy cradleboards and four dolls in dress attire. Lower left, rawhide gun case with mirror. Note clusters of feathers and cloth tied to butt of lance shafts.

fications and will be considered again further on. In 1884 the Mescalero boarding school was opened with accommodations for fifteen pupils. About this time the Apache were offered their first White medical assistance, and by 1886 all school children were being vaccinated. It was well that they were, for crowded dormitories and restrictions on movement caused the persistent spread of diseases for which even the Whites had no cure. Tuberculosis, among other afflictions, grew to alarming proportions.[22] Considering the schools themselves further, it is not a happy thought to recognize that from the beginning the policy was to use both the boarding and the off-reservation schools as a device to separate the children from their parents and thus to reduce the influence of traditional Mescalero culture. If parents were unwilling, students were seized, and then were kept from their parents year round and for as many years as possible.

Whatever is said about progress, significant improvements were painfully slow in coming. Fifty years would go by before distinct signs of advancement could be seen. In 1881, White leaders were still describing the Apache as "savages, pure and simple . . . it is worse than childish to believe they are being, or ever will be reclaimed."[23] Further, Americans remained convinced that their own way of life was the best and only way. But, they said, since Indians in general were incapable of ever becoming equal to Whites, the most one could hope for was to turn them into imitation Americans. Even this should be done with caution. The Whites were far more willing to spend money for military control than they were to aid the Indians economically or otherwise. Meanwhile, the frustrated Mescalero began to brawl among themselves, and several died.

Another disconcerting factor of some moment in this period was the discovery of gold in the northern part of the reservation, in 1882. Miners and prospectors ignored the boundaries and converged on the area in substantial numbers. When the Mescalero protested once more, the usual counterthrust of the invaders came in the form of demands for removal of the Indians. White justice did not vary. The dispute was ended by a revision of the reservation boundaries to accommodate the mining interests. It would not be the last time such adjustments would take place. In fact, total removal of the Mescalero from their beloved mountains remained a constant threat. Some respite from such pressures did occur in 1883, when 721 Jicarilla Apache were sent to live with them. But it was not a successful move for either tribe, and during the years 1886 and 1887 the entire Jicarilla group returned northward to their original New Mexican and Colorado range.[24] At this point there were only 438 Mescalero on the Agency roles, of whom 185 were males and 253 were females. Having no relief from the constant invasions and misuses of their land and property by Whites, the Mescalero repeatedly petitioned Congress for a clear title to their reservation. Yet not until 1922, after nearly fifty years of constant turmoil, would the government act finally be granted and the foremost Mescalero anxieties at last relieved.[25]

New problems were forthcoming. The rebellious Chiricahua Apache of Arizona had been forcibly removed from their original range to live with the Western Apache at San Carlos. It was an arrangement that both tribes resisted. Discontented Chiricahua groups left the reservation continuously after 1879, followed by immediate military efforts to intercept and return them. Both Chiricahua and Mescalero men were employed as scouts to assist in trailing and subduing the hostiles, who included the now famous Geronimo. A substantial number of Mescalero warriors responded to the numerous calls for their scouting services. By the time Geronimo's band had surrendered in 1886, more than half of the able Mescalero men were so employed at one time or another, and with serious consequences, for the campaigns were demanding and perilous, and many Mescalero lost their lives in battle.[26]

At the end of the conflict, all who could be identified in whole or part as Chiricahua Apache were taken into custody and shipped off to eastern prisons in Florida. With the move went the end of open Apache resistance to reservation life, White domination, and schools. Agents were able now to enroll younger children in reservation schools and send older children to off-reservation boarding schools. By 1889, three-quarters of the eligible children were enrolled. Also, White farming and dairy practices were encouraged with some results.

The full resistance of the Apache had by no means ended, though. Now it turned inward, and accordingly, the confines of the reservation continued to reap a heart-rending harvest. Cultural separation proceded apace at the schools. The frustrated Indian adults drank and fought among themselves, with numerous killings resulting. Charges of witchcraft and execution for it became more frequent. Agency attempts to persuade families to spread out as individual homesteaders brought traumatic pressures to bear on the traditional structure of the Mescalero local group, and it appears no effort whatsoever was made to understand either the Mescalero culture or the recurrence of certain social and religious traditions among them in response to new historical events.[27]

Inconsistencies in the management of all the Indian reservations, including the Mescalero, made further contributions to irritation, insecurity, and unrest. Constant recommendations by White pressure groups forced regular changes in policy. During one period it was thought wise to ask the various religious denominations to

Mescalero artifacts (DPL): Top, Mountain lion bow case and quiver; center, deer skin shaped to be worn on head; just above it, a beaded toy cradleboard with Mescalero designs but in the Plains style with pointed wooden boards. Left, gun case and top view of Mescalero saddle with flat cantle. Right, rare painted deer skin with horns, undoubtedly used by a medicine man. Bottom, deer hide bow case and quiver.

provide agents. When this idea proved faulty, school superintendents were called upon to assume the additional duties of agents as well. At other times, because of military pressure, army officers served as agents.

The first request for religious involvement went to the Society of Friends, and in 1869 the Quakers managed sixteen Indian agencies. In 1870 the invitation was broadened to include other denominations, and each agency was assigned to one of them. Their "duty" was to convert the Indians to Christianity, and to educate them in the ways of the White man.[28]

The Mescalero suffered especially under the military regimes, since most of these agents were either hardened against or insensitive to the important needs of the people. Best known for such an attitude is Lt. V. E. Stottler, perhaps the finest example ever of how not to deal with Indians.[29] Stottler arrived in December of 1895 and immediately demanded that the Mescalero men cut off their hair braids and exchange their traditional garments for White apparel, refusing to give them employment, food, and other necessities until they did so. Parents who were slow to send their children to school had their food supplies cut off, and if that were not sufficient, they were thrown in the guardhouse. Once in school, the children were kept from their parents, and cultural separation continued. The court of Indian offenses on which Mescalero judges sat was abolished as Stottler became his own judge and jury. Thereafter, any offense that touched the agent brought summary dismissal from jobs and a term in the guardhouse. All social events and ceremonies were banned as bar-

The Agency at Mescalero, 1908.
Photo by H. F. Robinson (MNMP).

Above: *Women bringing their children to the Indian school (MNMP).*
Left: *Women collecting rations (MNMP).*

Top: *The Agency at Mescalero, ca. 1900.* Above: *Mescalero child at the Agency, 1906. Photo by H. F. Robinson (MNMP).*

barous rites that needed to be suppressed. Tiswin parties were outlawed. Mescalero medicine men were permitted to minister to the sick only in cases where death was certain to take place. The traditional place and influence of the woman confounded the agent, and any mother-in-law who sought or was requested to play her customary role was immediately thrown into the guardhouse and supplies to the parents were cut off. The guardhouse was indeed a busy and well-populated place. Everything the Mescalero held dear was being destroyed.

Certain reforms by Lieutenant Stottler might be ranked as commendable, yet even these lost their force when his term as agent came to its end in 1898. He had erected a sawmill so that the abundant timber resources could be put to good use. Then he moved eighty-six Mescalero families from their tipis to the log cabins he had forced them to build. At the same time he attempted to make settlers, ranchers, and recreational developers pay for the privilege of using reservation land. To help the Mescalero become more self-supporting, he employed a scheme that combined blanket weaving by the women with sheep raising by the men. Five thousand sheep were purchased and distributed, a center was built where women could be taught to weave, and Navajo weavers were brought in to demonstrate the art. Some progress was made, enough so that when he retired, Stottler could boast that he had civilized the Mescalero.[30] Official praise came swiftly, and together with it the inevitable reaction of government in those times. In 1899 all ration supplies and financial help were terminated, except for the aged, blind, and infirm. The flocks of sheep deteriorated so quickly that the few remaining sheep were parceled out to those Apache who had shown some interest in raising them. The weaving ceased, and not a single known example of Mescalero blanket weaving exists today. Later on a class in lace making was begun for the women and an attempt was made to revive the weaving. Both efforts failed, and in the end no lasting economic improvements came to the tribe. The Mescalero also left the cabins when deaths occurred, and went back to using tipis so that they could move around more easily.[31]

The tight controls applied to the Apache were to remain for a long time however, and they are not really a free people, even today. The pass system was abolished in 1898, but agents continued to enforce stringent rules of conduct. In 1901 an agent named Luttrel established six feast days for the Mescalero, most of them coinciding with traditional American holidays such as the Fourth of July, Thanksgiving, and Easter. No thought was given to Apache feelings or traditions in this matter, and Luttrel was pleased to report that the Apache in his charge would now enjoy themselves in innocent amusement and recreation six times each year.

Luttrel's ideas were a perfect example of Indian policy in general at the time; in 1901, the Commissioner of Indian Affairs instructed all agents to direct their male charges to cut their hair and both sexes to adopt the White man's apparel. Traditional dancing and feasts were to be terminated. Convinced in ignorance that Indian face painting caused the blindness so common among Indians, the commissioner also called for an end to face painting. Agents were also, from that date on, to keep a permanent register of every Indian marriage on their reservations.[32] In sum, the plan, however well intended, was as always to strip the Indians of their ways of life.

During the troubles of 1880, some Mescalero had fled to northern Mexico. Opler states that in 1902 a small group of Apache discovered there were thought to be that remnant. They turned out to be Lipan Apache instead, but they were brought to the Mescalero reservation in 1903 or 1904 anyway.[33] Sonnichsen makes reference to thirty-seven Lipan, many of whom had intermarried with Mescalero, who were "allowed to come to the reservation from Mexico" in 1905.[34] When they came, they joined those already there in abject poverty. The Dutch Reformed Church, which had done missionary work among the Apache who were prisoners of war at Fort Sill,

The present tribal headquarters at Mescalero.

established a mission on the reservation in 1907. The Roman Catholic mission followed in 1911. By the early 1920s, approximately five hundred Mescalero were nominal Christians. Also, over one hundred Mescalero children were attending an inadequately staffed school.[35]

In 1912, New Mexico was admitted to the Union as a state. Negotiations were now under way to return the imprisoned Chiricahua to the West. In 1913, this movement became fact as 171 Chiricahua, after twenty-seven years of captivity in Florida, later Alabama, and then Oklahoma, were returned to live with the Mescalero.[36] Sonnichsen's figures differ slightly from those just cited. He states that 187 Chiricahua were moved to New Mexico, while less than a hundred remained in Oklahoma.[37] Whatever the case, now there were three poverty-stricken Apache tribes in residence on the Mescalero reservation. The willingness of the Mescalero (although they probably had little say in the matter anyway) to admit the others to the reservation was due in part to well-founded fears that the reservation would one day be taken wholly or in part from them. As late as 1922 legislation was still being sponsored to make the reservation into a public park. The Mescalero believed that cooperation and increased numbers might strengthen their case.

No question existed in Mescalero minds, however, that the land was rightfully theirs alone. Even today those bold highway signs at points of entry to the reservation proclaim it only as the "home of the Mescalero"; the others dwelling there are not mentioned. Even among their own kind the once-vaunted Chiricahua and the lesser-known Lipan remain the forgotten tribes. Perhaps this is because the arrival of the new groups engendered new tensions and added further complications to economic survival as well. It was not a good situation for any group. When Father Albert Braun arrived at the reservation in 1916, he found Mescalero, Chiricahua, Lipan, Comanche, and Mexicans included among the inhabitants. He also found that Whites were seeking to get the Apache to exchange their tipis for houses, to work for a living, and to give up such sacred ceremonies as the puberty rite.[38]

In 1917 the Americans entered World War I. Welcoming the break from reservation confinement and wretched conditions, a number of young Indian men enlisted. In gratitude, at the war's end in 1918, all Indians who had served in the armed forces were admitted to United States citizenship.

Another progressive step was taken in 1918, when a Business Committee was organized to govern the tribe. Since then, its president has been the principal officer and in most instances the spokesman for the Mescalero. Progress, however, was painfully slow. In 1918, tipis and wickiups were still being used for shelter. That same year a severe influenza epidemic struck the Mescalero. In 1922 Congress finally confirmed Mescalero title to their reservation. By 1923, a

cattle herd of six thousand head was begun for the Mescalero, and to ensure its success the grazing permits that had been issued to Whites since 1903 were canceled. In 1924, the Mescalero along with all other Indians were made citizens of the United States, and economic conditions improved somewhat as a five-year allotment program of sheep and goats went into effect.[39]

The national depression of the early 1930s reached the Indian reservations as well. Drought plagued the summers, and there were severe storms in the winter. New Mexico itself became a dust bowl, and along with everyone else the already destitute Indians were now in poorer straits. Disease, poverty, and hopelessness were the rule of the day. Because of this, President Roosevelt's New Deal included a massive program to assist the Indians. In 1933, an Indian Emergency Conservation Work (ECW) was formed to employ the Indians in the building of roads and facilities throughout the reservations. As ECW developed, it came to include the Indian Reorganization Act of 1934, which at last provided funds and instructors for economic, medical, and educational purposes. The Civilian Conservation Corps was formed, with a separate branch for the Indians. When John Collier became Indian Commissioner in 1933, the Indian situation altered dramatically. Attitudes became pro-Indian, and strong moves were made to respect and preserve what remained of the Indian cultures.

At last, anthropologists were invited to study the cultural heritage of the Indian and to do what they could to maintain it.

The tone and spirit of Indian treatment was measurably better now, but the truly critical matters for the Mescalero were not solved. For example, in 1931 it was revealed that monies being earned by the Mescalero from their timber holdings were being placed in the United States Treasury, from whence the Mescalero had to earn it back again by working on roads and other projects.[40] Whatever their own shortcomings, it was a vicious circle that sapped the vitality of the Indians and discouraged their desire to work. Thus, when government investigators came to the reservations and described them as lazy and unwilling to help themselves, the criticism was true, yet what they were seeing was in a large sense the product of their own handi-work.[41] Not until 1948 were the Indians of New Mexico given the right to vote.[42]

The Mescalero Tribe was formally organized in 1936. A constitution was adopted and a charter as a federal corporation was received. There is a Business Committee numbering ten members which acts as the tribal council. Each year, five of its members are elected by secret ballot for a two-year term. The committee elects its own officers—a president, a vice-president, a secretary, and a treasurer. Subcommittees are selected as required to act in the various areas needed to keep the reservation running smoothly.[43]

Opposite: The present tribal head-quarters at Mescalero. Below: The southern entrance to the Mescalero Reservation. Bottom: A meadow east of the town of Mescalero.

Mescalero fire crew.

2 Government and Social Order

It has been my custom to consider the Mescalero organizational structure in terms of *local groups.* Morris Opler favors the group terminology, and feels it is difficult to say with certainty, at this late date in history, whether there were bands or moieties (social and territorial units) within the tribe "larger than the local group."[1] In contrast, Harry W. Basehart has chosen to employ the term "bands" for "simplicity of reference." He also recognizes that historical reconstruction is "hazardous," but goes on to emphasize that in his view "bands were not local groups . . . and they exercised no control over a specific portion of land." Bands, he adds, tended to frequent recognized regions, and within these were "particular leaders and their groups who had favored camping places."[2]

I simply ask the reader to bear these views in mind, and to recognize that in many instances where I use the term *group,* it might properly be stated as *band.*

The Local Group

The Mescalero population was dispersed in separated and independent local groups over a large range, and as such centralized leadership was never required. No single man ever rose to a position where he was recognized and followed by all. Therefore, an Apache leader, one usually given the inappropriate title of "chief" by Whites, was simply a respected man with a carefully circumscribed position

310

within a local group. Since leaders were the contact points between groups, it was important that they fulfill their role well, for they gave the group its identity; the leader was the symbol of what they were. A leader wore no identifying or distinctive regalia, but his tipi would be noticeable, being located in the center of the camp.

The usual local group consisted of from ten to twenty families, and its status in the tribe was equal to that of any other group. Its minimum size was apparently determined by the number of people needed to fulfill the ordinary economic and military tasks, and its maximum size by the attractiveness of a given group at a given time. Families were free to relocate if they wished.[3]

When a task required greater numbers, as in the case of buffalo hunts and some war or raiding parties, local groups joined together to carry it out. In such instances, a local leader who had had prior successes with the job in question might be offered overall command on a temporary basis; but usually each local leader directed his own people. When the leaders held a conference, the members of each group still received their instructions from their own man. If ventures were successful and merited a celebration, sometimes one local group played host to the others. At other times each group returned to its own territory to celebrate.[4]

In most instances a local group was identified with a specific locality from which the group ventured out to hunt and to gather food. Most of these centers were in the mountains, and were originally selected because they provided either essential supplies and a natural defense, or ready access to the same things nearby. Local areas tended to have mutually recognized boundaries, and they were so spaced as to provide each group with enough room and the essentials for living. Boundaries did not overlap so as to provide serious problems, nor did any local group defend their property against the others. The entire range was open to all Mescalero, and within it all members had equal rights of access.

Local group membership was not hereditary and, as mentioned earlier, could be terminated at will. Nevertheless, strong Mescalero traditions born out of familiarity with their territory tended to make the local group a stable unit. In support of this assertion, certain Mescalero families have been identified with specific geographic centers for centuries, and this familiar pattern of identification is still used on the reservation today.[5]

The leader's role within the local group was to appraise the constant needs and wishes of his families, and then help them to formulate wise decisions. A primary responsibility was to soothe friction in the group by acting as peacemaker. By this he kept the group intact and working together, preserving at the same time his own position.[6]

Leaders were usually chosen for their maturity, experience, and common sense.[7] They must be aware of the Mescalero traditions and able to bring them to bear at the proper times in local life. They were expected to be generous and were not able to maintain the goodwill of the people without being exceptionally so.

The office was not hereditary, although in practice the son of a leader often succeeded his father, having benefited by the close association as the older man carried out his many duties. Often he quietly took over certain functions, and if he proved to be able, the group members transferred their allegiance to him at the father's incapacitation or death. On the other hand, if he failed to have the necessary qualities, he received little deference from the others, and another man who did was encouraged to assume the important role.

Since the Jicarilla, Lipan, and Chiricahua had well-defined band or moiety arrangements, researchers, as I stated earlier, have sought without success to determine whether the Mescalero had them also. Informants have made vague references to a "Plains" and a "Mountain" Mescalero, but attempts to develop the idea into a clear distinction of or between bands have thus far failed to bear conclusive fruit.[8]

311

The Extended Domestic Family

It was the Mescalero groom who was forced, by custom, to make the greater adjustments in marriage. Marriage was matrilocal, for the groom left his home and went to live in the encampment of his wife. The tradition served many valuable purposes for the wife. It kept her in familiar gathering territory and relieved her of having to familiarize herself with the material resources of another local group area; it permitted her to continue to share household and food-gathering tasks with those whose habits she knew well, requiring no serious adjustments in her work habits; it subordinated the husband to his new relatives, and assured, since they lived in the midst of the bride's family, that she would be treated well by her husband.[9]

It is plain that the Mescalero woman held a central place in the tribe, and one can see why girls were as welcome as boys at birth. Her contributions to the economy were extensive and reached into every area of life. Since women were more familiar with plants and their uses than men, herbal medicine for the treatment of minor ailments was largely in their hands. There were few things from which they were barred. They sought and obtained supernatural power as men did and shared in all celebrations and ceremonies. Many of the great shamans mentioned in Mescalero "power stories" are women. The mother of the male tribal culture hero rivals her son in importance. Opler points out that it is no accident that the girl's puberty rite is "structured so as to afford entertainment and bring benefit to the whole group."[10] The leaders of local groups were always men, and only men sat in council. But women were far from passive in family discussions and bore a strong influence on the men.[11]

The Mescalero man had far more adjustments to make than just that of moving to where the wife's family lived. Now he must hunt and work with his wife's relatives, and he was always at their beck and call. If he married outside his own local group, it meant familiarizing himself with new terrain and hunting grounds. He was considered a replacement for brothers his wife had lost through marriage, and he had to fulfill that role in every way, regardless of the burdens it imposed. To preserve these relative positions, he was to avoid coming face to face with his mother-in-law and his wife's grandmothers.[12] Sonnichsen adds that the rule supposedly cut down the number of family arguments and gave the bride's elder female relatives further influence over the groom.[13] Dorothy Emerson includes an informant's report that the rule was established to prevent a prospective groom from seeing and being attracted to a mother-in-law who might be more comely than her daughter.[14] Probably the custom included aspects of all three views. There were other behavioral obligations, which in sum amounted to conventions of behavior and speech that served as constant reminders of the man's obligations and relationship to his new family. In any dispute the son-in-law was expected to side with his wife's family. No reasonable request they made could be denied, and if ever the relatives decided a young husband was failing to measure up, he could be driven away and the result considered a divorce.[15]

At the same time, relatives understood that unjustified demands made of the new son-in-law would not in the long run serve their own best interests. Their safety and economic status depended heavily upon their ability to appear an attractive family and thus draw young men to the available daughters. A good worker was a special asset. They did not hesitate, therefore, to discipline a wife if she needed it, and pains were taken to support the husband in every way. In particular, they did not want to lose a good worker, hunter, and warrior, and they remained constantly aware that divorce was as available to the husband as it was to the wife.[16]

The social structure reached a long way. Even if the wife died, the husband was considered still to belong to his in-laws. If he had been a good husband they could invoke the *sororate*. Under this arrangement, he was expected to take a sister-in-law as a wife.

Mescalero customs prepared the way for this, since sisters were accustomed to working together and were familiar with each other's households. A woman could easily assume her sister's place. On the other hand, if the family had no marriageable girl to offer, an interval of mourning took place, presents and sentiments were exchanged, and the man was free to leave.[17]

One should not think that the lot of the Mescalero man was an unhappy one. He had important duties to fulfill and was easily able to hold a place of respect. The behavioral obligations he complied with did not trouble him, for he grew up in the midst of them and understood their purposes well. His own relatives expected him to cooperate fully with his in-laws. In any case, he was not isolated from his own family, for he usually lived near them and could visit them at will. Cooperation between local groups brought them all together at intervals for various purposes, so they were still together. And since it was he who had initiated the marriage in the first place, he selected a family with which he believed he could live in harmony.[18]

The wife in the marriage had few responsibilities to her husband's kin. A marriage was intended as a means of cementing bonds between families. If the newlyweds were of the same local group, everyone was well acquainted. On the other hand, if the man moved some distance away, his wife might never get to know her in-laws well. Nevertheless, a crisis was common cause, and something to be shared by related groups. Children tended to bring the families together, and often one family attended the celebrations and rituals of the other. If her husband died, the right of the husband's kin to invoke *levirate* came into play to safeguard the original marriage bond. A wife was automatically bound to her deceased husband's kin. But if his relatives had no marriageable man to offer her, or if they didn't want her, she was free to determine her own future

Opler states that a Mescalero man was allowed by tradition to take more than one wife, but it was usually all a man could do to provide for a single household, and the practice was seldom carried out. A few local leaders were able to manage it. Even then the *sororate* rule applied, and with the exceptions previously mentioned, the second wife had to be a sister or cousin of the first.[19] However, Sonnichsen includes some data that puts the situation as it existed in 1889 in a somewhat different light. It suggests that Apache men were not treating their wives very well and that there were a dozen instances of plural marriage. Divorce and remarriage was common, and many of the men and women had three or four former mates still living.[20] Perhaps the difference in the two views reflects changes that came about under reservation pressure.

Since children were raised in the midst of the mother's relatives, these played, understandably enough, the dominant role in the children's lives. The girl received her instructions from the women of the group, and the boy his training from the men. In time this schooling included his duty to make an honorable transition to his wife's family group, but even that was to be done in such a way as to reflect credit upon his own family for the way in which they had reared him [21]

3 Girl's Puberty Rite

The one ceremony which was (and is) considered to be a vital public and tribal event was the girl's puberty rite. By the early 1900s the rite was being held in the first week of July, at the feast grounds, which were located a mile or so above Mescalero. It lasted four days and nights, and was the most complex ritual event in the Mescalero repertory. I put this in past tense, but the rite is being done today much as it was in 1900. Therefore the description which follows includes information spanning the period from 1900 to the present.

The girl's elaborate dress was modeled after one worn by White Painted Woman during her stay on earth, and had to be made

Top: *The completed big tipi on the first
morning of the puberty ceremony (MNMP).*
Above: *Tipi being dismantled
as the girl prepares to run on the
fifth and final morning (MNMP).*

The round dance (after photo in Opler, Apache Life-Way, *p. 123).*

in a prescribed manner. Informants have told me that local group symbols are still affixed to each dress, and that the Mescalero can identify the group by the symbols. In the old days, when it was hoped that circumstances would be such as to permit every girl to have an opportunity to go through the puberty ceremonial, preparations for it were begun long before she reached the optimum age of twelve or thirteen years. While most of the family busied themselves with the collection of all that would be needed, one of the grandmothers, who saw in the girl a continuation of her own life, or a vicarious immortality, began to work on the buckskin ceremonial dress Some of these were splendid creations, with beautiful tanning, fringes, paint, and beadwork.

Three principal ceremonialists—an attendant, a singer, and a masked dancer shaman—were employed by each family of each pubescent girl who shared in the ceremony in any given year. A female ceremonialist was engaged to dress, advise, and care for each of the girls throughout the proceedings. She was known as "She Who Trots Them Off."[1] Her assignment included the ritual dressing, painting, massaging (to straighten out the girl's figure and life), and feeding of the pubescent girl. She also served as the girl's adviser, watched over her when she was not in the custody of the singer, and supervised the ritual runs to the east, which the girl made at designated points in the Sun Greeting Ceremony on the first and last days.[2] The final run was particularly significant. Before the sun rose on the final morning, the girls stood side by side facing the east. The entire tribe lined up before them to form a runway. Everyone waited expectantly for the life-giving sun to appear. As its first rays broke over the horizon, the girls raced toward it, expressing their own and the entire tribe's eagerness for new and promising life.

Catching the spirit of the event, and furthering their personal identification with the rite's benefits, everyone, men and women, girls and boys, ran just behind the girls. The girls ran to the east; then circled a basket filled with ceremonial items, such as pollen, paints, and feathers, and the sticks that had been placed around the fire pit; and finally returned to the hides that had been placed on the ground in front of the big tipi. The medicine man and his assistants sang four songs, and each time the girls ran, the basket was moved closer to the hides. During the final song the girls ran to the basket, took a feather from it, circled the basket, and then ran some distance to the east. On returning, they went to their own tipi, which was placed near the big tipi.[3] While the final running was going on, the big tipi was dismantled and the main poles were pushed over to the east; gifts were thrown to the spectators; and shortly thereafter the ceremony concluded. The guests returned to their homes. But the pubescent girls

Pubescent girls in the big tipi.
Photo by Blakely (MNMP).

were required to remain near their parents' tipi for four days and nights, during which time a number of ritual taboos were to be observed. They could not wash, and had to wear their costumes. They must also use the scratcher and drinking reed as they had during the ceremony, and they were each required to take a horse as a gift to the singer.[4] The poles of the tipi were left where they fell; they were not to be used for firewood.[5]

The bodies of the girls were painted yellow with pollen, considered a fertilizing color, and red, which symbolized blood and life. Two pubescent girls seen by Erna Fergusson in 1930 each wore two eagle feathers tied to the crown of the hair in such a way as to fall down behind.[6] A male ceremonialist was hired to sing a cycle of the songs of the rite at the proper times. These conducted the girl through the various stages of a long and successful life. Every growing thing, natural and human, was included, for the ceremony was a preparation for marriage and a prayer for a fruitful life as a woman and mother of the Mescalero. Taken as a whole, the songs pictured a long and successful life for each girl, so she danced to them for four nights in the tipi, and by so doing blessed in advance whatever she would encounter along the way.

The sponsoring family was required to build a big medicine tipi, which served as the place in which many of the ritual episodes took place. About forty feet high, it was constructed in a prescribed way four days ahead of the main ceremony. First, living pine trees were cut to provide the poles, which were erected at sunrise. In setting up the structure, the first four poles were raised and lowered

The clown performing for the amusement of the spectators at the puberty ceremony.

toward each other to the accompaniment of the singer, who sang sacred dwelling songs and sprinkled pollen on the poles. Once these were in place, eight others were spaced equally around them, to make a total of twelve poles. Originally buffalo skin, and later canvas, was used to cover the top half of the pole framework, and huge oak boughs were tied on horizontally to cover the lower portion, leaving an opening on the side facing the east. A row of thick young pines was placed at each side of the entrance. Next a firepit was dug in the center to the accompaniment of more songs, and the ground around it was covered with spruce needles, rushes, or cattail stalks. Later a

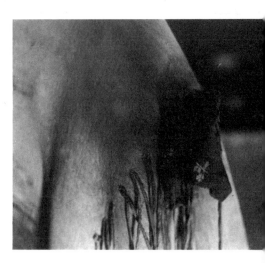

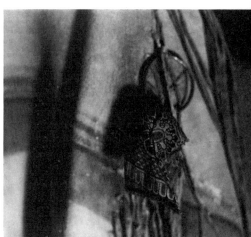

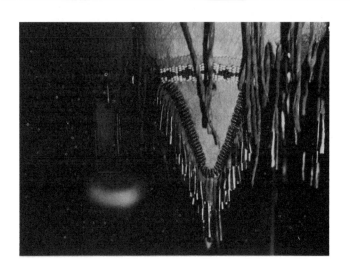

Above: *Puberty dress top or cape, front and back views (ALMN). Painted stripes at sides, fringed, with medicine bags containing mint or pollen attached. Certain Pueblo used bags like this of buckskin which contained red ocher.* Right top *and* center : *Details of mint bags made by wrapping mint in handkerchief and tying with buckskin thong.* Right, bottom: *Detail of beaded and fringed hem.* Opposite: *Front and back views of puberty dress top (MNCA). Fringed, with deer tail and tabs made from leg skins.*

fire would be kindled by the ancient friction method, and it would be kept burning continuously for the four days and nights of the puberty rite. It symbolized the sun, whose heat and light brought new life each spring, echoing in itself the very nature of the ceremonial.[7] Beyond building the tipi, the sponsoring family had to host and feed the many guests; the first such meal was for those who put up the ceremonial tipi.

The Mescalero believed that Mountain Spirits lived in the sacred mountains, from which places they acted to protect the people. Four impressive masked Mescalero dancers, properly known as Gans, and a fifth dancer known as the clown, and called the Gray One, impersonated these Spirits by coming down from the hills and dancing around a huge fire, located immediately to the east of the big tipi, on each of the four nights of the ceremony. Although their performance had some religious overtones, it was also considered social, a part of the entertainment. In effect, however, the presence of the Spirits was thought to safeguard the Mescalero from sickness and evil by keeping epidemic diseases away. Because of this, private arrangements could be made with the Gan shaman to have his group perform curing ceremonies away from the main ceremonial ground.[8] Therefore, social dancing to celebrate this fact always followed the Gan appearances at the puberty rite, and lasted all night. A medicine man who had the knowledge was hired as the third ceremonialist to paint and dress the masked dancers properly. He also sang for them while they dressed and danced.

The Mescalero (and also Chiricahua) Gan masks seem always to have been significantly different in style from those of the Western Apache. They employed the cloth (originally buckskin) head covering, but the basic wood parts were in a horizontal E-shape, formed by a horizontal board with three other boards projecting vertically from it; these in turn were adorned with smaller pieces set at right angles to the main boards. While the headdress of each Western Apache performer was different, those of the four Mescalero Gans were nearly identical in design. What variations there were appeared in the painted cloth part itself. Some had no paint on them, others had one row of white or yellow triangles, others had several rows plus a piece of seashell attached just above and between the eye holes. The headdress was always held toward the four directions before it was put on.

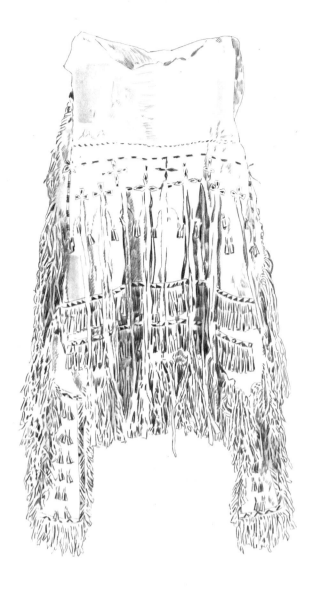
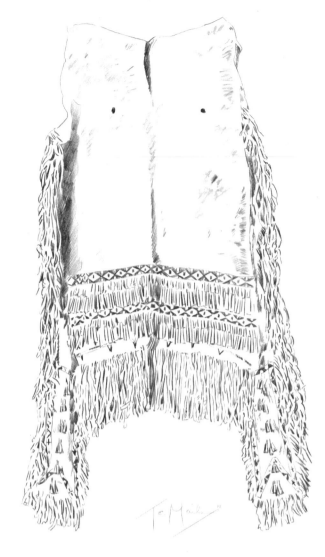

Top: *Front and back views of skirt used for puberty ceremony or by Gan dancer (ASM). Left: Detail of beaded symbols on front of dress. Above: Detail of beaded tab with tin cones.*

320

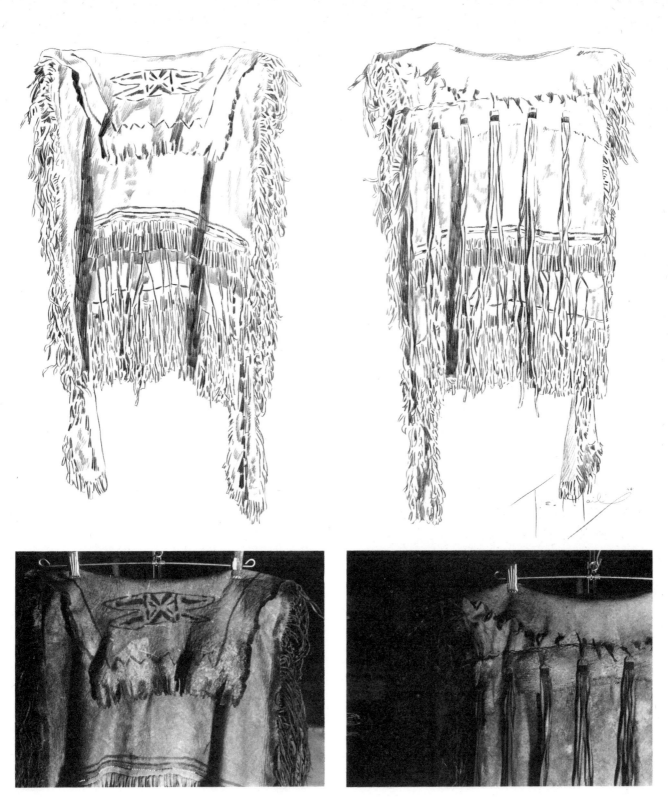

Top: *Front and back views of skirt used by pubescent girl or by Gan dancer (ALMN). The painted overhang on the skirt is unusual. Some photos show flaps like this on the front of the Gan performer skirts.* Above left: *Detail of painted flap at top of skirt front.* Above right: *Detail of top of skirt back.*

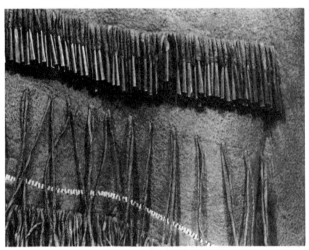

Top left *and* right: *Dew claw rattle of type used by Mescalero medicine men for puberty ceremony, front and back views (ASM). Above: Detail, skirt tin cones, beading, and fringing. Above right: Detail, skirt overlap, tin cones, and fringing.*

Above: *Mescalero Gan impersonators.*
Left: *Mescalero Gan impersonators*
(New Mexico State Tourist Bureau).

The upper part of the Gan's body and also his arms were usually painted black, over which symbolic designs were painted in yellow, white, or red. Dancers were painted differently for each of the four nights of the ceremony. They wore fringed buckskin skirts, decorated with tin cones and narrow lines of beading, and the traditional Apache moccasins with beaded or painted designs and usually the upturned toe. At times during the early reservation period they were able to obtain only scotch plaid trade shawls for skirts; later still they fashioned skirts out of canvas. Each Gan carried a long wand made of sotol stalk or yucca in each hand. The wands were painted with lightning lines and were pointed on the end opposite the handle so as to resemble a White man's sword. Only the leader's wand had a cross-piece on it near the handle. Their overall design was simpler in every respect than the Western Apache wand.

While the Gans performed on the first evening, the singer led the pubescent girls into the big tipi. There they knelt on hides of four-year-old blacktail deer, which had been placed there earlier (possibly originally buffalo, later on even cow hides, were sometimes used). Then, while the singer sang, using a rattle of animal hoofs for accompaniment, the girls arose one at a time and danced around the fire pit.[9] On the fourth night, the girls danced all night long. At the completion of each song, either the singer[10] or an old woman[11] drove an orange-wood prayer stick into the ground at the edge of the fire pit.[12] The sticks were placed in a clockwise progression. When all the songs had been sung, a circle of sticks enclosed the fire except for an opening at the east.[13] The Mescalero said that the most important parts of the ceremonial took place within the tipi.

At times during the ceremony, women who had had problems or tragedies with childbirth would kneel before the pubescent girls and ask them to bless their heads with pollen. Even young mothers who had had no such problems brought their daughters to be blessed in the belief it would guarantee the child's natural growth and fertility.

In summary, what I have seen indicates that the puberty rite is still being celebrated in much the same way today. But it requires only a little reflection to realize why the Mescalero's painful relationships with the Spanish, Mexicans, and Americans graphically interfered with the performance of the puberty rite and inevitably produced miseries and problems of every kind. As agents stifled the rite, they also stifled the beliefs of the tribe. Unlike the perceptive Father Braun, few White men saw that the songs were prayers, and that there was no wrong to be found in a ceremony which thanked God "in such a beautiful and forceful way for the great gift of procreation."[14]

4 The Individual Power Quest

The Mescalero believed that the universe was alive with a supernatural power that was eager to be involved in human affairs.[1] But this power had to reach man through some channel or supernatural helper, which could be a natural phenomenon, an animal, a plant, a rock—in fact any created thing. However, power could only be transmitted through the helper to believers, who would be receptive and responsive to it.

The Mescalero male in particular was taught that he could only cope adequately with danger if he had power, and the acquisition of power at some point in his life was considered a normal experience. In particular, the Mescalero held great reverence for the Sierra Blanca. It was where all things began. It was the home of game animals and birds and a source of water. It was also a natural fortress, to which local groups often retreated when hiding or under attack. When Apache boys were old enough to begin their training as warriors, they often came to this sacred mountain to fast and pray. If fortune blessed them, they would have a dream, which was interpreted

324

as a vision experience, at some critical point in their life. Ordinarily the "power" encountered in the vision changed into a person dressed as a Mescalero, and then led the man into a holy home, such as a cavern, somewhere in the mountains. Here he was given his own ceremony. Its proper uses were set forth, and its details, songs, and prayers were rehearsed until learned. As the man left, he was assured that his supernatural helper would appear to lend assistance whenever it was summoned by the songs and prayers. Such support and satisfaction were considered to be mutual. The supernatural power was believed to be pleased to have found a human collaborator through which its own full potential could be realized, and the man was glad that he had obtained a divine channel through which the supernatural power could respond to his needs.[2]

The relationship between men and their power differed from person to person according to what the person asked for and expected. Some asked little, others a great deal. In many instances the man might accept that help had been granted only for a limited time or purpose. At other times the power might be such as to lead the man to feel he was being given something special for the good of others as well as himself. If so, he might become a medicine man and participate in curing rites.[3]

It is important to understand that the medicine man or woman, often referred to as a shaman, was, and still is in the case of current practitioners, only the vehicle employed by the supernatural power in order to cure.[4] The man in and of himself had no such healing ability. The usual ritual he was to follow, as he still must today, required him to request that the patient offer four ritual gifts, such as eagle-down feathers, bits of certain stones or shells, and a small bag of pollen. These were presented to the medicine man, but were considered to be payment to the power itself. The act of offering was what invoked the presence of the power, and it was taken for granted that the power would comply. Once the power was present among them, every ritual act performed by the medicine man on the patient—such as brushing pain away with feathers, or sucking an object of some kind (which the healer had himself provided and concealed) from the patient—was simply a visible sign of the true healing being effected at the same time by the power.

Christians will see in the foregoing a close parallel to what. they believe—that faithful men and women frequently serve as the mediums through which God brings healing to pass. If the patient believes and understands this, it is accepted that the desired ends, and even miracles, will occur.

Women have always held a place equal to that of men in Mescalero ceremonialism. The peyote chief was a man, as was the leader or moderator of a peyote meeting, but women attended the ceremonies. While they could not impersonate the Mountain Spirits, they obtained ceremonies from them and directed the activities of the male impersonators. Women could not serve as the singer for the puberty rite, but they filled other equally vital offices. Men sought and still seek relief from their problems through the ceremonial abilities of power-filled women. Both men and women utilized plants and trees for medicinal purposes. To do so required a diligently acquired and specialized knowledge of plant locations, properties, and growth cycles, some of which was obtained by following injured or ill bears, badgers, and other long-clawed animals to discover what they, by instinct, ate. Other guidance was received in visions, and some discoveries were the result of trial and error—sometimes with drastic results along the way.[5]

Shamans frequently rose in reputation and just as quickly lost it. A series of failures would inevitably lead to dejection, rejection, and the abandonment of one's calling.

If the medicine man believed that his supernatural power was directing him to do so, he could perform his ceremonies during the day and for varying lengths of time. However, the usual form was to continue the rite over four nights, beginning after dark each night

325

and continuing until midnight. Where the urgency or seriousness of a patient required it, the treatment could be carried on until sunrise.[6] The shaman might also paint and costume Gan dancers and send them out to dance at a rite to cure the sick or drive sickness away.

Assumedly, supernatural power and a healing ceremony were given directly by a supernatural source to an individual. In actual practice, ceremonies were passed along to younger men who showed an interest in learning them. It was believed in such instances that the initiate's willingness was evidence that his supernatural power wished him to learn the rite and would be pleased to know that the power would continue to be used.[7]

In instances where ceremonies were not passed on, it was common practice for the shaman, when he knew that death was near, to carry his ritual items into the mountains, where he would hide them in a cave, hoping they would never be discovered by a foreigner, and knowing also that the Mescalero would leave them alone, as they believed that to violate them brought ghost sickness and punishment by the supernatural powers. The headdresses of the masked dancers were also hidden away after being used in a ceremony, along with dance skirts and other items employed by the Gans.[8]

Pollen was the most important item used in Apache rituals. The most usual source was cattail tule, but a medicine man's supernatural power might direct him to obtain pollen from certain other plants and trees.

Opler stresses the fact that Mescalero ceremonialism reflected "an anxiety that so often haunts a hunting and gathering people whose margin of survival is narrow—the concern over debility."[9] This accounts for the fact that, while rites were performed for many purposes, most of the ceremonies were curing rites. The Mescalero were conscious of the existence of evil, and they considered certain natural elements to be polluting agents: lightning could cause sickness by striking close to a person, a bear's odor could bring on another form of disease, owls were the embodiment of malignant ghosts, and a badger, coyote, wolf, or fox could cause the disfigurement of one who crossed his trail or touched his dead carcass. They also believed that supernatural power sometimes fell into the hands of malicious people, who manipulated the power in such a way as to cause sickness. Such people were considered witches, and much ceremonialism by shamans was devoted to exposing and frustrating them. Thus it was that whenever a particularly dark period came to pass in Mescalero history, charges of witchcraft and ceremonies to expose them increased considerably.[10]

5 Death and Burial

No formal rites were performed at death, for it was considered to be the final foe and not something to be celebrated. In the usual instance, burial in a shallow crevasse or grave covered by rocks was quickly carried out. The dwelling and other possessions of the deceased were burned, the grave was avoided, the name of the dead person was not mentioned again, and any references to the deceased were considered an insult to the relatives. There has always been a sharp cleavage between life and death in Mescalero thought.[1] Further, the ghosts of the departed might be employed by one kinsman to persecute another. If homes were not abandoned and possessions destroyed as convention demanded, it was believed that the ghosts of the departed, in company with other ghosts, would return to claim the items and at the same time afflict people who thought more of possessions than relatives with ghost or owl sickness.[2]

Mourning customs included an appropriate interval of lamenting, then the invocation of tribal laws regarding remarriage. The section on Government and Social Order contains a more comprehensive treatment of the subject.

Deborah Carter relates how, in 1879 or 1880, she had the opportunity to attend the burial "of an old [Mescalero] squaw who had no family to take care of her." Soldiers and Indians loaded the body, which in the custom of the time was wrapped "in her tent cloth," into a wagon and transported it to a mountainside. Here the Indians "scratched a level place in the side of the mountain, covered the corpse lightly with dirt, then with branches of trees to keep off the coyotes."[3]

Opler reports that according to the Annual Report of the Commissioner of Indian Affairs, the first Mescalero to be buried in a coffin, a little schoolgirl, was interred in June of 1888.[4]

Niño Cochise states that the Chiricahua wives and children of loved ones killed in battle went away to a private retreat to mourn. During such periods, widows cut their hair short and rubbed mud and ashes on their faces. It is suggested also that friends sought to help the mourners by presenting them with ideas that would turn their minds to other things.[5]

6 Division of Labor

Until recent years, Mescalero men and women observed a traditional and careful division of labor.

The woman's life was far from easy. She gathered the wild plant harvests, preserved the vegetables, and stored the surplus meat. She prepared the animal hides and fashioned them into the numerous items needed for storage, clothing, and shelter. She built the wickiups and ramadas, and she set up and took down the tipi. She gathered the firewood, carried the water, and prepared the meals. She wove the baskets and water containers and constructed the cradleboards. Her tasks included the brewing of tulapai, which was needed in quantity at important social functions. And while all of the foregoing was being done, she cared for and instructed the children.[1]

When the situation demanded it, men might help their wives stake out and flesh heavy animal skins. Old men and young boys might be called upon to watch the infants and very young children when the mother was busy with other things. But the man's foremost preoccupation was with hunting, defense, raiding, and war. Supplying the family with meat took a large share of his time. To maintain an adequate stock of horses he either had to obtain them by raiding or else catch and break wild horses. Other shortages had also to be replaced by raiding and stealing. Whenever his local group or other groups of the Mescalero suffered losses in war, he was expected to join revenge war parties. Except for special pieces constructed by shamans, each man made and maintained his own weapons, tools, horse gear, and ceremonial regalia.[2]

7 Dwellings and Sanitation

My studies indicate that the primary shelter of the Mescalero was a tipi of the Plains type with regular wind flaps and wooden pins. Far more of these are to be seen in camp photographs than, as some have accepted, the traditional Apache wickiups. Despite the fact that agents forced the Mescalero to build log cabins after 1895, only tipis and other shelters appear in photographs in the early 1900s, indicating that the log cabins were quickly rejected.

The Mescalero tipi may once have been as imposing, standardized, and well built as others common to the Plains area. Photographs taken of tipis erected at ceremonial gatherings and at fairs attended by the Mescalero would seem to substantiate this. Most of the earliest photographs, however, reveal that during the reservation period the ordinary tipi was carelessly made. Hide covers and dewcloths were soon replaced by canvas. Apparently the government agency was reluctant to give them new covers when needed, so the Mescalero patched and then patched again with any material at hand. Some covers eventually became little more than a sad assemblage of rags, and could only have served as the poorest of shelters to protect the confined Apache against the bitter winter storms of the high

*Mescalero woman tanning hide, using
beaming post and beaming tool,
1908 (MNMP).*

328

mountains. Moreover, the individual family member had only a single issue blanket for cover, so he must have suffered intensely. Dr. George Gwyther, in commenting in 1873 upon how the Indians were constantly being cheated, stated that blankets being sold to them by "crooked politicians" were thinner than those issued to the troops, yet cost them more than twice as much.[1]

The Mescalero used both the three- and the four-pole base for their tipis, and piled the other poles around these in varying numbers. There seems to have been no standard form of assemblage, and the diameter and height of the completed structure in the mountains was apparently dictated by the size and number of trees readily at hand.

Some army-type canvas-wall tents were given or sold to the Mescalero, and these also are seen in old photographs.

On the desert and in the mountains, the Mescalero did build wickiups similar to those of the Western Apache and Chiricahua. Pictures taken in 1900 and 1906 show them adjacent to the tipi and covered with canvas. In some instances they were set against the tipi poles, and the entire assemblage then covered with canvas so as to make a double lodge.

Besides the tipi and the wickiup, a brush ramada was usually constructed at the same time as the dwellings. This provided a comfortable and shady work area through which cool breezes would pass.

Early camp scenes show that villages were made up of mixtures of every kind of dwelling and work area just mentioned. Also, there were small corrals for horses; and whenever a Mescalero could obtain one, a flat-bed wagon, with sideboards and hoops for canvas covers, rounded out the scene.

Top: *Mescalero tipi, 1908. Photo by H. F. Robinson (MNMP).* Above: *Mescalero canvas tipis, 1906, showing exposed pole structure. Tipi cover being repaired in foreground, and tipi-shaped ramada in background. Photo by H. F. Robinson (MNMP).*

Deteriorating patched tipi cover, ca. 1908 (MNMP, Chapman Coll.).

Temporary shelters for the Mescalero when they were moving rapidly were brush wickiups on the desert and small eight-pole tipis in the mountains. Caves also served as shelters.

Shelter furnishings were few, light, as durable as possible, and always simple to replace. Individual pieces either were small or could be folded into a relatively small bundle. When they were available, metal pots and pans were purchased. The Mescalero made the pitch-covered tus common to all Apache, the traditional burden basket, and also tray baskets.

In prereservation days, when the Mescalero were free to move as they wished, camps were relocated at regular intervals and sanitation was seldom a problem. To relieve themselves even then, people often walked a mile or more from the campsite, avoiding at the same time some of the sickness that tends to spread more rapidly in confined conditions. The filthiness that Whites often complained about and associated with Indians came to pass in reservation times when few sanitary conveniences were provided; the Apache were not used to using them anyway, and they had no alternative but to reside in a mess.

8 Food and Drink

The economic pattern of the Mescalero was a triptych of hunting, gathering, and raiding. All three were considered essential pursuits in the maintenance of their life-way.

Unquestionably, before they obtained horses, the Mescalero employed the buffalo-jump techniques of the Plains Indians. Once they had horses, they foraged farther onto the Plains to the east and killed the buffalo in greater numbers. Such expeditions lasted two weeks or more, and the hunters returned with huge supplies of jerked meat, sinew, tallow, bones, and hides.[1]

Fruit, nuts, berries, and seeds had to be gathered when they were ripe; and between these and the buffalo hunts the Mescalero were kept constantly on the move. Indeed, it was a way of life they came to prefer and enjoy, for while existence was for the most part demanding and spartan, it was at least as free as one could expect, and ordinarily had its compensations for adversity.

The agave, or mescal, was the staple food, which the Mescalero women harvested and cooked in the same manner as the Western and Chiricahua Apache mentioned earlier. Mescal grew in the foothills and on the lower mountain slopes. They harvested at least two of its several varieties, and at times added sotol to it. Mescal plants are scarce on the reservation today, however, and about the only time the Mescalero attempt to have it is at the annual Fourth of July celebration, when the girl's puberty ceremony is held.

There was hardly a plant or animal the Mescaleros did not use in one way or another. They ate the stalks of bear grass and amole, yucca flowers and fruits, soapweed flowers, the fruit of various kinds of cactus, prickly pear tunas, mesquite pods, screw (or tornillo) beans, the pods and flowers of the locust, wild peas, wild potatoes, Indian potatoes, acorns, juniper berries, strawberries, raspberries, and every other kind of berry, sumac berries, cattail and tumbleweed roots, walnuts, piñon and pine nuts, and the inner bark of yellow pine, aspen, and maple. They made bread out of sunflower seeds and an unleavened bread from tumbleweed and other grasses, jam out of sumac berries, greens out of a number of leafy weeds, and chewing gum out of milkweed sap and pine gum. Mints, sages, and other herbs served as flavorings.

Besides the buffalo, the men hunted elk, deer, antelope, and bighorn sheep. Small game included rabbits and opossums. The various Mescalero divisions had different opinions about eating squirrel, prairie dog, ringtail, peccary, turkey, quail, and dove; but some did hunt and consume these. Bear and mountain lion were rarely eaten, being consumed for the most part in connection with ceremonies.

Some tribal groups refused to eat fish, and birds were rejected as food because of the things they ate and because of their associations with Mescalero rituals. One division of the tribe rejected jackrabbit, but even horses, mules, rats, and rattlesnakes were downed when hunger was severe enough.[2] Those who have studied the Mescalero and their gathering achievements always end up praising them for their ingenuity in the procurement of those things vital to survival. It was their key to life, and knowing that makes it easier to understand why confinement on the small reservation, with its limited resources, made things so difficult for them.

When a woman married, she erected a separate dwelling near those of her mother and sisters. There was no formal wedding ceremony. When all was in readiness, the groom joined his wife in the extended family encampment. All food was cooked at one place by the women in the family cluster, and then carried from the place of preparation by the wives to their husbands and children.

A noteworthy matter in regard to food was the Mescalero agreement with the typical Apache view that raiding was a normal business affair. While one's own people were to be treated justly, everyone else was fair game, to be deceived and preyed upon at will. Much of what they needed to exist was procured by raiding, and changing that point of view proved to be one of the most difficult problems the Spanish, the Mexicans, and the Americans had to face.[3]

A fermented drink could be produced from the mescal plant, but the Mescalero did not make it often. Their preferred liquid for social affairs was made from fermented whole corn sprouts, and was called tulapai by the Apache and tiswin by the Whites. Tiswin was made in large containers, and five-gallon cans became popular items with the Mescalero in reservation days. The corn was soaked until it sprouted and then crushed and placed in water. When it had fermented, the resulting beverage was like weak beer, but when drunk in great quantities it had powerful results, and caused so much drunkenness with so many disastrous consequences that agents were forever trying to stamp out its use.

9 Hunting

Like the men of other Apache tribes, Mescalero hunters sometimes employed head masks when stalking antelope or deer. Such a mask consisted of an actual antelope or deer head, with the horns attached. Deer were snared by hanging a string of head nooses along their favorite trails. On occasion, mounted men worked in relays to run antelope until they were exhausted and easily shot. Goddard claims there were communal hunts for elk and antelope in which the animals were driven along passageways and into corrals.[1] Usually, game was hunted by men who went out singly, in pairs, or in small groups, the exception being a buffalo hunt where great numbers would join together. Entire extended family or local groups also shared in rabbit surrounds.

The depth of Mescalero generosity—which undoubtedly had its roots in the survival of the tribe—was exemplified by certain hunting rules. If one hunter happened by accident upon another who had made a kill, the successful man had to offer a share to the fortunate arrival. If the newcomer's need was great, as much as half the kill could be taken. Common sense usually ruled in such claims, however, for the positions would probably be reversed another time, and the debt would have to be repaid in equal measure. In any case, the reputation of both men in the local group was at stake. Whenever a successful hunter returned to his camp, he was expected to be generous with the elderly, infirm, widowed, or orphaned—those who were not able to provide for themselves. If he neglected to go to them, they could come to him and make a request for a share. They were seldom refused.[2]

Buffalo hunts were cooperative affairs in which several local groups joined. There were two reasons for this: first, the manpower requirements demanded it, and second, the journey onto the Comanche-covered Plains was a perilous one. Buffalo hunts lasted two weeks or more, and required the help of everyone; therefore, this was one of the few instances when women accompanied the men. Research has failed to turn up any evidence that the Mescalero followed the stringent buffalo hunting regulations employed by the Plains Indians. Nevertheless, what has already been pointed out reveals that safeguards were in effect to assure that the fruits of such expeditions would be equally shared by all.

Since it was reported that the Mescalero lanced oxen to death during a raid, it is obvious they would use lances as well as arrows to bring down buffalo.[3] While their precise methods of hunting the animal are not known, it is reasonable to assume they adopted the Plains piskin, a method of stampeding the bison into a circular corral of sharpened posts set at an angle in the ground; that they used the buffalo jump, wherein the animals were panicked into running over the edge of a low cliff; and that when horses were obtained they rode among the herds using lances, bows and arrows, and, finally, when they were obtained, guns.

The women skinned the buffalo and cut up and jerked the meat. Probably they made pemmican as well, for the Chiricahua manufactured it, and it is reasonable to assume that what one tribe created in foodstuffs, another branch probably did also.[4]

10 Clothing

It is accepted that the traditional dress of the Mescalero, after they arrived on their original range some two to five hundred years before the Europeans came, was a buckskin outfit similar to that of the Great Plains tribes. The women wore a long skirt and a poncho-like overblouse or top. The men wore a Plains-style shirt, breechclout, and leggings. Male Mescalero footwear for everyday use may once have included the high-top Apache moccasins so familiar among the Western Apache, but if late photographs are an indication of earlier styles, the usual footwear came to be the familiar low-top Plains type, the traditional Apache moccasin with upturned toe-piece being employed only by the Mountain Spirit dancers. Indian agents finally forced all the Mescalero to change to White apparel, the most blatant example of this compulsion being the edict of Lt. V. E. Stottler, who demanded the change take place in 1896 and be observed thereafter.[1]

Even before Stottler instituted his reforms, many of the Mescalero women had adopted White trade goods and fashioned them into a style like that worn by the Western Apache women. (See the Mescalero drawings and photographs for verification, and refer to the clothing section of the Western Apache and the Chiricahua for details of manufacture.)

Deborah Carter found, in 1879, that despite a "lack of cleanliness and lack of civilization according to our standards, there was a definite innate artistic ability which was manifest in their beautiful baskets, marvelous beadwork decorating the moccasins, buckskin coats and head-dresses, worn for special occasions."[2]

Even thereafter, however, the male dress outfit was a combination of White and Indian styles. Today all Mescalero clothe themselves like other American citizens, except for the ceremonial garments used in the traditional puberty rite.

The raid and war outfit of the Mescalero male was Plains oriented in its makeup, showing influences in particular of the Cheyenne, Arapaho, and Ute Indians.

Leggings in post-White contact days were made of buckskin or trade cloth. In either instance they usually had broad flaps, like those on chaps, which were beaded with individual geometric designs. The photographs reveal that each man had his own pattern and that the styles were uniquely Mescalero. The leggings had no seat, the tops being cut off at an angle as on the Plains, and a small cloth breechclout covered the exposed areas. An alternate finish for leggings con-

*Mescalero women and children, 1906
(MNMP).*

333

sisted of either a very narrow beaded leg band with buckskin fringes on the outer edge, or a very broad beaded leg band with fringes on the outer edge. The broad bands had very bold patterns.

War shirts were mostly buckskin, with a medium-size triangular bib front and back, which was fringed. They were open at the sides. Some had narrow beaded shoulder- and armbands with inset geometric designs, and some had no beaded bands at all. Shirts were usually fringed at the place where the sleeve joined the shoulder and in short bunches along the back of the arm. Some shirts received an allover pattern of beaded designs such as circles. Some hide shirts had cloth bibs. Some shirts were rubbed with yellow and/or red paint. A brown stain was also used.[3]

Virtually every Mescalero warrior wore a turban type of war hat. Some had triangular pendant tabs of varying lengths which hung at the back or side. These were made either of trade felt or of animal skins; some of the later had the fur left on. They were usually adorned with beaded strips, symbols, pearl buttons, and down feathers. A few had one or two golden eagle tail feathers hanging from them so as to fall at the side of the head. The caps took various shapes, some like

Mescalero women and child at Agency, 1906 (MNMP).

Left: *Mescalero warrior wearing buckskin war shirt painted with symbols, in red paint. The necklace is Western Apache style.* Below: *Dress detail showing amulet bag for puberty dress made of handkerchief (MNCA).* Center: *Amulet bag made of hand-kerchief, containing mint leaves or herbs (MNCA).* Bottom: *Beading detail of woman's dress top or cape (MNCA).*

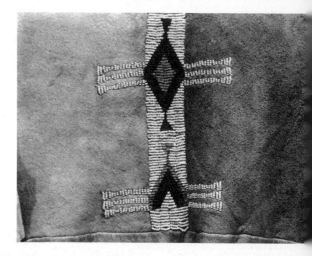

an inverted cup, and others with vertical sides. All but the cup styles were open on top.

Some warriors wore turban-style caps of thick fur, such as mountain lion, bobcat, beaver, fox, or wolf. Side views show that the tail was left attached to the hide, hanging as a pendant down the back of the head.

As mentioned earlier, men's moccasins were the low-top Plains style, sometimes ornamented with a V-shaped beaded stripe, whose point was toward the toe, and with short fringes, sometimes with tin cones added, at the outside of the beading and toward the outside of the foot.

A few Mescalero warriors wore a short version of the Plains-type bone breastplate, with the bones being angled rather sharply as compared to the fairly horizontal bone placement of the Plains style.

Numerous necklaces with amulet pendants similar to those of other Apache groups completed the outfit.

While most of the sewing was done with sinew, the fibers of the mescal plant also provided good thread and fabric. Sandals and bags were made from it, and some other desert plants were put to the same use.[4]

335

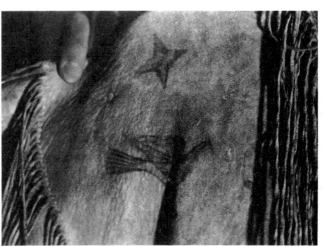

Top: *Mescalero buckskin war shirt,
front and back views (ALMN). Above
left and above right: Details of
painted symbols on war shirt.*

336

Left: *Nautzille, Mescalero chief (DPL).* Below: *Headquarters at Tertio Millennial, Sante Fe, N.M., 1883. Photo by Wittick (DPL). Note shields trimmed with cloth and feathers similar to Plains Indian style. Lance stack at right holds beaded quiver, turban hat, toy cradleboard, and bear skin. Post at tent holds toy cradleboard and turban hat made of bobcat skin, legs left on.*

Opposite top: *Mescalero warriors with lances, painted shields, and bows and arrows (MNMP). Note variety of hats and costumes. Opposite bottom: Mescalero in full dress. Photo by Wittick (MNMP), perhaps the best available of original costumes of men, women, and children. The boys at the left are in school uniforms. Note individuality of clothing, and painted and beaded buckskin dress tops of women. Below: Ignacio and son in war dress (DPL). Ignacio wears war amulet pouch on bandolier cord. Quiver and bow case are mountain lion.*

339

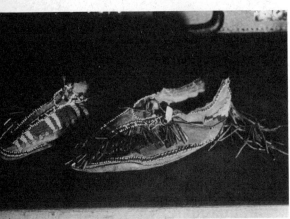

Right: *War or medicine bonnet (AF, Apache Coll.). Mescalero informant claimed it was "probably Mescalero." Cap and tail are red trade cloth; horns are cow; feathers are golden eagle tail. The horn tips are notched to be tied erect by a thong stretched between them.* Above: *Mescalero moccasins (ALMN).* Top: *Right side of medicine bonnet.*

340

11 Religion

Religion permeated most aspects of the Mescalero culture. However, as in the case of studies concerning the other Apache, views as to the real substance of Mescalero religion differ considerably.

Father Albert Braun, OFM, worked as a Roman Catholic missionary among the Mescalero for almost thirty years. Taking issue with even some other Roman Catholic missionaries, as well as with the Dutch Reform Mission, he saw the Apache ceremonials not as pagan rites, but as expressions of a fundamental belief in God. He discovered that the Mescalero had always believed in the existence of a God, whom they called Ussen, and that from their earliest memories they had prayed to Him.[1]

Opler refers to a small "pantheon of gods and goddesses" whom the Mescalero worshiped.[2] The main Supernaturals were the culture heroine, White Painted Woman, and her divine son, Water's Child, the culture hero. These two served as examples for the Mescalero and were frequently mentioned in prayers and ritual songs. Even then, they belong essentially to a mythological period—to the early days of Mescalero prehistory, when White Painted Woman gave birth to Child of the Water, who vanquished evil beings that were threatening the extinction of mankind. The Mescalero were preserved; the culture figures taught them their ceremonies and how to live wisely, and then left. After that they intervened very little in earthly affairs.

Opler also states that the word *Yus* or *Yusn* is a corruption of the Spanish term *Dios* (God). He sees it as a concept that was not original, but was absorbed into Mescalero religion as "just one more source of supernatural power."[3]

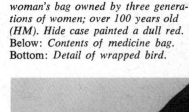

Below left: A Mescalero medicine woman's bag owned by three generations of women; over 100 years old (HM). Hide case painted a dull red. Below: Contents of medicine bag. Bottom: Detail of wrapped bird.

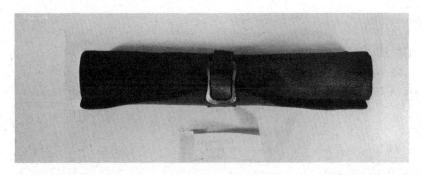

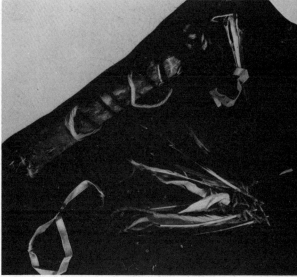

As with other nonagricultural societies, the vital Mescalero rituals were not scheduled to occur at specific plant-cycle times during the year. Instead, they were associated with the individual's life cycle and were designed to guide the child from birth to maturity.

There was a cradle ceremony, wherein the infant was placed in the cradleboard as prayers and appropriate ritual gestures were expressed.[4]

When children were able to walk, new moccasins were placed on their feet, and they were led along a trail of pollen to the east. This was symbolic of the long life everyone hoped would be theirs.[5]

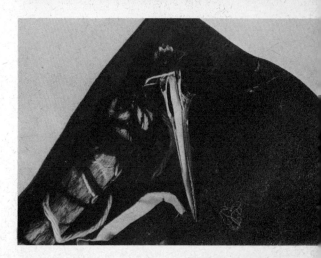

Shortly thereafter, in the spring when growth was apparent everywhere, the child's hair was cut short for the first time. Only a small amount was left to encourage what the parents believed would be luxuriant growth and would indicate vitality for the child in every way.[6]

Prior to the period of White control, the puberty rite could be held whenever the girl was ready. Later on, the full puberty rite for girls was only permitted during the first four days of July. Often it would be put off a year or more, until some practical time, and usually all girls who were ready went through it collectively. Therefore, a small feast as a token rite was often employed to mark the girl's first menstruation and entrance into womanhood.[7]

Each of the above was a personal matter pertaining to the individual child and his or her family.

The Jicarilla Apache

New Mexico

It is fitting that those who are among the handsomest Indians in North America have their reservation located in the midst of some of the grandest mountain country in North America. Dulce, the Jicarilla capital, is located north of Santa Fe, New Mexico, and west of Taos. An auto trip up the fine highways 84 and 17 takes one through an endless number of broad valleys, rolling hills, thick tree stands, and soaring rock areas.

I prefer going there in the spring, when the May flowers are in bloom, dotting the green landscape with clusters of red, blue, yellow, and white. The tall pine and fir trees are twenty or more shades of green, the streams are running full, and the stark white clouds billow up into fantastic forms and streaks that stand out sharply against a deep blue sky.

The horses, freed from the strictures imposed by the winter snow, cavort on the hillsides and race impertinently up to the fences to investigate any stranger who presumes to leave his auto and watch them.

Of course, the fall season is gorgeous too, as the aspen, oak, and cottonwood trees turn gold, orange, and then brown. But the mood is more somber in anticipation of winter. Of course, if one wants to see the Ceremonial Relay Race, September is the only time it is performed.

In May, the main highways and streets of Dulce pose no problem for the traveler, although chances are the side streets will be muddy, and offer the constant hazard of getting stuck. Yet even then the visitor will notice the neatness of the homes, and their ever-improving quality as the Jicarilla tribe moves with positive strides into the modern era.

The Jicarilla (pronounced "hick-ah-reel-yah") number about two thousand today. Their name comes from a Spanish word meaning "little basket," since they once made small baskets, a craft native to the tribe.

Opposite top: The Jicarilla Reservation country south of Dulce, May, 1973. Opposite bottom: Jicarilla country, 1973, at the eastern entry to the reservation, looking east.

343

The present reservation is approximately sixty-five miles long in the north-south direction and includes 742,315 acres. It was established in two parts, the northern half in 1887 and the southern half in 1908. The northern part consists of high mountains, deep canyons, and wide valleys. The southern part is marked by rolling hills, red and brown sandstone bluffs, mesa canyons, and wide valleys.

Nearly everything stated in earlier chapters about the economics of the other Apache tribes applies to the Jicarilla. The reservation is alive with trout streams and lakes, and hunters, fishermen, and campers find it a virtual paradise. The Jicarilla income is derived from natural resources, livestock, and tourism, about which more specifics will be given below.

The Jicarilla are a corporation, having a tribal council and an adopted constitution. The profits from tribal enterprises are used to train Apache personnel, to sponsor business, and to support education.

They give every evidence of being a happy and progressive people, although one must view the former from the Apache perspective. They are quiet and reserved around Anglo strangers, but when by themselves chatter endlessly in the Apache language in moderate tones, breaking now and then into spontaneous bursts of laughter.

As you drive across the reservation, one of the commonest sights will be two Jicarilla men or women going past you in the other direction in a late-model pickup truck, with both passengers in high spirits and obvious glee. And if you stop and wait a little while, you will see them returning to where they came from, still laughing and enjoying life together. Apparently, one of their supreme pleasures on a brisk spring day is that of driving out of Dulce for a few miles and then back. In these days, I can't help but think of what oil and fuel shortages might do to their favorite break in the work routine.

Mountain retreat area in New Mexico in original Jicarilla range.

Original Jicarilla range country as it looks in May.

The following story of the Jicarilla, which traces their development from early times to the present, is an outline history pieced together from government and state documents—such as the reports of the governors of New Mexico and the reservation superintendents —and from articles in the various magazines and newspapers of New Mexico, including the *Jicarilla Chieftain*. The bits and pieces, while brief, easily lend themselves to reading between the lines so as to enlarge upon the whole.

Insofar as childbirth, child training, and the mature activities are concerned, the Jicarilla were not so different from the other early Apache groups as one may first surmise from their continuing contacts with the Plains buffalo tribes and the Pueblo. Since this is so, there is no need for a duplication of such material. Instead, the concentration will be upon the major surviving ceremonial practices of the Jicarilla, for these, after all, are the extraordinary things in which everyone has a compelling interest. However, the Chiricahua Weapons Section and the General Section also contain some individual details about Jicarilla customs, and the picture captions supply additional information.

1 History

1540: The Jicarilla range covers southeastern Colorado, the central and eastern parts of northern New Mexico, and the Texas Panhandle. The Arkansas River is the northern boundary, the Canadian River the eastern limit, the region around Mora in northeastern New Mexico the southern boundary, and a line roughly extending north and south of Chama, New Mexico, the western limit. The Jicarilla hunt, gather plant foods, and travel throughout this territory, but confine their homes to an area bounded by the thirty-sixth and thirty-seventh degrees of north latitude, which extends no farther east than Springer, New Mexico, and no farther west than Tierra Amarilla, New Mexico.

The Jicarilla tribe is divided into two bands. The eastern band

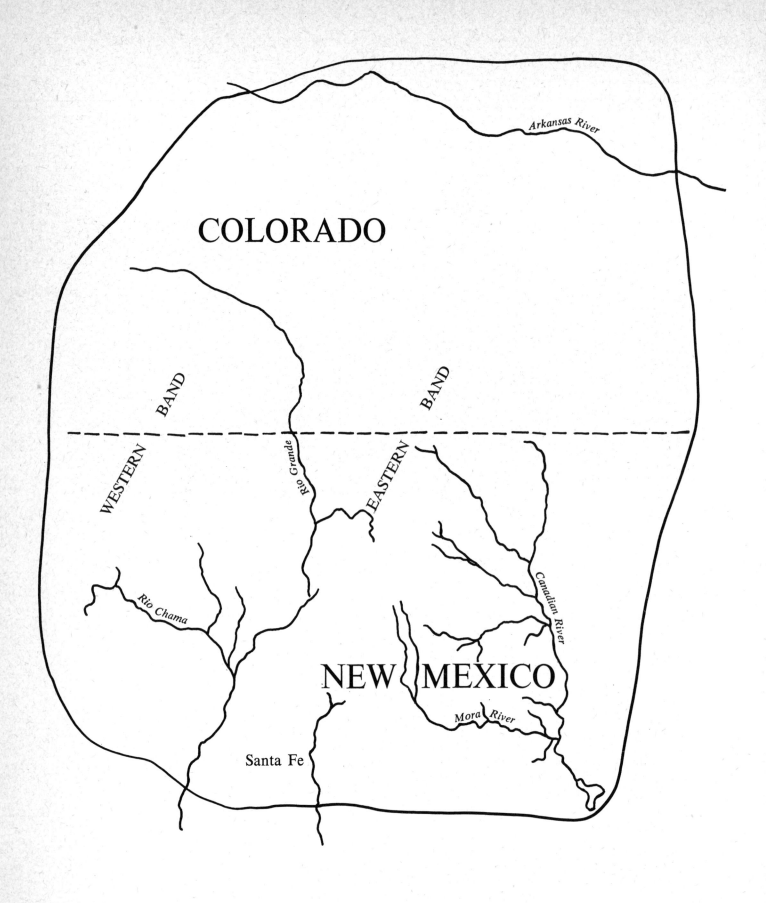

Original location of the Jicarilla bands.

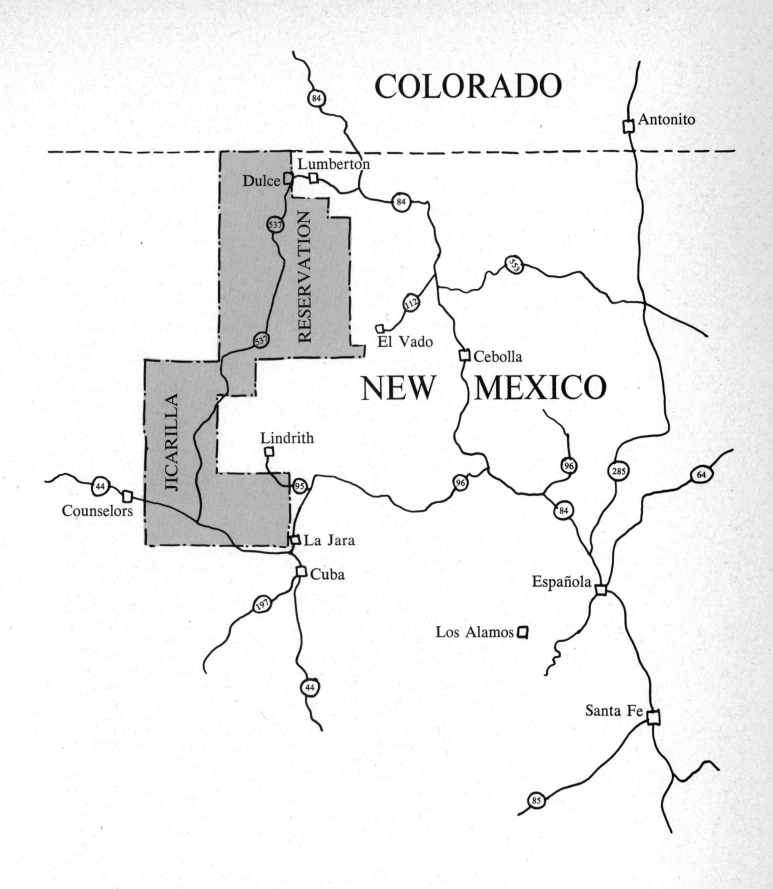

The present-day Jicarilla Reservation.

or "plains people," often called the Llanero, occupies the territory east of the Rio Grande, and their favorite retreats are in the Sangre de Cristo Mountains. The "sand people," who are often called the Ollero, live west of the Rio Grande. There are no cultural or linguistic differences between the bands, and there is intermarriage between their members, although marriage within the same band is more common. Since parents belong to different bands, the children, because of matrilocal residence, become members of the mother's band. The tribal bands serve to provide the sides for an annual ceremonial relay race held between the youths of the two bands, which in Jicarilla belief fulfills the purpose of assuring a plentiful supply of meat and plant food for the coming year. The two bands are further divided into local groups. These are clusters of individual families that result from blood relationships, marriage, common interests, or great friendship. Each of these centers around a geographic landmark under the guidance of a chief or leader.

At the time the first Whites arrived in the area there were approximately twelve local groups, six to each band. The primary unit around which social and economic life revolved was the extended domestic family with matrilocal residence. In the usual instance this consisted of a married couple, their unmarried children, their married daughters and sons-in-law, and the children of these. The extended family was the group responsible for the well-being and training of the child.[1]

Since they hunted buffalo and other large animals on the Plains and were in regular contact with certain Plains tribes, early Jicarilla material life was strongly oriented toward Plains culture. They used the tipi, the parfleche, the bow case and quiver, the usual buffalo hunting techniques, and the travois.[2] Their warpath and raiding customs also reveal a decided Plains flavor, and their garments were Plains in style. Much of this Plains-like appearance, however, was superficial and a part of their late history. Though most Jicarilla were using the tipi at the time of American occupation of the region, it is possible that the more common dwelling before that time was a dome-shaped frame wickiup covered with a thatching of leaves or bark.[3] And when the Jicarilla went to the Plains to hunt buffalo, they felt uneasy; they lost no time in finding the buffalo, securing the meat, and hastening back to the protection of their mountain territory. There was good cause for this, for in the open and level stretches of the east they were indeed vulnerable to the numerous Plains tribes. The need for horses forced them to go to the Plains on raids, but such expeditions were considered so dangerous that participation in them became as much a proof of bravery as a practical venture. Psychologically the Jicarilla have always been anything but a Plains people, and like the other Apache groups have always felt most secure in or near a country of mountains, forests, and streams. Frequent contact with Pueblo peoples of the upper Rio Grande also influenced Jicarilla ritual life and probably inspired the development of their agricultural complex. Besides this, Pueblo influence is seen in Jicarilla ceremonial life.[4]

In spite of the Plains and Pueblo influences, Jicarilla culture has remained in fundamental harmony with the beliefs, assumptions, and behavior patterns common to all of the other Apachean-speaking tribes of the American Southwest: the Lipan, Kiowa Apache, Mescalero, Chiricahua, Western Apache, and Navajo. Of the other Apachean groups, the Jicarilla were nearest in essentials and probably closest in historical relations to the Lipan. However, late secondary contacts and interchanges with the Navajo led to striking likenesses between the two tribes in mythology, ceremonial rites, supernatural beliefs, and agricultural practices.[5]

1598: Don Juan de Oñate is the first governor and first captain-general of the province of New Mexico. One of his immediate actions is to divide the province into mission districts. Fray Francisco de Zamora is assigned to serve the Jicarilla.

1629: Those Jicarilla living in close proximity to the Taos

Pueblo are at peace with them, and at this time exhibit their desire to make a similar peace with the Spanish. However, by Apache custom, the leaders speak for themselves and do not bring all of the people. The rest remain free to raid and make war as they please.

1706: Capt. Juan de Ulibarri is sent with a force of 140 men to warn the Picuris and the Jicarilla that further attacks on the Spanish settlements will not be tolerated. Ulibarri is kindly received by the first Apache he meets, invited to their camps, given food, and warned that the Comanche are waiting to attack him in Raton Pass. Moving on, Ulibarri meets other Jicarilla who greet him just as warmly and beg him to lead them in a war party against the Pawnee and the French. At this time the Jicarilla are also experiencing raids by the Utes and the Comanche. The Spanish government makes an alliance with the Jicarilla and the Cuartelejo to repel the Comanche invaders.[6]

Jicarilla man wearing beaded shoulder bands and beaded hair tubes.

Top: *The old mines east of the Jicarilla Reservation.* Above: *Abandoned mines in Jicarilla country, the cause of many difficulties for the Apache.*

1716: Some of the Jicarilla join the Spanish and the Pueblo in an expedition against the Faraon Apache, but the Faraon escape and the campaign is a failure.

1717: The Comanche are driving the Jicarilla from their homelands in Colorado and eastern New Mexico. Fighting and killing are increasing year by year, and the Jicarilla are desperate. Appeals for aid are made to the Spanish, who use their plight as an excuse to send missionaries among them to set them up as a buffer against the French. Antonio Valverde is the new governor, and in response to Jicarilla and Pueblo pleas he raises a huge strike force to attack the Comanche. The group includes 196 Jicarilla warriors. No contact is made with the Comanche, however, and the expedition force returns home. At this point the Jicarilla have large numbers of horses and are reported to be using red and white body war paint.[7] They are also fashioning crude crosses in an attempt to please the Spanish.

1720–1775: The Jicarilla retreat from the Plains under the massive onslaughts of the more numerous Comanche. The Utes also are extending their frontier, and now hold the entire northern area along the sources of the Rio Grande. Eventually, the Comanche control the southeastern Colorado, western Kansas, and the panhandles of Oklahoma and Texas. On the west the Navajo dominate a vast region from which constant raids are launched against the Jicarilla and the Spanish. Southward, matters are in constant turmoil as the rest of the Apache groups savagely resist the Spanish. It soon develops that the Spanish have encountered one of the strongest and most competent foes in their history. By 1775, the Jicarilla are remaining close to the presidios of northern New Mexico for protection, and some serve in the Spanish army.

1786: The Jicarilla are located in the Pecos and the lower Rio Grande regions, and now raid the crops near the new town of Belen and the horse and sheep herds near Socorro. Soon the raids extend as far south as Albuquerque. At times, alliances against common foes are made with the Ute, the Gila and the eastern Navajo. The New Mexicans develop a militia system to combat the Jicarilla, but trade between the two groups is so good that neither wishes to do serious damage to the other.

1803: The Jicarilla sack the Pecos Pueblo, inspiring retaliatory raids by the New Mexicans.

1804: The Jicarilla make a short-lived treaty with the Gila. The New Mexicans continue their attempts to catch and punish the Apache who are raiding to supplement their material needs. Governor Chacon makes a treaty with the Jicarilla to obtain their services as scouts for an exploration trip up the Missouri River. His campaign against the Navajo in August includes Jicarilla and Ute among the troops. By now the Jicarilla and one segment of the Ute are united and will remain so for a number of generations to come. Certain of the Jicarilla continue to raid, and are threatened by Chacon, who eventually makes a treaty with the Navajo that angers the Jicarilla. In response, they continue to raid the settlements. Chacon also asks the Comanche to help keep the Jicarilla in line. Some of the Apache are now serving as guides for the fur-trade trappers and perform exceedingly well in this capacity. But they are paid with whiskey. Some say this begins a situation wherein the Jicarilla in general develop a disasterous taste for whiskey, and their closeness to the settlements only aggravates the problem.

1810: The Jicarilla and Ute join forces for a buffalo hunt, and upon encountering the Comanche suffer a serious defeat. The New Mexicans make a treaty with the Comanche and the Kiowa to join in a battle against the Mescalero. The Jicarilla and Ute aid the Mescalero and are beaten again. It is enough, and in 1810 the Jicarilla sign a peace treaty with the Comanche. Relative peace follows for a time. With the outbreak of war between the United States and Mexico, along with other major problems confronting both countries, the Jicarilla are neglected, isolated, and miserable.

1834: Smouldering Jicarilla hostility toward the Americans

351

Jicarilla field camp. Canvas tents attached to tree. Photo by A. T. Willcox (DPL).

cause a few of them to steal some stock, for which they are pursued and attacked.

1846: The United States occupation of the area begins; Charles Bent is appointed governor and Indian agent. The Jicarilla are poverty-stricken, and beg for food and other material needs, promising they will be good and faithful citizens of the United States. Despite the danger, some buffalo hunts are still made. Differences with the Mescalero cause them to abandon their southern ranges. The tribe now numbers about five hundred. Bent proves to be anything but a friend of the Jicarilla, and in anger a group of them massacre the Joseph White family at a place called Point of Rocks. This is followed by an attack on a group of buffalo hunters. All licenses to trade with the Jicarilla are immediately suspended, and an army force which includes Kit Carson pursues and kills most of the hostile group. The Jicarilla in general are now looked upon as outlaws and, being forced away from the settlements, become desperate for food. The situation leads to a series of injustices on both sides. Troops are constantly in the field against them, and the Jicarilla and Ute carry out numerous attacks on wagon trains in the areas of Santa Fe and Taos. James S. Calhoun, the Indian agent, succeeds in signing a treaty with the Jicarilla that establishes a permanent home for them. He forwards it to Washington, but it is not acted upon and nothing comes of it. Hungry beyond that which they can bear, the tribe turns to raiding and warfare once again. In 1851, Fort Union is built to provide for control of the Jicarilla.

1852: The Jicarilla join with the Navajo and Ute for a war party against the Kiowa and the Arapaho, and instead raid the farms of settlers. Continued raids bring many complaints, and cause the assignment of the Jicarilla to the Albiquiu Agency. Here their crops are poor, they are fed wormy meat, and they are given meager rations. Soon they are in a destitute condition. Once again they resort to theft to exist.

1853: Kit Carson, serving under General Kearny, advocates agricultural schools for the Apache. He gains some influence with the Jicarilla and in time becomes a peacemaker between the warring factions.

1854: On Christmas Day, more than a hundred Jicarilla and Ute destroy a settlement on the Arkansas River, killing fifteen men, capturing women and children, and running off the livestock.

1855: In January, a retaliatory force of troops surprises the hostile Jicarilla and Ute in the midst of a war dance, killing forty Indians and capturing six children. In a second battle the Indians lose thirteen more warriors plus all their material possessions. Shortly after this the Jicarilla seek out the agent and beg for peace, explaining that they have only stolen because of want and promising to change their ways. Nevertheless, they withdraw to the mountains to regroup their forces and in a short while resume their raids. When twenty-four soldiers are killed in a battle with them, the governor of New Mexico declares that a state of war exists between the United States and the Jicarilla Apache.

1856: Kit Carson is made agent for the Jicarilla and the Ute. The Indians center their activities around Cimarron and work for L. B. Maxwell on his land grant as herders, hunters, and craftsmen. Carson and Maxwell manage to keep the Indians occupied and somewhat satisfied. The Civil War years are quiet ones for the Indians, and the abundance of new forts and uniformed troops helps to keep them subdued. Food is difficult to obtain, however, and some cattle are stolen by the Indians, who claim they are only taking supplies promised them by the government but not delivered. After the Civil War the Jicarilla are found to be naked, starving, and in ill health. They have received no rations for an entire year. Maxwell is their only source of supply. The government finally moves to assist the Indians as General Carleton orders that rations be supplied to them as long as they remain friendly. Several possible sites in Utah and Colorado are suggested as reservations for the Jicarilla, but they refuse to settle anywhere except their beloved New Mexico mountain home.

1869: The government terminates its ration program, and supplies are cut off at Cimarron as it seeks to force the Ute to break with the Jicarilla and to return to Colorado. The Jicarilla now go to the ranches and kill cattle, for their mood is such that they disregard the consequences. Gold is discovered on Willow Creek, and prospectors moving into the area bring forth still more anger from the Jicarilla. Only the presence of troops restrains them.

1870: Sale of the Maxwell Land Grant requires the removal of the Jicarilla and Ute, and their situation grows dimmer day by day. The Jicarilla population now numbers 864. Carson and Maxwell have moved away, and the present officials are not in the least concerned with Jicarilla welfare. Moreover, the White settlers are using every

Jicarilla camp, ca. 1900.

possible means to remove the Jicarilla from the Cimarron area. The Jicarilla retaliate with raids in Colorado and New Mexico.

1872–1874: Attempts are made to move the Jicarilla to Fort Stanton, New Mexico, for their own best interests, as settlers are demanding they be wiped out. Agent Thomas A. Dolan negotiates a treaty with the Indians in which they agree to give up the Cimarron area, but they let go reluctantly, continuing to roam that territory for some time thereafter. Most are allowed to go to the Tierra Amarilla on the northern edge of the territory. Here the government lays out a place for them known as the Tierra Amarilla Reservation, for the absolute and undisturbed occupation of the Jicarilla Apache, "except such officers, agents and employees of the government as may be authorized to enter upon Indian Reservations in the discharge of duties enjoined by law." The Jicarilla are attached to the Southern Ute Agency. They are to receive financial subsidies, provisions, protection, land allotments, and schools. Meanwhile, the Apache are being cheated by the contractors, who for several years have been giving them rotten meat and only half the rations paid for by the government. The Jicarilla have no recourse but to continue to roam, steal, and relieve their hopelessness with cheap whiskey.

1875: J. E. Pyle becomes the Jicarilla agent and recommends a school and teacher. Settlers do all they can to discourage this as they continue to press for Indian removal. It is proposed that the Jicarilla be gathered with the Mescalero at Fort Stanton.

Jicarilla loading rations, ca. 1900.

1876: The Tierra Amarilla Reservation area is turned over to the settlers as public domain in July. The Cimarron Agency is abolished in September on the excuse there are no funds for an agent. Efforts are renewed to move the Jicarilla to Fort Stanton, but when the special agent in charge of removal arrives, only thirty-two Jicarilla are ready and willing to go.

1880: Five Jicarilla chiefs go to Washington to plead their cause to remain in northern New Mexico. A new reservation is assigned to them on the Navajo River. Some do move there, but return to Fort Stanton in 1883. Others remain in the Cimarron area. The settlers continue to blame the Jicarilla for every problem arising as they seek their removal. Newspapers continually print sensational reports, which are totally false, about Jicarilla depredations.

1882–1887: The Jicarilla of the Taos and Cimarron areas are moved to the Mescalero reservation at Fort Stanton. Smallpox strikes on the trip, and six die, leaving 721 Jicarilla unhappily joined with 563 Mescalero. The Mescalero resent the numerical odds and even the very presence of the Jicarilla. The agent, Llewellyn, makes matters worse by forming a police force consisting only of Mescalero, and the Jicarilla refuse to obey them. Attempts at farming, cattle raising, and schooling meet with limited success. Tensions are constant, and in the fall of 1886, two hundred Jicarilla leave the reservation and settle at Sante Fe, refusing to leave until the governor listens to their grievances. The reaction of the alarmed citizens is such that the government, on February 11, 1887, issues an Executive Order to set aside a reservation in the Tierra Amarilla region. The return there is somewhat complicated by New Mexican settlers who have occupied land in the region under homestead laws, and now refuse to leave. The government begins to buy the land back, a process that will consume over fifty years. In May, 1887, the remaining Jicarilla at Fort Stanton are returned north and the tribe is finally united in a permanent home of its own.

1890: Tuberculosis infects the Jicarilla, taking such a heavy toll that if not stopped it will wipe out the tribe within a few years. The Presbyterian Church opens a mission and day school at Dulce and also strives to control the illness. It will remain in operation and render excellent service for twenty years. Even so, until 1920, there will be fewer births than deaths each year.

1892: The agent reports 515 Llaneros and 309 Olleros are living on the reservation. Some progress is being made in farming, and 36 children are in the government school in Sante Fe. Whiskey is a continuing problem, but the general conduct of the Jicarilla is good. They are tanning skins and making moccasins, baskets, and pots. The epidemic is being controlled, and the population is increasing slightly. Some Apache have begun raising sheep.

1894: The health of the tribe is good; the agent reports that the Jicarilla call upon the Agency doctor and that very few are patronizing the native medicine man. The desire for education is improving, and a request is made for a boarding school at Dulce.

1895: Jicarilla population is 845. Forty new log houses have been built. No disease is reported. Ranchers disturbed by Jicarilla straying off the reservation continue to press for their removal from the area.

The Indian Agency at Dulce, 1911.
Photo by H. F. Robinson (MNMP).

1896: The Jicarilla population is 853. Of the 42 deaths reported over the previous year, two-thirds are attributed to consumption. Requests for a boarding school on the reservation are renewed. Thirty-four more houses have been built, some log, some lumber, some adobe. The Jicarilla are adopting the White man's dress and living habits. Some are now eating foods formerly on the taboo list. Craftworks are increasing, as baskets, beadwork, and pottery are fashioned. Bows, arrows, and quivers are constructed for tourists.

1901: The size of the Jicarilla Reservation is set at 415,713 acres. Grain and hay are being raised with good success, and the agent suggests that the exceptionally fine timber of the area could be marketed and the proceeds used to buy cattle and sheep. Self-support is the ultimate aim. Fifteen thousand acres are fenced. There is an Indian court composed of three judges. More houses are built. However, the illegal sale of liquor by the Whites continues. A Methodist mission with a day school is established south of Dulce, but in ten years it will be destroyed by fire and not rebuilt.

1902–1903: Dr. H. M. Cornell comes twice a week to the reservation to minister to the sick. In 1921, he becomes resident doctor of the sanitarium and hospital, and through a fine health program and a staff of seven nurses, mostly from the Dutch Reformed Mission, finally conquers the tuberculosis. The first government school and hospital are built. Agency buildings are also erected. Schoolchildren are issued military-type uniforms to wear to school. The school has enrolled 132 pupils, but it closes for two months because of an epidemic of measles and smallpox. The boarding school will continue in operation until 1920, when the incidence of tuberculosis causes it to be changed into a sanitarium. Another boarding school will be begun in 1937, and in 1940 dormitories and a gymnasium will be added. In 1942 the sanitarium will be abandoned.

1906: The Wirt Trading Post is begun at Dulce, and Emmet Wirt extends unlimited credit to the needy Jicarilla. In all, he helps them to such an extent that he is known to them as a guardian angel. The pieces for the first wagons are brought to the Jicarilla, and cause considerable excitement as the Indians learn to assemble them and then master their use.

1907: The northern end of the reservation is voted for allotment to individuals by Congress, but the land will not be distributed until 1909. Every member of the tribe receives some land.

1908: The southern end of the reservation is added to provide more territory for grazing sheep and cattle. Sheep and cattle are issued, and paid for by the profits gained from them. The reservation has now increased to 722,303 acres.

1909: Irrigation systems are constructed at Dulce and other places.

1911: A sawmill is established south of Dulce. Dulce is now a center for the Denver and Rio Grande Railroad, and ties are purchased from the Apache.

1920: The annual per capita income of the tribe is approximately twenty dollars. Tuberculosis is still a problem, and children are dying from it in alarming numbers. In 1921, the government will issue sheep to the Jicarilla. Dutch Reformed Church missionaries have visited the reservation since 1914, and open a school at Dulce this year.

1929: There are 240 cases of TB, and the doctor makes 855 visits to homes. The Industrial Club is organized.

1931–1932: Permanent homes, half of them with wooden floors, now house 150 families. A terrible winter causes the Jicarilla to lose 72 percent of their livestock. Proceeds from the sale of timber are used to replace the stock. Only thirty-five Apache receive rations as non-self-supporting. Almost four hundred cannot speak English, read, or write. Not one is eligible to vote.

1934: The repeal of the Allotment Act restores the land to tribal ownership. The adoption of the Indian Reorganization Act calls for all the natural resources of the reservation to be developed for the

Jicarilla camp of traveling group, ca. 1910 (MNMP).

welfare of the entire tribe. Every Jicarilla proceeds voluntarily to return his land to the tribe.

1937: Tribal population is about 750. The Jicarilla are adopting the modern manner of dress. Men and women alike plait their hair in two long braids that fall over the shoulders in front. The men wear denim trousers with trade shirts of various colors and qualities, and all wear large black or gray stetson hats, cowboy fashion. Both men and women purchase shoes with low heels. Some men wear cowboy boots. The women continue to dress in voluminous calico skirts that reach to the ground, with loose blouses of the same colorful material. They sew their own garments and dress in this style for warmth and from a genuine sense of modesty. At the schools and around the agencies the younger girls wear shorter skirts, but on the reservation revert to the earlier fashions because of custom. The woman carries her child in the traditional cradleboard supported by a broad strap over her head. The Jicarilla remain a pastoral people. In winter they drive their flocks to the warmer open grazing grounds of the reservation and live in tents, log houses, or brush shelters. In the higher areas, at the northern end of their territory, they occupy small log or adobe houses, or more commonly square canvas tents. Almost none live in tipis or wickiups. In 1937, the Jicarilla become a federal corporation functioning under a charter and constitution.

1938: Only 12 percent of the population lives at Dulce. Emmet Wirt dies, and making use of the revolving credit fund established under the Reorganization Act, the Jicarilla borrow $150,000 of which $85,000 is used to purchase Wirt's business, lands, and other assets. They organize a cooperative, through which they purchase all goods for the tribe, market everything they produce, bank their funds, and borrow what they need. Their enterprise is an immediate success, and the government loan is retired in five years.[8] As late as the 1920s the Jicarilla have lived as government wards and prisoners, being sporadically rationed and severely repressed. Yet in just twenty-five years

Above: *Jicarilla temporary camp, ca. 1920–1930.* Below: *Camp scene, ca. 1936.*

since then they have risen to meet the challenge with quiet adequacy and are on their way to stability.

1944: The sale of livestock brings in $202,000. Non-Indians who do business with the Jicarilla are impressed with their industry and friendliness. Sixty young men are serving in the armed forces.

1946: Termination of the war brings new problems as wages from war work vanish. Dependency allotments sent home by armed service personnel end, and there is a downward trend in family income. Two-thirds of the families have annual incomes of less than $1,000, the rest less than $500. The demand for education and job preparation is accelerated.

1949: Tribal income from timber resources reaches $10,000.

1951: Tribal population has increased to over nine hundred.

Erna Fergusson visits the Jicarilla and comes away with an unhappy report. Dulce is a white clapboard town with modern houses for Agency people, a store, post office, and government offices. Few Apache live at the town. The Dutch Reformed Mission consists of a church, clubhouse, and homes for missionaries, but spreading missionary ideas is a disappointing labor. There are school buildings, with homes for doctors and teachers. The Apache live in widely scattered frame shacks and dusty tents. The tipi is gone. Furniture consists of dirty sheepskins and a few pots and pans. Flies, filth, and unwashed children abound. Water is scarce and must be hauled for miles. Most homes are not permanent; the people drift with the flocks. There is theft, and school teachers are skeptical of success. They claim that homes are beset with "immorality and filth, bickering and broken marriages." The old taboos that guided boys and girls are gone, and, the teachers assert, the Indians have not learned morality in the White sense. Strangely enough, most of the children continue to return home as soon as they can, preferring the supposedly troubled home to the school.

The Jicarilla are still adhering to ancient beliefs. Sometimes houses in which people have died are burned. The people dread ghosts, and they believe that witchcraft is being practiced. Even school children are seen with the red paint on their cheeks to protect against witches. Medicine men are being called upon to perform their services. Apache hesitate to kill even the coyotes who are after their sheep. Some belong to the Coyote People.

Jicarilla funds are in trust with the government, and the tribe wishes in vain to distribute a part of them for much-needed wagons, horses, windmills, and other necessities. The Agency people doubt the capacity of the Jicarilla to manage things well. In their view some Jicarilla with good incomes are putting their money to good use, but others are not.

All Jicarilla children attend a boarding school at Dulce, but the younger ones are housed in a miserable frame building. Those in the ninth grade and beyond must attend the Indian School at Sante Fe where they are kept segregated from White children. Only three have gone on to college. Police control is virtually absent, and the incidence of drinking by the young is rising.

1952: The tribe begins to make per capita payments, and in the next eight years over $4,000 will be paid to each member. Such payments reduce poverty, but they do not bring individual economic independence.

1956: The Dulce Independent School District is established.

1958: The Stanford Research Institute reports an investment return to the Jicarilla of approximately $55,000 per year from an educational trust fund being administered by the Albuquerque National Bank.

1960: The tribal charter and constitution are revised. The governing body is a tribal council of eight members, a chairman, and a vice-chairman, all elected at large. There are nine committees, covering all aspects of reservation life, who work well with the BIA. Law and order are handled by a tribal police force and a non-Indian judge from Alamosa. Every defendant has a right to trial by a Jicarilla jury. An Amended Family Plan is adopted to give all Jicarilla families an opportunity to better their living conditions.

1962: The *Jicarilla Chieftain* newspaper begins publication on January 8. It is the first Indian paper in New Mexico, and is run by an advisory board authorized by the tribal council. The list of churches includes the Jicarilla Apache Reformed, St. Anthony's Catholic Church, Church of Jesus Christ of Latter Day Saints, Dulce Baptist Indian Mission, and Dulce Assembly of God Mission. The tribe is seeking to recover forty million acres of land taken from it a century ago. Excellent highways now pass through the reservation.

1963: The BIA inaugurates an Adult Vocational Training Plan with a list of eighty-nine fields classified as to jobs on or near

359

the reservation. A Neighborhood Youth Corps is approved under the antipoverty program. Community rodeos and dances are being held. The First Annual Tribal Arts and Crafts Show is held. Almost a million dollars is disbursed to help families build new homes. A new telephone company building is built. There are now TV sets, some new cars, and new pickup trucks.

1964: Tribal population reaches 1,546, 80 percent of whom now live at Dulce. The twelve grades in the school district contain 700 students, 85 percent of whom are Apache. This year, two members of the Jicarilla tribe are elected to the school board. Oil and gas have been discovered on the reservation, land has been leased, and there are already 117 producing oil wells and 755 producing gas wells. The first jury trial is held this year.

1965: Per capita income from all known sources is approximately $1,000. The unemployment rate is high. While many students have started college and vocational schools and dropped out, the *Jicarilla Chieftain* reports that the tribe is looking forward to the graduation from college in December of the first full-blooded Jicarilla Apache. Principal problems are said to be a continuing lack of recognition of the importance of education, and an inability to speak English. An editorial calls upon the people to make Dulce the cleanest town in New Mexico.

1966: An Alcoholism Program is begun as a community action Project. Funds come from the Economic Opportunity Act.

1968: The population reaches 1,741. There are now many modern homes on the reservation, and numerous others have been remodeled. Several families live in new trailers. Water and sewer facilities have been improved, and stockmen are having good success with horses, cattle, and sheep. The climate and terrain make farming difficult. Efforts are being made by the tribal council to attract industries to the reservation.

1970: The population total passes the 1,800 mark. The reservation area is now set at 742,315 acres. The abundant wildlife, especially mule deer, and trout-stocked waters are attracting hunters, fishermen, and campers. Oil, gas, livestock, and tourism are providing income beyond government assistance. An arts and crafts program begun in 1962 is being carried on to regenerate interest in the ancient crafts. Some painting, basketwork, weaving, and beadwork are being done in both the Apache and Plains styles at a cultural center in an old house. It is called the Jicarilla Arts and Crafts Retail Shop, and it includes showcase exhibits of new pieces, as no ancient artifacts are available.

Opposite: *Camp scene, ca. 1930.*
Above: *Jicarilla camp, 1936, showing tipi pole structure used by the tribe. Note small wind flaps on tipi, a characteristic of Jicarilla dwellings. Meat drying rack at right. Photo by Margaret McKittrick (MNMP).* Left: *Jicarilla family at annual festival, ca. 1936.*

Right: *Jicarilla family at annual festival, ca. 1936. Below: Jicarilla woman, boy, and men. Photo by Rinehart, 1898 (DPL). Note hair ties, bandolier bands, Plains-type pipes, and beaded leggings. Opposite: Jicarilla women and horse gear.*

363

Right: *Jicarilla family (DPL). Note beaded blanket strip showing Plains influence. Woman's hair is tied with yarn.* Below: *Apache reservation police with two cattle thieves (SM).*

2 Apparel and Jewelry

The Jicarilla were in contact with the tribes of the central-northern and southern Plains, and adopted and utilized the styles of both in their prereservation and reservation clothing. The influence of the Ute and certain Pueblo tribes can be seen in their apparel.

The perferred material for early shirts and leggings was black-tail mule deer. The male shirts of the 1800s, until perhaps 1885, were a poncho with the sleeves attached and an especially long triangular bib, or neck flap, on both front and back.

The poncho was made from a doubled-over single piece of dressed skin, with the hair side out, and with narrow sleeves attached either by thongs or sewed with sinew. Some shirts were left plain with only the bib being painted. The principal decoration consisted of fringing, beadwork, pearl buttons, and the painting of the bibs with yellow ocher. Sometimes metal conches were tied to the bibs. In some instances tabs were made by cutting the hem of the shirt and the cuffs. The fringing was southern Plains in style of application, grouped in bunches on the sleeves and shoulder rather than running the full length of the sleeve. Yet the fringes were long, and of such quantity as to be northern Plains in character. The bibs were also fringed. The bead-work was done with sinew in lazy stitch. Shoulder bands were often broad and, as such, central Plains in style, but with the simple massive designs that were common to all but the southern Plains nations before 1850. They resembled in particular the beadwork of the Ute and some Pueblo. On the other hand, the narrow bands of beading employed were southern Plains in style. Colors of beads used included red, green, white, and varieties of blue.

In general, the comments regarding the shirt apply to the hide leggings. The leggings were relatively narrow and fitted to the leg. It was common to add a row of tabs to the bottom of the cuff—tabs similar to those employed by the Blackfoot, Ute, and the Taos and Santa Clara Pueblo. (Comparative drawings are included in the book to illustrate this.) The leggings were cut off at the top and attached to the belt with hide straps as was done on the Plains. A long breech-clout was worn with the leggings, and sometimes a shawl was wrapped around the waist.

Legging decoration consisted of side flaps, fringes, paint, and beadwork. Fringes ran around the cuff and almost the full length of the legging. Paint colors included yellow ocher and red, with stripes done in red, green, and brown.[1] Beaded leg bands might either be broad or narrow. The bead colors on a pair of leggings in the Denver Museum are red, white, yellow, light blue, and dark blue. The bead colors of an Arizona State Museum pair are white, two shades of blue, yellow, and red.

F. H. Douglas states that in general, Jicarilla beadwork from 1870 to 1930 is indistinguishable from that of the Ute, and that much of the beadwork found at the Northern Rio Grande pueblos was either of Ute or Jicarilla manufacture, or was patterned after Ute or Jicarilla prototypes.[2]

In the later 1800s the Jicarilla man's apparel began to shift to a combination of Anglo and Indian items. Photographs show men wearing traditional legging styles, but using trade cloth, and topping this with a trade shirt and vest, over which was worn broad otter skin bands decorated with mirrors and other objects, and also bone breastplates. They left the shirttail hanging out over the leggings.

The Jicarilla woman's dress of the 1800s was made of two blacktail mule deerskins after the fashion of the early Plains type. The skin of the legs was used to form the sleeves and was hardly trimmed. The yoke was made by sewing the two skins together a short distance from the top and letting the remainder fall or lap over. Such dresses also were common to the Ute and the Taos Pueblo.

Dress decoration consisted of paint, fringes, cut tabs, and beading. The yokes as well as the bottoms of the dresses might be

Jicarilla family (SM). Man holds shield, bow case, and quiver. Note face paint.

366

painted or rubbed with yellow ocher. Fringes were made either by cutting the skin itself or by attaching pieces. Most fringing was at the side seams and the hem. Double fringing was employed, as was common on the Plains. Beading was limited to symbolic designs, and the beads were sewed on with sinew. Colors included white, yellow, green, red, and various shades of blue.[3]

For ceremonial purposes, such as the Adolescence Rite, a gorgeous cape was added to and worn over the dress. Capes were also worn by the Mescalero, Chiricahua, and Southern Ute, but served as the upper part of their costume, being worn with the ends front and back; in contrast, the Jicarilla women wore theirs with the ends over the shoulders and also beaded them in a unique way. Jicarilla capes are especially hard to find today, and I am pleased to be able to include pictures of all that I discovered in museum collections. Some directors of museums who were without them told me they would give most anything to obtain just one.

Capes were made of the skin of the blacktail mule deer, and were decorated with yellow ocher and green paint, tabs, fringes, and beading. The beading was done in lazy stitch with sinew, and the colors used included red, yellow, black, varieties of blue, and white. Some capes had as many as 100,000 beads sewed on them.[4] The practice was also to tie amulets to the ceremonial capes, including buckskin and calico bags containing certain crushed leaves such as horse mint. A cape in the Denver Museum has a pouch with an antelope jaw in it, and Opler associates this with the part of the Adolescence Rite, where the boy goes out to look for objects to bring back to the girl.[5] Pieces of shell were also attached, as well as small bells and shaped chunks of quartz crystal.

My own research supports that of F. H. Douglas, who states that Jicarilla dresses are "in complete contrast" to those of other Apache groups, who used a two-piece costume of skirt and poncho, along with more beading and the tin cones rarely seen among the Jicarilla.[6]

Beading was also done on the bottoms of women's leggings, and beaded strips were appended to blankets for dress purposes.

A feature of note was the broad leather belt worn by the woman, to which her knife case, awl, and other utilitarian items were attached. Such belts ranged in width from ten to sixteen inches, and were decorated with brass tacks.

The Jicarilla men and women braided their hair in the Plains manner by parting it in the middle and drawing it to the sides. The braids of women were tied with buckskin or cloth, but usually not wrapped. Men sometimes wrapped their braids with deer or otter skin. When the hair was not braided, the men pulled it together and either secured it with a beaded hair tube or else tied it with pieces of trade cloth, leaving the ends hanging long.

Both sexes wore earrings, some of which were simple metal loops and others long loops of beads. A favorite type combined hair-pipe bones, loops, and beads, which together made a long pendant. Necklaces consisted of hair-pipe bone beads fashioned like a choker, with spacers of regular beads, and shells attached at the front. There were also chokers of round trade beads with the shell, which in each case represented the sun. Tubular white glass beads were used to make choker necklaces for both men and women and chest necklaces for women, where the beads were worn vertically. The men wore long strings of the beads looped bandolier-fashion over the right shoulder and under the left arm.

Both men and women wore bracelets and armbands that were beaded or were fashioned of trade brass or copper.

The Jicarilla man appears to have adopted for general use, in the 1870s and thereafter, the typical low-top Plains moccasin, which was beaded either with bands or an allover pattern on the instep. The older type of hide moccasin had a pointed toe and a slit down the center of the instep, which was perhaps unique to the Jicarilla. The woman's moccasin was ordinarily plainer, sometimes being entirely

Jicarilla dolls.

Woman's buckskin dress (SM).

without beading. Judging from photographs, some of the hides worn by women were scraped so thin they fitted the foot like a glove. By 1890 some women were wearing White women's shoes.

The Jicarilla war bonnets were of two types: one resembled the typical Plains bonnet of upright golden eagle feathers, with or without the full tail and with a beaded headband; the other was styled after the Pueblo models. The latter had a skullcap of cloth or buffalo hide over which passed a single row of upright golden eagle tail feathers that extended down to the middle of the back. One of the adapted Pueblo types had a row of metal conches around the headband, round side mirrors, and pendant down-feathers and trade ribbons. It also had split cow or buffalo horns at the sides. In later days the Jicarilla men adopted the black or gray stetson trade hat with broad brim, which is still seen on the reservation today.

Right: *Woman's belt and knife case decorated with brass tacks and buttons (SM).* Below: *Woman wearing buckskin dress and beaded cape, and carrying basket. Note jewelry and yarn hair ties. Photo by A. F. Randall (DPL).*

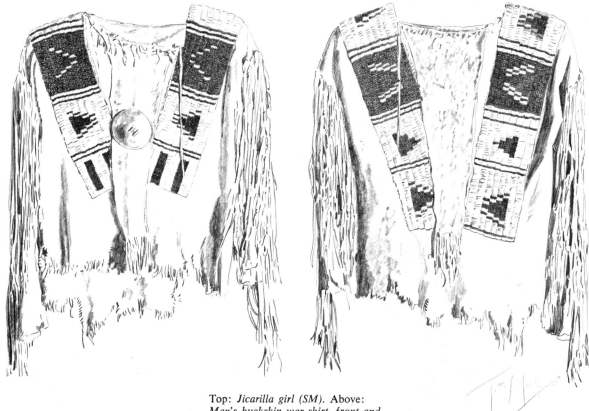

Top: *Jicarilla girl (SM).* Above:
*Man's buckskin war shirt, front and
back views (ASM). Note long bib
typical of Jicarilla shirts, and wide
style of beaded shoulder bands. Beads
are red, green, white, and blue;
concho is brass. Collected by John A.
Logan.*

370

Jicarilla family (SM). Man has fur
hair wraps, beaded blanket strip, and
holds Plains-type hand drum (SM).

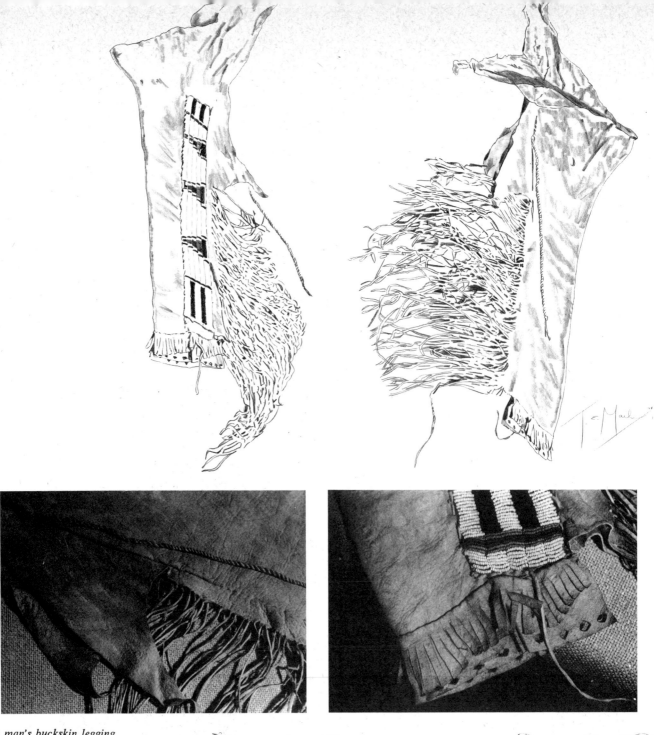

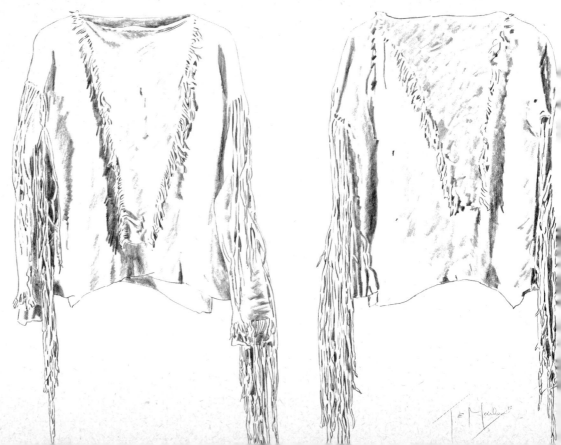

Top: *Jicarilla man's buckskin legging cut in traditional Plains style (ASM). Note tabs on legging bottom and long fringe. Beads are white, two shades of blue, yellow, and red. Length, 1.2 m. Collected by John A. Logan.* Above: left: *Detail of legging side flaps and fringe.* Above: right: *Detail of legging tabs and cutouts.* Right: *Man's daily-wear buckskin shirt (private collection).*

Augustine, chief of the Jicarilla.
Brass concho on bib front was typical
ornamentation.

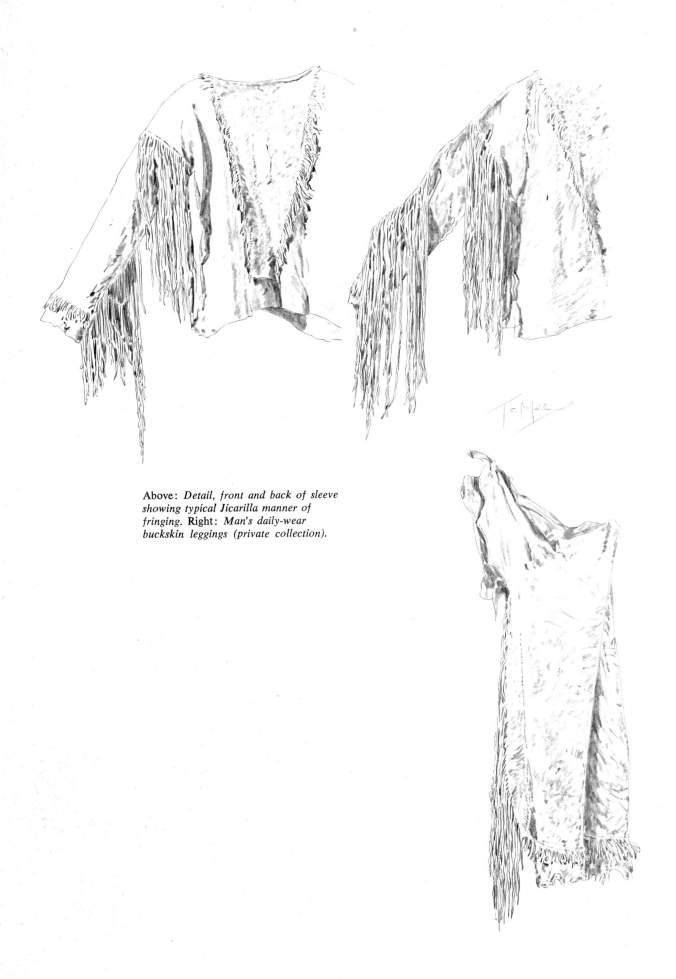

Above: *Detail, front and back of sleeve showing typical Jicarilla manner of fringing.* Right: *Man's daily-wear buckskin leggings (private collection).*

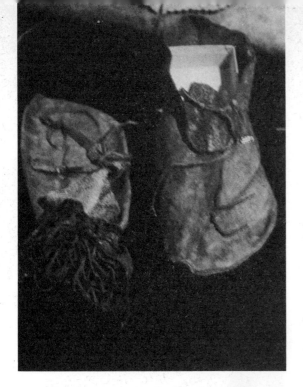

Above left: *Jicarilla rawhide moccasins,
top view (SM).* Above: *Moccasin,
side view.* Below: *James A. Garfield.
Photo by Hopkins (DPL).*

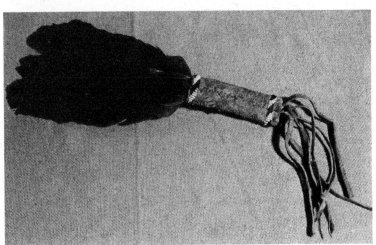

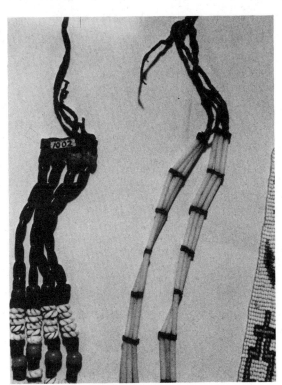

Opposite left: *Elote, after photo by Hopkins (DPL).* Opposite right: *Elote, side view (DPL). His war bonnet has a single line of golden eagle feathers modeled after typical Pueblo types.* Top: *Brass arm bands (ALMN).* Center: *Eagle feather ceremonial fan (ASM).* Above left: *Tube bead necklace.* Above right: *Thoket type trade bead necklace of style worn by Jicarilla and Chiricahua (AF).*

Opposite left: *Santa Clara Pueblo man in dress apparel, for comparison with Jicarilla costume (MNMP).* Opposite right: *Taos Pueblo man wearing leggings with beading and tabs similar to Jicarilla leggings (MNMP).* Left: *Ute apparel, for comparison with Jicarilla apparel (MNMP).* Below: *Ute men and women, for comparison with Jicarilla hair styles and apparel (MNMP).*

Jicarilla warrior in full war dress and holding lance or ceremonial staff (SM).

380

3 Religion

Jicarilla mythology is astonishingly complex and comprehensive. However, Opler, whose research is far more thorough than that of anyone else concerning the tribe—and to whom I am deeply indebted for much of the information in the ritual sections that follow—feels that it became so infused with influences from European and Pueblo sources that it is presently impossible to distinguish that which is entirely Jicarilla.[1] Further, the sacred myths, such as the origin story, have varied slightly, since they are employed as a base or storehouse from which the Jicarilla storyteller may draw at will for material to embellish his own version of a given myth.[2]

The myths include cosmology and ceremonial life and at the same time contain a surprising amount of information concerning nearly every aspect of life as it was lived in former times, some parts of which are adhered to even now.

Since the myths have always been thought of as the proper guide to life, their telling was an important undertaking. The long winter nights of earlier times were largely given over to this. The stories were of different kinds, some happy, some sad, and some frightening. The one at whose camp the people gathered gave a little feast, and about midnight they ate. "It is a sort of 'sacrifice', for they are talking of holy things, of the time when the earth was new and all were holy." When a man had a group of children listening to his stories, he gave them kernels of corn to eat, and then they never forgot what they heard.[3]

Opler also points out that written accounts of the myths cannot do justice to Jicarilla folklore. The people, he says, developed a vivid oral art in which gestures, pantomime, and the formation of words by using the natural sounds associated with the object or action involved carried much of the dramatic burden.[4]

The origin myth told about the creation of earth, sky, animals, and man. In the beginning there was nothing but Darkness, Water, and Cyclone. All the Hactcin, who were Supernaturals and personifications of the power of all objects and natural forces, were here from the beginning. They made the world first, and then the sky. The Earth was made in the form of a living woman and was called Mother. The Sky was made in the form of a living man, and called Father. He faced down and she faced up. They were the mother and father of the Jicarilla.

All kinds of Hactcin lived in the underworld, from whence the emergence started. Everything there was as a dream; the Jicarilla people were not flesh and blood, they were like shadows of things to come. There was nothing but darkness, and everything was perfectly spiritual and holy.

The leader, and most powerful Hactcin, was Black Hactcin, who made the world and all the animals and people. The names of the first two people were Ancestral Man and Ancestral Woman. The people dwelt in the underworld for many years—no one knows for how long—before they finally emerged and went looking for a permanent place to live on the surface of the earth.[5] Black Hactcin was the one the Jicarilla thought of as the Mexicans thought of Dios, or God. The next Hactcin after Sky and Earth were Sun and Moon. The child of Sun was Killer of Enemies, also known as Monster Slayer; his mother was White Painted Woman. The Moon's son was Child of the Water, also known as Water's Child; his mother was White Shell Woman.

The Jicarilla Hactcins, who, like the Gans of the other Apache, impersonated the Mountain Spirits, were begun by the Supernaturals, and in former times they impersonated the Hactcin to cure widespread epidemics and sickness. For a most interesting reason, the Jicarilla Hactcins have not danced for many years, and possibly will never perform again. Even when they did dance, no outsider was ever permitted to watch the ceremony. When smallpox threatened to wipe out the Jicarilla tribe, the people performed the Hactcin ceremony to aid their sufferings. But the White doctors opposed the idea in favor of vaccination. The Jicarilla leaders did not appreciate the challenge to their Supernaturals and decreed that anyone who was vaccinated could not impersonate a Hactcin. The result was that nearly all Jicarilla youth were disqualified from participating in the masked dancer ceremony.[6]

While there were many similarities between the Hactcins and the Gans, there were also significant differences. The one who made the dancers did not gain his power from the Hactcin. He received no message or instructions from them. He simply learned it from others, performed it, and knew it would do the sick people good.[7] The individual Hactcin impersonators were personifications of different and specific sources of power and more formalized than the Gans, and their activities even extended to rainmaking. As many as thirty-two men, including eight clowns, were made up for some Hactcin curing ceremonies.[8]

The clowns wore buffalo-hide caps, were painted with white clay and black stripes, carried deer-hoof rattles, and used sunflowers.

The Hactcins wore masks made of the hard-to-obtain hide of male or female mountain sheep. The masked dancers sprinkled cornmeal on the masks first and then motioned four times before putting them on, praying as they did so. The man who sang for the ceremony made the masks and kept them. If the ceremony was handed down from one man to another, the masks were given along with it.[9]

The ceremony took place in a huge corral about forty yards in diameter, called the sun, and the Hactcin home where the dancers were made up was a corral about thirty yards in diameter, called the moon. The big corral walls were made thick with brush so that no one could look in. The entrance faced east.

Inside each of the two corrals there was a central fire pit, and in the big corral there were four small fires on the south side and four on the north. The fires were lighted only at night.

The dancers and the people had to bathe before the curing ceremony, and the singer gave good advice to the people about their habits and conduct. The sick people sat out in the open between the two corrals without any covering. This conveyed the idea that they were abandoned until they were brought back by the four-day ceremony.[10] The ceremony itself was much like the Holiness Ceremony to be described. When it was done, the corral was left as it was, until it fell from decay.

4 Ceremonialism

According to Opler, the individual shaman, whose power was derived from a personal experience, has played a lesser or subordinate role in Jicarilla religion, with his ceremonials being performed for emergencies and minor crises. For the more important occasions, traditional rites, which had their origin in mythology of the people, were held. These were called "long-life ceremonies," and they involved careful planning and preparation.[1]

Over the years, the ceremonial life of the Jicarilla has been reduced to a few long-life ceremonies: the Holiness Rite, the Adolescence Rite, and the Ceremonial Relay Race. Some use is made of medicine men for curing today, although more regular use by far is made of the Public Health Service Clinic at Dulce.

The exalted status of the long-life ceremonies becomes evident as, in the Jicarilla view, shamans had to be transformed into a dance group which then did its most effective work by performing in the rituals.

Opler says that at the beginning of the ceremony, the four Holy Ones, or Supernaturals, painted and dressed twelve medicine men, known as the Tsanati, or Wonder Workers. A short skirt of yucca was made for each man, and spruce branches were stuck in around the waist. Yucca bands were tied around the wrists, upper

Left: *The clowns.* Below: *White Hactcin.*

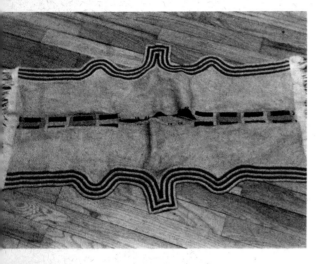

arms, ankles, and knees. Spruce branches were stuck under the leg bands and upper arm bands. Six of the shamans, painted blue from head to foot, represented the summer season; six represented winter, and were painted white all over. A vertical black line was painted on each cheek. Buckskin moccasins were worn, and a single golden eagle feather was tied in the hair on the top of the head of each man. The shamans held four kernels of blue corn, branches of spruce, and blades of yucca in each hand.[2]

When the Wonder Workers were finished, the four Holy Ones made six clowns, whose name in literal translation is "striped excrement." These were painted white all over, and had four broad black bands circling the body at the face, chest, thighs, and calfs. Each arm was also painted with four black stripes. Yucca bands were tied around the wrists, ankles, and neck. Two deer-hoof rattles were tied to the yucca ankle bands of each leg. The costume included deerskin breechclouts and moccasins. The long hair was gathered and formed into a "horn" on each side of the head. Each horn was painted white with four black stripes, and had an eagle-down feather at the tip.

In their right hands, the clowns carried "whips" made of the broad blades of yucca with eagle-down feathers at the tips. These were used to guard the holy places—the tipi erected at the west end of the corral—against menstruating women, whose presence was dangerous; they were used as weapons against sickness as well. In their left hands the clowns carried a branch of spruce, also used in curing stomach ailments.[3]

Opler adds that the clowns who would perform in the ceremonies for war parties were painted with six black bands, rather than four.[4]

Top: *Beaded cape (MNCA). Sinew sewn. Width at shoulders, 22½ inches; length without fringe, 28 inches; length of fringe on each side, 18 inches.* Above: *Beaded cape (MNCA). Sinew sewn. Width at shoulders, 23½ inches; length without fringe, 18 inches; length of fringe on each side, 25 inches.* Right: *Beaded capes, side view (ALMN, MNCA).*

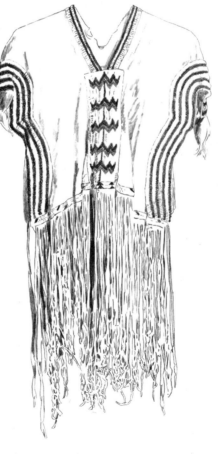

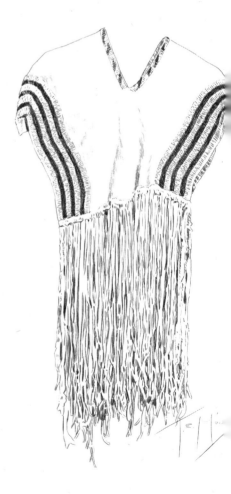

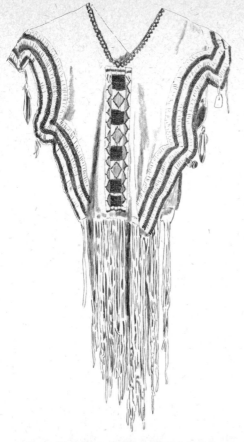
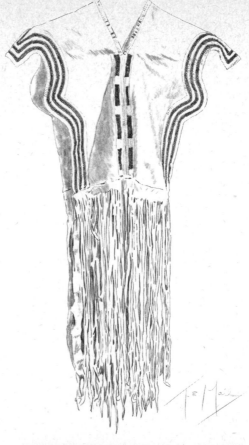

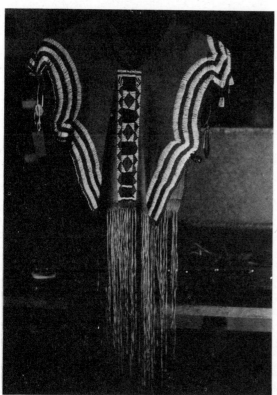
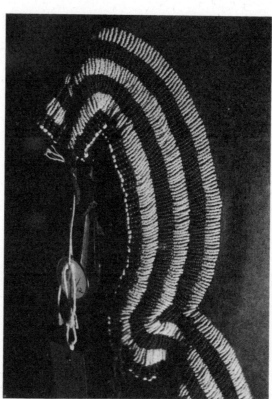

Top: *Beaded capes, side view (ALMN, MNCA).* Above left: *Detail of cape showing shells, crystals, and bells tied to sides as amulets.* Above: *Detail of cape beading.* Left: *Detail of cape fringing.*

5 Holiness Rite (improperly called Bear Dance)

The Jicarilla held a curing ceremony, or Holiness Rite, at the call of the shaman. Some feel it took the name Bear Dance from a Ute ceremony, although that ceremony had nothing to do with bears. The Jicarilla ceremony, in which sand paintings were made, was performed within a brush corral, while outside, women selected partners and danced with them. On the fourth night of the ceremony, a group of masked dancers, accompanied by sacred clowns, made a dramatic entrance. Present-day tourists are advised by those who know from experience to stay away from the Holiness Rite unless they understand what goes on and are ready for unique situations that may arise.

In the origin myth of the Curing Ceremony, Black Bear, Turkey, Rattlesnake, and all the animals living on the earth who were in charge of the various fruits gathered together in one place and celebrated the Curing Dance for the benefit of three sick men. A brush fence or corral was erected around the dancing grounds. A tipi or holy place was set up at the back of the enclosure. Then a hole was dug at the back of the tipi, a basket was placed over it, and a buffalo hide was put over the basket. The hole was dug deeper four times during the ceremony. The basket, hole, and hide symbolized bear and snake sickness.[1] The animals took the moccasins of the three sick men, tied them together, and used them to beat upon the basket. The chanter used a rattle made from a buffalo tail and the rattles of rattlesnakes. This was done for four nights.[2]

It was also said that a long time ago a curing ceremony of this nature was held west of Taos where the mountains stand near each other. The corral fence was constructed of brush, and no one was allowed to look through it from the outside. Some beat with the moccasins and others danced. When this part of the ceremony was done, a noise was made by rubbing the leg bone of a mountain sheep along a notched stick. The clowns and the Wonder Workers came in twice when they were rubbing the sticks. The men put corn, cherries, and the seed of the amole into a hole in the ground. They also put the tail of a rabbit in a clay pot. When they came in the fourth time, the amole and cherries were ripe, the corn was already hard, and a live rabbit jumped out of the pot. One man made a bow out of an arrow and shot another arrow with it without killing the rabbit. The men outside were curious enough at the commotion to look through the corral fence, and instantly turned into pine trees. This was why people were to not look from the outside through the corral fence when the medicine man was chanting. Stanley says that the mountains surrounding the holy site were given names: the first was called Nisdjatohi, the next was Isihiligigahi, and so on until forty-eight were named.[3]

The Jicarilla curing ceremony began with the erection of a corral and tipi, in which a white sand base was spread out and smoothed with eagle feathers. Around the border of the sand area, eagle tail feathers were placed in a circle. While the shaman prepared medicine with herbs, two men drew sand pictures of many kinds of animals. Cornmeal was sprinkled over the sand. For drawing, red, yellow, and white sand were used, as well as blue pollen. Four ground drawings were made during the course of the rite. A clay bowl containing water was placed in the center of the circle, and one person sat on one side of it and another on the other side. The medicine man then rolled around like a grizzly bear and made a noise like a bear grunting. At this point the healthy people sat on the painted animals, while the sick people for whom the ceremony was being performed sat in a row. The herbs were mixed in the clay bowl, and as the medicine man shook his rattle and sang bear songs, the patients began to make anguished cries, while their hands twisted, their feet became crooked, and their noses ran. These, says Stanley, were signs that the correct disease was being treated. As the shaman sang, he rubbed out the paintings with his feet. The medicine rattle was then placed under the feet and on the hands of the patients. This act pulled away sickness as the rattle was withdrawn. The medicine man embraced them, and they were "healed." The medicine was drunk by the patients and also rubbed over their bodies. In the full four-day ceremony corn mush and tiswin was made for the participants. The rest of the men and women danced for the four nights as a prayer for the sick.[4] Food for the feasting consisted of cherries and yucca, broiled rabbit and bread, and sometimes peas. In some rugged touches, dog dung was spread on bread as butter and clowns searched for menstruating women. The people were told to keep the bread, since it would be good medicine if one became ill and threw up from having unintentionally touched any kind of excrement and transmitted it to the mouth, such as dog waste on something used for food.[5]

According to Opler, the clowns and the Wonder Workers performed on the fourth night. Two tipis were set up outside the corral, and the performers were dressed and painted in these. The clowns entered the corral first and sought out women who were having their menstrual period, sending any they suspected out. Then the clowns and Wonder Workers came in an undulating line, as the snake moves. Then the two groups formed two lines, and the Wonder Workers showed their power by performing feats of magic. Then all formed a line, made a motion as if to drive the disease away, and left the tipi. After a basket dance, the ritual was repeated. Another exit, and the rasps were used. When the clowns and Wonder Workers returned the next time, the clowns did all the things people should not do at the ceremony, such as laughing, shouting, wrestling, and even pretending they were having intercourse. They alone could do this, because they were holy. In a final act the clowns and Wonder Workers performed dressed in their regular clothing.

On the fifth day the bird feathers were picked up, along with the two spruce trees with eagle-down feathers attached to their tips that had been used to flank the corral entrance, and everyone formed a long line. The line proceeded to the east to a young tree, the two spruces were placed there, and cornmeal was sprinkled on them. After this there was ceremonial racing. Then the shamans took the notched rasp sticks and, crossing them as the Gans did their wands, placed them on the bodies of the aged and infirm to disperse illness. Finally the entire group returned to dismantle the ceremonial tipi, which was built with a framework of twelve poles, just as were the big tipis of all the Apache puberty rites.[6]

The Holiness Rite was perhaps the most profound long-life ritual of the Jicarilla Apache, for the bear and the snake represented two great evil powers to be dealt with. The ritual could be learned only by those who had the power to heal. A special use of the ceremony was to cure those who were thought to be under the influence of a bear, a snake, or a witch. It could be held at any time of the year, although Jicarilla long-life ceremonies in general were usually set to coincide with the waxing moon, which was related to growth and fulfillment. While, as previously indicated, some call the ceremony the Bear Dance, and believe that in part at least it was borrowed from the Ute, Opler associates the ceremony with the Pueblo Indians, believing that since the Jicarilla had contact with the Pueblo for decades before making peace with the Ute it is more than likely that much of the ceremony came from the Pueblo.[7] In Opler's view, the name "Bear Dance" was given to the ceremony by White men, largely because a blackened and spruce-covered figure, symbolic of the bear, makes an entrance at one point during the ceremony.[8]

6 Puberty or Adolescence Rite

In the case of the Jicarilla, the word "adolescence" is perhaps more appropriate for this rite than the word "puberty," since the rite involves the participation of both girls and boys.

387

In the origin myth of this rite, as related by Opler, after the emergence and while the people were still traveling, two girls wandered away from the others. One day, while one of them was sleeping, the Sun lay with her. That night Water came to the other girl. The first girl conceived, bore the child who was named Monster Slayer, and became White Painted Woman. The second girl gave birth to Water's Child, the lesser of the culture heroes, and the boys who later participated in the Adolescence Rite were most commonly referred to as Water's Child. The second girl became White Shell Woman. The first Adolescence Rite was held over these girls. The same Jicarilla word means "shell" and "bead," and White Bead Woman is an equally good translation of the name and is favored by some authorities. One of Opler's informants said that a boy could take the part of Monster Slayer in a puberty ceremony more than once. He had been Monster Slayer four times. "They say it is better for a boy to have done it four times. Then he has long life."[1]

When it appeared that her first period was near at hand, a girl was fully informed of the numerous precautions she should take, and of the risks to which her carelessness might expose others. Boys, too, were made aware of the special dangers when menstrual blood was present. There was no segregation of the girl at the menstrual period, she was simply to be careful. She was told to keep away from food plants, for if she crossed a growing field the crop would be poor. If she walked through anthills her blood would stop up and cause her sickness. She should stay away from young men, for when a young man smelled the blood, he might double up, and get bloated too. It was not so dangerous for an aged man, since he was tough and experienced. Boys and men would become lazy if they had intercourse with a girl or woman who had not yet finished a menstrual period. Even a horse could become lazy if it walked where a girl had put her menstrual pad of antelope skin. To cure this, one cut all four of the horse's legs just above the hoof and let lots of blood out. This was done in the morning, and then strong medicine, like osha, was rubbed on hard. "Blood medicine" could be put on too. Therefore, menstrual pads should be buried far from camps or burned.

Some women wouldn't ride horses at this time, saying the horse smelled the blood and was no good after that. A woman who was menstruating should not watch a war dance, since it would make the men's legs stiff. She shouldn't visit a sick person, and she shouldn't attend any ceremony for the sick. In particular, she was not allowed in the corral on the last night of the Holiness (or Curing) Rite until the masked dancers had gone, for if she watched the dancers, their noses would bleed, and they might double up and go lame. If any of these things happened during a dance, a clown brought in a down feather hanging from the end of a yucca leaf. He went around and put it before each woman, and when he came to the one who was menstruating, the down feather would unerringly rise and point to her, and she was sent away. Indeed, it was the clown's duty to keep menstruating women away from ceremonial gatherings. Before a major rite got underway the clowns usually circled around with their yucca leaves and down feathers in an attempt to find and send away any woman who was menstruating. A girl who was menstruating was dangerous even for another girl or woman who was not menstruating, since they would become ill from smelling or touching her menstrual blood. The usual sickness resulting from this was rheumatism. The root of the blood medicine plant was chewed to cure it.

Since the expenditure in food and goods for the Adolescence Rite was a large one, and since some of the materials and objects required were difficult to obtain at short notice, the family began to get ready long before the time for the rite came. Unblemished deer skins were needed for the girl's dress and the boy's clothes, and hunters had the difficult task of taking the kill of a cougar or wildcat for the garments. A skin taken in this way had no holes in it from arrows and could be used for sacred purposes.

When a Jicarilla girl was thirteen or fourteen years old, she came of age. That is, she had her first menstrual period and became a woman. The day her first period occurred she told her mother, and her people took the final steps to ready themselves for her puberty ceremony, which would bring her good luck and a long life. They gathered large quantities of food and corn to make tiswin.

Opler's informants told him that while the others carried out their duties, the girl's father arranged for a singer. He made a cigarette with corn leaves and asked the singer to perform the ceremony by placing the cigarette on the singer's right foot. By picking it up, the man indicated his acceptance of the request. The cigarette was saved and used in the ceremony. In contrast to the Western Apache, Jicarilla puberty ceremonialists were not shamans. The traditional rite and its songs were handed down from the original ceremony and learned by one man from another.

The father also sought another participant, a boy of his daughter's age who would dance on equal terms with his daughter. This role was not considered a special favor, and no payment was rendered for it. The boy could be any youth except a relative. In the rite, he represented either Water's Child or Monster Slayer; it did not matter which he was called. During the ceremony the girl was called either White Shell Woman or White Painted Woman. It did not matter which; she stood for both, since the two holy women went through the first puberty ceremony at the same time.

For his own good, every boy was supposed to go through this ceremony before he grew to manhood. The boy's family assisted with the preparations. His relatives shared in the cooking and in the payment to the singer also, for the ceremony was for both young people. In the ceremony the singer sang over the boy, blessed him, and rubbed his head. He prayed for long life for him, for chieftainship, and for all good things. If this were not done and the boy attempted to accomplish these things, he would fail and became bald. According to Jicarilla mythology, that is why the turkey, the turkey vulture, and the eagle were bald. They had never taken part in this ceremony, yet when Monster Slayer asked who the chiefs were, they had stepped forward, and as soon as they did so their hair fell out.

The ceremony began at dawn on the day after the appearance of the new moon. The first act was the erection of the ceremonial tipi which served as the focal point for the ritual events. Twelve spruce poles were used for the framework. Unlike their Mescalero counterpart, the poles did not need to be freshly cut. Opler's informants said they could be poles that had already been used for a dwelling, and they could be used for the ceremonial tipi again and again. The singer sprinkled pollen in a circle to indicate where the tipi was to stand. A three-pole base like that of the regular home was employed, and certain plants were tied near the tips of the poles, at the place where they would come together when assembled. Grama grass was one of these, since it had pollen, and in addition, sunflower, wormwood, and snakeweed. The tipi cover was attached to the back pole, which was the last one placed in position. Sometimes the cover was new, but sometimes old ones were used. Formerly the cover, which was supposed to be made of buffalo hide, was cleaned and whitened with white clay. The entrance faced east, and the four pegs above the door were made of mountain mahogany wood. A turkey-down feather was tied to each side of the tipi, because the turkey stood for growing foods.

Inside, at the rear of the tipi, an elk skin or buffalo hide was laid on the ground for the girl and the boy to sit on. In the center a fire, called the fire from the north star, was kindled. When the tipi was ready, the boy and girl were dressed and painted. They entered the dwelling and sat behind the fire pit, the girl on the south side and the boy on the north. Their clothes were taken from them, and they sat with their feet stretched out before them. Then new garments were placed before them, arranged in the order they were to be put on. The girl's dress and beaded cape were of uncolored buckskin. The color of the cape was yellow; the moccasins and leggings were colored a deeper yellow than the cape, a color obtained by mixing red ocher

389

with the yellow ocher. The girls often wore shell earrings. The boy's clothing was of uncolored buckskin with two weasel pelts attached to the fringe at the shoulders. An Opler informant said that the pelts stood for the supernatural power of a shaman, and were like a prayer that the boy would get power. The boy also wore a wrist guard. The singer sprinkled pollen and specular iron ore on the clothes, and sang as the girl's mother dressed her, and a neighbor woman dressed the boy. First the right moccasin was put on the girl, and then the left. The right legging was put on, and then the left; then the dress, the fringed cape, beads, and a shawl. The boy was dressed in the same manner at the same time. First his moccasins were put on, then his leggings, then his shirt. Next, beaded armbands were put above his elbows on each arm, and a necklace of beads around his neck. A quiver of cougar skin with tail attached was hung on him too. It contained four arrows fletched with golden eagle feathers. A sinew-backed bow was handed to him.

According to the details gathered by Opler, then the mother of the girl daubed ashes or yellow ocher on the girl's eyebrows so they would come out easily, and pulled out a few bunches of hairs first from the right eyebrow, and then from the left one. The other woman did this for the boy at the same time. Usually only four bunches were plucked from each side; the young people could finish by themselves if they wanted to. A large, white, flat, disk-shaped shell with a hole through the center was used on the girl, and she wore it as a necklace during the puberty rite. It was rubbed under the girl's armpits and at her pubic region so that hair would not grow at these places. It was also rubbed on the places from which her eyebrows were taken. At the same time, a twig that had been made smooth by rubbing it against another branch of a tree was rubbed on the boy's face and at the same places on his body. In very early times, hard white stones were given to the girl to rub on her teeth and the boy's teeth. This was to make their teeth hard, white, and strong. Then the girl's mother tied two magpie or roadrunner feathers in her daughter's hair, and the hair was allowed to hang loose. The boy's hair was braided and bound with strips of otter fur with the tail attached, and two white eagle feathers were tied at the top of his head. After this the mother painted her daughter's entire face with yellow ocher, and the other woman painted the entire face of the boy with white clay.

After this, the singer gave the seated girl and boy wooden scratchers and reed tubes. These were to be used during the entire four-day ceremony, and the singer instructed the young people in their use. If the young people scratched themselves with their fingers during the ceremony, it would leave a scar like a burn and mar their looks. If they scratched their heads with their nails, they would get lice. They must use the tubes for drinking water so that water would not touch their lips.

Opler's informants told him that the instructions were as follows: the boy and girl were not to look up in the air or down into water, for then it might rain. They were not to smile after their faces were painted, or the paint would crack and they would have wrinkles before they got old. They could not lie flat on their backs at night with their faces to the sky, for it would rain if they did. Even though the tipi sheltered them, their heads must be turned to the side when they slept at night. The singer explained that the way they obeyed during the ceremony would decide their natures; if they were obedient and willing, they would be so throughout life. But if the girl became angry and scolded anyone during the four days, that would be her disposition during life. And if they failed to believe in the songs, the ceremony would not do them any good.

Directions were also given about food. Either the girl or her female relatives baked four round pieces of cornmeal bread in ashes, and these were brought in at this time and received by the girl. The singer told the two young people that they must not eat what the other people ate during the ceremony, but must divide one of these pieces of bread each day. This would be their only food, for eating anything sweet or sour at this time would cause their teeth to decay. When the instructions were finished, the two young people stood up and the mother molded the body of the girl with her hands so that she would be strong, healthy, and not bent over in old age. She also stood on the girl's feet and lifted her body upward so that she would grow tall. The other woman kneaded the boy.

After the kneading the singer led the way out of the tipi, with the boy coming next, and the girl following him. Then came the girl's mother, and finally the other woman. They proceeded to the front of the tipi, north of the door, and faced east. To the south of the door stood an old woman. The singer chanted four songs and then threw pollen in a line to the east as though making a trail. He did this four times, and the running began. The boy ran first, and the girl followed him. They ran to the east, circled clockwise (sunwise), and returned. While they were running, everyone else was kept away from the trail, since anyone crossing it at this time would get sick. When they were back in place again and facing the east, the old woman who was at the south of the door came to the girl and uttered a high-pitched, undulating call into her mouth or ear. Opler says this was the same call of applause women gave at the ceremonial race, the war dance, and the scalp dance. The woman who did this for the girl had to be old, could not be related to the girl, and was not paid for this service. To make themselves fast runners for life, the young people ran like this four times, each time going a little farther to the east. At the end of each run, the woman uttered the call of applause into the girl's ear. Then the two young people took their places in the tipi again. Formerly, the girl and boy stood on a buckskin and ran from there. When they returned to it for the fourth time, the girl shook it out to each of the four directions, beginning with the east and turning sunwise. This guaranteed that she would be a clean housekeeper.

To indicate their interest in the economy, a clay pot was filled with corn kernels and placed inside the tipi south of the door. This was brought out by the girl as the women lined up along the trail, facing the east. With a ladle of shell, gourd, hide, or buffalo horn, the girl gave out corn to each, beginning with the one farthest to the east. Opler's informants said this corn brought good luck to those who received it, for they mixed the corn with their seeds and were sure of good crops. Now the boy was ready to run to the directions. First he ran to the east and brought back whatever he found there, ranging from horse manure to wood to weeds. He gave this to the girl, and she put it inside the tipi on the east side. Then he walked sunwise to the south and ran to the south, bringing back something else to hand to the girl, and she placed it at the south side of the tipi. He then ran to the west for items to put at the back of the tipi, and in the same way to the north. The fourth time he ran to the north, she put what he gave her on the north side of the tipi. These things were left where the girl put them for the duration of the ceremony.

The rest of the day was devoted to practical tasks that added to the symbolism of the occasion. The singer sent the boy out to gather horses, which he was to take to a good grazing place and watch all day. This was done so he would arise early in the morning and do useful things. The girl remained inside the tipi most of the day, quietly grinding corn on a metate or working on baskets or moccasins. This was to make her strong and industrious. If she finished all the corn she had been given to grind, and the other tasks, the singer or a female relative painted her face a second time with yellow ocher, and she went to her mother's camp, which was nearby. The singer stayed in the ceremonial tipi all day.

On the first night of the ceremony, ritual songs were sung, the two adolescents danced, and a midnight feast was held for guests and relatives. A number of people gathered inside and sat along the sides toward the east end of the tipi. Sometimes pine, piñon, or juniper branches were spread around the sides where the people sat. The boy and girl sat in their usual places, facing the east. The singer was on the south side. The girl's father sat on the north side, in front of the boy. The girl's mother was usually busy cooking and taking care of the food. Special rules of conduct were observed. Anyone leaving the tipi must exit clockwise, the way the sun goes. Opler was told that a person could not cross on the west side of the fire pit so as to pass between the light and the ceremony without having bad luck or receiving punishment of some kind. Anyone who went to sleep in the tipi while the ceremony was in progress would age quickly. The singer smoked, prayed, and then chanted four songs to bless the ceremony. The first songs were for the directions; then there were two songs for dancing. During the dancing songs, the girl and boy stood and danced in place. The girl shuffled, and the boy used a high step. The girl had her fists doubled before her, and she moved them to and fro to signify action, so that she would never become lazy. The boy could do the same and would if he were not bashful.

After the first two dancing songs, the singer chanted four more songs for blessing, then two more for dancing, and so on till eight dancing songs had been sung. These songs varied according to the man who was conducting the ceremony, for there were eight or more different ways of doing it. Some singers mentioned the gods in their songs; some did not. They all sang of the "age stick," which were the sticks on which Ancestral Man and Ancestral Woman leaned when they made their way toward the place of emergence. They also sang the song of the Badger, who was among the first to come through the soft and muddy surface of the earth at the time of emergence. The singer usually sang two deer songs, to incline the deer favorably toward the boy when he became a hunter, as well as songs of the moon, the stars, and many different things.

Opler's informants said that songs were sung of White God, who had furnished the material out of which the sun was made in the underworld, and of Black God, who provided the substance out of which the moon was created there. These Supernaturals had central roles in the rites that made the emergence possible. Ancestral Man was the first of the people to emerge. He was followed by Ancestral Woman, his wife, the first woman to emerge. The dancing ended with a food song, which told how White Painted Woman gave out the food. Then the food was brought in. The mother and the other women carried it in and put the containers in a line running east and west down the middle of the tipi. Everyone, before eating, took a pinch of each kind of food and threw it to the four directions. With the feasting, the ceremony ended for the night. The visitors could either remain for the night or go to their camps, but the singer, the girl, and the boy had to sleep in the ceremonial tipi.

Except for an increase in the number of dance songs, the rite for each night remained the same until the fourth night. The girl spent the second day grinding corn and the boy tended the horses. Nothing but the blue cornmeal bread was eaten. On the evening of the second day they danced six times as twelve dancing songs were sung. The third day of the ceremony was the same, the boy and the girl dancing eight times.

The fourth night, the boy and girl danced in the tipi till morning, stopping only at midnight so food could be distributed as usual. Outside the tipi, the guests held social dances. On this night the singer used a kernel of corn to mark each song he sang. The first one was placed to the southwest of the fire, and the rest in sunwise fashion. At sunup the kernels were distributed to those present, and the people ate them to insure good health.

As the fifth morning of the ceremony arrived, most of the people returned to their homes, but the singer, the girl, the boy, and the close relatives remained. Opler was told that the girl's mother chopped up yucca root, removed the feathers from her daughter's hair, and washed her head. Another woman did the same for the boy. The yellow and white face paint was washed from them also. The girl's and boy's regular clothes were brought in now, and while the singer chanted one song the mother and her helper undressed and dressed them. The feathers were laid in front of the clothes that were removed.

After this the singer painted their faces red with black markings, using red ocher mixed with grease made from buffalo ears. The pollen he used throughout the ceremony was a mixture of different kinds—corn pollen, "pollen" from the wings of butterflies, pollen from western yellow pine, from limber pine, and from spruce. Opler states that the singer put red paint on one of his hands, and pollen and lines of pollen representing sun rays on the other. Then he rubbed his hands together and sang as the sun came up. Taking the boy first, he first put a little red on his forehead, the side of his nose, the side of his mouth, and on the sides of his chin. Then he smeared the red paint all over the boy's face. After this he did the same to the girl. He also put four dots of black specular iron ore on their faces, at the forehead, the cheeks, and the center of the chin. These stood for the sun, the moon, the north star, and the morning star. When the painting was done, pollen was put in the mouth and on the head of the boy and girl. Now all those who wished to have the same done to them came forward, and the singer painted their faces red too. This signified that they had joined the ceremony and would be blessed in the future. The people also made use of whatever paint, pollen, and white clay was left. They rubbed these on themselves, and believed this gave them good health and long life. Before he departed, the singer was paid, a horse being the accepted fee. He was also given any left over food.

After the Adolescence Rite, the girl was considered of marriageable age. She could dress her hair in a manner appropriate to mature women, using a hair form shaped like a bow or an hourglass. Her hair was folded at the back of her neck and covered with a rawhide hair form. Occasionally, to make the benefits more certain still, a second ceremony was held for the girl. It usually took place within a year of the first. If the family was poor, a boy did not take part and the ceremony was kept small. Only the rite of the first and last mornings was performed. A singer was hired, and the girl dressed up and worked, but that was all. The boy used the second time was not the original youth. The singers preferred to have both a boy and the dancing, and the family could hire a different singer for the second ceremony if they cared to.

7 Ceremonial Relay Race

Once a boy reached the age of puberty and while he was still unmarried, he was expected as a matter of religious responsibility to himself and the tribe to participate at least once in the annual Ceremonial Relay Race. Today the ceremony begins on September 13 and climaxes on September 15. In former times the dates and number of days were not so precisely set.[1] While the Jicarilla think of themselves as a united tribe, the geographic separation of the eastern and western bands provided the sides for the race and an opportunity for some enjoyable rivalry. The religious significance of the ritual is seen in the fact that the important thing is the holding of the race at the prescribed time. There is limited concern over who wins the contest.

According to Opler, one explanation of the origin myth of the relay rite goes as follows:

> The reason for the first ceremonial race was there was too much food of both kinds, meats and plants, at the same time. The food was all mixed up and people didn't know how to use it. The food did not come in season then as it does now. Sun and Moon decided that it must be divided up and that there should be seasons for the different kinds of food. Moon said, "I'll bet my fruits against you." Sun said, "I'll bet my animals . . ." So the sun won, and his side was able to hunt all kinds of animals and had a great deal of meat to eat that year . . . the sun and the moon agreed that they were going to

run like this every year for four years. The second year the moon's side won. The third year the sun's side won. And the fourth year the moon won again. The sun and moon took turns winning because people can't eat meat all the time, and they can't eat vegetables all the time. It was to insure both kinds of food for mankind. After the fourth race the ceremony was handed to these Apaches. They were watching it during these four years, so Sun, Moon, White God, Ancestral Man, Monster Slayer, and Water's Child decided to give it to them. They told the Apache: "This is your ceremony now. If you stop holding this ceremony you will starve." That is why the Jicarillas are afraid to stop holding this ceremony.

Over a long period of time, the Jicarilla became careless, and the ceremony had to be reintroduced to restore a balanced food supply for the people. In addition, two girls were offered in marriage as prizes. The four holy people, when the birds came to them with the request for this ceremony, selected the two girls and said, "One will stand for the fruits and the other for the animals." The winners of the race would marry the girls, raise children, and the people would increase. And the children, because the older people would not live forever, were taught this ceremony, so that people might continue to increase on the earth. And Water Beetle and Coyote raced against one another around the world so that the fruits and the animals would increase and be plentiful. And each year this had to be done or the fruits and animals would disappear and the people would starve.

A long time ago the people had forgotten about the ceremony and were not holding the race any more. Then some thought it was best to have it again; many wished to restore it. So all the Indians were called together. They began choosing sides. To one they said, "You will be Llanero," to the next, "You will be Ollero." This went on till the men were on one side or the other. In this way the Llanero and Ollero were formed, and they have raced against each other ever since. After that the two groups lived separately. The Ollero stayed on one side of the river, and the Llanero stayed on the other side. But the Jicarilla are all one people; there is no difference in customs, in language, or in anything else. Now we are all mixed up, the Llanero and Ollero.

The doctrinal reason for the ceremony is clarified by the myth. The contest is to insure a balanced and regular food supply. To accomplish this, Sun and Moon enlist the aid of the culture heroes, the other supernaturals, the animals, and such fast-flying birds as the sandhill crane, the cliff swallow, the falcon, and the hummingbird. Of the Jicarilla, the Ollero band represents the side of the sun and the animals, and the Llanero band takes the part of the moon and the plants. Opler says it is in terms of this conception that the behavior patterns and symbolism of the rite become intelligible. Whichever side wins the race, that which they represent will be more plentiful than the other foodstuff for the coming year. If neither side wins a decisive victory, it means that the fruit and the meat gained will be about even.

A number of features of the rite suggest it has been influenced by the nearby Pueblo tribes, notably the Taos, San Juan, and Picurís, who engage in similar ceremonial races. The corrals in which the Jicarilla runners are prepared are called kivas, a Pueblo term. The three days devoted to the ceremony are not typical for Jicarilla ritual. Also, the day of the racing has been named San Antonio Day, following the custom of the Taos, San Juan, and Picurís people.

Plans for the ceremony begin each year with the selection of the two men who will direct the activities of those on each side. Each leader is an experienced ceremonialist, and he needs assistants who also are well versed in the intricacies of the rite, to erect a sacred enclosure, to make an elaborate ground drawing for the race course, and to prepare paints, feathers, and other materials to costume the contestants. Opler was told that only men who have the right can cooperate in the making of the ground drawing, and the right comes only with learning. The leader asks the men with the right to work on the race with him by placing a cigarette on the foot of each one and saying, "You must come and help us paint."

The mastery of any part of the rite requires diligence and sincerity. It does not come through inspiration or divine favor, and as Opler states, the ceremony has no roots in shamanism. It is a traditional or "long-life" ceremony, handed down from the beginning of the world by one generation of practitioners to the next, and it is more highly regarded than medicine practice. The right to paint the ground drawing and to learn the songs has been handed down from the beginning, and is learned from one who knows the proper procedure. Once the right is given, the one who receives it can do it. The original songs and ground drawings were learned before the people emerged from below. They make the sun and the moon as the first ones were made by Holy Boy in the beginning, though his drawings were painted on buckskin. The sun is made round with four sets of rays, all of pollen. The moon is made in the shape of the full moon. The songs that are sung when they draw the sun and moon, which were given in the world below, tell how to make the sun. They tell how Ancestral Man and Ancestral Woman were formed and how the people traveled up to this earth on the ladder. There are life songs, too, about the food and the animals.

Opposite: *Spectators at the Ceremonial Relay Race, September, 1936. Photo by Margaret McKittrick (MNMP).* Below: *The Llanero shuffling down the relay track to meet the Ollero. The older men are followed by the runners. Photo by Parkhurst (MNMP). Certain Pueblo carry flag poles very similar to these as part of their Tablita Dance paraphernalia.*

Top: *The spectators watching the Llanero. Photo by Parkhurst (MNMP).* Above: *The Ollero coming to meet the Llanero. Photo by Parkhurst (MNMP).* Opposite: *The relay runners of the Llanero side.*

The group of boys from whom the two will finally be selected to run must heed certain taboos for several days before the tryouts; they cannot eat meat, they are to keep away from women, and they are not to smoke. These restrictions are kept until the ceremony is completed. Also, certain ceremonial practices are followed to add to their speed and endurance. Ashes from the burned stalk of the sunflower are placed on the inner side of the bottom of each foot. This makes the boys good runners and makes their joints move easily. Also the roots of the small sunflower are chewed, spit out in the hands, and the hands rubbed on the legs to make them good runners in a short time. The race is supposed to be held at the same location each year, for the kivas represent the place of emergence, and the racetrack is considered to be the spot from which the first race around the world for the plants and the animals began. Near the track is a body of water, symbolic of the traditional lake of the place of emergence.

The track must be repaired each year, and new corrals must be built. When the day nears for the start of the ceremony, the Jicarilla move to the site and establish temporary camps. The work on the racetrack and the corrals begins early on the morning of the first day. The track is smoothed off and the two kivas or holy places are built. The Llanero have their kiva at the west end and the Ollero have theirs at the east. Between the two kivas, starting at the farther end of each, is the racetrack, marked by four rocks of different colors which make a rectangle. The racetrack is divided in half, the Llanero caring for the west half, and the Ollero the east. The leader of each side tells his men what to do. The rocks at the ends of the tracks are black, blue, yellow, and white. The fresh feathers of fast-flying birds are placed under the rocks: feathers of the sandhill crane, cliff swallow, prairie falcon, hummingbird, tern, swan, black-necked stilt, robin, duck, bluebird, and dove are put there, all mixed together. They are left there all year long, and when the next annual race takes place the people bless them with pollen and specular iron ore. While the men are at work on the racetrack, the women are to keep off it,

396

since if a menstruating woman crosses it, it will affect the boys who run in the race.

As the track is taking shape, the leaders send younger men for small aspens and cottonwoods. Others are set to work clearing away the brush and weeds from the place where the circular kivas will stand. Once the ground is clear, a circle of holes is dug, clockwise, the holes spaced about two feet apart. When the holes are finished, the leader of each side goes around his circle of holes clockwise, praying and dropping pollen in each hole. Opler discovered that the pollens used are the sunflower, grama grass, limber pine, piñon pine, and wormwood. Now the helpers put small trees in the holes. The door of the Llanero kiva faces east; the door of the Ollero kiva faces west. The first two trees are placed in the hole to the south of the Llanero door opening. Then two are put in the hole to the north of the doorway. For the Ollero it is just the opposite. Then the rest of the trees are put in, moving clockwise around the circle of holes. A down feather is tied to the top of the trees that form the doorway as a guard to keep all women, especially any menstruating women, out. As the kiva is being built, one of the helpers digs a hole in the ground at the center for the fire pit. The leader kneels in front of this, prays, and

then sings. At intervals he motions to the directions. In front of him, on the west side of the fire, his helpers are sitting. Work continues on the kiva, and if the trees are not thick enough more are put in. Then boughs are worked horizontally, so that no one will be able to see into the holy place. Aspen and cottonwood trees are used for the kiva because they are light and stand for activity. Their leaves are always in motion, and this quality is transmitted to the runners.

No events are scheduled for the morning of the second day. Work on the corrals and the racetrack may continue, and visitors, including people from neighboring tribes, begin to arrive. At noon there is a feast. In midafternoon the ceremony proper is resumed. The leaders of the sides make the banner poles now. Each has a tipi pole, fourteen feet or so in length of aspen that was used in a home. Banners formerly were made of unblemished buckskin, although two I saw were made of cloth; that of the Ollero is white with a round yellow sun symbol in the center, that of the Llanero is dyed red and

The relay runner of the Ollero side.

has a yellow new moon in the center. These banners belong to the ceremony and are kept by the leaders till the next time the ceremony is staged. For the ceremony, the leaders tie the banners to the tops of the poles to show which side the men are on. Horizontal pieces of wood hold the banner out from the pole. Two eagle feathers and two ears of corn are put, like tall rabbit ears, above the banner at the very top of the pole, as well as a horizontal stick about two feet long. The leader prays and blesses them as he does this. The corn is arranged the way it grows on the stalk to show that a ceremony is being held for the fruits and growing things. The ears are not saved: fresh ones are used every year.

Opler learned that the black pottery drum for the ceremony in former days was covered with unblemished tanned hide from a buffalo. The Llanero drum has a new moon painted on the hide, and the Ollero drum has the yellow sun in the middle with yellow rays extending in the four directions. Today large wooden drums are used.

At this juncture a parade of the men of each band goes on horseback and on foot to separate racetracks to select the best runners for the contest to be held the next day. The banner and drum are carried ahead and the men go singing along to the racetracks that each band customarily uses for its tryouts. All they need are level places. The old men watch and pick the winners. They pick a first and a second, and the men of each side return to their kivas. The flag is set up at the right side of the door. The leader tells the men to enter the kiva, and get aspen and cottonwood branches and form a line, for now they are going to march and dance down the racetrack to the kiva of their opponents. They do this mostly for rivalry and pleasure, and the happy women and children assemble along the sidelines to watch. Inside the kivas fresh branches of aspen and cottonwood are handed to them, and they begin to dance and sing, moving the branches up and down. Circling clockwise, they exit from the kiva. Their leader takes the flag and stands in front of them. Next comes a man with the drum.

With the Llanero on the inside of the track, the two sides begin to shuffle toward each other, singing and drumming as they come. Each side sings its own song as the two lines come slowly toward each other. As they draw close the singing grows louder, until at last the singers shout. When they meet, they dance backward and forward three times and the fourth time pass each other, continuing until each side stands before the doorway of the kiva of the other, at which point they dance back and forth four times. Since the dance takes a long time and is tiring, the men rest for a short while before starting back. As they return the same marching song is sung by each side. As the two sides come together they shout at and joke with one another. Each side goes forward and backward three times, and they pass on the fourth time. On the way back, the Ollero pass on the inside of the track, and as they do so some try to pull their opponents off balance and strike in play with the branches. The sides continue into the kivas and circle them sunwise. The drum is placed on the ground and each man rubs his hands over the painted figure on the drum. Then he rubs his hands over his entire body. After this the men go to their camps.

The young people spend the second night in feasting and social dancing at the camps. While this is going on, the men who are in charge of the ceremony gather in the kivas and sing the traditional songs that will assure the effectiveness of the race to be held the next morning. And they sing for long life and for good luck. All join in the singing, and sometimes they sing all night.

Early on the third morning the men begin to gather at the kivas. Each holy place now has a door-keeper who puts a robe over the entrance and allows only those with specific work to do to enter. According to Opler, one man prepares paint. He smokes and sends smoke to the four directions before he begins his work. Then all the old men do likewise. Then the man throws pollen to the directions and prays for a long time. After this he prepares a small fire and burns sunflower stalk. The ashes and charcoal are mixed with water to make a black paint, and the other colors to be used are made in the same way. Other men bring the bodies of birds whose feathers are attached to the runners. Different feathers are used for this purpose; among them are those of the cliff swallow, red-headed woodpecker, duck, sandhill crane, bluebird, hummingbird, hawk, and eagle. The man in charge of the feathers and other appendages goes to the northwest point of the kiva where the drum sits and begins to drum and sing. When he is finished, he shreds some narrow yucca strips, which will be tied to the ankles and wrists of the runners to protect them from witchcraft. Aspen or cottonwood leaves will also be stuck under the yucca bands to help the boys run faster.

Opler states that the leader begins the ground drawing. First he sprinkles the fireplace with pollen and then spreads pollen over the place where the ground drawing is to be made. Sand is placed according to his directions and, employing a bundle of four eagle tail feathers as a broom, he levels the sand. Then he kneels, prays for a long time, and finally sings. Three helpers join him now, and the four men kneel and open up small buckskin bags containing ground colored rock that has been prepared in advance. A pinch of each kind is thrown to the directions, and as the men pray, pinches are dropped on the sand. The leader separates the four eagle feathers and gives one to each man to use as a brush. If four different figures are to be made, each man works on one, and the others give him advice and help. The figures need not be the same ones every year and are arranged according to individual judgment. The sun and the moon are always shown, and there are two swift birds, but there are many to choose from such as the sandhill crane, goose, swallow, hummingbird, and prairie falcon. The choices differ each year, with the sides changing so that each has different birds. Large birds are placed in front of smaller ones such as the hummingbird or cliff swallow. Sometimes the small ones are not drawn at all. In such instances some of the boys are made up to resemble the small ones. Meanwhile other men are completing their tasks. The preparation of paints continues, and the feather man pulls out feathers and shreds while he sings, and every so often beats the drum.

In 1934, Opler witnessed the making of a typical ground drawing and the preparation of the runners. Four drawings, each less than a foot across, were prepared. Each was about two feet from the others, and they were placed in a single line that ran from a spot about a yard from the door toward the northwest. This position made it possible for the runners to circle the kiva clockwise and walk on the drawings as they went out of the door. The drawing nearest the door was a realistic sandhill crane, done in white and showing an elongated neck. The next was a blue and white cliff swallow with a forked tail. Next was a round figure in solid blue with an outer edge of red and with four red rays extending toward the cardinal directions from it. Each side of it was flanked by a straight line that represented the moon. The blue symbolized the blue sky. The last figure was identical with the moon but had a yellow inner circle that represented the sun.

When all is ready the man in charge of the paints calls for the runners. These file in and undress. The man prays, makes motions over his paints, and then puts some of each kind on the feet of each boy, beginning with the right foot. Then the helpers paint each boy's body to resemble a bird which is representative of the different sides. The two winners of the tryouts on the Llanero, or moon's side, are dressed the same way. This side stands for the plants and for the water beetle, for Water Beetle ran against Coyote in the race for the girls in the beginning. The coloring suggests a beetle, and the two outspread feathers tied to the headband are the horns of the beetle.

The headband is of yucca. Attached to it is a small circle of yucca to which two feathers of the cliff swallow are tied. The boys' faces are painted with red ocher, and two slanting lines of black clay are made on their cheeks. They wear long earrings of shell or long slender pieces of bone. A leaf of narrow yucca is tied around their necks. A triangular-shaped area around the neck and upper chest is painted with white clay. A new moon is placed within this area and drawn in black outline. Except for the arms below the elbows and the legs from the knee down, the rest of the body is painted black. Prairie falcon down feathers are stuck at intervals and in lines to the black paint around the edges of the black area. The lower arms and hands, and the lower legs, are painted white, and over this a row of black dots. Strings of yucca are tied to the wrists and ankles.

The two main runners wear short buckskin skirts. The upper part is painted with white clay, the lower part with a dark yellow ocher. Pictures of plants and fruits—the chokeberry, a corn stalk, and a full-grained ear of corn—are painted in the white area on both the front and the back of the skirt. When a skirt is worn out, or if the boy who last ran with it dies, a new one is made with different designs. These runners never wear moccasins, since they stand for the plants and have no animal products to use. The backup runners wear dark colored cloth skirts, with edgings of different ribbon material.

The principal runners of the Ollero side are costumed in an opposite way. These represent the Coyote. Their headbands are buckskin, and fastened to each are two front wing feathers of the prairie falcon, to the tips of which are attached eagle-down feathers. These represent the Coyote's ears, and the spread of the feathers is symbolic of the bird in flight. One year the Ollero runners wear the headbands with the hawk feathers, and the next year they wear the bands with the cliff swallow feathers. The colors and other parts of the dress remain the same for a side; only the headbands are exchanged. The faces of the two Ollero boys are painted red with a blue slanting line on each cheek. The triangular space on the chest is blue, with a round white sun in the middle. The lower parts of the arms and legs are blue. The rest of the body is gray with black spots. White feathers are stuck in the wet paint, and when the boy runs the feathers fly off. White dots of paint are made in lines on the blue of the arms and legs, and feathers are stuck in them. Yucca strings are tied at the wrists and ankles. The skirt is painted a light yellow and animals are painted on it in white. A deer is always drawn. There is a belt of otter skin with tail attached. The Ollero runners who represent the animals wear moccasins, which are yellow except for some red at the top. The winners of the preliminary races are readied first and then the runners-up. Paints and feathers are employed to symbolize various birds. Down feathers are stuck to their bodies, and the sticky leaves of certain plants, such as blazing star and the yellow evening primrose, are moistened and stuck on their bodies also. To increase their speed and to hex their opponents, many of the boys wear amulets tied in their hair, some of which are bird claws enclosed in buckskin bags. An Ollero runner I saw wore two long yellow ribbons in his hair.

According to Opler, the last boy and the ground drawing are completed at the same time; and the final ceremonies to be conducted within the kivas takes place. The boys line up in two rows behind the ground drawing, facing it. The best runners stand at the head of each line, and beginning with those in front they are handed two short pieces of aspen wood and also branches of aspen to hold in each hand. These will help them when they run. The older men and the boys dance in place. The songs describe the race, and everyone shouts now and then. When this singing is finished, they all call out four times and the marching song begins. At this point the line closest to the wall of the kiva advances, with the fastest boy heading the line. He puts his right foot on the first drawing, his left foot on the second, and so on, till he gets to the door. Each boy, as he exits, is handed a down feather, which he blows toward the sun. His line follows him, and then the second line led by the second-best runner leaves the kiva in the same way. Opler says the same thing is taking place at the same time in the other holy place. When the runners have gone out, the older men use the rest of the paints and feathers and rub themselves with sand from the ground drawing for health and good luck.

Both sides now dance down the length of the racetrack as they did on the preceding day. According to Opler's informants, formerly, two girls, representative of the maidens who were pledged to marry the victor of the origin race of tradition, took part in the procession. (By 1936 this was no longer done.) Each girl, dressed in buckskin, led her side to the opposite side of the racecourse. In her right hand she carried an ear of corn and in her left a white eagle tail feather. Behind her was the leader of the side carrying the banner, and then a man carrying the drum. The singers followed him. Then came about a dozen older men who preceded the runners. These carried aspen and cottonwood branches in their hands. Heading each line of runners was a man with either a long feather or a wing of one of the four main birds in his hand.

Behind the boys come any who wish to join the procession. The sides dance forward and meet, dancing back and forth, passing each other and then repeating the act. The assembled spectators, with many of the people mounted on horses, shout and laugh with them. As they come together the fourth time they pass, with the White side (Ollero) passing on the inside toward the kivas. Each side continues to the kiva of the other. The Ollero put their flag up in front of the kiva of the Llanero and vice versa. Each side put its drum down by the kiva of the other, the Llanero placing their drum at the northeast rock and the Ollero depositing theirs at the southwest. When the race ends, those on the winning side will strike their opponents' drum four times, and if the boys become too tired to run any more and want to give up, the drum is used in the same way. A container of water is brought to the place where each drum is, to be used by the runners.

Now, half the boys who have danced to their opponent's kiva walk back to their own side. Opler's informants said that at this point the two girls who formerly led the dance would go away. The Llanero are now on the outside of the track and the Ollero are on the side toward the kivas. The two best runners of each side are at opposite ends, heading each line. They stand behind the rocks that mark the race course. These are small stones about two inches in diameter, set flush with the ground—not the large colored rocks that the runner must stay behind until his running mate has passed the large colored rock. Before the boys run, and when they are in line and ready, the leader of each side, or a man who has been given charge of them, strikes each boy on the leg with a sunflower stalk to keep him from perspiring or wearing out.

First a ceremonial run is made by four elderly men who are not competing with each other, to make a path for the younger men. They start from a place before the lines on the west side. They trot slowly and run the length of the track, crossing the colored rocks from the inside. Two other old men wait there, and run when the first two come past the rocks. They stay even with each other, for they are not really racing. They represent the four Supernaturals who ran this way in the ancient race, before the sun, the moon, and the fast birds began to do it. The moment the last two old men pass the rocks at the west end, the two young runners take off as fast as they can. The people make bets on the race, and everyone is considerably excited about it.

The Jicarilla women who sit on horses and watch the running cry out encouragement as the runners pass them. With the introduction of firearms, the results of the first lap are appropriately noted by a gun being fired by the side that is ahead. When the first two runners pass the large colored rocks, the second man on each side takes over; any one of the boys who are painted can take a turn running. The runners can compete in any order after the first two on each side have had their turns. A side which falls behind is even allowed to put its best man in again in an attempt to catch up. Some boys run as much as five times, some just once. There need not be the same number of runners on each side.

Two men on each side police the track to keep the people back and to see that the rules are obeyed. One from each side is at each end of the track. The two opposite each other in one half of the track are an Ollero and a Llanero. These mark the place where the runners will meet as they go in opposite directions. Their partners mark the place of meeting in the other half. Thus, as one side pulls ahead, the men in the two halves approach each other and, when one side has gained an advantage consisting of more than the length of half the racetrack, the men meet and cross, and the race is over. But the race must continue until one side either loses this much or gives up. The race usually gets underway about the middle of the morning and is over about noon.

The losers are expected to show sportsmanship and generosity, and the final hours of the ceremony are social, being given over to feasting, dancing, and other entertainment. After the race, the old men of each side, followed by the boys, dance to the middle again. Everyone gathers around, and as the women of the side that lost throw fruit, meat, blankets, and hides, all scramble for them. Then the members of each side dance to their kivas and go inside. They leave the drum in there, and the boys dress in their regular clothes. The buckskin, corn, and feathers are removed from the standard, and only the standard is left up. Opler says anyone can do this. A feast follows, and after this there is a war dance to the southwest, behind the kiva. Horse races can be held on the track at this time; and if desired a bucking horse contest. As the sun sets they eat again and afterward have a round dance that lasts all night. Sometimes the clowns perform on this last night, but not always. When morning comes the San Antonio feast is over. Opler states that the clowns were expected to perform at the ceremony held in 1934, but did not appear because one of the men who lived a long way off would not go back to get his cap. "They have a certain number of caps that the clowns wear and have to make that many dancers."

If general observations are valid, I would say that in the years since Opler's 1934 race, and in comparing recent races with 1936 photographs, the present costumes and painting of the runners are less elaborately done, indicating that attention to detail is waning. This also seems true of the race itself.

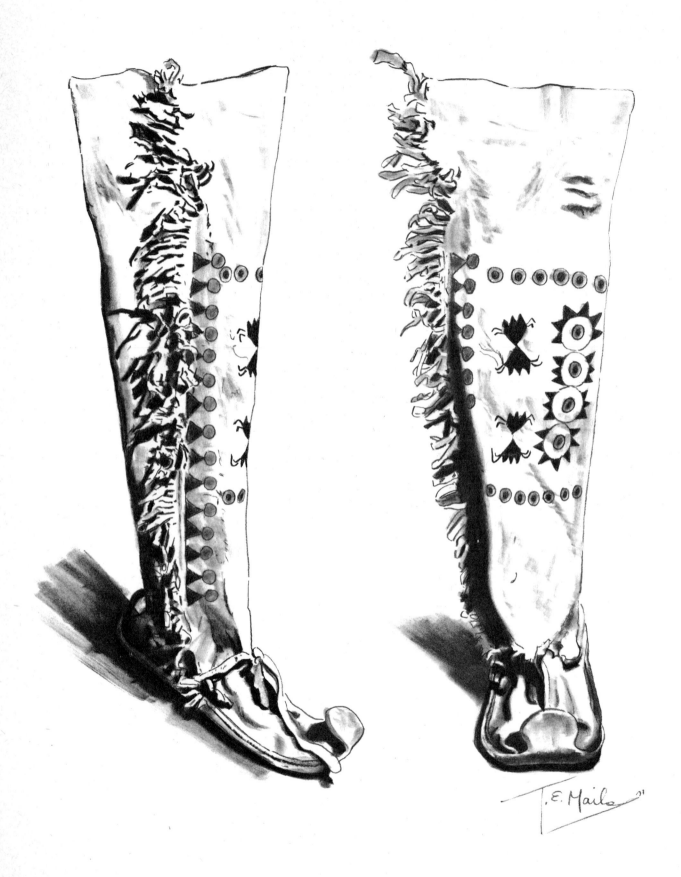

Side and front views of Western Apache painted moccasin (SM). Colors used are red and black.

Apache Arts, Crafts, and Games

The quality, variety, and productivity of ancient Apache arts and crafts in no way compares with those of the Plains nations. This can be attributed to two factors: first, there were perhaps only 10,000 or 12,000 Apache at any one time, not counting the Navajo, as opposed to perhaps 200,000 Indians on the Plains; second, the Apache were embroiled in raiding and warfare for over three hundred years, with few periods of peace for producing craftworks along the way.

Therefore, the total number of items crafted was relatively small, and the Apache life situation left little time for patiently done and innovative work. Perhaps this is why most researchers have paid but scant attention to Apache art other than baskets and have usually confined themselves to brief but vivid descriptions of ceremonial garments.

The nice thing about this is that it has given me the privilege of presenting herein the wealth of Apache creations that reside in Western museum collections.

Actually, as I stated in the Preface, there is more available than most people suspect, and some of it is splendidly done, as the paintings, drawings, and photographs of this book will indicate. The Apache collection of the Southwest Museum is particularly comprehensive, and it may be the best in the world.

Not the least of the Apache arts by any means was their ceremonial drama, as exhibited in the puberty and curing rites and in the war and social dances. Unfortunately, we can read only the few early accounts that were recorded; we must then attempt to imagine ourselves present at the great sacred performances. Samples of these may still be seen in contemporary rites, but it appears that the richness and reverence of former days is seldom duplicated today.

1 Painting

Perhaps the most overlooked ability of the Apache has been their painting, especially that of the Western Apache and Chiricahua. Other evidences of this skill are found on Mescalero and Jicarilla war shields. I suspect the reason for this neglect is that not much Western

Top: *The water bottle, or tus (AF).*
Center: *The water bottle carrying
strap.* Above: *Western Apache coiled
basket (AF).*

Apache painting has been seen and studied. What is astonishing about it is its delicacy, so surprising for a people so often classified as brutal, crude, and insensitive—a judgment that may well, of course, be called into question.

Most of all, the painting is uniquely Apache, so much so that a student should be able to identify it as such in the vast majority of instances. Unfortunately, so little has been recorded about it that it is difficult, unless tagged as it was collected, to state whether a given item comes from the San Carlos area, the Fort Apache area, or the Chiricahua. There are exceptions, since the form of a few pieces, such as the Gan masks, varied between the Western Apache and Chiricahua. But again, no one is actually certain what the prereservation Chiricahua Gan headdresses looked like. Some believe they were similar to the Mescalero, others that they had a character all their own.

While some war shirts and dresses were stained or rubbed with paints over large areas, the usual Apache painting was of religious symbols, which depicted the supernaturals, natural forces, and principal animals, birds, and insects through which the powers worked. In most instances the painting was done in delicate outline, usually blue or black, and the colors were filled in with muted tones. Exceptions to this were boldly done paintings with bright colors, and a medicine pouch of this nature is included in color in this book to demonstrate that the artists made a clear choice between bold and subtle tones.

The painting in historic times was done on both tanned skins and rawhide. In some instances the hide was either simply smoked to give it a beige tone or left its natural color; in other cases it was rubbed with yellow ocher. Over this base the artist, probably a shaman (although I can only guess at that), drew his outline and then filled in the colors with sticks, pointed bones, feathers, and fingers.

Painting was done on Western Apache medicine pouches, boot-length moccasins, war caps, war shields, saddlebags, medicine shirts, playing cards, and on medicine items such as puberty canes, hoops, crosses, and arrows, on Gan masks and wands, and upon the bodies of the Gans, the clowns, and the Hactcins. Besides these there were the dramatic sand paintings used for daytime curing ceremonials. Some war paint was applied to faces and bodies, but it was not of the quality associated with the other items mentioned.

Colors employed included red, black, blue, green, yellow, white, and brown. Walnut juice was used for brown; yellow ocher came from clays; yellow from soaked algerita roots and buds and flowers; red from mahogany roots, with such things as yucca leaves or ashes being added to change the tone; blue from clay; white from clay; green from combining yellow and blue; and black from charcoal and cactus juices.[1] Kluckhohn has given color information about the Navajo that is probably applicable to the Apache.[2]

The Apache drawings range from the extremely simple to the exceedingly complex, with some of the areas being covered with intricate figures, lines, circles, and crosses. In particular, medicine pouches, Gan masks, and Western war shields were impressively detailed.

2 Basketry
General

The Mescalero produced a twined burden basket, while the Western and Chiricahua Apache twined both burden baskets and water jars. All of the Apache groups used similar materials and methods to fashion the burden basket, the exception being that the wefts used at San Carlos were often wider than those of the other Apache tribes. In the early 1900s the best burden baskets were woven of mulberry by the White Mountain Apache, although common materials used included willow, cottonwood, and sumac.[1] Squawberry or sumac was used to make the tus, or water bottle. In crafting the burden baskets and water bottles, the whole withe formed the warp, but beginning at the heavy end, the weaver slit it three ways with her teeth and fingernails to make the wefts. Then she scraped them to remove the bark and to make them the proper thickness. Plain or twill twining or three-strand twining were used. As a rule, the tus was more coarsely woven than the basket. In twined weaving, two or more active elements passed over one or two passive elements, the active pieces going before and behind the stiff warp element, and over and under each other alternately so that they twined about the warp and at the same time about one another.[2]

The Western Apache and Chiricahua burden basket was mainly bucket-shaped, having a wide mouth, sloping sides, and a rounded or concave bottom. A buckskin or leather patch was often placed on the basket bottom to insure longer wear. The water bottle had a fairly wide mouth, while the body shape was any one of three types: a rounded body with a rounded bottom, a flat-shouldered type with a concave base, and a flat- or slightly round-bottomed hourglass shape. Since the weave of the tus was covered with a heavy seal coat of ground leaves and piñon pitch, little time was wasted on fine weaving. Ground juniper leaves and red ocher were rubbed into the surface of the tus, with the latter imparting some red color through the translucent, water-repellent pitch. Occasionally a black line or other limited geometric design was painted on the shoulder of the tus with soot, using the finger as a brush. The favored pitch was gathered from the bark of the piñon pine, where lumps had oozed from cracks or injuries, and was heated until it was soft. The melted pitch was swabbed onto the outer surface with a rag wrapped around the end of a stick. Pitch was then poured inside together with a hot stone, and the basket was turned until the entire bottle interior was coated.

The all-over weaving so typical of Western Apache water bottles was of a diagonal pattern. Variation in stitching commonly occurred as reinforcement at points of stress. The rim of the San Carlos tus was often finished poorly. Some jars were without specific finishing, and warps were simply close-cropped at the top. In such cases the pitch served to bind and complete the rim. In other instances, there may be a double coiled rim with the edge coil being finished with a crude false braid. A third type of rim finish was the plain coil. Stoppers were made of a bunch of grass or small brush, as needed. The largest tus would hold about five gallons.[3]

Burden baskets included more variety in their twining than did water jars. Sometimes they were woven in plain twining or in twill twining, while at other times the two methods were combined in a single basket. Workmanship varied from crude to the excellent items, which were used for special occasions. The San Carlos burden baskets were extremely well made, having more conical bases. The finer mulberry specimens were without the four heavy strengthening ribs common to other types, and often there was a diagonal slant to the weave.

As a general rule, the decorative bands in burden baskets were placed above center, and the twill-twined stripes that were interspersed between the wider areas of plain twining might be left undecorated or colored. Color alone was a popular type of decoration. For this, either native aniline dyes or the natural colors of the weft materials were used. Black, red, or reddish brown were the most common colors, and greater variety was attained by using commercial reds, greens, and blues.[4] Splints were sometimes dyed before they were woven in, while at other times the paint was applied after the weaving was completed. In either case, the designs were usually restricted to narrow positive or negative bands which incorporated simple geometric elements. Other decorations were added to the burden basket. The four vertical ribs were often covered on the outside with wide buckskin bands, to which clusters of buckskin fringes were attached, with tin cones added to the ends of the fringes. On occasion beads were strung on the fringes, and scraps of red cloth were added around the buckskin on the base.

The rims of burden baskets were finished in different ways. Two heavy coils at the edge were common, utilizing either the warp twigs from the body of the basket for the coil, or twigs with an addi-

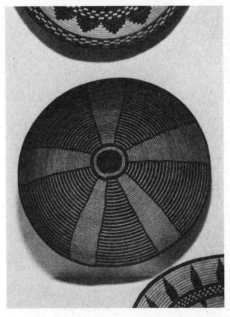

Top: *Coiled basket. The bottom one is Mescalero (AF).* Center *and above: Western Apache coiled baskets (AF).*

tional and heavy wooden hoop. The second coil might incorporate a heavy wire, either alone or as part of a bundle of native material. The first rim coil was poorly sewed and the edge coil generally showed better workmanship.[5]

In the rim of the twined water jar some false braiding was used. The sewing splint was drawn through the basket away from the worker, until the end had nearly disappeared. It was then pulled up over the rim toward the weaver and to the right, where it penetrated a second hole made for it above and to the right of the first holes. Through this it was pulled very tightly away from the worker, carried up again over the top of the rim towards her, and crossed the previous stitches nearly at right angles as it passed to the left. It was then carried down in front of the worker and passed through a third hole on a line with and to the left of the first. Then the process was repeated. Some rims were sewed entirely with devil's claw; others were made with alternating stitches of black and white or with alternating sections in these colors. When the alternating black and white was used the worker carried along two sewing splints at a time, taking a stitch with one, then the next with the other.[6]

Burden baskets and water bottles often had two loops attached to or woven into their outer walls for suspension. These consisted of buckskin or rawhide on the baskets and of the same materials or horsehair on the tus. In some cases three wooden loops were placed on the water bottle and were covered with pitch along with the rest of the container. A few Apache women still use the burden basket, which will sometimes carry a whole sack of grain, supporting it by means of a cloth or hide strap across the forehead. In earlier years it was the chief means of carrying objects and was frequently hung from the pommel of the saddle. It is always used at the girls' puberty rite.

As might be expected, there was considerable variation in size of both the burden basket and tus. Baskets averaged from twelve to fifteen inches in height. Tus heights varied more, since smaller ones were needed for canteens and larger ones for the storage of water or other liquids. Jars made for tiswin were usually wider and taller than those needed for carrying or holding water. Large, unpitched, wide-mouthed storage jugs were also made, ranging from one that held a few gallons to a fifty-gallon size.[7]

Western Apache Basketry

Western Apache baskets were by far the most complex and elaborate of all the Apache groups. A three-rod foundation was fashioned of slender twigs of willow, cottonwood, or sumac. The coil was small and round, and it provided an interesting textured surface, as well as rigidity, for the basket. The common stitching was of narrow and even sewing splints of the same material as the foundation. The black tones of the designs were obtained by using the martynia or devil's claw, and the rare touches of red employed came from the inner bark of yucca root. On occasion, weavers used red aniline dyes. Painted and dyed materials were not used on coiled work.[8]

Most of the baskets were open trays and storage jars. With some exceptions, the tray diameters ranged from eleven to fifteen inches. Although she was circumscribed by the demands of utility and tribal tradition, each weaver expressed herself as an individual in her baskets, a fact that led to an interesting difference in both form and design in basketry types. Depths varied from two to four inches, again with some variations. Most of the baskets counted four to five coils with thirteen to fifteen stitches per inch.

In constructing bowls, baskets, trays, and other flat objects, the close coiling technique was used. Virtually all of the coiling on shallow or flat objects was done in a counterclockwise direction, but some pieces were done with clockwise spirals.[9] Jars were coiled from right to left, yet they appeared to be just the opposite and clockwise, since the shapes were worked at from the outside, with the point of sewing on the curve next to the worker instead of away from her.

Top: *Western Apache coiled baskets (or tray bowls) (AF).* Center: *Western Apache coiled basket (AF).* Above: *Western Apache coiled olla, or water jar (AF).*

408

A few hours before the woman began a coiled basket, the foundation rods and sewing splints were immersed in water to make them soft and pliable. Sometimes they were buried in damp soil and drawn out one at a time as needed. An awl and a knife were necessary tools for weaving and were always close at hand. The woman spread a canvas or a blanket on the ground to sit on. Selecting three foundation rods, she held them at one end in the left hand, and allowed them to extend to the left. With the rods crossed, she took a sewing splint, laid one end across the ends of the rods on the side toward her, and held it with the left thumb so that the short end of the splint pointed upward and to the left. With her right hand she wrapped the splint around the rods five or six times, first under them and away from her, then up over them toward her, covering and fastening securely at the same time the end that was held by the thumb. The splints were wrapped around the rods a few times, and the rods were bent down and around to the right.

Then the unwrapped section of the rods was bent around the wrapped section, and they were all turned so that the loose rods were again to the left. After the sewing splint had been wrapped around the bend, it was passed through a hole made by the awl in the original wrapped portion, which was in turn passed through the middle of the top foundation rod, splitting it as it went between two rounds of sewing splint. The splint was pushed through the hole and then drawn away from the weaver on the wrong side. She pulled it tight and made another hole, to the left of the first one, while she held the splint end, which she brought up over the top of the bunch of rods, between her left thumb and forefinger. The splint was pushed through, again pulled very tight, and over the top. A third hole was made and the work continued until the original wrapped section was enclosed on one side. When the blunt end of the wrapped section was reached, the awl was pushed through the bunch of rods, just a little back of the first round of wrapping to enable her to get a firm hold. After the end was sewed in, the sewing continued along the other side of the wrapped part.

As the coiling continued, each spiral increased in size, and new foundation rods were added as the first ones were covered. Since these rods varied in length, it was seldom that two were covered at the same point, so it was easy to insert a new one by pushing one end of it against that of the one which preceeded it. The joints were covered with new stitches. When a new sewing splint was added, the old one was pulled through to the wrong side and left there until the basket was finished. It was then cut off so close to the coil that the end was almost invisible. The new one was drawn through the hole made for it, and the short end on the right side was held under the left thumb until covered by the following stitches. The same method was employed when working in colored splints for designs. The Western Apache woman usually finished the rims of her baskets with plain over-and-over sewing.[10]

Most of the Western Apache jars (ollas) were from eighteen to twenty-two inches high. The mouth diameters were all sizes, and in a few cases were greater than the jar height. There were several olla shapes. One had a flaring and fairly high neck, rounded body, and flat bottom. Another had a straight or gently inward-sloping neck, wide mouth, sharp or sloping shoulder, and flat bottom. A third form was constricted in the middle and had a small neck. There was also considerable individual variation within each of the three forms.

Designs used in coiled baskets in the first part of the twentieth century were varied and complex. Both geometric styles and angular life forms were used, with the latter being more common in Western Apache work than in any other coiled basketry in the Southwest.

The designs employed were animated and all-over patterns. Sometimes these were confined to bands, and other times they were interwoven. A solid black central circle or star was the origin point for most of the designs. Sometimes the outer edge of the circle and

Top: *Detail of coiled olla.* Center *and* above: *Jicarilla(?) coiled basket trays (AF).*

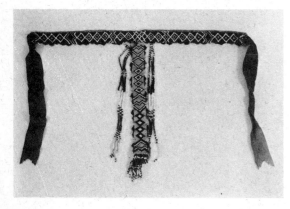

Top: *Jicarilla beaded horse amulet (MNCA).* Center: *Modern Jicarilla beadwork (MNCA).* Above: *Western Apache T-necklace worn by pubescent girl for Sunrise Ceremony (HM).*

the rim of the basket were combined to create a banded area. Designs were usually extended to the rim. Small blocks, squares, or rectangles made up the vertical, zigzag, diagonal, or other arrangements, with human or animal forms or small geometric elements being placed at various points. Geometric elements included checkerwork, squares, blocks, crosses, rows or diamonds, stars, chevrons, step figures, ladders, triangles, straight or wavy lines, four-direction symbols, and arrows, some of which were combined into various motifs. A broad variety of life forms was used, including plants, birds, dogs, horses, deer, cattle, men, women, men on horseback, and other things.

The designs employed for tray baskets are classified today as divided and undivided.[11] The divided layout was banded. The undivided class included four basic layouts: repeated, centered, circling-continuous, and radiating. In the first layout style, large elements were repeated within the area between the central motif and the rim. The centered style was accomplished by exaggerating the size of the central motif. The circling-continuous layout was obtained by using motifs to completely encircle the decorative area. Radiating designs extended from the central black circle to or almost to the rim. Several of the layouts were combined in some baskets to form composite styles.

Coiled jar designs varied to some degree. All jars had decorated bottoms. In some instances the bottom designs were independent, while in others they were fused with the wall design. Jar walls included all-over, spotted, and vertical layouts. All-over designs were made up of horizontal or oblique zigzags. Multiple zigzag lines were common, and they sometimes had life figures interspersed between them. Larger geometric and smaller life themes were often repeated on the body and neck of the vessel. Vertical layouts consisted of geometric bands of varying widths that reached from base to rim, with or without scattered life designs between them. The network style was formed by large crisscrossed bands, which made diamond-shaped areas in which life and geometric motifs were placed.

The considerable use of solids and heavy lines gave the Western Apache designs a substantial feeling. However, much of the heaviness was relieved by the use of thinner outlining lines, by a careful balance of dark and light in the mass areas, and by the judicious spotting of independent and small elements in the background. Perfect symmetry was often employed for the basic design. Designs were unified, often bold, and generally simple in a given basket. There was no rule regarding the number of divisions in a pattern, although four to seven divisions was the most common breakdown employed.[12]

Mescalero Basketry

The Mescalero worked the foundation elements in their baskets in an unusual manner. Irrespective of whether it was a two-rod-and-bundle, a three-rod-and-bundle, or a wide-slat-and-bundle, the whole was arranged in vertical fashion. This produced a wide and flexible coil that was distinctively Mescalero. There were usually no more than two or three coils to the inch, and the colors were restrained. The Mescalero used only white, yellow, or green yucca sewing elements, and the reddish-brown root of the narrow-leafed yucca. Massive simple design patterns predominated. Stars were used alone or in combination with stepped triangles, and there were terraced pyramids, diamonds, or squares in bands or spotted arrangements. Sometimes the pattern was done in solid green or yellow and outlined with reddish brown.[13]

Jicarilla Coiled Basketry

Jicarilla coiled basketry was sometimes of the three-rod type, and of a five-rod type that was unusual in southwestern Indian basketry. In either case, the foundation elements were arranged in a mass that resulted in a large coil. The rod material was willow, while the sewing materials were sumac, willow, and squawberry. In very early years a simple design in natural brown was common. Later on, red and green

410

were added. Today, aniline dyes of red, blue, turquoise, green, black, brown, and yellow are used. Although simplicity and massiveness characterized Jicarilla basket patterns in former years, a recent revival in the craft has featured more complex and smaller design elements and designs.[14]

There have been two forms of Jicarilla baskets: a deep tray-bowl, which in more recent pieces has handles, and a deep, straight-sided, flat-bottomed basket, which often has a lid. The Jicarilla make shallow round trays twelve to twenty inches in diameter, and also fish creels. Designs used for the first two forms include zigzag lines made up of stepped squares, single or multiple star patterns, terraced diamonds, crosses with little blocks at the corners, and large conventional animals. Most of these elements are arranged in bands of joined or isolated units.

The art of basketry virtually ceased in the 1950s. When the Jicarilla arts and crafts program revived it in 1962, it incorporated the aniline colors previously mentioned and a wider variety of designs, including deer, horses, floral themes, and conventionalized birds.

3 Beadwork

While some commercial glass beads were introduced into the Southwest by the Spanish around 1540, Feder is correct in saying that most of the Apache beadwork dates from 1850 on.[1] For the most part, Western Apache and Chiricahua beading styles were distinct enough to be recognized as Apache. But the Jicarilla and Mescalero were more influenced by the Plains tribes. In particular, one finds the Ute, Cheyenne, Kiowa, and Comanche influences in Jicarilla work, and Cheyenne, Kiowa, and Comanche influences in Mescalero items. Seed beads were the most used, and the preferred colors were black, blue, and white, although red, purple, orange, and yellow beads are also found among the Apache artifacts in museum collections.

The designs of early Apache beadwork were predominantly geometric, ranging from the early simple and slanting bands in two colors to the later ornate and complex styles. A variety of objects were beaded by the Apache, some being ornamented with beads and others made entirely of beads. These included awl cases, hatbands, bags, capes, dresses, war shirts, moccasins, war caps, medicine items, dolls, cradleboards, rattles, and various types of necklaces. A Jicarilla boy's shirt in the Denver Museum is entirely beaded on the front in black and white beads, and is dated ca. 1850. While the Western Apache beaded their moccasins with narrow lines and individual symbols, the Jicarilla and Mescalero sometimes outlined the edge where the side joined the sole with bands of varying widths of beads in several colors, and they sometimes added other lines and designs on the instep. On occasion, Eastern moccasins were elaborately ornamented with beads, short fringes, and tin cones.

The Jicarilla war shirts and leggings were sometimes ornamented with broad beaded shoulder bands and leg bands with very bold and simple patterns done in lazy stitch. The Mescalero beaded their war shirts with narrow lines of beads on the bib, shoulders, and arms, and their leggings on the sides and flaps. A late date and distinct style of White Mountain and San Carlos war shirt had lines of beading on it, as well as silver and brass conches and crosses of various sizes. The Mescalero, Chiricahua, and Western Apache also beaded their war turbans and caps with lines and symbols, and the few Jicarilla and Mescalero feathered bonnets also received some beading.

Beaded bags varied greatly in shape and decoration—so much so that I am including a number of photographs to illustrate this. As the Western Apache bag was commercialized in the twentieth century, it became more ornate, with scalloped beaded edges, floral themes, more colorful beads, and more elaborate designs.

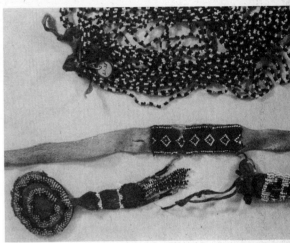

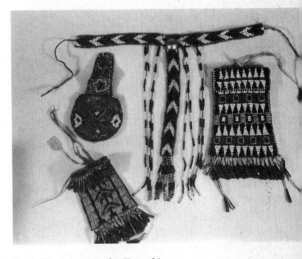

Top: *Western Apache T-necklace worn by pubescent girl for Sunrise Ceremony (MNCA)*. Center: *Beaded bags, neck band, and necklace (HM)*. Above: *Beaded T-necklace and bags (HM)*.

411

The splendid awl cases were not commercialized, and remained traditional in their decoration. Besides the beading, these were decorated with small tin cones suspended from short fringes of buckskin, and with brass and silver conchos. The awl cases also had long pendant tabs of various designs, and in all were an excellent and distinguished piece of art.

If pieces were to be made of beads alone, the Western Apache woman often wove them with commercial thread, on a loom that she made by nailing two short upright pieces of wood at the ends of a horizontal board.[2] Objects made solely of beads included in later years the T-shaped necklace, other necklaces, charms, medallions, hatbands, and solid bands, which were first woven and then attached to cradleboards and belts. The T-shaped necklace is commonly worn by girls in their puberty ceremony. Two bands, a vertical piece and a neck piece, are woven separately and sewed together to form it. The size of the vertical piece varies in length and width, and the designs are sometimes very elaborate, some including a stylized Gan figure. Many sell for more than one hundred dollars. Colors include yellow, red, violet, green, dark blue, and white. Designs include triangles, hexagons, diamonds, and other complex geometric forms. Besides the T-necklace, there is also an elaborate and delicate apron necklace worn by some girls in the ceremony.

In recent years necklaces have been made strictly for commercial purposes. Some of these are in styles long made by the Apache, consisting of a long narrow band with simple geometric designs throughout its length. A fringe of loose strings of beads hangs from the bottom, and just above the fringe is a round or other-shaped pendant. Others are short choker-type necklaces, which may be plain or have scalloped or pointed edges. Bolo ties are also crafted of a tube formed of rounds of beads, to make a circular slide and decorated with geometric designs.

The Apache are also crafting handsome sets of puberty dolls, which are carefully detailed to represent the pubescent girl and her sponsor. Besides these one can purchase beaded amulets for protection against harm.

4 Textiles

The Navajo were the only Apachean group to do any textile weaving of consequence. Except for a short-lived effort among the Mescalero, when an agent attempted to get the craft started among them, the Apache groups never did any. The Apache wore skin clothing until he encountered the White man. As a result of the Pueblo Rebellion of 1680, some Rio Grande Pueblo people lived with the Navajo for some time, and it is believed that the Navajo learned weaving from this contact. But since the Apache were seldom on good relationships with other tribes, there were few opportunities to learn weaving, and indeed they showed little inclination in this direction. Moreover, the southern groups with whom the Apache came most often into contact did but limited weaving.[1]

5 Pottery

The Apache made little pottery, although formerly all the groups made some crude cooking ware and a few bottles. Most of the pieces were of a dull gray or brownish tone and were left unpainted. The round-bottomed, open-mouthed cooking vessel sometimes received some decoration in the form of a raised and simple pattern, a fillet of clay around the rim. The Apache groups do not make any pottery today.[1]

6 Tools

In describing an instance in which they lived in the most primitive circumstances imaginable, Chiricahua informants spoke of sharp-edged stones that served as tools to shape materials and to build

Top: *Detail, beaded bag used for general purposes (HM).* Center: *Beaded amulet bags, front view (HM).* Above: *Beaded awl case (AF).*

412

wickiups. Stones were also used to strike sparks and to start fires. Once a fire was burning it was seldom allowed to die out.[1] Such stones were also used in early times to skin animals.

Tanning tools included a broad rib taken from a horse and used for beaming when hides were laid over a pole;[2] a fleshing tool, which was either a sharp deer bone, a sharp stone, or a metal blade; and large rough stones for pounding, thinning, and smoothing hides.

Deer leg bones were sharpened to make awls for sewing. Wooden awls were also made. Kaywaykla says that the women used a cactus thorn with the fiber attached for needle and thread, and also that the Apache carried in the folds of their moccasins the end thorns of a mescal plant with fiber attached for sewing the moccasin soles to the uppers.[3]

Smoothing stones were employed to smooth arrow shafts. These were grooved to receive the arrows, and were used either singly or as a pair which formed a complete round hole. (Please see the weapons section.)

There were various kinds of digging sticks, used for mescal gathering and planting.

Knives were common tools used by both men and women. The earliest were made of flint, later replaced by trade knives. (More data is available concerning these in the weapons section.)

When the Indians could get matches they used them. Next in preference were flints and steel to strike sparks. The use of the fire drill was known to all in former times. The fire drill consisted of a flat, soft piece of wood with a cup-shaped hollow in it. Wood shavings were piled around the hollow. A round, hard stick with a rounded end that had a little notch cut in it for better friction was then held vertically with the round end in the hollow and twirled between the palms of both hands. Friction caused the soft flat piece to smolder, then the shavings to glow. When blown upon the shavings burst into flame. An experienced man or woman could make a fire by this method in a few moments.[4]

7 Musical Instruments

Drums

One type of ceremonial drum consisted of a medium-sized pot covered with buckskin.[1] The pot usually had a sculptured neck forming a rounded groove. The edges of the wet buckskin cover were pulled tight far down enough to cover the groove, and were secured there with a buckskin thong. A pottery drum also had a handle. Water was put in the drum along with four pieces of charcoal, and four small holes were cut in the top for sound and ceremonial purposes.[2]

A loop drumstick, made of juniper, oak, or wild cherry, was used with the pottery drum. One end of a scraped stick was heated and bent to form the loop; the bent end was held in place by a buckskin wrapping.[3] The drum was struck at an angle, rather than straight up and down.

The other kind of ceremonial drum consisted of a flat piece of cowhide. The sticks were wooden switches. At Apache ceremonies the young boys of eight to twelve were often allowed to accompany the singers on the cowhide drums.[4]

Kluckhohn includes descriptions of the Navajo basket drum in his book treating the material culture of that tribe.[5] This drum was much like the one described by Stanley in his report of the mythological Jicarilla basket drum used in the Bear Dance (Holiness Rite). A buffalo hide was spread over a basket at the back of the tipi where a hole had been dug. The animals conducting the ceremony then took the moccasins of the three sick men being treated, tied them together, and used them to beat on the drum.

Rattles

The Apache made two kinds of rattles, one made from a gourd and one with dew claws.

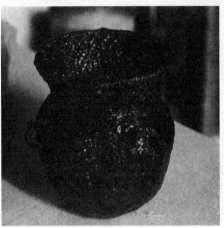

Top: *Beaded moccasins (MNCA). Probably eastern Chiricahua or Mescalero.* Above: *Pitch-covered basket (MNCA).*

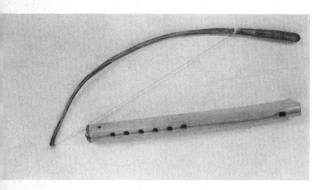

Top: *Fire drill demonstration at San Carlos in 1935. The drill was an 8- to 10-inch round stick made of sotol or juniper. The flat drill board was made of sotol and had cuplike notches to receive the drill and the tinder of juniper bark or dry grass. The drill was twirled rapidly between the hands to ignite the bark. Two men could do the work better than one man drilling alone. Photo by Margaret McKittrick (MNMP).*
Center: *Western Apache violin.*
Above: *Top, violin bow, bottom, flute (HM).*

Gourds grew in abundance in the Southwest, and several kinds were used to make rattles. Both ends of the gourd were cut off. The gourd was dried, pebbles were inserted and shaken around to loosen the meat and seeds, and then everything was dumped out. The gourd was then filled with sand and allowed to dry thoroughly. After the sand was poured out, rounded pebbles were dropped in and a long stick was inserted until it extended through both ends. The shorter end of the protruding stick was secured with piñon gum, and the longer end served as a handle. Some rattles were painted, some were not.

The hoof, or dew claw, rattle consisted of a short stick, some eighteen inches in length, which was covered with buckskin to which hooves strung on thongs were attached. Opler's informants spoke of deer or elk hooves, eagle claws, and mountain goat hooves used on the stick rattles.[6] The buckskin was also fringed and beaded. Stick rattles were used by the singers during the celebration of the girl's puberty rite at Mescalero.[7]

Stanley reports that the chanter for the Jicarilla Bear Dance used a rattle made from a buffalo tail and the tails of rattlesnakes. No details are given of its construction.

Violins

The violin or fiddle varied in length from one foot to more than two feet. It was made from a dead tree such as walnut,[8] or from the central stalk of the agave; the piece might be straight or slightly curved. Designs were sometimes partly cut out and partly painted, or were simply painted on. Some fiddles were intricately ornamented, and others were quite plain. Colors used were red, green, black, white, blue, and yellow.[9]

To make a violin, the tree limb was split down the middle, hollowed out, sound holes put in, and then the halves were tied together with deer sinew. The ends of the hollow agave fiddle were plugged, and several small round or diamond-shaped sound holes were made on top of the piece. Pegs were projected from each end to support the horsehair strings. Both single- and double-stringed fiddles were made, and a single peg controlled their tension and pitch. The bow was as long as the fiddle, of sumac, and curved. Its string was also horsehair. Opler is certain that the Apache violin was modeled after stringed instruments introduced into the region by Europeans.[10] Its use was social, and not ceremonial.

Flutes, Flageolets

The Jicarilla made a flageolet, and a flute—approximately 21 inches long and 1½ inches in diameter—that was closely associated with love and courtship. The flute had magic, and when played near a certain girl's home, would draw the girl to the flutist. The butterfly was connected with the instrument, and if a boy took pollen and traced a butterfly with it in front of the flute, the girl simply couldn't resist coming out.[11]

Rasps

The Jicarilla origin myth of the Bear Dance included the use of the rasp at one point in the ceremony. It consisted of the leg bone of a mountain sheep, and a notched stick along which the leg bone was rubbed.[12] This was probably an adaptation from the Ute, since they made considerable use of such an instrument. For optimum sound, one end of the notched stick was held in one hand while the other end was placed on a basket, gourd, or piece of rawhide, which served as a resonator.[13]

8 Games
Hoop and Pole

The hoop and pole game was religious in character, played only by men—women were not permitted even to watch it. No festivity was complete without the game, and it was played with great fervor and persistence. Only those medicine men deeply versed in their folklore and traditions could give a minute explanation of the original meaning and symbolism of this game, and they were exceedingly reluctant to part with their knowledge. It was said that one of the Gan taught the people the game in the beginning, along with an explanation of its symbolism. Several short prayers or chants, some sung and some spoken, were employed by players to neutralize the efforts of their opponents and bring success to themselves. The following is a typical example:

> The wind will make it miss yours;
> The wind will turn it on my pole.
> Today at noon I shall win all;
> At night again to me will it fall.[1]

Western Apache (White Mountain) Albert B. Reagan had the following to say about the hoop and pole game in 1901: "The pole game is the Apache national game. It is played by the men every day from early morn to late in the afternoon; sometimes to pass the time only, sometimes for 'medicine,' but almost always for gain. They sometimes bet all they have on it, in former times even their women and children."

The pole ground was a level space thirty-six yards long and six yards wide, laid off in a north and south direction. In its center was a base, usually a rock, from which the poles were hurled. Nine yards from this base, both north and south, were three hay-covered ridges, with the center ridge lying on the center line of the pole ground. Each ridge was three yards long, and the total width of the three was five feet. There were two narrow furrows between the ridges, into which a hoop was rolled.

The two poles were willow, about 15 feet long. They were made in three sections, which were spliced and tied with sinew. They tapered from a point to the butt, which was about 1¼ inches in diameter. The first 9 inches of the butt, called the "counting end," were marked with grooves. The counts on the butt were nine in number. The hoop was made of willow, about a foot in diameter, the ends bound together with sinew. A buckskin thong, stretched across the ring like a spoke, was wound for its entire length with cord. The center wrap was made larger than the others, and was called beads, because originally beads were used instead of the wrapping cords. The beads were counted to 50 in descending order on each side of the center. Sometimes there were more than fifty turns on each side, but only that number was counted. They were not touched by the hand in counting, but were pointed to with a straw by the player. They were always counted by twos. Together with the center bead, the 50 beads on each side made a total of 101 counts on the spoke of the wheel. The edges on both sides of the circumference of the wooden hoop were notched with 9 cuts, which, with the 2 sinew wrappings, were used in counting. The space between the places where the ends were lashed counted 1, and each of the notches around the ring, 1, making 11 counts in all, and a total of 112 counts on the hoop itself. Adding that to the 9 counts on the butt of the pole, there was a grand total of 121 counts in the game. Reagan says that the players learned to count, and that most of them were able to count to 1,000 in their own language.

The hoop was held vertically between the thumb and second finger of the right hand, resting on the extended index finger, over which it rolled when it was let go. If it was seen to be rolling wide of the furrows, it could be guided to its destination with the pole. As the hoop entered a furrow its speed was slowed by the loose hay and it fell over, only to be slid under the hay by a well-directed pole. If it failed to enter a furrow, it was brought back and rolled again. The first roll was always to the south and the next to the north, and so on for hours until the game was finished.

The poles were propelled by the right hand and guided with

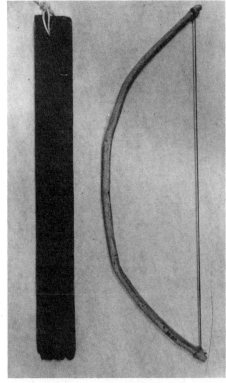

Top: *Violin (HM)*. Above: *Left, rhombus or bull-roarer; right, violin bow (MNCA)*.

415

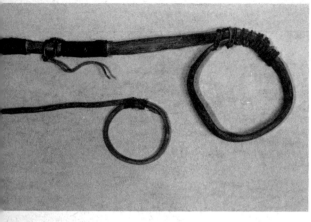

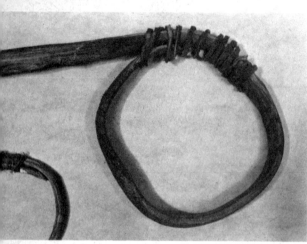

the left, the index finger of the right hand being placed against the end of the pole, which was held between the thumb and index finger. A successful throw slid into the furrow beneath the wheel, and stopped with its butt beneath it. If it passed entirely through the furrow or went to the side, the poles were taken back to the base and hurled again, the wheel being rolled as before. It took considerable practice and skill to hurl the poles successfully.

Poles being carried back after a throw were thrown over the right shoulder. They were then stood on end upon the ground for a moment only, after which they were hurled as before.

In counting, all points on each pole that fell on or within the rim of the hoop were counted, also all the points on the rim of the hoop and all the beads on the cord that fell within the edges of the pole. Once the points were totaled, the game proceeded as before. This was continued for hours, until one side or the other reached the number of points agreed upon as deciding the game. This could be any odd number from 37 to 1,001. The game was sometimes played for the best two out of three or three out of five rounds, and so on, with two throws south and one north constituting a play.

Reagan gives the following vocabulary of terms for the game in both English and Apache: let us play pole; the hoop; the counting end of the pole; hoop heads; the closely wrapped cord; the points on the hoop rim; the counting field; the three-ridged space; the pole ground; the base, or center, of the pole ground, from which the hoop is rolled and the poles are hurled; one of the wraps (beads) on the cord; the center bead on the cord.[2]

Capt. C. N. B. Macauley collected a hoop of sapling, ten inches in diameter, painted red, the overlapping ends lashed with cords, with a thong lashing between. A thong wound with cord was fastened across the middle of the ring, the outer circumference of which was notched with eleven notches equally disposed in the space between the lashings. He described the game to Stewart Culin as follows:

"Two men play. The ground is leveled and covered with hay or dried grass. One rolls the wheel and both throw their poles, points first, along the ground beside it, endeavoring to make the wheel fall on the butt of the pole. The counts are most intricate, depending upon the way in which the pole falls in reference to the wheel, the periphery of which is marked with rings of sinew. The details are so complicated that no civilized game nearly compares in complexity with this apparently simple sport."[3]

Rev. Paul S. Mayerhoff collected two jointed poles, each in three pieces, which when assembled were 14 feet and 15 feet 4¼ inches long, and a hoop made of sapling, 9¾ inches in diameter, the latter having a thong wound with cord stretched across the middle.

The game was played with two poles, each of which was made up in three sections, and a hoop. The butt end of each pole was marked off into 9 divisions or counters. The ring was also marked on its circumference with 11 divisions or counters. The spoke bisecting the hoop was wrapped with a cord and a bead was placed in its center. It was also used in counting, there being 104 winds of cord; when the knot or bead in the center was added, there were 105 in all. The total number of points on the pole and the hoop together was 125 in the average game, but it exceeded that in some. The two poles represented the two sexes, yellow representing the male, red the female. Their three sections were referred to as the butt, middle section, and tip. The joints were made by wrapping the pole with sinew.

The playing area was seventy-five to a hundred feet long, with the home goal marked by a flat rock midway between the two ends.

The ends of the court toward which the game proceeded alternately, as in horseshoes, were built up with hay or grass to form three parallel ridges and two valleys, eight to ten feet long. The hoop must be rolled and the poles thrown in such a way as to pass into a valley between the ridges and come to a stop before either object reached the extreme ends of the ridges. The throw counted only when the hoop fell upon the marked butt of the pole. In playing, one of the two opponents rolled the hoop forward from the home goal toward one of the ends; just as it began to lose its inertia the other man threw his pole in such a way that it would slide into the depression in which the hoop had rolled. The same procedure was repeated in the opposite direction. Then the next pair of players took their turn, and so on until all in the game had played. Then the first pair took another turn, and the rotation continued until the agreed number of points had been made by one opponent or one side.

The method of counting was simple. Each mark on the pole or hoop counted one point. If the hoop fell against the extreme butt end of the pole so that they just touched, it counted 1; if it fell somewhere on the butt section itself, as many points were counted as were enclosed by the hoop. For example, if it touched the first mark above the butt end, it counted 2; the next higher, 3; the next, 4; and so forth.

If the marks on the circumference of the hoop also touched the pole, points were added to the enclosed points already mentioned, 1 point if one mark, 2 if two marks, etc. And if the spoke of the hoop also crossed the pole, as many points were added to the throw as it took winds of the cord to cross the thickness of the butt. If the hoop fell upon the pole so that the spoke was exactly above and parallel with the pole, covering all the counters on the pole, that throw in itself won the game.[4]

Western Apache (San Carlos) S. C. Simms collected a hoop of sapling, 9¾ inches in diameter, painted red, divided in half with a thong wound with a buckskin cord, and having four equidistant notches on both faces on opposite sides of the median thong.[5]

Chiricahua E. W. Davis gave Stewart Culin an account of a hoop and pole game played by Geronimo's band at St. Augustine, Florida, in 1889. The game was played with hoops and poles, always by two men. The hoops were pieces of wood, with hide thongs tied to form a circle of about twelve inches in diameter. The poles were reeds ten or twelve feet long. A little mound of hay was placed on the ground and cleft in the center. The players stood about fifteen feet away, and each in his turn rolled his hoop into the cleft in the hay mound. When the hoop had nearly reached the hay, he would toss the pole through the hay, in the attempt to have the hoop encircle the end of the pole when the hoop reached the hay. The game was very difficult, and misses were more frequent than scores.[6]

Opler reports that the court was covered with something slippery, like pine needles, so that the hoop would roll. He states also that one of the poles was painted red at the butt end, and that an air of informality and good humor was always present. Often, musical instruments, such as the violin, were played during the games.[7]

Mescalero John C. Cremony says there were some games to which women were never allowed access. Among these was the one played with the poles and a hoop. The poles were generally about ten feet long, smooth and gradually tapering like a lance. They were marked with divisions throughout their length, and the divisions were stained in different colors. The hoop was of wood, about six inches in diameter, and divided like the poles, of which each player had one. Only two persons could engage in the game at one time. A level place was selected, from which the grass was removed to make a path one foot wide and from twenty-five to thirty feet long. The ground was then trodden down firmly until it was smooth. One of the players rolled the hoop forward, and when it reached a certain point, both threw their poles at it, overtaking it and knocking it down.

The graduation of count values was from the point of the pole toward the butt, which ranked highest, and the object was to make the hoop fall on the pole as near the butt as possible. The value of the part of the hoop that touched the pole was also counted. The two scores were then added together and credited to the player. The

Opposite top: *Drum sticks (MNCA). Top stick, 16 inches long; bottom stick 11½ inches long.* Opposite center: *Detail, showing method of tying looped end of stick with thong.* Opposite bottom: *Pottery drum and drum stick.* Above: *Playing cards (AF).*

417

Top: *Chiricahua men playing hoop and pole game (MNMP)*. Above: *White Mountain men thrusting the poles (DPL)*.

418

Top: *The release of the poles, Fort Apache (MNMP)*. Above: *Counting the score at San Carlos (DPL)*.

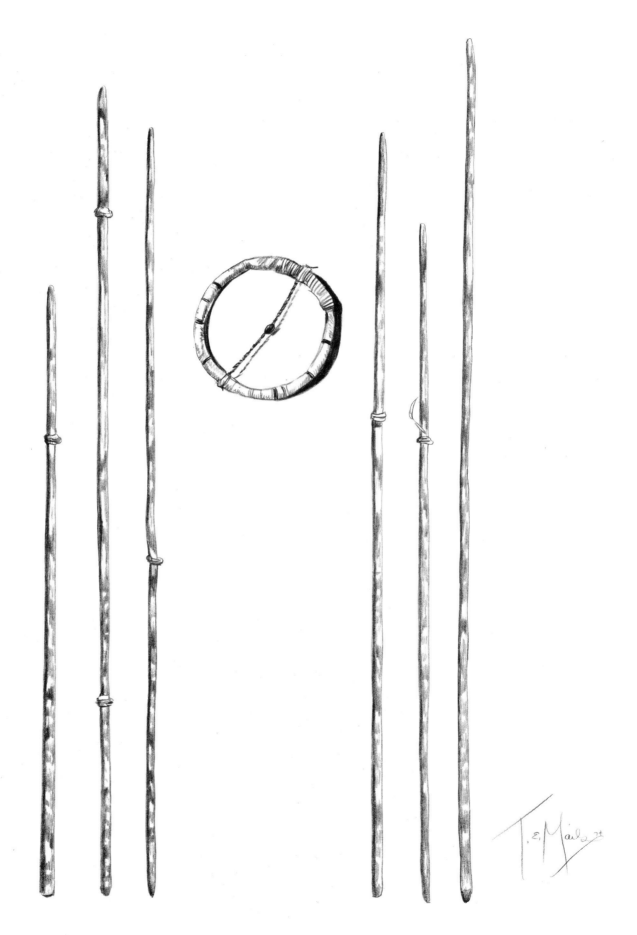

Above: *Hoop and poles for hoop and pole game (American Museum of Natural History). The poles are in sections.* Opposite top: *White Mountain mother and daughter playing dice game (MNMP).* Opposite bottom: *Apache men playing cards (SM).*

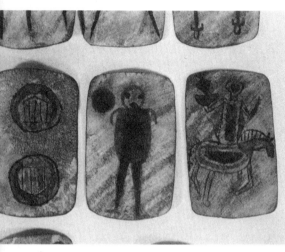

Top: *Playing cards (HM).* Center *and* above: *Details of playing cards, showing Apache art style.*

game was usually won by the first man to total a hundred points, but any number could be set by the players. When a game was going on no woman was permitted to approach within a hundred yards, and the men present were required to leave their weapons someplace else. When Cremony inquired as to the reason for these restrictions, he was told by some that they were required by tradition; but he was given another explanation that he believed was the true answer: When people gambled they became half crazy and were apt to quarrel. Since the hoop and pole game was the most exciting contest they had, and the players often wagered all they possessed on it, the loser was apt to get angry, and in early times fights resulted in which warriors were badly injured or killed. To prevent this, it was determined that no armed warrior should be present, and the game was always played at some distance from the camp, where arms could be found. Three prominent warriors were named as judges, and their decision was absolute. Judges were not allowed to bet while acting in that capacity. Cremony claimed that women were forbidden to be present because they always fomented troubles between the players, and created confusion by taking sides and provoking dissension.[8]

Jicarilla James Mooney reports that Jicarilla mythology described the wheel-and-stick game as having been made by Yolkaiist-sun, the Whitebead Woman, for her two sons, whose fathers were Sun and Moon. She cautioned them to not roll the wheel toward the north. They played for three days, during which time the Sun's son rolled the wheel toward the east, south, and west. His brother then persuaded him to roll it toward the north. An adventure with an owl followed, and the two boys were made to perform a succession of dangerous feats. When these were accomplished, they went to live in the western ocean.[9]

Hidden Ball

The only description of this game is set forth in the account of the Jicarilla genesis myth. It was a sort of shell game, in which one party hid the button under one of several wooden cups and the other tried to guess under which cup it was hidden. There was a score of 104 tally sticks.[10]

Foot Races

John C. Cremony, describing races he saw at Fort Sumner, New Mexico, among the Mescalero, said that racing on foot was a diversion frequently resorted to by the active, restless Apache, and added that the women generally won in mixed competition if the distance was not too great. In one instance, the officers at the post offered a number of prizes for races of different lengths. The longest race was half a mile, the next a quarter, the third three hundred yards, and the fourth one hundred. The races were open for men between fifteen and forty years old, and to girls from fifteen years to twenty-five. About a hundred Apache and Navajo entered, and practiced every day for a week. At the appointed time everybody in camp assembled to witness the contest. Among the competitors was a comely seventeen-year-old Apache girl named Ish-kay-nay. She had always refused marriage, and was the favorite runner among the Whites. "Each runner was tightly girded with a broad belt, and looked like a race horse." Ten entered for the half-mile prize, which was a gaudy piece of calico. At the word they went off like rockets, and Ish-kay-nay came in an easy winner, six yards ahead of all competitors. She also entered the quarter-mile race, but was ruled out by the other Apache, and their objections were allowed, it being decided that the victor in any race should not run in another.[11] Opler's Chiricahua informants told him that runners did not crouch at the start of a race. Also, when camps were fairly permanent, racetracks were made and also used for horse races.[12]

Shinny

A game of shinny was played among the Chiricahua. It was much like soccer, except that sticks were used, and both men and women played. It was a rough and taxing game. The shinny stick was forty inches long and hooked at one end. Some players carried a second, straight stick, for protection, which was used to ward off an opponent's blows. A small buckskin or wooden ball about half the size of a baseball, was used.

Each side had the same number of participants, each ranging in number from five to twelve. The playing field was almost a half mile long and any width, except the goal at each end was two trees, between which the ball had to go to score.

Once the ball was in play it could be advanced by kicking it or hitting it with the stick. Each goal counted 1 point. There were no fouls, and play continued until the sides were too exhausted to go on.[13]

Dice Games

Western Apache (White Mountain) Rev. Paul S. Mayerhoff collected three wooden staves, 10¾ inches in length, flat on one side, painted yellow, with a green band on the flat face. Using the name Throw Sticks, he described a woman's game that was played with great ardor. Three staves were used, eight to eleven inches long, and flat on one side.

The playing area was a circle about five feet in diameter. Its center was marked by a flat rock of medium size, generally from eight to ten inches in diameter. Around the circumference forty smaller stones were arranged in sets of ten, to be used as counters. Either two or four persons could participate at one time in the game.

In playing, the sticks were thrown on end on the rock in the center with enough force to make them rebound. Depending upon how they fell, flat or round face upward, the throw counted from 1 to 10, as follows: Three round sides up, 10 points; two round sides up, one flat, 1 or 2 points; one round side up, two flat, 3 points; three flat sides up, 5 points. If one of the players, in making her count, continued from her set of counters to the adjoining set of her opponent's and struck the place marked by the opponent's tally marker, it negated the opponent's count, and she had to start over. The first to reach 40 points won the game.

Mayerhoff collected pieces for another game, which he called Drop Sticks. There were four sticks, twenty-three inches long, with two having the round sides painted alike with four diagonal black stripes, and one with a broad red band in the middle and red ends. The first three sticks had flat reverses, painted red, and the fourth stick, with the red band, a black reverse.

Another set had three with round sides decorated alike with alternate red and black lines, and one with diagonal black lines. The first three had red reverses, the fourth a black reverse.

The Drop Stick game was played by both sexes together. There was no specific playing area. The playing pieces were four sticks, ranging from eighteen to twenty-four inches in length, round on the back, flat on the face. One of the sticks represented a man, the other three, women. The sticks were dropped and the points counted as follows: Four faces down, sticks lying parallel, 10 points; four faces down, pair of crosses, 10; four faces down, odd stick crossing the others, 10; four faces up, pair of crosses, 20; four faces up, odd stick crossing others, 20; three faces down, one crossed by the odd stick, face upward, 26; three faces up, one crossed by the odd stick, face down, 26; three faces up, crossed by the odd stick, face down, 39; three faces up, two crossed by the odd stick, face up or down, 39; four faces up, sticks lying parallel, 40; three faces up, one face down, lying parallel, 52; three faces down, one face up, lying parallel, 52; three faces up, one down, crossing one another six times, 62.[14]

Albert B. Reagan described the stick dice game as follows in 1901: This game was usually played by women only in their leisure hours. They wagered on it objects of small value, sometimes even money. When money was bet it was put under the stone on

Top, center, *and* above: *Details of playing cards, showing Apache art style.*

423

which the sticks were cast. The field was a leveled spot of ground with a small flat stone placed in the center. Other stones were then placed around this stone to form a circle 3½ feet in diameter, with four openings, ten stones being placed in each quarter of the circle. The openings corresponded to the northeast, southeast, southwest, and northwest directions. The circumference stones were of various shapes and sizes. A stick was placed in the opening at the northeast to indicate the starting point. In counting, a player moved his counting stick as many stones from the starting point as he had points to count, putting his marker in the space just beyond the last stone counted. If the count ended in one of the four openings, he put his marker in the next preceding space. The stones in each section were numbered. Those in the two sections on the right of the starting point were numbered from 1 to 20, and those on the left of the starting point in the same way toward the left.

The playing sticks were about a foot in length, and were the halves of green sticks about one inch in diameter. The bark was left on the rounded side and the split surface was marked across its face with charcoal bands about one inch wide. In throwing, the sticks were carefully held together in the hand, with the marked faces either in or out. They were hurled, ends down, the hand being released just before they struck the center rock, so that they were free to fall or bounce in any direction.

The counts were as follows: One marked face up, 2; two marked faces up, 3; three marked faces up, 5; three marked faces down, 10.

If a player scored 10, she threw again; otherwise she passed the sticks to the next player. When a player reached 10, she always said *yak!* and struck the center stone with the bunch of three play sticks sidewise before throwing them again. The number of players could be two, three, or four, the last-named number being the usual one. When four played, one sat behind each section of stones, facing the center. When more than two played, the two that faced each other played as partners. Partners always moved their counting sticks in the same direction. The player of the east section and her partner, if she had one, moved around the circle toward the south, and the player of the north section moved around toward the west.

If a player's count terminated at, or moved past, a place occupied by an opponent, she took her opponent's counting stick and threw it back, and the latter had to start over, losing all her counts.

A game consisted of three circuits, or 120 points. Each time a player made a circuit she recorded her score by placing a charcoal mark on a stone in her section.

The vocabulary used for the game was: "the stick game; let us play the stick game; the sticks used in the stick game; the game is finished, won; She, I have won the game."[15]

In 1903, Charles L. Owen collected thirteen wooden dice, 1⅜ inches long, flat on one side and rounded on the other, all painted black on the flat side, while three had reddish-brown backs and ten had white backs.

The game was played only by warriors. Thirteen—or, according to another informant, fourteen—dice were used. Two or four players participated. The highest possible throw was 20 points. The dice were shaken in a flat basket. The ground was hollowed out, lined with bear grass, and then covered over with a buckskin or blanket. This was to give elasticity and recoil to the dice when the basket was struck sharply. The method of shaking dice was to strike the basket, which was firmly grasped at two opposite sides, down upon the elastic blanket, the dice thereby being tossed upward and shaken well.

The score was counted as follows: Three white backs and ten black faces counted 12; three red backs and ten black faces, —; one red back and twelve black faces, 10; five white backs and eight black faces, —; seven white backs and six black faces, —; three red backs and ten white backs, 20;—red back,—white backs, 16; three black faces and ten white backs, —; three red backs, three white backs, and seven black faces, —; two red backs, ten white backs, and one black face, 5.[16]

Western Apache (San Carlos) S. C. Simms collected three wooden staves, nine inches long, the flat faces painted red, with incised cross lines painted black in the middle and end edges notched, and the round sides painted yellow; also, three wooden staves, eight inches long, identical with preceding except that the flat faces had alternate painted bands, black and red.[17]

Cat's Cradle

A cat's cradle was collected by Stewart Culin from a White Mountain Apache girl at Albuquerque. She called it *ikinasthlani*.[18]

Archery

E. W. Davis saw an archery game played by Geronimo's band of Chiricahua at St. Augustine, Florida, in 1889. It required considerable skill, and consisted of tossing arrows, point first, at a mark about ten feet away. The first man to throw his arrow attempted to land in the mark. If he missed, he got his arrow back, and this was the extent of his participation in the first round. Once an arrow was in the mark, however, the next player attempted to toss his arrow so that it would cross the first, and so on with the rest of the players. Sometimes all the players would toss their arrows without anyone winning. In this case, the arrows on the ground remained in the pot, and the play continued, with each player winning as many arrows as he could manage to cross with his own, until all the arrows had been removed.[19]

Bull-Roarer

The bull-roarer, used ceremonially by the masked dancer clown and by shamans, was also used as a child's toy.[20]

Wrestling

Men enjoyed wrestling, and some virtually became professionals at it, even contesting with men from other tribes. The object was to throw the other man off his feet so that any part of his body touched the ground. Large sums were often bet on these contests.[21]

Tug-of-War

There were frequent tug-of-war competitions. A variant was to fasten a rawhide rope around the waist of an especially strong man. Three other men then held the loose end of the rope, along which knots were tied to afford grips. A fourth member of the opposition assisted his team by attempting to hold the strong man down. If the man managed to arise, however, and to pull the other three adversaries forward, he was the winner.[22]

Cards

The Apache were such passionate card players that Al Seiber and his party once surprised a group of Chiricahua warriors in the midst of a game of Monte. They killed all the Chiricahua and took the cards. It was common for men and women to play cards, and large wagers were made on these games.[23]

It appears that the Apache card decks were adaptations of the standard Spanish-Mexican decks. They were hand-painted in typical Apache linear style on thin rawhide. There were four sets, with forty cards in each deck.

The usual colors were a greenish yellow, a dull red, royal blue or blue-black, and black. Both native dyes and commercial colors were used. There was no decoration on the backs of the cards. The designs were applied by individual artists, so that each deck was different from the others, although the suits and values remained constant. Some deck designs were strongly Apache in flavor, while others presented an interesting mixture of the Apache, Spanish, and Mexican cultures.[24]

Moccasin Game

The moccasin game which Geronimo says was called *Kah* (foot) was a religious game of chance that was played only in winter, when the snake and the bear were in hibernation, and at night. The story of the mythological origin of the contest could only be told in winter and at night also, or the storyteller would experience bad things, such as seeing a rattlesnake.

Both Chiricahua men and women participated. Sides were chosen, and a fire was built and lighted on a level place. Each side buried, on its side of the fire, four moccasins, which were placed in a row with only the tops showing. Then, while a blanket was held up as a shield between the sides, and while animal and bird songs, known as the legends of creation, were sung, one side hid a bone in one of its four moccasins.

The blanket was then lowered, and a member of the other team attempted to locate the hidden bone by striking with a stick the moccasin he thought contained it. If he guessed correctly, his side then hid the bone while the process was repeated with the other side guessing.

If he missed, his team was required to pay the opponents a number of yucca counters equal to however many moccasins the guess had missed by, and then his team had to guess again.

There was a set number of counters, and when one team had won them all, the game ended. The usual number was sixty-eight, of which four were worth 10 points each, and the rest 1 each. There were variations to the game, such as the guessing team attempting to just miss a moccasin to get the hiding team to give themselves away by their reaction.

The teams placed bets on each stroke of the stick and on which side would win. Geronimo says that a game usually lasted four or five hours. If the Chiricahua moccasin game had not ended by the time day broke, the teams had to blacken their faces with charcoal before continuing, because the original game had ended when the sun rose.[25]

While little information concerning the Apache moccasin game is available beyond the reports of Geronimo and Opler, Kluckhohn includes the details of the moccasin game, with its variants, as played by the Navajo. It was broadly similar to the Apache game, even to the painting of the face with charcoal at daybreak if the game was to be continued.[26]

Conclusion

It is remarkable to see how adverse situations can often work to contradict and confound their stated goals. Because of their negative historical factors, the reservations of Arizona and New Mexico have actually served to preserve the Apache as a distinct people. Captivity has perpetuated their unique language, heritage, and way of life, and the presence of these has assured that efforts to separate the people from their culture and environment by removal for employment and education would not succeed.

In spite of the suppression, abuse, poverty, social ills, and political conflicts, the reservations, located as they were within the larger territories of the original home range, provided the Apache with the important home places they needed to give them a historical and mythological identity. Even the well-intentioned educational program put forth by the Whites assured conflict and preservation rather than change. The schools compelled the children to learn English and punished them for speaking and thinking Apache, exposing them to books that portrayed their ancestors and parents as primitives, savages, barbarians, and pagans as opposed to the White man, who in spite of his conduct was always shown as civilized and enlightened. All too often their home environment was held up to them as degrading, ignorant, and fruitless. But the Apache children knew better, for at home on the reservation they learned to respect their heritage, language, and life-way. In consequence, the Apache simply withdrew and found security among their own.

Thus, while much of the early culture was smothered by strict federal rule and exposure to Anglo ways, the ancient Apache mentality, spirit, and traditions had the crucible they needed to survive insofar as they do today.

Debates among Anglos are constant as to whether or not the preservation of the Apache culture has been a good thing. The Apache themselves recognize that progress as a part of White society is contingent upon their command of industrialized skills and politics, yet there are few of them today who have found in what they have learned a sufficient reason to separate themselves from what they have been and are, "Apache."

In short, the Apache is justifiably proud of what he was and is, even though the combination of developments over the past eighty years may make it difficult for him to express this. Until the last decade, a history of grievous poverty, cultural disintegration, the gap between Apache and Anglo language and beliefs and values, drinking, and a lack of direction gradually infused his strength of former days with doubt and hesitancy. Now, though, the Apache have turned the corner, both with and without federal, state, and local assistance; and, displaying that spirit of survival which has characterized them from the beginning, they are making great progress. A visit to any of the four reservations makes this resoundingly clear to those who have followed and seen them over the years. The tribal management is positive and progressive, the services are improved, the homes for the most part are better, and the people are meeting well the delicate task of balancing between two valuable cultures. Hope and pride are back. The Apache have returned to the battlefields, but this time with a different purpose.

To say this is not to ignore the problems and needs that exist. Poverty as compared to average White circumstances is extremely serious in some instances. San Carlos in particular suffers greatly from it, and the aged people on all the reservations barely get by. In terms of education for growth and comfort in American society, the Apache still have a long way to go. Apathy and despair are by no means completely gone. Alcohol is a continuing menace of significant proportions.

Beyond this, other problems common to everyone have made their appearance on all the reservations. Divorce is becoming more and more common with its attendant consequences, and the ancient views regarding chastity are melting away. In the old days theft was never a problem, but now, said a friend, "We have to lock up everything when we go someplace. Last year we were robbed twice."

People who respect the ancient Apache life-way, and who find it very meaningful, often ask what of the traditional attitudes and rituals still remains.

Some reference has already been made to this. The Jicarilla hold the Ceremonial Relay Race, Adolescence Rite, and an occasional Holiness Rite. The Mescalero and Chiricahua celebrate joint puberty rites, and the Western Apache hold the puberty rite. I was pleased to learn that the number of Sunrise (Puberty) Ceremonies being held each year is increasing; informants at Fort Apache surmised that as many as fifteen rites were held there in 1973. However, even though they were well acquainted with what was going on, they were only able to guess at the actual number of ceremonies. This is a fact I find particularly interesting, since it suggests that the people do not always know everything that is happening on the sprawling reservation, and thus can give only approximate statistics to those who inquire.

Curing ceremonies are on the wane, but they are still being held. The Apache who live in the towns use the medicine men least of all, preferring to go to the public health facilities. People who live in remoter and more rural areas are sometimes inclined to call upon the medicine men. No Apache in my acquaintance seems to know exactly how many shamans there are on the various reservations today. Two of the best known at Fort Apache are Renzie Gordon and Ryan Burnette of Upper Cedar Creek. Renzie is an older man of some renown, a singer with an excellent voice. Ryan is a younger man of perhaps thirty years, who is also respected. Philip Cassadore holds an equal position at San Carlos.

While I have read that there are no living medicine men at Cibecue who have the power to perform puberty ceremonials, I was told recently that at the same time that rites were being held at Whiteriver and the known singers in that region were occupied, a rite was also being held at Cibecue, "So there must be a medicine man over there too." Of course, the Cibecue singer could have been recruited from some other place. The point is, there are several men practicing.

An informant also told me about a most interesting curing

ceremony that he witnessed near Whiteriver in 1972. The patient was an elderly woman who was in a rest home. But she had mental problems, so she was brought home for treatment. She was taken to a level place "down by the river," and the shaman and the friends of the family joined her there. The part of the ceremony witnessed took place in the afternoon.

The medicine man made a large imaginary circle by "praying with pollen" at the four corners. He began at the north and proceeded sunwise (clockwise), stopping at each cardinal direction as he moved around to the east, where he made an imaginary entrance. The woman was then taken in through the entrance to the center of the circle and seated there, "with someone there to help her." Since my informant was behind the medicine man when he touched the woman with pollen and prayed, he could not see exactly how it was done, but he thought it looked as if he touched her on the left shoulder, forehead, right shoulder, and chest.

Then a remarkable thing happened, for the Gans who were to dance later on came in their street clothing to do the same thing as the shaman had to the woman. They entered the imaginary entrance one at a time, with each man circling as the shaman did before applying the pollen. The remarkable thing is that the Gans came in regular attire, and thus would be known to all who were present. In the usual instance, their identity is kept secret, and even those who can tell who they are after they have been costumed and painted must not admit or indicate that they do.

At dusk a huge bonfire was built and kindled. When it was dark, the Gans came in full regalia and performed around and over the patient. Social dancing followed, and continued throughout the night. It was noted that the medicine man instructed the masked dancers to observe the traditional sacred rules for the four days immediately following the ceremony. These included an admonition to abstain from sexual relations with their wives.

A number of the ancient taboos are still observed. In giving an illustration of this, an informant spoke of certain camps near Fort Apache where long ago tuberculosis struck with devastating effect. Many died swift and agonizing deaths, and, abandoning the usual custom of burning the homes and property of the deceased, the living fled in terror as far away as possible into the high places in the hills. They never went back, and the bodies of the dead were left where they died on the ground in and around the wickiups. Their bones are there today. From then on, families who knew about this cautioned their children to stay away from "those places of death and ghosts." And if one should stumble inadvertently onto one of the places, he was to back out and circle around it in a certain way to avoid the various kinds of sickness it might bring. This had happened, and it was a "dangerous" thing to do, and there are those who even today circle the areas as they should. "The people are still afraid of those places."

It is frequently stated that Christianity has had little effect upon the Apache people. Since I am a Lutheran pastor, I always hesitate to address myself to this question, for my persuasion is obvious. On the other hand, I am at the distinct disadvantage of not knowing the religious orientation, or lack of it, of those who have made the assertions I refer to. I don't know how to judge them, and it seems it would be more fair if they declared themselves, since it would make an adequate evaluation of the worth of their views more possible. Also, some will insist that I have the supposedly compulsive need always to show the value of Christianity. Of course, I do accept its surpassing worth, else I'd not be a pastor, but the absolute fact is that I hold a profound respect for the Indian religions I have come to know well. And it seems to me that of all peoples, the Apache have learned to hold the two positions in good and common harmony.

Many Apache in my acquaintance appear to have relatively good understanding of, and appreciation for, the Christian religion. Yet at the same time they are able to respect and practice the traditional Apache customs, and they find no inconsistency in this. They say, and I believe them, that they simply understand Christianity from within the Apache view. And is that not what anyone does—sees his faith through the eyes of his own environment and culture?

In any case, I shall simply report some of what I have been told by the Apache, and leave the conclusions to others. At the very least the continuing reverence of the people, so clearly seen in their ceremonies, will be apparent:

"When I drive around the reservation early in the morning I see lots of people out praying."

"The old pray in the morning."

"The other day on Sunday morning I saw the medicine man out blessing a whole family while they were praying."

"Morning is God's morning. The Apache bury their folks in the morning. That's good luck. The afternoon is bad luck. If you bury anyone then, some others will die soon."

The following remarks were included in a letter received from an Apache friend at Christmas, 1973: "I have been pretty busy lately going here and there like last week we went to Paducah, Kentucky to this church there. . . . That's all for now hope to hear from you all soon, may God keep his hand upon you all." The writer is a Lutheran from San Carlos, and so are her mother and brother, who worship regularly.

Another good friend is an avowed and outgoing Christian who is completely immersed in the Western Apache traditions and is doing all he can to preserve and perpetuate them. Yet at the Christmas season recently he traveled to Haskell Institute to teach the Apache students to sing Christmas carols in Apache, and when I called one day after he had made that trip, he was off doing the same at a local Baptist church.

I am including here a reproduction of a page from the *Fort Apache Scout*, the newspaper of the White Mountain Apache tribe. It contains the Apache words for *It Came Upon a Midnight Clear*, and some drawings that appear to be more than adequate expressions of the Christmas event as seen through Apache eyes.

A final statement to bear in mind as one considers the impact of Christian missions is an excerpt from the editorial of the December 24, 1962, issue of the newspaper *Jicarilla Chieftain*.

When God blesses a home with a baby, the parents break the news to their friends by sending announcements. But when God chose to announce the birth of the Lord Jesus, He used a choir of angels. It was probably the most dramatic thing Heaven had ever done. Imagine that great choir singing with perfect voice, perfect harmony, in perfect song. It was as if there was a truth too great, too sacred, too divine for any imperfect mouth to utter. Heaven's joy was its greatest. It had to speak and broke forth in highest praise to God. The angels' message directs us to the heart of all true observance of Christmas. They sing not to the shepherds, Joseph, or Mary, but to God. To Him belongs the glory and honor of Christmas. God is first. "Glory to God." Only as God is put first and recognized as to who He is and what He has done in sending His Son can men know peace on earth. Does not this angelic choir show us that true worship of Jesus Christ is not sadness, but joy? The Christian life is not weeping but a song! In the darkest and most uncertain hours God may break through with music. Let us remember that God wants to Baptise us with the oil of gladness. A man's look, his manner, his work, his worship, should by God's grace all be cheerful. A Christian as no other man has a right to be in high spirits. "My mouth shall praise thee with joyful life."

Quite frankly, I've seldom read a more perceptive statement about Christ and the Christian life.

My point in bringing out the foregoing is not to show how

right or effective the Christian religion has been among the Apache, but rather to emphasize how the deeply religious nature of the people has enabled many of them to achieve an interesting combination of natural religion and Christianity without feeling that the ancient religious ways are either invalid or outmoded.

Having considered and appreciated the various reasons why the Apache groups drew apart and became separate entities in former times, we can still see, as their customs are studied in tandem, that remarkable similarities exist between them, and to such a degree that we cannot escape believing that at one time they had a very close relationship. Perhaps they were even united in one large block. We may then wonder whether the Apache might not benefit by combining their efforts today.

I asked this question of a friend at Whiteriver, and he replied that one day, when all spoke English, and perhaps became more Anglo in their ways, the Apache might get together. "When the Apache is gone from us it could happen." Yet he placed such a time in the distant future, if indeed it were to happen at all. "Right now," he said, "they are afraid to go there. They say, 'How can I go there?'" The import is apparent. For the majority, each reservation has become its people's security and home. While they experience, see, and hear about it, the outside world remains the vast and foreign unknown, which is menacing and uncertain. Those who have left the reservation and returned only reinforce that truth. This does not mean they are afraid to leave the reservation, for they frequently do, yet most venture forth in the confidence that they will touch the outside but tentatively, and then return quickly to the people and land they love.

People called them "Apache," which meant enemy. And they earned the name in every respect. Seldom has any people in history fought harder, man for man, woman for woman, and child for child, for the preservation of a territory to live in and a life-way of great value. Yet how things have changed, or at least how the direction of things has altered, in the last eighty years!

In my introduction to this book, I have stated my hope that readers would be moved to meet the Apache personally, so that we might all go in closer concert toward the future. Although I am well aware that the Apache feel the same way, I had not expected a written expression of this feeling. Thus it was especially pleasing to receive from my excellent friend Edgar Perry a letter dated January 3, 1974, which he concludes with these words: "We are happy and pleased with everything you have done for us. May our good Lord bless you and keep you as we look forward to a better future for our country, and thank you again."

"Our country!" One has only to consider that phrase in the light of history, to imagine what it means to have an Apache say it. And that awareness causes me to wonder once again why it has taken so long to consider the American Indian as what he is, part of the very fabric of this nation. How long will it be before history textbooks consider even the Indian wars as part of what has taken place within this country—that is, as civil wars rather than wars against foreigners? If foreigners were involved, the Anglos were the invaders, not the Indians.

Today, however, we have become one. The past has merged into a common history, into a time when it is necessary for us to say that those whose descendents are now citizens in common once fought against each other. What is needed is a change of perspective, so that the Indian life-way is considered as what it is, a regular part of the historic development and future of the United States.

The event that prompted Edgar Perry's letter was a Christmas, 1973, trip to Old Fort Apache with a huge load of gifts from my congregation in California. This was brought about not by our charity, but by the great pleasure we derive from sharing things and moments with a people we have come to care for a great deal. The Apache also had gifts for us. Accordingly, we shall remember for a long time the aged people assembled at the Culture Center, who repeated over and over again, "We sure do thank you."

My thoughts at the time were traveling in an opposite direction. I was saying in my heart, "I sure do thank you," for having treated me to an attitude, a nature, and a life-way that has meant more and done more for me personally than I can ever express.

To the Apache I say then, in the White Mountain Apache tribe language, "*Ashoog*," thank you with all the sincerity I can muster!

Left: *Jennifer, San Carlos, 1973.*
Above: *Page from* The Fort Apache Scout, *December, 1973.*

432

Bibliography

"The Apaches." *Arizona State Teachers College Bulletin*, vol. 20, no. 1.

Arizona, Legislature of the Territory of. *Memorial and Affidavits Showing Outrages Perpetrated by the Apache Indians, in the Territory of Arizona during the Years 1869 and 1870.* San Francisco: Francis and Valentine, Printers, 1871.

Arnold, Elliot. "The Ceremony of the Big Wickiup." *Arizona Highways*, August, 1951.

Baldwin, Gordon C. *The Warrior Apaches.* Tucson: Dale Stuart King, 1965.

Ball, Eve, with James Kaywaykla, narrator. *In the Days of Victorio.* Tucson: University of Arizona Press, 1970.

Bandelier, Adolph F. *The Southwestern Journals, 1883–1884.* Albuquerque: University of New Mexico Press, 1970.

Basso, Keith H. *The Cibecue Apache.* New York: Holt, Rinehart and Winston, 1970.

——. *Western Apache Raiding and Warfare: From the Notes of Grenville Goodwin.* Tucson: University of Arizona Press, 1971.

——. *Western Apache Witchcraft.* Anthropology Papers of the University of Arizona, no. 15. Tucson: University of Arizona Press, 1969.

——, and Opler, Morris E., editors. *Apachean Culture, History and Ethnology.* Anthropology Papers of the University of Arizona, no. 21. Tucson: University of Arizona Press, 1971.

Beeler, Joe. *Cowboys and Indians: Characters in Oil and Bronze.* Norman: University of Oklahoma Press, 1967.

Betzinez, Jason, with Nye, Wilver Sturevant. *I Fought with Geronimo.* Harrisburg, Penn.: The Stackpole Company, 1959.

Bleeker, Sonia. *The Apache Indians.* New York: William Morrow & Co., 1951.

Bourke, John C. *The Medicine Men of the Apache.* 9th Annual Report of the Bureau of American Ethnology, 1887–1888. Washington, D.C.: Government Printing Office, 1892.

——. *On the Border with Crook.* New York: Charles Scribner's Sons, 1891.

Burlison, Irene. *Yesterday and Today in the Life of the Apache.* Philadelphia: Dorrance & Co., 1973.

Carter, Deborah. "Adventure among the Apaches." *New Mexico Magazine*, December, 1958.

Clum, Woodworth. *Apache Agent: The Story of John P. Clum.* Boston: Houghton Mifflin Co., 1936.

Cochise, Ciyé "Niño," as told to Griffith, A. Kinney. *The First Hundred Years of Niño Cochise.* New York: Abelard-Schuman, 1971.

Collier, John. *Patterns and Ceremonials of the Indians of the Southwest.* New York: E. P. Dutton and Co., 1949.

Colyer, Vincent. *Peace with the Apaches of New Mexico and Arizona.* Washington, D.C.: Government Printing Office, 1872.

Cremony, John C. *Life among the Apaches (1850–1868).* Glorieta, N. M.: The Rio Grande Press, 1970.

Cruse, Gen. Thomas. *Apache Days and After.* Caldwell, Idaho: The Caxton Printers, 1941.

Culin, Stewart. *Games of the North American Indians.* 24th Annual Report of the Bureau of American Ethnology. Washington, D.C.: Government Printing Office, 1907.

Curtis, Edward S. *The North American Indians.* Vol. I, 1907. New York: Johnson Reprint Corp., 1970.

——. "Vanishing Indian Types; The Tribes of the Southwest." *Scribner's Magazine*, May, 1906.

Davis, Britton. *The Truth about Geronimo.* New Haven: Yale University Press, 1929, 1968.

Dedera, Don. "Fire in the Tonto." *Arizona Highways*, September, 1960.

——. "Is Geronimo Alive and Well in the South Vietnamese Central Highlands?" *Mankind Magazine*, August, 1971.

Dorsey, George A. *Indians of the Southwest.* Passenger Department, Atchison, Topeka and Santa Fe Railway System, 1903.

Dutton, Bertha P. *Indians of the Southwest.* Santa Fe, N.M.: Southwestern Association on Indian Affairs, Inc., 1965.

Eggan, Fred. *Social Anthropology of North American Tribes.* Chicago: University of Chicago Press, 1972.

Emerson, Dorothy. *Among the Mescalero Apaches: The Story of Father Albert Braun, OFM.* Tucson: University of Arizona Press, 1973.

Ewers, John C. *The Horse in Blackfoot Indian Culture.* Smithsonian Institution, Bureau of American Ethnology, Bulletin 159. Washington, D.C.: Government Printing Office, 1959.

Feder, Norman. *American Indian Art.* New York: Harry N. Abrams, 1969.

Fergusson, Erna. *Dancing Gods.* Albuquerque: University of New Mexico Press, 1966.

Forbes, Jack D. *The Indian in America's Past.* Englewood Cliffs, N.J.: Prentice-Hall, Inc., 1964.

Fuchs, Estelle, and Havighurst, Robert J. *To Live on this Earth: American Indian Education.* Garden City, N.Y.: Doubleday and Co., 1972.

Geronimo. *His Own Story.* Edited by S. M. Barrett, 1906. Newly edited with an introduction and notes by Frederick W. Turner III. New York: E. P. Dutton & Co., 1970.

Getty, Harry T. *The San Carlos Indian Cattle Industry.* Anthropology Papers of the University of Arizona, no. 7. Tucson: University of Arizona Press, 1963.

Goddard, Pliny Earle. *Indians of the Southwest.* New York: American Museum of Natural History, 1931

Goodwin, Grenville. *The Social Organization of the Western Apache.* Tucson: University of Arizona Press, 1969.

Greene, A. C. *The Last Captive.* Austin, Texas: Encino Press, 1972.

Guenther, Rev. Arthur. "50 Years in Apache Land." *White Mountains of Arizona*, vol. no. 17 (Fall, 1971–Summer 1972).

Hafen, Leroy R. *The Indians of Colorado.* Denver: State Historical Society of Colorado, State Museum, 1952.

Haines, Frances. *The Buffalo.* New York: Thomas Y. Crowell Co., 1970.

Herbert, Charles W. "Land of the White Mountain Apaches." *Arizona Highways*, July, 1962.

Herbert, Lucile and Charles. "The Old Gentleman Missionary." *Arizona Highways*, May, 1963.

Hoijer, Harry. *Chiricahua and Mescalero Apache Texts.* With ethnological notes by Morris E. Opler. Chicago: University of Chicago Press, 1938.

Jefferson, James; Delaney, Robert; and Thompson, Gregory C. *The Southern Utes, a Tribal History.* Ignacio, Colo.: Southern Ute Tribe, 1972.

Johnson, Barry C. *Crook's Resume of Operations against Apache Indians, 1882–1886.* London: Johnson-Tauton Military Press, 1971.

Journal of Arizona History, vol. 14, no. 2, 1973.

Kaut, C. *The Western Apache Clan System.* University of New Mexico Publications in Anthropology, no. 9. Albuquerque: University of New Mexico Press, 1957.

Kluckhohn, Clyde. *Navaho Witchcraft.* Boston: Beacon Press, 1970.

——; Hill, W. W.; and Kluckhohn, Lucy Wales. *Navaho Material Culture.* Cambridge, Mass.: The Belknap Press of Harvard University, 1971.

LaBarre, Weston. *The Peyote Cult.* New York: Schocken Books, 1971.

Lindquist, G. E. *The Red Man in the United States.* New York: George H. Doran Co., 1923.

Lockwood, Frank C. *The Apache Indians.* New York: The Macmillan Company, 1938.

Lummis, Charles F. *The Land of Poco Tiempo.* New York: Charles Scribner's Sons, 1933.

Mails, Thomas E. *Dog Soldiers, Bear Men and Buffalo Women.* Englewood Cliffs, N.J.: Prentice-Hall, A Rutledge Book, 1973.

——. *The Mystic Warriors of the Plains.* Garden City, N.Y.: Doubleday & Co., 1972.

Mason, Otis Tufton. *North American Bows, Arrows and Quivers.* Smithsonian Report, 1893. Yonkers, N.Y.: Carl J. Pugliese, 1972.

Material Culture Notes. Denver: American Indian Art Department, Denver Art Museum, 1967.

Mooney, James. *The Ghost-Dance Religion and the Sioux Outbreak of 1890.* Annual Report of the Bureau of American Ethnology, 1892–1893, pt. 2, 1896. Reprint. Chicago: University of Chicago Press, Phoenix Books, 1965.

Newcomb, Franc Johnson. *Hosteen Klah, Navaho Medicine Man and Sand Painter.* Norman: University of Oklahoma Press, 1964.

Newcomb, W. W. *The Indians of Texas, from Prehistoric to Modern Times.* Austin: University of Texas Press, 1961, 1965.

Ogle, Ralph Hedrick. *Federal Control of the Western Apaches, 1848–1886.* Albuquerque: University of New Mexico Press, 1970.

Opler, Morris E. *An Apache Life-Way.* New York: Cooper Square Publishers, 1965.

——. *Apache Odyssey: A Journey between Two Worlds.* New York: Holt, Rinehart and Winston, 1969.

——. *Childhood and Youth in Jicarilla Apache Society.* Los Angeles: The Southwest Museum, 1946.

——. *Dirty Boy: A Jicarilla Tale of Raid and War.* Menasha, Wis.: American Anthropological Association. New York: Kraus Reprint Co., 1970.

——. *Grenville Goodwin among the Western Apache: Letters from the Field.* Tucson: University of Arizona Press, 1973.

——. *Myths and Legends of the Lipan Apache Indians.* American Folklore Society. New York: J. J. Augustine, 1940, 1969.

——. *Myths and Tales of the Chiricahua Apache Indians.* Memoirs of the American Folklore Society, vol. 37, 1942. New York: Kraus Reprint Co., 1969.

——. *Myths and Tales of the Jicarilla Apache Indians.* Memoirs of the American Folklore Society, vol. 31, 1938. New York: Kraus Reprint Co., 1969.

——. "A Summary of Jicarilla Apache Culture." *American Anthropologist*, vol. 38, 1936–1938.

Parmee, Edward A. *Formal Education and Culture Change: A Modern Apache Indian Community and Government Programs.* Tucson: University of Arizona Press, 1968.

Reagan, Albert B. *Notes on the Indians of the Fort Apache Region.* Anthropological Papers of the American Museum of Natural History, vol. 31, pt. 5. New York: American Museum of Natural History, 1930.

Roberts, Helen. *Basketry of the San Carlos Apache Indians.* Anthropological Papers of the American Museum of Natural History, vol. 31, pt. 2, 1929. Glorieta, N.M.: Rio Grande Press, 1972.

Santee, Ross. *Apache Land.* New York: Charles Scribner's Sons, 1947.

Schwatka, Fredrick. "Among the Apaches." *Century Magazine*, May, 1887.

Smith, Anne M. *New Mexico Indians: Economic, Educational and Social Prob-*

lems. Santa Fe: Museum of New Mexico, 1966.

Smith, Mrs. White Mountain. *Indian Tribes of the Southwest.* Stanford, Cal.: Stanford University, 1933.

Sonnichsen, C. L. *The Mescalero Apaches.* Norman: University of Oklahoma Press, 1958.

Stanley, F. *The Jicarilla Apaches of New Mexico.* Pampa, Texas: Pampa Print Shop, 1967.

———. *The Apaches of New Mexico, 1540–1940.* Pampa, Texas: Pampa Print Shop, 1962.

Swanton, John R. *Indian Tribes of North America.* Smithsonian Institution, Bureau of American Ethnology, Bulletin 145. Washington, D.C.: Government Printing Office, 1952, 1968.

Tanner, Clara Lee. *Southwest Indian Craft Arts.* Tucson: University of Arizona Press, 1968.

Terrell, John Upton. *Apache Chronicle.* New York: World Publishing Co., 1972.

Thrapp, Dan L. *Al Seiber, Chief of Scouts.* Norman: University of Oklahoma Press, 1964.

———. *The Conquest of Apacheria.* Norman: University of Oklahoma Press, 1967.

———. *General Crook and the Sierra Madre Adventure.* Norman: University of Oklahoma Press, 1972.

VanRoekel, Gertrude B. *Jicarilla Apaches.* San Antonio, Texas: The Naylor Co., 1971.

Villasenor, David V. *Tapestries in Sand: The Spirit of Indian Sandpainting.* Healdsburg, Cal.: Naturegraph Co., 1963.

Watson, Editha L. *Navajo Sacred Places.* Window Rock, Ariz.: Navajo Tribal Museum, 1964.

———. *Navajo History: A 3000-Year Sketch.* Window Rock, Ariz.: Navajo Tribal Museum, 1964.

Wayland, Virginia. *Apache Playing Cards.* Southwest Museum Leaflets, no. 28. Los Angeles: Southwest Museum, 1961.

Wellman, Paul I. *Bronco Apache.* Garden City, N.Y.: Doubleday and Co., 1936.

Wharfield, Col. H. B. *Alchesay.* El Cajon, Cal.: Col. H. B. Wharfield, 1969.

———. *Cibicu Creek Fight in Arizona: 1881.* El Cajon, Cal.: Col. H. B. Wharfield, 1971.

———. *Cooley.* El Cajon, Cal.: Col. H. B. Wharfield, 1966.

Whitaker, Kathleen. "Na Ih Es, an Apache Puberty Ceremony." *The Masterkey,* vol. 45, no. 1 (Jan.–March, 1971). Los Angeles: Southwest Museum.

White Mountain Apache Culture Center. *White Mountain Dictionary.* Fort Apache, Ariz.: White Mountain Apache Tribe, 1972.

"White Mountain Scenic Railroad." *Arizona Highways,* July, 1970.

Whitewolf, Jim. *Jim Whitewolf: The Life of a Kiowa Apache Indian.* Edited with an introduction and epilogue by Charles S. Brant. New York: Dover Publications, 1969.

Wright, Muriel H. *A Guide to the Indian Tribes of Oklahoma.* Norman: University of Oklahoma Press, 1951.

Wyman, Leland C. *The Windways of the Navajo.* Colorado Springs: Colorado Springs Fine Arts Center, The Taylor Museum, 1962

Apache Newspapers:
The Apache Drumbeat, San Carlos, Ariz.
The Fort Apache Scout, Fort Apache, Ariz.
The Jicarilla Chieftain, Dulce, N.M.

Government Documents:
The Reports of Agents to the Commissioners and the Governors of New Mexico, 1873–1965.
The Reports of Indian Commissioners and Superintendents of Indian Schools, 1883–1938.

Notes

INTRODUCTION

1 Terrell, *Apache Chronicle,* p. 20.
2 Opler, *An Apache Life-Way,* p. 5.
3 White Mountain Apache Culture Center, *White Mountain Dictionary.*
4 Terrell, *Apache Chronicle,* pp. 18–20.
5 Watson, *Navajo History,* p. 181.
6 Swanton, *Indian Tribes of North America,* p. 327.
7 Opler, *Myths and Tales of the Chiricahua Apache Indians,* p. 112.
8 Swanton, *Indian Tribes,* p. 330.

THE WESTERN APACHE

1—HISTORY
1 Goodwin, *Social Organization of the Western Apache,* pp. 66–71.
2 Ibid., pp. 63–68.
3 Ibid., p. 69.
4 Ibid., p. 70.
5 Ibid., p. 71.
6 Opler, *An Apache Life-Way,* p. 9.
7 Goodwin, *Social Organization,* pp. 85–86.
8 Ibid., pp. 83–84.
9 Ibid., p. 92.
10 Ibid., pp. 93–94.
11 Ibid., pp. 88–92.
12 Ibid., p. 94.
13 Lockwood, *The Apache Indians,* pp. 39–40.
14 "The Apaches," p. 6.
15 Arizona Legislature, *Memorial and Affidavits,* pp. 3–4.
16 Ibid., pp. 5–6.
17 Colyer Report, 1871, p. 14.
18 Johnson, *Crook's Resume of Operations against Apache Indians,* pp. 9–12; Terrell, *Apache Chronicle,* p. 286.
19 Johnson, *Crook's Resume,* p. 8.
20 Ibid., p. 11.
21 Basso, *Western Apache Raiding and Warfare,* pp. 22–23.
22 Davis, *The Truth about Geronimo,* p. 237.
23 Johnson, *Crook's Resume,* pp. 23–25.
24 Ibid., p. 12.
25 Ibid., p. 24.
26 Photos show the different costumes worn by scouts.
27 Basso, *Western Apache Raiding,* p. 21.
28 Thrapp, *The Conquest of Apacheria,* p. 100.
29 Goodwin, *Social Organization,* p. 61.
30 Schwatka, "Among the Apaches," pp. 41–52.
31 Dorsey, *Indians of the Southwest,* pp. 177–91.

2—GOVERNMENT AND SOCIAL ORDER
1 Goodwin, *Social Organization of the Western Apache,* p. 60.
2 Ibid., p. 11.
3 Ibid., p. 7.
4 Ibid., pp. 50–58.
5 Basso, *Western Apache Raiding and Warfare,* p. 14.
6 Goodwin, *Social Organization,* p. 10.
7 Ibid., p. 110.
8 Basso, *Western Apache Raiding,* p. 14.
9 Basso, *The Cibecue Apache,* p. 5.
10 Ibid., p. 8.
11 Kaut, *Western Apache Clan System,* pp. 63–64.
12 Goodwin, *Social Organization,* p. 97.
13 Ibid., p. 9.
14 Ibid., pp. 116–19.
15 Basso, *The Cibecue Apache,* pp. 9–10.
16 Goodwin, *Social Organization,* p. 44.
17 Ibid., p. 43.
18 Ibid., pp. 43–50.
19 Ibid., pp. 35–43.
20 Ibid., pp. 17–24.
21 Ibid., pp. 12–17.
22 Ibid., pp. 12–50.
23 Ibid., pp. 58–59.

3—CHILDBIRTH
1 Reagan, *Notes on the Indians of the Fort Apache Region,* p. 307.
2 "The Apaches," *Arizona State Teachers College Bulletin,* p. 15.
3 Ibid.
4 Ibid., p. 307.
5 Ibid., p. 308.
6 Ibid.
7 Ibid.
8 Ibid., p. 309.

4—CHILDHOOD, NAMES, AND TRAINING
1 Geronimo, *His Own Story,* p. 153.
2 Ball and Kaywaykla, *In the Days of Victorio,* p. 8.
3 Opler, *An Apache Life-Way,* p. 13.
4 Bleeker, *The Apache Indians,* p. 79.
5 Goodwin, *Social Organization of the Western Apache,* p. 434.
6 Opler, *An Apache Life-Way,* pp. 10–12.
7 Ibid., p. 14.
8 Ibid., pp. 14–15.
9 Ball and Kaywaykla, *Victorio,* pp. 66–67.
10 Opler, *An Apache Life-Way,* p. 13.
11 Bleeker, *Apache Indians,* p. 80; see especially Goodwin, *Social Organization,* pp. 523–35.

12 Bleeker, *Apache Indians,* p. 81.
13 Ball and Kaywaykla, *Victorio,* pp. 28–29.
14 Bleeker, *Apache Indians,* p. 82.
15 Opler, *An Apache Life-Way,* pp. 15–16.
16 Ibid., pp. 17–18.
17 Bleeker, *Apache Indians,* p. 84.
18 Clum, *Apache Agent,* p. 145.
19 Bleeker, *Apache Indians,* p. 84.
20 Ball and Kaywaykla, *Victorio,* p. 133.
21 Bleeker, *Apache Indians,* p. 86.
22 Opler, *An Apache Life-Way,* pp. 29–30.
23 Bleeker, *Apache Indians,* pp. 86–87.
24 Geronimo, *His Own Story,* p. 71.
25 Ibid.
26 Opler, *An Apache Life-Way,* pp. 34–36.
27 Bleeker, *Apache Indians,* pp. 91–92; Goodwin, *Social Organization,* p. 475.
28 Bleeker, *Apache Indians,* pp. 92–93.
29 Ibid., pp. 94–95.
30 Ball and Kaywaykla, *Victorio,* p. 113.
31 Bleeker, *Apache Indians,* p. 96.
32 In some instances only one raid was required; Goodwin, *Social Organization,* pp. 664–65.
33 Ball and Kaywaykla, *Victorio,* p. 17.
34 Ibid., p. 158.
35 Ibid., p. 159; Goodwin, *Social Organization,* p. 567.
36 Goodwin, *Social Organization,* p. 484.
37 Ibid., p. 485.
38 Ibid.
39 Ibid., p. 476.
40 Ibid., p. 477.
41 Ibid., p. 478.
42 Ibid., pp. 478–79.

5—GIRL'S PUBERTY CEREMONY
1 Reagan, *Notes on the Indians of the Fort Apache Region,* p. 309.
2 Ibid., p. 311.
3 Ibid.
4 Goodwin, *Social Organization of the Western Apache,* p. 477.
5 Basso, *The Cibecue Apache,* p. 55.
6 Ibid., p. 58.
7 Ibid., p. 63.
8 Ibid.
9 Ibid.
10 Ibid., p. 65.
11 Ibid., p. 64.
12 Ibid., p. 65.
13 Ibid.
14 Ibid.
15 Ibid., p. 66.
16 Ibid.
17 Ibid., p. 67.

18 Ibid.
19 Ibid.
20 Ibid., p. 68.
21 Ibid.
22 Ibid., p. 71.
23 Ibid., p. 72.

6—BOY'S MATURITY RITES
1 Reagan, *Notes on the Indians of the Fort Apache Region*, p. 309.

7—COURTSHIP AND MARRIAGE
1 Reagan, *Notes on the Indians of the Fort Apache Region*, p. 313.

8—DIVISION OF LABOR
1 Reagan, *Notes on the Indians of the Fort Apache Region*, p. 291.
2 Ibid., p. 296.

9—THE WOMAN'S STATUS
1 Goodwin, *Social Organization of the Western Apache*, pp. 539, 540.
2 Cremony, *Life among the Apaches*, p. 216.
3 Ibid., p. 244.

10—MOTHER-IN-LAW AVOIDANCE
1 Reagan, *Notes on the Indians of the Fort Apache Region*, p. 301.

11—PERSONALITY CHARACTERISTICS
1 Goodwin, *Social Organization of the Western Apache*, p. 556.
2 Ibid., pp. 556–57.
3 Ibid., pp. 540–41.
4 Burlison, *Yesterday and Today in the Life of the Apaches*, pp. 49–50.
5 Goodwin, *Social Organization*, pp. 547–48.
6 Ibid., pp. 550–52; Davis, *The Truth about Geronimo*, pp. 53–54.
7 Goodwin, *Social Organization*, pp. 555–56.
8 Ibid., p. 566.
9 Ibid., p. 569.
10 Ibid., p. 513.
11 Ibid., p. 515.

12—TAG-BANDS; ENGLISH NAMES
1 Goodwin, *Social Organization of the Western Apache*, pp. 190–91.
2 Ibid., pp. 523–25.
3 Getty, *The San Carlos Indian Cattle Industry*, p. 10.
4 Burlison, *Yesterday and Today in the Life of the Apaches*, p. 70.

13—CRIME AND PUNISHMENT
1 Reagan, *Notes on the Indians of the Fort Apache Region*, p. 301.

14—SOCIAL DANCES
1 Reagan, *Notes on the Indians of the Fort Apache Region*, p. 315.

15—SIGN LANGUAGE AND SIGNALING
1 Reagan, *Notes on the Indians of the Fort Apache Region*, p. 300.
2 Ibid.

16—SCHOOLS
1 Reagan, *Notes on the Indians of the Fort Apache Region*, p. 313.
2 Ibid., p. 314.
3 Ibid.

17—DWELLINGS, FURNITURE, AND UTENSILS
1 Reagan, *Notes on the Indians of the Fort Apache Region*, p. 291.

18—FOOD AND DRINK
1 Reagan, *Notes on the Indians of the Fort Apache Region*, p. 292.
2 Ibid.; Opler, *An Apache Life-Way*, p. 371.
3 Reagan, *Notes*, p. 293.
4 Ibid., p. 294.
5 Ibid.

6 Ibid.
7 Ibid., p. 292.
8 Ibid., p. 295.
9 Ibid.
10 Ibid., p. 294.
11 Ibid., p. 298.
12 Ibid.

19—AGRICULTURE
1 Reagan, *Notes on the Indians of the Fort Apache Region*, p. 297.
2 Ibid., p. 299.
3 Ibid., p. 300.
4 Bourke, *The Medicine Men of the Apache*, p. 502.

20—TANNING
1 Reagan, *Notes on the Indians of the Fort Apache Region*, p. 296.

21—APPAREL AND JEWELRY
1 Burlison, *Yesterday and Today in the Life of the Apaches*, p. 48.
2 Reagan, *Notes on the Indians of the Fort Apache Region*, p. 289.
3 Ibid.
4 Bandelier, *The Southwestern Journals*, p. 88.
5 Reagan, *Notes*, p. 289; Ball and Kaywaykla, *In the Days of Victorio*, p. 17.

22—HAIR DRESSING AND ORNAMENTS
1 Bandelier, *The Southwestern Journals*, p. 88.
2 Ibid.

23—TATTOOING AND BODY PAINTING
1 Bandelier, *The Southwestern Journals*, p. 88.
2 Dorsey, *Indians of the Southwest*, p. 185.
3 Goodwin, *Social Organization of the Western Apache*, p. 489.
4 Ibid., p. 511.
5 Reagan, *Notes on the Indians of the Fort Apache Region*, p. 290.

24—DISEASES AND CURES
1 Reagan, *Notes on the Indians of the Fort Apache Region*, p. 314.

25—SWEAT BATHING
1 Reagan, *Notes on the Indians of the Fort Apache Region*, p. 307.
2 Clum, *Apache Agent*, p. 144.
3 Ibid.
4 Santee, *Apache Land*, p. 10.
5 Goodwin, *Social Organization of the Western Apache*, p. 685.

26—RELIGION AND CEREMONIES
1 "The Apaches," *Arizona State Teachers College Bulletin*, p. 13.
2 Basso, *The Cibecue Apache*, pp. 40–41.
3 Ibid., pp. 38–39.
4 Ibid., p. 39.
5 Ibid., p. 40.
6 Ibid., p. 73.
7 Ibid.
8 Ibid., pp. 90–91.
9 Ibid., pp. 70–71.
10 Reagan, *Notes on the Indians of the Fort Apache Region*, p. 319; Bourke, *The Medicine Men of the Apache*, p. 583.
11 Basso, *The Cibecue Apache*, pp. 36–39.
12 Ibid., p. 47.
13 Reagan, *Notes*, pp. 319–27.
14 "The Apaches," p. 13.
15 Basso, *The Cibecue Apache*, p. 49.
16 Ibid., p. 51.
17 "The Apaches," p. 14.
18 Ibid.
19 Ibid., p. 15.
20 Bandelier. *The Southwestern Journals*, p. 193.
21 Watson, *Navajo Sacred Places*.
22 Reagan, *Notes*, p. 302.
23 Basso, *The Cibecue Apache*, p. 51.
24 Ibid., p. 98.

25 Goodwin, *Social Organization of the Western Apache*, p. 267.
26 Ibid.

27—THE GANS
1 Herbert, "Land of the White Mountain Apaches."
2 Reagan, *Notes on the Indians of the Fort Apache Region*, p. 335.
3 Opler, *An Apache Life-Way*, p. 104.
4 Ibid.
5 Herbert, "Land of the White Mountain Apaches."
6 Guenther, "50 Years in Apache Land," p. 78.
7 Goodwin, *Social Organization of the Western Apache*, p. 491.

28—MEDICINE MEN
1 Bourke, *The Medicine Men of the Apache*, p. 500.
2 Ibid., p. 452.
3 Basso, *The Cibecue Apache*, pp. 40–44.
4 Bourke, *Medicine Men*, p. 456.
5 Ibid., p. 458.
6 Ibid., p. 461.
7 Ibid., p. 474.
8 Ibid., pp. 452–63.
9 Ibid., pp. 594–95.
10 Ibid., p. 466.
11 Ibid.
12 Ibid., p. 467.
13 Ibid., p. 469.
14 Ibid., p. 470.
15 Ibid.
16 Reagan, *Notes on the Indians of the Fort Apache Region*, p. 306.
17 Ibid.
18 Bourke, *Medicine Men*, p. 473.
19 Ibid., p. 594.
20 Ibid., pp. 594–95.

29—SPECIFIC MEDICINE ITEMS
1 Bourke, *The Medicine Men of the Apache*, pp. 477–78.
2 Reagan, *Notes on the Indians of the Fort Apache Region*, p. 326; Bourke, *Medicine Men*, pp. 590–93.
3 Bourke, *Medicine Men*, pp. 580–81.
4 Reagan, *Notes*, pp. 326–27.
5 Ibid., p. 327.
6 Bourke, *Medicine Men*, pp. 479–80.
7 Ibid., pp. 588–89.
8 Ibid., pp. 550–56.
9 Goodwin, *Social Organization of the Western Apache*, p. 667.
10 Reagan, *Notes*, pp. 322–23.
11 Ibid., p. 340.
12 Ibid., p. 320.
13 Ibid., pp. 323–24.
14 Ibid., pp. 320–21.
15 Ibid., p. 327.

30—MEDICINE CEREMONIES, A GENERAL VIEW
1 Reagan, *Notes on the Indians of the Fort Apache Region*, p. 319.
2 Bourke, *The Medicine Men of the Apache*, p. 452.
3 Opler, *Grenville Goodwin among the Western Apache*, p. 30.

31—MEDICINE ITEMS AS LIVE OBJECTS
1 Reagan, *Notes on the Indians of the Fort Apache Region*, p. 303.
2 Ibid.
3 Ibid.
4 Ibid.
5 Ibid.
6 Ibid., p. 305.
7 Ibid., p. 304.
8 Ibid.
9 Ibid., pp. 305–6.

32—CEREMONIAL DANCES
1 Reagan, *Notes on the Indians of the Fort Apache Region*, p. 285.
2 Ibid., p. 328.
3 Ibid., pp. 340–41.
4 Ibid., pp. 337–38.
5 Ibid., p. 330.
6 Ibid.
7 Ibid., p. 336.

8 Ibid., p. 334.
9 Ibid., p. 333.
10 Ibid., p. 332.
11 Ibid., p. 338.
12 Ibid.
13 Ibid., p. 340.
14 Ibid., p. 341.
15 Ibid., p. 342.
16 Ibid., p. 344.
17 Ibid.,

33—DEATH AND BURIAL
1 Reagan, *Notes on the Indians of the Fort Apache Region,* p. 318.
2 Ibid.
3 Ibid., pp. 318–19.
4 Ibid., p. 321.
5 Goodwin, *Social Organization of the Western Apache,* p. 515.

34—CHRISTIAN MISSIONS
1 Herbert, "The Old Gentleman Missionary," p. 2.
2 Ibid., p. 3.
3 Herbert, "Land of the White Mountain Apaches," p. 41.
4 Ibid., p. 43.
5 Ibid.
6 Basso, *The Cibecue Apache,* p. 98.
7 Ibid.
8 Opler, *An Apache Life-Way,* pp. 194–95.

35—WESTERN APACHE LIFE, 1940
1 "The Apaches," *Arizona State Teachers College Bulletin,* p. 7. For detailed information regarding life in the 1930s, see Goodwin, *Social Organization of the Western Apache,* pp. 285–569.
2 "The Apaches," p. 7.
3 Ibid.
4 Ibid., p. 8.
5 Ibid., p. 10.
6 Ibid., pp. 10–11.
7 Ibid., p. 11.
8 Ibid.
9 Ibid., p. 12.
10 Ibid., p. 13.
11 Ibid., pp. 13–16.

36—WESTERN APACHE LIFE, 1973
1 Parmee, *Formal Education and Culture Change,* p. 4.
2 Ibid., p. 88.
3 Ibid., pp. 23–24, 28.
4 Ibid., pp. 27–28.
5 Ibid., p. 14.
6 Ibid., pp. 115–18.
7 Ibid., p. 31.
8 Ibid., p. 108.
9 Basso, *The Cibecue Apache,* p. 93.
10 Parmee, *Formal Education and Culture Change,* p. 25.
11 Ibid., p. 26.
12 Herbert, "The Old Gentleman Missionary," p. 15.

THE CHIRICAHUA APACHE

1—HISTORY
1 Opler, *Myths and Tales of the Chiricahua Apache Indians,* p. 15.
2 Opler, *An Apache Life-Way,* p. 1.
3 Ibid., p. 2.
4 Ball and Kaywaykla, *In the Days of Victorio,* p. xiv.
5 Thrapp, *The Conquest of Apacheria; Al Seiber, Chief of Scouts; General Crook and the Sierra Madre Adventure.*
6 Terrell, *Apache Chronicle,* pp. 198–99.
7 Ibid., p. 181.
8 Cochise and Griffith, *The First Hundred Years of Niño Cochise,* pp. 42, 100–101.
9 Ibid., pp. 100–101.
10 Opler, *An Apache Life-Way,* p. 4.
11 Terrell, *Apache Chronicle,* pp. 293–336.
12 Johnson, *Crook's Resume of Operations against Apache Indians,* p. 21.
13 Dedera, "Is Geronimo Alive and Well?" p. 29.
14 Ibid., p. 30.
15 Ibid.
16 Ibid., p. 31.

17 Ibid., p. 30.
18 Ibid., p. 32.
19 Ibid.
20 Wright, *A Guide to the Indian Tribes of Oklahoma,* p. 40.
21 Davis, *The Truth about Geronimo;* and others cite 187 as the number moved to Mescalero.
22 Wright, *Guide,* p. 41.

2—FOOD HARVESTS AND AGRICULTURE
1 Opler, *An Apache Life-Way,* p. 355.
2 Geronimo, *His Own Story,* p. 73.
3 Bourke, *The Medicine Men of the Apache,* p. 471.
4 Cochise and Griffith, *The First Hundred Years of Niño Cochise,* p. 32.
5 Betzinez and Nye, *I Fought with Geronimo,* p. 35.
6 Geronimo, *His Own Story,* p. 73.
7 Cochise and Griffith, *First Hundred Years,* p. 230.
8 Opler, *An Apache Life-Way,* p. 363.
9 Ball and Kaywaykla, *In the Days of Victorio,* p. 19.
10 Geronimo, *His Own Story,* p. 153.
11 Cochise and Griffith, *First Hundred Years,* p. 91.
12 Ball and Kaywaykla, *Victorio,* pp. 19–20.
13 Opler, *An Apache Life-Way,* pp. 364–65.
14 Ball and Kaywaykla, *Victorio,* p. 121.
15 Geronimo, *His Own Story,* p. 72.
16 Cochise and Griffith, *First Hundred Years,* p. 41.

3—HUNTING
1 Ball and Kaywaykla, *In the Days of Victorio,* p. 66.
2 Geronimo, *His Own Story,* p. 78.
3 Opler, *An Apache Life-Way,* pp. 316–17.
4 Ibid., p. 319.
5 Betzinez and Nye, *I Fought with Geronimo,* p. 31.
6 Geronimo, *His Own Story,* p. 78.
7 Opler, *An Apache Life-Way,* p. 319.
8 Ibid., pp. 320–21.
9 Cochise and Griffith, *The First Hundred Years of Niño Cochise,* p. 32.
10 Ibid., p. 41.
11 Ibid., p. 7.
12 Opler, *An Apache Life-Way,* pp. 325–26.
13 Geronimo, *His Own Story,* p. 78.
14 Ball and Kaywaykla, *Victorio,* p. 121.
15 Opler, *An Apache Life-Way,* p. 327.
16 Geronimo, *His Own Story,* p. 79.
17 Ibid., pp. 77–78.
18 Betzinez and Nye, *I Fought with Geronimo,* pp. 33–34.
19 Geronimo, *His Own Story,* p. 78.
20 Betzinez and Nye, *I Fought with Geronimo,* p. 30.
21 Cochise and Griffith, *First Hundred Years,* p. 99.
22 Opler, *An Apache Life-Way,* pp. 328–29.
23 Geronimo, *His Own Story,* p. 79.
24 Opler, *An Apache Life-Way,* p. 329.
25 Geronimo, *His Own Story,* p. 79.
26 Ball and Kaywaykla, *Victorio,* p. 121.
27 Geronimo, *His Own Story,* p. 79; Ball and Kaywaykla, *Victorio,* p. 55.
28 Cochise and Griffith, *First Hundred Years,* p. 126.
29 Ibid., p. 18.
30 Betzinez and Nye, *I Fought with Geronimo,* pp. 32–33.
31 Ibid., p. 33.
32 Cochise and Griffith, *First Hundred Years,* p. 230.

4—TANNING
1 Geronimo, *His Own Story,* p. 78.
2 Opler, *An Apache Life-Way,* p. 376.
3 Ibid., p. 377.
4 Ibid.
5 Ibid., pp. 378–79.
6 Ibid.
7 Ibid., p. 379.
8 Ibid., p. 380.

5—GIRL'S PUBERTY CEREMONY
1 Opler, *An Apache Life-Way,* p. 91.
2 Ibid., p. 89.

3 Ibid., p. 90.
4 Ibid., p. 83.
5 Ibid.
6 Ibid., p. 84.
7 Ibid., pp. 96–97.

6—RELIGION, COSMOLOGY, AND THE SUPERNATURAL POWERS
1 Opler, *An Apache Life-Way,* p. 195.
2 Ibid., p. 196.
3 Ibid.
4 Ibid., p. 197.
5 Ibid., p. 198.
6 Ibid., p. 199.
7 Ibid.
8 Ibid., p. 200.
9 Ibid., p. 268.
10 Ibid., p. 269.
11 Ibid., p. 276.
12 Ibid., p. 277.
13 Ibid., p. 279.
14 Ibid., p. 281.
15 Ibid.
16 Bourke, *The Medicine Men of the Apache,* p. 587.
17 Ibid., pp. 591–93.
18 Ibid., p. 593.

7—THE GANS
1 Bourke, *The Medicine Men of the Apache,* pp. 583–85.
2 Opler, *An Apache Life-Way,* p. 100.
3 Ibid., pp. 102–4.
4 Ibid., p. 104.
5 Ibid., p. 105.
6 Ibid., p. 106.
7 Ibid., pp. 105–6.
8 Ibid., p. 109.
9 Ibid.
10 Ibid., p. 110.
11 Ibid.

8—RAIDING AND WARFARE
1 Opler, *An Apache Life-Way,* p. 334.
2 Ibid., p. 337.
3 Ibid.
4 Ibid., p. 339.
5 Ibid., p. 342.
6 Ibid.
7 Betzinez and Nye, *I Fought with Geronimo,* pp. 113, 115.
8 Ibid.
9 Dedera, "Is Geronimo Alive and Well?" p. 30.
10 Betzinez and Nye, *I Fought with Geronimo,* p. 114.
11 Ibid., p. 131.
12 Ibid., p. 84.
13 Geronimo, *His Own Story,* p. 116.
14 Betzinez and Nye, *I Fought with Geronimo,* p. 55.
15 Ibid., p. 113.
16 Geronimo, *His Own Story,* pp. 89–90, 344.
17 Ibid., p. 90.
18 Betzinez and Nye, *I Fought with Geronimo,* p. 7.
19 Geronimo, *His Own Story,* p. 98.
20 Ibid., p. 90.
21 Davis, *The Truth about Geronimo,* pp. 188–89.
22 Betzinez and Nye, *I Fought with Geronimo,* p. 63.
23 Geronimo, *His Own Story,* p. 136.
24 Betzinez and Nye, *I Fought with Geronimo,* p. 95.
25 Ball and Kaywaykla, *In the Days of Victorio,* p. 102.
26 Cochise and Griffith, *The First Hundred Years of Niño Cochise,* p. 198.
27 Ball and Kaywaykla, *Victorio,* p. 13.
28 Betzinez and Nye, *I Fought with Geronimo,* p. 91.
29 Ibid., p. 13.
30 Opler, *An Apache Life-Way,* pp. 347–48.
31 Mails, *Mystic Warriors of the Plains,* p. 531.
32 Betzinez and Nye, *I Fought with Geronimo,* p. 137.
33 Ibid., p. 86.
34 Geronimo, *His Own Story,* p. 92.
35 Opler, *Apache Life-Way,* p. 349.
36 Ball and Kaywaykla, *Victorio,* p. 133.
37 Ibid., p. 13, 119.
38 Geronimo, *His Own Story,* p. 110.
39 Ibid., p. 12.
40 Betzinez and Nye, *I Fought with Geronimo,* p. 67.

41 Ball and Kaywaykla, *Victorio*, p. 12.
42 Ibid., p. 108.
43 Ibid., p. 43.
44 Geronimo, *His Own Story*, pp. 102–3.
45 Opler, *An Apache Life-Way*, p. 352.
46 Ibid., pp. 352–53.
47 Ibid., p. 354.
48 Geronimo, *His Own Story*, p. 108.
49 Betzinez and Nye, *I Fought with Geronimo*, p. 67.
50 Geronimo, *His Own Story*, pp. 89–92.
51 Ball and Kaywaykla, *Victorio*, pp. 73–76.
52 Ibid., p. 152.
53 Ibid., p. 4.
54 Ibid., p. 152.
55 Opler, *An Apache Life-Way*, pp. 215–16.
56 Basso, *Western Apache Raiding and Warfare*, pp. 270–75.
57 Goodwin, *Social Organization of the Western Apache*, p. 667.
58 Opler, *An Apache Life-Way*, pp. 215, 216.
59 Opler, *An Apache Life-Way*, p. 134.
60 Ibid., p. 136.
61 Ibid.
62 Ibid.
63 Basso, *Western Apache Raiding*, pp. 290–91.
64 Ibid., p. 289.
65 Opler, *An Apache Life-Way*, p. 137.
66 Basso, *Western Apache Raiding*, pp. 291–92.
67 Ibid., p. 292.
68 Opler, *An Apache Life-Way*, p. 138.
69 Geronimo, *His Own Story*, p. 155.
70 Opler, *An Apache Life-Way*, p. 139.
71 Ibid.
72 Geronimo, *His Own Story*, p. 155.
73 Opler, *Apache Life-Way*, pp. 134–39.
74 Bourke, *The Medicine Men of the Apache*, pp. 493–98.
75 Ibid., p. 493.

9–WEAPONS
1 Basso, *Western Apache Raiding and Warfare*, pp. 223–26; Betzinez and Nye, *I Fought with Geronimo*, p. 5.
2 Basso, *Western Apache Raiding*, p. 230.
3 Ibid.
4 Ibid., p. 231.
5 Opler, *An Apache Life-Way*, pp. 340–41.
6 Basso, *Western Apache Raiding*, p. 231.
7 Ibid., 224.
8 Ibid., p. 225.
9 Opler, *An Apache Life-Way*, p. 341.
10 Ibid.
11 Basso, *Western Apache Raiding*, p. 234.
12 Ibid.
13 Goodwin, *Social Organization of the Western Apache*, p. 93; Ewers, *The Horse In Blackfoot Indian Culture*, p. 201.
14 Basso, *Western Apache Raiding*, pp. 234–37.
15 Opler, *An Apache Life-Way*, p. 341.
16 Ball and Kaywaykla, *In the Days of Victorio*, pp. 13, 18.
17 Ibid., p. 153.
18 Basso, *Western Apache Raiding*, p. 236.
19 Ibid.
20 Sonnichsen, *The Mescalero Apaches*, p. 78.
21 Ibid., p. 57.
22 Basso, *Western Apache Raiding*, pp. 237–39.
23 Opler, *An Apache Life-Way*, p. 341.
24 Basso, *Western Apache Raiding*, p. 227.
25 Cochise and Griffith, *The First Hundred Years of Niño Cochise*, p. 7.
26 Ball and Kaywaykla, *Victorio*, p. 18.
27 Ibid.
28 Basso, *Western Apache Raiding*, p. 245.
29 Betzinez and Nye, *I Fought with Geronimo*, p. 84.
30 Ball and Kaywaykla, *Victorio*, pp. 13, 18.

10–HORSES, GUNS, AND HORSEMANSHIP
1 Ewers, *The Horse in Blackfoot Indian Culture*, pp. 331–35.
2 Ibid., p. 397.
3 Terrell, *Apache Chronicle*, p. 81.
4 Ibid., p. 82.
5 Ibid., pp. 27–29.
6 Betzinez and Nye, *I Fought with Geronimo*, p. 84.
7 Geronimo, *His Own Story*, p. 78.
8 Cremony, *Life among the Apaches*, pp. 203–5.

9 Cochise and Griffith, *The First Hundred Years of Niño Cochise*, p. 7.
10 Geronimo, *His Own Story*, p. 72.
11 Santee, *Apache Land*, p. 6.
12 Ewers, *The Horse in Blackfoot Indian Culture*, p. 84.
13 Thrapp, *The Conquest of Apacheria*, p. 352.
14 Opler, *An Apache Life-Way*, p. 396.
15 Ibid., p. 293.

11–TIME KEEPING, 1880s
1 Bourke, *The Medicine Men of the Apache*, p. 562.

THE MESCALERO APACHE

1–HISTORY
1 Emerson, *Among the Mescalero Apaches*, pp. x, 38.
2 Dedera, "Fire in the Tonto," p. 34; Wilma Van Doren, "Forest Firemen," *Indian Life*, Aug., 1961, pp. 10–15.
3 Smith, *New Mexico Indians*, pp. 74–75.
4 Ibid., p. 72.
5 Ibid., p. 76.
6 Ibid., p. 80.
7 Opler, *Apache Odyssey*, p. 26.
8 Ibid., p. 27.
9 Terrell, *Apache Chronicle*, p. 160.
10 Opler, *Apache Odyssey*, p. 27.
11 Ibid.
12 Ewers, *The Horse in Blackfoot Indian Culture*, pp. 229–322.
13 Opler, *Apache Odyssey*, p. 31.
14 Ibid., pp. 31–32.
15 Sonnichsen, *The Mescalero Apaches*, p. 134.
16 Ibid., pp. 151–52.
17 Carter, "Adventure among the Apaches," p. 32.
18 Sonnichsen, *Mescalero Apaches*, pp. 181, 184.
19 Ibid., p. 172.
20 Carter, "Adventure among the Apaches," p. 32.
21 Ibid.
22 Opler, *Apache Odyssey*, p. 33.
23 Sonnichsen, *Mescalero Apaches*, p. 208; Report of the Secretary of War for 1881, report of Gen. John Roper, p. 118, in ibid., p. 208.
24 Opler, *Apache Odyssey*, p. 33.
25 Sonnichsen, *Mescalero Apaches*, p. 237.
26 Opler, *Apache Odyssey*, p. 34.
27 Ibid., p. 36.
28 Stanley, *The Apaches of New Mexico*, p. 329; Sonnichsen, *Mescalero Apaches*, pp. 217, 267; Emerson, *Among the Mescalero Apaches*, pp. 46–47.
29 Sonnichsen, *Mescalero Apaches*, pp. 221–30; Opler, *Apache Odyssey*, pp. 34–35.
30 Opler, *Apache Odyssey*, p. 35.
31 Ibid.; Sonnichsen, *Mescalero Apaches*, p. 235.
32 Opler, *Apache Odyssey*, p. 36.
33 Ibid., pp. 36, 96.
34 Sonnichsen, *Mescalero Apaches*, p. 231.
35 Lindquist, *The Red Man in the United States*, pp. 255–60.
36 Wright, *A Guide to the Indian Tribes of Oklahoma*, p. 40; Sonnichsen, *Mescalero Apaches*, p. 206, gives 187 as the number moved to Mescalero.
37 Sonnichsen, *Mescalero Apaches*, p. 206.
38 Emerson, *Among the Mescalero Apaches*, p. 47.
39 Sonnichsen, *Mescalero Apaches*, p. 237.
40 Ibid., p. 244.
41 Ibid., pp. 241–44.
42 Ibid., pp. 233–43.
43 Smith, *New Mexico Indians*, p. 72.

2–GOVERNMENT AND SOCIAL ORDER
1 Opler, *Apache Odyssey*, p. 13.
2 Harry W. Basehart, "Mescalero Apache Band Organization and Leadership," in Basso and Opler, *Apachean Culture, History and Ethnology*, pp. 35–49.
3 Opler, *Apache Odyssey*, p. 12.
4 Ibid.
5 Ibid.
6 Ibid., p. 11.
7 Basehart, "Mescalero Apache Band Organization," pp. 43–46.

8 Opler, *Apache Odyssey*, p. 13.
9 Ibid., p. 14.
10 Ibid., pp. 15–16.
11 Ibid., p. 16.
12 Ibid., pp. 14–15.
13 Sonnichsen, *The Mescalero Apaches*, p. 24.
14 Emerson, *Among the Mescalero Apaches*, p. 17–18.
15 Opler, *Apache Odyssey*, p. 15.
16 Ibid., p. 16.
17 Ibid., p. 17.
18 Ibid.
19 Ibid.
20 Sonnichsen, *Mescalero Apaches*, pp. 218–21.
21 Opler, *Apache Odyssey*, pp. 18–19.

3–GIRL'S PUBERTY RITE
1 Opler, *Apache Odyssey*, p. 156.
2 Ibid.
3 Emerson, *Among the Mescalero Apaches*, p. 51.
4 Opler, *An Apache Life-Way*, p. 133.
5 Ibid.
6 Fergusson, *Dancing Gods*, p. 263.
7 Emerson, *Among the Mescalero Apaches*, pp. 49–51.
8 Opler, *Apache Odyssey*, p. 157.
9 Fergusson, *Dancing Gods*, p. 259.
10 Opler, *An Apache Life-Way*, p. 127.
11 Fergusson, *Dancing Gods*, p. 259.
12 Opler, *An Apache Life-Way*, p. 127.
13 Ibid.
14 Emerson, *Among the Mescalero Apaches*, p. 52.

4–THE INDIVIDUAL POWER QUEST
1 Opler, *Apache Odyssey*, p. 24.
2 Ibid.
3 Ibid., p. 26.
4 Ibid., pp. 24, 72, 109.
5 Ibid., pp. 25–26, 263–65.
6 Ibid., p. 103.
7 Ibid., p. 109.
8 Ibid., p. 251.
9 Ibid., p. 25.
10 Ibid., p. 117.

5–DEATH AND BURIAL
1 Opler, *Apache Odyssey*, p. 25.
2 Ibid., p. 253.
3 Carter, "Adventure among the Apaches," p. 32.
4 Opler, *Apache Odyssey*, p. 106.
5 Cochise and Griffith, *The First Hundred Years of Niño Cochise*, p. 14.

6–DIVISION OF LABOR
1 Opler, *Apache Odyssey*, p. 19.
2 Ibid., pp. 19–20.

7–DWELLINGS AND SANITATION
1 Gwyther, "An Indian Reservation," *The Overland Monthly*, vol. X (Feb., 1873), p. 129; Sonnichsen, *The Mescalero Apaches*, p. 117.

8–FOOD AND DRINK
1 Opler, *Apache Odyssey*, pp. 10, 19.
2 Ibid., p. 20.
3 Ibid., p. 11.

9–HUNTING
1 Goddard, *Indians of the Southwest*, p. 155.
2 Ibid.
3 Sonnichsen, *The Mescalero Apaches*, p. 165.
4 Opler, *Apache Odyssey*, p. 79, and *An Apache Life-Way*, p. 363.

10–CLOTHING
1 Sonnichsen, *The Mescalero Apaches*, p. 223.
2 Carter, "Adventure among the Apaches," p. 31.
3 *Material Culture Notes*, p. 128.
4 Sonnichsen, *Mescalero Apaches*, p. 20.

11–RELIGION
1 Emerson, *Among the Mescalero Apaches*, pp. 74–75.

2 Opler, *Apache Odyssey*, p. 21.
3 Ibid., p. 142.
4 Ibid., p. 23.
5 Ibid., pp. 221–23.
6 Ibid., p. 23.
7 Ibid., pp. 277, 60.

THE JICARILLA APACHE

1—HISTORY
1 Opler, *Childhood and Youth in Jicarilla Apache Society*, p. 3.
2 Ibid.
3 Ibid.
4 Ibid.
5 Ibid., p. 4.
6 The Jicarilla history section includes material drawn principally from: the Reports of Agents to Governors of New Mexico; the Reports of Indian Commissioners and Superintendents of Indian Schools; Stanley, *The Jicarilla Apaches of New Mexico* and *The Apaches of New Mexico;* VanRoekel, *Jicarilla Apaches;* and New Mexico newspapers.
7 Terrell, *Apache Chronicle*, p. 128.
8 Collier, *Patterns and Ceremonials of the Indians of the Southwest*, p. 85.

2—APPAREL AND JEWELRY
1 *Material Culture Notes*, p. 130.
2 Ibid., p. 133.
3 Ibid., pp. 49–52.
4 Ibid., p. 49.
5 Opler, *Childhood and Youth in Jicarilla Apache Society*, p. 111.
6 *Material Culture Notes*, pp. 121–22.

3—RELIGION
1 Opler, *Myths and Tales of the Jicarilla Apache Indians*, p. xvi.
2 Ibid., p. vii.
3 Ibid., pp. viii-ix.
4 Ibid., p. xviii.
5 Ibid., p. 1.
6 Ibid., p. xi.
7 Ibid., p. 160.
8 Ibid., pp. 162–63.
9 Ibid., p. 182.
10 Ibid., p. 183.

4—CEREMONIALISM
1 Opler, *Myths and Tales of the Jicarilla Apache Indians*, p. 14.
2 Ibid., pp. 17–18.
3 Ibid., p. 18.
4 Ibid.

5—HOLINESS RITE
1 Opler, *Myths and Tales of the Jicarilla Apache Indians*, p. 31.
2 Stanley, *The Jicarilla Apaches of New Mexico*, p. 200.
3 Ibid.
4 Opler, *Myths and Tales of the Jicarilla*, p. 36.
5 Ibid., p. 42.
6 Ibid., pp. 42–43.
7 Ibid., p. 27.
8 Ibid.

6—PUBERTY OR ADOLESCENCE RITE
1 The principal corroborative source for the details of the Adolescence Rite is Opler, *Childhood and Youth in Jicarilla Apache Society*, pp. 103–15.

7—CEREMONIAL RELAY RACE
1 The principal corroborative source for the details of the Ceremonial Relay Race is Opler, *Childhood and Youth in Jicarilla Apache Society*, pp. 116–34.

APACHE ARTS, CRAFTS, AND GAMES

1—PAINTING
1 Opler, *An Apache Life-Way*, p. 110.
2 Kluckhohn, et al., *Navaho Material Culture*, pp. 216–26.

2—BASKETRY
1 Tanner, *Southwest Indian Craft Arts*, p. 15.
2 Ibid.
3 Reagan, *Notes on the Indians of the Fort Apache Region*, p. 297.
4 Tanner, *Southwest Indian Craft Arts*, p. 18.
5 Ibid., p. 25.
6 Ibid.
7 Reagan, *Notes*, p. 297.
8 "The Apaches," *Arizona State Teachers College Bulletin*, p. 8.
9 Ibid.
10 Ibid., p. 9.
11 Tanner, *Southwest Indian Craft Arts*, p. 29.
12 Ibid., p. 57.
13 Ibid., p. 27.
14 Ibid., p. 26.

3—BEADWORK
1 Feder, *American Indian Art*, p. 68.
2 Tanner, *Southwest Indian Craft Arts*, p. 182.

4—TEXTILES
1 Tanner, *Southwest Indian Craft Arts*, p. 58.

5—POTTERY
1 Tanner, *Southwest Indian Craft Arts*, p. 175.

6—TOOLS
1 Cochise and Griffith, *The First Hundred Years of Niño Cochise*, p. 7.
2 Tanner, *Southwest Indian Craft Arts*, p. 182.
3 Ball and Kaywaykla, *In the Days of Victorio*, pp. 17, 86.
4 Betzinez and Nye, *I Fought with Geronimo*, p. 13.

7—MUSICAL INSTRUMENTS
1 Opler, *An Apache Life-Way*, p. 336.
2 Ibid., p. 262.
3 Kluckhohn, et al., *Navaho Material Culture*, pp. 354–56.
4 Goodwin, *Social Organization of the Western Apache*, p. 477.
5 Kluckhohn, et al., *Navaho Material Culture*, p. 231.
6 Opler, *An Apache Life-Way*, p. 262.
7 Ibid., p. 263.
8 Ibid., p. 451.
9 Tanner, *Southwest Indian Craft Arts*, p. 177.
10 Opler, *An Apache Life-Way*, p. 450.
11 Opler, *Childhood and Youth in Jicarilla Apache Society*, pp. 160–61.
12 Stanley, *The Jicarilla Apaches of New Mexico*, pp. 199–200.
13 Mails, *Dog Soldiers, Bear Men and Buffalo Women*, p. 361.

8—GAMES
1 Culin, *Games of the North American Indians*, pp. 453–54.
2 Ibid., pp. 454–56.
3 Ibid.
4 Ibid., pp. 450–53.
5 Ibid., p. 450.
6 Ibid., p. 449.
7 Opler, *An Apache Life-Way*, pp. 448–50.
8 Culin, *Games*, p. 450.
9 Ibid., p. 449.
10 Ibid., p. 345.
11 Ibid., pp. 803–4.
12 Opler, *An Apache Life-Way*, p. 444.
13 Ibid., pp. 445–46.
14 Culin, *Games*, pp. 86–88.
15 Ibid., pp. 88–89.
16 Ibid., p. 91.
17 Ibid., p. 86.
18 Ibid., pp. 762–63.
19 Ibid., p. 385.
20 Ibid., p. 750.
21 Opler, *An Apache Life-Way*, p. 443.
22 Ibid.
23 Wayland, *Apache Playing Cards*.
24 Ibid.

25 Opler, *Myths and Tales of the Chiricahua Apache Indians*, p. 26; Geronimo, *His Own Story*, p. 76.
26 Kluckhohn, et al., *Navaho Material Culture*, pp. 393–94.

Index

Figures in italics refer to illustrations. The page number given is the page on which the caption appears.

Adolescence Rite, 367, 382, 387–393, 428
  clothing, 389–390
  food, 390–391
  origin myth, 388
  ritual songs, 391–392
Adult education, absence of, 196–197
Adult Vocational Training Plan, 359
Aged person, treatment of, 90
Agriculture, *37,* 101, 188–189, 193, 291
  death custom and, 181–182
  food harvests, *98,* 225–227
Albiquiu Agency, 352
Albuquerque Indian School, 300
Albuquerque National Bank, 359
Alchesay, Chief, *47,* 183
Alchesay High School, 203
Alcoholism, 206, 351, 355, 359, 428
Alcoholism Program, 360
Allotment Act, repeal of (1934), 356
Altars and sacred places, 126–127
Amended Family Plan, 359
American Indian Exposition, 216
Amulets, *57, 84,* 123, 147, *243,* 335, *335, 410, 412*
  cradleboard, 59
  hunting, *148, 150*
  tzi-daltai, 241–243
  for warfare, *38, 169,* 253, *339*
Ancestral Man, 381, 395
Ancestral Woman, 381, 395
Animal homes, belief in, 240
Apache, meaning of, 13, 431
Apache Arts and Crafts Association, 197
Apache Culture Center, 35, 201, 206
Apache Drumbeat, 195–196
Apache Indian Mission, 183
Apache Life-Way, An (Opler), 236
  See also Opler, Morris E.
Apache scalps, Mexican bounty for, 293, 295
Apache scouts, *48,* 214, *293*
  clothing and equipment, 34–35
  enlistment of, 34
Apache-English dictionary, 35
Apparel, *see* Clothing
Appropriation Act of 1856, 298
Appropriation Act of 1857, 298
Arapaho Indians, 332, 352
Archery, 425
Arivaipa Apache, 37
Arizona:
  Chiricahua Apache, 207–283
  Peace Policy, 30
  Western Apache, 23–206
Arizona Citizen, The, 210
Arizona Highways, 133
Arizona State Museum, 7, 9, 365
Arm bands, *377*
Arrow points, kinds of, 264
Arrow poison, 264
Arrows, types of, 264
  See also Bows and arrows
Arts and crafts, 7, 35, 197, 360, 361, 405–414
  beadwork, *410–413,* 411–412
  basketry, *12,* 205, *406–409,* 406–411
  musical instruments, 413–414, *414, 415*
  painting, 405–406
  pottery, 412
  textiles, 412
  tools, 412–413
Arts, Crafts, and Bead Association, 35

Assembly of God, 290
Atchison, Topeka and Santa Fe Railway System, 40
Athapaskan-speaking peoples, 13, 23–24, 55, 287
  original range of, *14–17*
Augustine, Chief, *373*
Awl cases, *40, 224,* 233

Bald Mountain band, 55
Baldwin, Gordon C., 7, 8
Ball, Eve, 226
Bandelier, Adolph F., 103, 117, 119, 126–127
Bands, organization of, 53
Basehart, Harry W., 310
Basketry, *12,* 288, 406–411, *406–409*
  general types of, 406–408
  Jicarilla coiled, 410–411
  Mescalero, 410
  Western Apache, 408–410
Basso, Keith H., 8, 10, 76–82, 128, 184, 260
Bathing, 65
  shampoo for, 117
  sweat bathing, *120,* 120–122, 142, 144
Beaded capes, *384, 385*
Beadwork, 35, *410–413,* 411–412
Bear claws, 163
  necklace of, *228,* 229
Bear Dance, *see* Holiness Rite
Bear meat, religious objection to, 99
Bears, hunting, 228–229
Bedonkohe Apache, 210, 259
Benito, 214
Bent, Charles, 352
Bering Strait, 13
Betzinez, Jason, 228–229, 259, 281
Black Bear (Holiness Rite), 386
Black Hactcin, 381
Black One, 240
Blackfoot Indians, 365
Blanket trade, 255
Blasphemy and profanity, 89
Body and face painting, 119, *161, 366,* 384
  Adolescence Rite, 390
  Gan dancers, 133, 250–251
  puberty ceremony, 317
  war party, 255, *257*
Bonito, *45*
Born of Water, *see* Child of the Water
Bosque Redondo (Fort Sumner), 299
Bourke, Capt. John G., 8, 101, 125, 126, 142, 144, 145, 147, 148–149, 151, 155, 158, 160–162, 164, 241, 243, 244, 253, 255, 262–263, 283
Bow case, *301, 366*
Bows and arrows, 263–269, *264, 265, 267, 268,* 293, *339*
  construction of, 63–64
  quivers, 269, *269, 272*
  shapes of, 263–264
  strings, 264–269
  wristguards, 269
Brannan, S. S., 126, 127
Braun, Father Albert, 290, 307–308, 324, 341
Buffalo, 24, 227–228, 281, 291, 330, 352
  headdresses, 293
  hunts, 331–332, 348

Bull-roarer, *see* Rhombus, or bull-roarer
Burden baskets, *39, 40,* 406–408
Burial and death, 68, 179–182, 190, 326–327
Burlison, Irene, 88, 189
Burnette, Ryan, 428
Business Committee (Mescalero Tribe), 309
Bylas, 197, *205*

Cactus, as source of moisture and food,
    257, 330
Calhoun, James S., 352
Camp Apache, 35
Camp Goodwin, 29
Camp Grant, 30–31, 212
Camp Grant Massacre of 1871, 30
Camp McDowell, 35
Camp Verde, 30, 212
Canes, puberty, *70, 72,* 72–74
Captain Jack (medicine woman), 147
Cards, *417, 420, 422, 423,* 425–426
Carleton, Gen. James H., 298, 299, 353
Carlisle Indian School, 91
Carson, Kit, 352, 353
Carter, Deborah, 300, 326–327, 332
Cassadore, Philip, 428
Cat's Cradle, 425
Census of 1910, 13
Census of 1930, 13
Central Chiricahua band, 207
Century Magazine, 37–40, *169*
Ceremonial dances, 170–182
    See also Curing ceremonies; Dances
Ceremonial Relay Race, 343, 382, 393–403,
    395, 396, 398, 428
    origin myth, 393–394
Ceremonies for the Sick, 170
Chacon, 351
Cha-ja-la (Mountain Spirit Dance), 244
    See also Gans, dancers; Mountain Spirits
Changing Woman, 74, 76
Charms, 126
Chato, 214, *216*
Cha-ut-lip-un, 144
Cheyenne Indians, 332, 411
Chihinne Apache band, 210
Chihuahua, Chief, 210
Childbirth, Western Apache, 55–58
Child of the Water (Born of Water), 61,
    63, 76, 233, *237,* 237, 238, 239, 240–241,
    255, 341, 381, 388, 389
Children, 58–68, 190, 313
    boy's maturity rites, 85
    cradle ceremony, 59, 341
    first moccasins, 61, 341
    first steps ceremony, 61
    games and sports, 63–66
    misbehavior of, 62
    names, 60–61
    novice complex for raid and war, 255,
        260–262
    orphaned, 58
    parental care of, 58–60
    participation in ceremonies, 66, 68
    spacing births of, 58–59
    toys and play, 61–62, *66, 68, 222, 367*
    training of, 61–68
    twins, 59
    See also Adolescence Rite; Puberty cere-
        mony
Chilecon Apache, 37
Chino, Wendell, 289
Chiricahua Apache, 7, 11, 12, 24–25, 29,
    29, 30, 31, 34, 37, 59, 63, 64, *109,* 133,
    145, 207–283, *211,* 289, 291, 292, 302,
    307, 311, 348, 428
    amulets and phylacteries, 241–243
    camp, *220*
    enemies against power, 260
    flight from San Carlos, 31–32
    food harvests and agriculture, 216, 225–
        227

Gans, 243–252
    girl's puberty ceremony, 233–236
    history, 207–216
    horsemanship, 281–282
    hunting, 227–229, 281–282
    medicine shirts and sashes, 243
    novice complex for raid and war, 260–262
    population, 216
    raiding and warfare, 252–260
    range of, 207, *208*
    religion, cosmology, and the supernatural,
        236–241.
    scratching stick and drinking tube, 262–
        263
    surrender of (1883, 1886), 34
    tanning, 229–233
    time keeping, 282–283
    weapons, 263–281
        bows and arrows, 263–269
        guns, 281
        knives, 278
        lances, 273, *278*
        quivers, 269, *270–272*
        shields, 278
        stones and slings, 278
        war clubs, 273–274, *274, 275*
Chissay, 37
Chokonen Apache, 259
Chow Big, 37
Christianity, 182–186, *202,* 238–239, 240,
    304, 429–430
Church of Jesus Christ of Latter Day Saints,
    359
Cibecue Apache, 25, 27, 29, 30, 31, 32, 37,
    53, 55, 168
    range of, 92
Cibicu, Battle of, 92
Cibicu Valley, 92
Cimarron Agency, 354
Citizenship, 198, 308, 309
Civil War, 29, 298, 353
Civilian Conservation Corps, 308
Clan system, 54, 197
Clothing, 102–103, *108,* 188, *335*
    Adolescence Rite, 389–390
    Apache scout, 34–35, *48*
    Jicarilla, *349, 362, 364,* 365–369, *368–*
        377, 380, 384, 385
    Mescalero, 332–335, *339*
    mourning, 102
    puberty ceremony, *66, 68,* 74, *103–106,*
        236, *318–321*
    warrior, 25, *161*
    woman's, 102, 188, *218, 222, 290, 295,*
        333, 334, 339, 369
    See also Moccasins; War clothing and
        jewelry
Clown, 62, *66, 70,* 133, 172, 173, 174, 240,
    245, 317, 382, *383, 384*
    mask, *138*
    trident, *140*
Clum, John, 61–62, 121
Cochise, 148, 207, 210, *211,* 212, *213, 218,*
    259
Cochise, Niño, *see* Niño Cochise
Cocopa Indians, 144
Cody, 37
Coiled basket, *406–409*
Collier, John, 308–309
Colorado gold discovery, 298
Comanche Indians, 210, 216, 289, 349, 351,
    411
Controller of Water, 239
Cooking utensils, 188
    See also Food
Cooley, Col. Corydon Eliphalet, 37
Corn:
    cooking, 96–97
    harvesting and threshing, 101
Corn bread, 188
Cornell, Dr. H. M., 356
Coronado expedition of 1540, 23
Cosmology, 236–241
Courtship and marriage, 85–86

Coyote, 238, 394
Coyote People, 359
Coyotero Apache, 35, 37
Cradle ceremony, 59, 341
Cradleboard, 56, *57, 59, 218, 303, 337*
  carrying, *56*
  construction of, 59
  made for girls, *66*
  religious charms, 59
Crafts, *see* Arts and Crafts
Creator and Ruler, 252
Cremony, John C., 87, 281–282, *417, 422*
Crescent moon (design), 236
Crime and punishment, 91–92, *298, 364*
Crook, Gen. George, 29, 30–31, 32, 34, 35,
  45, 53, 145, 210, 212–214, 282–283
  Apache round-up campaign (1872–1873),
  31, 53
Cross, *154, 157,* 158–160
Crow Indians, 292
Crown Dancers, 130–134, 173–174
  See also Gans
Cry babies, strangling of, 57–58
Culin, Stewart, 416, 417, 425
Culture hero, birth myth, 237–238
  See also Child of the Water
Curing ceremonies, 66, 124, 170–182, 192,
  428–429
  Ceremonies for the Sick, 170
  Gan dancing, 130–134
  Holiness Rite, 386–387
  at nighttime, 37
  types of, 125–126
  value of, 127–128
  See also Medicine men

Dahteste, *215*
Dances:
  Adolescence Rite, 387–393
  ceremonial, 170–182
    Ceremonies for the Sick, 170
    Dance for Rain, 176
    Dance for a Sick Child, 175
    Dance for a Sick Woman, 174–175
    Devil's Dance, 173–174
    Ghost Dance, 179
    Medicine Disk Ceremony, 176–179
    Night Dance, 170–173
    Protection from Ghosts, 175–176
    Sickness and Death of Whistling Wind,
    179
    Thank-Offering Dance, 176
    Wheel Dance, 170
  Crown Dance, 132–134, 173–174
  Holiness Rite, 386–387
  Mountain Spirits myth, 239–240
  puberty ceremony, 68–71, 78–82
  social, *84, 92*
  war parties, 258
  See also Gans, dancers
Darkness, Water, and Cyclone, 381
Davenport, Catherine D., 10, 35
Davis, E. W., *417,* 425
Dawes Act of 1887, 195
Dean, Irma, 10, *200*
Dean, Jimmy, *203*
Death and burial, 68, 179–182, 190, 258,
  326–327
Deer-head masks, 227
Deguele, 241
Dekley, 37
Denver Museum, 365
Denver and Rio Grande Railroad, 356
Department of the Interior, 31–32, 35, 183
Depression of 1930s, 308
Desert Land Act of 1877, 299
Devil's Dance, 173–174
Diablo, 29, 91
Dice games, *420,* 423–425
Diseases and cures, 120
Divorce, 428

and remarriage, 312–313
Dolan, Thomas A., 354
Dolls, 35, *66, 68, 222, 367*
Dorsey, Dr. George A., 40–52, 102
Douglas, F. H., *365,* 367
Drinking tube, 74, *74,* 261, 262–263
Drinks, 330–331
  See also Tiswin; Tulapai
Drop Stick (game), 423
Drums, *371,* 413, *417*
Dulce Assembly of God Mission, 359
Dulce Baptist Indian Mission, 359
Dulce Independent School District, 359
Dutch ovens, 96, 188
Dutch Reform Mission, 341, 356, 359
Dutch Reformed Church, 216, 306–307, 356
Dwellings, *see* Tipis; Wickiups
Dye colors, 233

Eagle feathers, use of, 124, 126, 133, *154,*
  160, 228, 233, 252, *254, 257,* 273, *377*
Earrings, *37,* 60, 102
Ears, pierced, 60
Earth, The, 381
Earth Woman, 237, 241
Eastern Chiricahua Apache, 24, 207
Eastern White Mountain Apache, 55
Economic Opportunity Act, 360
Education, *see* Schools and education
Education Committee, 201
Effigies (medicine), 158
Elote, *377*
Emerson, Dorothy, 312
Enemies against power, 260
English names, 90–91
Eskehnadestah, 37
Ewell, Capt. Richard S., 273
Exorcising power, 126

Face painting, *see* Body and face painting
Family clusters, local group, 54
Family economic unit, 188–192
Family, extended domestic, 312–313, 348
Faraon Apache, 351
Father, The, 381
Feathers, ritual importance of, 228
Feeble children, killing of, 57
Feeble-minded, respect for, 147–148
Feminine characteristics, 88
Fergusson, Erna, 317, 359
First Annual Tribal Arts and Crafts Show,
  360
Flageolets, 414
Flood story, 238
Flutes, 414, *414*
Food, 96–100, 101, 205–206, 330–331
  Adolescence Rite, 390–391
  cooking, 188
  drying meat, *361*
  grinding acorns, *101*
  puberty ceremony, 74, *76*
  roasting corn, *97*
  staple supply items, 188
  supply, mythology of, 393–395
  for sweat baths, 121–122
Food harvest, *98,* 225–227
Food stamp program, 198
Foot races, 422
Fort Apache Reservation, 10, 12, 24–25, *26,*
  30, 32, 35–37, *43,* 101, 129, 166, 197,
  201–206, 212, 428, 431
  abandoned (1922), 35
  average yearly income, 189
  cattle associations, 190
  cattle owned by, 189
  established, 212
  government, 201–202
  graves of Indian scouts, *52*

industry, 202–203
location of, 201
Lutheran mission, 183–184
military cemetery, 35–37, *51*
schools, 93–94
Fort Apache Scout, 206, 430, *432*
Fort Apache Timber Company, 202
Fort Bowie, prisoners at, *32*
Fort Ord, 29, 35
Fort Sill, 216, 306–307
Fort Stanton, 297–298, 354, 355
Fort Sumner (Bosque Redondo), 299
Fort Union, 352
Fossil Creek band, 55
Free, Mickey, 144
Furniture, 94–96

Gambling, 192
Games, 7, 63–66, 190, 414–426
Gans, 66, 68, 124, 126, 129–134, 155, 158,
    171, 240, 243–252, *244, 247, 249, 251,*
    323, 324, 381, 382, 429
    belt, *133, 134*
    Crown Dancer curing ceremony, 130–134
    dancers, *133, 156,* 164, 173–174, 177, 178,
        205, 243–252, 319–324, *320, 321, 323,*
        324, 326
        body paint, 250–251
        Chiricahua, 243–252
    difference between Hactcin and, 382
    headdress, 133–134, *134–135, 139,* 173,
        243–244, 246, *246,* 319, 326
        horns on, *139, 140,* 251–252
        symbols of, 244
    mask of, 133, *138, 140, 245,* 246, *250,* 319
    medicine hoops, *158,* 158
    Mescalero, *18*
    origin of, 129
    positions of performers, *139*
    power of, 129
    puberty ceremony, *70,* 82, 319–324
    wands, 133, *140, 141, 324*
Geronimo, *20,* 58, 62–63, 207, *215, 218,* 226,
    227, 228, 229, 252, 255, 258, 259, 262–
    263, *264,* 302, 417, 426
    ability to predict events, 253
    death of, 216
    in prison, 214–216
    Sonora raid (1883), 214
    surrender of (1886), *32,* 214
Getty, Harry T., 8, 91
Giant, The, *237,* 238
Gila Indians, 351
Goddard, Pliny Earle, 331
Gonorrhea, treatment for, 120
Good-bye, saying, 61
Goodwin, Grenville, 8, 10, 23, 24, 28, 32,
    53, 54, 55, 61, 65, 71, 87, 88, 89, 90–
    91, 119, 121, 128, 134, 162, 164, 182,
    197, 260, 263, 264, 269
Gordon, Renzie, 428
Government, 53–55, 310–313
Grace Lutheran Church, 182
Grant, Ulysses S., 31, 299
Gray One, *244,* 250, 319
Green, Maj. John, 35
Greeting, 61
*Grenville Goodwin among the Western
    Apache* (ed. Opler), 165
Guadalupe-Hidalgo, Treaty of (1848), 297
Gud-i-zz-ah, *38*
Guenther, Pastor Edgar, 183–184
Guns, horsemanship and, 281–282
Gwyther, George, 329

Hactcin, kinds of, 381–382
Hair bow, *37, 119, 222*
Hair braids, 367

Hair dressing and ornaments, 117, *349,*
    362, 366
Hair styles, 188

Hair tubes, *349*
Haskell Institute, 430
Havasupai Indians, 27, 55
Headdress, *see* Gans, headdress
Hennisee, Lt. A. G., 299
Herus (folklore myth), 239
Hidden ball (game), 422
Hide-and-seek (game), 64
Hides, *see* Tanning skins
Hill, W. W., 8
Hoddentin, *74,* 101, 166
    See also Pollen, sprinkling of
Hoijer, Harry, 8, 13
Holiness Rite, 382, 386–387, 428
Holy Boy, 395
Holy Ones, 382
Home Finding Center, 184
Hoop and pole (game), 64, 414–422, *418,*
    419, 420
    Chiricahua, 417
    Jicarilla, 422
    Mescalero, 417
    Western Apache, 415–417
Hoops, medicine, 126, 158
Hopi Indians, 24, 55, 198
Horses and horsemanship, *45,* 281–282, 297
    gear, 282
    guns and, 281–282
Humor, 88
Hunting, 189–190, 227–229, 331–332
    amulets, *150*
    boy's training for, 63–64, 66
    hide sling for, 278
    horses trained for, 281–282
Hygiene, 120–122

Ignacio, *339*
Indian Agency at Dulce, *355*
Indian Claims Commission, 290
Indian Emergency Conservation Work
    (ECW), 308
Indian Office Report of 1937, 13
Indian Reorganization Act of 1934, 190,
    195, 201, 308, 356–357
Indian School (Sante Fe), 359
Indian shinny (game), 64
Indians of the Southwest (Dorsey), 40–52
Individual power quest, 324–326
Industrial Club, 356
Intchi-dijin (cross), 241
Intermarriage, 27, 53, 55, 348
Ish-kay-nay, 422
Isihiligigahi (holy mountain), 386
Itza-chu (eagle), 243

Jerked beef, 188
Jewelry, 102–103, *228,* 365–369
    See also Earrings; Necklaces
Jicarilla Apache, 7, 11, 12, 13, 24, 29,
    197, 292, 297, 311, 343–403, 428
    Adolescence Rite (puberty rite), 382, 387–
        393
    camps, *352, 353, 357, 358, 361*
    Ceremonial Relay Race, 382, 393–403
    ceremonialism, 382–384
    clothing and jewelry, *349, 362, 364,* 365–
        369, *368–376, 380, 384, 385*
    coiled basketry, *12,* 410–411
    history, 345–361
    Holiness Rite, 382, 386–387, 428
    range of, *343–347*
    religion, 381–382
Jicarilla Apache Reformed Church, 359
Jicarilla Arts and Crafts Retail Shop, 361
Jicarilla Chieftain (newspaper), 345, 359,
    360, 430

Jicarilla Reservation, 12, *343*, 343–345
  abandoned mines, *350*
  established, 344
  loading rations, *354*
  population, 360
  size of, 356

Johnson, Andrew, 34
Josanie, 214
Juh, 207, 210, 259

Kaut, C., 197
Kaywaykla, James, 60, 64, 65, 207, 226,
  273
Kearny, General, 352
Killer of Enemies, *237*, 238
Kinishba "Brown House" (Pueblo ruin),
  203
Kinship terminology, 89
Kiowa Apache, 7, 11, 12, 13, 24, 216, 289,
  292, 297, 348, 352, 411
Klij-litzogue (yellow snake), 243
Kluckhohn, Clyde, 8, 406, 413, 426
Knife case, 278, *278, 279, 369*
Knives, types of, 278

Labor, division of:
  Mescalero Apache, 327
  Western Apache, 86–87
Lances, 273, 293, *296, 300, 301, 339, 380*
Laurel, 142–144
Leggings, 332–334, *362*, 365, 367, *372, 374,
  379*
Levirate rule, 313
Life Giver, 240
Lightning and Thunder, religious beliefs,
  237–238
Lincoln National Forest, 289
Lipan Apache, 11, 12, 13, 24, 289, 291,
  292, 297, 306, 307, 311, 348
Lizards, 163
Llanero band, 348, 355, 394, *395*, 396, *396*
Llewellyn, W. H. H., 300, 355
Local groups, 53–54
  government of, 310–311
Lockwood, Frank C., 28
Loco, Chief, 207
Loco Jim, 176
Long Nose, 250
Love magic, 124
Lupe, John, 71
Lutheran Church, 182–184, *185*
Luttrel, 306

Maba (bear-hunting time), 228–229
Macauley, Capt. C. N. B., 416
McClellan saddle, *216*
Mangus Colorado, 207, 259
Mano (grinding slab), 96
Mansos Apache, 27
Maricopa Indians, 27
Marriage, 190–192
  and courtship, 85–86
  intermarriage, 27, 53, 55, 348
  matrilocal (Mescalero Apache), 312
  mixed, 193
  plural, 313
Masculine characteristics, 88
Masks, for hunting, 227, 331
  See also Gans, mask of
Maternity belt, 56
Matthews, Dr., 155
Maturity rites, boy's, 85
  See also Adolescence Rite; Novice com-
    plex
Maxwell, L. B., 352

Maxwell Land Grant, 353
Mayerhoff, Rev. Paul S., 416, 423
Mazatayal band, 55
Medicine bag, *42*, 85, *146, 148, 167, 231,
  233, 318. 341*
Medicine cap, *257*
Medicine cord, *38*, 160–162, *160, 161*
Medicine Disk Ceremony, 125, 176–179
Medicine hat, *144*, 155–158, *155, 158*, 167
Medicine hoops, 126, 158, *159*
Medicine men, 126, *143*, 142–149. *157*, 190,
  359, 428
  capabilities and training, 142
  ceremonies, 164–165
  childbirth ceremony, 56
  curing ceremony, 127–128
  for dispelling sickness, 144–145, 148
  engaging services of, 125
  items used by, 151–164
    cord, *38*, 160–162, *160, 161*
    cross, *156, 157*, 158–160
    hoops and effigies, 126, 158, *159*
    as live objects (1901–1902), 165–170
    lizards, snakes, bear claws, 163
    pillows and ashes, 163–164
    rhombus, 151, *151*
    roots, 164
    shirt, 151–154, *152–154*, 167–168
    wooden snake, 162–163
  names, 144
  painted bag used by, *167*
  payment to, 146
  powers claimed by, 142, 144, 146
  role of, 142–149
  use of sweat bath, 142, 144
  vocabulary of, 144
  war party, 144, 253
  women, 147, 312
  See also Ceremonial dances; Curing cere-
    monies; Religion
Medicine object (ancient), *168*
Medicine sash, *150*, 243, *243*
Medicine shirt, *143*, 151–154, *152, 153, 154*,
  167–168, 243
  designs for, *172*
Medicine women, 147, 312
"Memorial and Affidavits showing Outrages
  Perpetrated by the Apache Indians in
  The Territory of Arizona during the
  years 1869 and 1870" (Legislature of
  the Territory of Arizona), 29–30
Menstrual periods, 71
Mescal (century plant), 55, 97, 225, 233,
  255, 287, 330
Mescalero Apache, 7, 11, 12, 24, 29, 99,
  133, 197, 210, 285–341, *289–310, 321–
  341*, 348, 352, 354–355, 428
  basketry, 410
  clothing, 332–335
  death and burial, 326–327
  dwellings and sanitation, 327–330
  food and drink, 330–331
  girl's puberty rite, 313–324, *314–317*
  government and social order, 310–313
    extended domestic family, 312–313
    local group, 310–311
  history, 287–309
  hunting, 331–332
  individual power quest, 324–326
  labor, division of, 327
  range of, 291
  religion, 341
Mescalero Reservation, 12, 24, 216, *284*,
  285–290, *307–309*
  cattle industry, 308
  employment, 288, 289–290
  established, 299
  gold discovery (1882), 302
  industry, 288
  number of acres, 287
  pass system, 299, 306
  population, 289
  schools and education, 290
Mescalero Tribe, organized, 309

Mesquite, 225
Metate (grinding slab), 96
Methodist Church, 356
Mexican names, 91
Mexico, 25–29, 30, 297
  bounty for Apache scalps, 293
Midwives, 56, 57
Miles, Gen. Nelson, 214
Mimbres Apache, 37
Mint bag, *318*
Missionaries, 91, 182–186, 238–239, 297, 306–307, 341, 356
Moccasin (game), 426
Moccasins, 61, 103, *110, 111, 223,* 293, 335, 341, 366, *375, 404,* 413, *413*
Mogollon Apache, 37
Mojave Indians, 37, 144
Monster Slayer, 381, 388, 389
Moon, 381, 422
Mooney, James, 13, 422
Morning star (design), 236
Mother, The, 381
Mother-in-law avoidance, 88, 312
Mount Vernon Barracks, 216
Mountain Spirits, 63, 239–240, 295, 319, 332, 381
  masked dancer ceremonies, 239–240, 244
  See also Gans
Mourning for the dead, 68, 102, 180, 326–327
Musical instruments, 7, 413–414, *414–416*
Mythology, *132,* 381–382
  of Ceremonial Relay Race, 393–395
  "enemies against power," 260
  girl's puberty ceremony, 76, 84
  missionary influences on, 238–239
  water and lightning, 237–238
  See also Religion; Supernaturalism

Na-a-cha, 144, 160
Nah-leen (hair bow), *37, 119, 222*
Naiche (Nai-chi-ti, Natchez), 207, 216, *218, 235*
Nakai'dok-lin'ni, 170
Nalte, *38*
Names:
  calling another by, 60–61
  given to a child, 60
  medicine men, 144
  terms of greeting, 61
  on war party, 257
Nana, Chief, 207, 214
Nan-ta-do-tash, 155
Natchez, Chief (Naiche), 207, 216, *218,* 235
National Park Service, 203
Na-tuen-de, *68*
Natzele, *300*
Nautzille, *337*
Navaho Material Culture (Kluckhohn and Hill), 8
Navajo Indians, 7, 11, 13, 23, 24, 35, 53, 55, 88, 127, 142, 155, 166, 198, 212, 306, 348, 351, 352, 405, 412, 426
  blanket trade, 255
  scouts used in Apache campaigns, *51*
Necklaces, *37, 115, 117, 228,* 335, *335,* 367, *377*
  securing conchos to, *116*
  T-shaped, *410, 411,* 412
  war, *116, 224*
  war medicine, *145*
Nednhi Apache band, 210, 259
Neighborhood Youth Corps, 360
New Mexico, 23, 30, 297
  admitted to the Union, 307
  Jicarilla Apache, 343–403
  Mescalero Apache, 285–341
  Territory of, 297
Night Dance, 170–173
Niño Cochise, 227, 228, 252, 327
Nisdjatohi (holy mountain), 386
Noch-ay-del-Klinne, 31–32

Northern Tonto Apache, 30, 53
  range of, 54–55
Novice complex (for raid and war), 255, 260–262

Oak Creek band, 55
Obscene jokes, 89
Office of Indian Affairs, 212
Ojo Caliente, 30
Old age, 90
Old Jim, 121
Ollero band, 348, 355, 394, *395,* 396–399, *396, 398,* 401–403
Oñate, Don Juan de, 348
Opata Apache, 25
Opler, Morris E., 8, 24, 59, 63, 133, 164, 165, 186, 207, 236, 238, 240, 248, 250, 260, 261, 282, 292, 293, 295, 310, 312, 326, 327, 341, 381, 382, 387, 388, 389, 390, 391, 392, 393, 395, 400–403, 414, 417, 422, 426
Orphaned children, 58
Owen, Charles L., 424
O'zho (heaven), 180

Painting, 405–406
Pantheism, 186
Papago Indians, 30, 198
Parfleche (rawhide container), 229–233, *232*
Parmee, Edward, 195, 197
Peace Policy (Arizona), 30
Penseh (medicine hoops), 126, 158, *159*
Perry, Corrine B., 10, 35
Perry, Edgar, 10, 35, 431
Personality characteristics, Western Apache, 88–90
Pesh-chidin (witch, spirit), 144
Phratries, 54
Phylacteries, 241–243, *243*
Pima Indians, 27, 144
Pinal Apache, 37
"Plains people," *see* Llanero
Pneumonia, 120
Pollen, sprinkling of, 56, 57, *83,* 166, 170, 173, 174, 176, 181, 233
Populus tremuloides, 120
Pottery, *406,* 412
Poverty, 195–196, 289, 306, 308, 352, 359, 428
Presbyterian Church, 355
Program of Removal Policy (Department of the Interior), 31–32
Protection from Ghosts (dance), 175–176
Puberty ceremony, girl's, 68–85, *70, 81, 82–84, 92,* 124, 190, 192, 205, 233–236, *245, 258, 314–317,* 341, 428
  alcoholic beverages and, 84–85
  beginning of, 74–75
  body painting, 119
  cane, 72–74, *72*
  clothing, *66, 68,* 74, *103–106, 234, 235, 236, 318–321*
  Jicarilla, *see* Adolescence Rite
  Mescalero Apache, 313–324
  mock, young children's, 65
  myths associated with, 76, 84
  1901–1902, 68–71
  1920–1930, 71
  1930–1940 (Chiricahua Apache), 233–236
  1930–1970s, 71–85
  parts or phases, 76–82
    Phase I "Alone she dances," 78, *81*
    Phase II "Kneeling," 78
    Phase III "Lying," 78, *81*
    Phase IV "Cane set out, she runs around it," 78–79, *82*
    Phase V "Running," 79
    Phase VI "Candy, it is poured," 79
    Phase VII "Blessing her," 79–82, *83*
    Phase VIII "Throwing them off," 82

preparing food for, 76
ritual paraphernalia, 72–75
temporary dwelling for, 78
Public Health Service Clinic (Dulce), 382
Pueblo Indians, 23, 25, 291, 295, 300, 348, 351, 365, *379*, 387, 395, 412
Pueblo Rebellion of 1680, 412
Punishment, crime and, 91–92, *298, 364*
Pyle, J. E., 354

Quakers, 304
Quintero, Canyon Z., Sr., 10, 35
Quivers, *27*, 269, *269, 271, 272*, 293, *296, 301–303, 337, 366*

Races:
    between boys and fathers, 64
    foot races, 422
    See also Ceremonial Relay Race
Raiding and warfare, 28, 31, 252–260
    "enemies against power," 260
    in Mexico, 27, 28, 29
    novice complex for, 260–262
Ramada, or squaw-cooler, *32*, 96, 206, *289, 292*, 329, *329*
Ramon (medicine man), 244
Rasps, 414
Rattles, kinds of, *322*, 413–414
Rattlesnake (Holiness Rite), 386
Reagan, Albert B., 8, 56, 57–58, 68–71, 85, 86, 87, 92–93, 96, 97–98, 99, 101, 119, 125, 126, 127, 133, 147, 151–154, 164, 165, 166–167, 170, 173, 176, 179, 180, 181, 415, 416, 423–425
Reformed Church, 290
Religion, 122–126, 192, 236–243
    altars and sacred places, 126–127
    ceremonial rites, 124–126, 382–384
    cosmology, 236–243
    holy (*godiyingo*) powers, 122–123
    Jicarilla mythology, 381–382
    Mescalero culture, 341
    taboos, 125
    view of universe, 122
    witchcraft, 123–124
    See also Adolescence Rite; Curing ceremonies; Medicine men; Mythology; Puberty ceremony
Reservations:
    early period of, 31–32
    modern contact among, 24
    See also individual reservations: Fort Apache; Jicarilla; Mescalero; San Carlos; White Mountain
Rhombus, or bull-roarer (*tzi-ditindi*), 151, *151, 415*, 425
Rio Grande Pueblo, 25, 412
Roman Catholic Church, 142, 290, 297, 300–302, 307, 341, 359
Roosevelt, Franklin D., 308
Roots, use of, 164
Rope, John, 162, 260
Rosin, Pastor Henry, 183

Sacred places, altars and, 126–127, 145
Saddlebags, *42, 230, 231*
St. Anthony's Catholic Church, 359
San Carlos Apache, 24, 25, 27, 30, 37, 53
    bands of, 55
    range of, 55
San Carlos Indian Agency, *196*
San Carlos Reservation, 10, 12, 24–25, *26*, 31–32, 72, 186–192, *189*, 193–201, *190, 198, 199*, 205–206, 212, 302
    average yearly income, 189, 198
    cattle associations, 190

cattle owned by, 189, *191*
Christian missions, 182–186
congressional appropriations, 198
descendants living on, 37
dwellings, *190, 198, 199*
escape from, 212–214, 258, 259
fire drill demonstration, *414*
government, 198
life (1973), 193–206
packing up rations at, *34*
population (1972), 193
poverty, 195–196
schools and education, 193–195, 196, 197, 198, 201
unemployment, 193, 196
San Juan, Chief, *296*
Sand painting, 125
"Sand people," *see* Ollero
Sanitation, dwellings and, 327–330
Santee, Ross, 121, 282
Scalps and scalping, 257, 293–295
Scarification, 148
Schools and education, 62–68, 91, 93–94, 193–195, 196, 197, 198, 201, 203, 290, 300, *305*, 359
Scouts, *see* Apache scouts
Scratching stick, *74*, 262–263
Seiber, Al, 160
Sex, 89
Shamans, *see* Medicine men
She Who Trots Them Off, 315
Sheridan, General, 214
Shields, 278, *296, 300, 337, 339*
Shinny (game), 422–423
Shoulder bands, *349*, 365
Shoz-dijiji (black bear), 243
Shoz-lekay (white bear), 243
Shoz-litzogue (yellow bear), 243
Sickness and Death of Whistling Wind (dance), 179
Sign language, 92–93
Signaling, 92–93, 257
Simms, S. C., 417
Sioux Indians, 292
Sky, The, 381
Slavery, 30
Slayer of Monsters, 76, 260
Smallpox, 93, 354, 356, 381
Snakes, 163, 227, 228
    symbolism, 160
Social dances, *84*, 92
Social order, Western Apache, 53–55
Social Organization of the Western Apache, The (Goodwin), 260
Society of Friends (Quakers), 304
Sonnichsen, C. L., 8, 306, 307, 312, 313
Sorcery, *see* Witchcraft
Sororate rule, 312–313
Southern Chiricahua band, 207
Southern Tonto Apache, 30, 53
    range of, 55
Southern Ute Agency, 354
Southwest Museum, 8–9, 405
Spencer, 144
Squaw-cooler, *see* Ramada
Stanford Research Institute, 359
Stetson hats, 205
Stones and slings, 278
Storytelling, 63
Stottler, Lt. V. E., 304–306, 332
Stratton family, 57
Subtribal groups, 53–55
    bands, 53
    clan system, 54
    family clusters, 54
    geographic range, 54–55
    local groups, 53–54
    phratries, 54
Sun, The, 238, 381, 388, 422
Sun Dance, 295
Sun Greeting ceremony, 315
Sunrise Ceremony, 236
    See also Puberty ceremony, girl's
Sunrise Park (resort complex), 202–203
Supernaturalism, 236–243

power and healing ceremony, 324–326
Tzi-daltai amulets, 241
Swanton, John R., 13
Sweat bathing, 120–122
  medicine man's use of, 142, 144
  heating rocks for, *120*
Syphilis, treatment for, 120

Taboos, 125, 429
Tag-band system, 90–91
Tanning skins, 101–102, 229–233, *328*
Tatooing, 119
Taz-ayz-Slath, *218*
Texas, Republic of, 297
Textiles, 412
Thank-offering Dance, 176
Theodore Roosevelt Indian School, 35, 203
Thrapp, Dan L., 8, 210, 282
Thunder People, 237, 238
Tierra Amarilla Reservation, 354
Time keeping, 282–283
Tipis, *75, 314,* 327–330, *329, 330,* 348, 357,
  359, 361
Tiswin (drink), 120, 331
Tobacco, 226
Tonto Apache, *27,* 29, 30, 31, 32, 37, 53–
  55, 65, 144, 160
Tonto territory, discovery of gold in, 29
Tools, 412–413
Trachoma, 120
Tribal Alcoholism Program, 206
Tribal Business Committee, 289
Tribal Constitution (Fort Apache Reserva-
  tion), 201–202
Tribal Education Committee, 203
Tsanati (Wonder Workers), 382–384
Tuberculosis, 120, 302, 355, 356
Tug-of-war competitions, 425
Tuklonen, Emma, *234*
Tulapai (drink), 24, 92, 96, 120, 331
  drinking party, 99–100
  fermentation process, 99
  ingredients, 188
Turkey (Holiness Rite), 386
Turquoise beads, 124
Twin children, 59
Tze-go-juni (medicine woman), 147
Tzi-daltai (amulets), 241

Ulibarri, Capt. Juan de, 349
Unemployment, 193, 196, 360
United States Constitution, 201
United States Indian Office, 13
Uplegger, Alfred M., 182, 183
Uplegger, Pastor Francis J., 182–183
Usen (or Ussen), 63, 252, 341
  See also Yus
Ute Indians, 332, 349, 351, 352, 353, 365
  379, 387, 411
Utensils, 94–96

Valverde, Antonio, 351
Victorio, Chief, 207, 214, *255,* 258, 281,
  299–300
Vigilante groups, 30, 298
Violin bow, 414, *414, 415*
Violins, 414, *414, 415*
Virginity lapel, 117
Voodoo power, 124

Walapai Indians, 55
War clothing and jewelry:
  bonnet, *257, 258, 340,* 369, *377*
  cap, *27, 111–113,* 254
  hat, 261, 334–335
  necklace, *116, 145, 224*

shirt, *38, 107, 222,* 334, *335, 336, 370*
  See also Amulets, for warfare
War clubs, 273–274, *274–277,* 293
War dance, 252–253
War games, mock, 65–66
War paint, 255, *286*
War party, 24, *220,* 252–260
  dances, 258
  "enemies against power," 260
  face painting, 255
  izze-kloth cords, 162
  novice complex, 260–262
  preferred attack, 255–257
  prisoners, 257–258
  scratching stick and drinking tube on,
    262–263
  shamans, 253
  signs and signals to transmit messages,
    257
  traps to ambush pursuers, 257
  traveling, 253–255, 259–260
  victory celebration, 258
  women and, 253, 257–258
War shield, *279, 280*
Warm Springs Apache, 30, 210, 212, 214,
  258, 281
Warriors, *25, 161, 296, 300, 301, 335, 339*
Warrior Apaches (Baldwin), 7
Water Beetle, 394
Water Beings, 239
Water and lightning, mythological association between, 237–238
Water Monster, 239
Weapons, 263–281
  See also Bows and arrows; Guns, horse-
    manship and; Lances; War clubs
Western Apache, 7, 11, 12, 23–206, *29, 109,*
  291, 292, 299, 302, 348, 428
  agriculture, 101
  altars and sacred places, 126–127
  apparel and jewelry, 102–103
  basketry, 408–410
  boy's maturity rites, 85
  ceremonial dances, 170–179
  childbirth, 55–57
  childhood, names, and training, 58–68
  Christian missions, 182–186
  courtship and marriage, 85–86
  crime and punishment, 91–92
  curing ceremonials, value of, 127–128
  death and burial, 179–182
  diseases and cures, 120
  dwellings, furniture, and utensils, 94–96
  food and drink, 96–100
  Gans, 129–134
  girl's puberty ceremony, 68–85, 428
    1901–1902, 68–71
    1920–1930, 71
    1930–1970s, 71–85
  government and social order, 53–55
  hair dressing and ornaments, 117
  history, 23–52
  labor, division of, 86–87
  life, 186–206
    in 1940, 186–192
    in 1973, 193–206
  medicine ceremonies, 164–165
  medicine items used by, 151–164
  medicine men, 142–149
  mother-in-law avoidance, 88
  personality characteristics, 88–90
  religion and ceremonies, 122–126
  schools, 93–94
  sign language and signaling, 92–93
  social dances, 92
  sweat bathing, 120–122
  tag-bands, English names, 90–91
  tanning, 101–102
  tatooing and body painting, 119
  woman's status, 30, 87–88
Western Apache Raiding and Warfare (ed.
  Basso), 260
Western White Mountain band, 55
Wheel Dance, 170
Whistling Wind, 179

White, Joseph, 352
White Bead Woman, 388
White Hactcin, *383*
White Mountain Apache, 24, 25, 27, 29,
    30, 31, 32, 35, 37, *47,* 53, 65, 119,
    132, *161,* 200–203, *418*
    range of, 55
    in war dress, *18, 161*
White Mountain Apache Culture Center, 10
White Mountain Reservation, 31–32, 35,
    100
    division of (1897), 37
    established, 31
White Painted Woman, 233–236, 238, 239,
    241, 253, 313–315, 341, 388, 389
White Shell Woman, 74, 381, 389
Whoa (Juh), 207, 210, 259
Wickiups, *32, 94,* 292, 327–330
    building of, 94–96, 186
    furniture, 94–96, 186–188
    shape of, 94
    Western Apache, *30*
Wind, 238
Wirt, Emmet, 356, 357
Wirt Trading Post, 356
Witchcraft, 123–124, 144, 148, 303, 359
    accusations of, 89
    protection against, 124
Witches, classes of, 123–124
Women:
    childbirth, 55–57
    clothing, *see* Clothing, woman's
    collecting rations, *305*

hair dressing and ornaments, *37,* 117,
    119, 222, 349, 362, 367
immoral, cutting nose of, 91–92
labor, 86–87, 94–96, 101, 189, 327, *328,*
    332
    medicine women, 147, 312
    in Mescalero ceremonialism, 325
    midwives, 56, 57
    mother-in-law avoidance, 88, 312
    shamans, 312
    status of, 30, 87–88
    at the war dance, 253
    war party and, 258
Wonder Workers, 382–384
Wooden medicine snake, 162–163
World War I, 308
World War II, 358
Wright, Burnette, 10, *204*
Wristguards, 269

Yavapai Indians, 13, 27, 30, 31, 55, 119
Yellow Coyote, *220*
Yucca food, 225, 330
Yuma Indians, 13, 37, 144
Yuman tribes, 13
Yus (or *Yusn*), 341

Zamora, Fray Francisco de, 348
Zuñi Indians, 13, 24–25, 288

447

E   Mails, Thomas E.
99
.A6   People called Apache.
M35
c.1

N.H. COLLEGE LIBRARY

a 3 4 6 7 6 0 0 0 2 4 8 7 4 7 a

SHAPIRO LIBRARY
Gertrude C.

New Hampshire College

2500 North River Road

Manchester, NH 03104

DEMCO